W9-BFK-579

My father, William Douglas.

My paternal grandfather,
Alexander Douglas.

My paternal grandmother,
Martha Archibald Douglas.

The house on North Fifth Avenue.

My father's last pastorate, Cleveland, Washington.

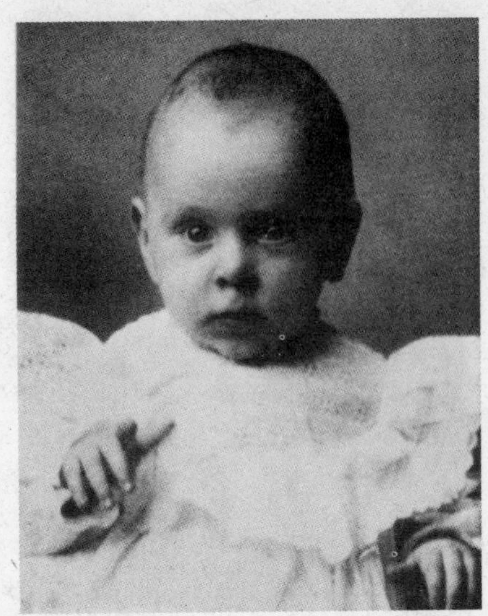

W.O.D. as an infant.

Martha, Arthur, and W.O.D.

Mother.

Mother and the three of us shortly after Father's death.

Yakima Avenue, east from
Front Street, about 1902.

Yakima Avenue, 1908.

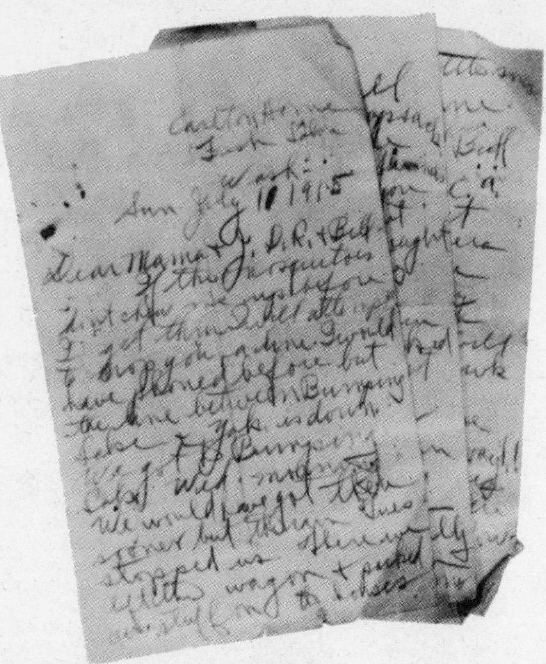

Sun July 11 1915

Dear Mama + J. D. R. + Bill

have phoned before but

the line between Bumping

Lake + Yak. is down.

We would have got there

sooner but

stopped us

all the wagon + packed

stuff on the horses.

The letter I wrote to Mother on a camping trip in 1915 (see page 19).

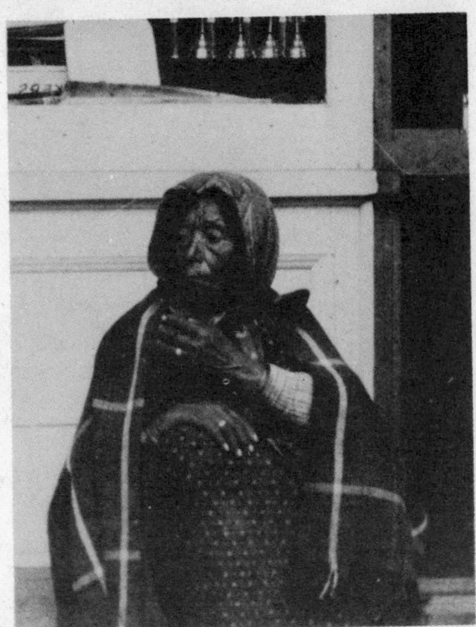

Yakima Susie.

Ringling Brothers Circus carriages being unloaded at the Yakima depot.

Eighth-grade graduation, 1912. Tommy Pickering is in the center of the first row, and Conrad Alexander, my other special friend, is in the second row, second from the right. W.O.D. is second from the left, bottom row.

This formal group photo was taken about 1910. I am at the left end and Tommy Pickering at the right end.

Art with the results of a boyhood fishing expedition.

Mother with the night's dinner.

In the wilderness with a friend, about 1913.

Hiking with a horseshoe pack.

The Yakima High School basketball team. Left to right: Leo Nicholson, Tommy Pickering, Orville Douglas, Arthur Darby, Bradley Emery.

My high school in Yakima.

MARTHA B.D.

W.O.D.

Smile.

MOTHER.

Martha and I at the Yakima railroad station about 1920.

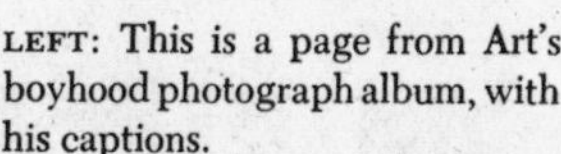

LEFT: This is a page from Art's boyhood photograph album, with his captions.

RIGHT: On a trip to the University of Idaho with the Whitman College debate team when I was a sophomore.

W.O.D. as a college student.

Whitman College.

Clerks at the Model Boot Shop about 1913: Lee Bruff, Henry Trauh and William O. Douglas.

Freshmen hazing at Whitman. I was hitting the water just as this picture was taken.

On the steps of Beta Theta Pi.

At a freshman kangaroo court. I am seated in the chair on the desk at the far left.

The author (lower right) and friends at Whitman.

WATCH YOUR STEP

From the day you violate these laws your days are numbered. The eagle eye of '15 and '16 is ever watching. The 40-watt Tungsten is hot and the waters of Lakum Duckum are cold and chill.

RULE 1

Wear the DINK on week days. No bare-head stuff goes. Fuss up on Sunday.

RULE 2

Lay off on the fried egg hat; the straw sailor or any other head piece that answers to the name of Stiff.

RULE 3

Forget your prep school stuff. Their letters and emblems don't count here. Leave 'em off.

RULE 4

Watch your manners. Touch your cap to the members of the faculty. Others do it. It won't hurt you.

RULE 5

Don't forget your station. Henceforward the Main entrance of Memorial Hall is not for you. Better crawl in a window than to come in by the Sacred Portal.

RULE 6

You are courting destruction if you are found in the vicinity of the Fussing Path from Memorial across the campus to Reynolds Hall.

RULE 7

Safety First

Don't get familiar with the Upper classmen. Obey the behests of the managers cheerfully. Show your pep and turn out for all activities and entertainments. Don't drag your feet.

The sudden changes in temperature referred to above will be applied to any Frosh who mutilates or tampers with this poster.

These rules mean NOW

'15
'16

Rules for Whitman freshmen.

President S. B. L. Penrose.

Dr. Benjamin H. (Daddy) Brown.

William R. Davis.

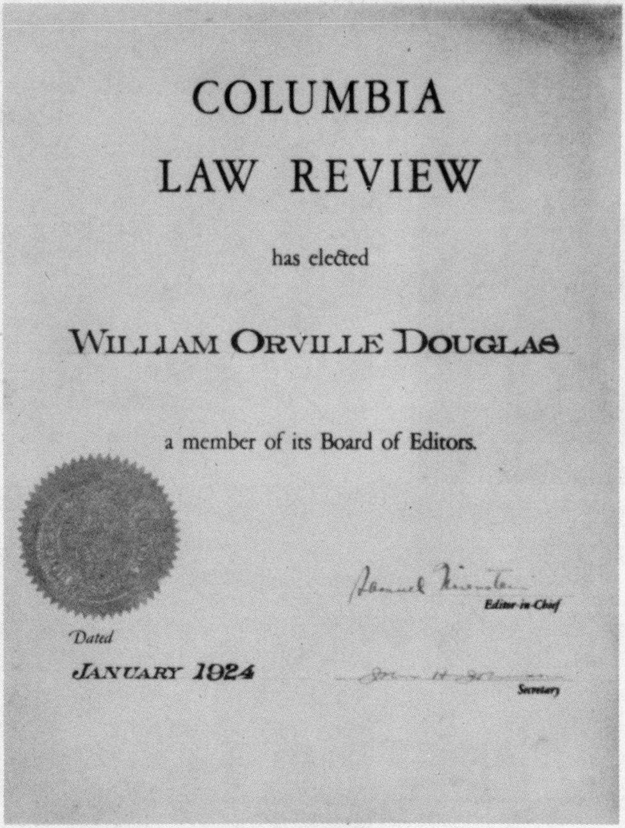

COLUMBIA

LAW REVIEW

has elected

WILLIAM ORVILLE DOUGLAS

a member of its Board of Editors.

Editor-in-Chief

Dated

JANUARY 1924

Secretary

Election to the *Columbia Law Review* in 1924.

Graduation from Columbia Law School, 1925.

The Yale Law School faculty in 1929 (Robert Hutchins is in the bottom row, third from the right).

With Millie and Bill, August 1940, in Astoria, Oregon.

Roundup with the Yakima Indians.

The SEC when I was made chairman. Left to right: Jerome Frank, Robert E. Healy, W.O.D., George C. Matthews, John W. Hanes.

With my brother, Art.

Prairie House, Goose Prairie, Washington.

The Supreme Court on April 17, 1939. Top row, left to right: Felix Frankfurter, Hugo Black, Stanley Reed, William O. Douglas. Bottom row, left to right: Harlan Stone, J. C. McReynolds, Charles Evans Hughes, Pierce Butler, Owen Roberts.

The official photograph at the time of my appointment to the Court.

Go East, Young Man

Go East, Young Man

The Early Years

The Autobiography of

William O. Douglas

Vintage Books
A Division of Random House
New York

First Vintage Books Edition, April 1983

Published in the United States by Random House, Inc., New York, and simultaneously in Canada by Random House of Canada Limited, Toronto. Originally published by Random House, Inc., New York, in April 1974.

The author wishes to thank those who generously contributed to the photograph section of this book:

My daughter, Mildred Douglas Read, my sister, Martha Douglas Bost, and my niece, Florence Douglas Persons, for family pictures.
Charlotte Mayerson for the picture of Prairie House.
The Yakima Federal Savings Bank for the old photographs of Yakima from their book, *As the Valley Was*, © 1968, Yakima Federal Savings and Loan Association, Yakima, Washington.
Harris & Ewing for the portrait taken at the time of my appointment.
The Supreme Court for the formal Court photograph.
The SEC for the picture of the Commission.

Grateful acknowledgment is made to the following for permission to reprint previously published material:

Janice L. Booker, "Justice William O. Douglas at Bat" from *The Shingle*, Vol. 36, no. 3, April, 1973. Copyright 1973 by Janice L. Booker. Reprinted by permission of the author and *The Shingle*, a publication of the Philadelphia Bar Association.

Felix Frankfurter, "Mr. Justice Roberts" from the *University of Pennsylvania Law Review*, 104/311, Copyright © 1955 by the *University of Pennsylvania Law Review*. Reprinted by permission of the *University of Pennsylvania Law Review* and Fred B. Rothman & Company.

Woody Guthrie, "Sharecropper Song"—12 lines. Copyright © 1947 by Stormking Music, Inc.; reprinted by permission.

Harcourt Brace Jovanovich, Inc., for permission to reprint an excerpt from "Chicago" by Carl Sandburg from his volume *Complete Poems*.

Harper & Row Publishers, Inc., for permission to draw material from *Of Men and Mountains* by William O. Douglas. Copyright 1950 by William O. Douglas. This material appears in the beginning chapters of this work.

Library of Congress Cataloging in Publication Data
Douglas, William O. (William Orville), 1898-
Go East, young man.
Includes index.
1. Douglas, William O. (William Orville), 1898-
2. Judges—United States—Biography.
I. Title.
KF8745.D6A3 1981 347.73'2634 [B] 81-40196
ISBN 0-394-71165-3 347.3073534 [B] AACR2

Manufactured in the United States of America

Cover photograph courtesy of the Supreme Court of the United States, Washington, D.C.

"All your anxiety is because of your desire for harmony. Seek disharmony; then you will gain peace."

—Jalal-Ud-Din Rumi
Persian poet 1207–1293

Contents

Preface

This autobiography was written in my spare time over the last ten or twelve years. The writing took place in the winter; the research, in the summer. While I have been blessed with a photographic mind, enabling me to work quickly, my memory is not always clear and lucid because I have a tendency to telescope events. So it was necessary for me to go back over old family records, to visit Nova Scotia and Maine, Minnesota, and to talk with my companions of the early years. Happily, quite a few have survived. Old mountain trails both in the Far West, in Appalachia, and in New England had to be revisited so that their detail could be recaptured. That meant retracing old paths to reactivate the "feeling intellect," as Wordsworth put it. It involved poring over old class records and scores of brittle, yellow newspapers.

The early chapters repeat a few of the episodes reported in *Of Men and Mountains* published some twenty-five years ago. Occasionally some paragraphs have been taken from that earlier volume merely because I found that the original mood and feeling were lost in a rewriting. Even the few paragraphs of the old book seem new, however, because they are in a different setting.

For the later years, research of a different character was required. Though I was at the SEC for five years, I found it necessary to reread all the public files—and my own private files—to be sure of my observations and to contact many of my old associates who worked in the same vineyard. And respecting the New Deal and FDR's record and the goings-on of the Harry Hopkinses, the Harold Ickeses, and the Jesse Joneses, I had to get acquainted with all the old diggings, including the Hyde Park Library, the *Congressional Record*, and books written by the main actors.

I never kept a diary and I am glad I did not. Those who did usually worked assiduously, like Harold Ickes, to revise and polish it so as to make his own record shine. Or they might, like Henry Morgenthau, record on tape every bloody conference so that no detail would escape history. Henry's dedication to detail led some of us attending his conferences to put into the record through the microphones, risqué stories, whether relevant or not, for in those swashbuckling days irreverence often possessed us.

In 1934 on reaching Washington, D. C., I did start a diary; and I made only one entry. It related how Harry Hopkins, "speaking for the Boss," as Harry said, asked me to overlook the sins of a mighty Democrat. I told him to go to hell; and that was the end of my diary and the end of a chance to become the buddy of Harry Hopkins, who threw sand into every competitor's machine. But I had an advantage, which few experience—the advantage of not ever having the Potomac fever, but only a desire to leave the city and get back to my woods and mountains as quickly as possible.

It was FDR who spoiled my plans. The reward of being on the Court was a rich one. Only a few of my Court experiences are in this volume, most of them being reserved for a later time. But the research on those thirty-five years was the easiest of all. For my notes and memoranda were copious and the Court decisions a living fabric of the law.

If the Court work were as demanding as some make out, I would not have had time for this and other writing projects. But it has never demanded more than four days a week. Even if only one day a week were given to outside writing, two would remain for hiking, rest, and reflection.

Holmes once wrote that his writings and decisions were "little fragments of my fleece that I have left upon the hedges of life." And so it is with this volume. "Would that my enemy would write a book" is not an idle wish. Yet one can never be sure that what he writes in complete sincerity is the full truth. For one can never be sure that it is not his subconscious which controls the pen.

My foreign journeys are covered by several hundred notebooks. So when I wrote about overseas affairs I took easy refresher courses through them. And the many Kodachromes and 16-mm colored films I shot prodded my jaded memory.

Overseas travels by a judge have a real leveling effect. In most countries judges are close to the bottom of the official totem pole; they are not independent but miserable, submissive creatures who know their master's voice. And that voice is not a Bill of Rights.

Even domestic travels into the back country can give a new perspective. For years I wore an old hat that had been sat on, slept on, and stepped on. It had been through storms without number and soiled beyond restoration. Byron Lockhart of Austin, Texas, who was with me on numerous trips in the Southwest, once introduced me at a lunch, saying, "If I should ever see this man's hat in a cow pasture, I'd step over it."

Jim Bowmer of Temple, Texas, and recently president of the Texas Bar, is a country lawyer and an ardent environmentalist whom I hoped Lyndon Johnson would name to our Court. Jim and I have been almost everywhere together. Once we stopped at a small village, Frijole, on the east side of the Guadalupe Mountains so far west in Texas that some of them are in New Mexico. We stopped to get some coffee before assaulting the massive limestone wall of the Guadalupes. In the coffee shop we met an old friend of Jim's, Noel Kincaid, who was the local justice of the peace. Jim introduced me as Justice Douglas. Kincaid, giving me a steely look, said, "Justice Douglas?" And turning to Jim, he added, "I've been here thirty years and I'd have sworn I knew every goldarn justice of the peace in these parts."

On another trip into West Texas to the fabulous Capote Falls, we left the Presidio and went many miles west on a dirt road before we came to Candelaria. Knowing this was the last outpost, Jim suggested we stop at the general country store and get some cheese, crackers, and soft drinks for lunch. It turned out that the store was run by two lovely, attractive sisters in their late thirties. We ate our meager repast, paid the bill, and started to the door when one of the ladies suggested we sign the guest book. We obliged her and in the column marked "residence" I wrote "U.S. Supreme Court, Wash., D.C." A year later we were back for another Capote Falls visit and once again stopped at the store. One of the proprietors said they had discussed all winter which one of us was Justice Douglas. So Jim suggested we line up, as the police line up suspects, and let the two ladies pick the guilty one. After viewing us for a few moments and after whispered conversations, one of the ladies put her hand on Jim's shoulder and said, "This must be the Justice." So Justice Bowmer and Bill Douglas, the law clerk, thanked them and walked out arm in arm.

In 1948, in refreshing my memories of Mount Adams, in my home state of Washington, I drove to a rendezvous on the south side of the mountain, a campsite that lies six thousand feet above sea level. From that point we would start the assault early the next morning. My car broke down in hot Pasco, Washington, where the asphalt pavements were soft under a 115° sun. It was a holiday and I had to walk several hours to find a mechanic. I wore my climbing shoes; but I did not have on the protective layers of two socks to prevent blisters. By the time my mission was completed I had an ugly blister on one foot and started looking for a doctor. At last I found one; and by the haughty attitude of the receptionist, I knew at once I was not welcome. I wore a tattered shirt and Levis so old that the blue had partly faded. When I walked into the doctor's office and told him my problem, he said, "We do not take care of the likes of you." I asked, "Why not?" "Because," he said, "there is a clinic a half-dozen blocks down this street that takes care of all the bums."

Reaching in my pocket I pulled out twenty-five dollars in paper money. Holding the bills out to him, I asked, "Will your charge be greater than this?" He quickly responded, "My dear sir, I apologize. Please sit down and I'll bandage your blisters"; and while he applied the bandages I told him quietly how the law was way ahead of medicine, how, if he were disbarred for malpractice and was indigent, the highest court in the land would take his case, would waive all filing fees and costs and name a lawyer—"as good as Bethlehem Steel has"—to represent him. "How do you know all that?" "Because, sir," I answered, "I seem to spend a lot of time there."

Before my appointment to the Court in 1939, the man in the judicial system who epitomized the values that FDR despised was a Wilson appointee, James Clark McReynolds of Tennessee. He was on the bench when I was sworn in; and though we were usually (although not always) at opposite poles, he and I had an unusually close relationship. That was due to the fact that we had mutual friends at the Harvard Business School, where I occasionally had taught. My talks with Old Mac, as we called him, were revealing to this innocent young neophyte. I knew that Justices had opposed views on the Bill of Rights and other legal issues. But I had naïvely assumed that they were detached free spirits like Holmes, Brandeis, and Cardozo. But Old Mac ushered me into reality. Every day he would speak with great emotion about FDR. "That man is really mad, is he not?"; "Do you think he'll have to be committed?" and on and on.

Writing an autobiography is in a sense giving a detailed account of the slow, step-by-step education of the author. The overall aim of this volume and the volume to follow is the hope that our people will come truly to love this nation. I hope it may help them see in the perspective of the whole world the great and glorious tradition of liberty and freedom enshrined in our Constitution and Bill of Rights. I hope they will come to love the continent, the most beautiful one in the whole world. I hope that before it is too late they will develop a reverence for our rich soils, pure waters, rolling grass country, high mountains, and mysterious estuaries. I hope that they will put their arms around this part of the wondrous planet, love it, care for it, and treat it as they would a precious and delicate child.

William O. Douglas

Go East, Young Man

Chapter I

Birthplace

My mother, Julia Fisk Bickford, was born in 1872. She was one of a set of twins, and was the smaller of the two, weighing under two pounds at birth. The wedding ring she wore as a grown woman would have gone over her fist and her head would have fit into a teacup. She was so small that for months she was dressed only in a blanket and carried on a pillow. She was three before she could walk, and in those days, had the nickname "Mite." Mother was never robust, but by the time of her teens she was athletic, with the reputation of being able to run "like a deer"—an image she proudly recalled in later years when varicose veins in her legs almost crippled her.

Mother was born in Maine, Minnesota, shortly after her parents migrated there from Vermont. Her father, Orville Fisk, was born in Moreton, Vermont, and is the grandfather for whom I was named. He was barely sixteen when Lincoln was elected in 1860 but answered the call to arms and ended up with Grant at Vicksburg.

Mother's mother, Salome Bickford, was from Newport, Vermont. Salome's New England roots were strong, going back on both sides to the early colonists of Massachusetts. Salome's mother, Rebecca Thompson, was the sister of Daniel Pierce Thompson, the Montpelier, Vermont, editor who wrote *The Green Mountain Boys* in 1839, a novel recounting tales of Ethan Allen. Daniel Thompson was a man whose interests in some ways paralleled mine; he was an author, a lawyer, a judge, a participant in abolitionist causes, and even a schoolteacher at one time. He worked hard for his education, and his biographer has described him as an ardent fisherman who wandered through the Vermont mountains taking notes for the books he would write.

When Orville Fisk returned from the Civil War, he brought with him a bad case of malaria from which he never completely recovered. Orville married Salome Bickford Richardson, a widow with two small sons, Elmer and James. (James was to be the first in the family to settle in the Far West; he went to Yakima, Washington, and later became Superintendent of Schools there.) The Fisks lived in Vermont for several years after their marriage, and then left in 1872 for Ottertail County, Minnesota, to establish a homestead under the veterans' land grant, near the little town of Maine. They crossed the Great Lakes en route, an experience which caused Grandmother Salome to vow she would never again set foot on any boat! Since she was carrying twins at the time, the experience was probably extremely traumatic.

Maine, Minnesota, is in the western part of the state, near Fergus Falls and Battle Lake, and not far from the North Dakota line. The countryside is rolling and wooded, dotted with small lakes. My grandparents cleared the land and established a fine working farm where they eventually grew a large crop of wheat. Orville Fisk became very active in local politics, serving as both county clerk and a member of the school board. He was a staunch, unregenerated Republican and, from all accounts, a man of few words. He died in 1885 at the age of forty-one; I never knew him.

I did know Salome Fisk, for she lived to be eighty, and died in 1912 when I was fourteen. She came west to Yakima to visit us while she was still in her seventies. I marveled at how one so small and slight could have plowed and harvested, raised six children, cooked for that household, fed the horses, milked the cows, put in a vegetable garden, cut firewood, and done all the other ranch chores she was responsible for when her husband was incapacitated by malaria. My life at times seemed hard, but whenever I started feeling sorry for myself, I thought of my grandmother and her burdens.

Orville and Salome Fisk had six children, including my mother Julia. The twins, Julia and Jennie, both grew up to marry ministers. Jennie married a Baptist, and Julia married a Presbyterian, my father, William Douglas.

The Douglas branch of my family was, thank goodness, no kin to the Stephen A. Douglas who beat Lincoln for the United States Senate in 1858 and who defended the continuing existence of slavery in the South.

My Douglases did not come to the United States until the 1890's. They had first settled at Alma, Pictou County, Nova Scotia, while Canada and the United States were still colonies. Father's grandfather, Colin Douglas, arrived with his family in 1773 on the famous ship *Hector*. The landing is memorialized by a statue in Pictou, showing a Scot in kilts, his hat at a rakish angle, his gun in his right hand, his left holding an ax on his shoulder, his powder horn hanging free.

On the *Hector* were some thirty-odd families—about one hundred and eighty people—all Highlanders. Of these passengers, all but one were Presbyterian. How that one survived the eleven-week sea voyage without being converted remains a mystery. But I always maintained that the Highlanders knew such discrimination back home that they practiced latitudinarianism abroad. In time sects multiplied, and even the Presbyterians became bifurcated. Those with conservative political leanings formed one church; the so-called liberals another.

Colin settled on the east side of Middle River, taking up a homestead that ran all the way from the river to the top of Green Hill some miles distant. It was pleasant, rolling country, with many heights of land that overlooked distant views of the Straits of Northumberland, where Pictou is located. Moose and Virginia deer were abundant and wild turkey too, and the waters were filled with salmon. Though the land is beautiful, with gentle hills, the soil is rocky and it would be hard even to scratch out a few potatoes from it. This place of my ancestors is very close to starvation land.

The first winter was an ordeal, provisions were in short supply, and there was no such thing as food reserves. So Colin and another man traveled forty miles to Truro, an earlier settlement, demanded a "lend-lease" arrangement, and returned to Pictou with the required food and other articles. They jokingly comment in Pictou today "and the Douglases have been stealing ever since." Not so. Colin returned to Truro after the next year's harvest and returned an amount of provisions equal to what he had taken.

By the second year a few broad fields had been cleared. The Frasers, McDonalds, and Rosses joined the growing town of Alma. In time, a church—Presbyterian, of course—was built and a one-room schoolhouse that covered eight grades. Apple trees were planted early in the nineteenth century, and some old gnarled monarchs are still standing on the thirty-five-acre tract where Father was born and which I later acquired. The family later kept sheep and dairy cows, and the Douglases remained agricultural people until Father's time.

Colin Douglas, the original settler, had two sons, John Alexander and Alexander. The former was the grandfather of John T. Douglas, who now lives in New Glasgow and is an enterprising contractor. Alexander, who was my grandfather, married Martha Archibald. My father, William, was their only child, since his mother died shortly after he was born. Alexander then married Elizabeth Ross, who gave him two more children, Lewis and Maude.

The tract of land owned by Alexander was a part of what is known as Green Hill—a long, low rounded hill that was cleared by hand and planted to gardens and to grass. Sheep and cattle and milk cows were raised, and by dint of the hardest kind of work, a living was eked out. This country was covered with hemlock and black spruce, decorated by stands of aspen and dotted with white birch. A pulp mill buys the wood these days, but there were few cash crops at the start.

By the time my father finished the Alma school, there was an academy in Pictou which gave the equivalent of a high school education. Father attended the academy. As a young man he was tall, with a high forehead, warm blue eyes, and a full beard. He was early caught up in church work and gained a reputation as an accomplished singing evangelist.

His half brother, Lewis, once told me that he felt Father had been a fool to leave Nova Scotia. "I attended his evangelical services and when the hat was passed you could hear the silver dropping." But Father wanted to be a Doctor of Divinity. Some Pictounians went to Scotland for that purpose, but by the 1890's, more and more were going to the States, and that is where Father headed. "The American migration from Nova Scotia took our best brains," Pictounians say to this day.

Father attended Rush and the Moody Bible Institute in Chicago, and was ordained a Presbyterian minister at Crockton, Minnesota, on April 6, 1898. His first regular pastorate was at Maine, Minnesota, where the Presbyterian Home Mission had a church and a parsonage. He had two other churches—at Maplewood and Battle Lake. Father served two congregations on Sunday and one on Thursday night, traveling to them by horse and buggy.

He arrived in Maine, Minnesota, for his field work in the ministry in 1895 and he married my mother, Julia Fisk, in 1896. Mother was a slight girl, about five feet four, weighing perhaps 110 pounds, with blue eyes and reddish-brown hair. She was musically talented and played the organ in the Maine church both before and after her marriage. Two children were born to my parents in Maine—my sister Martha, in 1897, and I, in 1898. My brother Art was born in California four years later. One's birthplace is like a shadow following wherever one goes. Once, when I was returning from an overseas trip, at four o'clock one morning a sleepy immigration officer asked me, "Where were you born?" My answer was, "Maine, Minnesota." He retorted, "Make up your mind, buddy. Them are two different states."

How Maine got its name, I do not know. It still flourishes, with a new Presbyterian church, a new Presbyterian parsonage, and a filling station, of course. Opposite the Presbyterian church is the little graveyard where my maternal grandparents lie. It was a Republican town then, and is now. Orville Fisk was the Republican town clerk, and it followed that my mother was Republican by birth. She took her politics seriously and was a party worker in Yakima, where I grew up.

My first consciousness of politics and political parties came in 1911 and 1912 while I was in my early teens, when the Republican party represented by Taft and the Bull Moose defection headed by Teddy Roosevelt were front-page news. Wilson was emerging as the Democrat, and I asked Mother about the contest. When we got into a discussion of the merits of the various parties, she made clear that her resolute commitment was to the Republicans. When I pressed her, she finally said that the Republicans represented the Rich, who hired the entire labor force. "If the Rich are disenchanted, then we are all unemployed" was her comment. I was hardly fourteen, but I knew the Rich who were the pillars of Yakima. I did not hate or despise them but I had no love or respect for them. They treated labor as scum; they controlled the police; some of them even had investments in Yakima's brothels. They went to church and were "godly" men; but I had nothing in common with them.

Mother felt differently; she was a faithful Republican watcher at the polls, making sure that no undeserving Democrat ever voted. I would chide her in good humor about it, but she was adamant in her philosophy that if we, the workers, wanted jobs, we must all vote for Republicans. Sixty years later—in 1972—I sat at a counter in a Washington, D.C., restaurant having a cup of coffee, and the waitress who served me told me the same thing. Mother had been upset when Wilson was elected; this waitress was overjoyed that Nixon won, for the Rich would stay in power and her job as a waitress would be secure. Even at the age of fourteen I did not buy that theory, and I soon became an ardent Wilson protagonist.

Mother was a robust Republican up to the day Franklin Roosevelt named me to the Supreme Court. She was living with Martha in Chicago at the time and came to Washington, D.C., when I took my oath. At a luncheon that day she announced, "You know, I think this man Roosevelt has got something to him after all." And when in 1940 many of us doubted the wisdom of FDR's running for a third term, Mother was clear. Of course he should run. Of course he would win. Mothers are indeed wonderful.

Mother died in 1941, and FDR sent a solid wheel of red roses to Yakima, where the funeral service was held. My little mother, who knew poverty in the Middle Eastern, African, and Latin-American sense of the word, would have been overcome with joy to think that any President—particularly FDR—would remember Julia Fisk Douglas.

My days in Maine were not many, for my father decided to move to California and warmer weather when I was only a few years old. Nova Scotia has long winters, but they are not nearly so cold as those in Minnesota, the Dakotas, and Montana. Nova Scotia weather may drop to zero occasionally, but the winter days are usually in the thirties. Winter in Minnesota bears down hard and stays a long while. California and its sunshine beckoned.

I was about three years old, but I left Minnesota with great sadness. I was greatly attached to Grandmother Fisk and I cried when we left her. I cried most of the way across the country in a dirty, rickety Pullman car. I remember vividly the moment the train pulled into San Francisco and we took the ferry to the city. That was my moment of greatest anguish and I recall it every time I enter San Francisco. The train had somehow become my link with Grandmother, and now that it was gone, the tie was broken. I was desolate and did not get over my sorrow for days.

I have only vague memories of Maine: sawdust pitched high around the foundation of our house for winter insulation, melting snow, the first new shoots of spring, an early yellow flower, and a black cat. I called the cat Black Me, childish shorthand for "It's black and it's mine." But polio—which I had while we still lived in Minnesota—laid me low at the age of about three. In my childish associations, I somehow blamed my polio on the cat, which I had loved but which I believed also betrayed me by proving unlucky. As a result, black cats became a bad omen for me. Years later I was deep in Australia, at Alice Springs. My Australian cobber, the late Bill Harney, and I were returning to our hotel from a barbecue on the fringe of town. On that dark spring night a black cat suddenly ran in front of us. To Bill Harney's amusement, we had to walk about eight blocks to keep from crossing that cat's path, for the pestiferous animal kept following us.

Father's pastorate in California was at Estrella, in San Luis Obispo County. Estrella is a small town not far from Paso Robles. It was warm in the winter and hot in summer, and the sun was so glaring that it soon affected Father's weak eyes. He had to spend hours each day in the dark cellar of the house, dictating sermons and letters to Mother, who was his faithful secretary. They had no typewriter; Mother wrote the dictation out in longhand, and many of Father's sermons were in her hand.

There was a public school at Estrella that agreed to take me in, though I was not yet old enough for the first grade. The day I walked into that school was one of the proudest days of my life.

Whenever I smell overripe bananas, a picture of the hot, shaded streets of Paso Robles where the family shopped comes to mind. As they shopped, I would wander among the fruit stands, which were permeated with the powerfully attractive banana aroma.

Another permanent love born in Estrella was for the dry, rolling hills dotted with oaks. They were brown in the high heat of the day but purple at sunset. They were moody, like people, and by Easter they were covered with a nap that was a most delicate shade of green. To this day, whenever I reach the Southern California coast and see its barren hills, I feel at home. This feeling of security is rooted in Estrella, where love cemented our home into an unconquerable castle.

It was in that home that I got the first beating of my life. When Father asked me to shut a door in the living room, I shook my head. He asked again. I still refused. Standing up and pointing at the door, he said, "Close it or I'll whip you." I refused to close the door. He grabbed me with one hand and a board with the other and let me have it. In the confusion that followed, I was rushed off to my bedroom—and the door was never closed.

The hot climate of Estrella was too severe for Father; so, after my brother Arthur was born, the family headed north to the state of Washington. En route to Father's new pastorate, we stopped in Yakima, the nearest small town, where Mother's sister Mae lived. It was my first glimpse of the town I was later to live in, leave, and in a sense, come back to.

That night a soft, warm southwest wind was blowing over the ridges of the Cascade Mountains. Spring was coming to the Yakima Valley. I felt it in the air. It was after midnight. The houses of Yakima were dark. The streets were pitch-black. Only the flickering streetlights marked the way. As we walked from the station, tired from the long train trip, Father was up ahead with the suitcases, walking with giant strides. Mother came next, with Arthur, a lad of a few months, in her arms. My sister and I brought up the rear.

There were strange noises from the trees and shrubs that we passed, creepy sounds from the grass and the irrigation ditch that ran along the sidewalk. I wondered if they were from snakes or lizards or the dread tarantula that I had been taught to fear in California. Maybe snakes were sticking out their forked tongues as they used to do under the steps of the house in Estrella. Maybe a tarantula would lie in wait and drop off a tree and get me when I passed. Maybe lizards in Yakima were giant lizards. And then there were the dread rattlesnakes that Mother spoke of with fear and trembling. Did they gulp young boys alive, like the snakes in the picture book that could swallow a whole sheep? Was the rustle in the grass the rustle of a rattler? These were alarming thoughts to a boy of five.

I looked anxiously over my shoulder. The trees and bushes with the strange noises in them seemed to take the form of monsters with long arms. I ran to catch up. Then, by the time I had once more looked furtively over my shoulder at the shapeless pursuing forms of the darkness, I discovered that I was far behind again. Why did Father walk so fast? And so, block after block, I alternately lagged behind and ran, fearful of being lost and swallowed up in the night or grabbed by some demon of the dark.

Father walked west from the Northern Pacific railroad station, up Yakima Avenue. At Fifth Avenue he turned north, looking in the darkness for the house where our relatives, the Pettits, lived. He apparently did not have their exact address, or having it, was not able to read the house numbers in the dark. He stopped several times to arouse a household, only to find he had picked the wrong place.

At one house he had hardly entered the yard before two great dogs came racing around opposite sides of the house, barking and snarling. I was frozen with fear, but Father did not hesitate. He continued on his way, speaking to the dogs in a voice that was firm and which, apparently, to the dogs as well as to me, seemed to have the authority of the highest law behind it. The dogs became silent and trotted out to investigate us. They circled and sniffed me, putting their noses right into my face. I can still feel their hot, stinking breath. They seemed to be awful monsters that had come to hold me for ransom. I wanted to scream. But the crisis quickly passed. Father was soon back. He dismissed the dogs with ease, resumed his search, and presently found the house we wanted. A friendly door soon closed on all the strange noises and on the dangers of the outer darkness.

The new pastorate was at Cleveland, Washington, located in the hills north of the Columbia River and not far from the present town of Roosevelt, in an area known as Horse Heaven, so named because of its good grass. This was not barren country dotted with oaks like Estrella; it was semi-wooded, with streaks of pine running out into the grasslands. There was good water for stock, and the altitude gave it the cooler climate which the doctors had recommended for Father.

Mother always felt that Cleveland was a healthy place in other ways too. The people were the most hospitable she and Father had known. They were wheat farmers and cattlemen, with large farms, running from six hundred to six thousand acres. Though the people were scattered over many square miles, they formed a compact community in spirit. They were neighborly folks. Perhaps it was the character of the people. Whatever the reason, they were friendly and cooperative. In time of need they came from all points to lend a hand, whether to raise a church or a barn, move a house, put out a fire, or dig a grave. Some of them were small and selfish men, but Mother said that most of them were God-fearing folk—honest, warm-hearted, humble, and dignified.

In 1904, when we lived in Cleveland, it was a lively village of a hundred or more inhabitants. There was a church and school, a post office, stores, and several boarding houses. A half-dozen miles to the south was a small settlement appropriately called Dot. Three miles to the east was the town of Bickleton. Father had the pastorate at each of these three places, riding to preach in each at least once a week, and preaching in two churches every Sunday, a physically arduous routine.

Bickleton is still a small, thriving trading center for farmers. Dot today is hardly identifiable. In those days it had only a church, a simple one-room building where father held a Thursday night service for people from the outlying ranches. His first service at Dot was disappointing, as only one man appeared. Father waited awhile but no one else showed up, so he opened the service with a prayer and a hymn. Then addressing the lone man in the audience, he said, "Since there are only two of us present, I wonder if I should continue the service or wait another week until word of my arrival gets around." The man arose and said, "Reverend Douglas, I'm not a preacher, only a cowboy. All I know is this: if I had forty horses and a load of hay and went out to feed them and could find only one horse, I don't think I'd let that one horse go hungry."

Father got the message and settled down to an hour-long sermon. When the service was over and he shook hands with the lone member of the audience at the front door, he asked, "How did it go?" The man replied, "Reverend Douglas, as I said, I'm only a cowboy. But if I had forty horses to feed and went out looking for them with a load of hay and found only one horse, I don't think I'd give the whole load to that one horse."

At Cleveland, I had as a teacher Mrs. McCurdy, who was one of the finest women I ever knew. In later years I used to visit her frequently, recalling the early days as we sat in the shade of an ancient yellow pine. On one of these visits, I met a lady who told me how disappointed she had been at my father's arrival in Cleveland. News of his coming was that he was a single man, so the young lady went out and had some captivating dresses made. To her consternation, she discovered that the new minister was married, had three children, and was very much in love with his wife.

Father liked Cleveland and enjoyed ministering to its citizens. There was no reason why he should not have thrived there, living a long and useful life. But the family was to lose him soon. In less than a year a strange accident took him away from us while he was in his forties and I was not yet six.

Father had stomach trouble—ulcers, the doctors said. In 1904 surgery was the only answer, though thirty years later other remedies might have been used. I remember the day he was carried from Cleveland to Portland, Oregon, for the operation. I also remember the day word came that he had died. The news brought a very special shock, because the operation had been successful and we had been told he would be back with us shortly.

Instead, he never returned. He was present one day and then he was gone forever. There would never be another to lift me high in the air, to squeeze my hand and give me masculine praise. There were no longer any pockets I could search for nuggets of maple sugar. The step in the hallway, the laugh, the jingle of coins in the pockets—these had gone as silently as the waters of the great Columbia. He never would return. At first I could not believe his absence was so complete.

Father died on August 12, 1904, at the North Pacific Sanitarium, Portland, Oregon. Mother wrote her own mother on the thirteenth: "He knew me yesterday morning. I asked him if he knew me. He tried to say yes. I said to him, 'Do you know me, dear?' and he spoke so I could understand him. 'Yes,' he said. I said, 'Do you feel better since I came?' and he said, 'Yes.' Oh, it is so hard. You don't know how lonesome it is without him."

Speaking of her children, she said, "I want to bring them up so they will be good children and do as much good in the world as Mr. D. did."

Mother cried intermittently for days and nights on end. She was crushed for years. We left Cleveland and settled in Yakima, not many miles away. The reasons we went there were several. First, we could not afford to return to Minnesota. Second, mother's older sister Mae, Mrs. A. C. Pettit, was in Yakima. Third, Father was to be buried there and Mother wanted to be near his grave.

It was at Father's funeral that Mount Adams made its deepest early impression on me. Indeed, that day it became a symbol of great importance. The service was held in Yakima. Inside the church it was dark and cool, and the minister's voice rolled around like an echo in a cavern. It was for me meaningless and melancholy. I longed to escape. I remember the relief I felt in walking out onto a dusty street in bright sunlight. There were horses and carriages; and then a long, slow trek to the cemetery. Dust, the smell of horses, and more dust filled my nostrils.

It was a young cemetery. The trees were saplings and there was only a little green grass. Dust seemed to be everywhere and I heard hard, dry lumps of dirt strike the casket. The cemetery became at once a place of desolation that I shunned for years. As I stood by the edge of the grave a wave of lonesomeness swept over me. Then I became afraid—afraid of being left alone, afraid because the grave held my defender and protector. These feelings were deepened by the realization that Mother was afraid and lonely too. My throat choked up and I started to cry. I remembered the words of the minister, who had said to me, "You must now be a man, sonny." I tried to steel myself and control my emotions.

Then I happened to see Mount Adams towering over us on the west. It was dark purple and white in the August day and its shoulders of basalt were heavy with glacial snow. It was a giant whose head touched the sky.

As I looked, I stopped sobbing. My eyes dried. Adams stood cool and calm, unperturbed by the event that had stirred us so deeply. Suddenly the mountain seemed to be a friend, a force for me to tie to, a symbol of stability and strength.

Father was one of the few truly good men I ever knew. Like St. Francis, he loved people and went humbly among them. Spiritual reward, not monetary gain, was his desire. His values were reflected strongly in the sermons which Mother preserved and which I read as a boy. His salary never amounted to more than six hundred dollars a year, though that was handsome by Nova Scotian standards, since in those days a schoolteacher in Pictou County earned only a hundred and fifty dollars a year.

The clergymen I came to know in Yakima after my father's death reflected neither immorality nor pretense. Their only vices, by my standards, were their mediocrity and the remoteness of their religion from life. There was, however, one exception—Dr. William D. Robinson, a Congregationalist. Once I went to a Sunday evening service he conducted, and was so attracted to the man, I found myself more and more in the Congregational Church, less frequently in the Presbyterian.

Robinson's appeal was in his application of the teachings of Christ to the problems of life—and in particular, to those of the Yakima Valley. The other preachers talked about "love" in the way the American Legion talked about "Americanism"; but when they came down to an earthly application, they seemed to be defenders of the status quo and against the rabble. The rabble were the hundreds of itinerant workers who came north with the sun, picked Yakima's fruit, and moved on to Canada's wheat harvest. Some were IWW's (Industrial Workers of the World); others were families traveling by jitney from valley to valley in pursuit of a livelihood. Dr. Robinson pricked the conscience of Yakima when he talked of them. The other local ministers treated them as scum. Vagrancy was a crime—how much of a crime, I was to discover years later.

In the early years my father and William D. Robinson were my heroes among the churchmen. They were to be joined later in my life by Bishop Bernard Sheil of Chicago, Rabbi Stephen Wise of New York, and A. Powell Davies, the Unitarian minister of Washington, D.C., whose papers I prepared for publication after his death. Bishop Sheil incurred ecclesiastical displeasure by carrying Christian concepts to the Catholic Youth Organization in Chicago's slums. He was removed from his post and relegated to a nonexistent bishopric in Asia Minor. Rabbi Wise, who started his career in Portland, Oregon, had the keen conscience and the thundering courage of the Prophets. These led him to search out the social injustice in his own neighborhood and rally public opinion behind reforms. Davies, the Unitarian, looked affluent Washingtonians in the eye and asked them from his pulpit what they were doing about *their* slums, *their* second-class citizens, *their* law-enforcement abuses, *their* own juvenile delinquents.

As I started to move around the world, I discovered that the Church —whatever creed or faith it espoused—was usually aligned with the Establishment. Few clergymen were relating the teachings of their church to the marketplace. There were exceptions. In Latin America, where the banks function exclusively for the benefit of the Establishment, I saw Maryknoll Fathers going about the job of creating credit unions and for the first time providing consumer credit at the village level, where the poor congregated. On the other hand, it was also in Latin America, in Ecuador, that I heard how a priest did in two UNESCO workers. They had come to advise the peasants on how to improve the plots of land they worked as serfs. To put an end to such "progress," the priest whispered that they were "communists." The villagers became aroused and one day closed in on the two UNESCO workers, who fled the mob and sought sanctuary in the church. They were killed at the altar.

In the Middle East, I saw the mullahs brigaded with the landlords to keep the serfs subdued. Moslem mullahs, like Christian clergy, assure the downtrodden that their rewards will come in the Hereafter—if they maintain an attitude of charity and meekness before the Establishment.

In India—where I could smell a village a mile distant before the marvelous village reconstruction program got under way—life was so filled with despair for the average person that the Hindu priests made a religion out of the renunciation of life.

In my early years in Afghanistan, I found an editor on trial for publishing an article whose theme was "It's time for the legislature to appropriate money for schools rather than for the church." The crime, of course, was "sacrilege"; but he was convicted only of "vagrancy."

In this country I saw most churches—Catholic, Quaker, and Unitarian excluded—regard mixtures of whites and Blacks in one spiritual community as a serious ecclesiastical faux pas. And I saw lawsuits started when it was proposed to lay an Indian or a Black alongside a Caucasian in a graveyard for that eternal sleep.

On Park Avenue, in New York, I heard sermons as unctuous as any pronouncement of John Foster Dulles. Their main import was to ease the consciences of the Establishment and to assure their members' entrance to the Heavenly City. Park Avenue churches were almost never concerned with the problems of the cancerous growth a few blocks to their north, in the ghettos of Harlem. How could they be? Those ghettos are tied into New York finance and the New York real estate Establishment, and all the building inspectors and police that those powerful people corrupt to keep illegality "legal."

My point of deepest depression about the Church came in Washington, D.C., at the United Presbyterian Church on a Communion Sunday. A well-known right-wing Republican came down the aisle as an usher, passing trays of wine and bread. I was seated on the aisle, and as he started one tray down my row, he whispered, "Imagine me sharing Communion with a rank New Dealer such as yourself."

Yakima churches mirrored world views when it came to the attitude of the clergy to social problems. Everyone was being prepared for the After Life. The Here and Now of existence was up to the individual. The Protestant ethic of hard work, frugality, and honesty would see one through.

These views changed somewhat with the coming of the Big Depression and mass unemployment. The manner in which everyone had become a victim of some Establishment became obvious to more and more people. The prosperity of recent years has seemed, however, to revive some of the old smugness, and by 1972 a majority apparently preferred a Billy Graham to a religion with a social conscience.

But for me the Protestant ethic, although still a part of my character, was never enough.

Chapter II

Childhood

When Father died he left Mother, three children, and $2,500 in life insurance. Mother spent $600 of that sum in building our five-room house in Yakima. The balance of the money was invested by Mother's lawyer, James O. Cull. He put it in an irrigation project in the Moxee area of the valley—a project of which he was a promoter. A lawyer who did such a thing today would be disbarred, for it violates basic fiduciary standards. The project was not fraudulent, but was highly speculative. It was designed to bring water to the dry sagebrush lands lying to the east of Yakima—a scheme later brought to fruition under a vast federal project that bears the name Roza. The project our money was in failed completely.

Soon after the Moxee debacle, James O. Cull went through bankruptcy. He was to me in those days the devil incarnate, for he was the start of all our woes. He caused us to start life penniless at 111 North Fifth Avenue. My brother Arthur, who was four years old at the time, later carried his full share of the family's responsibility, but it was my sister, Martha, age seven, and I, a year younger, who felt the brunt of this newly arrived poverty. It was the ten cents or fifteen cents that we brought home each evening that often meant the difference between dinner and no dinner.

As a boy I tended a few yards; I washed store windows; I swept out retail establishments in the early morning. In the summer, first Martha and I, and later Arthur, too, went into the lush berry patches in the valley and worked as pickers. Berries were followed by cherries, and cherries by apricots and peaches. They gave work opportunities that were golden and we exploited every possible hour to earn a dollar.

My proudest achievement was the day I picked four hundred pounds of a small black cherry called the Black Republican and earned the handsome sum of four dollars. I was fifteen then. My saddest day was when I was seven or eight and was discharged as a berry picker. We were in strawberries, my sister and I, and the farmer fired me because my boxes had berries so hurriedly picked they were mutilated. We were paid by the box, and I, interested in pennies, went in more for quantity than quality. That day I cried the whole way home.

The most grueling work for me was in the peach harvest. Peach fuzz set my skin aflame, and even one day's work picking peaches would give me a burning rash.

My small earnings in the winter months were gleaned largely from scouring alleys and garbage cans for burlap sacks which I sold at produce houses, or searching for scrap iron for which a junk dealer might pay a pittance. Years later, in Washington, D.C., I saw the junk collectors with their two-wheel carts slowly making their rounds in the early morning hours. They were usually Black men and I felt sorry for them, recalling my own experience.

Mother brought us up as Father would have wanted her to do. Our clothes were threadbare but we were neat and our shoes were polished. We were chastened without mercy if we showed any signs of dishonesty or tattling or cheating. We attended Sunday School at 9:00 A.M., church at 11:00 A.M., Epworth League at 5:00 P.M., and church again at 8:00 P.M. There was also Thursday evening prayer meeting that we never missed.

Mother had a keen sense of humor. That and her religious faith carried her through long years of severe poverty. There was a story she loved to tell about a woman who had arthritis for years. This woman saw an advertisement for a cathartic, say Pluto Water, and sent for some. After a week she wrote a testimonial to the company: "Before taking Pluto Water, I had been bedridden for years. Since taking Pluto Water, I've not been in bed for more than ten minutes at a time."

The local minister made a monthly call, and Mother in her best bib and tucker would serve him tea. We had only one rocking chair and one of its rockers had been broken, leaving only a short piece of wood. A robust person, bent on rocking, soon would find himself on his back. One day the minister got the rocker, and Mother, somewhat ashamed of our decrepit furniture, hesitated to warn him. But all of us were on edge the entire half-hour, holding our breaths as the divine rocked clear to the edge but never went over.

Mother, God rest her soul, was one of the most frightened persons I have known. She was afraid of the dark, of electrical storms, of the woods, of all wild animals, and of snakes. But her greatest dread was of bears. Where she acquired that phobia, I never knew. The only animal Mother felt comfortable with was a cow. She was adept at milking, and one winter she demonstrated her skill when an uncle, James Thompson, kept a cow in our woodshed.

It was Mother's fears that decided me to raise my own children without fear. They learned, I think, that the wilderness and all its inhabitants were to be worshipped, not feared. How Mother tolerated my later back-pack trips into the Cascades is a mystery. Every summer, starting at the age of eleven, I disappeared into the wilds of the Cascades for three weeks. Even I did not know where I was going. During those absences, Mother must have died a thousand deaths, and if the following letter is typical, the news I sent home was scant comfort:

Carlton Pass
Fish Lake
Wash.
Sun. July 11, 1915

Dear Mama and J.D.R. and Bill*

If the mosquitoes don't chew me up before I get them I will attempt to drop you a line. I would have phoned before but the line between Bumping Lake and Yak is down. We got to Bumping Lake Wed. morning. We would have got there sooner but the rain stopped us. There we left the wagon and packed our stuff on the horses to Fish Lake 15 miles above Bumping. I am now 75 miles from Yakima in the pines and freezing without a coat on. We started at Bumping at 2 p.m. Wednesday and traveled about 11 miles, when we came to the fork of two trails and went off on the wrong one and got lost. We wandered around until about

* J.D.R. was my nickname for Martha. She had a passion for new shiny ten-cent coins, which were made famous by the first John D. Rockefeller, who made a habit of handing them out to the poor. So Martha was given the nickname, at least by me and Art, of "J.D.R." I addressed by brother Art as Bill, because I liked him as much as I liked the name Bill, the name I would have liked to have been called instead of Orville. By the end of the next school year, my last in high school, I refused to answer anyone who called me Orville.

8 p.m. and struck the right one and went back to the fork. There we stayed out in the rain all night and got to Fish Lake Thursday—safe and sound. Now we are in a log cabin enjoying life and feeling good. Rich is going to Bumping tomorrow to get some supplies and will mail this letter. I did nothing today but lay around and read. The rest fished. We are planning to leave here Friday and get home Sunday p.m. about 3 o'clock. I do not want to but of course I can't boss them around. But the two fellows want to stay longer and start home one week from tomorrow getting home Wednesday. So if I am not home Sunday I probably won't be home till Wednesday. They don't know yet. I will try to get home Saturday or before so Bill can have camera and knapsack Sunday. It's cold up here. If you wear your plaid coat and mackinaw you will shiver. I haven't fished much. Only caught *1* fish but hoping for more. We are all right now. There is a telephone locked up in an iron box about ¼ mile down trail belonging to the ranger and if I can see him I will phone you.
Gee but I am *cold*. It is cloudy and a chilly wind is blowing. I am still looking for my bear, cougar and rattlesnake.* If I am not home Sunday or Saturday and if Bill is going on Y.M.C.A. camping trip let him borrow a camera from Ed Hill. He could if necessary get along without a knapsack. But I will try and get home one week from today.

Carnsarn those mosquitoes any way! ! When the mosquitoes get any larger up here they turn to meadow larks. I have climbed up to Carlton Pass 5947 ft. and am going up again to take some pictures. Well don't worry. I am safe and sound. Will be home soon. The country is fine here but it's cold. I haven't sweat yet. Am going to bed about 8:30. It's now 7 p.m.

So Long
Orville D.

Despite our troubles, the early years in Yakima were happy ones for our hard-working family. We had an old pump organ that Mother played, singing hymns and folk songs. Though dancing was taboo, and also all card games, checkers became our dish. Comic books were tolerated, but books that appealed to the prurient interests of a boy had to be seques-

* My emphasis in the letter on wild animals (which I never saw on this trip) and the cold of the wilderness was because bears, cougars, snakes, and coyotes were Mother's greatest fears and cold weather was in her estimation a major hazard of the woods.

tered in the woodshed. There were family taffy pulls in the kitchen, and church picnics and an occasional concert of sacred songs to attend.

There was a sunrise Easter service we never missed. It was held on the roof of the six-story Miller building, the highest one in town. Mother's contralto voice led the singing, and to this day the sight or smell of Easter lilies brings back memories of asphalt rooftops.

Though it was nip and tuck for Mother, feeding and clothing three children and setting enough aside to pay the real estate taxes, there was a camaraderie about the family that made it a real joint venture. Every new job—even the routine of the old ones—caused a sense of excitement, for each meant a conquest of a problem that might engulf us all. We never felt sorry for ourselves; we never felt underprivileged. Class distinctions were nonexistent in our eyes: we went to the same schools as the elite; we competed for grades with them and usually won. We went to the same church.

Because of our poverty, we did occasionally feel that we were born "on the wrong side of the railroad tracks." We had only a small tree at Christmas time and the Presbyterian Home Mission sent a Christmas box each year. It was filled with secondhand clothing which we resented. One year when I was in my teens a beautiful coat with a big patch on the right elbow arrived. I liked the coat, but my pride was too great to put it on.

Ever since then, Christmas has seemed to me to be a grubby occasion. For many it is the time to give "welfare" to the people, although welfare should be of concern 365 days a year. I always felt Christmas ought to be the special occasion for expressing one's admiration, respect, affection, or love for a particular person. A Christmas gift should be, I thought, a highly individual expression of interest or concern. An apple might serve the end. The ideal gift, however, would be one that the donor had created —like a book or a slingshot or something else resulting from his own efforts. Kloochman Rock near Yakima, that rises to a sheer height of eight hundred feet, has on its ledges a rare species of penstemon. One of these flowers—tenderly collected and carefully pressed—would make a Christmas gift unequaled.

As I look back, I feel that the patched coat that came from Philadelphia or New York was a perversion of Christmas. The donor gained merit by his generosity in disposing of his cast-off clothing. This charity was the beginning of the end of personal relations. It was a miniature of the foreign aid program of the United States in the post-World War II years —a project designed essentially for the welfare of the United States, as evidenced by the fact that out of every five dollars we advanced, we received four back in the form of interest, repayment of principal, or dollars expended here.

Whatever the merits of that patched coat, it transformed Christmas into something offensive to me. Christmas eventually became a virtual monopoly of the Establishment whereby retail sales mounted. It almost seemed as if it were the duty of all Americans—measured by the GNP—to give at Christmas freely and fully. It mattered not whether the gift was cigars, lingerie, neckties, or booze—so long as one spent money. As the years passed, I came to hate the holiday more and more.

I loved the advent of the chinook wind, which meant the arrival of the kite season. It was quite a hobby around town and a special one for Arthur and me. We made our own kites of thin strips of wood, glue, paper, and string. The golden age of kites was prior to the advent of power lines and telephone lines. Before they invaded the sacred precincts of North Fifth Avenue, we had few obstacles to clear. The locust trees were all young and we sailed kites with impunity. We even invented a glider and put it together with painstaking care. With this at one's back, one could, we thought, soar for hours over the Yakima Valley with the help of the chinook wind. That was our theory, and we convinced our older sister, Martha, who was much lighter than we, to be the test pilot. Her take-off was from the gable of an old shed. After much persuasion and a slight push she took off into outer space; but much to our chagrin she landed smack on the ground at our feet, smashing the glider to smithereens. A very mad Martha burst into tears.

Martha, a redhead, was very precocious but never athletic. She worked extremely hard from the time she was a small child. As I have said, she and I picked fruit in the orchards together, and she took on all sorts of jobs to support herself and the family. She worked her way through college, first Whitworth College in Spokane, Washington, and later, Whitman College in Walla-Walla. In time, Martha went into personnel work in large department stores in the East and Middle West; after reaching retirement age, she was retained to advise the stores on problems of the elderly, making herself a reputation as a geriatrician. Mother lived with her in her various posts, and Martha did not marry until some time after Mother's death in 1941. Very sadly, Martha's husband, Dale Bost, who was a well-to-do investment advisor, died only a few years later.

My younger brother Arthur was a brilliant extrovert. He and I were always extremely close friends and companions. Arthur was athletic, playing both football and tennis very well. He had, from the start, a knack for turning a penny. He always seemed to find a discount, whatever the purchase. Like me, he worked his way through Whitman College and Columbia Law School, and also practiced law in New York City. Arthur was the only one in the family who had the skill for making money; he began his career as a young lawyer with John Harlan in a large Wall Street firm, and eventually went from general counsel for the Statler Corporation to president of the entire Statler chain of hotels.

Despite his money and position, Arthur's loyalty to me remained unchanged: once a Douglas, always a Douglas. A few days after I issued a stay of execution in the Rosenberg case in 1953, Art was on the train he took daily from Scarsdale to New York City. Another commuter came down the aisle, and stopping at his seat, asked, "Is your name Douglas?"

My brother nodded, and the man said, "Are you the brother of the son-of-a-bitch who issued the stay of execution in the Rosenberg case?"

Arthur, always quick to defend any slur on the Douglas clan, got to his feet and asked, "What did you say?"

The man repeated the question. Arthur—a tall, broad-shouldered, powerful man—hit the stranger right in the mouth with a blow that would have felled an ox. The man went down and five of his teeth fell out. The contest over, a terribly contrite Arthur got down on the floor and helped his victim look for the teeth.

The stranger sued Arthur for $50,000—"$10,000 for each tooth," as Art put it. The case was eventually settled.

Arthur died prematurely in 1958 at fifty-six, about the time that Hilton acquired control of the Statler chain. He made a million dollars, all honestly. He left his wife, Florence Peebles Douglas, and three young daughters: Florence or "Fluff," who married a New York lawyer named John Persons and lives in Scarsdale; Nancy, a beautiful, sensitive dark-haired girl who grew up to get a Ph.D. and practice psychiatry in San Diego; and Mary, also beautiful, creative, and inventive, who got a master's degree in social work, married Peter Miller, and now practices psychiatry in Indiana. Arthur's death was a terrible loss to me, a loss which I still feel.

In the early years of the century when we first moved to Yakima, the land around town was mostly bleak sagebrush, occupied only by jackrabbits and rattlesnakes. With scant rainfall, the land had the semi-arid quality of a desert, and only with the gradual introduction of irrigation was the valley transformed into orchards and vegetable gardens. Hot, dry summers were common; there were many days of ninety-degree temperatures, and once in a while the thermometer went as high as a hundred and ten. The sun was then searing. I noticed it especially while picking cherries, thinning apples, or picking peaches. Sweat came profusely—sweat and orchard dust. But one was never soaked through, as the humidity was nil and evaporation very fast.

Though the sun was hot, the shade—where it existed—was cool. Art and I planted locust tree saplings in the front yard that eventually grew to magnificent proportions. The sweetish odor of locust blooms and the tantalizing scent of lilacs, like those that grew at the side of the house, still create a strong nostalgia.

Trees, once started, grew easily in town, for the Yakima officials, with a discerning look to the future, had brought two water systems to each lot. One system was for drinking, one for watering. The city also planted maples and locusts along all the public streets, and in time, these small seedlings became large enough to make Yakima an oasis of green.

In the early years, however, these trees were still small, and the relative lack of shade was offset only by the still unobstructed view of the mountains. With no trees to block the view, we could look west from our front porch on the outskirts of town and see thousands of sunsets over the Cascades—sunsets which tinged the dominant glaciers of Adams and Rainier with reds and golds as if some artist of Paul Bunyan-like proportions were using their ice fields as canvas. And on hot summer days I often looked longingly at both snow-capped peaks, imagining they were great ice cream sundaes, with vast tongues of creamy chocolate lava flowing down over vanilla ice cream.

But despite my fantasies, the heat remained uncomfortable. Night—usually a cool relief—sometimes failed to bring a breeze, and I'd toss for hours before falling asleep. This was, of course, long before air conditioning; and while electricity in time came to our home, we were too poor for electric fans. To Mother—who suffered greatly from the heat—even an electric light seemed to make a room hotter.

The sunshine and heat of the day brought rich rewards to the ranchers. On the average, the skies were clear of clouds two-thirds of the daylight hours when the fruit was growing—an average far above what either Virginia or New York can boast. The result was particularly pronounced in case of apples, which, thanks to pure sunshine, took on a remarkable color and taste.

The winters were usually open. But when an infrequent snow melted or when a rain came, there might be a freeze. Then the puddles in the dirt streets would turn into ice. While we had no skates, we improvised and would convert a sheet of ice twelve feet by three feet into a rink.

Not much snow ever came to Yakima, though occasionally we did have a foot or two. In anticipation, Martha, Art, and I pooled our resources and bought a sled. There were only a few hilly streets for coasting, so we got our rides by tying onto the bumpers of automobiles, undaunted by the exhaust fumes. Tragedy, however, awaited us. One evening my brother and I had hooked onto a car coming west by tossing our rope over the bumper and hanging onto the loose end. Everything went well until we came to North Fifth Avenue, where we lived. We cast off, but a knot in the rope caught on the bumper of the car, the sled was pulled out from under us, and in spite of our screams and shouts, our precious possession disappeared up West Yakima Avenue, never to be seen again.

The first automobile in Yakima did not have a gas engine. This first auto that I ever saw was a wood burner, a Stanley Steamer, and quite a thing for a boy to behold, especially on North Fifth Avenue, decidedly on the wrong side of the tracks. The driver wore a long "duster" that buttoned around his neck and reached his shoe tops. He wore a cap and huge sunglasses. The Steamer made a soft, pleasant hissing sound as it passed along our street.

For my own transportation, I saved my pennies for several years to get a bike and finally sent off to a mail-order house for one. When it arrived, I went to the freight office, uncrated the bicycle, and then walked it home. The problem was to ride it. Fifth Avenue was unpaved, and the sidewalks were rickety wooden ones. I was terribly embarrassed to be seen practicing. I had many spills, each time feeling humiliated. But soon I caught the knack of it, and once that happened, life had new dimensions. Now I could go with the wind—and I did.

We always had a vegetable garden, devoted mostly to potatoes, carrots, onions, parsnips, rutabagas, and, of course, pumpkins. The predominant place of root vegetables in our diet helped set, I suppose, eating habits and preferences for a lifetime.

Mother was a good cook. On meatless days she produced wonderful vegetable dishes; even the lowly rutabaga was transformed into a delicacy. She had a recipe for potatoes and peas, cooked in milk, which was exquisite, and her white layer cake with soft chocolate frosting was a joy. Of all her pies, mincemeat was probably the best. Mother would tell a story about an old lady in Minnesota who baked two pies—apple and mincemeat. For easy identification she made the mark TM in the dough covering the mincemeat pie—TM meaning "'Tis mince." She then put TM in the dough covering the apple pie—TM meaning "'Tain't mince."

In those days it was common to have several itinerants a week knock at the door and ask not for handouts but for a meal they would pay for by chopping wood, mowing the lawn, or washing the dishes. We used tail-end pieces of wood from the local mill, so the reduction of them was hardly worthy of a woodchopper. And our lawn was too small for a mowing rewarded by food. But Mother would occasionally feed one of these drifters, if he looked like a "good" man and did not have alcohol on his breath, and let him repay by washing the dishes.

There was a very kind man by the name of Krauss who lived opposite us. His eyes were warm and his mind was bright. He had humor, wit, and gentleness, but he was also a drunkard. What beset him, I do not know. At night I would often hear him coming up Fifth Avenue, singing and shouting in the pitch-darkness. "Demon rum," Mother would say. "Let that be a lesson to you." One night, when I heard Mr. Krauss singing, I went out to watch him. It was moonlight and I could see his figure weaving up the rough, uneven sidewalk. As he neared his house, he veered too far right and fell into a ditch that was part of our open irrigation system. Happily, since the ditch was filled with water, Krauss fell on his back; but unhappily, he got stuck there and could only holler. So I ran over, gave my alcoholic friend a hand, and helped him out. He never remembered my act of friendship. But real friends never keep strict accounts, anyway.

In Yakima, we grew our own pumpkin for Halloween, which was a very special occasion. As a prank, we took the wooden spool that thread comes on and cut notches in each rim. Using a nail as an axle, we would wind a cord around the spool, place it against a windowpane, and pull on the cord. The noise to the occupants of the house was terrifying. These were the days of portable wooden sidewalks, and on Halloween, children of the neighborhood made a community project of piling them in the middle of the street.

Our favorite Halloween target was the outhouse, and legend had it that the outhouse was a special target in Pictou, as well. An old Scot had had enough of pranks and one Halloween sat in his outhouse with shotgun across his knees waiting for the boys. When the children appeared, he frightened them terribly, but they begged him to get his fiddle and play some tunes. He allowed one child to go to his house and fetch the instrument. Exchanging the shotgun for the fiddle, he sat in his outhouse playing his best for an admiring audience. Then, as he reached a crescendo, over went the little structure with him inside.

Our backyard neighbor on Sixth Avenue was a man whom we disliked. He was small and wiry, and thoroughly obnoxious to us. We spent hours each Halloween in wait for him to leave his home and enter his outhouse. Once we heard the latch click, we would give one big heave and push it over with the door down, leaving him two possible exits. We met with success year after year. I did not understand the German he spoke, but I could tell the substance of the imprecations coming from the pushed-over little house.

The arrival of a sewer line was front-page news in Yakima. When finally a toilet and tub were installed in our house, we had arrived. No more nervous trips to the outhouse at night; no more scares for a young boy who had not yet learned to appreciate the beauty and wonder of the stillness of the night. The bathtub was a revolution, too. Prior to that time Mother heated water in a tub on the kitchen stove after dinner on Saturday night. She bathed first, then Martha and then Art. I always brought up the rear. Out of that experience grew two permanent habits: an aversion to bathing and a restriction of the habit to Saturday nights.

When electricity came to North Fifth Avenue, another new age unfolded. The smelly, smoky kerosene lamps with their weak yellow light passed into the technological limbo. Their greatest nuisance was during our nightly studies. We usually used the dining-room table for doing our homework, and frequently we had rows over the location of the lamp. With electricity, those quarrels ended, the overhead bulb serving each one equally. Now the house could be instantly lighted by moving a switch, as contrasted to the nervous lighting of a kerosene lamp in the dark. The exciting nights were finished, when Mother in her nightgown carried a kerosene lamp in her left hand and a butcher knife in her right as she tracked down nocturnal noises, looking for a prowler.

The Columbia Grade School was across the alley from our home. I attended it for eight years. And I went through the high school located some six blocks distant on South Seventh Avenue. They were excellent schools, so far as teachers and library facilities were concerned. I have been grateful, many times since then, that they were there to shape my early life.

Tom Pickering, one of my close friends in grade school, went to the same high school and the same college. He later was an official in the Morris Plan Bank in the New York City area. Another was Al Egley, who now runs a clothing store in Yakima. My long-term friends from grade school and high school days were not numerous. Elon Gilbert, orchardist, cattle breeder and specialist in Arabian horses, traveled much of the world with me. Doug Corpron, after twenty-five years of medical service in China, practiced medicine in Yakima—and still does. Roy Neilan is still a businessman in Yakima. Conrad Alexander, talented newsman who later worked on the *Wall Street Journal,* was also in this select group. Brad Emery, with whom I did most of my early back-packing, worked on the Yakima *Herald-Republic* to retirement, and then moved to California. We were both over sixty when I asked him to go on a reunion back-packing trip with me. He laughed and said, "I took my last hike with you when I was eighteen and have turned down every offer since. It's time someone else does the hiking."

Entertainment in Yakima was not common. Perhaps that is why we valued it so much. The circus, the county fair and an occasional vaudeville show became important counterpoints to the ordinary routine of daily life.

I remember a theater where occasional vaudeville teams and musicales appeared. At one of these, I saw an artist manipulate a concertina with great skill, and I vowed to make it one of my hobbies. I always wished I could play a musical instrument. I tried the organ and the piano as well as the concertina, but I didn't have it. Nothing came out through my fingers, to my great disappointment.

The coming of the circus was always an excitement and the love of the circus has continued throughout my life. To this day I look forward to circus time every spring. In Yakima, the large circus train usually arrived late at night; the animals were unloaded at the crack of dawn. Filled with a boy's eagerness and joy, I went down early to the yards. There were a few jobs for the first arrivals, and watering the elephants was the prize task. These elephants were mangy and forlorn compared with the wild species I saw in later years roaming the savannas of East Africa. But to me and my companions, the elephants were exotic creatures to behold and admire. We formed bucket brigades, and after filling up at a spigot, hurried as best we could to our assigned animal. An elephant seemed to suck one bucket dry in a jiffy, making us hurry to get a new supply of water. Occasionally the beast, after loading his snoot with water, would spray the donor, thoroughly dousing him. But that only added to the prestige of the job.

There were camels, too, and zebras. I had lingering doubts about the zebra's stripes, half convinced they were painted by man.

In Yakima, I always longed to ride a camel, but I never realized this ambition until I reached the Gobi Desert in Outer Mongolia in 1961. A decade earlier I had been a passenger on an elephant in India. But those were experiences I never could have foreseen during the poverty-ridden years in Yakima.

Yakima was a whistle stop for Presidential campaign trains, and one morning in 1912 there must have been several thousand of us waiting to greet Teddy Roosevelt, whose gleaming teeth, bushy mustache, and waving arms we had seen pictured many times. But when his train pulled in, it was an anticlimax; the charisma which we had expected was missing. There was no loudspeaker and only those in the front rows could hear what he said from the rear platform of the Pullman car. Voiceless, Roosevelt was no magnet, no charmer, and we went away disillusioned.

The county fair lasted a week, and farmers, housewives, merchants, and the forerunners of Future Farmers of America worked hard to display their handiwork, their crops, and their livestock. The county fair had side shows, and we got to know their personnel better than we ever knew the circus people. Year after year I found employment among these side shows, usually taking tickets at the Tunnel of Love, the Lady and the Tiger, or the Educated Horse. The latter was my favorite. I sometimes took to the stand and acted as the barker, extolling the virtues of the animal. This horse could "read, write, and do arithmetic." He would count by pawing a board a designated number of times. An attachment to his hoof held chalk with which he would make strokes on a slate, changing two plus two to four.

The barkers who sold snake oil were the most versatile and accomplished. Their spiels were works of art. Years later I tried to reconstruct them and recapture their magic, but time had made my memory of them too elusive to recall in detail.

One skillful concessionaire sold pieces of fried chicken and a small container of French fries. The chicken sizzled on a hot griddle. The concessionaire made it interesting for goggle-eyed youngsters. He was a bit of a ventriloquist and made the leg of a chicken or a breast cackle, whistle, and talk back to him. The odors of the food stands where chicken, hamburgers, popcorn, and coffee were vended were tantalizing. Even to this day, those odors, whether in Siberia or San Jose, California—both of which have outstanding fairs—bring back the memories of those early Yakima county fairs.

My favorite hero of the fair was the man who painted his face black and stuck his neck through a hole in a canvas, while a barker sold three baseballs for a dime to the public. The idea was to hit this man. One hit fetched a prize—a Kewpie doll or a lampshade. Two hits in a row produced a better prize. Three hits in a row won a cash prize. I saw my friend nicked once, but never squarely hit. One fall he returned wearing leather headgear, and when I asked him about it, he said that the sharpshooters were getting better.

Our conversation ended with his wry comment: "What a hell of a way to earn a living." To which I had no rejoinder.

An aura of tragedy enveloped the county fair the last time I worked there. A stunt flier appeared in an old-fashioned biplane. Aeronautical engineering was in its infancy and its products were primitive. This daring man climbed to a thousand feet and then plummeted to the ground, like a rock. Never before had death, as a physical reality, seemed so close to me.

The people of the side shows were a sad group who lived out of suitcases, had no homes, and were drifters on a lonely sea. But they were, I thought, fine people, and the magic which they brought to Yakima will always remain a bright memory.

Chapter III

Polio

There was a driving force that took me first to the foothills and then to the mountains, though I myself did not recognize it for what it was until years later. From the time I was about eleven years old I took every occasion to slip out of town for hikes into the foothills just above Yakima. The occasions were not frequent, for each day after school I delivered newspapers and on Saturdays I worked in stores, creameries, and cold-storage plants. In the summer months I worked in the packing houses and orchards at all the jobs that were available—thinning fruit, spraying, irrigating, picking, making boxes, packing fruit, icing and loading refrigerator cars. There was a regular sequence of fruit during the summer—cherries, apricots, peaches, pears, and apples. But there were gaps between the crops. And in the fall, winter, and spring, there were Sunday afternoons, holidays, and occasional evenings when I would have a few hours free to explore.

I would leave the town and head toward Selah Gap, the point of the hills nearest my home on North Fifth Avenue. There I would test my legs and lungs against the hillside. It was hard work: two miles at the fast pace of perhaps five or six miles an hour; the climb of a hillside five hundred feet or more in elevation; then a return to home and bed, dead tired, every muscle of my legs aching. Time and again I followed this routine, turning my back on more pleasant diversions that Yakima offered.

It was infantile paralysis that drove me to the outdoors. The disease

I had as a small child in Minnesota, and its aftereffects, haunted me for years. Before the vaccines were developed in 1953, polio was a crippling and deadly disease. The victims I later came to know were tragically affected by it. Among them were the daughter of a good friend in Yakima, young and beautiful Jennifer Gilbert, who died, for it affected her respiratory organs; and Franklin Roosevelt, the most prominent victim of those earlier days, whose legs became paralyzed. That was also how the disease affected me. Roosevelt caught polio in the 1920's when he was nearly forty; whereas I was only two or three years old when it struck me.

At the turn of the century, when I became sick, the medical profession knew little about polio. I ran a high fever for several weeks and for a long while my life seemed to be in danger. The country doctor who attended me was pessimistic. He thought I would lose the use of my legs, which I could not move, and predicted I would not live beyond forty. He had no remedy for the short life; his prescription for the legs was frequent massage in salt water, a prescription hardly improved upon by the medical profession even years later.

Mother kept a ceaseless vigil to maintain the routine the doctor had ordered. She soaked my legs in warm salt water and rubbed it into my pores, massaging each leg muscle every two hours, day after day, night after night. She did not go to bed for six weeks. The fever passed, but the massages continued for weeks thereafter.

I vaguely recall the ordeal. I lay in bed too weak to move. My legs felt like pipestems; they seemed almost detached, the property of someone else. They were so small and thin that one of Mother's hands could go clear around them. She would knead them like bread, pushing her hands up them and then down, up and down, up and down, until my skin was red and raw. But she would not stop because of that. She said she wanted me to be strong, to be able to run. She told me that when she was a girl she could run like the wind; no one could catch her. She wondered if I would ever be able to do so. And then she'd laugh and rub my legs—rub and rub and rub—and two hours later, rub some more.

One day when the doctor came, I sat on the edge of the bed. I could not stand alone. I reached for Mother's hand, pulled myself up, and stood there weak and unsteady. I tried to walk, but could not. I saw tears in Mother's eyes, and she and the doctor went away to have a whispered conversation.

The massages were continued. I lay in bed most of the time. Each day I tried to walk a bit. The weakness in my legs gradually disappeared.

My feet would flop a bit; the muscles of my knees would twitch; curious numb sensations would come and go. But before many months I relearned to walk, and the worst effects of the paralysis seemed to pass. Someone said that the salt water and massages had effected wonders. Mother was silent awhile and then said, "So did my prayers."

But the ordeal had left its scars. There were staggering obstacles ahead. An enervating weakness remained for years. I had no endurance in my legs. They tired easily, and when I exercised even mildly they would ache and twitch all night. I had no medical advice, no lay adviser, no confidant as I was growing up, who could allay some of the worries about my legs.

That, however, was only one of my problems. A more serious one, as time showed, was the great solicitude of my mother and her pampering of me. Afraid of the doctor's prediction about my life span, she set out to guard my health, to protect me against physical strains, to do all sorts of favors designed to save my energy. Though I worked at hard jobs from the time I was very young, at home I was waited on hand and foot. Worse than that, I began to hear what Mother was saying to others: "He's not as strong as other boys; he has to be careful what he does—you know, his legs were almost paralyzed."

This solicitude set up a severe reaction. It seemed to me I was being publicly recognized as a puny person—a weakling. Gradually there began to grow in me a great rebellion. I protested against Mother's descriptions of me. But I believe the protest, although partly against her, was mostly against the kind of person I thought I was coming to be. Yet, I was indeed spindly. Concentrated exercise, like sprinting or wrestling, made me feel faint; and sometimes I'd be sick at my stomach or get a severe headache. I was deeply sensitive about my condition and used many a stratagem to conceal my physical weakness.

The severest crisis, however, came when my own generation started snickering. That was a time when boys in their early teens wore knee breeches and black stockings. One day as I was en route to school, carrying a pile of books under one arm, a group of boys my age caught up with me. One of them, whom I did not know, commented jeeringly, "Look at that kid's skinny legs. Aren't they something? Did you ever see anything as funny?"

The others laughed; then a boy said, "Sure would cover them up if they were mine."

The words were a lash across my face. The laughter burned like an iron on my neck. I was humiliated and ashamed. I wanted to retort. But I trembled and my throat became dry, so I could not answer. Then, as quickly as a flash flood, came tears. As I turned away, it seemed to me that by crying I had not only confirmed but had proved the charge twice over.

I was depressed for weeks and months after that episode. I wanted to quit school and go into hiding. I begged Mother for long trousers, an idea which she pooh-poohed. I became a semi-recluse, staying indoors as much as possible. I felt ashamed of my appearance, becoming self-conscious and shy, quite irritable and sensitive to all criticism.

The idea that I was a weakling festered and grew in my mind. Had I had a wise adult counselor, it might have been dispelled; but I had no such perceptive confidant, no father. There was no one to whom I could express my inner turmoil and tension. So I grew inwardly more and more rebellious.

In retrospect, I see that this period is when I became a loner. Throughout my life I have enjoyed company but seldom sought it out. I preferred to eat lunch alone. I preferred to walk or exercise alone. I became a very lonely, introspective person. While I enjoyed select boyhood friends, I was not a bit gregarious. And that characteristic carried through all my life. I often went alone, even on the treacherous 250-mile crossing of the Himalaya in 1951, and on my long hike of the 2,100-mile Appalachian Trail from Vermont to Georgia in the early sixties.

But my rebellion, at twelve, had more immediate objectives. I decided to prove my superiority over my contemporaries in other ways. Even a boy with weak and puny legs can get straight A's, I said to myself. No one would excel me in school. So I threw myself into that endeavor, and came very close to making the perfect scholastic record which I had set as a goal.

Yet even this achievement was not enough. The physical world still loomed large in my mind, reinforced by what I had read in school about the Spartans of ancient Greece. They were rugged and hardy people, the kind that I aspired to be. As I searched out the literature that described their toughness, I found in Plato's *Republic* a passage that shattered my morale. Plato talked of the dangers to the race through propagation of the "inferior" type of person, those who were physical weaklings, or deformed; he recommended simply doing away with them.

It was oppressive to think that I would have been destroyed by the Spartans to make room for some hardier boy. For by boyhood standards,

I was still a cripple, unable to compete physically. I had read what happened to cripples in the wilds; the crippled deer or fawn or bird did not have much chance to survive its natural enemies the coyote, the hawk, the cat. Nature protected only the strongest and best, and man, including myself, was much the same, I thought. Only strong men could do the work of the world—operating trains, felling trees, digging ditches, managing farms. Only robust men could be heroes of a war.

By these standards, I was a failure. If I were to have happiness and success, I must get strong. And so I searched for ways and means to do it.

I got myself a set of barbells and practiced day after day, trying to strengthen my legs, back, and arm muscles. Even so, strenuous exercise still made me feel faint. Sometimes I would vomit, sometimes I'd get a severe headache. So I decided to start hiking the sagebrush hills that rim Yakima. That idea came to me from Kenneth Coonse, a strapping boy who had had a touch of TB. After his hospitalization his doctor had advised hiking to develop his lungs and legs.

After talking to Kenneth, I made an instant decision, one which made me feel much better. I, too, would make my legs strong. Thus I started my treks, and used the foothills as one uses weights or bars in a gymnasium. First I tried to go up them without stopping. When I conquered that, I tried to go up without a change of pace. When that was achieved, I practiced going up not only without a change of pace but whistling as I went.

I always went alone. The hills to the north of Yakima were only about two miles away. I often crossed the Yakima River on the Northern Pacific Railroad bridge (where later I was to spend much time with hoboes and Wobblies) and then went up the hill.

That fall and winter the exercise began to work a transformation in me. By the time the next spring arrived, I had found new confidence in myself. My legs were filling out. They were getting stronger. I could go the two miles to Selah Gap at a fast pace and often reach the top of the ridge without losing a step or reducing my speed. Following these hikes the muscles of my knees would twitch and make it difficult for me to sleep at night. But I felt an increasing flow of strength in my legs, and a growing sense of contentment in my heart.

Only years later did I learn that polio had taken its toll in another way, apparently infecting the lining of my heart. Dr. Bernard Lown of Harvard had discovered in the 1950's the Lown syndrome, and in 1968 my Washington doctors diagnosed that syndrome in me.

The Lown syndrome* in lay terms is the phenomenon whereby the heartbeat drops, say, to thirty-two when the normal beat should be sixty; then it suddenly races, say to a hundred and eighty to compensate, then drops back to sixty. This arrhythmic condition—seemingly traceable to an earlier virus infection, such as polio—presents no great problem in an age of drugs which can suppress excess heart activity. But as one gets older, the conversion back to sixty (my normal heartbeat) often presents problems, as when the heart skips a few beats or a whole series. The danger then is that when the heartbeat drops, the cycle will not straighten itself out.

Apparently my heartbeat had dropped to thirty-two all my life when I was asleep, presenting no problem and offering a refreshing slumber. But by the time I reached seventy, the Lown syndrome had appeared, and that is why a pacemaker was installed—a pacemaker that is set to keep the heartbeat from dropping below sixty. At first the press was filled with stories about my "heart condition." But my heart itself is basically healthy, and after the pacemaker, as before, there is no limit on my physical activities except age. Over the years I continued to hike wherever I happened to be—city, country, or mountains—and the habit of walking regularly probably contributed a great deal to my good condition. But from seventy on, my generation must take for granted that "all mountains are getting steeper."

I took my early hikes into the hills to try to strengthen my legs, but they were to strengthen me in subtler ways. As I came to be on intimate terms with the hills, I learned something of their geology and botany. I heard the Indian legends associated with them. I discovered many of their secrets. I learned that they were always clothed in garments of delicate hues, though they seemed to be barren; though they looked dead and monotonous, they teemed with life and had many moods.

It was a real ordeal for me to walk the hills in the dead of summer, for then they were parched and dry and offered no shade from the hot sun and no springs or creeks where thirst could be quenched. Then the rattlesnake seemed to thrive. But in the spring, fall, and winter, there were interesting places to explore; my walks then were more fun than ordeal.

When I tramped the foothills in dead of winter, the pulse of life on the

* The full name of the syndrome is the Lown-Ganong-Levine syndrome. There is a technical account of it in *V Circulation,* p. 693 (May 1952).

ridges was slow. The wind swept down from Mount Adams and Mount Rainier, cold and piercing, and I would find some black rimrock where I could sit, my back to the rock, protected from the wind, hoping the warmth of my sagebrush fire would not awaken a den of rattlers with the false message that spring had arrived. And when I turned around and started home, the same strong wind at my back made me feel as if the strength of giants was in me. I strode along the barren ridge with ease, commanding the city that lay at my feet.

Sometimes the chinook, the soft and balmy breeze from the west side of the Cascade Mountains, would blow. With the chinook came a light and gentle rain; and as it swept across this desert area it always carried the refreshing smell of dampened dust and the pungent but delicate odor of sage. Often I walked at night, when the chinook blew hardest and the outdoors always seemed most alive.

When I stretched out on the ground and listened, I could hear the cheatgrass singing softly in the wind. The sage, too, would join the symphony. The legend is that as the wind goes softly through the sage, it sings in memory of the Idaho Indians whose plains it covered as far as the eye could see and whose mountains it decorated far above the deep-snow line. And the verse of its song is always the same, "Shoshone, Shoshone."

I discovered, too, that if I looked carefully I could find a variety of wildflowers surprising in so arid an environment. I remember looking down one spring afternoon, fresh from the man-made gardens of the valley, and seeing at my feet among the sagebrush a scattering of delicate pink. It was the rock rose, or bitterroot, a gentle membrane that the Creator seemed to have fashioned from bare rock-dust simply to decorate desolate places. A low plant, with waxy pale-pink flowers ribbed in a darker hue, the bitterroot has a translucent quality that makes it look as fragile to the touch as the gossamer wings of a tropical butterfly. Its leaves, I later learned, dry and vanish when the flowers appear, and its blossoms open with the sun and close with the darkness.

But the bitterroot is sturdier than it looks, and useful as well as decorative. The plant was collected by Lewis at the mouth of the Lou Lou Fork of the Bitterroot River in Montana. Its roots are the spatlum known to Indians, explorers, and early settlers as valued food. They contain a rich supply of starch, slightly bitter, thence its name. I never see the bitterroot blooming among the sage without feeling that I should take off my hat and stand in adoration at the wondrous skill of the Creator. I'll always remember the words of the artist who said, "I have grown to feel that there is nothing more amazing about a personal God than there is about the blossoming of the gorgeous little bitterroot."

I do not envy those whose introduction to nature was lush meadows, lakes, and swamps where life abounds. The desert hills of Yakima had a poverty that sharpened perception. Even a minute violet quickens the heart when one has walked far or climbed high to find it. Where nature is more bountiful, even the tender bitterroot might go unnoticed. Yet when a lone plant is seen in bloom on scabland between batches of bunch grass and sage, it can transform the spot as completely as only a whole bank of flowers could do in a more lush environment. It is the old relationship between scarcity and value, one of the lessons which the foothills of Yakima taught me.

There are two early trips that stand out especially in my memory. One was in the coolness of early spring. I left town before dusk and climbed the barren ridge west of Selah Gap. On the way up I had crossed a draw and caught the sweet odor of the mock orange. In the darkness I could vaguely see the lone shrub that filled this draw with the fragrance of its blossoms. It stood six feet high, and in this barren ravine the delicacy of its fragrance seemed strangely out of place.

The night was clear and the moon had just reached this horizon. Mount Adams loomed in the west, "high-humped," as Lewis and Clark aptly described it when they saw it on April 2, 1806. Along the ridge of the Cascades to the north was Mount Rainier, cold, aloof, and forbidding. Below at my feet the lights of the town had come on, blinking like stars of a minor firmament. A faint streak of light, sparkling in the moonlight, marked the course of the Yakima River as it wound its way across the valley, through dark splotches of sumac, cottonwood, and willow.

Above the dark rim of the foothills were the stars of the universe. They were the same stars that saw these valleys and hills and mountains rise from the murk of the ocean, reaching for the sun. They saw the Columbia lava, hot and steaming, pour in molten form across this land again and again, scorching to cinders everything it touched, burying great ponderosa pine four and five feet thick under its deep folds, and filling the sky with smoke that finally drew a curtain over the sun. They saw a subtropical land touched by the chill of the Arctic and rimmed with ice and snow. They saw the mighty Columbia and the Yakima grow from driblets to minor drainage canals to great rivers. They saw the glaciers recede and floods come. After the floods they saw the emergence of a desert that some unseen hand had sown with fragrant sage and populated with coyotes, rabbits, kangaroo rats, sage hens, sage sparrows, desert sparrows, bluebirds, and doves. They saw the Indians first appear on the horizon to the north, spreading out to all parts of the continent in their long trek from Asia. And thousands of years later they saw some newcomers arrive, the ones that fought, quarreled, and loved, the ones that built houses and roads and planted orchards, the ones that erected spires and lifted their eyes to the sky in prayer.

I think it was that night that I got my first sense of Time. I began to appreciate some of the lessons that geology taught. In the great parade of events that this region unfolded, man was indeed insignificant. He appeared under this firmament only briefly and then disappeared. His transit was too short for geological time to measure.

As I walked the ridge that evening, I could hear the chinook on distant ridges before it reached me. Then it touched the sage at my feet and made it sing. It brushed my cheek, warm and soft. It ran its fingers through my hair and rippled away in the darkness. It was a friendly wind, friendly to man throughout time. It was beneficent, carrying rain to the desert. It was soft, bringing warmth to the body. It had almost magical qualities, for it need touch the snow only lightly to melt it.

It became for me that night a measure of the kindliness of the universe to man, a token of the hospitality that awaits man when he puts foot on this earth. It became for me a promise of the fullness of life to him who, instead of shaking his fist at the sky, looks to it for health and strength and courage.

That night I felt at peace. I felt that I was a part of the universe, a companion to the friendly chinook that brought the promise of life and adventure. That night, I think, there first came to me the germ of a philosophy of life: that man's best measure of the universe is in his hopes and his dreams, not his fears, that man is a part of a plan, only a fraction of which he, perhaps, can ever comprehend.

Another trip into those hills marked a turning point in my life. It was April and the valley below was in bloom, lush and content with fruit blossoms. Then came a sudden storm, splattering rain in the lower valley and shooting tongues of lightning along the ridges across from me. As the weather cleared, Adams and Rainier stood forth in power and beauty, monarchs to every peak in their range.

Away from town, in the opposite direction from its comforts, the backbone of the Cascades was clear against the western sky, the slopes and ravines dark blue in the afternoon sun. The distant ridges and canyons seemed soft and friendly. They appeared to hold untold mysteries and to contain solitude many times more profound than that of the barren ridge on which I stood. They offered streams and valleys and peaks to explore, snow fields and glaciers to conquer, wild animals to know. That afternoon I felt that the high mountains in the distance were extending to me an invitation to get acquainted with them, to tramp their trails and sleep in their high basins.

My heart filled with joy, for I knew I could accept the invitation. I would have legs and lungs equal to it.

Chapter IV

The Cascades

During the summer months of the following ten years I made many trips, usually of a week or two or even longer, into the Washington Cascades. On these treks I almost always had companions, my good friends Bradley Emery, Elon Gilbert, Douglas Corpron, or my brother Arthur. We usually went on foot, carrying our supplies on our backs.

In this way I hiked through much of the wild country between Mount Adams and Mount Rainier on the eastern slopes of the Cascades. I walked most of the trails, climbed most of the peaks, explored the ridges, fished or looked down into practically all of the numerous lakes, camped in dozens of the meadows, and sampled the trout in almost every stream in that vast watershed.

One of my earliest trips was into the beautiful Klickitat Meadows (Klickitat in Indian language means "galloping horse"; and if the word is repeated rapidly, it is easy to see why). This trip was more luxurious and more painful than most—luxurious because I had less to carry, painful because it involved my first mountain experience on horseback. As it turned out, the word "Klickitat" came to have special significance for me.

The plan was that I would meet my friends Elon and Horace Gilbert and their cousin Gilbert Peck near the top of Darling Mountain and we would proceed together from there to the meadows by horseback. Because I had to work, they were to leave a few days earlier than I, taking with them the horses and gear. I would catch up with their slower packtrain by hiking quickly.

On the Saturday in June when we were to meet, I left Yakima in the early morning. I went by stage to Tampico, twenty miles up the Ahtanum River, and walked the seven-mile dirt road to Soda Springs. Without the hindrance of a pack, I could keep an even pace of four or five miles an hour, taking long steps and feeling the stretching of muscles at the back of my knees. It was good to keep the rhythm of the walk, never losing for a second the cadence of the swinging pace.

In less than two hours I came to Soda Springs. Here, in a grove of pine and green grass, was a bubbling soda spring. I associated the term soda water with drugstore counters where sweet, cold drinks could be had, so I made at once for the spring in the grove. I found an old tin cup on the grass, dipped myself a full measure of the water, and started to gulp it down. It was bitter, sulfurous water which I spit out at once. "Medicine," I muttered in disgust, as it brought back unpleasant memories of the sulfur compound Mother concocted each spring.

I did not tarry long in the cool ponderosa grove. The easy part of the hike was behind me. I had about ten miles to go before I met Elon and the others, over a trail that climbed a few thousand feet quite sharply.

When I left the road at Soda Springs, I was at once in a deep forest that no ax had ever touched. Great yellow pine reached to the sky, one hundred, two hundred feet. This was the dry eastern slope of the Cascades. There was little underbrush; the woods were open, not dense. The sun came streaming in, as if it were pouring through long narrow windows high in a cathedral. The soft notes of some bird—a thrush, I believe—came floating down from the treetops. As I listened, it was as though the music came from another world.

I had not gone a quarter-mile when I felt the solitude of the mountains. I had been in them before, but this was the first time I had been alone. This was the first time I had felt the full impact of their quietness.

It was so silent I could almost hear my heart beat. No moving thing was in sight. The quiet was so deep that the breaking of a twig underfoot was startling. I was alone, yet I felt that dozens of animals must be aware of my presence and watching me—hawks, flycatchers, hummingbirds, camp robbers, bear, cougar, deer, porcupine, squirrels. Yet when I looked, I could see nothing but trees and sky.

Then I became aware of the fragrance of the trees. The ponderosa pine towered over all the others, and I began to see the scatterings of other conifers: black pine and whitebark pine, white and red fir, and the tamarack or larch. I stopped, looked up, and took a deep breath. Then I realized I was experiencing a great healing. In Yakima, I suffered from hay fever. Suddenly it was gone. My nose wasn't stuffy. My eyes were clearing. I breathed deeply of the fragrant air again and again, as I lifted my face to the treetops.

I had been hurrying, tense and strained. I was alone and on my own in unexplored land. I was conscious of being exposed to all the dangers of the woods, a prey for any predatory man. But now, strangely, that apprehension fell from me like ashes touched by a wind. I suddenly felt that these pine and fir that had greeted the early explorers were here to welcome me, too. These trees were friends—silent, dignified, and beneficent. They were kindly, like the chinook. They promised as much help and solace to me as had the sagebrush and lava rock of the foothills.

I felt peace spread over me. I was at ease in this unknown wilderness. I, who had never set foot on this particular trail, who had never crossed the high ridge where I was headed, felt at home. One who is among friends, I thought, had no need to be afraid.

It was about nine miles to Cultus Hole; the trail had an easy grade, and I do not think I took three hours to reach it. I stopped here to rest about noon and ate the sandwiches Mother had made for me that morning. The meadow was ablaze with wildflowers: blue lupine, red paintbrush, and splotches of yellows and other blues which I had not yet learned to recognize. I lay down on my stomach and drank deep of cold water running from unseen snowbanks in ravines somewhere above me. For two hours or so I had been in the deep woods, unable to see any horizon. Now I could tell where I was. Below me to the east the Ahtanum was beginning to drop away fast. The contour of an opposite ridge was starting to take shape. Ahead of me was a pitch of hillside that promised a stiff climb to the top.

The trail rose sharply in a series of short cutbacks. It wove around giant tamaracks that were standing on this ridge even before the First Congress met. Here were white-bark pine that knew America long before Jefferson sent Lewis and Clark on their explorations.

It was hard going and I took my time, stopping every dozen steps or so. It was perhaps a mile to the top, which I covered in about thirty minutes. I was ahead of time for the rendezvous.

This saddle on Mount Darling was partially open, with scattered clumps of trees. As a result, Mount Adams loomed up right in front of me before

I had gone far in a westerly direction. To its left was Mount Hood, to its right was Mount St. Helens. Stretching away to the northwest were the rugged Goat Rocks, their dark basalt cliffs streaked with snow. One comes upon this view so suddenly that it is breathtaking no matter how often he walks the trail. These snow-capped peaks are so close it seems they can be touched. They rise abruptly, tower high, and are incredibly majestic.

This day I sat on a rock waiting for my friends in something of a reverie, until suddenly I was aroused by the pounding of hoofs. They appeared in a rush, with whoops and hollers, on horseback and leading a horse for me. There were shouts of greetings, a short account of my trip, a description of plans that had been arranged, and then we were off.

I had driven horses in the orchards, and I had ridden workhorses bareback from field to barn, but I had never been in the saddle. I hardly had my feet in the stirrups and the reins in my hand before my friends were off for camp, four miles distant on the Klickitat Meadows.

They rode like madmen. There was no more holding my horse than turning the tide. He was not to be denied the companionship of the other horses or the prospect of early grazing in the lush meadows. The first half-mile led through willow and aspen and low-hanging fir. I lost my hat and almost my neck on overhanging branches.

On a swerve in the trail on a downhill pitch, I lost my stirrups. I regained them only to lose them, again and again. But I never let go the reins or the horn. I "pulled leather" all the way, with no control whatever of the horse.

It was a gentle downhill slope, which my horse took on a dead run. As he raced on and on in his mad way, I bounced to the rhythm of his pounding hoofs. He ran like a demon through a stand of giant tamarack and into a sizable grove of aspen. The leaves of the aspen trembled as if they were cymbals in the hands of some weird dancer. Those who had preceded us in earlier years had carved their initials and the dates of their journeys into the white bark of these trees. Those cuts had healed, leaving dark scars, and the scars, combined with the natural dark splotches on the trunks of the aspens, took fantastic forms. They formed faces—grotesque and distorted. They are leering at me, I thought. They are laughing—laughing at my bouncing. And as I raced by, tossed about in the saddle, the quivering of the leaves of the aspen, the laughter of their scarred trunks made it seem as if the trees themselves were twisting and weaving in some strange dance of a dervish.

My body beat the saddle incessantly as I bounced up and down, so hard I jarred my teeth, so hard I was constantly winded. I could not have yelled a command to the fleeing Indians had I been in earshot and had my life depended on it.

And then there was the pain in my legs. The legs that I had thought were getting strong and hardy had collapsed on me. Sick and puny? Legs like pipestems? Not as strong as other boys? Those were questions that pounded in my head. This was prophecy come true. The shooting pain in my legs was not imagination. No one was shouting at me derisively about them. Now my weakness appeared in a tangible form. In only a few minutes my legs had crumbled.

Through history books I had read of tyrants putting men on the rack for torture. Maybe this was it, the rack with all its promise of anguish fulfilled. I later learned that the hips, the knees, and the ankles are all springs which, when rightly used, make the saddle as comfortable as an armchair. But there was no coordination among the springs that day. Indeed, the springs were not functioning; they were out of order.

The hips were the first to go; they froze in excruciating pain. Each lunge of the horse made it seem as if the muscles in my hips were being torn asunder. I felt like a man who was being quartered. The pain shot down my leg to my knee. Knees and ankles ached under the hammering from the saddle. Each movement of the horse was like a knife thrust in my thigh. There was no relief. On and on we went, through patches of willow where the branches raced across my cheek, cutting hard into the skin.

On and on my horse raced, like a demon through a wilderness. Shortly we came to Coyote Creek, a yard or so wide with a dark lava bottom. He vaulted this as if he were winged, landed on the other side, and kept going at his terrible pace without missing a beat. He galloped recklessly through rock fields. Then he started to scrape the trees as if to be rid of his helpless, frightened rider.

The "whoas" had long ceased. I was silent and grim. For me the problem was one of survival. Leaving the horse safely by my own volition was out of the question. My legs were paralyzed. I could not have dismounted by myself had the horse been standing still. To fall under these pounding hoofs was a frightful thought, but even more frightful was the thought of losing face before my pals.

How I hung on I never knew, but hang on I did. It was not over twenty minutes, I suppose, though it seemed an eternity from the time we started until we reached the meadows. Then we shot through a grove of fir and were at the edge of a beautiful expanse of green grass, a half-mile wide and a mile and a half long. It's all over, I thought. I finally made it.

Not so. We were at the meadows, but off to the left I saw the disappearing tail of Elon's horse. The gang was heading for another camping place. So on we went, still at a dead run, for another half-mile. My anguish was only increased by the respite that had come so close but been denied.

At last I saw the camp. It was at the junction of Coyote Creek and the Little Klickitat near the lower end of the meadows. As my horse slowed to a trot and then to a walk, I became as nonchalant as I knew how. Easing him over to a high rock, I stepped gingerly out of the saddle. I stood there regaining my poise as we bantered back and forth. I was so lame I could hardly walk, and that lameness I could not conceal. But even cowboys limp, and my limping did not cause me to fall from grace.

My legs, however, ached and trembled. They seemed paralyzed, and I wondered if the old trouble had returned. The answer was not long coming. For I wiggled my toes and knew at once that I was all right.

Those worries were overshadowed by one that was even more serious. My posterior was in a most painful condition. I could not conceal it much longer. The four-mile gallop had worn raw spots on my buttocks—raw burning spots that clung to my trousers. I needed medical attention badly and I announced the fact. While my announcement produced great merriment, there was no ridicule. I was a casualty and some casualties were expected.

Off came my trousers for an inspection. The decision was that I was to lie on my stomach and receive medication. A large rock, as big as a grand piano, stood near the junction of the two creeks. On that rock I lay while my three youthful pals gleefully attended to my wounds and in due course patched me up in commendable style.

I remember that we had a wonderful supper that night. We also had a big campfire in the open grassy flat that lies in between the mouths of the Little Klickitat and Coyote Creek. There were delicacies from home, cookies and cake. Since the food had come by horseback, too, there was no stinting.

The sixteen-mile hike and the four-mile gallop had made me very hungry. I ate my fill and excused myself from kitchen duty that night, promising to do double duty the next day. I was sore and weary and tired beyond compare.

I put my bedroll down on the grass by the Little Klickitat, and as I slipped between the blankets, Elon came over to me. My friend was of slight build and not more than five feet six. His hair was brown, his eyes hazel. He always had a cheerful word for everyone, taking pains to see that his companions were comfortable, seeming to find joy in doing little things for his friends. Then his eyes would dance and a note of tenderness would come into his voice. This night he leaned down close to me and quietly said, "Say, fella, you're okay. You sure can go it the hard way."

I swallowed a lump in my throat and murmured thanks. Pride swelled in my heart as I lay for a moment looking at the myriad stars that hung so close to earth it seemed they could be touched. The Little Klickitat sang softly to me. I went to sleep triumphant. Those whose opinion I valued so highly had rendered their verdict.

The hikes which I shared with my brother Art helped to build a bond of respect and affection between us that was to last all our lives. Although he was the younger, we were fairly evenly matched in physical strength because it took me most of my teens to overcome the effects of polio.

One of our trips, when I was about sixteen and Art twelve, turned almost into an endurance contest before we got back home. We had been out for a week and were on the ridge of the Cascades, on what is now known as the Pacific Crest Trail. On this August morning it was slow going up a 450-foot pitch. The horseshoe packs that we carried on our backs weighed thirty pounds. Mine hung over my shoulder like a weight of lead, feeling twice as heavy as it really was, for I had not yet mastered the technique of the rest step, which is necessary if you are to make a steep grade with ease. Instead, I climbed the hard way. I suspect I practically lunged at the hillside; at least I went in spurts, taking a dozen steps or so and then stopping to pant. In this way Art and I took almost two hours to master the ridge.

As we climbed, the sweat welled up under our packs and rolled down our spines. I saw it dripping from Art's nose. Our shirts were wet through. When we stopped to get our breath, we bent over and leaned forward toward the hillside, silent and bowed like beasts of burden. We expected each small shelf we came upon to be the top, and we were completely exhausted by the time we reached the true one. There, beside a spring under an ancient western hemlock, we dropped our packs and rested. I was proud of my legs. They had given me no particular trouble.

Art and I lay perhaps a half-hour while we rested from the climb. Then we moved along to the west toward Dewey Lake. This was easier going; since there was no substantial gain or loss of elevation, a steady pace could be maintained. We stopped often, however, to pick the low-bush huckleberries, which were at their peak. We had been without sweets for a week and we craved the sugar in the berries.

As a result of the morning's slow pace, and our afternoon loitering, we decided to make camp a few miles short of where we had planned. We were drawn by the magic charm of a small shelf below us and we descended to explore it.

No more perfect place to camp on a clear August night could ever have been found. Here was a spring with clear, cold water. The shelf had a carpet made of alpine bunch grass, heather, and moss. Balsam fir, with its needlelike spires, rimmed its edge. There was a scattering of dry wood for a campfire. The western rim of the shelf dropped off a thousand feet or more in a steep incline to a tangle of wilderness. Mount Rainier rose over us. We commanded the whole scene as if we were on the spire of a cathedral. Here we threw off our packs.

We did not pitch the pup tent that night, as there were no trees on which to stretch the ridge rope. Luckily, there was no threat of inclement weather. We did not seek boughs for our bed; the meadow seemed soft enough for two tired lads of twelve and sixteen to rest. So we by-passed the chores of making camp, and simply cooked our evening meal. For supper, Art and I had oatmeal, scrambled eggs—tasteless because made out of powdered eggs—bread, and coffee and ended up gnawing on dried prunes for dessert.

The sun was setting when supper was over and dishes were done. I walked to the edge of the shelf to watch the last light leave the cold shoulders of Rainier. The mountain rose up, up, up, eight or nine thousand feet above me. Its eternal ice fields looked down, threatening and ominous because of their nearness. The great dark shoulders of lava rock that crop out among its ice and snow stood stark and naked in all their detail —mightier than any fortress, bigger than any dam or monument that the hands of man could erect.

Alongside that view I always feel as if I were no more than the pint of ashes to which some day every man will be reduced. That dust, scattered on the gargantuan shoulders of Rainier would be as insignificant as a handful of sand in an endless ocean.

It is easy to see the delicate handiwork of the Creator in any meadow. But perhaps it takes these startling views to remind us of His omnipotence, to make us realize that vain, cocky, aggressive, selfish man never conquers the mountains in spite of all his boasting and bustling and exertion. He conquers only himself.

By the time we turned in, the wind was blowing on us from the ice and snow fields in the distance. The sun, which had sprayed these glaciers with the colors of the spectrum, had now set. Rainier stood alone in silhouette, bleak and gray in the dusk. The mood of the mountain took hold of me.

I slept fitfully. I had thought my legs stood up well during the day, but now they twitched behind the knees. Moreover, the wind never died, and our bed was drafty no matter how we arranged the blankets. During the dark hours I sat up a dozen times, tucking them in. Each time before I settled down again, I looked once more at Rainier—a sentinel of the night, a mother watching her brood.

We were up at the first streak of dawn. Within the hour we had breakfast: more prunes (which we had put to soak the night before), more oatmeal, more tasteless scrambled eggs, and thick pancake bread, which we washed down with strong black coffee. In less than an hour, camp was broken, the coals of the fire were out, and we were ready for the rest of the trip to Dewey Lake.

Before we started, we sat down to study our contour map. We were in new terrain and we wanted to be certain we did not get off onto false trails. As we studied the map, we noticed that we might save half a day by using a certain shortcut, and so we decided to take it, even though it meant leaving the easier trail and beating through several miles of trackless forest.

The first part of the descent was gentle. After that, it became more precipitous. You quickly learn that carrying a heavy pack can make going down a mountain more dangerous than going up. A man with a pack on his back is like a horse with a rider—he has an element of imbalance that must be reckoned with in every step. Momentum is easy to gain, and hard to lose. Loss of balance even for a second can spell disaster. Moreover, two or more men working their way off trail down a steep mountainside owe a special obligation to keep either bunched together or widely scattered so that rocks loosened by one will not come pounding down to kill or maim the other. Even a sprained ankle might be a calamity when one has only limited food supplies and is several days from civilization.

Art and I had slippery pine grass under us for about the first five hundred yards, and so we went slowly, digging our heels in at every step. Below us was a yawning pit, heavily wooded, with occasional outcroppings of basalt. For several hundred feet we worked our way through shale rock and around cliffs. After that, there was a field of boulders to cross, great rocks perhaps loosened by frost from some crag high above;

and after that, gentler slopes on which we could make faster progress. All the way down we saw many fresh bear tracks, deer prints, and the mark of porcupines.

Presently we heard the murmur of the stream that ran down the ravine to the Rainier Fork of the American River. We made our way to it over downed timber and through a thick stand of fir. There on a spit of sand we threw down our packs, lay on our stomachs, put our faces into the clear, cool water, and drank like young animals. It was a fast-water creek running over rocks into clear pools. We sat on the sand bar, resting and listening to the murmur of the stream. A light wind was in the treetops, making them sway and sing. All else was quiet.

Opposite us, on the other bank, was a great mass of Canada dogwood, or bunchberry, a plant only six inches high, with creamy flowers. It covered the bank thickly, as ivy does. Mixed with the dogwood was a scattering of pure white alpine beauty, a fragile ladylike flower with thin, soft leaves. The two flowers together made the stream a place of enchantment. The reward of our descent was already great. The loveliness of these flowers and alpine beauty had filled the canyon for centuries. Yet we were probably the first humans ever to enjoy it.

This was the unexplored wilderness—no roads, no trails, no blazes, no signs. This was domain even far off the beaten path of Indians. This forest was primeval, untouched, unseen. Trees fell, and in a generation or more were turned into duff. New trees sprang from fallen seed, reached with their thin tips through a colonnade of evergreens for a slit in the sky, pushed lesser trees aside, and in time were reclaimed, as man is reclaimed, by Mother Earth.

A trail, like a road, brings a sense of ease and relaxation. Men have passed by here before, one says, so all is well. But a journey on foot through the untrodden wilderness brings different impressions. Man is now on his own. No one has gone ahead. This is new, untouched domain, full of hazards. On this trip Art and I had looked for some visible sign of danger—a bear coming through the brush, a cougar slinking along the creek bottom, a bobcat lying watchfully on an overhanging limb, even a porcupine waddling up a hill. But we heard or saw nothing but pine squirrels and chipmunks. The unexplored wilderness, as usual, held no danger but the traveler's apprehension.

I think I captured, that August morning in this unchartered canyon, some of the feeling that Daniel Boone, Lewis and Clark, Jim Bridger, and other early travelers must have had in their explorations beyond the frontier. Under those circumstances man walks quietly, his nerve ends alert to pick up even slight warnings. In that environment he returns to primitive man, who stealthily walked the ridges and traversed the canyons, who hunted and was hunted, and yet survived all others to rule the universe.

We did not tarry long at the creek, but pushed on rapidly, avoiding thick brush and working our way down to the junction of Rainier Fork. We reached that point two hours after leaving the top; and in another hour we found the place where Morse Creek joins the American River. We crossed it and shortly came to the trail that led down to the Naches to home, though we still had more than seventy miles to go.

While Art and I were eating lunch at the place where we rejoined the trail, I made a secret resolution which was quite unfair to him. I had been thinking about my legs. I knew they were improving; the day before, apart from the twitching of the muscles, they had stood up well under the pull out of Fish Lake. I was stronger each summer. But how much stronger? I wondered.

As I studied the contour map I estimated we had come about ten miles that morning. I knew there was an excellent campground at Indian Flat, a good fourteen or fifteen miles away, and my resolution was that we would camp at Indian Flat that night.

"We must get going if we are to make camp by dark," I said to Art, without telling him what I had determined to do.

It was about two o'clock when we headed down the American River on the Normile Grade. It was not water-level travel all the way; there were ups and downs. But it was an old, narrow miners' road, easy by mountain standards. We had good footgear: thick socks, closefitting shoes more than ankle-high, and hobnails. I set the pace at five miles an hour—a fast one even without a pack.

How long I maintained that pace I do not know, probably not many minutes. The muscles along my shinbones set up a protest. There was a caustic tone in Art's words "Where's the fire?" The pace soon slackened to perhaps three miles an hour. But once that speed was set, I tried to hold it all afternoon. We walked until dusk with no interruptions except for stops to drink at pools along the river. The pace was steady; we never relaxed even for a moment.

It was a long and weary trail, and dusty too. Fine particles rose with every step and eventually sifted through all our clothes and filled our nostrils. There was no breeze; the sun had baked all moisture out of the hillside and it bore down on us, hotter and more stifling as we worked steadily down to lower elevations. All conversation ended. I could hear only the roar of the river, our footsteps, the rattle and clanging of the utensils tied on our packs. Mile after mile we trudged, looking neither right nor left, alert not to lose by some careless step the rhythm of our long stride. I was in the lead; Art kept close on my heels. We had gone about six miles when we came to Pleasant Valley—an excellent camp.

"Why isn't this okay?" Art asked.

"There's a better one down the line," I said.

So we swung through Pleasant Valley without breaking our walk. Then he inquired how much farther we had to go that day. I was noncommittal. After another half-mile he asked again. When I dodged a reply, he pressed me.

"Just a few miles," I answered. As we trudged on, the inquiry "How much longer?" became more frequent, the tone of his voice more dissatisfied.

I knew how he felt. A great weariness had overtaken me too. But I had made my resolution, and for me it was do or die. My light-hearted responses to his constant question concealed my own feelings. I too was exhausted, and it took self-control not to be curt and sharp.

By late afternoon the questions had ceased; we now had a second or third wind and were traveling on some hitherto undiscovered sources of energy. The pack was hanging more heavily than ever on my shoulders. A numbness began to creep through my back muscles, as if they had received a light injection of some anesthetic. As the shadows in the valley lengthened I walked like an automaton. My legs seemed more like stilts than part of me; they were almost without feeling. And my feet seemed weighted down by heavy clogs.

I remembered, as we pushed along, a chapter in one of Cooper's books. It told of the pursuit of a frontiersman by Indians: how he kept his pace all through the heat of the day, and finally, by sheer endurance, eluded his pursuers in the dusk. My pursuers were the lengthening shadows. By dark I would be encompassed, and there would be no escape because of my fatigue.

The pace continued to be a frightful one, though actually it may have dropped to a slow walk. The shin muscles of my legs were aching like a tooth with an exposed nerve. A small pain commenced above my eyes, and soon the pounding of my heels echoed in my head. I longed to stop and rest; I wanted to sleep and never move until the next day. But I pushed on.

After a while my legs and head became impersonal objects, like things belonging to someone else. So I went on, my eyes on the trail, my head down. I was almost unaware of my surroundings. On and on, mile after mile.

At the junction of American and Bumping rivers we struck the dirt road. One more mile to our camp.

"How about here?" said a tired voice in the rear.

"Not yet," I said.

On we went, until at dusk Indian Flat loomed up as if out of a dream. We dropped our packs and lay on them, exhausted, until we were aroused by a tantalizing smell—bacon, flavored with wood smoke. Another party was making camp across the meadow.

It was dark by the time fir boughs were gathered for our beds and wood collected for the fire. We were far too tired to spend much time in cooking, though normally we'd have caught a mess of trout for the frying pan. We were tempted to beg a meal from our neighbors, but pride or some standard of independence was a barrier. Because we carried only light rations, our supper was frugal: only the usual oatmeal, pancake bread, and dried prunes. The smell of our neighbor's bacon almost made our own food unpalatable—and worse, the oatmeal was burned.

I woke with a splitting headache. I lay for an hour, hoping it would cease, but it continued unabated. When I got up and walked about, I felt sick to my stomach. The exertion of the day before had contributed to my suffering, but the headache must have been compounded by inner tensions. Dreams vaguely horrible had occupied me in my sleep. All night I had seemed to be hunted by some evil pursuers. There were boys my age peering at me and taunting me, and older people watching and nodding their approval. I would almost escape the scene, and then these pursuers would catch up with me—and I would be too weak in the knees to get away.

I lay down on my fir-bough bed, too ill to move. Soon my brother, whose spirits I had sustained the day before, awakened. Even as a youth he was tall and rangy, headed for six feet or more. His legs were long and agile. This morning his light brown, almost reddish hair was in a tangled mass. He had slept long and hard and now was refreshed and hungry as a bear. I was secretly proud of his performance and envious of his strength. Art had outdone me.

He cooked himself a big breakfast, did the dishes, and put the beans to boil. I did not feel like eating. The only food I wanted was soup. That's it, tomato soup, I thought. My longing for soup was so acute, it became an obsession. We had no soup of any kind. I asked my brother if he would try to borrow some from the neighbors.

Art disappeared, and was gone an interminable time. I was at first annoyed at his delay, and then anxious for him. An hour later he arrived, breathless and excited, and told me he had been chased by a bull.

"What did you do?" I asked.

"I went up a tree," he said. "That's where I've been all this time." His blue eyes glistened in his excitement.

"And the soup?"

Triumphantly he pulled out from under his shirt a can of tomato soup. As he heated it, he told me of the bull that chased him: the roar of the beast, the quivering nostrils, the horns, the red eyes, the pawing hoofs. Art's description was so vivid that I, too, could see the flames coming out of the monster's nose.

I drank the soup—every drop of it. And having drunk it, I fell asleep. I woke at noon, hungry for beans and heavy food, ready to push on, refreshed, and neither stiff nor sore.

Though in later years I hiked mountain trails with a pack up to forty miles a day, this one day I had walked twenty-five miles with a thirty-pound pack. My legs had stood up. I had conquered my doubts. I knew that I was now free to roam these mountains at will, to go on foot where any man could go, to enter any forest without hesitation.

Chapter V

Coming of Age in Yakima

My love of the mountains, my interest in conservation, my longing for the wilderness—all these were lifetime concerns that were established in my boyhood in the hills around Yakima and in the mountains to the west of it.

Of course, it was not only the natural surroundings of Yakima which influenced me, although my fellow townsmen sometimes denied responsibility for me. When I was named to the Supreme Court by President Franklin D. Roosevelt in 1939, the Yakima *Daily Republic* wrote an editorial entitled "Yakima Not to Blame." The editorial first praised the local schools and their superintendent, A. C. Davis, a very superior man. Next it listed the roll of teachers one by one under whom I had studied, and said good things about each. Finally it stated that if I were judged solely by the education I had received in Yakima, I would have in me nothing but pure strains of Americanism. But alas, noted the writer, I had developed symptoms of strange *isms* that were not compatible with Americanism. Where I got infected with these *isms* was not known; perhaps in Washington, D.C. The conclusion was, "We want to go on record as saying that Yakima is not to blame."

The *Daily Republic* was owned by W. W. Robertson, a most reactionary man. The editorial was written by N. K. Buck, one-time police judge and later mayor. Buck wrote editorials and small news items for Robertson, and their styles were remarkably similar. But this column about me was written with particular verve and feeling, for Buck disagreed violently with what he thought were my political and constitutional views. The piece delighted me no end, and I foolishly carried it in my wallet for so long that it finally crumbled away. Unfortunately, someone destroyed that entire edition of the paper after a few hundred copies were run off, and apparently no copies are extant.

The conclusion of the editorial was humorous, but wrong. The Yakima system was in large measure responsible for the kind of person that I became, in the sense that its teachers were quickening influences that helped me see the dimensions of the world of that day. In the Columbia Grade School, under Grace Shrader and Pearl Hibarger, I first became aware of the beauty and power of words. They read poetry and made it musical. They read prose and brought to it magical qualities. We were much too young then to learn how to put prose or poetry to effective use ourselves, but life acquired new dimensions when the dictionary became an instrument of conquest and we discovered how to appreciate the words of others.

Louise DeGraff, in my eighth grade, taught American history with emphasis on the economic system. We did not learn much about depreciation or depletion or the relation of wages to profits. But we got some glimmering of the problems of costs and profits and the historic place of business in the American scheme. Miss DeGraff neither made business a graven image to worship nor did she make us think it was suspect. Rather, she taught what business was and some basic things about its anatomy and how it had helped shape the American destiny. I was to learn about the robber barons later. Under Louise DeGraff, I made my first distillation of facts; and from her I received, I think, my first lesson in the nice distinction between the relevant and the irrelevant in any analysis.

Yakima High School, which I entered in the fall of 1912, was a joy. A. C. Davis was then principal; Susan Anthon (later a columnist for the Yakima *Daily Republic*) taught botany; C. A. Palmer, physics; Lucille James and Elizabeth Pryor, English; Lillian Wheeler, Latin; and Rose M. Boening, history. As a newspaperwoman, Susan Anthon came to represent a conventional point of view, yet she pleasantly tolerated me in later years. As a teacher, she introduced me to a new world of flora, where I discovered that many flowers, trees, and shrubs of the Pacific Northwest had marched all the way from Asia to become established here. From Mr. Palmer we learned about some of the phenomena of physics in our daily lives. From Lucille James, I acquired a love of Latin and gained such proficiency that I could converse or orate in that tongue by the time I was a senior.

From her also, and from Elizabeth Pryor, I discovered great tides of history in our literature and learned something of their meaning.

Miss Pryor also taught public speaking and debate; in retrospect, I marvel at her ability to take a slightly crippled, nervous, frightened young man and give him poise and stage presence. I became such an excellent orator under her tutelage that I was selected for the school finals in my sophomore year. I had a beautiful oration and I practiced it to perfection. When the big night arrived, I walked onto the platform with the two other contestants, sure of victory. The others spoke first, increasing my confidence. But as I was being introduced, my mind went blank. I could remember only the first sentence of my speech. I stood in the spotlight, saying it over and over again, each time with more emphasis. The rest was utterly gone. I had learned to speak only from memory, not yet knowing how to extemporize. After what seemed an eternity, I gave up, tears welling to my eyes. I left the platform in utter humiliation, disappeared into the darkness of the night and did not return home for hours. By the end of another year, however, Elizabeth Pryor had not only restored my confidence but also introduced me to the rough and tumble of debate—a contest that I greatly enjoyed.

Lillian Wheeler and Rose M. Boening were also inspirations. Miss Wheeler made Latin a thing of beauty, and she tidied up our minds, making perfectionists of us. Miss Boening, in history, emphasized not *what* happened but *why* it happened. She made the question *why*? ring in our ears. America now turned on a different axis for me, as ambition, greed, self-sacrifice, lust for power, face-saving, all these and many more motives gave new dimensions to the history in our texts. Years later I was to discover Thorstein Veblen and John Dewey, Underhill Moore and Karl Llewellyn at Columbia, Robert M. Hutchins, Thurman Arnold, and Charles E. Clark at Yale, asking the same questions about law. I have always thought that Miss Boening of Yakima started my bent toward what was later dubbed "sociological jurisprudence."

Mr. Palmer, the physics teacher, coached track as well. By the time I was a junior, my slightly impaired physical condition had pretty well gone, so I went out for track. I chose the mile run as my specialty. I never came in better than third and I never quite broke five minutes. Years later Paavo Nurmi of Finland became my hero when he set the world's mark at 4:10:4. Once when I was in Helsinki, I walked the city over trying to locate him to express my admiration, but I never did meet up with him. When Roger Bannister of England broke the four-minute barrier in 1954, I was amazed. When in 1962 Peter Snell of New Zealand ran it in 3:54.4, I was dumbfounded. And when in 1967 Jim Ryun lowered the outdoor mile to 3:51.1, I gave up wondering. My own five-minute time was to me the outer limit of endurance.

Another powerful force in my high school days was Tony Savage—football and basketball coach. I was too skinny for the former sport, but I had fair success as a basketball center. Tony, who was a hero just out of the University of Washington, became a god to us. He was kind but outspoken, quick to criticize and slow to praise. His tap on the back that meant "well done" was a tremendous reward. His quick, soft reprimand could be crushing. I never felt the full force of it, though my pal Elon Gilbert did. Elon was a quarterback, and try as he did, he never could satisfy Tony. In desperation Tony took Elon aside so that no one else could hear, and said, "Elon, if anyone ever says you played quarterback for the Yakima High School, deny it." Nothing worse ever happened to Elon.

There was a beautiful, wholesome girl in my class whose name was Fern Graham. I was much too busy ever to date her, but she stayed in my thoughts for years. On a debating trip to Ellensburg, I met another lovely young girl, Mildred Barton, with whom I was deeply enamored. Ellensburg was nearly forty miles to the north, however, and I did not see Mildred Barton again until thirty-five years later, when I was autographing my book *Of Men and Mountains* in Seattle. Much to my regret, I went through high school without the benefit of women.

I won many honors in high school, and when our class graduated, the prophecy about me in the yearbook was that I would be President of the United States. Grace Rhine, who made the prophecy, recorded this "vision":

> Scene IX—Presidential Parade
> President—Orville Douglas, in small automobile
> Secret Service Men: Russell Nagler and Elmer Carlsen
> Senators: Kenneth Coonse,* Warren Chase
> Representative: Henry Hughes
> Reporters: Conrad Alexander and Agnes Scott. Show great excitement and take down items on shorthand pad.

* Kenneth Coonse, the boy who had first suggested walking the hills to me, later became a famous Boston surgeon.

Directly following: George Butler leading great crowd and carrying an I.W.W. banner.

Secret Service Men come back to arrest George, accusing him of attempting a riot.

George denies the charge, saying that they intend to be peaceable.

Reporters rush back madly to get all the news.

Curtain

I graduated first in my class, and while being valedictorian brought me a scholarship to Whitman College, there was another honor that pleased me even more. During my last three years I was in charge of the alarm that brought students to classes, that adjourned classes, and that was used when fire drills were held. The alarm was a huge iron triangle that hung from a rope, and I wielded the iron rod that sounded the alarm and played the tunes. It was a coveted position, for it excused the gong-ringer from the end of every class a few minutes early, and allowed him to arrive a few minutes late. I enjoyed it immensely.

Not all my days in Yakima were quite so glorious. When I was thirteen I became a carrier for the local newspapers—the *Morning Herald* and *Daily Republic.* On Sunday, I handled the Seattle *Post Intelligence,* too. My employment as carrier for the *Herald* and *P. I.* was somewhat irregular, but I stayed with the *Republic* for some years, delivering it on a scheduled route six afternoons a week for $1.75 a week. When I was in the fruit harvest, I left the orchards to meet the paper's deadline; and in due time, when I went to college, Arthur inherited the same route.

Part of that route was a business section on the east side of town, north of Yakima Avenue between Second Street and the railroad track; the other part was residential, extending from North First east to North Tenth, and north about nine blocks: an area of about eighty-one square blocks. The carrier in those days was a newspaper employee. Should his rolled paper hit a puddle or should he miss the porch, leaving the paper concealed in bushes, the irate householder would call the paper, in which event the company would send a paper out by Western Union at a charge of ten cents, which was deducted from the carrier's weekly check. It did not take many deductions to leave little of $1.75. A severe man—a Mr. Guthrie—supervised us, and we all thought he enjoyed docking our weekly pay check, though we doubtless did him a disservice.

One of my jobs was being pin boy in a bowling alley. This was a job for Friday and Saturday nights. The game was tenpins; and the mechanical pin-setter had not been invented. As I remember it, my fee was ten cents a game. The trick was to get one's feet and legs up quickly, on a ledge above the backboard, for the balls came hard and the pins flew. I watched how skilled bowlers knocked one or more pins down by bouncing another pin off the backboard, but in spite of my early experience, I never amounted to much as a tenpin bowler.

One summer I worked in an ice cream plant, and forever after did not care for ice cream. The men who ran the vats where the ingredients were mixed chewed tobacco, and when either had collected a mouth full of juice he would let go into the vat, saying, "That should beef it up a bit."

While there were many children's parties in Yakima, we were never invited to a single one, and we were far too poor to have one in our own home. We grew up never seeing the inside of another home. In the after years I thought it was a blessing that I had not. For if I had been united with the elite of Yakima even by so tenuous a cord, I might have been greatly handicapped. To be accepted might then have become a goal in later life, an ambition that is often a leveling influence. To be accepted means living in the right area, wearing the right hat, thinking the right way, saying the right thing. What it means in the law is a Dean Acheson or John Foster Dulles or a reactionary president of the Bar Association. They cause all the beauty to disappear in a pontifical emptiness.

One experience of my adolescence enforced my feeling that I had been born on "the wrong side of the railroad tracks." A prominent churchman in town, the father of one of my friends, was bent on ridding Yakima of prostitutes and bootleggers. The prostitutes were scattered in brothels along South Front Street in establishments that advertised "Rooms" or "Hotel," most of which have now been reclaimed as "Gospel Missions," carrying luminous signs: *Jesus Saves*. The bootleggers were supposed to operate there, too. At that time Yakima, having the benefit of local option, allowed beer to be sold but no hard liquor. The bootleggers, however, brought the whiskey to everyone, including high churchmen and other members of the elite.

This particular reformer had several sons, my age and older, and he and they would have made an admirable vice squad. But as he told me, he would have none of that; he wanted to "save" his sons from being polluted by these evil people. That is why he approached me. Would I, for one dollar an hour, spend Saturday and Sunday nights "working Front Street"? My instructions were, "See if you can get a woman to solicit you.

See if you can buy a drink from someone. When the night is done, check in at the office, execute an affidavit, and the police will move in."

And so a teen-age boy became a stool pigeon in a red-light district. Never did I have such a shabby feeling, and in the end, never did I feel sorrier for people than I did for those I was supposed to entrap. I met voluptuous women whose faces were etched in sorrow, suffering and fear. Their tears never seemed very far beneath their coarse laughs and dirty stories. The men who brought "white mule" in gallon glass jars for sale to these brothels were shadows respected neither by the prostitutes nor by themselves. They had hunted looks; they swore softly under their breath; their eyes never met mine. I shamefully bought "one shot" glasses full of the fiery stuff for a dollar each, putting it to my lips and then tossing it into a basket or potted plant or under a sofa when no one was looking.

In time I came to feel a warmth for all these miserable people, something I never felt for the high churchman who hired me. They were scum that society had produced—misfits, maladjusted, disturbed, and really sick. What orphanages had turned them out? What broken homes had produced them? Which of these prostitutes had first been seduced by her father, causing all standards of propriety and decency to be destroyed? Which of them had turned to prostitution and bootlegging as a result of grinding poverty?

As much as my family needed the money, a few weeks of this job were all I could endure. As the evening hours passed along South Front Street, I heard stories about my employer whose sons were too precious to expose to crime and criminals. South Front Street did not know that he was financing stool pigeons; it heard, however, of his other doings. He had put enterprise after enterprise together, including many orchards, in his own lawless way—ruthlessly foreclosing mortgages, ruthlessly forcing competitors to the wall, ruthlessly reducing wages. I went to South Front Street to entrap a low, petty class of criminals; I discovered on South Front Street that on the day of the final reckoning there was one high churchman who would have to make a more severe accounting than they.

From this experience two impressions burned themselves into my memory. First was the only class consciousness I ever had. Most of my own experiences prior to this one and virtually all of them subsequent to it, spelled equality as the dominant American theme. But South Front Street in Yakima made me realize that there were those even in this free land who thought that some men were more equal than others, that their sons were to be preferred over the sons of other people less worthy. Second was a residue of resentment of which I have never quite got rid—resentment against hypocrites in church clothes who raise their denunciations against the petty criminals, while their own sins mount high. This feeling somehow aligned me emotionally with the miserable people who make up the chaff of society. I never sought their company, nor engaged in their tricks or traffic, nor spent my hours with them. I think, however, that I have always been quicker to defend them than I would have been but for the high churchman of Yakima.

Later I had an ice route that included South Front Street. I drove a one-horse wagon filled with three-hundred-pound blocks of ice that I sawed, then cut with a pick to fit each box. Once, when the tailgate was down and I was inside serving a customer, the horse got frightened and bolted away, strewing ice cakes down the middle of the dirt road for the next two blocks.

Usually the job was simpler—removing food from iceboxes to make room for the ice and then repacking the icebox. The "girls" in these "rooming houses" along South Front were friendly and garrulous and very unattractive. They had somehow or other missed out on love and security. "Bring on your ice, honey," one would shout, "and I'll throw open my community chest." Yet they "belonged" to their group, and that fact of belonging produced a keen sense of togetherness. There was friendship and compassion in these houses of ill repute. The women were vulgar in one sense, but they were also kind and tolerant and tender. I saw more of those qualities there on South Front Street than I later found on more sedate avenues.

The story goes that one of these Yakima prostitutes finally decided to leave the "house." She had been there twenty years and had made many friends. The prospective parting promised to be sorrowful. So the "girls" decided to give her a farewell sociable. There was much merriment at the party, the cheap booze flowing freely. At the end the heroine was in tears.

"Then why don't you stay?" her associates importuned.

"I love you all. I enjoy the work. Everyone has been very kind to me. But my legs and my arches are getting me. I can't climb those damn stairs any more."

The memories of the brothels of Front Street in Yakima came back to me years later during my travels. On a visit to Casablanca, I saw a lovely Moorish town with white adobe houses where the Establishment, then French, lived; down below were the miserable huts, made out of pieces of tin and packing cases, of the poor majority. The French word for the area was Bidonville, meaning the oil-drum slums. High on the hill overlooking the squalor was what a Frenchman called "the best investment in North Africa." It was a brothel whose tentacles stretched into the elite of Paris and her institutions. I saw the same in Saigon, where French development projects exalted two things: plush gambling casinos and deluxe brothels. These too were owned by the Establishment in Paris. The influence corrupted both Casablanca and Saigon, tying into the underworld, putting petty local officials on its payroll, and corrupting the police.

I learned that this industry was not a French monopoly. The Chinese had similar rich projects in the sector of free enterprise in Southeast Asia, notably Singapore. America had a like bent. In Cuba we built brothels of splendor and American finance reaped huge dividends. We paid off Batista for his cooperation, and we made our Havana brothels "first class" by barring Cuban males from them, though staffing them, of course, with Cuban girls.

On my later world travels I learned that slavery still thrives in the world. In the 1960's there were probably four million slaves, white, brown, black, and yellow. Of these people, the women have usually been kidnapped. They fill the brothels of Turkey and Iraq. In Damascus, I was offered by a broker not only a mistress but a cook, a housemaid, and a chauffeur from the black market for slaves.

What I had seen as a boy in Yakima, I later saw on a vast scale across the country. Our brothels are financed by our banks and protected by real estate lobbies and owners who reap huge profits. That means a close working relationship between the underworld and our Establishment. If anyone doubts it, talk to the mayors and governors who tried to close these places down and found out from what sources the great opposition came.

I was too naïve to know these things as a boy in Yakima. But since then I have often wondered who owned and financed the Front Street houses. My crusading friend who hired me did not last long. His campaign fizzled out in a few months. I now suspect, though I do not know, that the financial and real estate Establishment bore down on him.

Charles Darwin wrote that "a man who dares waste one hour of time, has not discovered the value of life." It was, I think, the same idea that kept me out of the pool halls of Yakima. After visiting them a few times, and finding only indolent men with empty talk, I put these places behind me forever. The Yakima public library was much more interesting. In this squat, square building, donated by the Eastern philanthropist Andrew Carnegie, I was introduced to all sorts of new books by the lovely Lucille James, my former English teacher, then serving as the librarian. Darwin, Perry, and other great explorers could be read, Shakespeare consumed, and American history absorbed here.

These were the years, too, in which I began to read newspapers regularly, and to take an avid interest in politics. It was the era of the muckrakers, and of such giants as Bryan, Borah, Johnson, and Pinchot. My appetite was whetted by the very real three-way fight over the Presidency in 1912, and I came to regard myself as a Woodrow Wilson progressive, a stand I later regretted when I saw Wilson's repressive policies in the area of civil liberties.

An earlier Democratic standard bearer, William Jennings Bryan, became my hero for a while, although disillusionment eventually set in. Bryan was probably the first national politician I ever saw in person. I remember hearing him speak at a chautauqua in Yakima.

In those days chautauquas were an important summer forum. They had spread from Lake Chautauqua, New York, where they were originally a sort of vacation camp assembly for Bible study and incidental visting speakers. Chautauquas came to the Far West, where they were very popular. Bryan often toured the circuit, and usually kept his audiences spellbound.

The big brown tent where Bryan spoke was hot that summer I heard him, and the great man perspired profusely. To keep himself going during the two hours he spoke, he relied upon a pitcher of ice water and a huge handkerchief with which he wiped his brow. I do not remember much of what Bryan said; his ideas were largely lost because I became mesmerized by his voice. It was deep and solemn, with a wide range, and he could make it soft and pleading or angry like a torrent. I tried to follow his words for sentence structure, for grammar, for figures of speech, but I remember only his general tirades against rum and whiskey, and the tones in which he extolled the virtues of water.

I found this excerpt from what must have been a typical Bryan speech:

> Water is the daily need of every living thing. It ascends from the seas, obedient to the summons of the sun, and, descending, showers blessing upon the earth; it gives of its sparkling beauty to the fragrant flower; its alchemy transmutes base clay into golden grain; it is the canvas upon which the finger of the Infinite

> traces the radiant bow of promise. It is the drink that refreshes and adds no sorrow with it—Jehovah looked upon it at creation's dawn and said, "It is good."

In later years a man who talked two hours would be deserted by his audience, but in those days Americans were not in such a hurry. Radio and TV had not arrived. The human voice, always entertaining, meant listening to a live speaker. There were no amplifiers; a man had to have lungs and larynx to match. Bryan kept the tentful of people so quiet on that blistering day, one could have heard a pin drop, and the admission price was so low that even we could afford to go. It was only years afterward that I wondered whether his ideas had any relevance to the world I knew.

In the meantime, Bryan was very influential in the choice of Woodrow Wilson as the 1912 Democratic nominee, and Wilson made Bryan his first Secretary of State. Bryan, who was greatly interested in foreign affairs, had always been anti-colonial and anti-tariff; now, in his new position, he tried to negotiate treaties providing cooling-off periods for disputes among nations, and arbitration by international commission. I had admired his earlier speeches for his style, rather than his substance; reading about him in these years left me with a more favorable impression of the man.

Although Bryan resigned from Wilson's Cabinet in protest over the President's second war note to Germany, he did not really fall from grace in my eyes until he prosecuted John Scopes in Tennessee in the 1920's for teaching Darwinian theory. Years later I found Bryan preaching under palm trees in Florida, and at the end of his sermon, selling municipal bonds to hapless investors. These bonds and their committees I investigated while with the Securities and Exchange Commission. Bryan, my idol, turned out to be nothing but a bag of wind, after all.

Hiram Johnson, another one of my heroes, was different. Bryan was once asked who was the greatest speaker, he or Hiram Johnson. Bryan replied, "When I speak, I can draw ten thousand persons and so can your governor. When I speak in an arena, I can fill the arena and so can your governor. But when Governor Johnson speaks, the people believe him."

I never heard Johnson speak, but his ideas had wings. As governor of California, when he issued his famous proclamation summoning the people of that state to enact massive reform measures in 1911, he was a knight in shining armor to a fourteen-year-old boy. He inveighed against the Southern Pacific. He proposed the initiative and referendum, free schoolbooks, a workmen's compensation law, a railroad commission to put an end to oppressive practices, a limitation on hours of work in mines and other industries, a child labor law, and a law restricting the hours of work for women. Hiram Johnson got these laws passed. He also promoted and obtained a law prohibiting employers from putting discharged employees on black lists. I did not understand all the nuances in his proclamations nor did I thoroughly comprehend all his measures, but he was a thundering voice that I admired more than I did the Establishment in Yakima.

Hiram Johnson was a Republican, and in 1912 he ran as Vice-President with Teddy Roosevelt on the Bull Moose ticket, which he had helped to form when his wing of the party split off from the more conservative Taft. This did not diminish my admiration for Johnson, however, and I was pleased when in 1916 he was elected to the United States Senate from California, serving nearly five terms and dying in office in 1945. As a young senator, Johnson opposed conscription for the Armed Forces. He denounced those who "with great enthusiasm" would "send men into battle" and "blow to pieces humanity" while at the same time professing the "most tender regard for individual rights" and "descant upon the fundamental principles of the nation" when it comes to "property rights of the individual." Hiram Johnson also led the fight against the regime of censorship in 1917. I was to meet him years later in Washington, D.C.

A boyhood hero who was to play an important role in my life many years later was William E. Borah of Idaho. Borah was elected to the Senate in 1906, and served until his death in 1940. I did not know him personally while I was growing up in Yakima, of course; I only read about him.

I knew that Borah had championed the cause of an unpopular minority, the Mormons, and that he had led the fight to bring them full suffrage. My first impression of Borah was not entirely favorable, however. Shortly after taking his seat, he was appointed special assistant to the prosecutor in the trial of "Big Bill" Haywood, an early labor organizer accused of the 1905 bomb murder of the governor of Idaho. Darrow defended Haywood.

The trial, held at Boise, Idaho, in 1907, was big news throughout the Northwest, and dominated all the newspapers of the region. I was only nine years old at the time, but I remember the flavor of the stories. The actual assassination had been a tragic episode in the ongoing conflict between the Idaho mine operators and the mine workers, and actually,

Haywood was only one of four men allegedly involved in the crime. Haywood, already denounced by President Teddy Roosevelt as an "undesirable citizen," had been secretly indicted in Idaho. With the connivance of Colorado officials, Haywood was arrested in Colorado late at night when the courts of that state were closed. He was denied access to counsel, then rushed to Idaho by a special train that stopped only at isolated spots to take on water and fuel.

The trial was a tense affair. Absentee mine owners, bitterly opposed to unionism, were on one side. On the other side was the Western Federation of Miners, who were fiercely opposed to the management. Haywood was their militant secretary. The clashes between the two groups had been numerous and bloody. Management had often called out the militia on its side, and sometimes the miners had retaliated with violence. Blood had run on both sides. The murdered ex-governor had used the National Guard to break a strike some six years earlier, and when he was killed, people concluded that the miners were "getting even." Haywood however, was probably innocent.

Borah's side lost its case against Haywood; Darrow won. I remembered both men for their stature and courage. I remembered Darrow for his defense, which was unusually eloquent. Darrow, too, became an early hero; my admiration for his skill and courage in taking on unpopular causes grew as the years went by.

At about the same time, as a result of an episode which took place in Nampa, Idaho, Borah acquired in my mind some of Darrow's stature. There were then not many Blacks in the Pacific Northwest. One young Black was the mascot of a baseball team in Idaho which played a game at Nampa, a railroad town twenty miles from Boise, the state capital. He had shot and seriously wounded a policeman, claiming the officer had kicked him off the sidewalk. The Black was jailed, and word came to Borah in Boise that a lynching was being readied. Although there were no scheduled trains that would get him there, Borah immediately persuaded a train crew to rush him to Nampa, where he raced from the station directly to the jail, and mounting the steps, addressed the crowd. Though repeatedly jeered, Borah was persistent and kept on orating. As he talked, an ally of his obtained the jail keys from the constable. Unlocking the jail, the ally appeared with the young man, and while Borah pleaded with the mob, the Black was marched through the crowd to the train in safety and taken to the security of Boise.

Years later I met Senator Borah in Washington, D.C. When I was being considered for a seat on the United States Supreme Court, it was Borah who claimed me as a Westerner, and thereby smoothed the path to my nomination. My tie to him went deep.

A fourth boyhood hero was Gifford Pinchot. He was Chief of the United States Forest Service when I was young. Pinchot and Teddy Roosevelt were in my eyes romantic woodsmen. I did not then know about Pinchot's "multiple use" philosophy, which, as construed, allowed timber companies, grazing interests, and even miners to destroy much of our forest heritage under the rationalization of "balanced use." I only knew that Pinchot was a driving force behind setting aside wilderness sanctuaries in an effort to save them from immediate destruction by reckless loggers. I was so thrilled by Pinchot's example that I perhaps would have made forestry my career had the choice been made in my high school days. I kept vaguely in touch with Pinchot in later years, admiring him for his role as governor of Pennsylvania in the twenties and again in the thirties.

I was to meet Pinchot in Washintgon, D.C., and of my boyhood public heroes—Hiram Johnson, William Borah, and Gifford Pinchot—Pinchot was the most enduring influence in my life.

Chapter VI

Minorities

As I grew up in Yakima, discrimination against racial and ethnic minorities was barely under the surface. There were no ugly actions against anyone like the incident in Nampa when Senator Borah had come to the rescue of the Black threatened with lynching. But the attitude of unfriendliness was there. An Italian was a dago and the word was spoken in a venomous way. A Pole was a Polack, and he too was looked down upon. We would take our lunch to school and scatter into small groups to eat our sandwiches. A Polish boy at school always had a sandwich made of white bread with the filling a good quarter-inch or more of lard. His lard sandwich was treated derisively by the rest of us. Poles came to have a connotation of half-civilized people in Yakima—an attitude that still brings me a feeling of shame whenever I meet a Pole, particularly a distinguished musician, scientist, or diplomat.

There probably was discrimination against Blacks in Yakima as I was growing up, but I was unaware of it. In high school, a Black student, Ira Simons—who later had a distinguished career in the postal service in Seattle—was pretty much of a hero. Without Ira our football team could not win a game; with Ira we seemed to be champions. And I have admired him over the years, not only for that boyhood reason, but for his high standards of citizenship.

Of course, when I was a boy, there were only about a hundred Black families in town. Today, there are nearly a thousand, and the feeling of racial discrimination is closer to the surface. In recent years Thelma Petrillo, who had been a licensed real estate broker from Los Angeles, wrote to an established agent in Yakima to inquire about a job. He wrote back telling her to come, that there was an opening for someone of her qualifications with his firm.

When Miss Petrillo walked into the man's office, sometime later, he was flabbergasted because she was a Black. He told her his own situation had changed and that he no longer needed anyone. Then he sent her to his colleagues in town to look for a job.

Eventually, after Miss Petrillo had made a futile round of Yakima real estate firms, she went back to the man who had encouraged her to come in the first place. He confessed that she could not get a job because local people were afraid she would sell what was considered "white property" to Blacks.

Thelma Petrillo never did get a real estate job in Yakima. She surrendered and left the business, despite the Supreme Court ruling that restrictive covenants were unconstitutional.

Discrimination against Indians, in earlier years, was perhaps more overt, although we did not think of the situation in those terms. The valley where we lived was the ancestral home of the Yakima tribe, and a large area of land running from the rich bottom lands south of town to the berry patches of Mount Adams had been set aside for them. People who were raised in town did not know the Yakimas well. Most of them lived on the reservation, and their children did not go to school in Yakima. Not living with them or playing with them, we felt them to be strangers.

As a young child, I saw Indians only on the streets or in the stores. Yakima Susie—an aged Indian squaw—stood on the corner of Yakima Avenue and First Street begging for money. She was a lonely pathetic figure who had many reasons for suspecting the whites. The boys of my age teased and taunted her, dragging pennies tied to a piece of string in front of her, only to pull the penny away when with her failing eyesight she finally saw it and bent over to try to pick it up.

Mother, God rest her soul, had what was probably the then-prevalent view of Indians. She knew nothing of the awful deeds committed by whites against the Indians, which were recounted only by later historians. But as a little girl on the Minnesota frontier, Mother had heard of massacres and attributed all the fault to the Sioux. I was to learn a different view of Indians; my first lesson was taught me in the mountains west of Yakima, where I began to hike as I grew older.

We never saw many Indians on these early pack trips. Once in a while there would be some women picking blueberries, filling dozens of five-gallon kerosene tins and packing the berries out by horse. We seldom saw Indian men, except during the salmon-fishing season when the salmon came upstream from the ocean to spawn. Then the men would spear the fish, fillet them, lace them to willow frames, and smoke them against a willow or alder fire.

On one of my trips to the Tieton Basin, I made friends with a young Indian whom I had seen there several times before. I was fishing for trout, and he offered to show me his salmon. On another trip into these lovely McAllister meadows (now flooded by an irrigation reservoir) I screwed up my courage and inquired, "Could you teach me how to spear a salmon?"

My heart overran with joy when he said he would. He took a green willow bough five or six feet long, peeled and scraped it until it was smooth, and tapered it at each end. He had with him an extra tip made of deer bone and an extra leather thong to fasten the tip of the shaft. He soon had the shaft fitted into the socket of the bone and the thong tied fast to the bone and the shaft.

We went along the Tieton until we came to a likely pool. The young Indian put my spear in the water, showing me how it appeared to be broken and saying I must therefore aim several inches above or beyond where the salmon seemed to be. We stood still as statues. He had my spear poised. My heart pounded with the excitement of the moment. Soon there was a flash and my spear in his skilled hands lifted a salmon.

I could hardly wait to try my own hand. He gave me the spear and told me to stay at this pool. He went upstream, and I felt more comfortable with him around the bend of the river. His expert eye on my amateurish performance would be most embarrassing.

I waited, my spear poised to strike, my eyes on the water. Minutes passed. Then there was a flash. My spear drove home, but I hit only the bottom of the river. I readjusted the bone tip and waited again. In a half-hour or so there was another flash and my spear hit the water another time. Once more I speared the bottom of the Tieton. Again it happened, and again.

I decided I needed more instruction. So I went upstream a quarter-mile or so and found my friend. He had speared three salmon since I saw him. I stayed with him for about an hour, watching him spear two more. By then I thought I knew the technique, so I went upstream and found water that seemed ideal.

Here was a clear pool with a sandy bottom where a salmon could easily be spotted. The pool was about five feet deep, a dozen feet across, and about twenty feet long. There was brush on each side which made handling the spear difficult, but a log fallen across the river at the head of the pool made access easier. Above the log a great deal of driftwood had collected, much like a beaver dam.

I worked my way carefully out on the log until I was over the middle of the stream. Then I crouched down to watch the water like a hawk, my spear lifted in my right hand. From my vantage point it was easy to see any fish that entered the pool.

I had not been on the log many minutes before a salmon darted in. I drove the spear down toward him with all my strength—and lunged right into the water. In those days, I could not yet swim, and my legs went rigid with fear as I grabbed the overhanging brush. Luckily, I caught hold of some willows and pulled myself to shore, shivering and shaking.

I looked across the river. My Indian friend was there, doubled up with laughter. He had retrieved my spear, and he shouted to ask if I wanted it back. I finally saw the humor of the situation, but I made a gesture indicating I never wanted to see the spear again. I shouted thanks for all he had done and started for camp to dry out. I had gone about fifty yards or so when I heard a yell. I turned around and there was my friend holding up the biggest salmon yet. It came from the pool in which I had been doused.

That night as I lay under the blankets listening to the wind in the tops of the pine, I thought about the young Indian. Some called his race inferior. Perhaps, with his lack of formal education, he would not do so well in my Latin class but in the woods he was a champion who walked in the footsteps of great ancestors. He was from a race that lived in a world full of spirits. Every manifestation of nature had a hidden meaning. I did not know much about ecology then, but I learned from watching him and others that although the Indians took their living from the wilderness, they left that environment virtually intact. The Indians had trails, but their trails were not defacing. At times they used fire to clear thick stands so that shrubs, bushes, and grain would come in, attracting game, especially deer and bear. Indeed, their judicious use of fire was a technique that ecologists were to adopt years later. From my chance encounters with these Yakimas, I began to get faint glimpses of the idea that their relationship to the earth was wiser and healthier than those of the sheepmen and loggers.

I learned from this same friend, on other trips, some of the legends of his people. Many of these involved rocks and mountains that I had climbed, and so were of particular interest. His philosophy was absorbing, and I remember him saying in roughly these simple terms: "It takes many different shrubs, and trees and grass to make a forest. It takes many kinds of animals to fill the woods. The bear, goat cougar, coyote, deer and elk are all different. Wouldn't it be too bad if all the animals were alike? It takes many races to make the world. Wouldn't it be bad if all people were the same?"

I got other glimpses of Indian life, including one which I did not fully appreciate until much later in life—about the sweat houses, the small wigwams where young men foregathered at the start of the hunting season. Hot rocks were placed in the center of the tent, covered with dirt, and drenched with cold water. The men sat in a circle, letting the steam cleanse their bodies. My friend said the cleansing had a special reason, not exactly related to our purpose of bathing. The Indians considered deer, on which they were greatly dependent, to be sacred, and cleansing the hunters was part of the ritual of taking the deer as food.

In 1855, long before my meeting with this young Yakima, Seattle, chief of the Duwamish tribe on the west side of the Cascades, sent a letter to Franklin Pierce, then President of the United States. The letter, too long to reprint in full, is a moving document:

> There is no quiet place in the white man's cities. No place to hear the leaves of spring or the rustle of insect's wings. But perhaps because I am a savage and do not understand, the clatter only seems to insult the ears. And what is there to life if a man cannot hear the lovely cry of a whippoorwill or the arguments of the frogs around a pond at night? The Indian prefers the soft sound of the wind darting over the face of the pond, and the smell of the wind itself cleansed by a midday rain, or scented with a pinon pine. The air is precious to the redman. For all things share the same breath—the beasts, the trees, the man. The white man does not seem to notice the air he breathes. Like a man dying for many days, he is numb to the stench . . .
>
> What is man without the beasts? If all the beasts were gone, men would die from great loneliness of spirit, for whatever happens to the beast also happens to man. All things are connected. Whatever befalls the earth befalls the sons of the earth.

In later years I came to know Alba Showaway, son of Alec, the chief of the Yakima tribe. It is a large tribe, with 6,047 members. Of these, only 706 are full-blooded; some of the others had, by the time I knew the tribe, blue eyes and flaxen hair. To qualify as a Yakima, one had to have only one sixty-fourth Indian blood.

Alba was a bright-faced, industrious chap whose friendship I prized. Through him I would purchase moccasins and soft riding gloves made by the Indian women. These leather goods were priceless for their durability, but they had one unusual characteristic: a pungent odor, traceable to the urine in which the leather was tanned. At the invitation of Alba and his father, Elon Gilbert and I would ride the reservation, helping with the September roundup of cattle. Each Indian cattleman had grazing rights for fifteen hundred head, and the roundup was a serious but festive affair.

At that time, there were also about five thousand wild horses running loose on the reservation. Several young tribesmen would supplement their living by roping these horses, running them into improvised corrals, and breaking them to ride. Out of those roundups came some wonderful saddle horses. One of these young entrepreneurs was Mr. Robert Jim, present chief of the Yakimas.

Mr. Jim's predecessor, persuaded by the Bureau of Indian Affairs (which was more white-oriented than Indian-dedicated), had allowed helicopters to be used to hunt the horses. Machine guns were fired into the racing herds from the air, and most of the horses were killed. The ostensible reason was to conserve grass on the reservation for cattle. But the Indian community was outraged, and Mr. Jim ran for office on a platform that promised conservation of the wild horse. Those who had planned to wipe out the horses were unsuccessful when Mr. Jim won; and out of the stock of one hundred or so which were left when Mr. Jim took office, the wild horses made a comeback. Today the reservation is their refuge.

In recent years Chief Jim discovered the bones of a horse deep down in an eroded stretch of the banks of the Yakima River. Extensive digging recovered the entire skeleton, which was shipped off to Whitman College at Walla Walla. Dr. Richard H. Clem, Professor of Geology at Whitman, had to determine whether these bones were from a horse of the Pleistocene period that had flourished on this continent and then became extinct, or whether they were from a modern horse. Carbon 14 tests apparently are not very useful on bones, so Dr. Clem had to make his judgment on the basis of the kind of soil and rocks above and beneath the buried skeleton. He wrote me in 1973 that "based on circumstantial evidence" the horse was a "modern" horse probably fifteen to twenty thousand years old."

I was raised on the theory that horses came to America with the Spaniards and slowly worked their way north. But this new evidence indicates that when the Indians came from Siberia (perhaps 18,000 B.C.) they rode horseback over the land mass that then connected Asia and this continent, where the Bering Sea now is.

Chief Jim's eyes brightened when he brought me the story. Though the Indians, like other humans, had their faults, they were not the thieving monsters who raided south of the Rio Grande to steal horses.

As a young man I had read the journals of Lewis and Clark, written when they crossed from St. Louis, Missouri, to Astoria, Oregon, in 1803. They had stopped at the confluence of the Yakima and Columbia rivers, and Clark describes the scene vividly. He found Indian women cooking fish in pots made out of woven reeds, and the astounding thing was that they were waterproof. They could not, of course, be set over a fire, but the water was heated by putting hot rocks in the reed pots and replacing them when they cooled off. In that way the water could be kept hot enough to cook salmon, trout, and venison.

Through the years I looked for pots of the kind Clark described, but to no avail. Finally, in the early seventies I wrote Chief Jim asking if he knew where I could find a reed pot. Weeks passed, and one day he came to my chambers at the Court with the news that the art of weaving waterproof pots was not lost. The older women could still do it, and inspired by my inquiry, they had instituted classes to teach the young girls how to make these pots. He brought with him one that was finished except for the top row, whose ends hung loose. "We kept the pot unfinished," he said, "because the work of the Yakimas is unfinished—and so is the work of the Court on Indian matters."

By the time my teen-age years ended, I had met a different group of outcasts, who made a very deep impression on me. They were the Wobblies, or IWW's, of the Far West—the Industrial Workers of the World. Though Yakima denounced them as criminals, I came to know the Wobblies as people who deserved more than our society had meted out to them. During vacations I worked with harvest crews in the wheat lands of eastern Washington. This is checkerboard land, alternate fields lying fallow for a year. It is winter wheat land: the seed is sown in the fall, the September and October rains give it growth, and by November a soft green nap spreads over the land. When the heads are ripe in early summer, these fields are pale yellow, and the ripples from the wind make them a sea of gold.

When I was working for Ralph Snyder, who had a big spread near the town of Washtucna in eastern Washington, I was in an accident with harvest equipment—an accident that might have been fatal. In those days the separator was stationary; the wheat was cut by a reaper and traveled from the reaper up a spout on a belt into a header-box pulled by four horses. The problem of the driver of the header-box was to keep the wagon under the spout, an easy matter on level ground but difficult on steep terrain. (The wheat price was then so high that even marginal land, producing six bushels an acre, was planted. These marginal tracts included steep rocky hillsides.) One day I was below the header on such a slope when the wheels of the wagon I was driving caught on some rocks, causing the wagon to turn over. I jumped free and watched the wagon and four horses go over and over into a deep ravine. Much damage was done to the wagon, though no horse was badly hurt.

As I jumped, my shirt, the only one I owned, caught on a nail and ripped in two. A man named Blacky was with me on the crew. I never knew his full name, but I knew he was a card-carrying member of the IWW. In recent years he would doubtless have been a target for every Un-American committee. Blacky kept all of his worldly possessions in an old, battered suitcase. They were a pair of high-heeled shoes that he had bought for a girl friend in Seattle and one shirt. After the wagon accident, Blacky gave me the shirt and would accept no compensation for it. The shirt was a gift to a person in need. That act of generosity built the first bond between me and the men who rode the rods and camped under railroad bridges, a tie that deepened and has lasted through my life. I never would wear the cast-off clothing sent by friendly people to the Presbyterian church, but Blacky's gift of a shirt was on a different plane. It was a gift from the heart, and I thought it was the most precious thing I had ever received.

Blacky was perhaps thirty. He was slight, swarthy, with fingernails always dirty. Where he came from, I never knew. He was a part of the jetsam in the stream of life that poured over the Pacific Northwest in those troubled days. He talked mostly of women and of his hunger for them. He wondered if he could ever be a gynecologist. And when I explained to him the work, study, application, and the long years through college, medical school, and internship that would be necessary, he threw up his hands. That was no dish for him. The idea had merely caught his fancy because being a gynecologist would give him access to women, and access was what he desired above all else.

The most interesting encounter I ever had with a rattlesnake happened when I worked in the wheat fields with Blacky. The separator would blow out the chaff, and we used it to make a pile about four feet high and long and broad enough for two bedrolls. When Blacky and I put our bedrolls down and got inside them, the chaff would settle into a rather thin but comfortable mattress. One bright moonlit night I was wakened out of a sound sleep by a blood-curdling scream from Blacky. I sat up and saw him somewhere in the air between me and the moon. When he came down, he did not stop running until he reached the header-box. Only when he was safe did he explain what happened. In language unfit to quote he said that a rattler had crawled in bed with him and wrapped itself around his feet.

"He was just trying to get warm," I shouted.

Blacky's reply is not fit for print, either. Thereafter he never, never slept on the ground.

There was no drive or ambition in Blacky. But there was kindness, compassion, tenderness, and a desperate loneliness. I had seen that same loneliness under the railroad bridge over the Yakima River north of the city, where I used to sit with restless vagabonds, sharing coffee and stew, while the wrath of their discontents against society bubbled out. Their lives were mostly empty and filled with despair. I had been raised to believe in the Puritan ethic—that right was right and wrong was wrong, and that man, endowed with free will, could choose which he preferred. It was all a matter of good and bad, sin and righteousness, reward and punishment. Criminals were the product of the wrong moral choice. The poor were the product of lack of desire, energy, and will power. The rich were those who took advantage of their opportunities.

Young as I was, I began to doubt the accuracy of this ethic. I sensed in this restless, lonely community, constantly pursued by the forces of law and order, personal tragedies that had somehow or other fragmented them.

I traveled extensively with the IWW's and came to know them as warm-hearted people who, it seemed to me even then, had higher ideals than some of the men who ran our banks and were the elders in the church. A hungry man was always welcome under that railroad bridge; not only was he offered food, but there he could feel that he was an equal with everyone. And almost always, these drifters left the area cleaner than they had found it. As Dan Carlinsky, a latter-day hobo, observed in his book, "A real hobo takes care of the jungle."

It was under bridges like the one in Yakima that Carl Sandburg spent his wandering years, listening to the folkways of the people and later making the musical transcriptions that in time appeared in his book *The American Songbag.*

Many of these wanderers had real grievances, and responded by protesting, sometimes crudely, sometimes eloquently, that their plight was serious, the injustices heaped upon them real. They sang, they swore, they did outrageous things at times. But they were seeking a place of some security in a free society.

I knew my vagrant friends not as thieves, but as the underprivileged who had only crumbs from the table of our affluent society. By then I had experienced South Front Street and had come to compare the ethics of those at the top with those at the bottom of Yakima society.

The police, in my view, represented the ultimate personality of the Establishment that owned and ran the Yakima Valley. They were harsh and relentless and bore down heavily on the nonconformist. They caused a close sifting of loyalties in a young man who felt the roughness of their hand. I knew their victims too intimately to align myself with the police. My heart was with the impoverished, restless underdogs who were IWW's.

Most of the IWW's had no criminal records and engaged in no lawless conduct. Yet, though few who rode the rods were criminals, we were all treated as outcasts or vagrants; we were even fired on by the police in railroad yards.

Traveling on freight cars in those days was like hitchhiking at present. Those too poor to pay a rail fare waited in the yards for a freight train to make up and pull out. I rode the rails not as a sightseer, but to get myself to places where it would be likely that I'd find work; I used the freight cars to move back and forth across the valley, to and from school, to and from jobs.

Riding in open gondola cars was one way of getting where you wanted to go. But, like riding on top of a freight car, it had disadvantages, for the brakemen who patrolled the train would detect the passenger and either eject him or try to shake him down for a fee. If you were lucky, you might spot an open boxcar. You'd hop in, find yourself a nice corner, and travel in style. On clear days, in friendly country—where there were no police—you could sit on top of a car or on a flatcar, in a hidden nook or cranny of a large piece of machinery.

"Riding the rods" was surer, because you were safe from detection on a moving train. Though freight cars have changed over the years, in the days when I was a boy, there were two rods which ran under most of these cars. They were two or three feet apart, about eighteen inches beneath the car and about ten inches from the ground, running under the car for almost its entire length.

The trick was to get a couple of boards and lay them across the rods to form a small platform. We'd lie on the boards, on our stomachs, our heads on our arms and our eyes tightly closed. It was a miserable place to ride because the suction of the train kept dust and cinders constantly swirling. Unless you fell asleep, it wasn't particularly dangerous, although you did come out pretty grimy. Even the nights were hot and the sand stinging.

A faster way to travel was "riding the blinds," because only the passenger trains had blinds, and these trains of course made better time than freights. But riding the blinds was much more dangerous. At the place where the coal car backed up to attach itself to the mail car, there would be a piece of heavy fabric, arranged like an accordion, which locked the cars together. This was the bellow-like "blinds," and when the engine first pulled against the dead weight of the train, these blinds would separate, so that a man could slip inside. Then, as the train picked up speed, the fabric would close up, and one would be stuck there until the train once again slowed down, only to start up quickly. The passenger had to be alert to these changes in pace to get either in or out in time, and he had to get out on the far side of the train lest he be apprehended on the station platform. The blinds were also a risky place to hide because they were close to where the mail was being sorted, and because if an occasional fireman or brakeman came through, one was trapped.

This danger of apprehension, on both passenger and freight trains, was especially acute at Pasco, a railroad junction where the Snake River joins the Columbia in Washington. The railroad company had many "yard bulls" at Pasco and they met every train, deploying on both sides. They fired at us frequently, but happily they were poor shots. Our practical philosophy toward them was summed up by Dan Carlinsky, who wrote: "A hobo should never get tough with a railroad bull. The railroads don't hire kindly old gentlemen."

The "bulls" were widely resented, however, and in his book *Calked Boots,* Bert Russell of Idaho tells how one night he and some others found a famous railroad "bull," whom I did not know, though he had the name of Yakima Bill. They met him at a barn dance, alone and without a gun. They showered him with beer bottles, then took away his pants, and roared with laughter as he ran away "drawers flapping."

Traveling with these migrants was not always an experience in camaraderie. Some of these men were neither Wobblies nor men who shared the ideas of the Wobblies. There was light-hearted conversation and much storytelling around campfires under the railroad bridges. On the freight trains I was pretty much a loner, preferring to be by myself. Sometimes, though, I had no choice but to climb aboard inside a boxcar, which usually meant company. The folk stories of boxcar travel were filled with accounts of how one set of "passengers" ganged up on another, frisking them and tossing them out the side door or even killing them. I always got in a dark corner of the car and sometimes went to sleep. One night, however, I was uneasy about the demeanor of some of the other "passengers," and though exhausted, I managed to stay awake until dawn brought us to the town where work was to be found. I never was harmed inside a boxcar, but I lived on the theory that it was wolf eat wolf in those dark confines.

Eventually the wrath of Washington, D.C., and of Woodrow Wilson was turned on the IWW's. The Immigration Bureau also descended on them, sorting out aliens for deportation. These IWW's were herded like cattle into cars and carried across the country for internment, while not a single lawyer in Washington State spoke up in protest.

Felix Frankfurter, whom I knew in later years, did speak up. He did courageous work in the field of civil liberties in 1917 when he was counsel and Secretary of Wilson's Mediation Commission, an agency created to facilitate the settlement of labor disputes. He traveled extensively in the West, investigating a copper strike in Arizona, an oil-field controversy in California, and logging problems in Oregon and Washington. Frankfurter denounced the illegality of wholesale deportations of striking miners from Arizona to New Mexico. His was, indeed, one of the few voices raised on behalf of my IWW friends. He felt, as he wrote much later, that "but for an almost negligible percent, all labor is patriotic, is devoted to the purpose of the war and its prosecution" but that some "industrial conditions" needed remedy and that "the masses insist upon an increasing share in determining the condition of their lives."

That was a view with which I would have agreed at the time I worked with the Wobblies, and that was the view of the Mediation Commission, which placed most of the blame on the employers whose bitter opposition to unionization "had reaped for them an organization of destructive rather than constructive radicalism." The commission, reflecting Frankfurter's views, went on to say that "sinister influences and extremist doctrines may have availed themselves" of industrial unrest but that "they certainly have not created them."

In time the logging companies, the mine owners, and the large ranchers joined forces with the United States Army in one of our ugliest unconstitutional programs. The Army, in effect, displaced the courts, and handled the IWW's exactly like the Soviets handle ideological strays. One of the most disgraceful episodes took place in Centralia, Washington, on Armistice Day, 1919.

Centralia was a small lumber town where the IWW's had a foothold. As fear of the Wobblies mounted, tempers became inflamed, and in the summer of 1919 a Citizens Protective League was organized to "combat radicalism." The chief of police in Centralia insisted that the IWW's had a legal right to exist. That displeased the lumber operators, and rumors spread that extra-legal measures would be undertaken to combat the Wobblies. The IWW's got out a leaflet entitled "To the Citizens of Centralia We Must Appeal" which exhorted the townspeople to oppose violence against the organization. But, as planned, members of the American Legion, on Armistice Day, 1919, made a rush for the hall where the IWW's were located. This hall became a battleground. The barricaded IWW's defended themselves, opening fire and killing three members of the Legion and wounding two others. Another legionnaire was killed by a war-veteran member of the IWW's whom he was pursuing. Finally the IWW's were overcome and thrown into jail.

The foregoing is one historical account of what happened in Centralia. But when I read about it at the age of twenty-one in the papers of eastern Washington, my impression was that as the legionnaires were parading peacefully, they were wantonly shot down by the IWW's. There was a parade, but whether it broke up opposite the hall to raid that building or was broken up by the IWW's was certainly not clear from the newspaper account; this became a crucial issue in the trial that grew out of the episode.

It was not until much later that I learned the actual facts. The night of the shooting, Centralia was in darkness. A mob broke into the jail and lynched a prisoner. The incident rekindled hatred for the IWW's. Wholesale arrests were made. The local Bar Association pledged its members not to defend an IWW no matter what the charge. A Seattle paper, called the *Union Record*, pleaded for common sense and urged that IWW's be allowed to present their side of the case. This led to the arrest and indictment of four members of the staff of the paper by the federal government and the closing down of the plant by the federal authorities. The rest of the Seattle press thereupon opened an indiscriminate attack upon all organized labor, and in one of the Seattle papers, an advertisement was run which advocated mob rule and lynching.

Ten IWW's involved in the Centralia episode were tried the following March. The courtroom and town were filled with legionnaires in uniform. The federal government had two dozen or more troopers present. When the jury returned a verdict, finding two of the defendants guilty of manslaughter, the judge refused to accept the verdict because it was not stiff enough to suit him. On further deliberation, the jury acquitted two, found one to be insane, and found seven guilty of second-degree murder. The jury recommended clemency, concluding there had been a conspiracy to raid the hall and that the defendants had acted in self-defense. The jury also protested that the IWW's did not receive a fair trial. The trial judge, however, disregarded the jury plea for clemency and imposed maximum sentences ranging from twenty-five to forty years. The Washington Supreme Court affirmed that verdict. I thought then, and still think, that our record as a nation against the IWW's was disgraceful.

There were many other dramatic episodes at this time. In Oregon, Washington, and Idaho, many IWW's were sentenced either under criminal syndicalism statutes or under vagrancy laws. The great bulk of the prosecutions, however, took place in California. For seven long, terrible years the IWW's felt the full force of governmental prosecution.

Near Pasco, in eastern Washington, a wheat rancher went into town to get a crew for the harvest. Of the twenty men he hired, the dominant members were IWW's. When the men arrived at the ranch, some eighteen miles east of Pasco, they struck for higher wages. The rancher angrily refused their demands, ordered them to leave the ranch, and told them to walk back to Pasco. With that announcement he roared out of the place with his truck to go back to town and find another crew. While he was gone, the discharged men found paint, brushes, and ladders and painted on each side of his white barn the letters IWW. On his return trip, the rancher passed the discharged crew as they trudged the hot, dusty eighteen miles into Pasco. When he saw the mutilation of his barn, he became doubly indignant; roaring back to Pasco, he got the sheriff and a posse to meet the crew and lodge them in jail for defacement of his property.

The literature of the IWW's usually had as a preamble: "The working class and the employing class have nothing in common." But the IWW's were not out to overthrow the government; they sought to improve working conditions in the logging camps, in the wheat fields, in the coal mines. They were part of the tide of hungry, restless, bitter people who moved south to north along the West Coast, seeking employment wherever they could find it. I heard from their lips unvarnished stories of privations and sufferings.

Some logging camps, in the forested mountains of the west side of the state, were in those days as bad as slave-labor camps in other countries. Wages were pitifully low, food was atrocious, the logger's bunk was crescent-shaped, made of metal, and stacked in tiers of three. In the east side of the state, migratory workers in fruit, berries, and wheat were equally badly treated. The ultimate goal of the Wobblies was to form a single big union of all these workers: loggers, migrants, miners, regardless of race, sex, origin, craft, or type of work.

The migrant laborers were, of course, not all IWW's, though the latter were prominent among them. Local people, like the young Douglases, helped make up the force. Whole families moved north with the sun, camping in the fields, cooking in the open, tending sick and squalling babies, living in filth. They were looked down on as scum and treated as such by the Establishment.

They were part of the migrant labor force that John Steinbeck later depicted in *The Grapes of Wrath.* They started working in the fields in Southern California and Arizona in late spring; they reached Oregon and Washington by June in time for berries and cherries; they stayed for the soft fruits; some then went to the wheat harvest, others thinned apples; most of them joined hands to harvest the pears and apples before moving on to later crops in Canada.

Years later I learned that the East, too, has migrant workers. They move north along the Atlantic to harvest potatoes. Some linger on in the winter after the harvest to pack the potatoes. They live in miserable camps, some of which are owned by labor contractors.

In the late sixties proposals were at long last being made, to the effect that laborers who harvest food are as worthy of a subsidy as the food itself. Profits from federal subsidies go into the farmers' pockets. The human machines that work in the fields need like protection.

Woody Guthrie wrote a song about these people:

> Quit beating that woman, Officer! We're peaceable folks

Out on the hunt of a job of work.

Thirty days we go to spend in jail
'Cause we spoke at a union and we ain't got bail.

Come on, black man! Come on, white!
Show these rich how the poor can fight!

Stand up, woman, and meet a man!
Gonna make this country the promised land!

Gonna have a house with strawberry pie!
I aim to live some before I die!

Gonna have a meeting and all talk free!
Come on, you cops, and be like me!

At the time I was working in the fields and orchards, there were no Blacks among the migratory workers in my region. There were, however, many Chicanos, whom I came to love. By and large they worked in family units, and their grandchildren make up a sizable community in the Yakima Valley today. Among the drifters who rode the freight trains with me, there were few, if any, Chicanos; but the ones I knew and worked with in the fields were good, hard-working, God-fearing laborers. The local people treated these Chicanos as though they were afraid of them, as I guess they were. But why this nation of foreigners should be afraid of foreigners, I could never fathom.

It would be over forty years before Cesar Chavez would organize these farm laborers into unions. While Chavez was attempting to do so, Humberto Fuentes of Idaho was forming migrant councils to provide the Chicanos and others with services in education, economic development, and housing. Day-care centers for children were also part of the program. These councils used federal money and fought against federal domination.

Chavez and Fuentes have worked on different segments of the same problem—the elimination of discrimination against a minority. Tremendous progress has been made since my time, though the Chicanos still get the rough backhand of the elite. The fear and resentment was evidenced by the fact that in Yakima a Chicano who could not write or read or speak English could not vote, though he might be literate in Spanish. The courts have now ended that particular kind of discrimination. Today migrant workers in Yakima have fairly respectable campgrounds and clean water. In my day they had nothing. They were despised and denounced by the growers, who, however, could never have got their crops in without them. The situation was the American equivalent of the nineteenth-century British factory system which I read about in school in Dickens, our most popular author. Later, as I traveled the world, I discovered that the conditions under which migratory laborers of our Far West work were only a microcosm of those that plague the earth.

I remember, in about 1917, standing beside the railroad tracks in Yakima, when word came that there was to be a big roundup of IWW's. The newspapers carried the story that the government was coming through with a train full of them. I went down to the railroad and waited for hours.

The train that passed through Yakima was not carrying men on display. These were *sealed* boxcars carrying human beings, thirty or forty in each car. The authorities were taking outcasts through our city. There were no toilets, no food, no water, just sealed boxcars with these poor bastards inside.

I walked home with tears in my eyes. I thought of all the pompous members of the Establishment of Yakima who should have been in those cars. The men who were there had only tried to increase the benefits to working people. They got rid of the bad food and the crescent-shaped beds that working people had to sleep on, on which you would crawl through the rear and lie on a piece of tin. As one example of the work of the IWW's, the men in the forests lived better; they had fruit and liver or beefsteak, whereas before they had been fed crusts of bread or porridge and coffee.

Having been one, I have an enduring love for migrant workers. They are still looked down upon as we were. Yet they are wonderful people who take care of their children and their wives and they are the direct descendants, spiritually, of our working people of the beginning of the century.

I have had experiences with vagrants throughout my life. In Tucson, Arizona, in the forties, I discovered a tent city up on the hill above the town and was told that it was for men who came through the city and didn't have any work. The local Sunshine Club had established what was called the Tucson Hilton, where the court would send those men simply for not having any money.

Charles Ares, my law clerk at the time, did some research into the matter and the two of us together wrote and published an article about it. It expressed the opinion that the vagrant is a man whose only crime is that he does not have any money. A publisher of a Tucson newspaper, however, thought I was Public Enemy Number One during this period and he wrote an editorial saying that "Justices should stick to their last." Tucson, two or three years later, repealed its vagrancy law. And about twenty years later, when I was making some speeches in the Southwest, the people of that city became so enthusiastic that a Tucson paper wrote "Mr. Justice, we are proud."

During the FDR period, a local ordinance was passed in Washington, D.C., making it a crime for anyone to come into town without visible means of support. The bill came to FDR for approval and he vetoed it. The talk around Washington called the bill "the Jimmy Roosevelt Law," a comment on the working habits of the President's son. FDR said, "Why the hell are they after Jimmy? If this law passed, half of Washington would be in jail."

Chapter VII

World War I

The war in Europe seemed far away to a boy in Yakima in 1914. I was fifteen that summer, and about to begin my junior year in high school. Just before school opened, and after the cherry, apricot, peach, and pear crops had been picked, I saw a chance to get away for a few days of back-packing.

I wanted to see the fall colors of the high lake country in the area of Mount Tumac—the willow, Douglas maple, and tamarack in their various shades of yellow and orange. So I caught the train up to Naches and hiked from there along the Tieton to the headwaters of Indian Creek. I went alone, carrying my usual horseshoe-shaped pack.

I imagined I would run into a sheepherder in the high country, and since sheepherders those days were very isolated, I decided to take some recent issues of newspapers and magazines with me. By mid-September, a sheepherder who had been on the high ridges all summer would have been away from the world for over three months and he would be hungry for news. There were no radios then, and whatever information he received would have been brought by "shoe telegraph," as they say in Iran. So I put several issues of the Yakima *Daily Republic* and a recent issue of the weekly *Outlook* in with my blankets. All carried front-page stories of the war which had broken out and spread through Europe in the previous few weeks.

A few days out, I spotted a sheep camp on the edge of a meadow in high country east of Cowlitz Pass. The smell of sheep was everywhere.

A curl of smoke and a half-dozen yapping sheepdogs came out of a clump of fir. It was only two hours before sundown and I was overjoyed, because a sheep camp at that time of day meant a wonderful meal.

The sheepdogs quieted at the voice of their master, and the sheepherder who greeted me was a middle-aged man with a full brown beard and blue and kindly eyes. His face was bronzed, and when he took off his hat I could see that his tan ran up his massive forehead and into the bald spot on the top of his head. He looked a little as I imagined Walt Whitman must have looked: tall, long-legged, long-armed, a wiry, rangy man who appeared to be equal to any challenge of the mountains. His voice was resonant, with powerful carrying qualities even in ordinary conversation. It was a voice that came back to me four years later as I drilled and marched in the uniform of the United States Army.

He greeted me with "Hi ya" and extended a hand as gnarled and tough as the alpine fir that dotted the ridges to the west. He invited me to his camp on the far side of the grove of fir. It faced the edge of a smaller meadow I had not seen from the trail. Firewood had been split and piled near his tent. There was a crude table of small pine and fir logs.

As I walked into camp, two or three camp robbers, birds which apparently had been stealing bread from inside the tent, flew up. My host turned his dogs on them, and they went through the futile exercise of pursuit, with much barking and wagging of tails. Then at a soft, almost inaudible command, something like "All right, boys," they stopped and curled up in the shade.

It turned out that the packer, the man who ran the pack train and kept the camp provided with food, had left on the previous day for supplies. He would be back in two days, when camp would be moved beyond Cowlitz Pass to the west. The sheepherder, whose name I never knew, had come back to camp to start a fire and cook supper. I was invited to share it with him.

"I haven't seen a paper for four months," he said. "So you will have to bring me up to date."

He lit a fire and started to prepare the food. I brought him cold water from a fast-flowing spring that fed a rivulet winding its way through this small meadow for a hundred yards or so and then pouring out into a soggy, swampy expanse of grass and reeds. I made my camp close by the sheepherder's big tent and collected white fir boughs for my bed.

By that time the sheepherder had his pots on the fire. I handed him the Yakima papers and magazines. He thanked me, saying after a pause, "Will you do me a favor? Read me the paper while it is still light."

So while he cooked supper, I read the most recent paper, headlines and all, starting with the left-hand column on the front page. Most of it was news of war—the Kaiser, the Huns, the English Channel, Flanders, the Rhine. It was deep dusk when I finished the first page. Supper was about ready.

"Thanks, son," he said. "Now bring your plate and get some mutton chops, potatoes, and peas. There's bread and butter and jelly in the tent. Do you like your coffee real stout?"

When I started to eat, he left with his dogs to tend the sheep. He was back in an hour or less. As he was filling his own plate, he said, "Son, do you think you can see to read me some more?"

So I lay on my belly by the campfire and read on and on as he ate. When he had finished, we did the dishes.

"Now we'll build up this fire a bit and hear the rest of the news," he declared.

It was a still, clear night. There was a touch of chill in the air. I sat close to the fire. He cross-examined me. He not only wanted to know about the war, he wanted to know about baseball, the price of hogs, sheep, cherries, and hay, the news of the valley, of Woodrow Wilson, whom he admired, Congress, Teddy Roosevelt, and Pershing. I could not answer all the questions he asked, though I tried to give him a synopsis of the events of the summer of 1914.

After he had pumped me dry, there was silence—not even a murmur of wind stirred the tops of the fir that guarded the camp. Only the crackling of the fire and the faint sound of the snoring of one of the dogs could be heard. All else was quiet. The stars hung so low that they almost touched the firs.

My heart was filled. There was hard work in the valley, and freedom in the mountains, and, it seemed, endless opportunities ahead. I saw my future shaping up in vague outline. I had some family responsibilities, but I had no worries or doubts or fears. I felt a place awaited me in America. I felt I belonged here and that I was part of something exciting and important.

The war in Europe was as remote as the typhoon that swept bare an island in the South Pacific whose name I could not even pronounce. War in Europe? That should not concern anyone here. Hasn't Europe always had wars? Even a Hundred Years' War? The war was remote, as foreign as a flood in China or a revolution in Persia.

That is why, I think, the evening in the meadow below Cowlitz Pass remains so vivid in my mind. For as I sat in silence, thinking of the war as something wholly removed and apart from our world, the sheepherder spoke, "Well, you boys may have to finish this."

I was startled. I plied him with questions. Why should a war in Europe affect us? How could fifteen-year-old boys finish a war? Why would America want to fight in Europe?

We talked into the night by the campfire on the edge of the lonely meadow in the high Cascades. My host did not have much formal education, but he was informed and highly intelligent. He could make a complicated thing seem simple; he had the capacity of putting seemingly irrelevant things into a pattern. Or perhaps it was an ability on his part to make one see things his way. He was indeed exciting. He gave me my first seminar on war. He told me why it was that this war would soon be "our war." He said the war was a maelstrom that no Big Power in the West could avoid, and predicted that we would soon be sucked into it. Man was warlike and war ran in cycles, he said; citing American history, he pointed out that each generation on this continent had had a war. And because we had not had a conflict since the Spanish-American War, it was time for another. "There's nothing like martial music to stir people up," I remember him saying.

This was the most unsettling talk I had ever heard. I was back on the trail early in the morning, striking down toward Indian Creek, Klooch-man Rock, the Naches, and home. As I swung along in silence, the words came back to me: "You boys may have to finish this."

Brad, Elon, and I? Perhaps my kid brother Art, too? Would we have to kill people with knives and guns? We fifteen-year-old boys, who loved everything that moved in the mountains, who swore we never could kill a doe or a fawn, would be killing people soon? The guy must be nuts! Another daffy sheepherder!

Then I remembered the last scene with him. He had cooked me a great breakfast—ham and eggs, potatoes, hot cakes with butter and syrup, and coffee. I had washed the dishes and assembled my pack. I stood on the edge of the meadow facing the east as I said good-by. There was gentleness in his voice. He placed a hand on my shoulder and stood in silence a moment. "You will make a good soldier. A kid that can lug a pack over these ridges can go anywhere Uncle Sam wants to send his army."

Then I picked up the cadence—one, two, three, four; left. left. left-right-left—as I marched down the trail to home and to my junior year in high school, and out of the Cascades on the last wholly carefree trip I ever had in the high mountains.

Two more summers went by, and in the fall of 1916 I entered Whitman College. By the end of my freshman year the United States—in April, 1917—had entered what would become the First World War. War fever swept the campus.

Men in uniform became a common sight. Some of them were upperclassmen back at the fraternity house for a weekend before leaving for some unknown destination. Friends with sealed orders in their pockets were saying good-by with moist eyes. There was much swearing and boasting and bravado. America was going to "clean up a few alley rats." It wouldn't take long. The Kaiser was probably "shaking in his boots already"; the "Huns will be mighty sorry they started this fight." The general attitude was "We'll teach them."

I wanted to join the Marines. One afternoon I lay on my back on our lilac-lined lawn in Yakima looking at the clouds and trying to fit my life into World War I. The obstacles were great; Mother was dependent on me, and after talking with the recruiting officers, I could not see how I could be sure of sending her the necessary twenty dollars a month. As I lay there, watching the sky, the clouds seemed to form the Marine symbol and I wondered if it were an omen. But it was not.

I applied for service in naval aviation and passed all my examinations up to the final one, which was the color test. In those days a box of yarn was used, and I was asked to pick out Old Rose. The recruiting officer, anxious to have me, was very patient. But over and over again I picked the wrong piece of yarn, and finally I was rejected.

I went to the stores of Walla Walla and collected clippings from spools of yarn. I practiced day after day with friends who were not color-blind, but I got no better. In desperation, I consulted a biology professor who knew about color-blindness. After giving me tests, the biologist classified me as "green-red" color-blind—an affliction that curiously never bothered me with traffic or other lights, only with fabrics and the landscape.

By 1918 my sister Martha had taken over the responsibility of supporting Mother. I applied for Officers' Training School—and once more I faced the color test. I was in a group of thirty taking the physical exam. Since I undressed the fastest, I was examined first and had my clothes back on first. The examiner, whom I knew, saw me standing by and asked me to go into the next room to give the other boys the color test as they came through.

I asked each man to pick out Old Rose and gave every one a mark of one hundred. Then the examiner came in, and noticing the written entry by each name except my own, said, "Now I'll give you the color test."

"You mean the guy who gives it has to take it?"

"Okay, put yourself down for a hundred," he said wearily.

And I was in the Army!

We were sent to the Presidio, in San Francisco, then a place with open fields and few buildings. As I marched in that training camp, drilled by an old Army sergeant, I remembered Logan Wheeler, the first of my friends to die in France, killed in action at the Meuse-Argonne. Logan had worked in his father's creamery. He had wavy chestnut hair and brown eyes with joy and laughter in them. He was full of life and walked as if there were springs in his heels. He was always on the run, always cheerful and friendly.

A few days after news of Logan's death reached Yakima, I met his girl friend, a lovely creature, on South Third Avenue. She was coming from a store, a package under her arm. Grief had marred her beautiful face. She walked as if wounded. I choked up, stopped for a second, touched her arm, and hurried away without speaking. As I passed, she broke down and wept. It was then I realized for the first time, I think, what it meant when a war became "our war."

From the Presidio, I went back to the ROTC unit at Whitman College, and from there I was directed to report to Camp Taylor, Kentucky. Before the travel orders to Kentucky could be effected, however, the Armistice was announced, and a few weeks later I was discharged. So World War I had no dislocating effect on me.

Several episodes during the war made an enduring imprint on me. While I was at the Presidio the good people of San Francisco opened up the doors to their homes and showed us servicemen wonderful hospitality. On most of these occasions I was on edge, for I gathered from the talk of these affluent people that the war was being fought to make the world "safe for banks and for bankers." "Let's include the migrant workers and the IWW's," I would suggest, but that idea was met with alarm. I left San Francisco suspecting that World War I was being fought for the Establishment, which was not greatly concerned in maintaining an open society where those at the bottom could rise to the top and where the underdogs had equal civil rights.

At the college ROTC we had a colonel obsessed with two ideas. First, we must become "leaping jaguars," ready with bayonet in hand to run any German through. Second, we must be in the right mood for our role and learn to hate the Germans. How was that to be achieved? By bayoneting dead horses, pretending they were Germans. I had more disgust for the colonel than I had hate for the Germans.

When the flu epidemic hit, in the fall of 1918, I was still an ROTC private at Whitman waiting to go to Kentucky. I was the acting sergeant in our company, and one of my main jobs was to take the men out at 5:30 A.M. for calisthenics. I used the cross-country run as a regular feature of those morning exercises, and soon found that two of the men could outrun me. One of these was Art Jacobson. So when the fleet-footed Art was about to pass me, I invoked the sergeant's prerogative and blew my whistle, bringing the whole company to a halt. The flu, then, began to take its toll, and the number running grew smaller and smaller. Private homes were enlisted, nurses requisitioned, and cots shipped in by the dozens to take care of the ill. Some of the men died, and among the first was fleet-footed Art, one of my dear friends. Finally, only one member of the company was left healthy. He and I escaped the flu, and as he was one of those I could outrun, morning exercise went on uninterrupted despite the ongoing epidemic.

When the Armistice was signed, I was still in Walla Walla. My orders to report to Camp Taylor, Kentucky, for artillery school had been held up for days, probably because someone high up knew that the end of the war was near. On the day of the Armistice the commandant ordered us out, and we paraded down the streets of Walla Walla. I felt for the first time a mob's hysteria. The crowd was, of course, happy and relieved that the battles were over. People had lost sons and relatives, and many wept. Women broke ranks and rushed into the street to embrace us. I was sad and embarrassed. We were far from being heroes. We had never been under fire. We had never even heard the distant cannon roar. I wanted to escape and hide, to free myself from the cheering, weeping, exultant crowd. But on we marched, and then back to the barracks.

Despite my eventual misgivings, I got out of the war experience a new sense of pride in our flag which was to stay with me through the years. When it rippled in the wind, I was always deeply affected.

Years later I was sick at heart when another kind of mob, a crowd that was marching to object to one of our overseas commitments, burned an American flag in New York City. I understood these people who were opposed to the war in Vietnam, but I was shocked when they actually destroyed the flag.

The burning of an American flag is a crime under certain laws, but it has a more sinister aspect than most violations of law. Our flag is not just a piece of cloth, nor is it the personal emblem of the party in power. The American flag does not belong solely to whoever may be in the White House. The American flag is symbolic of *all* of the free institutions represented by our way of life.

Under our Bill of Rights every person is guaranteed the right peacefully to assemble and peacefully to petition his government for the redress of grievances. It gives the citizen the privilege of parading and making known his protests. This First Amendment privilege is unknown in most parts of the world. In many countries the right to assemble, to parade and to petition are subject to the whim and caprice of the man or the party in power, who decides who shall and who shall not speak up.

The right to assemble and to use the public streets for protests—so basic to the United States—has a long and bloody history. Many men and women, including the Quaker William Penn, suffered grievously for exercising this right, and the attempted suppression of it led to the American Revolution. These lessons were foremost in the minds of Madison and Jefferson when they drafted the first ten amendments.

The American flag to me is symbolic of the right to assemble and the right to petition our government for the redress of grievances. It signifies equal justice under law and the right to a fair trial. It stands for the right of any person—whatever the color of his skin or whatever his creed or national origin—to enjoy the public facilities of our nation. It represents free elections and an independent judiciary. It is symbolic of all civil liberties that the American tradition honors and respects.

These were my thoughts that day in New York when the flag was burned in public.

When I expressed these sentiments in a Washington, D.C., drawing room, the hostess smiled rather dryly and said, "But you taught them that disrespect." What she referred to was the second Flag Salute case in the 1940's when the Supreme Court held that schoolchildren, when motivated by religious scruples prohibiting "worship" of any secular symbol, need not salute the flag. But there is, of course, no tolerable religious dogma that would sanction flag burning or flag desecration any more than it would sanction human sacrifice.

Back in college after the war I was caught up with the proposal for the League of Nations. I felt that organization was necessary if World War I was indeed to be the war to end all wars. But the opponents of the League were so strong, I suspected that as my sheepherder friend had said, war was an institution that people like. The newspapers were filled with stories of men being sent to jail for saying that the war was a munitions makers' war, that it was an instrument to make some people rich. Slowly I became completely disillusioned.

Moreover, my own experience in the Army taught me that it was largely the "doughboys" who made the supreme sacrifice. For many of the regular officers, the war had been a way to get promoted. It was the peace that was anathema to the officer corps. I also began to have grave doubts about top generals such as "Black Jack" Pershing, who headed our forces in World War I. I was not sorry to leave the Army.

During World War I about twenty-four million men were registered for the draft. Of these, nearly 338,000, or 1.41 percent, sought to evade the draft, or desert once they were in. Though, as I have said, I had misgivings about the war, I never could have evaded military service. For I had a passionate love not only for the mountains, but for our nation and its institutions as well.

Chapter VIII

Whitman College

I went to Whitman College, Walla Walla, Washington, in the fall of 1916 because Whitman gave me a scholarship. Most of my high school friends were going to the University of Washington in Seattle, but there was a program at the time whereby the valedictorians of certain public high schools across the state—and I was one—were offered full tuition scholarships of one hundred dollars a semester to Whitman.

Fortunately, I preferred the east side of the state to Seattle, which was across the Cascades to the northwest. It would be harder to get to than Whitman, which lay down the valley from Yakima along the rail lines to the east. I thought, also, Seattle would be large and crowded, with less opportunity for part-time work; and although I'd never even set foot in a city up to that time, I was sure I would not like it.

In between fruit crops that summer I rode the rails to Walla Walla to scout out employment possibilities. Even with the tuition scholarship, I knew I could not go to college unless I earned all my living expenses and sent Mother twenty dollars a month. I decided at once that Walla Walla was a sleepy town where I would have to struggle for existence, but I found what seemed to be an anchor—Falkenberg's jewelry store, which is still there.

I met the owner, Kristian Falkenberg, a Norwegian not long out of the gold fields of Alaska; Philo Rounds, his assistant; and Jerry L. Cundiff, then a clerk, now the proprietor. They offered me a job at ten cents an hour. After checking with the college registrar's office, I learned I could have all my classes from 8:00 A.M. to noon, leaving five hours for work at Falkenberg's in the afternoon.

Fifty cents a day was not enough, however, so I also found an early-morning job as janitor of an office building and of a candy store, which I could do from 5:30 A.M. to 7:30 A.M., making up the needed twenty dollars for Mother. A third job as a waiter in a "hash house," a boarding house for working people, gave me my main two meals each day. So armed, I went back to Yakima, finished my farm work, and left for Walla Walla by bicycle (which I wanted to keep on campus) in September. It was a 165-mile ride.

I shared the janitor job with another student named Harper Joy. Harp had been in vaudeville with a "black-face" act and had also been a clown in a circus. In later years—even after he had become a respectable investment banker in Spokane, Washington—Harp often took his vacation with a circus, still playing the role of clown and loving every minute of it. Harp had stage presence and real ability. I think his musical scores of old-time vaudeville songs are one of our best collections, even to this day. Harp was the spark plug that brought the Whitman Glee Club to a new high. The singing was excellent, and Harp and his cohorts filled in with vaudeville acts between musical renditions. He played the role of Madame Zenda, who, though blindfolded, knew all and saw all. A sidekick worked through the audience, holding up a lady's scarf, a man's wristwatch, and the like. "What do I have in my hand, Madame Zenda?" always brought the correct response. What the clues were, I never knew.

Sometime later in our college careers, Harp and his Glee Club went on a successful tour, their last performance being in Spokane. The group included my brother Arthur, who by then was also a student at Whitman. They returned to Walla Walla by train, and they filled an entire Pullman car, except for one lower berth which the railroad had foolishly sold to an elderly couple. When Harp's crew took over the car, someone produced whiskey, and soon all hell broke loose. The elderly man in the lower berth complained, but to no avail. The party grew in noise—the noise of singers on the loose, the noise of collegians making merry. No one slept that night.

The reckoning was not long in coming. The elderly couple complained to S.B.L. Penrose, Whitman's president, who was so severe and straight-laced that he once threatened me with expulsion from college merely because I had the habit of whistling when I walked on campus or down the hall outside his office.

The Pullman car party brought the wrath of Penrose down on Harp, who admitted the charges and apologized. Nonetheless, Harp, my brother Art, and the others were expelled from college. Harp asked for a hearing before the Board of Trustees (of which he later became a member) and was granted one. What he said to the Board is not extant. I heard at the time that it was a moving, eloquent plea: he had a mother to support; he was poor as a church mouse; he was not a "rounder" or a "boozer." Harp's plea hit home and he and the others were reinstated.

The versatile Harp, whom I met six mornings a week, often sang as we worked. One song, or remnants of it, lingers on in my mind. The title was "You Can't Float on Every Instrument in the Band," and the song started off:

> My father was a musicker
> When he was but a boy,
> And he played the big bass fiddle in the band.
> He always wanted to be a
> Violiner when a kid,
> But he had too many k-knuckles on his hands.

In the later verses Father was stuck with the bass fiddle, and it saved his life when the band sank while on a ferryboat. The "flute had holes, let the water in"; the drum collapsed as the drummer was about to "beat his way home" on it. The fiddle was too small to be of any use. The only useful instrument was the big bass fiddle that Father played.

"Oh, I'd like to be a fiddler," sang poor Father, "But I ain't. So here by my big bass fiddle I must stand, and play nothing but those bass strings if my feet will just hold out." Then came the key to the refrain: "You can't float on every instrument in the band." But Father floated to shore and was the sole survivor.

After our morning tour of duty Harp and I got coffee and doughnuts and made our 8:00 A.M. class. I attended classes until noon, waited on tables at the "hash house" for my lunch, worked at Falkenberg's all afternoon, waited on tables for my dinner, and then studied feverishly from about eight o'clock until my nine o'clock bedtime hour. This regimen was rudely interrupted near the end of my first school year when I was given a big bowl of hot beans to put on the dining table of the boarding house. There was no room on the table itself and no sideboard where I could set the beans down. I shouted at the men but they did not hear, or, at least, pay attention. The heat on my bare hands was so intense, I had to drop the bowl of beans on the floor, and my career at that place ended literally with a crash.

During my first year at Whitman, I pitched a tent near a little brook that now runs by the girls' dormitory, and lived there for some months. Then, at the insistence of the college, I moved into a ramshackle dormitory. I still brushed my teeth and washed in the creek every morning.

Being in the dormitory created new problems. I would lock my door at night, only to have "friendly" people break it down just for the fun of hearing the sound of crunching timber. I owned only one pair of dress shoes; my only other pair was the work shoes I wore on my daily rounds. One night I came back to the dormitory to discover that my "friendly" neighbors had taken spikes and nailed my good shoes to the floor.

Next I moved into the Beta Theta fraternity house, sleeping on an open porch or in a tent in the fraternity backyard. In time, I came to regard college fraternities as a handicap, because they tend to create clannish attitudes at a time when one needs to break down all barriers and search to the outer limits for interesting people. I concluded that fraternities were a form of feudalism and that feudalism on a college campus paid few dividends.

But while I was at Whitman my fraternity had many redeeming qualities. We had for years the best choral group in the Far West. Our glee club was indeed superior. Better still, years before the other fraternities integrated, this group of mine had no racial or religious restrictions on membership. This problem was later to plague the other Whitman fraternities in connection with Jewish students, and Orientals particularly. (The first Jew I ever knew was Hyman (Shorty) Neslin, who was born in Russia. He ran a men's clothing store in Walla Walla, which I swept out in the early mornings. I learned to admire and respect both him and the group of which he was a member. Shorty Neslin seemed on a closer wave length with humanity than many of the other people I knew in Yakima or Walla Walla.)

My wages at Falkenberg's increased until, when I was a senior, I earned fifty cents an hour. I became janitor, then window washer, and finally clerk. My other jobs also varied. I attended furnaces in private homes, mowed lawns, swept out retail stores, and did other similar chores. I seldom had an evening for a movie, dance, or a musical. I had no time for browsing in the library, no time for intellectual discourse with the faculty, precious little time for serious talk with anyone.

One year I joined the debate team, adding it to my long hours of work. We met the University of Washington, Washington State College at Pullman, and the University of Idaho at Moscow. We never had much problem winning, except at Moscow. "Those Idaho juries are always stacked against us," we bitterly complained.

These out-of-town trips cut into my income-producing hours. Sleep was short, extra jobs had to be taken on to make up for lost income. I remember the end of one debate season when we returned from Moscow and Pullman dead tired. There was a dance that night and I had a date to go. By dinnertime I was so tired, I asked one of my friends if he would stand in for me. He agreed and I went to bed. I was so exhausted I slept all Friday night, all day Saturday, and all Saturday night, finally waking at seven o'clock Sunday morning thinking it was Saturday.

College-on-the-run had so many disappointments for me that I decided, rightly or wrongly, that no child of mine would have to do an hour's outside work while he was going to school.

Somewhat similar sentiments were expressed by a coal miner during Jack Kennedy's primary campaign in West Virginia in 1960. Kennedy had been accused of being the son of the wealthiest man in the United States, of having been surrounded by luxury, of never having to do a day's work. He was standing at a mine shaft shaking hands with miners as they came up at day's end. One miner looked him in the eye and said, "Is it true you're the son of our wealthiest man?"

"I guess it is true."

"Is it true you have never wanted for anything and had everything you wished?"

"Yes, it's true."

"Is it true you've never done a day's work with your hands all your life?"

"Yes, that's true also."

"Well, let me tell you this: you haven't missed a thing."

Today I feel somewhat differently. Whether the Great Society can be born by paying everyone's way through college is doubtful. Still, while it is easy to say that we worked our way through college or law school and that the younger generation is too lazy to do so, the fact of the matter is that six hundred dollars covered my annual board and tuition at Whitman College. Though I worked hard to support myself and send money to my mother, I never earned more than fifty cents an hour. I could never have managed the four or five thousand dollars a year it now takes to go to most colleges in this country. I would have been dependent on scholarship money or tuition grants, as students are today. I must say, however, that I feel the circumstances which led young people to support themselves and to pay their own way seems to me better, both for the schools and for the long-term good of the young people.

Although there were good times and fun, we were very serious people at Whitman. We debated politics, made speeches for our candidates, and worked, worked, worked.

It is important to understand that *most* of us at college were poor. I was not the only one; most of my classmates had to work to put themselves through school. The few who did not work were the social outcasts. We felt that the fellow with the rich father and the fancy clothes had a dim future. We believed that "civilization was the sound of heavy boots going up the stairs and satin slippers coming down."

Still, I would not recommend the pace at which I went through Whitman. I suppose you might say I went through college at a dead run.

I was working on the outside too many hours a day to get involved in many collegiate activities on the Whitman campus. Some could not be avoided, like the annual battle between the frosh and the sophomores. The frosh, of course, had to wear little green caps on penalty of being tossed into a campus pond, known as Lakum Duckum. On an appointed October night, when I was a freshman, the men of the two classes met in combat. I was hauled from the tent I then lived in and at once was locked in combat with a stranger. The idea was for one of us to tie the other up, take him to the pond, and throw him in. The sophomore got a scissors hold on me, almost causing me to lose consciousness. So I was led away to the lake and tossed in, hands tied behind my back.

Another day we had to engage in a tug of war with the other class, a rope being stretched across the pond. Two years in a row of this juvenile stuff almost made me leave Whitman. The difficulty was that as far as I could find out, the other schools in the Northwest were as bad, if not worse. And years later when I was on the faculty at Yale, I discovered that the scions of the First Families performed in the same way, though in a more sophisticated manner.

There were also the awful fraternity initiations—being blindfolded and forced to eat raw hamburger flavored with asafetida; standing for hours before blinding lights; being forced to steal milk bottles at dawn. There were rumors that one group actually required initiates to kill an animal and make a sacrifice in the custom of the ancient Greeks; whether true or not, I did have to go through a form of hazing when I became a Beta.

Students have always had their protests, and my generation at Whitman was no exception. Most of us started with a dislike of President Penrose and his pompous manner. He was a good Christian man, with a William McKinley type of political and economic philosophy, who would have fitted snugly into any sector of the Establishment across this broad land. He was a pseudo-intellectual with the instincts of a stuffed shirt. We did not kidnap President Penrose or seize his office or lay siege to his home. Our peak of reaction against him personally was an episode during an outdoor opera held on the campus pond.

President Penrose was coming across the pond in a skiff, his fine baritone voice resounding across the water. The boat put up at an improvised dock. Still singing, Penrose prepared to leave the boat by mounting a few steps on a short staircase built to the water's level. But we had sawed the step, and our president's baritone was quickly muffled by the murky waters of the pond. He came up puffing and filled with a mighty rage at the inefficient carpenter who had built the dock and the steps.

We had a specific complaint against the athletic director, Nig Borleski, who we maintained played favorites, not allowing on the first team any men who did not belong to his fraternity. Armed with a well-prepared case about this discrimination, a committee of three, which I headed, called on the president one Sunday afternoon in his home. We wanted Borleski fired. Whether we were right or not, we had a complaint within the zone of legitimate student interests. The result, however, was that Borleski stayed on, and we were the ones who were almost expelled for daring to exercise our First Amendment rights in such fashion.

In athletics Whitman took on all comers, although in later years the college joined a smaller league. In my days we played an annual football game with the much larger and more powerful University of Washington. One year there were only thirteen men on the Whitman squad; Washington had at least thirty-three. The game was played at Seattle. One of our members had the flu, and the only other extra man took the place of a first-stringer who had broken his leg. These eleven played the entire game, which Whitman lost 120–6. But on their return to Walla Walla, the student body gave them a rousing welcome. The six points gained under those odds gave us a moral victory.

In basketball we were whiz-bang, having outstanding teams. In tennis we were only fair. My favorite sport next to basketball was tennis, and during my first year in college I somehow made time to compete. I met

Robert Porterfield in the finals for campus champion and was narrowly defeated. In the ensuing college years work piled up much too high for any sport.

Some of our protests were more effective than the one against the athletic director. We had one professor who though conscientious was very dull and boring. His class started at eleven and was scheduled to last until five minutes of twelve, when a bell would ring. Someone obtained an alarm clock with a very loud ring, placed it in a drawer in the professor's lectern, and set the alarm for eleven-thirty. When it went off, twenty-five minutes before the scheduled bell, the entire class would rise and walk out. One day I was the last to leave, and the professor said to me, "Douglas, the older I get, the quicker these fifty-five minutes seem to pass. I don't understand it."

In another escapade, my class managed to get a cow to the belfry atop the Memorial Hall tower. She was sad and lonely as we tied her there, and she let her feelings be known to the janitor who came on duty a few hours later. Our applause was reserved for him. For how one person brings a cow down winding turret stairs remains a mystery.

I did not much enjoy the social side of college life, but I later realized that most American colleges and universities at the undergraduate level stressed this aspect. Going to college was a social badge; graduating from college was a prestige matter. Exposure to the world of ideas was not too welcome. The college and the university were not great seedbeds of dialogue and discourse; they were the centers of social activities to which aspiring parents could send their children with the hope that somehow or other a college degree would give their offspring a better foothold on the economic and social ladder than they themselves had.

Whether everyone should go to college is doubtful. Better to give everyone a B.A. at birth, I have often thought. Then college years need not be ruined by social strivings or by all the collateral activities that make "the search for knowledge" a secondary pursuit.

At Whitman, on one of my work assignments, I met the first homosexual I ever knew—and I came to know him well. I liked him for his humor, friendship, and helpfulness. I had only normal feelings toward him, and I suppose that if in those days I had been asked to name the ten men I most admired, he would have been on the list. One day when we were working alone he grabbed me and expressed his sexual interest in an unmistakable way. I pushed him away and left, and I avoided him thereafter. I was not angry, I was only sad.

Years later I discovered from legal cases and from books the nature of the "disease." I knew one United States senator who was reputed to be homosexual and one Undersecretary of State. I understood that Lafayette Park, opposite the White House, where my old friend Bernard Baruch used to sit in daylight hours and "hold court" over matters of state, became at dusk the meeting place for homosexuals. Friends of mine, innocently relaxing there, had been accosted. I later learned that the District of Columbia hires twelve men whose sole job is to patrol parks and men's rooms trying to induce homosexuals to solicit them—a practice I once described in an opinion.*

I saw these miserable people hounded and solicited by the police; many were driven out of the lower echelons of government. I learned that the condition is not explicable in terms of the Puritan ethic. I also learned that some who denounce homosexuality the loudest and proclaim against it the most vociferously may be the ones closest to being its victims. I knew none of these things, however, as a lad at Whitman.

There was one period at Whitman when the bottom dropped out of my world. Funds were badly needed at home, and I could send no more than the twenty dollars I was already remitting, so the decision was made that I should drop out of college. That night I walked the campus for hours, while a full moon rode high. There were tears in my eyes and my heart was heavy. For I felt that if I now turned aside, I might be forever relegated to menial jobs around Yakima. That fate would have been as miserable as being in a pot of glue, barely able to move and certainly unable to escape. The next day's mail brought news that the crisis had somehow been resolved, and that I could stay on in college. Thereafter I walked with springier steps.

At Whitman, I came under the influence of two powerful professors—Dr. Benjamin H. Brown, who taught physics and geology, and Dr. William R. Davis, who taught English. Daddy Brown, as we knew him, lived at the cosmic level, not the ideological one. Russia had gone Red in the revolution of 1917, but Daddy Brown knew that come spring, the fields of Russia would be alive with the brilliance of wildflowers. Creeds and dogma come and go, but planetary life goes on undisturbed. He taught us man's small role in the universe, the immensity of the Glacial Age, the magnitude of the Pleistocene, and so on. He taught us to observe the winds and the rocks. Rocks became round by rolling, and that was all

* *Osborn v. United States,* 338 U.S. 323 at 343.

we needed to know to find old watercourses. Wind carried dust. Who loses the dust? Who gets it? Solve that, and you know what lands are becoming poorer, what lands richer. That lesson was useful to me years later in North Africa.

Daddy Brown had an earth's weighing machine in the basement of Billings Hall. A select few of us were allowed to weigh the earth. The job could be done only after 2:00 A.M. or before 4:00 A.M. when there was no traffic on the street. By two o'clock the nighthawks were home, and no milk vans started on their way until four. No vibrations reached the delicate machine. Precisely how it worked I do not know, but one time, we were all able to say, "We only missed the weight of the earth by six hundred pounds."

Life after death? The loveliest image Daddy Brown could draw was illustrated by a skull he had unearthed near an apple tree. The root of the tree had grown through the eyes of the skull, sucking up into the tree the entire brain of the deceased. "How wonderful to become an apple tree!" he exclaimed. "Can anyone think of anything more choice for an afterlife?"

Father would have been shocked, but I shared Daddy Brown's feelings.

Dr. Davis, like Elizabeth Pryor at Yakima High, taught literature as a mirror of history, sociology, economics, politics. His counterpart at the University of Washington was Vernon Louis Parrington, whose *Main Currents in American Thought,* published after I finished Whitman, in addition to Veblen's *Absentee Ownership,* were, in my estimation, classics.

Davis was an inspirational man who had a knack of worming his way into another's life. In a few years he became indispensable to me. He was, indeed, a second father. If I had a speech to make, Davis heard me rehearse it at the crack of dawn in the outdoor college amphitheater. If I had a personal problem, he was my confessor. As a result, Davis became so powerful in my life, that when I graduated, I had almost decided to make English literature my career.

Whitman has always excelled in science. By the 1960's almost a hundred percent of her graduates in biology went on to graduate school. The median score of recent Whitman graduates in the Graduate Record Examination in science was in the ninety-ninth percentile in national competition. Whitman was high by all scholastic standards, but it was quite parochial while I was there; its students were almost entirely white, almost all from the middle class, almost all of American birth.

There was one Chinese girl—Grace Lee of Yakima—who had been

second to me in high school grades. Grace Lee was a brilliant person and later ran a Chinese restaurant in Baker, Oregon, taking over after her husband died. Grace was badly buffeted by prejudiced Americans. Because she was Chinese, it was impossible for her to obtain a teaching position in any school in the Far West. She had the finest credentials, but she was turned down over and over again, and finally gave up in disgust. Jingoism and talk of the "yellow peril" have always been present on the Pacific Coast. Brilliant, dedicated, vivacious Grace Lee was its victim in my time.

The first institute for Oriental studies was established at the University of Washington before World War I. Edmond Stephen Meany was its founder. In the sixties that university's Far Eastern Institute was probably one of the best in the nation, though it probably represented Formosa in its thinking rather than China, and was CIA-minded rather than geared to creating a cooperative society between East and West. The Pacific Coast still is lacking in international dimensions in its thinking, but when I was at Whitman there was no international dimension at all on the campus; and without that dimension, there is no adequate education likely for world affairs and world crises.

After the Armistice of 1918 Soviet Russia loomed large on the scene. It did not take much imagination to believe she would be a Great Power in our time. So I concluded that I would learn Russian. Since no course was offered at the college, I searched Walla Walla, looking first for a Russian scholar, then for a Russian. I found neither. Today we have the Berlitz records and various learning aids; then there were none. So I sent away for a correspondence course. The Russian grammar book was good, but I had no way of training my ear to the correct pronunciation. After a month or so of intensive study, I threw in the sponge. Thirty-five years later, when I crossed the Caspian Sea from Persia and landed in Baku, the only Russian word I remembered was *nyet*.

I helped organize the Woodrow Wilson Club at Whitman. I was aroused mainly by the dream of a better world, which Wilson hoped to achieve through the League of Nations. I espoused the League and denounced its opposition.

It was Article X that defeated the League—the guarantee against external aggression against the boundaries of the various nations fixed by the Treaty of Versailles. Hughes thought that that commitment was inexorable, that the dynamics of history often made it desirable that boundaries be adjusted through mediation, conciliation, or arbitration, Article X with its flat guarantees would lead nations not to permit peaceful adjustments of boundary questions. In my youthful enthusiasm I did not appreciate that defect which I later did understand. I, in time, came to believe that Wilson's insistence on Article X was the beginning of the opposition to the League, the opposition hardening and extending to other aspects of the League as the months passed.

My platform performances were lively affairs, one of which almost cost me student status. The college president, S. B. L. Penrose, was a cousin of Boise Penrose, who had been aligned against Wilson and the League. One night I undertook to dissect Boise Penrose piece by piece before an audience that included President Penrose, and I was called on the carpet for conduct unbecoming a student. I apologized lest any innuendoes were cast on the president, since such was not intended. But I stuck by my guns on his cousin Boise, and won a small fracas in the cause of civil liberties.

Years later, after I met Charles Evans Hughes, whom Wilson had defeated in 1916, I wondered about my early enthusiasm for Wilson. Hughes, in the 1920's and later on as well, was the great civil libertarian, not Wilson. Wilson was, after all, responsible for the famous "Red Raids" under his Attorney General, Mitchell Palmer, and Wilson was also an all-out segregationist. As President of the United States, he was probably ill-suited to head a multiracial nation, and eventually I concluded that Woodrow Wilson had done incalculable damage to our democratic idea. But young men and women often go off on false trails.

When I read, in 1971, *America's Reign of Terror* by Roberta I. Feuerlicht, the events she wrote about hit me hard. Many of these instances of persecution of minorities took place during the Wilson years, and when I was growing up I had personal experiences with the Wobblies and migrants similar to the episodes she describes. Through the newspapers of the time, I was aware of the other events as they happened. While at Whitman, I did not have all the details contained in her book, but a reading of it brings back freshets of vivid memories.

There were religious activities at Whitman but I participated in few of them, except for a short stint one winter. Three of us students volunteered to conduct services at several churches in the vicinity of Walla Walla, after the president's office had requested help. One of the volunteers was Louis Gaiser, the only student in my time who kept a bottle of whiskey under his mattress. Louis was the offbeat whom we tolerated, and he vowed that whiskey sharpened his tenor voice. The second of the two was Irving Jones, whose nickname was Cooley City because that was his hometown.

When we went out to hold Sunday evening services, Louis Gaiser would boom out in his sonorous voice, and if his throat was also properly tuned with a little lubrication, Cooley City Jones would join him. I was the presiding officer. Either Louis or Irving did the praying. Louis led in the singing. Irving preached the sermons and proclaimed a Fundamentalist creed, and the good people of Touchet and Dayton loved us. When Irving became an undertaker rather than a minister, and Louis hid his bottle and became a teacher, I felt that organized religion had lost two bright prospects.

The apogee of my exposure to theological dogma, as distinguished from faith, had taken place about the time I was seventeen. A revivalist of renown came to Yakima, not Billy Sunday but one of his type and caliber. A temporary canvas "temple" was put up on West Yakima Avenue, the portable seats resting on the ground and a "sawdust trail" leading up the center aisle to a crude, improvised platform. There was an American flag on the platform, a pulpit and two chairs, side by side. A man with a tuning fork hummed, raised his arms, and brought a male chorus into full voice. It was the best all-male rendition of religious songs that I heard until years later when I attended a Baptist Church in Alma Ata, Soviet Russia.

After the singing the revivalist strode onto the stage with the dignity, poise, and suavity of a hypnotist—which he turned out to be. He talked of God, of the Bible, of Jesus, of the devil, of heaven and hell. The chair on his right was the force for "good"; the one on the left was "evil." This went on for fully an hour, when he reached his peroration. Draping the American flag gently over "good," he praised all the virtues. Then he took "evil" and smashed it to smithereens. After the collection plate was passed, he called everyone "to come to Jesus." Most of us went, each being blessed by a touch of his hand on the head. Then there was a prayer, and we melted away into the darkness of Yakima.

On the way home that night I puzzled over what had happened. I realized that the men and women who walked that "sawdust trail" had made no commitment to stop whatever practices blighted their lives. They had experienced an orgasm. They were motivated by fear—fear of punishment in the hereafter. As a boy, the virtues of heaven and the horrors of hell had been pounded into me and I took the existence of those two "places" for granted the same as I did the existence of Chicago and New York City, also unseen. In those terms, each of the revival participants had bought a ticket to heaven, where he would find peace and security.

As I viewed the people of Yakima and of Walla Walla in the months that followed, I realized that most members of the Establishment had received tickets to heaven merely for being pious on Sunday. Heaven became in my mind a lovely pink cloud occupied by those who had made the greatest contributions to the church. I began to think how dreadful it would be to sit on that pink cloud with all those people, who were not only a thieving lot, but hypocrites, and above all else, dull, pious, and boring. There was no one I could talk with about the quandary I was in, for I was thinking heretical thoughts. But I was distressed that in this revivalists' heaven there would be no IWW's or any of those I really and truly admired as warm-hearted human beings. I kept all those thoughts to myself.

Finally I took the Apostles' Creed, a regular ritual in the Presbyterian church, and underlined in ink the parts—the only parts—in which I truly believed. And what is printed below has in italics those underlined words:

> *I BELIEVE in God the Father Almighty, Maker of heaven and earth; and in Jesus Christ* his only Son our Lord: *who* was conceived by the Holy Ghost, Born of the Virgin Mary; *Suffered under Pontius Pilate, Was crucified, dead, and buried*: He descended into hell: The third day he rose again from the dead: He ascended into heaven, and sitteth on the right hand of God the Father Almighty: From thence he shall come to judge the quick and the dead.
>
> I believe in the Holy Ghost: the holy Catholic Church; the Communion of Saints: *The Forgiveness of sins*: The Resurrection of the Body: *And the Life everlasting.*

As I began to travel the world, I became more critical of those early religious assumptions. When I rubbed shoulders with our own poor and saw the awful poverty of the Middle East and Latin America, I realized that heaven and hell were instruments whereby the clergy maintained the security of a static society. As stated by a Maryknoll father, wise in the ways of Latin America: "The peasants are in the field, the destitute in the slums, the students in the classroom, the rich in their castles, and God is in His heaven."

In other words, a peasant, who went to bed hungry and whose babies died for lack of any medical care, suffered greatly on this earth but got his reward in heaven. Religious superstitions thus became a way of keeping the masses subservient and the rich secure in their monopolies of wealth and political power. A Catholic prelate in Latin America put the same idea in trenchant words: "Poverty is the most certain road to eternal felicity. Only the state which succeeds in making the poor appreciate the spiritual treasures of poverty can solve its social problems."

In later years I came to know several Americans who I felt had greatly dishonored our American ideal. One was Cardinal Spellman of New York; the second was J. Edgar Hoover of the FBI; the third was John Foster Dulles, who in time became Secretary of State. By all assumptions and conventions those three would certainly end up in heaven. I could perhaps endure them for an evening. But to sit on a cloud with those three through eternity would be to exact too great a price. So I dismissed heaven completely as a theological creation—and hell, too.

Many people, however, take their creed seriously, and one who trenches on it is in trouble. Profanity and sacrilegious talk were crimes under colonial law when New England was first settled. Since I was a son of the manse, I knew that tradition and respected it. Mother's remedy for a child who swore was to wash out his mouth with soap and water. Both Charles Evans Hughes and Hugo Black had the same Puritan tradition—as did Frank Murphy, Wiley Rutledge, Harold Burton, Harlan F. Stone—none of them ever swore.

My friend Saul Haas, whom I met long after I left Whitman, was of a different tradition. His capacity to swear had monumental and, at times, artistic aspects. But Saul's tolerance did not always carry him through crises. Saul had a radio station in Seattle and later a TV outlet, and in the early radio days his station KIRO put on a weekly Sunday morning hour-long program called *Church of the Air*. The program was made up of records which an attendant put on a phonograph after making a short statement that KIRO was now on the air.

This particular Sunday the attendant arrived at the station with an awful hangover, barely able to make the announcement, and put on the record. He waited a few minutes to make sure the machine was working properly, and then went downstairs and up the block to a café for hot black coffee, which he desperately needed. Half an hour later he returned to the radio station to find the entire switchboard flashing the message that incoming calls were being made. Each time he plugged in to answer, an irate housewife or a gruff male was denouncing him and KIRO. He went into the broadcasting room, only to discover that the needle had stuck in the middle of a prayer, with the result that the record was saying over and again "Oh, Jesus Christ" . . . "Oh, Jesus Christ." He instantly got the needle out of the groove and the *Church of the Air* continued. But the listeners were so upset, Saul, despite his own relaxed attitude, had to announce publicly that the man had been fired, which he was. But Saul instantly rehired him under another name, for he was a good radio man.

The subject of revivals arose when in Washington, D.C., I came to know Senator Sam J. Ervin, Jr. of North Carolina. Senator Ervin, a distinguished lawyer and jurist before he came to the Senate, was a great champion of the Bill of Rights and is perhaps best known for his part in the Watergate investigation. He is also a storyteller *par excellence*. Senator Ervin had yarns concerning the Billy Sunday type of revival meetings that came to his town. A trumpeter would precede the evangelist, and by the time of the revival he would get the singers and musicians in the community organized. The big meeting ended with a plea for all to come forward, confess their sins, give testimonials, and say what the good Lord had done for them.

On one such occasion everyone came forward except Uncle Ephraim, who with difficulty walked with a crutch under his left arm and a cane in his right hand. He was plagued with arthritis, old injuries to his hips, and had a touch of the gout. The evangelist, learning Uncle Ephraim's name, called out for him to come forward and make the testimonials unanimous. With great difficulty Uncle Ephraim hobbled to the front, and the evangelist said, "Now tell us, Uncle Ephraim, what the good Lord has done to you."

Uncle Ephraim raised his aching head and said, "He just about done me in."

Years later in Washington, D.C., I had many talks about God with my ear and nose doctor—the late Sam Alexander. Once when he had given me a shot of penicillin and had me wait fifteen minutes to see if I developed a reaction, I put to him the question, "Why do you believe in God?"

His answer came as a surprise. "Because of ear wax." In his eyes, ear wax was the ultimate gift to man, the wax that later was the key to the discovery that the American Indian was indeed of Mongol stock, because both the Indians and Mongols have "dry" ear wax, while the Caucasians and Blacks have "wet" ear wax. To Alexander, ear wax could not be explained except in terms of a divine gift.

And the more I traveled the world and saw its unfolding wonders, the more overwhelmed I became. There was no way to explain the beauty and interlocking dependency of all life except in terms of a divine power, whether one studied the propagation of lichens or the fertilizing of waters by the manure of the hippopotamus.

. . .

One awful consequence of my early religious training was fear of supernatural punishment. Every child has a sense of guilt. The guilt may be groundless; the transgression, if it be such, may be trivial. Nonetheless it exists, and the church exploits this guilt to regiment children. I was taught—or led to believe—that lightning was the hand of God, that the bolts would hit the guilty. In my young mind, when the heavy electric storms came, a vengeful Jehovah was searching out the sinners. I was filled with fright beyond understanding. I actually tried to hide, though I had been told that no one could hide from God, that he would send the bolt of lightning under the bed if necessary.

It took years for me to rid myself of this fear, and eventually to appreciate the beauty and grandeur of electrical storms. The day came when I could sit in my tent on a mountain ridge and enjoy a storm as one does a symphony. There is a majestic quality about the big storms when seen in the open. A smell of ozone is sharp when a bolt hits a mountain peak. A great conifer that is hit lights up instantly like a match. Once when a plane I was traveling in was hit by lightning, the electricity rolled off the wings like golden water. But there was a vast gap I had to bridge between enjoyment of that experience and the early teaching about the hand of God.

As the years passed and Buddha, Zoroaster, the Bab, Mohammed, Confucius, Joseph Smith—yes, and Gandhi too—came into view, I realized that they, like Jesus, were also sons of the Lord, sent to do his business. My "awakening," which really took years, dated back to the hypnotic revivalist I met in Yakima, and I was always grateful to that showman for revealing what a fraud he was.

My whole faith was regenerated when in 1951 I crossed the Himalayas, and near the end of my journey, stayed three days at a Buddhist monastery, named Hemis, where I heard a story I liked to believe was true. Jesus, I learned, had been on the monastery's faculty for ten years—the ablest teacher in its long and illustrious history. He had indeed gone east—not into outer space—after the Resurrection, following the caravan trails where the Persian empire had made Aramaic the common language of tourists.

The Eastern philosophies have respect for all forms of life, animal as well as human. Behind these philosophies are deep-seated animistic beliefs. In the Himalayas, altitude sickness is attributed to the god who rules over the pass or the peak. The aboriginals of Australia, who, like the Hawaiians, probably come from Malay stock, are associated at birth with a wild animal, bird, or fish, which becomes the child's guardian and which that human being, in turn, honors or protects. I know a family in Hawaii that for centuries has had the shark as its guardian.

This identification of people with animals, creating a community relation with a particular animal, means that a species of brotherhood is also created. Man is not on earth to dominate, destroy, and kill for the sake of showing off his superiority. Man becomes one with the life of his area of earth.

I came to believe that Jesus was, like other men, the son of God, that, as Alan Watts wrote, he had "intense experiences of cosmic consciousness—of the vivid realization that one's self is a manifestation of the eternal energy of the universe, the basic 'I am.'" The powerful lesson of the New Testament is that if Jesus could identify with God, every person can do the same. The Hindus and Buddhists believe that. Each of them can say "I am God" without being guilty of subversion or blasphemy. For that represents the striving for a goal of which all people are capable of seeing, understanding, and fulfilling in part.

With the passing of the years after my graduation from Whitman, I came to feel that something more than sentiment was needed to keep our colleges going. It is my coldly objective consideration that colleges have not filled an important role and in their existing form are by no means indispensable to "education." They are cluttered with youngsters caught up with problems of adolescence which their parents hope to avoid having to solve. More important, there are few students who have any real intellectual interest in specific areas. Many are floaters; many look on college merely as a status symbol. Ivan Illich, in *Deschooling Society*, describes how schools train only (certainly mainly) for life in the existing order of things, not for critical analyses of the strengths and weaknesses of it and of the needs of government and of people in the fast ongoing changes in societies. His criticism extends, of course, to most schooling, including colleges.

Colleges, whether private or public, are extremely expensive institutions to operate. The amount of money invested in facilities is great and the output in terms of educated men and women is not commensurate. My thought has been that a new approach should be taken.

One suggestion is the British Open University, which uses radio, television, tape cassettes, and printed material to offer a college education through home study. No formal academic requirements would be needed. Those who did the work would take an examination, and if successful, get college credit.

My preference is for a tutorial system where students would report regularly to a tutor, and the tutor, say, in English literature or economics, would lead a group in a discussion of the questions raised. Each student would be geared to his own pace, going as fast or as slowly as his abilities and energy permitted. He would work on his own, using the assignment sheets of his tutors and taking examinations at stated times.

Whatever system was used, the average student would end his academic career with junior college. The new tutorial institution would be geared for the exceptional student, usually aiming at some specialty requiring graduate work.

Excellence would be the standard. Full development of the idiosyncrasies of the individual would be the aim. The tutorial system would eliminate the leveling influence of the college. The tutorial institution would be aimed not at standardizing ideas, but at releasing the creative potential of every individual.

We might then in the end have a real aristocracy of talent drawn from the vast democratic pool of peoples of all races and all faiths and all standards of living.

I have always had a sentimental tie to Whitman that goes very deep. Among the Douglases in my family who have graduated from Whitman, besides myself, are my brother Art, my sister Martha, and my son, Bill. My first grandaughter, Leslie Lee Wells, came from England in 1971 to attend Whitman College for a time.

As Daniel Webster said in arguing the classic Dartmouth College case a century ago, "It's a small college, but there are those who love it." Certainly that is the way I felt about Whitman when I graduated in May of 1920, at the age of twenty-one.

Chapter IX

Small-Town Teaching

When I finished college, Mother was still having financial trouble. Martha, who had dropped out of Whitworth College to help support the family while I went through Whitman, now wanted to get her own degree. Moreover, Arthur would start college that fall and would need help. I went back home to Yakima and got a job teaching English, Latin, and public speaking at the Yakima High School, a position I kept for two years.

Before reporting to the high school for work, I bought an automobile in Walla Walla for forty dollars. It was an early, decrepit Dodge that had immortality. No car was ever more solidly built or more serviceable. It rode the ruts of the dirt roads of that day with ease. (Ten years later that car was a bright memory when I was working as a lawyer in Wall Street. Charles Schwartz, whom I will mention later, got an option on Mrs. Dodge's stock and sold it to Dillon Reed, investment bankers, for a reputed five million. Dillon Reed then proceeded to reorganize Dodge Motor Company, taking out as its fee about thirty million dollars. That was a common practice of predatory finance in those days; and I knew as I studied the anatomy of that operation that the quality I saw in my early Dodge would suffer. That quality did in fact disappear for some years.)

One holiday Arthur was back in Yakima from Whitman and borrowed the old Dodge to visit a girl friend in the Lower Valley, the flat, rich, irrigated land below the gap south of Yakima. He had not returned by early the following morning, and I was disturbed. I did not have long to wait. A note came to me by a courier from the Yakima City jail, saying Art was being detained. I went there at once, and learned that Art had been picked up for speeding late the night before and had insufficient cash to deposit for bail. When I reached him, Art was in the bullpen, a room perhaps twenty by thirty feet, which was a temporary place of detention. Art, never one to let a moment go idle, had organized the dozen or so nondescript inhabitants of the bullpen, and had them marching in unison—first clockwise and then counterclockwise. They all happily reacted to Art's cheerful command, and were sorry to see him leave when I deposited the fifteen dollars collateral.

During my days as a high school teacher I filled in occasionally during spring vacation at a one-room school at Wiley City, where the teacher taught eight classes. The first day I had trouble with a "bully" in the eighth grade. Though I subdued him, he threatened revenge. Sure enough, the next morning he arrived with his father, who insisted on a fist fight. Only when I in turn subdued the father did the son settle down.

While teaching in Yakima, I spent some time with the Boy Scouts. During my own young years in Yakima, I never had time for Scout work. I knew the woods, but I was my own instructor. That experience had made me wholly sufficient in the wilderness; I had no fear of the woods, I felt at home there. I could live on the land and start fires without matches. The loveliest orchestration I knew was the music of the wind in the conifers and the roar of mountain brooks. So it was that in my teaching years in Yakima, I was approached by Scoutmasters to help them on their hikes and camp-outs; and sometimes I went along to try to introduce the boys to the woods in a civilized manner, putting them on speaking terms with all of the wonders of the out-of-doors.

Those seminars were interesting to me, the instructor. Scouting was in those years a "high-minded endeavor," as it still is in a few parts of the country. But American scouting has changed a great deal. Boys no longer go to the woods to classify plants, to learn the tracks of animals, to study zoology, or to indulge in geological hunts. Many of them go to Scout camps to be entertained, to play games, to indulge in horseplay. I visited such camps and saw how the role of Scoutmaster has deteriorated. The Scout camp, like the kindergarten, is a place for parents to dump their children for a few weeks, so that they need not be bothered themselves. The Scoutmaster is chosen not for his Daniel Boone or Gifford Pinchot abilities, but for his geniality. He performs no educational functions; he is a chaperon; his task is to keep the boys happy. And as I roamed these places, I saw the tragic consequences.

"What have you learned this summer?" I would ask a Scout.

"How to smoke, how to drink, how to steal" was not an uncommon reply.

I also became the debate coach at the Yakima High School and traveled across the state with a fired-up team of two girls—Margaret Trout and Lorna Defoe—and two boys—Wayland Chase and Waldo Gedosch. Changing sides on the issues every day we were out, we won the state championship!

After I was on the Court, I was making a speech in Spokane. A nice-looking, middle-aged woman came up to me and said, "I'll bet you don't recognize me, Mr. Justice." I looked into her eyes that had not changed and said, "You're Lorna Defoe." She had been on the debate team at Yakima High all those years before.

I enjoyed contacts with the students, but high school teaching was not entirely satisfying. When I finished college I had been undecided as to my career, and the indecision gave me a feeling of insecurity. My classmates were clear as to what they would do in life. Why wasn't I? I leaned toward English literature, but law also had a strong pull. If I had had to make a final decision in the fall of 1920, it would have been English literature. Indeed, I applied at that time for a Rhodes scholarship in English literature at Oxford. My credentials were excellent, and I appeared at the office of Dr. Henry Suzzalo, president of the University of Washington, in Seattle, at noon on the designated day. I and a dozen other applicants sat in an anteroom for hours. Some were closeted with the committee an hour or more. I was called last, and by the time my name was announced, it was six o'clock. I finished my interview before six-five, and as I staggered limply out, I knew that the selection was wholly political—that I had no chance. The committee asked me only two questions, which I easily answered:

"What is the difference between a demagogue and a statesman?"

"What did Wordsworth mean by a 'feeling intellect'?"

Forty years later I met the man who had won out over me for that scholarship. He had studied law at Oxford and later in this country, and became a professor of government. He was one of the most conservative influences I have known. Perhaps he was born that way, but I have wondered ever since whether his Oxford experience blighted a promising young man and whether it would have done the same to me.

Fifty years after my interview the Rhodes scholarship committee was still struggling with the problem of elitism in the choice of its candidates.

I was interested to read a *New York Times* article announcing some of the winners for 1972; among them were a biology graduate who reportedly grew up in the Bronx, a young man who worked with prisoners in New Mexico, and a cadet who organized a week-long Black Arts festival at the Air Force Academy, which he attended. According to the *Times*, the stereotype of the "well-rounded, Establishment-oriented, athletic, brainy, and well-connected individual" sought by the committee was beginning to change. Now they might accept as an athlete a strong hiker or back-packer; and being a social activist would not necessarily disqualify a man. But of course, many of the candidates were still from the same old mold.

Rejection by the Rhodes scholarship committee did not turn me immediately to law, but it did dampen my enthusiasm for English literature as a career. Two years' experience in teaching English, Latin, and public speaking did the same.

Moreover, my growing awareness of the American Legion, its intolerance and its injustices, also helped turn me closer toward the law as a safeguard of freedom. When I was teaching at Yakima High, I joined the local branch of the American Legion, but I did not long remain a member. I do not recall whether I resigned or whether I let my membership go by default. The barrage of intolerance that soon was laid down by the national organization made me think that the Legion was at times the most un-American of any group.

The American Legion in its Minneapolis Convention in November, 1919—its first national convention—had resolved in favor of the exclusion of Japanese and other members of the Oriental race. The Legion demanded that no foreign-born Japanese be allowed to become naturalized. It demanded that Congress prepare an amendment diluting the Fourteenth Amendment by making it read that "no child born in the United States" of "foreign parentage" shall hereafter be eligible for citizenship "unless both parents were so eligible at that time." The Orientals whom I knew were a credit to our country, and the Legion's drive against them was a real affront to me.

The Legion at that first national convention in 1919 also resolved to combat "all anti-American tendencies, activities, and propaganda." It resolved "to organize immediately for the purpose of meeting the insidious propaganda of Bolshevism, IWWism, radicalism, and all other anti-Americanisms by taking up the problem of: . . . detecting anti-American activities everywhere and seizing every opportunity everywhere to speak plainly and openly for 100 percent Americanism and for nothing else."

The Legion further resolved that there existed in the country "various organizations and isms whose ultimate aim is the destruction of the principles of law, order, and true democracy"; that the Department of Justice has "a great mass of facts and evidence regarding these activities, especially those of the so-called parlor socialists and Bolsheviki, which our organization considers by far the most dangerous, for they, under a mask of respectability, insidiously inject infamous teachings into the minds and thoughts of our citizens."

The Legion recommended that the Department of Justice be changed "from a passive, evidence-collecting organization to a militant and astute group of workers, whose findings shall be forcefully acted upon by this, our American Government."

To me, this sounded like an espousal of the police state. The "Red Raids" which accompanied World War I and its immediate aftermath were the product of this kind of thinking. It was many years before I learned the details of these raids, which were made a matter of public record by a courageous judge, George W. Anderson of Boston. What Judge Anderson found shows that as a government we acted dishonorably under Mitchell Palmer and his field man, J. Edgar Hoover, who was one day to rise to an eminent position. Innocent men and women, whose only crime was being foreigners, were descended upon by the FBI in the wintertime, loaded into lorries, moved onto islands off Boston, and placed in houses that had no heat, no blankets, no food. We temporarily made intolerance of the alien our god and dishonored our Constitution by practicing un-Americanism of the worst kind in disrespect of the rights of nonviolent, peaceful minorities.

The American Legion which I repudiated early in the 1920's continued to maintain its rightist stance on many major issues. In 1967 a Legion circular came to my desk, reading: "R. J. Reynolds Tobacco Co., makers of CAMEL-TEMPO-WINSTON-SALEM cigarettes use COMMUNIST TOBACCO." On the reverse side, the pamphlet read: "TRADE GIVES AID. The makers of CAMEL, TEMPO, WINSTON, and SALEM should face reality, as an increasing number of loyal American firms are doing, and refuse to be a part of aiding the Communists in Europe while our GI's die fighting Communism in Vietnam. WHEN WE HELP A COMMUNIST FORM OF GOVERNMENT WE UNDERMINE THE SECURITY OF OUR OWN COUNTRY."

This attitude has been reflected throughout the years by the Legion's attitude toward conscientious objectors. As early as 1919 the Legion, in its first national convention, condemned the restrained treatment of conscientious objectors, "many of whom were naught but enemies of this country, hiding behind the cloak of religion."

That phrase "hiding behind the cloak of religion" was to become familiar as I discussed it as well as a host of other subjects in Yakima, in 1921, with a new friend, O. E. Bailey. Like my feelings about the Legion, Bailey's views on the clergy, morality, and the law also helped lead me to a legal career.

During the time I taught in the Yakima High School, I became greatly attracted to Bailey, an insurance agent representing Sun Life Insurance Company. I do not recall exactly how I met him, but I believe he sought me out as an insurance prospect. He was such a good salesman that he signed me up to sell insurance for him in my spare time. My interest in insurance soon waned, for the first policy I sold was to a man who within a few days tried to commit suicide. I had cheerfully advanced the first year's premium, taking the insured's note, which of course he never paid.

My acquaintance with Bailey flowered into a warm friendship. We sat long into the night in philosophical, political, and religious talk. His mind was keen. His horizons were wide. He was a man without formal education who was as eager for knowledge as anyone I have known. His laughter started quietly, rose quickly, and exploded in a crescendo. He turned a phrase neatly and used earthy anecdotes to enliven his serious talk. O. E. Bailey was the product of the wind-blown, poverty-ridden dust bowl of North Dakota, living there long before shelter belts were planted. As a boy, he knew cow-chip fires and sunsets reddened with dust. Somewhere along the line Robert G. Ingersoll had entered his life, and he read the man's works avidly. He could quote Ingersoll for hours on end and he usually cited him with approbation. Bailey was probably an atheist, though he never proclaimed the fact. If he had a God, it was not the God of the Establishment. Bailey had little praise for dogma. The Immaculate Conception was, to him, the clergy's invention. He mocked miracles and made light of saints. Before Sinclair Lewis had written of the lecherous Elmer Gantry, O. E. Bailey had long criticized the clergy for preaching morality and practicing immorality.

Bailey was not a lawyer, though he knew about law. He was the first person I met who had actually seen the Supreme Court in session. Bailey described the Court so that it—and its tremendous potential for righting or ignoring human grievances—came alive for me for the first time. His terms were solemn, and his words are still powerful in memory. For this was the "final court from which there is no appeal," he said. And he added, "Sometimes the Court errs."

That last I knew, for the Court's treatment of Eugene Debs had been a disgrace in my eyes. Moreover, the Court had never been a bastion of liberty in America's "Reign of Terror," the period that roughly started with Debs and ended with Coolidge. I began to put together what the Legion was doing with what O. E. Bailey observed, and decided that perhaps one trained in law could be an effective voice for human rights.

My only real contact with the Supreme Court up to that time had been rather a tenuous one. William Howard Taft, who was appointed Chief Justice of the United States in 1921, had visited the Whitman campus a few years earlier while I was still a student there. At that time Taft was not yet Chief Justice. He had served as a federal judge shortly before the turn of the century and had been President of the United States from 1909 to 1913. Taft was then on the Yale Law School faculty, and he and I were destined to have one other thing in common: each of us was named to the Court from Connecticut. The only other such Justice was Oliver Ellsworth. When we students saw Taft at Whitman, we were not allowed to meet him or ask him questions. My only impression of the man was that he was greatly overweight.

I began to frequent the courtrooms in Yakima. I attended many trials in the state courts and got a measure of the lawyers who practiced there. I had enough confidence to feel that I would be a match for any of them.

I used to walk into the federal courtroom in Yakima and listen to proceedings before Judge Frank H. Rudkin. He had his roots in Yakima, having practiced there. Then he became a Superior Court judge in the Washington state system, and from that bench, went to the State Supreme Court. In 1911 Rudkin was named to the federal District Court, where he served until 1923, at which time he went to the Court of Appeals in San Francisco and departed the Yakima scene. From 1920 to 1922, however, he sat in Yakima and I saw him from a distance many times. He had a receding hairline, with a shiny, white pate and a full black beard. His voice was cavernous, and when he spoke he seemed to have the power of the Prophets in him. How great a judge he was I never really knew, but he became to me the embodiment of the law.

Slowly I cast my vote for law and against English literature, Mother's objections notwithstanding. She wanted me to stay in Yakima and become a high school principal because that sounded like a secure future to her. But I tended more and more toward law school.

By the spring of 1922 I had written Harvard Law School to apply for admission and I received notice that I had been accepted. It was May and I had been at the YMCA exercising. After a shower I went to the reading room and had an experience that shows how accidental some good things are. I barely noticed a man sitting opposite me, also reading. If either one of us had read faster than the other, we probably never would have met. But it so happened that each of us threw his magazine on the table at precisely the same time.

That started a conversation. He was James T. Donald, just arrived in Yakima to practice law. I expressed the hope that in three years I would perhaps join him at the Yakima Bar. He asked where I would study law, and when he learned I had applied to Harvard, he added, "I hope you have a lot of money." I told him I did not have a cent, that I'd have to work my whole way through.

"Then go to Columbia," he said.

We settled down for a long, serious talk. He had worked his way through Columbia and "knew the ropes" and he would help with letters and advice. The next day I canceled out at Harvard and applied for Columbia. Jim gave me letters to the Columbia dean, Harlan F. Stone, with whom I was later to serve on the Court; to Miss Breed, head of the Appointments Office; and to others. By a chance meeting, my entire career was changed. And but for that chance meeting, my life would probably have centered in Yakima, for I probably could not have worked my entire way through Harvard and in time probably would have drifted back to the Washington public school system.

That chance contact was also the start of a warm friendship with James Donald that lasted until his death. He moved to Baker, Oregon, and practiced law, where I almost joined him. We became fast fishing friends, taking to the high country by pack train and searching for trout in remote lakes and streams both in the Cascades of Washington and in the Wallowas of Oregon.

Jim and I made up in enthusiasm what we lacked in skill. Our camps were filled with great talks about the nation and the world, our Happy Hours were seasoned with humor, our fishing was marked with high strategy.

One of Jim's partners in these later days was Blaine Hallock, who had served in my ROTC company in 1918. The three of us made Izaak Walton history of our own. Blaine was a talented dry-fly fisherman. He tied his own flies and made a study of the habits of "fresh-water trouts," as he used to call them. He was an artist with a fly rod, and it was a joy to see him cast. He did everything with finesse; he was a perfectionist.

For years Blaine's wife begged him to take her fishing. Once he succumbed and they fished an Oregon lake from the same boat. Each had a strike and hooked a trout at the same time. Blaine, who was busy with his own line, kept saying over his shoulder, "Now remember what I told you, honey." His wife reeled in vigorously, and instead of playing the fish and giving it line, pulled it in until its nose was touching the end of her pole. Then she said, "What do I do now, honey?"

Blaine turned, and seeing what she had done, replied, "So far as I'm concerned, honey, you can go straight to hell."

He never took her fishing again.

And so it was that a casual encounter in the YMCA at Yakima in May of 1922 brought me great dividends. I was to learn that one cannot make a chart of one's life in advance and expect to follow it. Chance enters into it; the only sensible planning is to try to keep midstream while history is made.

Chapter X

Law School and Law Practice

In September, 1922, having decided to go to Columbia Law School, it was time to go East. After two years of teaching I had saved seventy-five dollars and, of necessity, my transportation across the country was to be by freight train. I had arranged to go to Wenatchee, Washington, to take over two thousand sheep owned by a Yakima firm and see them safely on the Great Northern Railroad to the Chicago stockyards.

The night before I left, Mother, my sister, my brother, and I gathered for a final evening together. I remember sitting on the stool by the organ that Mother often played for us, my heart heavy. This seemed like a permanent parting of the ways, as I would be gone three years. There were tears in my eyes as I took an old battered suitcase with a suit and change of clothes in it and left by the back way to the railroad yards, where I would catch a freight to Wenatchee.

I made my rendezvous with the sheep, and rode in style in the caboose. As the train pulled out of Wenatchee in the late afternoon, I climbed to the top of a car and faced the setting sun. Soon the orchards of Wenatchee were swallowed up and we entered the sagebrush, rattlesnake country of the Inland Empire. This was long before Grand Coulee Dam had made it possible to irrigate this potentially rich country of volcanic ash. A quarter-century later irrigation water would run into the old bed of the Columbia, and not only turn a wasteland into a garden, but, to the surprise of the engineers, fill many an ancient pothole with water from subterranean channels. Blue-water lakes and rich green fields would transform the desert we crossed that night. Now it was dry and unproductive.

Those matters, of course, were no part of my dreams. Mine were vague, like those of any boy going into battle in a strange and faraway place. I was this night concerned only with getting away from Yakima.

Why did I leave? What was the source of my confidence that, even penniless, I would succeed? I do not know, though I have often wondered about it. In Yakima, I had a feeling of being caught; escape was essential. And yet there was a feeling of guilt too—guilt for leaving an impoverished mother, who by that time had decided that if I applied myself, I could in another ten years become principal of the high school.

The impulse to leave had won out. I had the fear of being trapped into a dull and listless life. I had come to dislike the place; its environment was oppressive. Ideas were not congenial to Yakima. The pulpits—with the one exception I mentioned—were filled with Billy Grahams. Later I was to become very homesick for Yakima as the rough environment of New York buffeted me, but the night I left I was filled with the happiness of one who after a great ordeal escapes a prison. The clickety-click of the wheels of the old freight and the cool night air made these early hours of my escape exquisitely serene.

We had not yet left Washington State before the railroad strike of 1922 was upon us. The train was at once sidetracked, high and dry, and we stayed on a siding over twenty-four hours. I knew enough law to know that carriers had feeding and watering responsibilities to livestock in transit. "My sheep will die," I told every railroad employee I could reach. Hours passed, and finally a switch engine appeared and hauled us to a town that had pens for feeding livestock. There we stayed another day, waiting to be carried East.

This was my first long journey both in miles and in time. It took almost two weeks to reach Minneapolis. Whenever the freight train was moving, I was in the caboose. It had a coal stove in the middle and a long, narrow bench on each side. My hat and my coat were my pillow for the few hours of sleep I was able to get at night. Lying there, or sitting, I loved the familiar, rhythmic click of the wheels as they passed over the links in the rails. I also admired a tobacco-chewing brakeman, who could spit like nobody's business. He would sit opposite me and shoot a wad across the caboose, over my prostrate body, and out the open window. He never missed.

It took us three days to reach Miles City, Montana, where we stayed all night in a pouring rain. I spent the night in the freight house with a railroad employee who had a Ph.D. in Philosophy from Harvard. Somewhere along the line he had lost out, with a probable assist from alcohol. We talked all night, dissecting the universe while my sheep bleated.

The immensity of my country came home to me as we cleared the Rockies and entered the Great Plains. Dust storms were making up every day and beginning to cast a pall over the land, the situation that came to a crisis under FDR years later. I was soon to find full confirmation of what my Yakima friend, O. E. Bailey, who grew up in North Dakota, had told me about the privation of the farmers who settled west of the rich Red River Valley. As a consequence of their suffering, North Dakotans had rebelled, formed unorthodox political parties, and turned socialistic under such leaders as William Langer, whom I was to meet years later in Washington, D.C., when he became a senator. In 1920 the U.S. Supreme Court had sustained in a unanimous opinion the constitutionality of the socialist program. On this freight train ride that offbeat program gained new meaning in my mind. My reading of Thorstein Veblen had taught me the manner in which the Establishment was exploiting our material and human resources, and this situation suddenly came alive for me. I began to see, in the rawness of North Dakota, the stuff out of which great reforms were being created.

When we reached Williston, North Dakota, we were sidetracked a mile from the station. Hours went by, and it seemed as though we never would get clearance to go ahead. By that time ten days had passed since I had left home, and I had had little sleep and little to eat. Assured by the crew that we would not leave for some hours, I crawled under and over a dozen or more trains to get to the lunch counter in the station at Williston. I ordered several dollars' worth of food—oranges, sandwiches, peanuts, and candy—which the waitress put in a big paper bag, and I bought an apple pie, which I held in my left hand. I had just left the station when I heard a whistle and saw my freight train on the far sidetrack pulling out and going East. I raced like mad. It would be a close call. Just as I reached the train, the caboose was entering the main line, going ten miles or more an hour. The paper bag burst, strewing my provisions along the track. I had time only to step aboard with my apple pie. Climbing on top of the caboose, I sat there eating every last morsel of it. No pie ever tasted better.

Not long after that, we reached Minot, North Dakota, where there were feeding pens but no food. To save the sheep, I herded them across the plains for one entire day and then back to Minot at night. I had no dog to help me, and no other assistant. At dusk I brought the sheep down the main street, where the store folk came out to cheer me. I loaded the animals in the cars—all but one. A ewe escaped, and to the delight of the people of Minot, she ran all over town, with me in pursuit. She finally got stuck under a warehouse platform and I went in and got her, dragging her out and carrying her in my arms to the freight yards.

Three days later we were in Minneapolis, where a wire from the owner of the sheep awaited me. I was to deliver them to such and such a broker, which I did. Not one sheep was lost, though each had lost weight. My job done, I had only to get to New York City.

On the trip from Minneapolis to Chicago I paid my toll to the crew of the freight train—fifty cents apiece, as I recall. When we came to a new division point, I discovered that the new crew was also collecting fares. I was easy prey, for I was on a flatcar—the only available space, except underneath on the rods or on top of the boxcars. This was a loaded and sealed train, carrying for the most part fruit in refrigerator cars. When the new brakeman came along, he asked for a dollar, and I paid him. Nothing more happened for a long time. It was three or four o'clock in the morning on a clear, cold night when the train's conductor came by and also asked for a dollar; he said there were yard bulls ahead, he did not want me to get into trouble. For the dollar, he would see that the bulls did not arrest me. It was the same old story.

I was silent for a while, trying to figure how I could afford to part with another dollar. I had only two or three. I had not had a hot meal for seven days; I had not been to bed for thirteen nights; I was filthy and without a change of clothes. I needed a bath and a shave and food; above all else, I needed sleep. Even flophouses cost money. And the oatmeal, hot cakes, ham and eggs and coffee—which I wanted desperately—would cost fifty or seventy-five cents.

"Why should I pay this guy and become a panhandler in Chicago?" I asked myself.

He shook me by the shoulder and said, "Come on, buddy. Do you want to get tossed off the train?"

"I'm broke," I said.

"Broke?" he retorted. "You paid the brakeman and you can pay me."

"Have a heart," I said. "I bet you were broke sometime. Give a guy a break."

He roared at me to get off or he would turn me over to the bulls. I was silent.

"Well, jump off or I'll run you in," he said.

I watched the lights of Chicago come nearer. We were entering a maze of tracks. There were switches and sidetracks, boxcars on sidings, occasional loading platforms. And once in a while we roared over a short highway bridge. It was dark and the train was going about thirty miles an hour. The terrain looked treacherous. A jump might be disastrous. But I decided to husband my remaining dollars. I stood poised on the edge of the flatcar, searching the area immediately ahead for a place to jump.

Suddenly in my ear came the command: "Jump!" I jumped.

Something brushed my left sleeve. It was the arm of a switch. Then I fell clear, hitting a cinder bank. I lost my footing, slid on my hands and knees for a dozen feet down the bank, and rolled to the bottom.

I got slowly to my feet as the last cars of the freight roared by and disappeared with a twinkling of lights into the East. My palms were bleeding and full of cinders. My knees were skinned. I was dirty and hungry and aching. I sat on a pile of ties by the track, nursing my wounds.

A form came out of the darkness. It proved to be an old man who obviously also rode the rods. He put his hand on my shoulder and said, "I saw you jump, buddy. Are you hurt?"

"No, thank you," I replied. "Not much. Just scratched."

"Ever been to Chicago?"

"No."

"Well," he said, "don't stay here. It's a city that's hard on fellows like us."

"You mean the bulls?"

"Yes, they're tough," he said. "Maybe they have to be. But it's not only that. Do you smell the stockyards?"

I had not identified the odor, but I had smelled it even before I jumped. "So that's it?"

"Yeah. I've worked there. The pay ain't so bad. But you go home at night to a room on an alley. There's not a tree. There's no grass. No birds. No mountains."

"What do you know of mountains?" I ventured.

My question led to his story. He had come, to begin with, from Northern California. He had worked in the harvests, and as he worked he could look up and see the mountains. Before him was Mount Shasta. He could put his bedroll on the ground and fall asleep under the pines. There was dust in the fields of Northern California, but it was good clean dirt. People were not packed together like sardines. They had elbow room. A man need not sit on a Sunday looking out on a bleak alley. He could have a piece of ground, plant a garden and work it. He might even catch a trout, or shoot a grouse or pheasant, or perhaps kill a deer.

I listened for about an hour as he praised the glories of the mountains of the West and related his experiences in them. I asked what had brought him to the freight yards at this hour of the morning. He said he had come to catch a westbound freight—back to God's own land, back to the mountains.

Dawn was breaking, and now I could see the smoke and some of the squalor of which my friend spoke. Lonesomeness swept over me. Never had I loved the Cascades as much as I did that early morning near the stockyards of Chicago. Never had I missed a snow-capped peak so much. Never had I longed more to see a mountain meadow filled with heather and lupine and paintbrush. I could see smokestacks everywhere, and in the distance, to the east, the vague outlines of tall buildings. But there lay before me nothing higher, no ridge or hill or meadow—only a great monotony of cinders, smoke, and dingy factories with chimneys pouring out a thick haze over the landscape.

The old man and I sat in silence a few moments. He said, "Do you know your Bible, son?"

"Pretty well."

"Then you will remember what the psalmist said about the mountains."

I racked my brain. "No, I don't recall."

Then the old man said with intonations worthy of the clergy, "'I will lift up mine eyes unto the hills from whence cometh my help. My help cometh from the Lord who made heaven and earth.'"

There was a whistle in the East. A quarter-mile down the track a freight was pulling onto the main line.

"That's my train," he said. "That train takes me to the mountains." He took my hand. "Good luck, son. Better come back with me. Chicago's not for us."

I shook my head and said good-by with sadness.

He smiled. "Stay clear of the flophouses. They'll roll you when you're asleep. Go to the YMCA. It's cheap and clean and they're on the level."

The engine went by. The passing train was picking up speed. The old man was more agile then he looked. He trotted easily along the track, grabbed a handhold, and stepped lightly aboard on the bottom rung of the ladder. Climbing to the top of the boxcar, he took off his hat and waved until he was out of sight.

I watched as the freight disappeared into the West. That old man had moved me deeply. I recognized his type from the hobo jungles I had visited between Yakima and Chicago. I felt the jungle companionship in this old man of the stockyards. He was a vagabond, but he was not a bum. He had made me see, in the dreary stockyards of America, some of the country's greatness, kindness, sympathy, selflessness, understanding.

I sat watching the sun rise through the smoke and haze. Even though Chicago's environment was depressing in 1922, it had not yet reached the stage of deterioration which was achieved by 1972. Not all its waters were open sewers; smog had not possessed the city; industrial poisons had not yet taken over the Great Lakes nor made Lake Erie a fire hazard. Yet there was a smell in the air that even the touch of the sun could not cleanse. There was not a tree or shrub or blade of grass in view.

That morning I saw none of the gracious, warm-hearted people I later came to know in the city. Nor did I see the Chicago that Carl Sandburg painted in his robust lines of *Chicago Poems.*

That morning I had only a distorted and jaundiced view. I was hungry, dead-tired, homesick, broke, and bruised. I had a great impulse to follow my vagabond friend to the West, to settle down in the valley below Mount Adams and to live under its influence. Most of my friends and all the roots I had in life were in the Yakima Valley. There would be a job and a home awaiting me, and fishing trips and mountain climbs and nights on the high shoulders of Goat Rocks. It was a friendly place, not hard and cruel like these freight yards. People in the West were warm-hearted and open-faced, like my hobo friend. I would be content and happy there.

Then why this compulsion to leave the valley? Why this drive, to leave the scenes I loved? To reach for unknown stars, to seek adventure, to abandon the comfort of home? But what of pride? What would I say if I returned? That I didn't have the guts to work my way East, to work my way through law school, to live the hard way?

It was too late to go back. Law school would open in a week. There was still a challenge ahead. New horizons would be opened, offering still untested opportunities.

I turned my face to the East—toward my convictions—and walked along the railroad track, headed for the YMCA, as my friend had recommended. I would sleep the clock around and then return to the freight yards to catch a ride to New York City and Columbia Law School. The bath at the Y was a very enjoyable physical experience, and the long sleep was refreshing—all for fifty cents.

When I finally pulled into the freight yards in New York City, I had only six cents of my seventy-five dollars left in my pocket. I was grimy and weary, and I'd had very little to eat for several days. I had had no bath since Chicago, no change of clothes, and doubtless looked like a bum. My clothes were tattered, my hat was nondescript, my battered brown suitcase was held together by a piece of rope. I was utterly lost. As I walked along a broad avenue lined with tall apartment buildings, I tried to stop a man, asking, "How do I get to Columbia?" His eyes swept by me and he kept going. Over and over again I tried to stop people to ask directions, and each time I was rebuffed. No one would even speak to me. It would have been different in Yakima or Walla Walla. The stranger who asked a native for directions might even end up as a luncheon guest. Not so in New York City. The stranger—especially the one with no badge of affluence—knew only the rough back of the hand. I quickly saw the cold side of New York City and I never got over it.

Somewhere in my suitcase was a slip of paper on which I'd written the address of the New York headquarters of Beta Theta Pi. After untying the rope that held my bag together, and rummaging around, I found the address and, eventually, made my way to the staid and rather elegant Beta Club.

I went up to the clerk, told him I was a fraternity member, and asked, "Do you have a room for the night?"

The fellow took one look at the dust-covered specimen before him and answered with an abrupt "No." Furthermore, he didn't believe I was a member of the fraternity.

As we stood arguing, a Whitman friend, William M. Wilson, came down the stairs. He was passing through New York on his way to Johns Hopkins University in Baltimore to study medicine.

I greeted Bill with great joy, and in high indignation turned to the clerk and said, "Ask *him* who I am."

Bill Wilson said, "This is my friend Bill Douglas, from the Whitman College chapter of Beta. Put him up."

In addition to that intercession, Bill loaned me seventy-five dollars as seed money to get me started in New York.*

The next day I registered at the Columbia Law School and was assigned a room in Furnald Hall. Then I scurried around to try to find work. In this hungry time, I often had only one meal a day. I sold newspapers and waited on tables, but I still could not get far enough ahead to pay my tuition and my room rent at Furnald Hall.

Miss Breed, head of the university's employment agency, tried to help

* Wilson (whom I shortly repaid) later became an eminent gynecologist in Portland, Oregon.

me. She was perhaps in her thirties, an exceedingly attractive brunette, well educated and adroit with people. She carefully interviewed each student who sought work. I gave her Jim Donald's letters, but she had few doors to open for me. Finally the bursar of Columbia called me into his office and said, "You have not paid your tuition or your dormitory rent. I have consulted the regulations of the university and learned that I will violate none of them if I drop you from the Law School."

I was stunned and saddened. Now it seemed that my legal career would have to wait. But before accepting that, I thought I would get advice from the dean, who was then Harlan F. Stone. I went to Dean Stone's office and was ushered to him at once. I would never have given credence to anyone who would have prophesied that he, an eminent law teacher, and I, fresh from the freight yards, would, in seventeen years, be sitting together on the Supreme Court. Of course, there was no such prophet.

Years later, on the Court, I told Stone of my arrival at Columbia by freight. He asked the name of the railroad. I said it was the Great Northern most of the way to Chicago. "Then you should always ride the Great Northern, paying first-class fares." After a pause he added, "Come to think of it, why not send them a check for your Law School transportation?"

Stone, then as later, was a portly man with a broad face and twinkling eyes. A mop of hair usually hung down his forehead. All in all, he had somewhat the appearance of a farmer. His voice was soft and he was patient with people. He never begrudged an hour with a student, mulling over personal problems. He talked to me as a father, and I listened as a son. His advice was to drop out, get a job, save my money, and come back in a few years. He had nothing to offer in terms of a scholarship or a loan.

So I went from the dean's office across to New Jersey and got a job as a teacher of Latin and English in a high school. I packed my bag, said good-by to a few friends, and left Furnald Hall. But on my way to the subway and New Jersey, I made one last stop at the Appointments Office. "Not a thing," said Miss Breed. "Now wait a minute—what's this?"

Picking up a memo, she read a message from her assistant. A man with offices in Columbus Circle ran a correspondence school. He was doing well with various courses, including one on hemstitching. Now he wanted a course in law. Could a third-year law student be sent down to help him?

"I'll go," I said.

"But you're not a third-year man," Miss Breed said.

"Let me try," I implored.

She gave in, handed me a note of introduction, and agreed to keep an eye on my bag while I visited Columbus Circle. I reached it by subway in less than a half-hour. The proprietor did the talking, and in five minutes I realized that I knew more law than he did. He handed me a textbook on business law, saying he thought he would start with that.

"Let's be modern," I said. "Let's make it a case law course. We'll divide the book into fifty parts and prepare fifty lessons."

The idea had suddenly come to me to assign five pages of text, say, for Lesson No. 1, sending each student a true legal problem taken from a prominent New York decision. The student would read the text, study the question, and write his answer, returning it for grading. We would give the citation to the law report so that he could, if he wished, go to a library and read it. In thirty minutes we agreed on this format. He would sell each course for twenty-five dollars—five for the book, twenty for the questions and answers. Did I want a part of the profits?

"No," I said, and quickly adding up my cash requirements for the year, I announced I would do it for a flat six-hundred-dollar fee, but I needed a two-hundred-dollar advance. Within the hour I walked out of the office at Columbus Circle with a check for two hundred dollars and a contract that would pay me four hundred dollars more on delivery of the manuscript within six weeks.

I repaired at once to Columbia, paid two hundred dollars to the bursar, picked up my bag, moved back into the dormitory, and canceled my New Jersey employment.

Preparation of the correspondence course was such a formidable undertaking that I did not go to law classes for six weeks. I spent practically every working hour of every day in an alcove in the library of old Kent Hall putting my case material together: finding the best illustrative cases and making digests of them. At the end of six weeks I had finished the job and resumed classes, working feverishly to catch up.

When I turned in the manuscript and received the balance of the fee, I realized what a foolish bargain I had made. The proprietor had already sold a thousand courses on which I could easily have had a quarter or more interest. For a while I graded the papers for him at a normal hourly rate. Then I got others to do it, for soon I was in big-money tutoring. I saw my correspondence-course friend frequently. He was making money fast and never realized that the chap who had prepared his course in law had had less than six weeks of legal education.

I was in New York City for six years altogether; I attained considerable professional achievements there—as a student, as a practitioner, and as a teacher. So logically, perhaps, I should have only happy associations with New York. But those six years developed in me a deep dislike for the city. That feeling goes back, no doubt, to my early reception when I first walked Park Avenue. Later, I was often feted in New York apartments and came to know the warm-hearted people who live there. But though warm-hearted, they are still far, far removed from the miserable people of the ghettos that surround them. New York City is highly stratified, as are most metropolitan areas, and it is run largely for the middle and upper classes. During those first few miserable, starving months in New York, I saw the ugliness of the city.

Moreover, I felt alien to the city because I came from the wide-open spaces, where only the haunting call of the coyote or wind in the pines broke the stillness of night. Now whenever I awoke, I heard nothing but the roar of traffic. This constant noise always grated on my ears. In one of my early years in New York, I had a room looking onto an air shaft. The only green thing in it was a miserable geranium plant struggling to survive. The sun touched the shaft only briefly each day and never reached the room. For me this was as depressing as I imagine a prison would be. Even when I acquired a sunny room, the depression never left me. The din of the city was still present. The only bird I ever saw was a pigeon. I longed for the call of the meadowlark, the noisy drilling of the pileated woodpecker, the drumming of the ruffed grouse. I would sleep well, I thought, if I could only hear the music of a wilderness creek flowing over ledges. But all I ever heard above the distant rumble of the city was the dripping of a faucet.

I needed grass and earth under my feet. But unless I traveled far—either west or north—all I found was concrete. I saw block after block of apartment houses—some standing in splendor, most in squalor—with no tree, no touch of grass to adorn them, no playground except a paved one, no nature trails.

The earth and all its wonders were too much a part of me to shake off. I needed them as a daily diet. When I thought of the babies being born and raised in these unlivable concrete prisons, I became even more depressed.

I was able to live very cheaply in New York, though it was supposed to be an expensive city. I found real warmth in places like the Horn & Hardart restaurants. Until recently, they had food on display in machines with glass doors that could be opened with a coin. For ten cents I could get a dish of pork and beans; for five cents, a glass of milk, or bread and butter, or a piece of apple pie. That was a good twenty-five-cent supper, which carried me through many a day during the first few rough months of my first year in Law School. The food was good and it was nourishing, as good and as nourishing as the twenty-five-dollar meals that I later ate in Sardi's or the Oak Room at the Plaza or other high-class restaurants where the head waiters would bow and scrape.

I liked the people who ate at Horn & Hardart. Most of them were open-faced and friendly. I always seemed to be on the same wave length with them.

There was a Child's Restaurant at Broadway and 110th, where one day by chance I met the famous John Bassett Moore, leading international-law expert who taught at the Law School. I met him only because the sole empty chair in the crowded restaurant was at his table and he asked me to join him. That was the beginning of a warm friendship. He was short and rotund and bald, and at the time, sported a gray goatee. His eyes always seemed to dance to the excitement of his ideas as he talked.

There were, of course, other kind people in New York City. One of the friendliest was a chap, also in Law School, who had the room next to me in Furnald Hall. He was so friendly that he barged into my room full of talk all night long. It was not long before he was marched off to a mental institution as a psychotic.

A tall amiable chap counted the prices of the items on our trays at the university cafeteria and always gave me a wink as I said "Touch me lightly, Joe."

The decrepit man who sold roasted chestnuts and pine nuts on Broadway at 116th Street reminded me of my old Wobbly friends. He was a compassionate person with wide interests in politics and literature, a man who never made the grade due to some idiosyncrasy that I never comprehended.

There was much sadness among the people I knew. I had known Jews in the West; and some of them were my dear friends. But the Jews in New York City were more numerous and inclined to be clannish. They faced the problem of discrimination organized in a way that I had never seen before. The power structure was against them.

There were six Blacks in my class, Paul Robeson being the most memorable. Paul worked his way through Law School by boxing professionally. The Blacks, of course, knew severe discrimination, but their organized opposition to it had not yet jelled.

One of my classmates in Law School was Carrol Shanks, later to become president of the Prudential Life Insurance Company. Alfred McCormack, who later nosed me out as Justice Stone's law clerk, was a warm friend. So was Tom Dewey, who had a fine baritone voice and worked his way through school by singing at the Cathedral of St. John the Divine.

Another close friend was Simon Rifkind. My friendship with Si has been long and enduring. Si, too, worked his way through school, and after graduation, became a partner of Senator Robert Wagner of New York. He later served as district judge in New York from June 6, 1941, to May 24, 1950, making a very outstanding record on the Bench, as he did before and afterward at the Bar. It was Si who nearly fifty years later represented me in impeachment proceedings launched in 1970 by Nixon, Agnew, and Gerald Ford.

Hiram C. Gill had been a turbulent mayor of Seattle from 1910 to 1918, and when I was in Law School, his widow moved to New York City. Her son, Stanley Gill, was in chemical engineering at Columbia. Howard Meneely, later president of Wheaton College, was working for his Ph.D. in history; Delbert Obertauffer, later head of the Department of Physical Education at Ohio State, was getting his M.A.; George C. Watson of Petersburg, Virginia, was at the Columbia Business School. The five of us used to gather at "Miss Gill's" almost every Friday night for a home-cooked meal and poker. The poker I later played with FDR in Washington, D.C., I learned at Columbia.

Later, I made the acquaintance of other classmates, among them Hal Seligson, Law Comstock, Arthur Schwartz, and Alvin Sylvester. In time I came to be on intimate terms, although still a student, with Dean Harlan F. Stone, Professor Underhill Moore, and Professor Huger Jervey. These three were the ones to whom I turned for advice when my financial problems seemed insoluble.

Up to the time I went to Law School, I never drank beer or hard liquor. It was never quite taboo, but it was not fashionable in the West. In New York City, drinking was *the thing* to do. So I started taking a few drinks, mostly of miserable gin.

After I got to Columbia, I also tried very hard to learn to smoke cigarettes. I had never smoked before coming East, but I noticed that everyone—almost everyone—in Law School smoked. I had the foolish idea that if I were to succeed at the Bar, I, too, would have to smoke. So I purchased a pack of Tareytons, lit up, inhaled deeply, and almost passed out. The next day I tried again, and the next day, and so on. It took weeks for me to master the "art" of smoking cigarettes because I really disliked the taste and the sensation, but I felt it was a skill I had to learn.

Eventually I became addicted to the weed, though I could scarcely afford the expense. Added to that was the financial drain because of my friends who, it seemed to me, were always "bumming" *my* cigarettes. To solve the problem, I went to a tobacconist who had a shop near 110th Street on Broadway and asked him, "What is the worst cigarette you have?" I filled my pockets with the brand he pointed out and handed them out liberally to anyone who asked. The experience broke the cigarette habit of several of my friends and saved me money I badly needed.

Having acquired the habit, however, I became an inveterate smoker. I smoked not Tareytons but Camels, and became so accomplished that I could smoke three packs a day. I finally gave up, twenty years later, only when a wise doctor—Ralph Fenton of Portland, Oregon—detected the first warning signals a person gets on the start of cancer of the lung. There is now a name for it, but in those days Fenton had learned from observation that when the mucus membrane of the throat acquires a certain hue, cancer of the lung has started.

Once my tutoring jobs began, they seemed never to stop. I prepared students for college-entrance examinations for Princeton, Yale and Columbia. To obtain my services, or the likes of them, students needed to be both stupid and rich. My boast was that I never failed to get even a dumb student into Princeton. None of my students *ever* failed, except one in law. And as my success mounted, my fees rose. I started at five dollars an hour and got as high as twenty-five. The latter was paid by a lady who ran a boys' school in the South. She was out of date when it came to elocution. She and her husband had a suite at the Waldorf-Astoria, and it was there that I had her recite again and again before her husband and me "The Cremation of Sam McGee." She demanded a certificate of proficiency. So I had one made of sheepskin that looked like a genuine diploma but was only a personal citation.

I took on another project while I was at Law School—a job in a settlement house on Henry Street on Manhattan's Lower East Side. The name of the house was DYNT (Do Ye Next Thing). It was a small establishment as settlement houses went, run by a very fine woman. We served an Italian community, and my job was to organize boys who were in their teens. The boys and I got along famously and organized the Yakima Club. We had social meetings every Friday night, where they learned about

Indians, spearing salmon, fly fishing, climbing mountains, camping out, and so on. Weekends we spent hiking.

One favorite place was in Rockland County. We would take the train to Tarrytown, New York, and from there, hike an old easement that overlay water pipes for some thirty miles. It seems as if my life is always going full cycle, for it was only a few years ago that some Rockland County people got me to visit them and lead a march to promote a project of turning that very easement into a public hiking trail.

Other outings of the DYNT group were on the New Jersey seacoast. At that time New York City took its garbage to sea on barges and dumped it. The tides carried it to New Jersey, and my Italian boys and I had the greatest difficulty in finding clean waters for swimming along the New Jersey coast. Crates, cabbage heads, orange peels, dead dogs and cats, and all the junk one can imagine were washed up there. The sight was unseemly and popular indignation finally reached a boiling point. New Jersey at long last sued New York in the United States Supreme Court, and in 1931 an injunction was obtained forcing the city to acquire incinerators.

This DYNT club brought me some of the happiest associations I had in my many years in New York City. The boys blossomed and matured as they got on understanding terms with Mother Earth. They escaped the dirty alleys into the sunlight of woods and waters. They grew to be fine citizens, and over the years they wrote me personal, affectionate notes.

All of these early experiences came back to me recently as I was backpacking in the Olympic Mountains in the State of Washington. I came across a group of twenty young men, members of student conservation camps. They had been recruited from cities and were a summer adjunct to the National Park Service, building or repairing trails. I camped with them one night and began to talk to one lad from the Bronx. I asked him how he liked the job. What he told me was most revealing. His first few nights on the ground were sleepless ones, for he was deathly afraid of the night noises. He was frightened of the woods—of bear, elk, porcupines, coyotes. He was scared of the dark. He shook and trembled night after night. After about a month, however, he became adjusted, and laughingly added, "You know, I never knew until I came West where milk came from. In the Bronx, I assumed it was manufactured, like beer and whiskey."

. . .

I fear that my negative reaction to the city was once reflected in a judicial opinion. Internal Revenue had taxed an insurance agent who won a contest and got his wife's and his own expenses paid from Texas to New York City for a long weekend. Those expenses, it was charged, were taxable income, and the Court so held. The theory was that it was a great reward to come to New York City. (370 U.S. 269)

I dissented, saying, "If we are in the field of judicial notice, I would think that some might conclude that the weekend in New York City was a chore and that those who went sacrificed valuable time that might better have been spent on the farm, in the woods, or along the seashore."

The *New York Herald Tribune* replied editorially to my dissent:

> Not being versed in legalities, we have no opinion on a Supreme Court decision wrestling with the question of whether a prize-winning insurance agent's visit to New York from Dallas, Texas, should have been counted by the tax people as a pleasure or a business trip. However, we cannot help being taken aback by Justice Douglas's opinion, expressed in passing, that "some might conclude that the weekend in New York City was a chore and that those who went sacrificed valuable time that might better have been spent on the farm, in the woods, or along the seashore."
>
> Now, these are hot days, not to mention trying times, in New York, and when a Supreme Court Justice begins picking on us, it requires all our sang-froid and philosophic outlook to shrug it off. After all, we could mention that New York does have a pretty good farm (in the zoo), several sets of woods (Central or Prospect Parks), and seashore galore (from Coney to City Island). Furthermore, we doubt whether Mr. Justice Douglas is quite as much a hayseed as he sometimes makes himself out to be.
>
> Anyhow, Judge, why don't we conclude that it's hot in Washington, too, and that there are times when even a Supreme Court Justice wishes he could go climb a mountain, or a tree, or something. As a matter of fact, we were just going to suggest it.

A few of my early feelings about New York never entirely left me. Whenever I go to that city, I always try to leave that same day, so as to escape spending a night there. I sleep only fitfully in New York. It has great rewards in music, art galleries, the theater, the Yankees, Mets, and the Giants, but for me none of them is worth a weekend.

. . .

The days were long and the nights short at Columbia. I worked all the time, just to keep going, but I would save my pennies and every once in a while amass enough to go to the Ziegfeld Follies and see W. C. Fields or some other favorite.

I discovered Will Rogers on Broadway at the *Follies*. He had a shock of tousled hair, and he chewed gum and whirled a rope as he talked, carrying off the cowboy role with suitable Oklahoma attire. I remember a few of his quips. He was talking about flying and mentioned that one pilot gave him cotton to put in his ears. He sighed, "I only use cotton in my ears when I go to the Senate Gallery."

One night members of the American Bankers Association were in the audience. Rogers said, "Loan Sharks and Interest Hounds, I understand you have ten thousand here; with what you have in the various federal prisons that must bring your membership up to around thirty thousand."

He talked about the removal of Senator Truman Hondy Newberry from the Senate: "I wonder what he will do now. Guess he will about go back home . . . and turn honest. You know that may be just the makin' of that man, to catch him before he gets too deep into politics. You can save 'em sometimes if you get 'em early enough. 'Course, where I blame him is buying a seat in that body of men. That's like payin' admission to go in a jail. Who did they put in to take his place?"

When Will Rogers died with Wiley Post in 1935 in an airplane crash in Alaska, an important influence went out of American life. Apart from FDR, there have been no Presidents in this century who could make America laugh. We need laughter for good health. I have left my saddle to the Will Rogers Memorial in Oklahoma.

Another Ziefeld *Follies* star I admired, but never knew, was Eddie Cantor, who stole the show one winter with his song "I like them wild, weak, warm, and willing or I don't like them at all." In the same troupe was W. C. Fields. "A man cannot be all bad who hates little children" was among the first of his sayings I heard.

The Metropolitan Opera was high on my list of places to visit when I reached New York City. Mother had mentioned it often because of her interest in music. She had a lovely voice, though it was wholly untrained, and she accompanied herself on our old, old pump organ. It was for her sake that I saved my nickels and dimes in the winter of 1922–1923 and finally had the price of a ticket in the second—perhaps it was the third—balcony. My seat was way up under the eaves and I sat looking down, waiting expectantly. I forget the name of the opera, except that it was Italian and the great Enrico Caruso was in the cast. I, of course, did not understand a word, and the action seemed so agonizingly slow and ponderous that I wearied very fast. In fact, I left before the end, resolving, as I used my last nickel to get on a subway heading north, that I would never go to another opera. It was a promise I have faithfully kept for over fifty years.

Through my tutoring service, I struck it rich at Columbia. I not only paid all my expenses, I also banked a couple of thousand dollars, enough so that in 1924 I was, for the first time in my life, fairly well set up financially. That summer I returned West and married Mildred Riddle, graduate of the University of Oregon, resident of LaGrande, Oregon, and Latin teacher in the Yakima High School, where I had met her. She was related on her mother's side to Thomas Stone, one of the signers of the Declaration of Independence.

While we were living in New York, Mildred taught in suburban schools around the metropolitan area, though never in the city itself. We lived in New York during the school year, but would spend part of each summer on the small farm of Mildred's parents in Oregon.

She was a lifelong scholar of Latin and rated high in the teaching profession for her achievements in that area. She had teacher's certificates in Oregon, Washington, New Jersey, and New York and she taught Latin for a while in a private school in Connecticut before the children were born. She was a quiet, retiring lady of beauty who liked to sit in green meadows beside purling waters; but she never really enjoyed the hard exhausting journeys into the high wilderness.

If someone had told me then that I would be divorced, not once, but three times, I would have been horrified. Divorce was, in my Presbyterian heritage, a sin, and I looked down on those who had gone that way. It is, it seems to me, the worst ordeal a man can suffer and it has for me a strong sense of shame—shame because of great failure. There is nothing in life brighter than a lifelong marriage. Yet often the mysterious amalgam is lacking, and when that happens, no one is at fault. Over the years I saw couples who were complete misfits but whose religion or stubbornness or weakness held them together—at least formally. Sometimes the husband, sometimes the wife, became alcoholic. Sometimes one or both were on the "make," seeking sub rosa partners. Sometimes the mounting energies were expended in outside endeavors and projects which left the home empty, and made it necessary for the children to shift for themselves. It took years for me to resolve that those conditions were much worse than divorce, that divorce, especially for the young wife, can well be the beginning of a new, full life.

. . .

At the end of my first year in Law School, I made the Columbia *Law*

Review, then, as now, a student publication. We had rooms in the basement of Kent Hall and there edited eight issues a year. We wrote unsigned student "Notes" and "Comments" and polished up or revised articles submitted by outsiders. When I joined the *Review*, Samuel Nirenstein was editor in chief, and during my third year, Alfred McCormack held the post. Never, up to then, did I have a brighter, happier moment in my life than the day I received notice that I was an editor of the *Review*. That achievement turned not on pull, family, influence, or politics, but on grades alone. But the burden it added to an already busy life was considerable, with the result that my second happiest day was when we put the last issue of the *Review* "to bed" and turned over our jobs to the oncoming group of eager-beaver second-year men.

I got my law pretty much on the run during those three years at Columbia. In addition to the *Law Review*, which demanded time, during my last two years I tutored, and also worked for one of the professors, Underhill Moore.

Underhill Moore's mind had a cutting edge, sharper than any other. He was in the field of commercial law, and a year at his feet was a prodigious experience—in the exactitude with which he dealt with minutiae; in the broad dimensions of the practical world where he framed his questions; in his concern with the roots of the law and their modern incidence. Moore was Teutonic in appearance. He was almost bald, which helped emphasize his massive appearance in head and shoulders. He was Teutonic in method also, very demanding and very precise. He had a thundering voice and he emphasized his points by pounding the table with his fist.

Trade associations were at the time under fire from the Department of Justice for antitrust violations and some cases involving their practices were before the U.S. Supreme Court.* It looked as though the cement associations would be next. So the industry hired Underhill Moore to write them a treatise. He took me as his assistant, and we not only did library research and economic analysis, but toured the East as well. We went by car, visiting all the cement plants and interviewing executives. We had an expense account and this was the very first time in my life that I knew what "eating high on the hog" meant.

On one leg of this junket, Moore and I were somewhere in Maine riding a caboose, the only way to reach a remote cement plant. It was a warm spring day and Moore sat by an open window. The benches in the caboose, as usual, ran along each side of the car. Moore sat with one leg under him and *The New York Times* held by his two hands in

* *Maple Flooring Assn. v. United States*, 268 U.S. 563.

front of him. He was absorbed in reading when the brakeman, sitting opposite, let go a wad of tobacco juice that passed between Moore's face and the newspaper and went smack out the window. Moore ruffled his paper and muttered something inaudible and returned to his reading. In a few moments the brakeman let go another wad of tobacco juice, and it also passed between Moore's face and the paper, neatly clearing the open window. Moore, flushed with anger, turned to the brakeman and shouted, "What goes on here?" The brakeman rose to his feet, cleared his throat, and said, "I'm sorry, sir, if I upset you. But I think you must admit it was some spitting." I could no longer contain myself and broke into loud laughter, to which first the brakeman and then Moore succumbed.

The men on the Columbia Law faculty were mostly hard-hitting teachers with sharp minds. They were not lecturers but teachers who used the Socratic method, a brand-new technique in my experience.

Stone himself was an excellent teacher in this method; no one was better at it than he. He never made an affirmative statement as to what the law was. Not once did he put into black type, so to speak, any fundamental principle of the subject matter. All he did was question, question, question. Finally, one caught on—at least those who did well in the course—to the stages in the law's development by the intonation of Stone's voice. The way he would say "So you think, Mr. Douglas, that such and such is the governing principle" was the only guidepost through his course, except the voluminous materials, including cases, which he assigned for reading.

Herman Oliphant, with his pointed nose and piercing eye, had an incisive mind. He had the skill of a brain surgeon in dissecting a legal problem. It was Oliphant who, on my very first day in Law School, embarrassed me before the class of 365 students. He came into the room, placed his notes on the lectern, polished his glasses, and then paced the room—up one aisle, around in back, down the center aisle where he stopped at my row. I was on the aisle and, therefore, an easy victim. He asked my name, had me stand, and then asked, "Mr. Douglas, what is an estoppel?" My mind was a blank. All I could say was, "I know it's not anything you find in the woods. Whether it is a legal principle or a disease, I haven't the least idea." I sat down, crushed and humiliated, certain that I was doomed as a lawyer, though by term's end I had earned myself an A in Oliphant's course.

Young B. Smith—bright, affable, and conservative—taught Torts.

Later, when I was elected to the Columbia faculty, he was to be my nemesis, as I shall describe.

Harold Medina, who later served on the Court of Appeals for the Second Circuit, taught New York Practice. Medina was bright, able, and a ham actor. One shining principle was his admonition: "When you practice law, get a piece of wood that you can force into the letter slot on your door, so you won't be served with a subpoena when out to lunch."

Medina had a cram course preparing one for the New York Bars—which we all took at the end of our third year for fifty dollars apiece, and which made Medina a small fortune.

Ralph W. Gifford's courses were Criminal Law, Wills, and Evidence. He, too, was an actor who could turn the class into stitches over a juicy sex case.

Richard Powell was a terrier who taught Property and was expert at resolving such mysteries as limitations on cross-remainders.

Huger Jervey taught Personal Property, Trusts, and Mortgages. Jervey was so bored with his duties that he hired me to correct all the examination papers in his classes—at fifty cents a paper. I read at least six hundred for him every May.

Professor George Folger Canfield taught Corporations. He was old and feeble and his classes were very disrespectful of him. Eventually, the time came for him to retire. A few of us passed the hat and bought him a lovely pipe set at Dunhill's. Then, at the end of the last class, we had a little party and I presented the gift to the old professor. I made a little parting speech of appreciation and Canfield was so touched he cried. The next day the dean thundered at me, "What did you do to Canfield?" When I told him, the dean shouted, "I've been trying to get rid of Canfield for years. Now he says he's going to stay on. Why in hell do you go around giving no-good people presents?"

Thomas Reed Powell, who was to become a spokesman for the Establishment when he reached Harvard in 1925, was then an iconoclast. He was the offbeat intellectual who could cut the Supreme Court into ribbons in any field of constitutional law. I had taken his course in my third year in Law School and turned in a paper feeling completely confident I would get an A. It might, I thought, turn out to be the best paper I had ever written. To my surprise, I received a C. I was both stunned and humiliated. Years later, when I was named to the Court, Powell wrote a congratulatory note in poetry, the first stanza of which was a reminder of that grade:

In days of yore
In old Kent Hall
He took some law from me.
And rumor has it
That his grade was just a
Modest C.

I replied in a long, rambling poem, the last stanza of which read:

Yes, when I am not one of five
But only one of four
Then truth and light will go for naught
As once it did before
When at the feet of T.R.P. I only got a
Modest C.

Meanwhile, I had formed the Powell C. Club. Combing school records, I collected the names of men who had received a C from Reed Powell and who later became prominent in the law. One, I recall, was Wesley A. Sturgis, who was a Yale Law professor of note and later dean of that school. These men and I formed the club, elected officers, and had stationery printed. For a few years we had an annual powwow, the guest of honor being Reed Powell. Our purpose was to remind him of his fallibility in handing out grades in constitutional law.

I did not learn until years later, when his daughter Mary Lee wrote me an amusing letter, that Powell, when a student at the University of Vermont in 1898, got a C in history!

While several of my classmates, like Si Rifkin, were extraordinarily able, on the whole, the intellectual competition at Columbia was not as keen as I had expected.

This is not to say I did not have to compete. In fact, to my everlasting chagrin, I graduated second in my class, having lost out on first place to Al McCormack. The two of us, throughout Law School, constantly tried to edge past each other, but we remained good friends. In fact, I was later to be best man at his wedding.

Al was a poor boy, with brains and ambition, who was determined to make good. He married a girl whose family was said to have fifty million dollars, and I had the feeling that her father looked askance at his daughter's penniless groom.

To add to the father's discomfort, on the day of the rehearsal for the wedding, those of us in the wedding party took an alcoholic bracer to prepare ourselves for the coming ordeal. We were, I'm afraid, late in arriving, and by the time we approached the church, Al's future father-in-law was in a fury, standing at the top of the stairs waiting for us. As Al went to greet him, the bride's father grabbed him by the collar and the seat of the pants and threw him down the steps.

We were outraged. We threatened to kidnap the bride and run away to Cuba, and later proposed that the matter needed third-party negotiations. In general, we thoroughly riled the dear man.

Al eventually became wealthy and his political views tended to become more conservative. Al, however, always defended me against those who disliked my views and one of his sons has grown up to be a liberal whose politics are very different from those he saw around him as a child.

Still, I was terribly hurt that when we graduated, Al was selected as Justice Stone's law clerk. Stone had left the deanship of the Law School for a partnership in Sullivan and Cromwell in the summer of 1923. When the Teapot Dome scandal broke in Washington, D.C., and Henry M. Dougherty, the Attorney General, resigned under fire, President Coolidge, who had gone to Amherst with Stone, called Stone to take over that office. So Stone went to Washington and became Attorney General of the United States in 1924. The action at the Department of Justice for which Stone is best remembered was his appointment of J. Edgar Hoover to head the FBI.

Shortly thereafter Mr. Justice McKenna died and Coolidge named Stone to the Court, where he took his seat March 2, 1925.

Stone decided to take, each year, a Columbia Law man as his clerk, and I thought surely I would be chosen. But Al McCormack nosed me out. The news reached the Law School in April, and I was so unhappy that for two weeks the sun never came out for me. The world was black and I was unspeakably depressed that for all those years and all that work, I had so little to show. The one opportunity I had wanted had passed me by—a year in the nation's capital before I went West to practice law.

Grant S. Bond, a lawyer in Walla Walla, had a partnership waiting for me. But he graciously said he would hold it for me when I decided to stay in New York City for another year to sample law practice there. So I started to walk the city streets, looking for a job. I made the rounds of the Wall Street firms, covering many of them. I was interviewed by Emory Buckner, an eminent trial lawyer, spending an hour with him after he returned from lunch. I decided against Buckner because I could smell liquor on his breath, and I did not think liquor and the serious business of law mixed. I saw John Foster Dulles and decided against him because he was so pontifical. He made it appear that the greatest favor he could do a young lawyer was to hire him. He seemed to me like a high churchman out to exploit someone. In fact, I was so struck by Dulles' pomposity that when he helped me on with my coat, as I was leaving his office, I turned and gave him a quarter tip. I finally signed up with Cravath, deGersdorff, Swaine, and Wood at 15 William Street, because everyone there seemed earnest and frank, and not at all pretentious. I took and passed the New York Bar examinations.

When I graduated, the faculty at Columbia asked me to teach three courses—Bankruptcy, Damages, and Partnership. I agreed, and worked it out so that I could meet these classes in the early morning and get to Cravath's by nine-thirty or ten o'clock. That meant teaching law and practicing law on the run. Of the three courses, I had taken only Partnership, so there was a lot of digging to do, for which I had very little time. As a result, I barely kept one hour ahead of my Columbia students.

I was terribly nervous as I entered each classroom to give a course. Law as taught at Columbia University was not the gentle discourse of English classes at Whitman. The students were the lions and the teacher was the tamer. Utter precision was demanded and sarcasm plus occasional humor was the technique. I got no calmer as the year progressed. So I stopped Oliphant in the hall one morning and asked him what to do about nervousness just before combat with the students. "I wish I knew," he replied. "I have been teaching twenty years and the palms of my hands are always moist when I meet my class." After a pause, he added, "The truth is that if you're not nervous, you're no damn good as a teacher." I found out that he was right.

My brother Art came to Columbia after I graduated. He inherited my tutorial business, which put him through school as it had paid for me. By the time Art arrived, the tutoring service was "big business."

Art took my course in Damages, and was surprised when he got an A.

Our offices at Cravath's were small cubicles opening on an air shaft—two desks, two telephones, two chairs. The desks were side by side or back to back. It was a noisy alcove, as the telephones were always ringing. My first roommate was John J. McCloy, who later was to serve with distinction in the federal government in Washington, D.C., as High Commissioner in West Germany, and as Chairman of the Board of the Ford Foundation.

Night after night I worked until eleven o'clock or midnight, and often until 2:00 or 4.00 A.M., returning to my desk by nine-thirty or ten in the morning, but before that, teaching an eight o'clock class. I learned in those long nights that some men preferred law practice to love, compassion, family, hiking, or sunsets. The partner for whom I worked usually took me to the Savarin Restaurant in the Wall Street area for dinner. Dinner talk was always shop talk, never about running fast waters in a canoe or the problems of unrest in India or the "red hunts" in New England.

I had a long series of nights working with H. A. Moore, an excellent lawyer of the old school and completely dedicated to "the law." He wore a green eyeshade and smoked cigarettes incessantly.

One night the telephone rang and he answered in an angry voice because he resented the intrusion, "What? The house is on fire? Why in hell bother me? Call the Fire Department."

Hanging up the phone with a bang, he said to me, "Can you imagine that? My wife calling me from Long Island to tell me our house is on fire. Hrrmmph!"

I saw him some years later. He was gaunt and gray, only a shadow of the man I once knew. He had never had the time to get to know the flight of the whistling swan or the call of the loons across northern waters. He had given his all to "the law" and it had squeezed every other interest out—even listening to the music of Mozart, which he loved.

I worked closely with Donald C. Swatland, a younger man who was fiercely intent on every job, extremely able and very high-principled. Late one night he and I completed a draft of a document transferring title to a vast empire from him and his partner, Robert T. Swaine, to a new corporate enterprise. My job was to take the draft to Ad Press, read proof on it, approve the final copy, pick up fifty execution copies at nine in the morning and have them in Don's office at nine-thirty. My proofreading job was finished at four in the morning, I picked up the execution copies promptly at nine, and I had them at the office at 15 William Street at nine-thirty. I proudly handed them to Don, who scanned a copy with his eagle eye and then picked up all fifty copies and threw them at me. I asked what was wrong. He screamed at me that his name was Donald C. Swatland, not Donald Swatland. The names—Robert T. Swaine and Donald C. Swatland—had appeared a dozen or more times as "parties of the first part," and sure enough, the "C" had dropped out in one sequence.

"I'll put it in in ink," I said.

"Not in this office," he shouted.

So back I went to Ad Press. And so it was that while I had come to honor precision as an intellectual habit, thanks to Don, I at last came to honor it as a professional habit.

I carried the briefcase for Bruce Bromley at the trials of a few cases. I thought at the time that he was a superb trial lawyer as well as a generous human being. Then I lost track of Bromley for years as our trails diverged. Later he was to serve briefly as a member of the Court of Appeals in New York. I can give no account of his services there, as I did not follow his work, but afterward I knew him well as an appellate advocate.

Some day I will write a story on advocacy before our Court. I will say then that Bruce was one of the ten best that ever appeared there in my time. He gave little emotional content to his argument, and he was wise, for the appearance of emotion tends to discount the appellate advocate. He was utterly factual, and he had sifted his facts through a fine sieve, which made them highly pertinent. Whether he won more than he lost, I do not know. Anyway, those statistics are irrelevant. The power of advocacy is presentation of a cause in its raw basic form and an exposure of the policy issues that point one way or the other. In that respect Bruce was preeminent.

One of my duties those days was to attend stockholders' meetings in Hoboken, New Jersey, or in Wilmington, Delaware. I would go with a briefcase filled with proxies. A secretary of the corporation was also present, another officer, and myself. Motions were put and I would cast all 900,000 votes or all 1,900,000 votes for those motions. Once in a while a minority interest would appear—perhaps two or three people, plus their lawyer. I still cast my briefcase of proxies for the management and against the dissenters, for I was only a courier, a ministerial agent.

I often wondered what injustices, if any, were being perpetrated and why the corporate system did not provide a better mechanism for airing these complaints and processing them. Little did I realize that in another ten years or so I would be drafting laws and regulations that would make that not only possible, but necessary.

There were a lot of my friends practicing law in the Street in the mid-twenties, among them, Thomas E. Dewey, who had been my classmate at Law School. Tom had worked his way through by singing and might have had an illustrious vocal career on the stage. Tom and I often had lunch together and talked of the future. We seriously considered forming a Douglas-Dewey law firm, or perhaps it was Dewey-Douglas. We discussed it on and off for several years. I finally told Tom that my decision was against it. When asked why, I explained that I was certain I would be left high and dry with a law firm because he would run for public office. He laughed at the idea. I was a good prophet. In 1931 he was chief assistant, U.S. attorney, then a New York district attorney, then Governor, and then Presidential candidate in 1944 and in 1948.

As the years passed, Tom and I did not see much of each other. But he kept touching base with me. When I was at the SEC he was N.Y. district attorney, and when he and his wife Frances had a chance to get away in the dead of winter he'd call asking for my suggestions. Once I recommended the country club at Charlottesville, Virginia, noted for its cuisine and hospitality. So Tom and Frances went there for a week or so. Shortly after his return to New York, I had reason to call him and asked, incidentally, how he enjoyed the club. He was not exuberant in his praise and I asked if anything had gone wrong. "Oh, no," he replied. "It's just that only one person asked me for my autograph during one whole week." And that was one measure of his virtual addiction to politics.

Also among my friends were Stanley Fuld, later chief judge of the New York Court of Appeals, and Si Rifkind, later U.S. district judge and the one federal judge whose records coming to us for review were the best of all, reflecting great craftsmanship. Si—who later left the Bench to practice law to support a growing family—became one of the few top advocates ever to appear before the Court in my time.

John Harlan, later to be on our Court, was at the Root-Clark firm. The big firms in those days held an annual party, a stag affair in a suite in some midtown hotel. Cravath's parties were friendly but sedate, but John Harlan used to tell, with humor mixed with chagrin, of a party his firm had in the Commodore Hotel. They ordered up a piano to make the occasion more festive, and by four in the morning every sliver of the piano—every key, every string, every screw or nail, every bit of wood—had been thrown out the window. Thus did robust unregenerate Wall Street march to the Great Depression.

There was a distinguished group of federal judges in Manhattan in those days. I knew only the district judges. Learned Hand, erudite, with a yen for off-color stories, and a wonderful companion; John M. Woolsey, who was to write some of the first opinions clearing pieces of literature from the charge of obscenity; and William Bondy, named by Harding—sturdy, resolute, and eager to strike a blow for liberty. He was, however, deaf, and a primitive hearing aid did not help very much. So he caused problems to the lawyers who appeared before him. In one case, Si Rifkind moved for a modest $5,000 fee in a bankruptcy case. He presented his motion with dignity and persuasion. When he finished, Bondy leaned over and said, "Mr. Rifkind, I have been thinking for some time about your case and I agree with you that your fee be set at five hundred dollars." Years passed and pressure on Bondy to retire increased. One day he said to a friend of mine, "They say I should retire because I am deaf. Don't they know I have always been deaf?"

In time he did retire, and lived, as I recall, to be eighty-eight. By that time life had passed him by; his old friend Cardozo had died, but he did not remember it. He was having lunch with a friend of mine in a restaurant. Though they were at the same table, my friend had to shout to make Bondy hear. So what he said resounded throughout the restaurant. "How is Cardozo?" Bondy shouted. "Cardozo is excellent," my friend roared in return, bringing all conversation in the restaurant to a halt.

When I practiced at 15 William Street, I was exposed for the first time to the corruption of Tammany Hall. Young lawyers were deputized as attorney generals to be watchers at the polls in state and federal elections. I volunteered and was assigned to a precinct on the Lower East Side, where I spent the whole day from eight in the morning to six at night. My instructions were to challenge suspect persons, making them prove identifications of their names and residence. Everything went well until about five-thirty. Suddenly a line of twenty-odd characters formed, wearing caps and sweaters. They were young men and looked to me as if they had been imported into this precinct to vote at this election. I stepped forward and challenged the first man. The second man put a gun in my ribs, and all was silent for a moment. Then I stepped back and let the line pass through. Discretion won out over valor.

Six o'clock came and the polls closed. The precinct captain asked me for the key to the voting machine. I refused to give it to him. He called a policeman, who told me to turn over the key. I refused. My position was that the machine had to be kept intact, so that the total vote minus the twenty-odd "ringers" would be known. If the machine were opened, the totals could be manipulated after I left. I wanted the machine delivered intact to headquarters with my certificate of irregularity. The precinct leader finally broke down and confessed that they were "ringers," adding, "But they did not change the result; they merely swelled the total of Democratic votes so I could make a better showing to the boss." I did not give in, however, and finally got a police escort to the subway, returned home with the key, and submitted my report the next day.

In New York City, I learned about the devilish work of the police. The police of Yakima had always been picked for their brawn, not their brains. At that time New York followed the same pattern. The third degree flourished. When I practiced in Wall Street, the police were obtaining confessions by tying suspects in dental chairs and drilling their live teeth. It was a technique Hitler later used in Germany. When I discovered it in New York City, my respect for police practices dropped even lower than it was when they were shooting at us in the freight yards of Pasco.

All of my own early experiences in the law came tumbling through my mind years later when in 1969 my wife, Cathleen, decided to study law. Law practice, I had learned, was at times grubby business and at times as exhilarating as reaching 22,000 feet in the Himalaya without oxygen. But I did not bare my soul to Cathy when she made her decision, for it was her life, not mine, that was at stake. She started with a much more romantic attitude than I had ever mustered.

As Cathy went along and began to understand the new world she had entered, she had hours of doubt as well as energizing days. She was able to read, relax, and reflect in ways I never experienced, and she grew in stature with each passing month. I taught her only one thing—that contests in the law should never be at the emotional, but only at the intellectual, level. It is the strength of the mind and the will that carries one through dark days and that cautions against exuberant celebrations of victories. The study of law exposes all the ugly corrupt forces that have cast so many laws and reputations into disrepute. But it also exposes the shining moments when the spirit of a people is exalted and conscience is triumphant.

The law, however, is a narrowing experience in the sense that it enslaves one because of its exacting demands. I urged my wife, therefore, to develop hobbies and many outside interests that would keep her from becoming a dry husk when she reached seventy or eighty.

It was a proud day for me when Cathy graduated with honors, for she had survived the cutting comments from competitive students who implied that it was my influence that had brought her prestige. I was also proud when she passed the D.C. Bar and was sworn in by Chief Judge Gerry Reilly of the D.C. Court of Appeals, an old friend of mine.

When I studied law, there were some women in school, yet they were tokens only. By the seventies the tide had turned and women in large numbers were at the Bar. That, I thought, was healthy, not because women were a cure for the mediocrity of the profession but because many have distinct contributions to make in the law. And furthermore, it is important that they be liberated from the caste system that has plagued most societies.

The work at Cravath's was challenging and exciting, and the Cravath discipline was exacting. By the end of the first year I asked Grant S. Bond in Walla Walla if he would give me a further leave of absence. Bond could not wait, but I stayed on in New York anyway, deciding to go to Yakima instead of Walla Walla the following year.

Hearing that I planned to leave, Robert T. Swaine, one of the name partners in the firm, took me on top of the mountain and showed me the promised land of Wall Street, My starting salary had been $1,800 a year, a very good salary for those days and the top Wall Street law clerk pay of that time. After one year I was earning $3,600. Now Bob Swaine came to me and offered me $5,000 and a "future" with the firm.

Swain said, "You've spent your life in the second balcony and I am introducing you to the orchestra." I was to be advanced at once to $5,000 and rapidly thereafter. He had a full expectation that in a few years I would be a junior partner, and from there on, the world was my oyster.

I was flattered and pleased. Yet I had made my decision, and it was based on other values. In this and in other law firms, many young men, within ten years of my age, had been passed by for unknown reasons. They were capable but perhaps not liked by an important client. Some, though they were making $25,000 a year, were on the shelf, with no important work, collecting ulcers. One man I knew was turning to alcohol. Even those who made the top did not seem to have much left at sixty-five. If I walked their paths, I'd never be able to climb another mountain or wade a trout stream. Those men were spent before their time. When they reached the end of the corridor and were ready for retirement, they seemed to have no intellectual interests aside from the law.

I looked around at the older men in my profession and I knew I didn't want to be like *any* of them. They couldn't climb a mountain, couldn't tie a dry fly; they knew nothing about the world that was closest to me, the real world, the natural world.

New York City had a few advantages, of course. I enjoyed the theater crowds and Times Square at midnight. I enjoyed the smell of chestnuts roasting on a pushcart. I searched out the street vendors who sold the nuts of pinyon pine of the Southwest. I discovered Babe Ruth and Lou Gehrig at Yankee Stadium and McGraw's Giants at the Polo Grounds. I liked the waterfront and the sight of vessels clearing the harbor for Europe. But I was filled with a longing for open fields, rolling ridges, and high mountains.

I think that an important influence on me at the time was my correspondence with a boyhood friend, Douglas Corpron. Doug and I had climbed together when we were youngsters. Now, while I was in corporate law in New York, Doug was a medical missionary in China. He would write me about his work and the poverty and the great need of the people. His letters helped put my New York life into perspective and made me more aware that I did not want the kind of success I saw around me.

In Yakima, I thought, I could hike my beloved hills, fish my trout streams, hunt pheasant in the lower valley, mow my lawn, revel in sunsets, and keep alive my botanical interest in the amazing wildflowers that the volcanic Cascades produce each year. The canyons of Wall Street seemed barren in comparison. Money did not seem important. I had gone hungry and at times was filled with despair, but that seemed far behind me. With my law degree and my admission to the Bar came a new sense of security. I did not want to be rich; I only wanted to escape dire poverty. Now I knew I would. It was for those reasons that I declined the overtures of the gracious Mr. Swaine and left for Yakima.

After I left Wall Street, in 1926, I went briefly to Seattle, with the idea that perhaps I'd practice there. But the big Seattle firms didn't seem much different from those in New York. In fact, the main difference seemed to be that whereas I'd been offered $5,000 in New York, the highest salary suggested to me in Seattle was fifty dollars a month. That offer was made to me by Frank Holman, later president of the American Bar Association and a bitter critic of the Court. He was so bitter that I never had the courage to remind him that he once had offered me a job.

What I was looking for out West was a personal country practice. So in Yakima I became associated with James O. Cull—the lawyer who had misappropriated my mother's small inheritance. I did not seek him out. He urged me to come with him.

He suggested that I move into his office and get started. He had just emerged from bankruptcy and was trying to get a new start in life. He wanted me as his associate; he wanted to atone for what he had done to Mother. He said he hoped to be able to pay me fifty dollars a month. But he could make no promise. I was to move into his office on the second floor of the Pagor Building, 11 Second Street. So I threw in my lot with him on a temporary basis only, and our association was to last even more briefly than I imagined it would.

My first legal assignment in Yakima was drafting a mortgage on a farmer's chicken pens. I worked assiduously on it, spending most of one day, as I recall. The last mortgage I had drawn was on the Chicago, Milwaukee & St. Paul Railway Company when I practiced in Wall Street. My chicken-coop mortgage had a like detail and finesse. I took it into Cull's office, and he first complimented me on it, then admonished: "Our fee for this is fifteen dollars and you have put in at least fifty dollars' worth of work."

I asked him what he would have done differently.

"Out here we have a simple mortgage form that is printed. There are spaces for the names of the parties and a description of the premises. You could fill it in in less than fifteen minutes."

And so I had my first lesson in country law practice.

Yakima law practice meant tough digging. Not many people in town made $5,000, the salary Swaine had offered me. It was an impecunious practice, to say the least. I averaged about twenty-five dollars a month in fees. I saw years of work ahead of me before I could even think of buying a house.

Still, "every devil loves the marshes where he was born," and I liked being back in Yakima. I could always get away to the mountains and hike. Though Yakima practice seemed a treadmill, each day had its exciting problems, and I was resigned to taking the Washington Bars the following spring and making Yakima my permanent headquarters. But my Yakima practice ended in a few months. A telegram came from Columbia with an offer of a five-thousand-dollar assistant professorship for full-time teaching.

I did real soul-searching. I asked my friend Elon to talk the problem out with me. We sat on a lava cliff high above town one night and discussed the matter from top to bottom. Before I returned home that night, I had made my decision to return to Columbia. I did not know it at the time, but I was about to reenter one of the mainstreams of American life.

Chapter XI

Columbia and Yale Faculties

My return to Columbia marked the first time in my life when I had leisure to study. From the first grade through high school I had been trotting while I learned, work on the side consuming most of what should have been my study hours. In college I had no more than a hour a day to prepare for classes. In my first year at Columbia Law School I had missed six weeks while I holed up preparing the correspondence course. After October my outside activities left not more than an hour or two for studying after classes. When I practiced law and taught, I was always rushing. I never had a chance to read, reflect, reread, study, converse at leisure. I always had to live on an intellectual subway, racing from point to point as I tried to absorb a book on the way.

As a result, I developed a photographic mind, being able to take in a page at a glance, but it was not learning in depth. My years of teaching law, first at Columbia and then at Yale, produced the opportunity to probe deeper into various problems that interested me.

My new leisure gave me time to reflect on my past and future and put current problems in perspective. For the first time I had the chance to browse in libraries. Now my intellectual perspective began to acquire new dimensions. I made many friends in other fields—Stanley Gill at the Engineering School, John Dewey in Philosophy, James Bonbright in the Business School.

At Columbia, revolt against the traditional approach to law was now under way. Underhill Moore, Herman Oliphant, Hessel Yntema, Karl Llewellyn, and Walter Wheeler Cook were the renegades. I joined their ranks. We picked up another renegade from the History department, Julius Goebel, and one from Political Science, Thomas Reed Powell. We wanted to discover whether the law in books served a desirable social end or should be changed. We were dubbed the leaders of "sociological jurisprudence."

We wanted to join forces with other disciplines at Columbia—such as business, economics, sociology—to examing an entire area. We wanted interdepartmental fertilization of ideas—a process that critics later dubbed interdepartmental "sterilization" of ideas. In finance, we wanted to teach the anatomy of finance as well as the rules of law. In criminal law, we wanted psychiatry as well as the criminal code. In credit transactions, we wanted to explore all the institutions of credit as well as the commercial code. The same was true of almost every other subject. The teaching of law in other fields was largely unrelated to the sociological, economic, or financial data with which that branch of law dealt.

Law had become a compartmentalized specialty, quite remote from the actualities of life. If we could integrate the various disciplines, we could learn what the law should be, by learning the problems with which it must deal. To do that we had to reeducate the teachers, making them familiar with each field. And I was to discover that reeducating teachers was the major stumbling block.

Such a program required a great faculty effort. Most law professors did not want to throw away the notes they had been using for years. They were not concerned with, nor did they discuss with their students, the bias in existing laws and whether they truly served the public interest. We wanted a dean at Columbia who would be interested in that approach and give us, in time, a capable faculty.

We were blunt and outspoken in our demands. One of our more acid-tongued members was Herman Oliphant, later general counsel to the U.S. Treasury. I had known him as a severe teacher, now I came to know him as a human being and as a friend.

Karl Llewellyn was a nonconformist, interested in commercial law, who was not satisfied with reciting "what the law is." He wanted to know how it got that way, whose ends it served, why it should not be changed, and the lawyers' and judges' roles in changing it.

Another member of the Columbia Law faculty, Julius Goebel—soon to be our foremost legal historian—liked to prick the Establishment's favorite balloons. He delighted in showing the silly, foolish purposes some laws had been designed to serve. He had many enemies, the most violent dubbing him a Katzenjammer Kid.

Underhill Moore, who taught Sales, and Walter Wheeler Cook, who taught Equity, were fireballs. They were legal nonconformists. Moore, as I have described, was a teacher *par excellence* who kept every student intellectually honest and tidy. He zeroed in on every bit of loose talk and drove the speaker into the open for annihilation. Cook was similar. They both disliked intellectual arrogance—and Nicholas Murray Butler, president of Columbia, was the epitome of that.

In banking transactions Underhill Moore wished to consider not only "the facts of the case" as developed in the record, but also "the relation between judicial behavior and institutional ways of behaving in the contemporary culture of the place where the facts happened and the decision was made." (38 Yale L.J. 703,705) His pursuit of that study as revealed in his reports (41 Yale L.J. 1109; 45 Yale L.J. 1, 260) produced great guffaws among some of his colleagues at Yale, and ridicule by Frankfurter at Harvard. But as Moore told me before he died, "It may take a thousand years for the idea to take hold. But custom—not only the dry 'facts' of a case—is a powerful conditioner of the law, operating perhaps subconsciously."

I have said enough about our revolutionaries to indicate how dangerous they sounded to President Butler, whom we had dubbed "Nicholas Miraculous." He was so terrified at the prospect of Columbia being dominated by "sociological jurisprudence" that he appointed a dean, Young B. Smith, without consulting the Law faculty. I had nothing against Smith. He was a fine man but he was the antithesis of what we wanted: he represented the past. Under him our educational venture was doomed. We had been working with John Dewey and James Bonbright, trying to bring into focus the various disciplines that bore on legal issues. We hoped to open the law to reexamination in the light of philosophy, sociology, and history, and Smith was utterly opposed to what we were trying to do.

So I wrote a letter to President Butler. It had only one sentence and it said in substance: "In view of your appointment of a dean of the Law School without consulting the faculty, I tender herewith my resignation." My resignation was never formally accepted.

Not many months had passed before a committee of the Law faculty urged me to return to Columbia. I said I would consider it when Butler retired as president. They whispered that he would retire the following June. I replied I'd believe it when it happened. Butler did not retire until

1945; had I returned to Columbia, I would have been under his unfriendly wing for an additional seventeen years.

I was the only one to resign from Columbia in 1928, but the following year Hessel Yntema, Underhill Moore, and Walter Cook all resigned.

Forty years later Columbia was to suffer a serious blow. The office of the president remained the same old voice of the Establishment. The presidents who followed Butler had all emulated him. Like the men in Wall Street, they were talented but lacking public consciousness; they bowed to the Pentagon and the CIA. The students and many faculty members finally rebelled, and virtually paralyzed the university. What they did was excessive, but the rebellion was long brewing; my encounter with Butler in 1928, when he emasculated the Law School, was by no means the beginning. Columbia seemed to have had the curse of the Establishment on it for decades. Harlan Stone had in fact resigned as dean of the Law School several times as a result of Butler's machinations.

When I resigned that spring of 1928, it looked as if my law-teaching career had come abruptly to an end after only one year of full-time teaching. I began to make plans to return to practice.

About that time I met Carl Sandburg in Pelham, a suburb of New York, where I lived. I do not recall the occasion that brought him there, but we had a long evening together, just the two of us. Even then, Sandburg ended his day at 4:00 A.M. I had always been on a different time schedule from Carl's, getting to bed early and getting up early, but I broke my routine to spend at least a part of a night now and then with him.

On this night Carl walked me home, strumming his guitar and softly singing some of the folk songs he had just published in his book *American Songbag*. When we arrived at my apartment, he stopped at the entrance and sang me one last song, making sure that his voice and guitar were muted so as not to disturb the neighbors. The moon was high, and in its light I could see that his face was beaming. A long lock of unruly hair—not yet gray—hung over his forehead. Our friendship had begun with the realization that we both had once ridden the rods, and it was sealed this night with music. That common bond lasted throughout the years.

Much later I was on a program with Carl Sandburg in Chicago. It was a memorial dinner for John Peter Altgeld, the courageous governor of Illinois who in 1895 had pardoned some of the Haymarket rioters. I spoke first, Carl following. We were on the air, and when it came his turn, he faced the microphone, burst into tears, and for a few seconds was inarticulate. I teased him about it when the committee and the panel assembled for a reception after the program, and he told me an interesting story. When he was a boy he sold newspapers on a Galesburg street corner. Some of those Haymarket rioters had been executed, and the papers, reporting on it, were dropped at his corner. As he unwrapped them and saw the headlines, he was overjoyed. Illinois was now a safe place for boys. Years later, when Altgeld issued the pardons, he realized that innocent men had been executed. The thought that he, Carl Sandburg, had exulted at the event, filled him with remorse, and that remorse came flooding back at this Altgeld memorial.

Carl Sandburg was our greatest twentieth-century humanist.

James T. Donald, who had steered me to Columbia and away from Harvard, had moved from Yakima to Baker, Oregon, and asked me to join his prospering law firm. I was attracted by the offer not only because of Jim, but because of his partner as well—Blaine Hallock—who was with me in the same company in World War I. But I finally decided to return to Yakima, my first love. And so the decision stood, until a night in May, 1928, when Richard Walsh, head of John Day Publishing Company, invited me to spend an evening with him at his club in Pelham, New York. I had met Walsh in Pelham, and through him, his wife, Pearl Buck, from whom I learned much about the Far East, particularly China.

The guest speaker that night at dinner was the attractive and brilliant dean of the Yale Law School, Robert M. Hutchins, who was then in his late twenties. We met in a foul-smelling locker room of the country club, that being the meeting place because only there could bootleg liquor be served. I was with the committee that put Hutchins on a New Haven train very late that night.

The next morning I was awakened by a call from Hutchins, always an early riser. He told me he had summoned the Yale faculty to a nine o'clock meeting and they had elected me to the faculty. My first question to him was almost insulting: "Where is Yale?" I was so ignorant of the East that I actually did not know where that university was. There were other questions, too, all of which in time were satisfactorily answered. And so, by September, 1928, I was ensconced in Hendri Hall as an Associate Professor of Law. In 1929 Hutchins left Yale to become president of the University of Chicago. He asked me to go with him to become dean at Chicago.

The top salary in law at Chicago was $10,000. Hutchins persuaded his board of trustees to offer me two and a half times that amount, saying that I was "the most outstanding law professor" in the nation. That eloquent statement insulted many law professors who defected as friends of Hutchins. Moreover, although I accepted the Chicago appointment, I never taught there. I stayed at Yale and became Sterling Professor of Law until 1934, when I went to Washington, D.C.

The president of the University was James Rowland Angell, broad-gauged, tolerant, and fastidious when it came to academic freedom. The dean of the Law School after Hutchins was Charles E. Clark, who later graced the Court of Appeals for the Second Circuit and left behind a glorious record of liberalism.

My days at New Haven were happy ones. Both my children were born there—Millie in 1929, Bill in 1932. Bill was born at 6:00 A.M., and I was not very sharp at my eight o'clock class that morning. Eight o'clock was for me the prize time to teach, because it left the rest of the day free.

New Haven was a relaxed, easygoing college town. Its physical beauty and intellectual grace made it an ideal habitat. People were intimate and friendly. Although there were undercurrents of a minor antagonism between Town and Gown, Yale produced a lively social atmosphere and in some departments a lively intellectual climate. Yale College, however, was filled with sons of the elite who lived in a warm glow of easy scholarship, easy living, easy work. They were the "chosen" who in time would run the nation. The college professors dealt kindly with them; they were spoon-fed, coddled, pampered. I early discovered that they were unused to intellectual discipline, for the Yale College men in my law classes were waiting for someone to fill their heads with knowledge. Yale, in those days, was notorious for being that kind of filling-station.

When I was at Yale, I carried into the classrooms the teaching techniques I had acquired at Columbia. In retrospect it was a rather hard-bitten approach, fashioned on the Socratic method and based on the premise that in the forums of the law the soft-spoken, philosophical advocate had no high place. So I bore down hard, treating each student as if it were irrelevant that his father or grandfather was a "great man." I tended to treat the class as the lion tamer in the circus treats his wards. Soon the class was in protest, sending a committee to Dean Hutchins to have me fired. Hutchins called me in to his office and told me what the committee had said.

I replied that the students were grandsons of very eminent and at times disreputable characters, and that as a result of the wealth of their ancestors, the students had been spoiled all their lives. I said I thought it was time they learned that when they stood before a court or a jury, they would be judged by their perception and fidelity to the law, not by their ancestors.

"It's fine with me if you fire me," I said.

"Don't be silly. I'm merely passing the complaint on to you," Hutchins told me.

"I am inclined to bear down even harder on the spoiled brats."

"That would be revolutionary and wonderful."

And so I stayed on at Yale.

By the time I had reached Yale and had time for reflection, I was, in a way, sorry that I had turned to law. I had seen enough in New York City and in the State of Washington to realize that the practice of law required predatory qualities. There seemed to be recognized prices for nuisance value in the law—prices at which groundless suits could be settled. Finance was predatory and many men who managed it had predatory proclivities. Their lawyers took on the coloration of their clients and designed ways and means of accomplishing certain projects that should have been beyond the pale. I had seen that Wall Street had its Augean stables, and many of the caretakers were lawyers. The great names in the law were, with few exceptions, attached to men who exploited the system but brought very few spiritual or ethical values to it. Those who reached sixty-five years of age might be wealthy, but as I observed in New York, they were mostly shriveled men with no interests beyond the law. Few had rendered public service, and those who did used that front merely to get more business.

At Yale, Bob Hutchins and I often sat around talking of these things. There was no one on the professional horizon whose example we wanted to emulate. The small-town lawyers tended to be heavy-footed pettifoggers whose energies were expended on small things. Those of New York City were more suave, sophisticated, and deft. But they added up to the same total score.

Teaching was only a stone's throw away. Why spend one's life teaching bright youngsters how to do things that should not be done? Why teach them to be cleverer than their fathers? Or, on the other hand, why not practice and use the new-found finesse for one's own benefit?

These were problems we explored; most of us did not resolve them, but ended with doubts and misgivings about law as practiced, wondering whether English literature, philosophy, or conservation might not have been a better dish. In general, during and after my days in New York, most of my friends were not lawyers but biologists, botanists, geologists, ecologists and the like.

In the late twenties and early thirties there were very few creative forces in the law. Law faculties were encrusted with heavy-footed traditionalists. Hutchins worked hard to get rid of two such men who had come to Yale from Harvard—Edward S. Thurston in Torts and Warren A. Seavy in Evidence—by subtly indicating to Harvard that they wanted to return, implying that he would view the event with sorrow. Sure enough, Harvard rose to the bait and made them offers which they accepted.

Some of us at Yale were trying to do what we had been unable to do at Columbia—make the law more relevant to life. To what extent is it based on institutional practices? To what extent does it serve consumer interests? Forty years ago there were a few legal aid societies, but "public interest" law firms were far in the offing.

Robert Hutchins taught Evidence and had a psychiatrist join him in examining old rules of law for their validity in light of modern knowledge and insight. What he did in that field some of us were doing in other fields. Charles Clark was pioneering in Procedure, and his activities had ended, by 1938, with the Federal Rules of Civil Procedure, drafted by his committee for the U.S. Supreme Court and the Congress. Thurman Arnold was teaching and writing his *Folklore of Capitalism.* Hutchins, to enliven the subject of Torts, brought Walton Hamilton, an economist, to the Law faculty, now that Thurston had left.

Hammy had never studied law but he had a wonderfully creative mind and put old principles into brand-new bottles—not only in Torts, but in Business Regulations, Patents, and related fields. (In time Hammy was called to Georgia for consultation on economic-legal problems and the governor of Georgia, Ellis Arnall, was so impressed that he made Hammy a member of the Georgia Bar. Being a member of a state Bar, he could in three years become a member of the Supreme Court Bar. And that happened.)

Another Yale law professor who was opening up new vistas was Wesley Sturgis. His field was arbitration. Harry Shulman was doing the same with labor. Richard J. Smith was bringing common sense and the British experience to bear on public utility rate regulation. Arthur L. Corbin, Edwin Borchard, Gus Lorenzen, William R. Vance made up the stalwarts. Harold Laski of the London School of Economics was there off and on.

Arthur Goodhart of Cambridge was present for a visit. The Yale Law campus was filled with a fervor that no other law faculty experienced.

Felix Frankfurter, who flitted on and off the Yale campus, was a brilliant traditionalist. We had been with him a hundred percent in his advocacy of the cause of Sacco and Vanzetti, two hapless foreigners who were unfairly tried, unfairly convicted, and cruelly executed. Frankfurter's book on the case, first published in 1927, had been our bible. Clark and Hutchins at Yale, and I at Columbia, had promoted its cause. We had written letters, spoken at meetings, and circulated petitions—all to no avail.

Carrol Shanks had graduated with me from Columbia and was practicing in Wall Street when I went to Yale. We induced him to join the faculty and work with me in the field of corporate finance. He spent a year at Yale, only to find practice more to his liking, but during that year we started a project that ended with several Douglas and Shanks casebooks.

Walter Nelles, brilliant but little known, was on the faculty, and he was probing delicate areas of civil rights in the late twenties and early thirties. Edwin Borchard claimed international law; but two of his outside interests made enduring impressions. Borchard was almost a one-man lobby to push through the federal Declaratory Judgment Act, and he also wrote *Convicting the Innocent*—case histories of innocent men found guilty of major crimes. It was that book which quickened the conscience of America in regard to legal injustice.

Thurman Arnold was one of my closest friends at Yale. Thurman was an unorthodox, nonconformist, unpredictable man with an extremely sharp mind and an unusual wit. He was a brilliant lawyer and a wild and wonderful companion.

Mrs. Arnold's finest hour came one night when she and Thurman were giving a dinner party. Thurman and I lived in the same block on Willow Street, about two miles from the Law School, and often walked home together. That night we were in the midst of an exciting conversation when we reached his house, and I suggested we continue it in my home, where I would pour him a drink. So the two of us settled down in my living room. The time passed more quickly than either of us realized. When he finally looked at his watch, he jumped to his feet and said. "Frances will be angry. I'm already an hour late for dinner."

"Don't worry," I said, "I'll handle Frances." So we walked up the block to his white house. The moon was high and the evening air crisp. As we stopped on the sidewalk, Thurman said, "An ideal night to see the mortgage on my house." Pointing to the sky, he outlined the mortgage —its size, its thickness, its durability. With that explained, he hurried up the steps, saying, "Leave Frances to me. I know how to deal with her."

I stood at the foot of the steep stairs that led to their porch. As Thurman reached the door, Frances appeared. With her left hand she seized him by the collar. With her right she took him by the seat of the pants, and literally threw him into the street. Shaking her fist, she shouted, "And I'll do the same to you, Bill Douglas."

I picked Thurman up, and taking him by the arm, walked him back to my home, saying, "We must find more friendly people." With that consolation he finished the fifth of bourbon and said, "Friendly attitudes —that's the thing this city needs. Come with me."

Foolishly I got into Thurman's car and went off with him. I soon discovered that, distracted by his own exciting monologue, Thurman had left the street and was driving down the sidewalk. With that corrected, he drove from house to house, announcing as the host answered the door that he headed a good-will mission aimed at generating a more friendly attitude among the people of New Haven. All told, we visited a dozen homes, where Thurman delivered his own version of the Sermon on the Mount and left, pleading for better human relations in the city.

At each stop, the wife of the house would instantly call Frances, and it was only a matter of time until she caught up with Thurman and took him home. Both of us sent flowers to Frances the next day. But it took some weeks before normal relations, even with Thurman, were restored.

Thurman, usually absent-minded, would walk into class with his hat still on, sucking his pipe, and leading Duffy, his dog, on a leash. He conducted his class in that manner, saying to his stumped students that unless they all did better, he'd have to ask Duffy to supply the answer.

Thurman Arnold, wit, after-dinner speaker, advocate, and poet, backed the streetcar company in New Haven when it sought to raise its rates from five cents to a dime. He made speeches about it, saying that unless the rates were raised, respectable people would find themselves riding to work with the hoi polloi. "Nothing," he shouted, "would be more humiliating to the intellectuals of Yale than to find themselves in streetcars filled with ordinary common people."

Thurman also designed a get-ahead system. To get ahead, one had to have points. One got points by getting publicity—favorable publicity preferably, but any publicity was better than none at all. There were five points when one got one's name in the New Haven *Register*; ten points in *The New York Times*; twenty-five points in a national magazine; fifty points in the rotogravure section of the *Times*; a hundred points in a *Times* editorial. One night Arnold was speaking in New Haven while Wesley Sturgis spoke in Bridgeport. We arranged with Western Union to send them identical telegrams, signed with their respective names. Each, as he rose to speak, got the message from the other: "I would appreciate it if you would mention me in your speech tonight." Both were so annoyed, they would not speak to each other for days.

When we were at Yale Hutchins and I thought—and I still do—that training lawyers as mechanics are trained is fatal to the concept of a university. The body of "knowledge" pounded into the heads of law students does not survive long after Bar examinations are passed. Law, like engineering, changes fast. The so-called "practical" facts soon become obsolete. The only knowledge of permanent value—in law as elsewhere—is theoretical knowledge. Theoretical knowledge, critical judgment, and the discipline of learning are the only enduring aspects of legal education which make the individual readily adaptable to changing situations and problems.

Law schools then—as now—had become trade schools. Students were taught to memorize rules and manipulate them, as one does a deck of cards. Alumni pressure to this end was great, as was the pressure from Bar associations. The result was that at Yale, as at Columbia, the Law School become an isolated and insulated compartment of the university. Though the Law School dealt with sociological matters, it had no ability even to converse with the Department of Sociology. Though it dealt with matters of economics, business, political science, psychology, and the like, it had no nexus with those disciplines.

Dean Hutchins and I wanted interdisciplinary studies and projects. It was precisely the kind of approach some of us had undertaken at Columbia, only to be thwarted by President Butler. We wanted the university to be an intellectual community in which the law group would be enlightened by others as well as enlightening them.

While Hutchins was still at Yale, he raised five million dollars to found the Institute of Human Relations, which was to study such issues. I associated with Dorothy Thomas of the Institute of Human Relations in making further studies of aspects of business failures, some of which studies were published.

One other professor, George Dession, joined the Institute. He worked in the field of criminal law with psychologists and psychiatrists in an interdisciplinary project. Dession continued with his provocative criminal law work until his untimely death.

The whole Yale Law project gradually faded. The total effect of the institute and of all our efforts was zero, because we could not find enough people who were willing to devote effort to such matters. The same problems are still being discussed in the law schools to this day, as well as in the legal profession. Yet almost nothing has been accomplished in all these years.

Hutchins left Yale to go to the University of Chicago in 1929. Dession died. I left for Washington, D.C., in 1934. Meanwhile, the momentum of tradition had taken over, aided and abetted by infiltration from Harvard, where the idea of a how-to-do-it trade-school type of law school flourished.

My years at Yale disillusioned me concerning the law as an instrument of power for the social good.

Years later Hutchins put the early concept for which we had worked in eloquent language: "If we see the university as a center of independent thought and criticism and the law as an ordinance of reason directed to the common good, we understand how the two come together and how the one requires the other. The intellectual community has to think together about important matters: the law is the application of thought to what is perhaps the most important of all matters, the regulation and direction of the common life. Law teaches us how to lead the common life and disseminates newly discovered moral truths.

"The law becomes a university subject, as distinguished from one appropriate to a multiversity, when it is seen not as a collection of coercive rules to be manipulated by the technician, but as a body of principles of the highest moral and pedagogical value. The task of the university law school is the clarification and refinement of these principles, which are relevant to the life and to the study of everybody inside and outside the university. Since law is architectonic, which means that it shapes the conduct of society, everything in the society is relevant to it."

Charles E. Clark who, as we have seen, became dean at Yale after Bob Hutchins departed, was a seminal influence in the law. As dean, however, he was a stickler for the proprieties, took offense readily, and regularly wrote critical notes of faculty conduct and attitudes. "Charlie's notes" became the subject of light-hearted comments, and a competition set in to see who had the most distinctive collection. When it came to students, Charlie exacted very high standards.

One day in May, Clark called an early-morning faculty meeting, at the time of the start of final exams, not long before graduation. It seemed that the leading student had been apprehended in his dormitory room with a woman. The nightwatchman faithfully reported the episode to Charlie, who, being a Puritan at heart, instantly responded by convening the faculty. Charlie presented the case in detail and with meticulous care, mindful of the student's rights. But he thought that an issue of morality was involved, that Yale should never compromise with a moral issue, and therefore he had most reluctantly concluded that the student should be dismissed. That action would be a professional blow to the man, but the morality issue was an overriding consideration to Charlie.

The discussion went around the room, professors speaking in order of seniority. As I recall, eight or more had agreed with Charlie when it came my turn. I said that I disagreed with the majority, that I had a different view. "From what Charlie has told us, the man is undoubtedly quite superior. We should therefore elect him to the faculty."

It was Thurman Arnold who tossed the big bomb. Thurman had talked with the student and learned that the girl was dancing in a chorus that was performing locally. She had come to the dormitory for a quiet and decorous hour. The student played Tschaikovsky's *Nutcracker Suite* for her. Then they played a few hands of gin rummy and the young lady was sent back to her hotel.

Thurman addressed the faculty as follows: "All the evidence is in. The campus policemen examined the suite of rooms where all this occurred and have assured us that nothing untoward went on; a victrola and records were in the center of the room; cards were on the floor; there was no evidence of any wrongdoing. Everything is exactly as the boy represented. Now, gentlemen, we have a case here of a perfectly normal, healthy young man who escorted to his dormitory room at near midnight a lovely young lady from the Paramount Chorus. They remain there for an hour and a half. And what do they do? They play Tschaikovsky's *Nutcracker Suite*. That's what they did, and that's *all* they did. In light of this, I say again that we don't really need this boy at Yale, and I say this not because of what he *did* do but because of what he *didn't* do!"

The student was not expelled. He went on to graduate with honors, and before many years, headed his Bar Association.

One day Thurman and I were riding the New Haven Railroad, seated in the smoker near the men's room. A sign on the wall said: "Passengers will please refrain from flushing toilets while the train is standing in or passing through a station."

Thurman and I got the idea of putting these memorable words to music, and Thurman quickly came up with the musical refrain from *Humoresque*:

Passengers will please refrain
from flushing toilets while the train
is standing in
or passing through
a station.

Thurman at once addressed the passengers in the parlor car and taught them to sing this song in unison. After many attempts, they were able to make a perfect rendition. Thereafter, it was common on the New Haven to hear people singing the song.

The railroad was pretty annoyed and changed its signs to read. "Don't flush toilet while train is in station." Thus did Thurman make a "constructive" dent on a bureaucracy.

The Wickersham Commission (National Commission on Law Observance and Enforcement) rendered a voluminous report in fourteen volumes in 1931. Thurman and I were brought in to make a report on criminal statistics. We got ourselves a Hollerith machine and made some wondrous computations. The commission printed our report, and we were so mesmerized by what we had produced that each of us ordered a hundred copies of the reprint, making sure we could supply the insatiable demand. Thirty years passed and I refreshed Thurman's mind, telling him that recently I had counted my copies and I still had ninety-nine. "Ninety-nine?" he exploded. "You must have given one away, I still have my original hundred."

At about this time, Sherwood Anderson had caught my fancy with his book *Dark Laughter*, published about 1925. He seemed at that time to be a symbol of what we would call today the New Left, so I eagerly invited him to a cocktail party after a Yale football game. I had just repapered the living room, making the downstairs of our house resplendent. Anderson was standing in a corner surrounded by guests and holding a martini in one hand and smoking a cigarette with the other. After lighting a new cigarette on the old, Anderson, to my consternation, put the old one out by crushing it against my new wallpaper, and then he casually tossed the butt on my carpet. My hero instantly became an uncivilized boor, and I never saw him again.

During this period I struck up warm relations with Dean Wallace B.

Donham, Donald David, and George E. Bates of the Harvard Business School. That group had explored with the Harvard Law School the idea of a joint law-business course. In the commercial field the two facilities covered much of the same ground. Why not meet intellectually and integrate the courses? The Harvard Law School would have none of it, having too great a vested interest in its own patented disciplines. So the Harvard Business School turned to Yale.

I taught at the Harvard Business School from time to time and found it the liveliest intellectual center on the Harvard campus, apart from the Philosophy department. Bates, from Harvard, taught at the Yale Law School off and on. As a result, Bates and I put together a law-business course intended to take four years. It was approved by both faculties. A student who finished it got both law and business degrees. Our first outstanding student of the joint course was Eugene Zuckert, later to become Secretary of the Air Force under both Kennedy and Johnson.

I had an extraordinary group of students, of whom I will mention only a few. Quigg Newton later became my law clerk at the SEC and went on to a great public career. Howard Marshall did creative work in the petroleum field and became a specialist in that area. Thomas I. Emerson wrote for me the most provocative original examination paper I ever did read. Tom ended up a member of the Yale Law faculty and the outstanding authority in the nation on the First Amendment.

Fred Rodell went from his studies at Yale Law School to Harrisburg, Pennsylvania, to work with Governor Gifford Pinchot for a few years. Later, he worked on *Fortune* and *Life*, and soon he was ensconced on the Law faculty at Yale. He never was a conformist; never a quiet, submissive man; never a spokesman for the status quo. Fred was a rebel in the Jeffersonian sense; he promoted many causes, took many public positions, and wrote many articles, all of which were offensive to the Establishment. He was an excellent teacher and shaped the thinking of hundreds of students. He joined me on many of my wilderness expeditions in the Far West and we remained warm friends through the years.

Fred was always a prompt defender when I was under attack. I recall one fiery letter he got off to *Life*, which had denounced me for going through a divorce. Preceding me in divorce had been Douglas MacArthur, the great general. Why, Fred asked, was MacArthur great in spite of the divorce, while I was disreputable because of it? Fred's work on the Court, entitled *Nine Men*, was to be succeeded by a volume on the so-called Warren Court. He finished the chapters on Warren and Black, and was in the midst of one on Frankfurter when he was laid low for years with a debilitating malady. Fred was one of the original minds emerging from the 1930's.

Another brilliant student of mine at Yale was Abe Fortas, later to bring high distinction to the Bar in Washington, D.C., and still later to join me on the Court. As a student, Abe spent one hot summer pounding the streets of Chicago, and got good credits for an outstanding piece on loan sharks and consumer credit, published in the *Yale Law Journal.** Though written in 1933, the paper still reads with alarming relevance.

While I was on the Yale faculty, I sent prize students into the markets, into the highways, and into the back streets to find out how rules of law looked in operation. One had to examine credit laws in the light of whose interests they served as well as in their application; and certainly such a legal device as garnishment fell into sociology more than the law. I tried to get students into the field to pursue these issues, and though the overall effect was practically nil, a few talented students, like Abe Fortas, did interesting work.

I enjoyed my years at Yale because they gave me great freedom. I never taught more than five hours a week, though it took me eight hours to prepare for each class. That is because I would start out each teaching year fresh, without any "leftover" notes, teaching each course as if I had never taught it before. The light teaching schedule left much time for research.

In later days it came to pass that a professor could not think unless he received a research grant from a foundation. The years 1928 to 1934 preceded that corruption of universities and colleges. We had no funds for field work, but we were filled with research desires. So we did much on our own. I became interested in the actualities of corporate receiverships —their causes, the administration of the receiverships, and the ultimate outcomes. I launched a Connecticut study of that character, and published some of the results in the *Connecticut Bar Journal.***

During these years I made bankruptcy studies in Connecticut, in New York, and in New Jersey. I arranged with Judge William Clark of the U.S. Federal District Court in Newark for permission to interview his bankrupts every Monday morning, and held a bankruptcy clinic. I would make the 5:15 A.M. train out of New Haven on Monday mornings, arrive in Newark by eight o'clock and interview bankrupts all day, and return

* 42 *Yale Law Journal* 526.

** 4 *Connecticut Bar Journal* 1 (1930).

to New Haven late the same night. I conducted similar studies in New Haven and in Hartford on receiverships.

There were mounting bankruptcies under Herbert Hoover, and at about that time a well-known attorney, William "Wild Bill" Donovan, who was to head OSS in World War II, was asked by the Hoover administration to conduct a study of the problem. By then, bankruptcy was becoming a fairly common daily occurrence, and I would go to New York a couple of days a week to join forces with Donovan in this work.

I went to Washington now and then while I was still at Yale to work with Julius Klein, Secretary of Commerce under Herbert Hoover, who had asked me to come down there on a consultant basis to work on the problems of bankruptcy. I researched, I lectured, and I published articles in that area, and by the time Roosevelt was inaugurated in 1933, I had acquired a reputation in the field—a reputation that was shortly to bring me to Washington, D.C.

Never did I dream that I would live to see the day when a court held that a person could be too poor to get the benefits of bankruptcy. Yet, in 1973, the Court in *United States v. Kras* (409 U.S. 434), held by a five-to-four decision that an indigent who could not pay the bankruptcy filing fee could not be discharged of his debts. As the dissenters said, "Some of the poor are too poor even to go bankrupt." (*Id.* at 457)

Chapter XII

George Draper

At Columbia, I had met George Draper, a Professor of Clinical Medicine and the brother of the famous dancer Ruth Draper. He practiced on the side, and for a while was my physician. I kept up my contacts with him after I went to Yale, seeing him socially when I was in New York City and consulting him when I was indisposed.

We became fast friends and developed almost a father-son relationship. He introduced me to the world of psychosomatic medicine, in which he was a pioneer. He had been psychoanalyzed by Jung and had probed deeply into Freudian mysteries. His book *Human Constitution* is a classic.

I can never forget the beautiful painting in his office dating back to fifth-century China. A venerable Chinese doctor stood on the edge of a lake, looking up at the rising moon. "If I could only collect the moonbeams, I could cure all the ills of mankind" was the title.

I saw the painting the first day I went to consult Draper. My problem was migraine headaches, which threatened to ruin my career. I had gone to several New York specialists, paying the last one six hundred dollars. He had said as I left, "Call me sometime when you are quite sick, maybe I can come up with something." I had heard Draper's name mentioned at the Columbia Faculty Club and called for an appointment. As I walked into his office, there was a fire in the fireplace, the Chinese painting hung over it, and Draper was at his desk. Tears filled my eyes, for I knew intuitively that I had come to the right man.

"It is the imponderable that causes much illness," said Draper. Draper eventually psychoanalyzed me and helped me discover and understand the stresses and strains that produced the headaches. Once I faced up to them, the migraines disappeared. Draper cured ulcer patients without surgery or hospitalization and successfully treated people with high-blood pressure. He helped men of small stature to avoid Napoleonic complexes by realizing how they were overcompensating for their deficiency.

Richard E. Byrd, during the winter of 1934, stayed by himself in the remote Advance Base in Antarctica, an experience he later wrote about in his book *Alone*. Parts of Byrd's experiences reached the press by radio, including the account of how he was nearly asphyxiated by carbon monoxide from an engine. It was a grueling account of a man in a hole deep under the snow and ice of a hostile region. Draper used the account as illustrative of the urge of some men to return to the womb, to escape the adversities of life, and to find security—only to realize there is no escape from life except through so-called "nervous breakdowns," insanity, or death.

When it came to his interest in "disease tendencies," Draper was not exactly a pioneer, because Hippocrates had gone into the same field, as had many subsequent students both here and in Europe. But while many urged the medical profession to study the physical constitution, the interest of the profession in considering the mind and body together greatly waned. Draper thought that possibly when Pasteur revealed the vast and mysterious world of microbes as the cause of disease, the entire thought of the medical world, or most of it, was deflected from the study of the human constitution to the study of the external causes of disease. Draper sounded the call to the medical profession to look at man as a whole, not as a thumb, wrist, elbow, head, stomach, liver, or neck. He was interested in diagnostic clues.

Draper rebelled because he realized that while disease could be understood only in the context of the whole man, disease more and more was being considered in separate and discrete aspects. There were now nose specialists, foot specialists, kidney specialists, heart specialists, and so on. Draper gave extreme examples to illustrate his point. "How can a thumb expert know about its problems unless he knows the whole man?" he'd ask me.

He thought that personality types were representative of tendencies to certain types of disease—heart trouble, ulcers, high-blood pressure, and the like. Once I remember he corrected me when I said that a friend of mine had a tumor. He said, "That is the typical error that my medical friends continually make." I asked what was wrong with that observation, and he said, "You should not say Mr. Jones has a tumor. The correct statement would be, 'Mr. Jones is a tumor.'" That was his dramatic and exaggerated way of emphasizing the point, and it was that bluntness and iconoclastic approach that made him almost *persona non grata* with his contemporaries.

He identified disease not only by the human psyche, but by physical tendencies as well. The thorax of gall-bladder people, he said, was both deep and wide, and relatively deeper than it was wide. The thorax of ulcer people was flat and narrow. The thorax of those with pernicious anemia was deep and wide, relatively deeper in respect to its width than is the case in other disease groups. The thorax of hypertensive people is long, but of medium depth and width.

He did not think that those physical manifestations were the end of the problem. He used them only diagnostically and then only in stubborn cases. Yet he did not need a laboratory measurement, say of the thorax, to "size up" a patient and predict with uncanny accuracy his problem or the area in which his problem lay.

The mechanistic approach to medicine—greatly influenced he thought by Rockefeller and other foundation grants—had sent doctors off on the wrong trail by establishing taboos against the powerful force of the human psyche. Yet one's psyche, he explained, was an important and very potent element of an individual's inherited characteristics and played a prominent part in many diseases.

The hours with George Draper were scintillating. He was strong in intuition, insight, and gentleness. He lived a generation too early, largely denounced by his contemporaries. But he had the distinction of being the father of psychosomatic medicine in this country.

Draper and Franklin D. Roosevelt had been to school together. They were both members of the Eastern aristocracy. Draper had been FDR's personal physician when Roosevelt was stricken with polio in the early 1920's; and he saw the President through that ordeal.

As FDR convalesced, the contest between mother and wife became intense. Sara Delano, FDR's mother, whom I later knew, was strongly masculine and iron-willed. She wanted her crippled son on the front porch at Hyde Park, blossoming as a stamp collector. Eleanor, the wife, and Draper, the physician, thought that course would be tragic.

"Why are your legs important in speechmaking?" Draper would ask

FDR. "It's your heart and your mind that are important in politics, not your feet."

This was the theme on which George Draper hammered away. He knew that a man like FDR, who accepted the fact that he could do nothing because he was crippled, would in time be crippled in spirit as well as in body. The healthy course was to get into the stream of life. "Become governor," Draper urged. Eleanor Roosevelt took the same tactic. They had strong support from Louis Howe, FDR's wise and faithful secretary. When they won and Roosevelt resumed an active life, Draper considered it a great victory over Sara Delano.*

When Roosevelt was elected President by a landslide, Draper urged me to join FDR in Washington. He thought I belonged in the public arena. My only ambition up to then had been to teach and practice law and maintain hiking, fishing, and conservation hobbies. But as the Washington scene began to unfold, my interest in it increased, and one morning at breakfast, while I was reading in *The New York Times* of some monumental financial skullduggery, my decision was made. I wanted a job in the nation's capital.

My own experience with polio put me on FDR's wave length and he was my hero long before I met him. Draper, knowing of my decision to join the President's troops, urged me to get close to him and stay close. "Tell him of your own polio experience," Draper would advise me. But I never did. I felt it would be like talking to the President about his own illness, and I never mentioned that either directly or indirectly. So far as I know, FDR was never aware of the fact that I went through as a boy what he experienced as a man.

Draper was in the capital on numerous occasions but he never did call FDR or drop by to see him. Draper was an extremely sensitive man, and I think he felt that his appearance at the White House would be upsetting to FDR, taking the President back to the days of his illness and his dilemma—whether to follow the urgings of mother or the advice of his wife. I thought Draper was far too sensitive on that matter, but he was so shy and so easily hurt that, after urging him occasionally, I ceased to press the matter. I do not believe he ever saw FDR after the 1932 election, and I never talked to FDR about Draper.

As the years passed, I became embroiled in Washington affairs, and Draper became more and more interested in the people, like John L.

* In *FDR, The Beckoning of Destiny*, Kenneth Davis gives a faithful account of the bout FDR had with polio and the roles that Eleanor, Draper, and Louis Howe played during that time.

Lewis, who dominated the scene. After I had written this chapter I came across an old letter Draper had written me in the forties, long after my analysis. He had seen a friend whom I had sent to him for consultation. This chap had a father who, unlike mine, had not been gentle and perceptive but antagonistic to the son. Crisis after crisis had occurred, in some of which physical force was used. The son's reaction was to seek comfort from his mother. Eventually a pattern developed where he baited and challenged and aroused his father in order to satisfy the subconscious urge to seek maternal solicitous care. The result in the man's adult life was that he became a kind of John L. Lewis, a man constantly defying authority. Thus, Draper said, did infantile patterns mold the man and make him an obnoxious person. His reference was not to John L. Lewis but to the kinds of forces that sometimes produce a John L. Lewis.

Draper and I remained very close friends. I would see him, or at least call him, whenever I was in New York. Once, in the early forties, just after I went on the Court, I invited him to come spend a month in the Wallowas with my family and me. He agreed, and at the appointed hour he arrived at LaGrande, Oregon, by the Union Pacific train.

I drove him to Lapover, where I had built three cabins in the early 1940's, the main one being constructed of large tamarack logs. There was running water piped to the cabin from a creek, a septic tank, a wood cookstove, and a fireplace. There was also a guest cabin, where Draper stayed.

Draper had never seen an area so wild and untouched as the Wallowas of that day. He did not ride a horse, and he had no desire to cross the high ridges that rim the Lostine Canyon. He walked up and down the river, took naps, and sat in the shade reading all day. He talked eagerly with everyone who came up or down the trail and was fascinated by the mountain men he met—a species wholly unknown to Manhattan Island.

One weekend Sandy Balcom, the great fisherman, came for a visit, fishing by day and telling his stories by night. Sandy is a cross between Danny Kaye and Groucho Marx with a touch of Jack Benny added. At the end of the third day Draper took me outside and said, "For three days now I have laughed. I have never before laughed continuously and so long. I have laughed so much I am totally exhausted. Either Sandy must go or I must go."

I told him to relax, that Sandy was leaving at dawn. When Sandy departed, Draper embraced him as though he were saying farewell to a son. As we walked back to the cabin Draper said, "Never have I seen a genius of that dimension."

Draper had been married to the famous interior decorator Dorothy Draper. She reflected other pressures of the times and pushed him toward a Park Avenue practice, a high income, and a social life. During that August visit many of Draper's personal problems surfaced and we talked at length about them. He treated me as a sounding board and I respected his confidence. The episodes he related in the vastness of the Wallowas made me realize that his knowledge of the human psyche was not merely the result of an intellectual specialization, it also reflected his own troubled days. Out of his own torment and pain he had gained understanding of the crisis of other people.

I never met a more daring intellect than Draper's, and I never knew anyone whose insight into other humans was more revealing and sympathetic. He was a great physician in the largest sense of the word.

In sum, the main seminal influence in my life was Dr. George Draper. He did not, of course, know about law and perhaps if he had been a lawyer, he would have taken quite a different position on issues over the years than I. He was, however, a seminal influence because having discovered that I had been launched in life as a package of fears, he tried to convince me that all fears were illusory. He went about it in various ways. "People will say you are nuts. But remember, no one is nuts if he can find a responsible person who agrees with him. That is man's way of establishing a rational relation with the universe."

Another time he would say, "Find your kindred spirits in the law and they will help you find your lodestar."

Yet again he said, "You'll see lawyers—perhaps judges too—panic at taking the final step. Why this fear? The mind is supposed to make us all free. Brilliant patients of mine have walked out of this office on bright, sunny days and told me on the next trip that the sky had been dark. You see, they were not yet whole, completely integrated. Some complex of fears made them shun reality. Face the cosmos. Its inhabitants are gruesome. But the cosmos is challenging. We know so little; yet by cosmic potentials anything is possible."

In these early years I met six seminal forces in the law who shaped my life, thanks to Draper. Though he knew only one of them, I list them in the chronology of their entrance into my life. They were followed by many others; but the first six were Robert M. Hutchins, FDR, Ben Cohen, Jerome Frank, Louis Brandeis, and Hugo L. Black.

Chapter XIII

Fear

"The only thing we have to fear is fear itself."

These words of FDR, spoken at his 1933 Inaugural, reflected—to me—the wisdom of George Draper. By the time FDR made this speech, I had learned from personal experiences that he spoke the truth.

Stark, naked fear is the most devastating force man knows. I knew this, to some extent, as a boy, but it came to full consciousness only as a man when I was psychoanalyzed by George Draper. All of my residual fears of the elements were at long last isolated, but they were not as important as those that lay under the surface of consciousness.

Fear is man's worst enemy, and many of his fears come from imponderables that the victim often does not even suspect. The person who cannot without great apprehension enter an elevator or an airplane or other locked vehicle may be a casualty of a severe birth trauma. Fear of water, fear of lightning, fear of the darkness, fear of animals, fear of open spaces can also be real and forbidding.

I suppose few people started life with more fears than I—and few reached the thirties with less. The best way of riddance is talking with a knowledgeable person. I had few of those opportunities as I grew up, since I had no adult confidant. Most of my fears were resolved by confrontation and rationalization—the hardest but certainly the most enduring way.

Since I had no father to guide me as I grew up, I became much too dependent, emotionally, on my mother. As a result of my bout with polio, Mother pampered me during my early childhood. As I grew up, I was torn between wanting to be tied to her apron strings and rebelling at the very thought of it. Why did I suddenly get on a freight train and, wholly penniless, head East for the law? I had had a job of sorts, one that brought in a hundred dollars a month. That was affluence to Mother, who up to that time had no more than twenty-five cents a day for food for her family. It was therefore with a great sense of guilt that I left her and the job. and struck out on my own. This feeling was compounded as I grew older. And it seized on apparently random elements for exploitation.

Mother had a younger brother named Milo Fisk who died of peritonitis when he was fifteen or so. Her half brother, James Richardson, who had moved to Yakima to try to rid himself of asthma, told me about Milo. So did Mother. One said that he died because he ate a green plum and a tomato. Another said that he was stricken either because he had sinned or because God was resolved to make someone who was very fond of Milo suffer because of her or his sins.

As a result, I grew up with a phobia about intestinal pains. Like lightning, they were one way through which Jehovah worked his will. Moreover, the story of Milo and my liking for baked beans, my favorite dish to this day, were mysteriously and inextricably interwoven. When my polio fever broke, I craved baked beans. Baked beans became a symbol of my return to a haven of security, which of course was my Mother. But in my association with Mother, I subtly became Milo, who also had been frail and weak. And the fate of Milo was all too plain.

This infantile, nonsensical fear grew and grew, reaching a climax the day Rudolph Valentino died in 1926. Valentino, like Milo, died of peritonitis, and I at once developed all the symptoms. That episode and my migraine headaches drove me to all the expensive doctors in New York City, who understood nothing but money, and finally to Draper.

The sessions with Draper probed deeply into many fears. The toughest, the most intractable, and yet the puniest were infantile fears. Others of course also came to the surface. My fear of water was very great. Mother continually warned against the Yakima River, which was indeed treacherous, and she kept fresh in my mind the details of each drowning in the river. But the pool at the YMCA in Yakima was safe and offered the opportunity to learn to swim. The YMCA pool was only two or three feet deep at the shallow end, and while it was nine feet deep at the other, the drop was gradual. When I was ten or eleven years old I got a pair of water wings and went to the pool.

My aversion to the water had started when I was three or four years old and Father took me to the beach in California. We stood together in the surf. I hung on to him, yet the waves knocked me down and swept over me. I was buried in water. My breath was gone. I was frightened. Father laughed, but there was terror in my heart at the overpowering force of the waves.

My introduction to the YMCA swimming pool revived unpleasant memories and stirred childish fears, but in a little while I gained confidence. I paddled with my new water wings, watching the other boys and trying to learn by aping them. I did this two or three times on different days, and was just beginning to feel at ease in the water when a misadventure happened.

One day I went to the pool when no one else was there. The place was quiet. The water was still and the tiled bottom was as white and clean as a bathtub. I was timid about going in alone, so I sat on the side of the pool to wait for others to show up.

I had not been there long when in came a big bruiser of a boy, probably eighteen years old. He had thick hair on his chest and was a beautiful physical specimen, with legs and arms that showed rippling muscles. He yelled, "Hi, skinny! How'd you like to be ducked?"

With that he picked me up and tossed me into the deep end. I landed on the water in a sitting position, swallowed what felt like half the pool, and went at once to the bottom. I was frightened, but not yet frightened out of my wits. On the way down I planned: when my feet hit the bottom, I would make a big jump, come to the surface, lie flat on it, and paddle to the edge of the pool.

It was a long way down. Those nine feet seemed more like ninety, and before I touched bottom my lungs were ready to burst. But when my feet finally hit, I summoned all my strength and made what I thought was a great spring upward. Instead of coming to the surface like a cork, I rose slowly. I opened my eyes and saw nothing but water—water that had a dirty yellow tinge to it. I grew panicky. I reached up as if to grab a rope, and my hands clutched only at water. I was suffocating. I tried to yell, but no sound came out. Then my eyes and nose emerged from the water—but not my mouth.

I flailed at the surface, swallowed more water and choked. I tried to bring my legs up, but they hung like dead weights, paralyzed and rigid.

A great force was pulling me under. I screamed, but only the water heard me. I had started on the long journey back to the bottom of the pool.

I struck at the water as I went down, expending my strength as one in a nightmare fights an irresistible force. I had lost all my breath. My lungs ached, my head throbbed. I was getting dizzy. But I remembered the strategy; I would try again: spring from the bottom of the pool and, hopefully, to the surface; lie flat on the water, strike out with my arms and thrash with my legs. Then I would get to the edge of the pool and be safe.

I went down, down, endlessly. I opened my eyes. Nothing but water with a yellow glow—dark water that one could not see through.

And then sheer, stark terror seized me, terror that knows no understanding, terror that knows no control, terror that no one can understand who has not experienced it. I was shrieking under water. I was paralyzed under water—stiff, rigid with fear. Even the screams in my throat were frozen. Only my heart and the pounding in my head said that I was still alive.

And then in the midst of the terror came a touch of reason: I must remember to jump when I hit the bottom. At last I felt the tiles under me. My toes reached out as if to grab them. I jumped with everything I had. But it made no difference. The water was still all around me. I looked wildly for ropes, ladders, water wings. Nothing but water. A mass of yellow liquid held me. Now terror struck deep inside me, like a great charge of electricity. I trembled with fright. My arms wouldn't move. My legs wouldn't move. I tried to call for help, to call for Mother. Nothing happened.

And suddenly, strangely, there was light. I was coming out of the awful yellow mass. At least my eyes were. My nose was almost out too.

Then I started down a third time. I sucked for air and got water. The yellowish light was going out.

All effort ceased. I relaxed, even my legs felt limp. A blackness swept over my brain. It wiped out fear; it wiped out terror. There was no more panic. It was quiet and peaceful. Nothing to be afraid of. This is nice . . . to be drowsy . . . to go to sleep . . . no need to jump . . . too tired to jump . . . it's nice to be carried gently . . . to float along in space . . . tender arms around me . . . tender arms like Mother's . . . now I must go to sleep.

I fell into oblivion, and the curtain of life fell.

The next I remember I was lying on my stomach beside the pool, vomiting. The chap who threw me in was saying, "But I was only fooling."

Someone said, "The kid nearly died. Be all right now. Let's carry him to the locker room."

Several hours later I walked home. I was weak and trembling. I shook and cried when I lay on my bed. I couldn't eat that night. A haunting fear was in my heart. The slightest exertion upset me, made me wobbly in the knees and sick to my stomach.

I never went back to the pool. Now I truly feared water.

A few years later, when I came to know the waters of the Cascades, I badly wanted to swim in them. But whenever I did—whether I was wading the Tieton or Bumping River or bathing in Warm Lake of the Goat Rocks—the terror that had seized me in the pool would come back. It would take possession of me completely. My legs would become paralyzed. Icy horror would grab my heart.

This handicap stayed with me as the years rolled by. In canoes on Maine lakes fishing for landlocked salmon, bass fishing in New Hampshire, trout fishing on the Deschutes and Metolius in Oregon, fishing for salmon on the Columbia, at Bumping Lake in the Cascades—wherever I went, terror of the water followed me. It ruined my fishing trips, deprived me of the joy of canoeing, boating, and swimming. I became convinced it had something to do with my puny legs, since they became useless once I got into deep water. That fact puzzled me. I often said to myself, "It's funny that I can walk and run and climb with my legs, but not swim with them." But once the panic seized me in the water, I had no command over them.

The phobia grew and grew. It made every expanse of water a source of anxiety, and yet, a challenge. It was at once an invitation to overcome the fear and a fear that I would never succeed in doing so. My aversion to water was, indeed, mixed with a great attraction for it. Often I would be mesmerized and would stand on the edge of a pond or a pool, looking into the water as if to draw from its depth the secret of its conquest of me. It was the master, I was the servant. That created a deep and unreasoning resentment, and the more helpless I was in conquering my fear, the more intense the resentment became. The waters of the rivers and lakes tempted me, but as one can have an appetite for food to which he is allergic, so the waters to which I was drawn filled me with apprehension.

My fears, of course, went back to the day I almost drowned. For many years I thought it took only will power and courage to overcome any fear. It was from Draper that I learned that the early fears of childhood work through the sympathetic nervous system, which does not depend on will power for its functioning. When the man says "Yes," the sympathetic nervous system will often say "No" and send him helter-skelter in the direction opposite from where he believes he has decided to go. If this goes on long enough, a man can end up frustrated and in the grip of an illness that no medicine can cure.

By the time I reached Yale in 1928, I decided to conquer that fear. I reported to Bob Kipmuth, Yale's famous swimming coach, and he laid out a plan for me. I went to the Yale pool and practiced five days a week, an hour each day. The instructor put a belt around me. A rope attached to the belt went through a pulley that ran on an overhead cable. He held on to the end of the rope, and we went back and forth, back and forth across the pool, hour after hour, day after day, week after week. On each trip across the pool a bit of the panic seized me. Every time the instructor relaxed his hold on the rope and I went under, some of the old terror returned and my legs froze. It was three months before the tension began to slacken. Then the instructor taught me to put my face under water and exhale, and to raise my nose and inhale. I repeated the exercise hundreds of times. Bit by bit I shed the panic that seized me when my head went under water.

Next he held me at the side of the pool and had me kick with my legs. For weeks I did just that. At first my legs refused to work. But they gradually relaxed, and finally I could command them.

Thus, piece by piece, he built a swimmer. And when he had perfected each piece, he put them together into an integrated whole. In April he said, "Now you can swim. Dive off and swim the length of the pool, crawl stroke."

I did. The instruction was finished.

But I was not finished. I still wondered if I would be terror-stricken when I was alone in the pool. I tried it. I swam the length up and down. Tiny vestiges of apprehension returned. But now I could say, "Trying to scare me, eh? We—ll, here's to you! Look!" And off I'd go for another length of the pool.

This went on until July. But I was still not satisfied. So I went to Lake Wentworth in New Hampshire, dived off a dock at Triggs Island, and swam two miles across the lake to Stamp Act Island. I swam the crawl, breast stroke, side stroke, and back stroke. Only once did I feel fear. When I was in the middle of the lake, I put my face under and saw nothing but bottomless water. The old sensation returned in miniature. But I laughed and said, "Well Mr. Terror, what do you think you can do to me?" It fled, and I swam on.

Yet I had residual doubts. At my first opportunity I hurried West, went up the Tieton to Conrad Meadows, up the Conrad Creek Trail to Meade Glacier, and camped in the high meadow by the side of Warm Lake, where I had panicked as a boy. The next morning I stripped, dived into the lake, and swam across to the other shore and back—just as Doug Corpron and my other boyhood friends used to do. I shouted with joy, and Gilbert Peak returned the echo. I had conquered my fear of water.

The experience had a deep meaning for me, as only those who have known such feelings and conquered them can appreciate. In death there is peace. There is terror only in the fear of death, as Roosevelt knew when he said, "All we have to fear is fear itself." Because I had experienced both the sensation of dying and the terror that fear of it can produce, the will to live somehow grew in intensity.

At last I felt released. By immersing myself in water and coming to know that medium of life as well as the medium of air, I conquered that fear.

Fear of lightning was another force in my life, originating in religious dogma. I overcame that by reasoned exposure to the danger and by talks with Draper. The arrival of a sure-cure against the fear of lightning was marked by an airplane incident. I was flying over Colorado in a heavy electric storm. Lightning hit the wing just outside my window and for a few seconds rolled in fiery waves along its surface before disappearing in the void. I experienced wonder and amazement but not fear.

Fear of inadequacy because of my weak legs as a result of my bout with polio was another overwhelming force. In retrospect I realize I probably overcompensated for that fear in many ways. But when I could hike and climb with the best of them, that fear dissolved just as a white cloud on a summer day slowly disappears when it encounters a cold air stream high in the sky.

But my rebellion against the shame of being called a weakling had lasting effects. As already noted, it caused me to become very much a loner. Moreover, it inured me in a subtle way to all criticism. Not that I enjoyed criticism, I certainly did not, but criticism never made me turn tail and run. Rather, it impelled me forward into the thick of the fight.

My fears included the fear of wild animals, or at least some of them. As a boy I never encountered a cougar face to face, though in later years I saw cougars in the wild many times. I learned then what I did not know when I was young, that a cougar, unlike a tiger, goes away from man and seldom attacks unless wounded or cornered.

My first experience with this animal was when I, as a boy, took a back-packing trip with my brother Arthur. We got lost in a side canyon below the Pacific Crest Trail (now a National Trail by Act of Congress) south and west of Dewey Lake. We made camp on a spit of white sand in thick brush along Panther Creek. We built a fire and cooked supper, and after the dishes were done, sat around the small fire, talking. It was a pitch-black night and after a while we felt uneasy.

Suddenly out of the brush came the most frightening cry in the mountains—the screech of a cougar. The cry was close by, so close that I thought the creature would be on us any second. Shivers passed through my body. I think my hair stood up. Art's face looked white as a sheet.

When I recovered my wits and reflected, our situation seemed hopeless. We were trapped. The brush was impassable. We could not escape over the two-thousand-foot barricade of the mountain. We could not even hide, for the brush was on three sides of us and it concealed the cougar.

The ten-foot spit of sand was our cage for the night. The situation of a zoo had been reversed. The cougar could roam at will and survey the victims cornered in the cage by the creek. He could stalk us—then pick us off, one by one, whenever he chose. He would probably wait until we were asleep and then spring on us. These were the fearful thoughts in my mind.

Now the cougar screeched again. It was bloodcurdling—a cry that could pierce the heart and create a state of near-panic in the uninitiated. The screech seemed to come from behind our pup tent. My fright was increased by the realization that we had no weapons, except jackknives.

Then Art and I thought of the fire. All animals were supposed to be afraid of fire. If we kept one going and stayed close to it, we'd be safe. So we decided to build our fire as big as we could and feed it with wood all night.

Wood was our problem. We went to the creek's edge and cautiously looked up and down. We saw some timber along the shore not more than twenty-five feet away. Keeping together, we cautiously waded the creek and dragged a quantity of limbs and logs close to our tent. We moved the fire as near to us as we dared and then retired. Art and I took turns replenishing the fire throughout the night.

The screech of the cougar came again and again. It sounded closer and closer, until he seemed to be right next to the tent. I imagined I heard his catlike steps. I even imagined I felt his breath against the canvas walls.

Many times since I have awakened to find the tracks of a cougar not far from my bedroll or tent. But I did not know in those early days that a cougar is the most difficult of all animals to approach in the mountains and rarely attacks man.

The night was endless. I kept an open jackknife in my hand all night long. We got no real sleep until the first streak of dawn was in the sky. Then we slept hard for several hours and woke relieved that the menace of the night had passed.

The screech of the cougar is enough to unnerve anyone. Some say I am wrong, that these animals do not screech. But they do, and theirs is the bloodiest of all the noises in the wilderness.

Bears—Mother's pet fear—were, in my amateur experiences as woodsman, animals one could forget. In all my journeys into the wilderness on foot or horseback, I have rarely seen a black bear. They have a keen sense of smell and sharp hearing and go away from man. The only dangerous black bear is one who has lost his fear of man, and they do get that way. In Yellowstone they learn to like the "goodies" that garbage cans and tourists offer. At a cocktail party in Washington, D.C., I was appalled when a lady said, "You know, Mr. Justice, last summer in Montana, I got so friendly with a bear, I could hold a piece of bread in my mouth and he'd take it from me. Wasn't that cute?"

She was shocked when I told her she should be committed to St. Elizabeth's. One pat of that bear's paw would have sent the lady into oblivion.

Grizzly bears are, of course, different. They are vicious if attacked or wounded. In the fifties I was with the Olaus Murie Biological Mission in the Brooks Range, Alaska—land of the grizzly bear—and came to know something of their habits. Bob Krear went out one bright day for photographs and came across a grizzly asleep on a slope. Bob walked to within a hundred feet of the animal and snapped a picture. The noise of the camera click awoke the bear and he immediately charged. Even at a hundred feet a man probably looks like a caribou, for grizzlies are plagued with near-sightedness. Bob was quick-witted enough to realize he was downwind from the grizzly, so he ran a half-circle, the bear in hot pursuit. When he reached a point in the arc when he was upwind, the bear was twenty feet or so from him. As Bob relates the story, he was sure his end was at hand, and his heart was reacting accordingly. When the bear, however, smelled Bob or saw him, he came to a grinding stop and made a quick getaway. For the scent or sight of man is a signal of danger, one that comes to a grizzly in that remote land only rarely in a lifetime. Bob was so shaken he did not have much of an appetite for three days.

Tossing a rock at a grizzly is a very dangerous thing to do, as some college students discovered at Glacier Park; and many people have been injured or killed at provocations as slight as that. One of the boys at Glacier Park was mauled, chewed, and almost killed by a she-grizzly and was saved only by the arrival of a Park Ranger, who shot the animal. The boy fortunately lived, but required extensive plastic surgery. But my friend John S. Crawford, famed outdoor photographer, spends weeks a year with grizzlies, photographing them, making sure, however, that no movement of his can be considered as an act of aggression.

"One never knows," John tells me. "Perhaps I've just been lucky."

But I have learned that one who is in transit usually only has to cough or sneeze once to send even a grizzly the other way.

The rattlesnake in the Yakima area is the Northern Pacific (*Crotalus viridis oreganus*). They are abundant below three thousand feet above sea level. While they never frightened me, I came to respect them. The rattlesnake was as common to Yakima as the sagebrush and lava rock. I grew up hearing much folklore and nonsense about them. I supposed that the rattler changed his skin every year; that is, however, more likely to happen several times a year. The number of rattles, we were told, grew, one for each year; a rattler, in fact, gets a new rattle every time he sheds his skin. The rattler, we thought, was blind right after shedding; he is, however, only slightly blind prior to shedding. Tobacco juice, we were told, was the best cure for a rattlesnake bite; that is pure buncombe.

Eastern Washington, where I grew up, is ideal rattlesnake country: dry, with not much rainfall and no great extremes of temperature. It is lava-rock country, whose ledges stay warm on bright sunny days. The rattlers love to coil there when the sun is not too hot. Hikers and fishermen climbing these lava outcroppings get negligent and reach for a handhold without first looking. That is when they get hit by a rattler. Horses, mules, and cows usually get hit on the nose as they graze. People wearing sneakers or low shoes walking nonchalantly through bottom lands get hit around the ankles. Those who know the region take precautions—they keep their eyes alert as they climb and they wear ankle-high boots.

Even so, one sometimes has a lapse. I was hiking a canyon rimmed at various levels with lava ledges. It was October and I had put rattlers out of mind because usually by then they have denned. But this was a warm autumn day. I had stopped to rest when suddenly I heard a rattle; the snake lay on the ledge about shoulder-high on my right. I saw it as it struck, and at that instant I jumped. I felt its hot face next to mine, but it missed me. My jump was so excellent I hit the down slope and rolled perhaps fifty feet.

East of Yakima, in the great Inland Empire, are vast wheat ranches which in the old days were harvested by header boxes that stayed under the spout of the reaper until filled and then swerved to carry the grain to the stationary separator. (Nowadays the entire operation is usually done by one huge combine.) When I worked on the wheat ranches during college vacations and drove the header boxes, I'd see rattlers occasionally come into the box with the wheat. They usually left with the wheat as the nets lifted it into the separator, where they would be chewed to pieces. The presence of rattlesnakes in header boxes made every driver I knew nervous. Invariably we'd sit on the side of the box, our feet hanging on the outside.

There are numerous and varied species of rattlesnakes, and it is not often that any one of them is more than two feet or so in length. But east of Yakima out on the breaks of the Columbia, I have seen them eight feet long and as big around as a man's arm. I once mentioned that in Texas, and it brought on a sharp and continuous argument with my friend Byron Lockhart of Austin, Texas, who claimed that Texas was the only state that had rattlers eight feet long—an argument that only Laurence M. Klauber, who wrote the authoritative work on rattlesnakes, *Rattlesnakes, Their Habits, Life Histories, and Influence on Mankind,* could settle.

As a boy I learned about the denning of rattlers. A road was being built through the canyon leading north from Yakima to Ellensburg. Many dens of rattlers were uncovered by the blasting; and in my mind's eye I can still see the writhing mass of hundreds of snakes wrapped together in close embrace. And I can still smell the rancid mass.

So far as the woods of this continent are concerned, only a few basic fears have survived for me. One of them is the fear of avalanches; the second is the fear of falling trees; the third, the fear of forest fires.

Once when I was on horseback in eastern Oregon on a steep slope of the Wallowas, a huge boulder came hurtling down just below Frances Lake, probably loosened by some animal. It careened one way and then another, its course unpredictable. To run was foolish. So I dismounted and stood still. My horse was frantic, but I managed to hold him. In a few seconds the huge rock roared under his belly at a faster speed than he could ever run.

Snow avalanches are ominous for one going cross-country on skis or snowshoes. One February, Elon Gilbert, Cragg Gilbert, and I were on skis going into Gold Hill from Morse Creek in the Washington Cascades.

There had been a sharp rise in temperature and the snow was very soft, slowing our travel. In the darkness of this night we heard a great roar ahead. Realizing it was an avalanche, we turned back. When we returned the next morning, we discovered that our slow pace the previous night had saved our lives, for the avalanche was several hundred yards wide and had carried with it huge pine and fir trees as though they were matches.

Another time I was leading a packtrain across a slope of large, loose rocks below Old Snowy in the Goat Rocks area of the Cascades. While the trail across this rocky slope was plain to see, it seemed treacherous to me. So I dismounted, leading my horse, King. We were halfway across when the vibration of the packtrain caused the whole slope to move downward. The horses did not panic, but they were visibly alarmed. In a few seconds the whole trail had slid down three feet or more. Then a larger slide occurred, carrying us down another six feet or so. I turned King and the packtrain loose and stood above them. Though the horses were in real panic as the trail slid yet another six feet down the mountain, no ropes were broken and no horse bolted. When they reached terra firma they immediately started grazing. They came through the ordeal less shaken than I was.

As a boy, the danger of forest fires struck terror in me, particularly a crown fire, which in a forest of conifers jumps from treetop to treetop, at a rate which has been estimated to be thirty miles an hour.

In long periods of drought the trails in the Cascades lie thick in dust, ankle-deep and as fine as flour. Pine and fir needles become as combustible as paper. A campfire, unless circled with a trench, can spread along and under the surface. The chain that drags a log in lumber operations may scrape a rock and make a spark, igniting a whole forest almost at once. A cigarette or match carelessly tossed by the side of the trail can do the same. Lightning can make a flaming torch of any resinous evergreens. Even one spark can cause irreparable damage—a smoldering fire whipped to a blaze by a slight wind, racing up trees and through forests faster than a man can run, filling all life with its hot tongue, leaving behind desolation and a sterile earth that will not produce crops of timber for a generation or more.

Rangers, guards, and lookouts of the Forest Service are on edge in these dry spells. Douglas C. Ingram was a grazing examiner of the Forest Service in the twenties. He was an outstanding field botanist. One day Ingram sent in to Washington, D.C., from southwest Oregon a new species of silene, a wildflower of the pink family. The species he sent is the handsomest of the western silenes—gray-green leaves topped by deep cherry-red flowers. On August 17, 1929, the late William Dayton—chief dendrologist of the Forest Service—had this wildflower named for Ingram: *Silene ingrami.* Ingram never knew this, for a few days earlier he had died fighting a forest fire.

The fire was on Camas Creek in the Chelan National Forest of eastern Washington. Lightning had struck a pine tree. A trench was put around the fire after it had burned a hundred and sixty acres, and it seemed that the danger was over. But the next day the wind picked up live embers and carried them across the trench. The embers fell within a few feet of the fire fighters. The freakish wind whipped the fire so crazily that the men could not stop it. Before morning the fire had covered five thousand acres and was still raging.

A large crew was brought in, including my friend Glenn Mitchell and Ingram. When the fire trapped a dozen of the men, Ingram led them into a small clearing and sat whittling sticks and telling stories. His cool leadership banished their panic and restored reason, but all this time the fire was leaping toward them. This was not a ground fire; it was a crown fire, and often this kind of forest fire goes faster than a horse can run. If the men had run, the flames would have curled around their shoulders and burned them to cinders. Ingram was ready for the emergency. As the fire sped toward them, Ingram had the crew lie flat. The fire leaped over them and went its mad way. Then Ingram led the men safely to camp.

A couple of days later it looked as if the men were about to be trapped again. Ingram pulled them out of the area and took them to a high ridge to eat lunch. Since conditions had not improved, he then sent them back to camp. Ingram and another fire fighter, Ernani St. Luise, remained behind to look for Glenn Mitchell, who, they thought, had gone down the ridge. They had not traveled far when the wind blew up the fire which was below them. An inexperienced person would probably have retraced his steps. But as Glenn Mitchell told me, "Anyone who has fought fires knows that they run uphill whenever there is a chance." Mitchell knew what a forest fire would do, for this same day a crown fire had made a fast run up the ridge where he was working. A hot wave of flame and smoke barely missed him.

Ingram also knew forest fires. His decision was to get around the end of the conflagration and below it. But as Glenn Mitchell said when he told me about it, "This was one of those phenomenal instances when the unexpected happened." The fire did not travel uphill or down. It burned a strip about a mile wide and three miles long on a level contour. It was going faster than Ingram and St. Luise could walk. Hurry as they did, they could not get ahead of it. Progress was slow because of the rough terrain and downed timber. The freak wind increased to a gale and whipped the fire toward them. It came with a roar, curling over the trees and along the tops. Its long hot tongue licked the earth and turned it black.

Ingram and St. Luise saw it coming. They picked out a fairly open yellow-pine slope where there was not much to burn. They lay down together, faces to the ground. A wall of fire and smoke, fifty or more feet high, raced up the slope and lay over the men for a second or two like a fiery blanket, burning their clothing and blackening their skin. It killed these two grand men. Then it was gone in a flash, roaring like a winged inferno to the top of the ridge.

Ingram and St. Luise probably were suffocated from lack of oxygen, perhaps even before the fire reached them. A near-vacuum, with the heat of a furnace, is often formed in the path of a raging forest fire.

That is the way millions will die when the atomic war starts. The scientific way is to explode the bomb miles above the surface. The eruption will suck the oxygen upward, leaving the people to suffocate, and those who do not die that way will be seared and reduced to ashes by the ensuing heat.

It was only later in life that I learned that fires could be beneficent influences in the wilderness, as beneficent at times as sunshine and water. I had seen how the Indians burned patches of trees to encourage growth of grass where game would forgather, but as a boy I thought that was a custom not compatible with forest management.

When I did my field work on the Everglades National Park, recounted in my book *My Wilderness,* I discovered that fires set by the National Park Service were part of an essential control of the hardwoods, which otherwise would in time choke out the Caribbean pine. A devastating fire in Oregon in the thirties wiped out 250,000 acres of the Tillamook State Forest. Everyone bemoaned the tragedy. It later appeared that no game was destroyed, as the animals went out ahead of the flames. Moreover, the fire bestowed many blessings. It cleared out the ground debris that interfered with the growth of plants on which the game fed, and it killed a dry land snail that was a source of lung disease in deer.

Falling trees are another fear of mine, wholly imaginary, since I have never experienced them. As a boy I saw what spring twisters had done, toppling huge pine and fir trees into patterns of discord no one could predict. To be present in that Armaggedon would indeed be terror. So, as boy and man, when the wind picks up and the trees start creaking, I instinctively quicken my pace or that of my packtrain to put the hazard of falling trees behind me.

But forest fires and falling trees have been theoretical fears. I was never a victim—or even a near-victim.

Our home at Goose Prairie, however, came close to being a victim in 1968. It is bordered on the north by the U. S. Forest lands. I have on that side a series of tanks holding propane gas that run our generator for the electricity needed to light the house and to bring water from the deep wells. In April, 1968, a small twister came down the mountain, breaking off a huge tree on the Forest Service land behind us. It fell our way, crushing our fence. But it fell neatly between two propane gas tanks, the clearance being not more than an inch on either side.

1968 was a rough year for me, what with open-heart surgery and other major operations. So at Prairie House we always say, "1968 was not altogether a bad year. Some kind spirit steered the falling tree between our two tanks."

As a result of many alpine adventures, I had no fear of great heights, especially after I learned how to use crampons and ice axes on glaciers. I now know what a boy could not know, that the fear of death is made up of all other fears. I know now that long years ago in the rugged Cascades I had begun to shed that great, overpowering fear.

Many people have phobias that doom them to exile from the mountains. Though I believe I could walk the cornice of the Empire State Building without qualms, I understand the panic that seizes some of my friends at the very thought of looking down a sheer wall. One friend was so obsessed by fear of heights, he could not sit in the balcony of a theater, his urge being to jump or throw himself over the balustrade. Another friend could not travel by car a canyon road where there was a drop-off of a few hundred feet. Still another could not stand to go near the rim of the Grand Canyon. The saddest case was he who did not even dare get into an airplane for fear of going berserk.

I experienced briefly in later years some of these fears. An auto accident in Washington, D.C., resulted in a severe blow to my head, which apparently caused injury to the inner ear—a concussion in the labyrinth, the agency that controls one's balance. A few hours after the accident I was walking a corridor of the Supreme Court Building, headed for my office, when suddenly the entire corridor seemed to turn over from left to right. I grabbed at the wall and hung on for dear life. Anyone who saw me would have sworn I was intoxicated. By hugging the wall and walking gingerly, I made it to the office, where I became violently ill. These attacks came and went, and seemed endless. They lasted nearly two years, until the blood clot in the labyrinth had been absorbed. During that time I could not drive a car and many of my accustomed activities were curtailed. Up to that time I could walk a log across a roaring creek even with a heavy pack on my back—an ability which I later reacquired—but during those two years I was so unsure that I dared not venture to do this. I then understood for the first time the gripping fear which heights generate in some people—a phobia that produces somewhat the same effect on the labyrinth as my concussion did.

I have no fear of riding horseback, even though a freakish accident in the fall of 1949 nearly took my life. I still ride regularly every summer up and down the trails of the Cascade Mountains surrounding my home. Billy McGuffie, an old sheepherder friend, was at Tipsoo Lake on the morning of October 2, 1949, when my old wilderness companion Elon Gilbert and I started on horseback up Crystal Mountain. Mount Rainier stood naked in all its grandeur across from us. Billy hailed me, and I stopped briefly to talk with him before I took to the trail. He was lighthearted as he pointed out all the meadows and basins on the slopes of the mountain where he had once herded sheep. How Billy happened to be at Tipsoo this morning, I do not know. "Providence sent him," Jack Nelson whispered to me a few days later in a Yakima hospital.

I had been into that country on skis and snowshoes when it was under thirty feet of snow, but there was much of the countryside which I had not seen in summer or fall for over thirty years. This would be the ideal day to see it. There was not a cloud as far as the eye could see. The Oregon grape had turned to a deep purple, the huckleberry to blood-red, the mountain ash to a rich cranberry. The willow, maple, and tamarack were golden splashes across dark slopes of evergreens and basalt. As we skirted a steep and rugged shoulder of rock, I sensed a quiet air of waiting. It was as if the mountain were gathering itself together for the winter's assault.

Then the accident happened. I had ridden my horse Kendall hundreds of miles in the mountains and found him trustworthy on any terrain. But this morning he almost refused to follow as Elon led the way up a steep sixty-degree grade. Feeling that my saddle was loose, I dismounted and tightened the cinch. Then I chose a more conservative path up the mountain. Keeping the mountain on my left, I followed an old deer run that circled the hillside at an easy ten-degree grade. We had gone only a hundred yards or so when Kendall—for a reason which will never be known—reared and whirled, his front feet pawing the steep slope. I dismounted by slipping off his tail, landed in shale rock, then lost my footing and rolled some thirty yards. I ended on a narrow ledge lying on my stomach, uninjured. As I started to rise, I glanced up and looked into the face of an avalanche. Kendall had slipped and fallen, too. He had come rolling down over the same thirty precipitous yards I had traversed. There was no possibility of escape. Kendall was right on me. I had only time to duck my head. The great horse hit me. Sixteen hundred pounds of solid horseflesh rolled me flat. I could hear my own bones break in a sickening crescendo. Then Kendall dropped over the ledge and rolled heavily down the mountain, ending up without a scratch. I lay paralyzed with pain—twenty-three of twenty-four ribs were broken.

I could not move or shout. Would Elon ever find me in the brush where I lay concealed? Elon did—in twenty minutes that seemed like a century. Then, marking the spot where I lay, he raced down the mountain to find help. Again it seemed an endless wait, but in less than an hour there were sounds of men thrashing through brush—the rescue party that Billy McGuffie had organized. Soon there were strong arms lifting me gently onto a litter. Then a warm, rough hand slipped into mine, as I heard these whispered words: "This is Wullie McGuffie, my laddie; noo ever'thing will be a' richt."

First I feared I would die; then, as the pain continued unabated from the broken ribs, I feared I would not. The ambulance that reached Chinook Pass was accompanied by a state police car. These police were most solicitous and kind, and I pleaded with them to shoot me, the pain was so unbearable. As we raced the sixty miles to Yakima, a young intern riding the ambulance gave me a huge injection of morphine; and then and there, in spite of the awful pain, I had my first lesson in allergies.

I had never been administered drugs before and it turned out that morphine was poison to me. It was as if I had been sprayed with gasoline and then ignited. After fighting it awhile, I became unconscious, and was in and out of consciousness for five days. During the first few days in the hospital it seemed that whenever I opened my eyes—night or day—Doug was by my bedside. Douglas Corpron, my boyhood friend from Yakima and a companion on many early hikes had, as I have related, studied medicine, gone to China as a medical missionary, and returned to Yakima as a physician and surgeon. Then one day he stood over me with a grin on his face. There was a note of bravado in his voice as he said, "That was another tough climb we had together. But we made it, just as we once conquered Kloochman."

When I came to after about five days, the nurse said much mail had arrived and asked if I would like her to open some of it. The first letter she read was from Joseph Kennedy, containing a check for $2,500. Joe said that I was headed for a mountain of medical and hospital bills and that he wanted to help out. The letter brought tears to my eyes, for although Joe and I were far apart ideologically, friendship comes first with the Irish. Shortly before this accident I had been visiting him at Palm Beach, Florida, when he said, "I must be nuts. The two men in public life that I love the most are Jack and you. And I disagree with you guys more than anyone else. What's wrong with me?"

In due course I got a letter off to Joe, thanking him for the check and enclosing a promissory note for its repayment. By return mail came a gruff communication from Joe that contained the note torn into tiny pieces and telling me to go to hell.

October and November passed and I was still in the Yakima hospital, flat on my back on a board, waiting for the ribs to heal. A sneeze or cough was like a new injury. I could not even read, lying in that position. Since I slept only fitfully, it seemed as if I were constantly awake. One day I remembered Donald Culross Peattie's book *An Almanac for Moderns,* in which he made a botanical entry for every day in the year. It occurred to me that I should make an entry every day for some historical item on human rights. So I searched my memory, and each day came up with one or two. July Fourth, marking our independence, was obviously page one in my new book. January first was, of course, the Emancipation Proclamation. By the end of November, when the doctors —Schuyler Ginn, Joseph Low, and Doug Corpron—shipped me off to Arizona for a long convalescence, I had collected sixty or seventy significant dates in the political history of the Western world. Thus was *An Almanac of Liberty* conceived and born.

After a month or six weeks in Tucson, I decided to get back on a horse. I loved horses and wanted to rid myself of fear of them. A neighbor had a gentle animal and saddled him up for me. With trepidation, I approached the horse, caressed it, walked around it, and hesitated. Finally I put my foot in a stirrup and swung aboard. I broke out into a cold sweat and shook all over. So I dismounted. The next day and the next and the next, I did the same, until I no longer panicked. Then I had the horse walk; soon I was trotting; a month later I was at a full gallop.

I thought my fear had been conquered, but I was in error. The following summer I was back in the Wallowas of Oregon, riding my old favorite, Dan—the horse that would swim a river with me, go cross-country, travel a dark night through—when we came to a stretch of trail where the steep slope on my right was a close replica of the one near Chinook Pass where I nearly met death. The cold sweat and panic returned momentarily. It took some years for the last vestige of it to disappear; it finally evaporated after exposure to those danger points over and over again.

My accident with the horse led indirectly to the production of another book. The broken ribs had punctured my right lung, leaving a great deal of scar tissue. For climbing or other exercise, the right lung was for all practical purposes dead. Moreover, the thirty-eight fractures in the twenty-three ribs threw out spurs of calcium to such an extent that the spurs tied together all my ribs. The result was that I no longer had any lung expansion—not even part of an inch.

The consequence was that all my deep breathing had to be done by the diaphragm, which of course slowed me down on the slopes of mountains. The doctors concluded that my mountain-climbing days and my days at high altitudes were over.

To see whether or not the doctors were correct, I decided to cross the Himalayas in India. I sent my camping gear ahead and flew out. I organized an expedition under the auspices of the Himalayan Club, picking a distinguished Central Asian scholar, Ram Rahul, as my companion and interpreter. On arrival in New Delhi, I had lunch with Nehru, an old friend, and told him of my plans. He advised against certain routes, as the Chinese army was penetrating to the south. So I moved west on my maps and picked my course, starting in the Kulu Valley and going north to Leh, capital of Ladakh, roughly 250 miles. The story is told in *Beyond the High Himalayas.* We went over Rothang Pass (13,200 ft.), Baralacha Pass (16,200 ft.), Gongrechen Pass (16,500 ft.), La Chulung La Pass (17,000 ft.), Pagmur Pass (16,500 ft.) and Staglang La Pass (17,479 ft.). We were at 15,000 feet for over a week. I was, of course, short of breath in the thin air, and we had no oxygen. I made it, however, as well as the Indians and Tibetans that made up my party. So I knew that my doctors were wrong.

That expedition was made in 1951, and in the ensuing years only age, not my lungs or diaphragm, curtailed my mountaineering. All of which proves, I think, that given time and patience, the body can make great and profound adjustments if one chooses to live to the full.

Once I wrote: When man knows how to live dangerously, he is not afraid to die. When he is not afraid to die, he is, strangely, free to live.

With the passage of time, I would state the basic idea a bit differently. Death is inevitable, but the thought of it usually breeds fear. Yet the fear that is truly debilitating is the fear of the unknown in the environment around us. When we rid ourselves of that fear, we are free to live and can become bold, courageous, and reliant.

Chapter XIV

Conservation

Colin Turnbull in *The Mountain People* tells how one African people, the IK, had survived by putting every person—man, woman, and child—on his own, tossing out the window familial love and community cooperation, a phenomenon that startled me even though I had long had a hunch that we already were drifting in that direction.

De Tocqueville wrote in 1857 that "Christianity has obviously tended to make all men brothers and equal." I have seen very little of such a result in daily life. What I have seen is that the Judaeo-Christian civilization conditioned men to fight each other and despoil the earth.

Even "Love thy neighbor" never became a robust creed. Religious wars, the Inquisition, and even the song I sang as a boy, "Onward Christian Soldiers," were proof enough. "Love thine earth and its wonders" was never promoted by the Christian philosophy. It was, however, a part of the Zoroastrian faith. Care of the soil, the vegetation, and the waters was part of the basic doctrine.

It is an oft-told tale that the Bible speaks of the "wilderness" and its dangers, perils, and hardships. Scholars have analyzed the etymology of the word with its various implications. It was often used in the sense of dry, arid country, but it was also the place where evils and curses prevail and where man is likely to be destroyed.

It was seen as a place the good Lord had created in which to punish the sins of the people. In it were demons, devils, and evil spirits. The wilderness was a disciplinary setting where people were humbled and made ready for the land of milk and honey.

The Bible contains no references to the wilderness in terms of a conservation ethic. There was no fondness for it. In the early years of Christianity it remained pretty much the enclave where forces of evil lived. The wildlife that inhabited the wilderness was inferior and apart from man. St. Francis thought otherwise, and treated birds and other wild creatures as his "brothers," but his view did not prevail in his time. Religious books taught that man should not enjoy the scenery of valleys and mountains but should look inward and concentrate on his own salvation. That is why Petrarch on a fourteenth-century alpine ascent became ashamed when he found himself admiring the view from the top of the peak instead of thinking of his own soul.

The Christian—and the Moslem too— was interested in being "saved." His salvation turned on his article of faith, which in turn had no relation to the earth, the air, the waters, or the wildlife. His faith entailed a belief in a Supreme Being, and by that faith, he could, without fear, poison the waters, pollute the air, level the forests, and despoil the land. For he would in time pass through the portals leading to the Heavenly City, no matter what he did to the earth.

That Christian conditioning of the minds of our people had important consequences. It put man and the wilderness at war with each other. It explains the almost messianic drive of our early settlers to level the land. Laying waste the wilderness, driving out the Indians, felling trees, harnessing rivers, building cities became almost a religious rite. It still affects much of our thinking about the wilderness and the need to subdue it.

Since man was above all other forms of life, there was no respect for the community of birds, fish, deer, elk, wolves, bear, and the like. For they were separate and apart, made by God for destruction by man. The upshot was that Christianity conditioned men to be vandals interested in converting everything—from alligator skins to plumes of the ibis, to sparkling blue waters to mountain ranges—into dollars. Man took the wealth and left only the ashes of the wondrous earth for those who followed.

The American Indian, on the other hand, seems to have had an Oriental reverence for the land and its life, and when I was exposed to Hinduism and Buddhism in Asia, I realized that Eastern thought had somewhat more compassion for all living things: man was a form of life that in another reincarnation might possibly be a horsefly or a bird of paradise or a deer. So a man of such a faith, looking at animals, might be looking at old friends or ancestors.

In the East the wilderness has no evil connotation; it is thought of as an expression of the unity and harmony of the universe. Eastern religions, by linking all life together, foster love for the wilderness rather than suspicion and hatred.

In the Hindu and Buddhist philosophies there is no beginning or end, only a circle of life. Every life is related to another. An Indian ambassador in Washington, D.C., confided to me that he would never kill a fly or a mosquito for fear he was swatting an ancestor or departed friend. I was greatly influenced in my thinking by an Indian botanist whose experiments showed that the growth of plants can be accelerated or retarded depending on the type of music to which they are exposed. Man and flowers, as well as deer and ground squirrels, have a "being." That idea became an article of faith that greatly altered my relationship to the outdoors.

For years I, too, was a hunter of sorts, going for doves and grouse and ducks. I also trudged the high ridges of the West for deer and elk. I specialized in all the fresh-water fish from East to West—trout, bass, perch, pickerel, land-locked salmon, wall-eyed pike. I consorted with those who made hunting and fishing an art.

There were several events or experiences that radically changed my attitude to all forms of wildlife. First was a fishing expedition I shared with Hill Carter, my Washington, D.C., physician. In the late forties we fished on opening day in Virginia. We parked our car at 4:50 A.M., and as we were getting out, I noticed what looked like hundreds of men and boys converging on this creek, or "run" as they call it in Virginia. It was so small, a person could easily jump it. Big fat men with two hundred dollars' worth of shiny, new equipment, little boys with cans of worms and willow sticks, men in hip boots, with big creels, jars of salmon eggs, hats that were pincushions for flies, nets large enough to land a pickerel—all of these were headed for the run. When Hill and I reached the creek, we discovered there was standing room only, each fisherman actually being three or four feet from a neighbor on both sides. The state had planted the trout the previous day. The largest fish caught was eight inches long, and they were all caught by eight o'clock.

This hunger of people to fish, the great display they put on, the tremendous energies expended proved, I guess, that deep in all of us is a predatory instinct. That day, however, I realized there were more people than fish, and before long I found myself on the side of the fish.

My aversion to hunting began in the fifties when I spent the night at the Cardinal Club in Maryland, an expensive membership club where wild turkeys were raised. On a certain spring morning the birds were released by the gamekeepers on the east side of a low ridge while the members, ready with loaded shotguns, lay low on the west side.

I missed the actual shoot at the Cardinal Club, but that night after dinner an officer of the club showed us movies of prior shoots. The slaughter was sickening. Most turkeys were shot after having flown all their lives not more than a hundred yards. Thereafter I found myself reaching for my camera rather than my gun in duck blinds; and soon I gave up hunting altogether.

In America there were a few people who appreciated this viewpoint. The turning point was made by Henry David Thoreau, who said in 1851, "In wildness is the preservation of the world." Thoreau's philosophy was not that man should take to the woods and live in primitive fashion, but rather that wilderness should offset cities, that men needed retreats from urban life, that the wild spaces and the cultivated ones should be balanced, that the harmony in the out-of-doors should be preserved.

John Muir was this century's powerful promoter of the Thoreau philosophy, and I thought so well of Muir and his works that in 1961 I wrote a book about him—*Muir of the Mountains*. But it was the work of Aldo Leopold, whom I knew only through his book *Sand County Almanac*, which taught me man's responsibility to the earth. He emphasized ecology —the interdependence of all living things in a given environment. He transformed conservation from an economic to an ethical problem. Leopold talked about the "impertinence of civilization" in laying waste to land, polluting waters, and exterminating species of wildlife. He realized that unless we changed our attitude toward the earth and its life, we would have sick communities. He taught that it was a moral wrong for man to regard his natural environment as a slave. Man should not be a conqueror of land but a member of the land community. Leopold articulated the need for a land ethic—a challenge that consumed much of my energies in the latter part of my life.

In my time Walt Disney did more than anyone to distort and deprecate our wildlife. He had a wolverine fight a bear to the death. Animals, other than men, do not follow that course. They have conflicts but soon withdraw. Disney got the wolverine to fight the bear by starving both animals for weeks in a Los Angeles zoo. The battle actually took place in a movie set in that city.

Disney showed rams of the mountain-sheep family charging each other, their foreheads clashing to the tune of the "Anvil Chorus." Rams never do such silly things. They charge, of course, but in between charges they rest, walk around, paw the earth, and the like. They do not follow the pattern of a Hollywood dancing troupe.

Disney had lemmings commit suicide by leaping off cliffs into the Arctic Ocean—which they never do. The pictures were fakes. What seemed in the deepening dusk to be lemmings were pieces of cotton batting shot from concealed airguns.

We, the so-called civilized people, have moved into what Michael Frome calls "a shell of artificial, mechanical insulation." We have lost touch with our environment. We allow engineers and scientists to convert nature into dollars and into goodies. A river is a thing to be exploited, not treasured. A lake is better as a repository of sewage than as a fishery or canoeway. We are replacing a natural environment with a synthetic one.

My old hero, Gifford Pinchot, once said, "Conservation is the foresighted utilization, preservation and/or renewal of forests, water, lands and minerals, for the greatest good of the greatest number for the longest time."

But he left behind a group of "experts" who specialize in conquering nature. One who watches the "experts" in Washington, D.C., who are supposed to be guardians of the "public interest," will conclude that we have no conservation ethic. Individuals in the bureaucracy understand it; but few bureaus practice it. America is dedicated to the dollar sign and the pressure of the Establishment on any of these bureaus is overwhelming.

We get our oxygen for breathing from the green plants. Who is the guardian of the rate of combustion versus the rate of photosynthesis? Certainly no one in Washington, D.C.

Conservation early became a major interest of mine. By the time I was in my teens the Cascades of Washington—public lands—were being cruelly destroyed by sheep, cattle and lumbering. The grazing was cruel and prolonged. Lazy sheepmen kept flocks in meadows much too long. Sheep with their sharp hoofs and close bite can destroy a sanctuary as they work hard to get every blade of grass. When I was a boy some alpine basins were already dotted with hummocks of grass where wind erosion did the rest. This was a public subsidy to an irresponsible sheep industry.

Much the same happened when cattle were turned loose. They left their droppings in every campsite and turned high lakes into muddy wallows.

The lumbermen were the third curse across the land. They built roads and clear-cut entire sections, taking every tree down. The ensuing erosion was calamitous. Clear blue streams became muddy watercourses, ruining salmon and steelhead fishing. If the clear-cutting is high up, sluiceways of dirt and gravel are built that wash dreadfully. After clear-cutting may come new growth, usually berries in the early years. Bears come for the berries and occasionally strip a fir and hemlock seedling for the sweet cambium layer of bark. So the lumbermen insist that there be an open season on bears. That came to pass in the State of Washington. The lumber companies sent their hunters into the woods, and the result was the virtual extermination of the black bear in the Pacific Northwest.

I have hiked practically all the mountains of this country, and I saw the tragedy of sheep, cattle, and/or lumbering repeated over and again. The public domain was up for grabs and its riches were being dispensed by the federal (in Texas, the state) bureaucracy to a favored few.

The heads of the federal agencies are nominees of Cabinet officers. When they take action, the public has no right to be heard even on vital issues; the bureaucracy is a powerful steamroller. The agencies are headed not by ecologists but by men trained in forestry or livestock management or who are tuned to those interests. The Congress passes laws making those public lands subject to "multiple use"—to watershed development, wildlife, recreation, wilderness, and the like as well as timber and grazing, but the Forest Service and the Bureau of Land Management largely forgets the word "multiple" and turns the public domain over to the exploiters. And they are rewarded; a high percentage of retired Forest Service personnel go to work for lumber companies.

During my early days in the East I discovered New England and its trails. The Long Trail in Vermont is a favorite hiking trail of mine. It joins the Appalachian Trail—now a National Trail by Act of Congress—which starts at Katahdin in Maine and meanders 2,100 miles to Georgia.

I followed that trail south through the Berkshires of Massachusetts and all the way to Georgia. But the Tennessee and North Carolina segments topped them all for sheer beauty of distant views and for the variety of life, both fauna and flora. Midway down the Blue Ridge a side trail much too precipitous for horses drops several hundred feet to a damp, dark den where only shafts of sunshine penetrate. A two-hundred-foot waterfall fills the small enclosure with a roar. I am especially proud of the Blue Ridge because that waterfall is named for me.

I made the circuit of huts in the White Mountains of New Hampshire, establishments run by the Appalachian Mountain Club and manned by college boys. Of the eight huts, Madison (4,825 feet) was my favorite, perhaps because of the steep climb up King Ravine to reach it. I fly a flag over the Supreme Court one day each year and then mail it to Madison Hut, called *Chez Belle* by the hutmen, where it expends itself in the fresh winds off Mount Washington.

It is only by foot that one can really come to know this nation. That is the way to find the fisher, a member of the weasel family that is one of the most ferocious hunters we know. His choice diet is porcupine, and after that, squirrel. The woodcock—unknown in the West—is one of the glories of creation. And then there is the moose. It had been almost a mythical figure to me. I knew the elk of the Far West, but I was not prepared for the gargantuan appearance of the moose. His tremendous spread of horns was part of it, but part also was the stance of this herbivorous animal in the bogans of New England, where he eats plants under the water! The bull moose became in my mind something more formidable than Teddy Roosevelt had ever imagined.

We of the Far West have conifer forests of which only the tamarack or larch is deciduous. They, plus the willow and vine or Douglas maple, give touches of color to our mountainsides. But the hardwoods of New England produce a rare dramatic effect in the fall. The birches, beeches, maples, and oaks produce the most beautiful color. Yellow, gold, crimson, red, russet create a symphony that has no equal in nature. People make pilgrimages to see this sight, pilgrimages as sacred as those to Medina. One late weekend in October I confidently counted a million people in and around Gatlinburg, Tennessee, who had come to pay their respects to the fall colors.

I learned in New England that a people's love of the mountains can be a powerful and contagious force. That section of our country was cruelly exploited by lumbermen. It was reduced to stumpage where previously majestic white fir and stately hemlock grew. New England loggers and New England pulp mills were no less avaricious than the Western ones. But when the work of the despoilers became clear and the population increased and the recreational demand on each acre multiplied, the civic response was considerable. Today the legend persists that it was the dedication of Harvard professors to conservation that turned the tide.

There is much to be said for that view. Harvard professors certainly became active in White Mountain affairs, and it is to them largely that we owe the debt for what we have today in recreational resources in the Mount Washington area. In time the entire community joined forces to preserve inviolate the recreational potentials of New England. There was no more resounding declaration than that of the people of Maine to make the Allagash a scenic river—protected its entire length by a six-hundred yard sanitary corridor in which no structure could ever be erected.

Over the years I wrote and spoke a great deal about the reforms that were needed to correct these evils. The eastern and southeastern parts of the United States, where I hiked during my early days in the East, were not bothered by depredations of sheep and cattle. The threat of the lumbermen was different from that of their Western counterparts. In the East the desire was to harvest all the hardwoods, which grow slowly, and replant with pine, which grow much faster. Another threat was advancing "civilization." Roads were built everywhere. Housing projects encroached on land whose most desirable use would be for recreation. And then there was the problem of industrial and sewage pollution, which was a result of the crowding of people.

My first experience with water pollution occurred in the forties. Stanley Jewett, of the Fish and Wildlife Service, and I caught a mess of rainbow trout, put them in a wire cage, and lowered them at the confluence of the Willamette and Columbia rivers at Portland, Oregon. The Willamette was then heavily polluted by seven pulp mills, whose refuse contaminated the waters in that part of Oregon. I do not remember exactly how long the trout lived in water with practically zero oxygen, but it was not long. Eventually, the people of Oregon agitated to correct this condition.

Industrial pollution was followed by municipal pollution, and as I traveled I kept my own inexpert account of the slow decline of our natural resources, predicting by some years the demise of Lake Erie. I saw lovely pristine lakes in Wisconsin turn sour under the accumulation of sewage. The Potomac, Missouri, the lower Yakima, the Hudson became open sewers, and we raced merrily on, bragging about our *Gross* National Product when we should have been worrying about our *Net* National Product, that is, what would be left after we deducted what was needed to clean up the mess.

I became disillusioned with the government bureaus in control. I saw that our federal agencies were at times the worst offenders. Army installations often dumped raw sewage into rivers. The Navy did the same in

San Francisco Bay. So did the first federal building erected in Knoxville, Tennessee in the 1870's.

Under FDR and the New Deal, dam building received a great impetus. George Norris, Republican senator from Nebraska, was spiritual head of the hydroelectric school of thought. I remember him pointing at cascades in the Potomac and saying what a shame it was that they went to waste when they could be generating electric power.

I had taken a dim view of dams, however, ever since an experience on the Tieton. There was a meadow in the Cascades where the North Fork and South Fork of the Tieton River met. It was known as McAllister Meadows and it was a lush place, resplendent with flowers and rimmed with pine and fir; willows grew along its banks. The meadow was ideal for a boy, with small streams and no great hazards. It was as idyllic a place as I ever knew.

Early in this century a dam was placed across the Tieton at a point where it enters a narrow gorge, and McAllister Meadows was buried forever. The water that filled the reservoir was milky from the fine glacial grist and was a source of supply to farmers down below whose lands needed irrigation. But the loss of McAllister Meadows, I thought, was too great a price to pay. Some other valley—and there were plenty—should have been used, where the loss of the river bottom would not have been tragic.

So I did not share the enthusiasm for dams that FDR and George Norris kindled among people. On the Columbia River the new dams did great damage, not to river bottoms but to salmon and steelhead that go up the river to spawn—usually in some tributary but sometimes in the bed of the main river itself. As a boy I speared salmon in McAllister Meadows, many hundreds of miles from the ocean. Most of the Columbia dams had fish ladders—a series of pools which a migrating salmon or trout could easily negotiate. Coming down toward the sea, the young salmon fry would have to go through the turbines. So there was some loss there, but the greater losses came as a result of the accumulation of nitrogen in the pools which could cause the blood vessels of a fish to break.

None of us knew about the nitrogen hazard at the time the Columbia River dams were built, but we did know about the other risks to the migratory fish. I was so concerned that I visited the dams to see how the fish ladders were working, and on seeing FDR after one of those visits, I asked him for the job of counting the fish at Bonneville, the only job which I ever asked him to give me. He took it as a joke and roared with laughter, saying "You've got yourself a new job."

As the dams on the Columbia grew in number, the damaging impact on salmon and steelhead increased. Finally, when the Corps of Engineers announced plans for the Benjamin Franklin Dam above Hanford, Washington, we formed a protest group and wrote and spoke extensively against it. That dam, which was finally shelved, would have wiped out the spawning grounds for a great deal of the fall run of Chinook salmon. It would also have buried numerous islands where tens of thousands of ducks winter and where several thousand Canada honkers congregate.

I joined conservation groups in opposing the Corps plans for twelve dams on the Potomac, and succeeded in defeating them. Its largest one would have been at River Bend, a huge structure that would back the water up into an eighty-five mile-long reservoir, flooding the prize farm lands of Western Maryland. The river fluctuates so much that the down-pull would leave hundreds of acres of stinking mud flats exposed. One of the chief purposes of the dam was to provide a head of water that would flush the Potomac of sewage. We proposed instead an amendment to the law which would authorize the Corps to build sewage disposal plants. Congressman Henry Reuss of Wisconsin introduced the necessary legislation. Shortly, at Washington, D.C., social events one began to hear, "Think of all the generals whose names could be attached to sewage plants. For whom should we name the largest one?"

In 1954 the C&O Canal, which runs west from Washington, D.C., for a hundred and eighty miles to Cumberland, Maryland, seemed doomed as a recreational area. Plans had matured to turn it into a freeway. A few of us—thirty-seven in number—felt that the old canal deserved a better fate and proposed that it be made a national historical park. We went on a protest hike in March, 1954, catching a train to Cumberland and walking back in eight days. Our easiest day was twenty-one miles and our longest twenty-seven. The radio and TV networks covered the event because it apparently was newsworthy that people were still walking.

Almost every town we passed sent delegations out to meet us. The hike heightened public interest in the canal as a recreational property. People began to express themselves in favor of its preservation. In time the *Washington Post,* which had once sponsored the freeway, came out for the national park. The National Park Service reversed its position and opted for the national park. The sentiment on the Hill also crystallized that way, and a bill passed the Senate but could not get through the House. Just before leaving office, Dwight Eisenhower made the canal a National Monument. The idea of a national historic park was renewed under Kennedy and Johnson, but Stewart Udall, Secretary of the Interior, sabotaged it. Finally, under Nixon, the much-maligned Walter Hickel, briefly Secretary of the Interior, took hold of the proposal and sponsored it. The bill finally passed both the House and the Senate in 1970 and became the law in 1971.

Meanwhile, I took part in almost innumerable crusades across the country to save a river here, a lake there, a bit of woods somewhere else. The culprit was at times an industry. More often than not it was a municipality or other branch of local government. Even more frequently it was a federal agency, and over the years we began to rate such agencies as public enemies.

Number One was the Corps of Engineers, obsessed with building dams. We went to eastern Kentucky to help save the Red River Gorge—a genuine piece of Daniel Boone country—from being flooded by another Corps dam. We ran the Buffalo in Arkansas to dramatize the need to preserve its wonderful river bottom from a needless dam. We went to Allerton Park in Illinois to try to prevent the Corps from building a dam on the Sangamon, its purpose—again—to flush the river of sewage. Beyond that the Corps would have channelized the river below the dam, putting it in a flume and spraying the spoil banks with herbicides to keep another river bottom from developing.

The story was the same all over the country. River bottoms full of game, trails, picnic grounds, swimming holes would be lost forever. "How can the benefits be rated so great when the costs are so enormous?" we would ask. But the loss of a river bottom was never listed among the costs of so-called "progress."

Number Two on the public-enemies list was the Bureau of Public Roads, which until the seventies had no conservation standards and which ruined probably more trout streams, scenic ridges, and fertile valleys than any other agency. Its motto was more and more roads, when it should have been sounding the alarm over what the price of these roads was in terms of ecological values.

Number Three was TVA, also dedicated to building ruinous dams. The battle for the TVA in the early days was almost a holy cause for the liberals. The issue was public power versus private power, and it was assumed that public power would shed all of the malpractice of private power. But as time passed and the new bureaucracy fastened its hold on Tennessee and on the people, TVA became a sacred white cow that did untold damage to the environment. We fought to save the little Tennessee River from a TVA dam, which was needed neither for flood control nor power. Turning the Little T into a lake was supposed to add new industrial sites with cheap water transport down the Ohio River system. But we counted over eight hundred unused industrial sites that TVA already had.

This was a poor excuse for flooding forever some of the choice farmlands of the South, wiping out ancient Cherokee village sites and ruining the finest trout stream in the Southeast. Brown trout in the Little T ran as high as twelve pounds. I floated on it and fished it and camped on its shores—and I wrote and spoke against the dam. It was saved temporarily by the Vietnam war, because of lack of funds, but TVA goes merrily on its way, an ensconced bureaucracy—a principality, if you please—where Parkinson's Law operates to perfection.

TVA is shattering the dream of FDR and Norris in another way. It is the greatest strip miner in the nation. TVA, originally designed to preserve the land, is now despoiling it. It has eleven coal-burning steam plants. It uses about thirty-two million tons of coal a year, half of it strip mined with the modern shovels which often remove fifty to a hundred feet of the top of a mountain to reach a seam of coal. The earth and rock reserve spill over the side of the hill. Rains cause severe erosion and floods. Rocks and shales adjacent to coal produce pyritic rock, which is a potent producer of acid, iron, and other pollutants. The acid kills all fish in the drainage streams and most of the plant life. There is no effective reclamation after this has happened. I think it was Congressman Ken Hechler of West Virginia who said that the reclamation being done was "like putting lipstick on a corpse."

Number Four on the public-enemies list was the Bureau of Reclamation, which, like the Corps of Engineers and the TVA, operated under the pressure of Parkinson's Law and so kept its engineers busy building dams in marginal areas where drainage turned the run-off into salt water. Exhibit A is the Colorado River, which by the sixties delivered only salt water to Mexico, though our 1944 treaty guaranteed that Mexico would receive annually 1,500,000 acre-feet, *viz.* 1,850,234,000 cubic meters (except for an extraordinary drought or serious accident to the delivery system in the United States, in which event the consumptive use in each nation was to be reduced in equal proportions). Everyone thought, of course, that the water to be delivered would be usable water.

Number Five was the Soil Conservation Service, which, again like the Corps, was obsessed with converting rivers into flumes or sluiceways, keeping the spoil banks sprayed so that no new river bottom would be created. Coastal states lost their wetlands. So did interior states whose potholes were breeding grounds for waterfowl. Creation of flumes to replace rivers kept engineers busy and insured the destruction of our waterways. By 1971 SCS had completed 284 projects and approved 1,033 more, its aim being to channelize 11,000 streams, substituting sterile ditches for pleasant, meandering streams.

Number Six was the Fish and Wildlife Service. It has poisoned or helped to poison most every section of land west of the Mississippi. The poisons are in killed animals put out for predators, primarily coyotes, but also for eagles. Any predator that eats off the carcass of a poisoned animal also dies. So the chain of food poisoning increases to include even magpies, crows, and ravens. The poisoning is so extensive that on a ten-day trip in the Wind River Mountains of Wyoming we saw almost no living thing—no animal, no bird, only a marten. The poisons work faster than animals can breed. We are being deprived of all our meat-eating wildlife so that a few sheep and cattlemen can be appeased. Genesis told man to "have dominion . . . over every living thing that moveth upon the earth." The federal agencies have given Genesis an evil twist by filling the public domain with poisons for predators.

Number Seven was the Atomic Energy Commission, an active promoter of pollution by radiation. Scientists are divided on whether or not radiation from nuclear-energy plants will be harmful to humans. Those who mine uranium are, of course, subject to special risks. The nuclear plant in operation emits radiation; its waste materials must be transported and buried; and there is always the danger of an operating accident. These are highly dangerous elements, so dangerous that at the rate at which we in this country—and in Europe—are erecting nuclear energy plants, some think the germ plasm of man is being jeopardized.

Number Eight was the Park Service, which built cities inside the sanctuaries of the parks (witness, Yellowstone) and crisscrossed most of the wilderness areas with highways; or built funiculars so that the public could get into the wilderness the easy way. By 1970 Yellowstone National Park, believe it or not, was beset with smog, like Los Angeles.

Number Nine was the Forest Service, which listened attentively to the lumbermen's talk and cut, cut, cut for commercial purposes. There were left, to be sure, a few "wilderness" areas, but they were much too small for the population in the 1960's, not to mention the 2000's.

These agencies were all protectors by statute of the "public interest." Yet in practice they were the great despoilers, competing with the moguls of industry to flatten, grind up, pollute, and destroy the earth.

But the conservation groups battled on, doomed to defeat by the pressure of population and by the pressure of lobbies. Planning could have kept highways and the crowds of people on the perimeters of these sanctuaries. Planning could have preserved most of our free-flowing rivers. But there were no plans, not even regional ones.

Coolidge, and later Hoover, had a cabin on the Rapidan River in Virginia at the junction of two streams—Mill Prong and Laurel Prong. That old cabin has been restored and is maintained by the National Park Service. It is still a quiet, serene place, miles from all noise and from all civilization. Coolidge used to fish there, Vermont style—that is to say, he used worms to catch rainbow and brook trout. Two Secret Service men accompanied him—one to bait the hook, the other to remove the fish. On one July day he caught eleven trout out of one pool, and still kept casting—without further success.

Finally one Secret Service agent summoned enough courage to say, "You have caught eleven out of this pool, Mr. President. Shouldn't we try another pool?"

The sardonic reply was "Well, they put twelve in, didn't they?"

That comment represents in a nutshell modern man's dedication to the conversion of every part of the earth into money or into fun. There is no place in America where that cause is more reverently respected than Texas, as I recounted in my book *Farewell to Texas*. Everything in Texas will be converted into dollars, except perhaps the sunsets, and I would not be surprised to find some syndicate that had designs on them.

The disease is not peculiar to free enterprise. It is found in Russia under a socialistic regime. It is found in authoritarian states, as well as in mixed systems. It is not a manifestation of modern technology. The industrial state, as we know it, has merely broadened the dimensions of exploitation and made it an easy, almost effortless process.

The root of the disease is in man's obsession with the GNP. A continuous rise in the Gross National Product means an increasing conversion of natural resources into dollars, rubles, francs, and so on. The search is on for these resources.

He who stands up to defend the last untouched granite cliff of Yosemite (which can, by the way, be ground up and used to produce energy), or the last acre of redwoods, or the last pristine lake in Vermont (which would make a cheap bathtub for new industrial wastes), or the rolling grasslands of eastern Montana (being converted into badlands by bulldozers in search of coal) will in time be denounced as un-American.

So many federal agencies are enemies of the environment, it is easy to despair. Moreover, Washington, D.C., is filled with lobbyists for every special interest that is trying to make a fast buck out of some piece of the public domain. The alliance between lobbyists and agencies is so close that the prospects of keeping our part of the hemisphere habitable is very chancy. Only an aroused and revolutionary attitude by people can save the day.

In the thirties and forties I had viewed the creation of an agency as the solution of a problem. I learned that agencies soon became spokesmen for the status quo, that few had the guts to carry through the reforms assigned to them. I also realized that Congress defaulted when it left it up to an agency to do what the "public interest" indicated should be done. "Public interest" is too vague a standard to be left to free-wheeling administrators. They should be more closely confined to specific ends or goals.

All agency heads, I thought, should be confirmed by the Senate—the Chief Forester, the director of the Park Service, the head of the Bureau of Land Management, and the Bureau of Reclamation, the Chief of the Fish and Wildlife Service, and all such officials. They formulate policy, and their predilections, background, and experience should be tested in the crucible of Senate hearings.

Beyond all that is the need for public participation in agency decisions of an administrative character. The people are as sophisticated and knowledgeable as the bureaucrats. They know whether an alpine basin should be sprayed to kill sagebrush with the hope that more grass will grow for the permittee, a cattleman. They know the scourge of poisons set out for predators. They know the likely effect of the cutting of a virgin stand of timber on runoffs, on the quality of a stream as spawning grounds, and so on.

I concluded that the so-called experts had come close to ruining our environment, that a return to common-sense judgments of laymen was essential.

Chapter XV

Outdoorsmen

During my days at Yale, I had gone with the family to Square Lake, Maine, near the Canadian border and fished at Gordon Frazier's place for landlocked salmon.

Gordon Frazier ran a comfortable fishing camp on Square Lake. He was a slight man, short and wiry, with friendly gray eyes, and was as much a part of the Maine woods as the deer and moose who lived there.

When I later went to Washington, D.C., I arranged with Frazier to wire me when the salmon fly hatch started in late May or early June. Then I would catch a noon train out of Washington, transfer in Boston to an overnight sleeper, arrive at Guerette, Maine—a stop on the B&M—by eleven o'clock the next day, and be fishing by noon.

In those days I spent the hot summers in Washington, D.C., and was often on my feet eight hours or more a day examining witnesses. Perspiring depletes the supply of adrenalin due to the loss of salt and Draper suggested I take a teaspoon of table salt in a glass of warm water before every meal. It was a distasteful prescription but I routinely followed his instructions until salt tablets came on the market.

So when I woke one morning on a sleeper crossing Aroostook County, Maine, I dressed, proceeded to the dining car, and when handed a menu by the waiter, said, "I'll start with a glass of warm salt water."

The waiter gave me a queer look but shortly returned with a glass. My practice was to take the salt water in a gulp, and that is what I did this morning, only to discover at the end that he had given me a stiff dose of Epsom salts.

"Enough to ruin any fishing trip," Gordon Frazier said.

Once Gordon and I fished a distant lake, crossing Square Lake and leaving our canoe on the far side for the return trip. We were delayed and started our return crossing at dark. A sudden storm came up and with it a strong headwind. Lightning was hitting all along the shoreline and the rolling thunder seemed endless. I was in the bow, and we paddled hard to get into water deep enough and clear enough of logs to start the outboard motor, which sputtered and sputtered as we drifted back into the dangerous shallow water. So we had to paddle hard again to be clear of the shore. This time the motor started and Gordon stood up in the stern to see better, keeping the steering handle between his legs.

It was an eerie trip, the only light furnished by flashes of lightning. The waves were so high, I soon became soaked, and I spent most of my time bailing. All shore lights were invisible and time seemed to stand still. I had just learned to swim and was not yet fully at home in the waters. Preparatory to what I thought was an inevitable swamping of the canoe, I took off my heavy hiking shoes and my heavy jacket. I carefully stored in one pocket a waterproof watch case and my reliable jackknife. Come what may, I was ready. But we landed safely, Gordon with unerring instinct putting the canoe right alongside the darkened dock. I embraced him, vowing to have a Gordon Frazier Medal struck off.

He was an accomplished woodsman. I had gone cross-country in the Cascades many times, and reaching a height of land, could get my bearings. The Maine woods, however, were brand-new to me. The trees were thick, the underbrush lush. The interlocking branches of trees cut out the sun. It was difficult to tell which way you were going—unless, of course, you had a compass. Gordon Frazier never carried one; he taught me to tell where north was by the shape and location of moss on the trees. He knew his own domain, of course, well enough to mark directions also by the flow of little creeks and deer runs that he frequently traveled.

The Big Depression was on us when I first met Gordon Frazier. He showed me his squirrel rifle, rubbing it gently as he talked. "I could line up thirty or more men with rifles as good as this one and we could march on Washington, D.C."

"Why?" I asked.

"To get some political action if it's not coming real soon."

He talked many hours about the anxiety of people at the bottom of our society. A real pinch was being felt. Some were hungry; many were out of work. The forces that Gordon Frazier represented put FDR into the White House. I once told Roosevelt about the Gordon Frazier "brigade" in northernmost Maine.

He laughed, saying, "We may need them yet."

I learned at the time of the 1932 elections that it takes something as basic as hunger to send people flocking to the polls. Hunger or fear—those are the ingredients of landslide changes in political America.

At Kidney Pond in Maine, which is almost under the shade of Mount Katahdin, I learned, thanks to Ray Bardeen, the art of canoeing. He and I spent many hours together in Maine waters, Ray always in the stern of the canoe. I saw moose feeding in bogans and came to know the guides who would call moose with a horn made of white birch bark. Ray Bardeen told of one experience calling and calling across a lake while his hunters sat quietly in the canoe. Ray, to simulate a female urinating, filled the horn with water and poured it from a height back into the lake. Pretty soon the series of calls, plus the pouring of the water, produced a result. Sure enough, a big bull moose could be heard coming nearer and nearer. It was by then growing quite dark and Ray's hunters were getting anxious. He whispered to them not to shoot until the big bull got really close.

In a few minutes Ray started to laugh. His calls and the sound of falling water had elicited a response not from a moose, but from another group of hunters whose caller was a neighbor of Ray's. Thus did two experts outdo each other.

One spring Ray Bardeen drowned in Kidney Pond, and I could not go back there. Nearly thirty years passed before I returned to Maine, whose woods and people I dearly love.

Jake Day, an artist, had a group of outdoorsmen called Jake's Rangers, and they took me in as an honorary member. We hiked, back-packed, and camped all around Mount Katahdin and way into the north country. We climbed Katahdin and hiked across Baxter State Park, which was created out of logged-over land. I could see the great regenerative power in Maine that would once again produce a mighty forest of Eastern hemlock and white pine.

Our group tracked down the woodcock, not to kill but to photograph. I discovered the fiddlehead ferns, and I learned from Jake the recipe for cooking them. They and square-tail trout make the most tantalizing dish in the woods. Maine woods can be very wet, and I learned from the Rangers how to start a fire under such conditions.

Another son of Maine who honored me with his friendship was Willard Jalbert, affectionately known as the Old Guide and the wisest of all men with a canoe. In the roughest of water he would stand in the stern and tip a canoe loaded with six hundred pounds on its side to clear a rock and then quickly and gently tip it back. He called it "rolling her through." The Old Guide loved the canvas canoe and despised the new aluminum ones. The latter, he claimed, always got stuck on a rock; his canvas canoe never did get stuck. He was the champion who had two trained legs that functioned perfectly in his mid-seventies. I learned from the Old Guide the love of fast waters and got from him a partial picture of their great mysteries.

Olaus Murie was a biologist who knew the anatomy of our woods more thoroughly than anyone. His book *A Field Guide to Animal Tracks* is a classic; he also wrote articles and gave many speeches. He and I were on numerous trips together—once in the Brooks Range of Alaska, where he was trapping lemmings, examining their scat, and studying their migration. Olaus joined us on the 180-mile hike from Cumberland to Washington, D.C., in 1954 along the C&O Canal. He was a good hiker, but always brought up the rear because he went in an unhurried way so as not to miss a flower, or the track of an animal, or the flight of a bird.

One day on that Canal hike, Aubrey Graves of the *Washington Post* trucked up from Virginia a Mexican burro, and it walked a few miles with us before it was loaded on the truck and taken home. Some of the hikers waited for Olaus, planning to trick him. As he approached, they pointed to the track of the burro and said, "What is it?"

Olaus got down on his knees, examined the track closely, said nothing, got up and walked away. The inquirers caught up with him, and pointing to another track of the burro, repeated the question. Olaus again got down on his knees and examined the evidence carefully. Looking up, he said, "I know what it is but I also know it's impossible."

"Then what is it?"

"Why, it is obviously a Mexican burro, but there is none anywhere near this place."

They all howled with laughter.

Once I was with Olaus and Carroll Noble on a trip into the Wind River Mountains of Wyoming. This was in the late fifties or early sixties when the federal poisoning program aimed at predators was reaching its peak. The dreadful Chemical 1080 was laid out for coyotes in pieces of meat. The coyote died, but so did the hawk or eagle or raven that ate off the dead animal. The fox and rabbit also died, as did any critter that touched the carcass. Olaus took a careful look at every footprint on or near every mile of trail, and found only one living animal in the Wind River Mountains—a pine marten, who hunts mostly from treetops.

Olaus was so full of ideas about things that should be done to correct the growing problems of the wilderness that he had nearly six books under way in his study at Moose, Wyoming, when he died, leaving them for his wonderful wife, Mardy, to finish.

Harvey Broome, a lawyer of Knoxville, Tennessee, had as his first love the Great Smokies. He and his wife, Anne, probably covered every nook and cranny of these wonders of nature. They also hiked in the other mountains of this country, as Harvey wrote in his last book, *Faces of the Wilderness*. They were with me on a long hike down the Olympic Beach in the State of Washington, protesting against bringing a road and hotdog stands into the wilderness beach, one of the few remaining in the country. Harvey also joined us on the C&O Canal towpath protest march. He was a favorite around the campfire, giving excellent talks on the dimensions of the problems of protecting the outdoors.

Professor Fred Rodell, of the Yale Law School, was one of the half-dozen truly great teachers in that school in the five decades I knew it, but he was much too liberal to have a Yale chair assigned to him. A discerning barber in New Haven, however, had one of his chairs named for Fred, and that was more appreciated than one from Yale itself.

Fred had an innate love for the wilderness, particularly for streams. His passion was delicate fly-fishing, and in that department he ranked with my friend, Blaine Hallock. Fred's other passion was outdoor photography. He had a sensitive eye, which I, a disbeliever at first, became convinced was as effective as a light meter. Fred and I took memorable trips, both in the wilds of the Wallowas of Oregon and in the Snowmass area of the Rockies in Colorado.

Dick Neuberger—newspaperman and United States senator from Oregon—was pretty much of a drugstore cowboy. Though he himself would not have been comfortable alone in the wilderness, its values were prized by him, and some of our best wilderness stories came from his pen. He floated Fall River with me only to get the feel of a river, to know its life, to unravel some of its mysteries. He later wrote me that he wanted to see the Wallowas in order to write a piece about them, adding that he had only three days to do the field work.

I got hold of two top Forest Service men, Chet Bennett and Wade Hall, and they were eager to take on the trip with us. The four of us gathered at my Wallowa cabin and started off on horseback at 7 A.M. On our shortest day we covered twenty-six miles; our longest, forty miles. The weather was perfect; the scenery superb. We slept the first night at Tombstone Lake. Dick managed a smile in spite of his lameness after the long ride, walked painfully to a grassy spot in the meadow by the lake, lay down on his back, and whispered "Put the tombstone at my head." It was a great article he wrote after recovering from the trip.

Ben Hur Lampman of the editorial page of the *Oregonian,* Portland, Oregon, was an old friend of mine. He was a quiet, philosophic outdoorsman with the eyes of a botanist and biologist, which gave meaning to all the wonders he found in the woods. One of his famous books was *The Coming of the Pond Fishes.* His editorial pages were garnished with stories of the woods, of fishing, of cooking fish in heated sand. He described how the coals are raked aside, the fish wrapped in damp paper, put into the hot pit, and covered with sand and embers. Then in time the whole fish is removed and "the viscera compacted are removed" with adept movement of the point of a knife. This is fish, he said, in agreement with Izaak Walton, that is, "too good for any but anglers or very honest men." The "source of hunger," he maintained, "doth surpass all else."

I never went fishing or camping with Ben except vicariously. He deftly took me to task once for exalting the dry fly and pooh-poohing bait.

> But the associate justice neglects, we think, to consult a most distinguished precedent which in piscatorial matters has all the weight of the English common law. The authority is one that cannot properly be ignored in the handing down of such a ruling, for surely it is generally conceded to govern these instances, and the name that it bears is warmly luminous in English letters. It may seem tedious to cite Izaak Walton, but none the less there is a duty in the instance, for Walton is Walton, as one might say Blackstone is Blackstone, and not to be altered by individual prejudice or personal inclination. This ethical pillar of what one might term the common law of angling, the veritable father of the code, sets the associate justice, one fears, at naught.
>
> We have no intent to reverse an associate justice of the highest tribunal, nor should we know how to come about it with privilege and decorum, but it ought to suffice to refer to the code of the angler as written by Master Walton, wherein a considerable part of the chapter on trout fishing is devoted to the employment of baits, which portion takes precedent over equally authoritative discussion of using the artificial fly. Izaak Walton was lyric in his praise of the gentle, which is the common, maggot, and of the

> dewworm, the lobworm, the brandling, the marsh worm, the tag-tail, the flagworm, the oak worm, the gilttail, the twatchel and many another. He gives explicit and well-nigh affectionate instructions for their culture and care before he turns, with scarcely less of delight, to treating of the grasshopper, the minnow, and the caterpillar. All these, and their manipulation, are in the classic corpus juris of the ethics and practice of trout fishing. (*People v. Trout, 1 Walton 78*)
>
> It seems, clearly enough, that in his ruling on fly fishing, the associate justice is reversed by a still higher court . . . The error is not in individual election of a certain method, which is as may be, but rather in the implication that trout may be honestly acquired in no more than the one manner. And Master Walton is so obviously to the contrary.

Whenever I am in camp and we sit toasting or eating bread I think of a poem in Ben's editorial column:

> Be gentle when you touch bread
> Let it not lie uncared for, unwanted—
> Too often bread is taken for granted.
> There is such beauty in bread;
> Beauty of sun and soil;
> Beauty of patient toil;
> Wind and rain have caressed it,
> Christ often blessed it—
> Be gentle when you touch bread.

Ben was a gentle, perceptive soul who would have been an ideal companion in the woods, but he died before we could arrange a trip.

E. Palmer Hoyt, publisher first of the *Oregonian* and then of the *Denver Post,* was a man born to the woods. He managed a camp as he would a paper, putting each of us on assignment. He was cook extraordinary. He never complained, not even when the saddle on his favorite horse, Dynamite, came loose, putting E.P. beneath the horse. Riding horseback, however, was not his dish; after a brief stop he'd get ready to mount and say to the horse, "Dynamite, roll out the torture, here I come."

With E.P. in camp, we were never without fish, for he had an affinity for those finny creatures.

Elon Gilbert, my old companion, brought friendship and compassion on many arduous trips and lifted tired feet with kind words. Once we were camped high in the Cascades, and the combination of high altitude and an unaccustomed alcoholic drink caused him to collapse. He was almost in the fire when I came to his rescue. He whispered to me, "Please do not let my nephew, Cragg, see me in this condition." Cragg almost collapsed from laughing, as he was the one who was holding his uncle up.

Most of the men I spent time with in the outdoors were conservatives by political philosophy. Jim Donald saw social security and mounting income taxes as the beginning of the end of economic freedom for the majority of people. "How can we make enough for our retirement?" he'd ask over a campfire.

"You cannot do it," I'd reply.

"Why?" he'd ask.

"Because they are going to give you a number, put you in a computer, and pay you ninety dollars a month when you are sixty-five."

"That's the bloody end of all of us," he'd say. "It's socialism."

"Yes," I'd answer. "It's an American version of socialism. But it is not socialism for the poor." And since Jim was counsel to one railroad company and other Northwest industries, I added, "It's socialism for the rich too." And I'd remind him of the billions that the RFC or other federal agencies were ladling out to business. And so another fishing trip would be ruined for Jim.

Jim was an easy victim of practical jokes. We were once camped at Long Lake in the Wallowas of eastern Oregon. I always rose early to start a fire, make coffee, and prepare breakfast. One morning I could tell by the muttering from Jim's sleeping bag that he had a bourbon hangover. So I prepared a big steaming cup of hot black coffee, putting in a fishhead with the two eyes looking upward. Jim thanked me profusely as he bemoaned his indiscretion of the night before. The coffee was the best he ever did taste. "You saved my life," he shouted. In a few moments, however, there were anguished cries from a bitter man as he saw two fish eyes glaring up at him from the bottom of the cup.

His partner, Blaine Hallock, probably held the same views that Jim did. But he had a philosophic bent and realized that what was happening in the United States was merely a small straw in the world-wide sweep of events.

Merle Chessman, newspaper publisher and TV and radio owner from Astona, Oregon, was very active in Republican politics and a doer, not a worrier like Jim, or a philosopher like Blaine. But each one of them had a clear understanding of our constitutional commitments and stood firmly against the search for the dissenter that became popular after World War II, the witch hunt that possessed us in the fifties, the bugging and other forms of pervasive surveillance that were practiced in the sixties and seventies. They were for the status quo, but they allowed for "play in the joints," as Mr. Justice Holmes once put it. They would be called reactionaries by today's liberals, but they were strong in the Jeffersonian tradition when it came to speech, press, ideas, and beliefs. Each in his own way promoted some phase of the conservation movement that was gaining momentum after World War II.

Sandy Balcom, a poet, fisherman, and humanist, was also identified with the status quo, but was apolitical. He never discussed politics, economics, or sociology in the woods—confining himself to fish. He was a humorist of note, telling classical stories in the area of sex. He was an actor by instinct, a manufacturer of pipe organs by profession.

Once Sandy and I fished Silver Creek south of Haley, Idaho, which is not far from Sun Valley. We registered at the hotel and in the cool air of the evening walked down the street to a restaurant. As we walked in, he pushed me aside, walked up to the hostess, and pointing to me, asked her, "Do you know who he is?" She shook her head. "Ever see his picture?" Again she shook her head. "Well, let me tell you something. He often pretends he's Justice Douglas, but he's not. I'm Justice Douglas."

"Glad to meet you, Mr. Justice," she said to Sandy.

"When do you get off work?" he asked.

"At midnight."

"My room is three-oh-nine," he said, giving her my number. "I'll be waiting for you."

There were knocks on my door all night long. I never responded, but if I had opened the door, it would probably have been Sandy standing there in his long red underwear.

Henry and Leland Hess of Portland, Oregon, were my frequent fishing companions. They were lawyers from eastern Oregon and were active in Democratic party affairs. Under Truman, Henry was U.S. Attorney for some years in Oregon. He was a crusading liberal of the 1930 and 1940 vintage. A delegate to the Democratic Convention in 1944, he swears to this day that if he had been given the nod, he would have put me in nomination for the Vice-Presidency in a speech that would have swept the convention.

Henry, like my other fishing companions, was bred on the Constitution. He pinned his faith to the First Amendment. The independence of the judiciary was his creed. For years he had headed Edith Green's Congressional campaign in Oregon, but when in 1969 she said she thought that I should be investigated for possible impeachment, Henry and Leland resigned, gave her no support, and ever after voted for someone else. The Hess commitment was a type of friendship that began to disappear in the fifties and that suffered severe setbacks in the sixties and seventies.

The Hesses are stout people. In the early sixties Wayne Morse, senator from Oregon, was under great pressure from his constituents to oppose a Forest Service plan to log the Minam River in eastern Oregon. The Minam is one of the last free-running, unpolluted rivers in Oregon. Its water is clear, flowing over rocks and white sand. As a result, it is a very sensitive river to fish, as exposure is great and man and fish are highly visible to one another. Salmon run the river to spawn, and after the salmon come the trout to feast on the salmon eggs that are laid in the gravel banks. Elk range the upper sections; deer and bear are more widely scattered. It is beautiful ponderosa pine country, and farther up it is adorned by Douglas fir and Engelman's spruce.

Boise Cascade, the lumber company, wanted to log the forty-mile stretch, and the Forest Service agreed. What the terms would be no outsider knew, but the story was that Boise Cascade would get a million dollars to build the road. Forest Service officials were ecstatic when they talked to me about it. They described the campsites that would be built, the fireplaces, the parking lots for cars, the toilets.

Those who loved the wilderness, almost everyone who had hiked this wilderness, were greatly opposed. Wayne Morse called Orville Freeman, Secretary of Agriculture, who supervised the Forest Service, and Senator Henry Jackson, who was chairman of the Senate Subcommittee on wilderness areas. Morse pounded his desk and demanded a public hearing before the Minam River was ravished. The hearing was held in LaGrande, Oregon. The Forest Service thought it would be a *pro forma* hearing of a few hours. It lasted, however, for two days, one hundred and twenty-five witnesses appearing, all of them testifying for preservation of the Minam.

Representatives of Boise Cascade did not appear, but it asked Leland Hess to testify on its behalf. The company was confident about Leland, for the Hess family had operated lumber mills in eastern Oregon for two generations. Leland agreed to testify as the anchor man, the last witness at the hearing.

In due course he was called and testified in substance as follows: He had hiked the Minam many times, fished its many pools, camped on its white sand spits, and hunted its canyons. He loved the Minam and its beauties. It is true that the Hess family was in the lumber business, that they logged many tracts in eastern Oregon. But, he said, before a Hess was party to the destruction of this wonderful wilderness, the family would prefer to go through bankruptcy.

Thus was the Minam River saved, and in due course it was declared a wilderness, which by definition is a roadless area.

Gene and Frank Marsh were lawyers from McMinnville, Oregon, and active Republicans. Gene was Speaker of the House. They were twins, and it took me much time to tell them apart. Their wives would telephone every day to tell each other what her husband was wearing, so every morning or evening they appeared dressed exactly alike. They were great outdoorsmen and wonderful companions. I once asked Dorothy, Gene's wife, how she could tell the difference between the twins. She whispered, "I have a secret way that I can't tell you."

Gene's Swedish dialect stories were outstanding. His best was a theological one, on the difference between the Swedish Evangelical Church and the Swedish Lutheran Evangelical Church. Ole is the narrator and in inimitable dialect pointed out the following difference between the two creeds.

"The Swedish Lutheran Evangelical Church believes that Eve seduced Adam. The Swedish Evangelical Church believes that Adam was a son-of-a-bitch from the beginning."

Saul Haas, newsman and radio and TV proprietor from Seattle, was bred to apartment life, not to the woods. He was not athletic at all, but he enjoyed being in the wilderness and soaking up its wonders. The problem was getting him there—by boat or by horse. Once settled in camp, he was content, and he enlivened our hours with lively talk and reflections. He made fun of the "purists"—the fly fishermen—and contended that what fish wanted and deserved was a juicy worm. So on our many trips he worked hard to prove that worm fishermen were better than those who cast a fly.

Saul liked to bet against fly fishermen. One day on the Lostine in eastern Oregon he pointed to a pool and said, "I bet there are no trout in it." I got my rod and asked how much he'd bet. "Twenty dollars that you can't hook and land three trout in five minutes." On my first cast I got myself a trout. On my second cast I got a strike, but missed. On my third I landed a second trout; and on my fourth, a third. I still had nearly two minutes left. Saul paid his bet promptly and with the twenty dollars I bought a chair—the Haas chair—for my cabin, and on later trips he always sat in it to ruminate on the thesis that it never pays to gamble.

Saul always wanted to see Frances Lake, which is about 9,200 feet up in the Wallowas. The trail in those days was a winding sheepherder's trail that went up the steepest slope. I put Saul on a horse named Steel (which in Russian is Stalin), who was strong and reliable, and off we went. The trip up was appalling for Saul, but the trip down was devastating. His knees would not hold up, so he sagged in the saddle like a bag of oats. The look downward was a glimpse of a darkening abyss, and Saul became frightened. Somehow or other he dismounted, and after dismounting, fell under the horse. But Steel stood still. Saul tried to walk a spell, but kept falling. By some miracle he got back on Steel and made it back to the valley.

I had gone ahead, but in a short time, became worried. I was about to return up the mountain when faithful Steel appeared with his rider. It took two of us to lift Saul from the saddle. When we finally got him to bed, he refused even a drink, let alone food. But his knee ached badly and my hot packs did not seem to help. So we got some horse linament from the barn and massaged the knee with it. In a few minutes Saul was screaming that his leg was burning up. So though crippled and non-athletic, he jumped from his bed of pain and raced to jump into the river, where I found him fairly bellowing with pain. The moon was high and the night cold. And in later years I always told him that when those conditions recurred, I could always hear his shouts echoing off Flagstaff high above the cabin.

Saul was a "great trooper," as we used to say. He loved salmon fishing in the Pacific. Sometimes he and I went alone, sometimes with large groups, the four rods off the stern changing hands every fifteen minutes or so. Once, when it was Saul's turn, he said he wanted to rest and asked me to take over his rod. I did and landed the largest salmon of the day. There was a modest bet on the largest fish, and Saul claimed he had won and I had lost, because while fishing, I was merely his agent. The controversy hung fire for years and was never resolved, but he managed to get away with the fish.

One day Saul and I fished for salmon off Astoria, Oregon. I left my catch at a cannery to be cooked and canned. He took his salmon, around forty pounds, with him. We traveled by car to Portland and stopped at the prestigious Benson Hotel, where I had a room. Saul had no reservation but said he would manage it. We opened the trunk of the car, he took out the big salmon, laid it across his arms, and walked with it to the desk, where he put it down and said, "I want a room for me and my fish."

I have been on many hunting trips, but I have never killed a deer or an elk or a bear. They are, in my eyes, as close to man as the coyote, who has always had a very warm place in my heart. In the fifties I used to try to escape Washington, D.C., in February and go to the clear air and warm sun of Arizona. Dick Jenkins—who ran the La Osa Ranch near the border town of Sasabe—used to go into Sonora, the northern province of Mexico, and hunt. Mexican ranchers have man-made waterholes for their cattle and horses, some of them being small ponds. Ducks would settle there to feed, and Dick loved to crawl up the bank to get one shot of ducks on the wing. I let Dick get the ducks and I concentrated on doves, which came to the watering place about dusk. Dick dubbed me "the dove's best friend in Sonora" because I usually seemed to miss.

I did, however, hunt the mountain lion in Arizona, and my guide and companion was Marvin Glenn of Douglas, Arizona—tall, lean, with quick movements and little bent for conversation—an ideal companion in the woods. We hunted in the rough and rugged Chiricahua Mountains, north of Douglas near the New Mexico line. There are sheer cliffs, razorback ridges, treacherous slopes of loose rock, and little water. This ancient home of the Apache Indians is now a national forest, crisscrossed by trails, but even in wintertime there are not many travelers who go into the deep recesses of this wild tangle of ridges and canyons.

Our purpose was not to kill mountain lions but to bring them back alive, for Marvin had standing orders from zoos for the cougar. Marvin's dogs were amazingly efficient. In the fifties they were selling for as much as fifteen hundred dollars. They were "broke" to the false trail of bobcats and deer. Unlike many hounds, they never wasted a hunter's time by chasing these animals for hours on end. So when Marvin and I left camp on horseback and heard the hounds baying way up ahead, we knew they had got the scent of the right prey.

On one trip we had breakfast by 6:00 A.M. and were saddled and on our way before seven. We had no sooner left the camp behind, when we heard the lusty baying of the hounds, indicating a fresh scent. It was indeed fresh, for by the time we caught up with the hounds, they had treed the cougar. We were finished hunting by eight that morning.

Another year we left camp early, following a trail for over ten miles. Topping a ridge, the hounds got their first scent and away they went, not down the trail but cross-country, through the roughest terrain I had ever traveled. The going was slow, and the cat, knowing he was being pursued, stayed clear of grass and brush and moved over high rocky escarpments largely devoid of vegetation. The hounds lost much time there and Marvin had to dismount to look for a paw print in patches of sand. In time he found one, and figuring the direction of the cougar's course, he reset the hounds on their trail and off they went. The sun was getting low when we came off the ridge to a valley strewn with rocks, where the hounds once more lost the scent. Marvin said to me, "It will be dark in half an hour and we are fifteen miles from camp. So let's give the dogs only ten more minutes, then call it a day. For we should get out of this hole before dark, if possible."

The wind came up and I was shivering as the dogs worked round and round in ever-increasing circles. Suddenly the bitch leading the pack let go with her tremulous baying, and off we all went through the brush in the valley right below us. In a few minutes we knew from the sound of the dogs that the cougar was treed. We had to work fast because darkness was not many minutes away. Then I learned how to catch cougars alive.

Marvin took his rope from his saddle, put a noose on a forked stick, and climbed up the tree far enough to reach the cougar with the noose on the stick. The cougar batted it away several times, but shortly the rope was around the animal's neck. Marvin came out of the tree, saying that cougars choke easily and we must be careful not to injure the creature. My job, he said, was to grab the cougar by the tail when it hit the ground—and in a matter of minutes, that's what I did. Marvin kept his rope taut and we turned the animal on its back. Then, tying the rope to a tree, Marvin produced two short ropes with nooses. The idea was to drop a noose over one paw and put a half-hitch around the other, pulling the two together. It was not easy to do, because the paws were slashing furiously. But Marvin finally had the two front legs secure. Then he moved to the rear and finally completed the process there. There remained the most dangerous weapon of all—the mouth with its flashing fangs. For that Marvin produced a stout stick and a piece of malleable baling wire. He offered the stick to the cougar, who took it ferociously. Quickly Marvin twisted one end of the wire onto one end of the stick and then rapidly wound the wire around the animal's jaws, finally twisting it tightly to the far end of the stick.

Now, horses normally bolt at the smell, not to mention the sight, of a cougar. But Marvin's horses were "broke" to cougars, and he had one precious mule who did not mind if a live cougar rode on its back. So Marvin and I placed the cougar on the mule's back, covering all but its head with a canvas and then putting on a diamond hitch.

These last steps we took with the aid of flashlights, and then started the long fifteen-mile journey to camp in the complete blackness of night. It was a cold, uneventful ride, which we made in silence. The dogs were dead-tired and we and the horses were too. I could not even see my horse's ears. Branches of shrubs scratched my face and I felt tree trunks scraping my legs. Yet it was glorious to be abroad on a night so filled with mystery. I was proud to know a man who could find his way through this Apache wilderness in the dark of night. I learned from him what his love of cougars meant, how deep it was; and, through Marvin, the cougar who had frightened me to death when I was back-packing in the Cascades as a boy, became a new wilderness friend.

The man who—literally and spiritually—towered above most of the Western outdoorsmen who helped educate me was Roy Shaeffer of Lostine in eastern Oregon. Roy was literate, but largely uneducated. He was, however, extremely intelligent and thought long and hard about the pressing problems of the day. For example, when penicillin first came on the market, a doctor prescribed it for one of his daughters, but Roy could not afford to buy it. The next summer he told me the story and asked, "Is penicillin just for the rich? Since it saves lives, why do not the poor get it for nothing or at least for the small price they can afford to pay?"

Roy had started life as a sheepherder; in later years he ran a dude ranch at Lapover on the Lostine River in the Wallowas. He rented horses or took out parties who wanted to fish or hunt in the high mountains—or just sit and contemplate the solitude of the wilderness.

It was an education in the art of survival to be with Roy for a week or so. He knew the habits of fish, and one day at Long Lake while I was preparing to go fishing, he asked me to leave my rod in camp and come with him. We walked to a grassy meadow through which a small creek ran to the lake. The creek had a deep quiet stretch of water, and stopping about fifty feet from it, Roy said, "If we walk any closer, the fish will hear us and disperse. They are right under the near bank. The water has washed under the turf, leaving a hollow cave where the fish congregate in midday, feeding on whatever comes down. Go on tiptoe, kneel down, put your hand deep in the water carefully and move your fingers slowly. Soon you will touch a fish. Do not try to seize it. Rub his belly for a few moments and then you can lift him out of the water without a struggle."

I followed Roy's directions and in five minutes had a one-pound rainbow on the grass.

Roy knew miner's lettuce and how to prepare it for a tasty dish at a campfire. He, like the porcupine, knew that the spring beauty had a potato-like root, which when baked is very delicious. He knew how to cook trout on heated flat rocks. He knew the one tree in a forest most likely to shed the rain in a two- or three-day storm.

"Animals are much, much smarter than men," he would say. "All except the porcupine."

He showed me how a coyote teaches her pups to handle a porcupine. The quills, of course, are the great danger. So the coyote circles the porcupine over and again, first one way and then another. All the while the coyote pretends to charge the porcupine. It may take an hour for the porcupine to react as the coyote has planned. But when the coyote finally charges, the porcupine will stand up on its hind legs, exposing the soft underbelly, which the coyote instantly seizes. The fight is over, and the feast is ready for the pups.

Roy had a healthy respect for horses and mules and their ability to forecast the weather. Mac, the mule who lived to be thirty-seven years old, was, according to Roy, the smartest of all. Mac could predict an oncoming blizzard, and, if turned loose, always went home the safest, most comfortable way.

Roy was an expert shot with a rifle. He would shoot at coins or cartridges that someone would toss in the air. He excelled with an ax, cutting logs and hewing them so they would fit neatly together. He was a leather-tanner, and he could make soap out of ashes. He was indeed as versatile as Daniel Boone.

A huge man, he stood well over six feet and weighed probably 250 or 260 pounds. His hands were like hams and he had the strength of ten men. When the Oldsmobile of a friend of mine got stuck in a ditch on a steep mountain road, Roy got two friends, and with Roy at the front and the other two at the back, they carried the car back to the road.

Roy was a bootlegger in Prohibition days and kept eastern Oregon well supplied with a whiskey that had the reputation of being A-Number One. He was tried three times, but no Oregon jury would convict him, because they liked him and because his liquor was superb. When the revenuers came, Lucy, his wife, would see them from the cabin on the hill and break any jar that contained whiskey. So the officers found it difficult to get evidence. Roy never lost his coils either, and when I asked him how he managed it, he told me the story. Annamay, his lovely daughter, was very large—due to some glandular disturbance. "All I had to do," said Roy, "was have Annamay sit on the coils. Her skirts covered them up, and the officers were too polite to look underneath."

Roy drank a lot, but he was not an alcoholic. He started nipping when he got up in the morning and in that way finished a quart of whiskey every day. Once, to keep a dude from getting drunk on a pack trip, Roy drank the man's last fifth of Scotch, stopping only once for a breath of air. Then Roy cooked dinner, did the dishes, and was the first one up the next day.

I was deeply shocked when Roy died in his sixties. And the doctors seemed puzzled as to the cause of his death, until they performed an autopsy; then they told me that his aorta, the artery to his heart, was as hard as solid rubber.

"What caused it?" I asked.

"Well, during his lifetime he either drank too much milk or too much whiskey," one doctor said.

Roy was buried in the little graveyard at Wallowa, Oregon. The day was clear and beautiful, but the valley was filled with sadness. Roy did not have an enemy in the county. Everyone loved him.

FDR was Roy's hero and he came to Washington, D.C., for FDR's inauguration in 1945, traveling by railroad coach clear across the country. He wore cowboy boots, Pendleton pants, a loud plaid shirt, a mackinaw, and his ten-gallon hat. I had no idea he was coming, but he got off at Union Station with a battered suitcase, stepped into a cab and told the driver, "I want to see Bill Douglas." By some miracle he ended up at my home.

The highlight of Roy's visit was, of course, the inauguration of FDR for the fourth term. As FDR took the oath at the rear of the White House, Roy stood, with head bared, on the grounds below. That was his proudest day.

We talked of these things during Roy's last days. We did not think he would die, for he had always seemed indestructible, a towering man of great strength. We had counted on Roy being with us for so many more years that the funeral had a special sadness for us. Henry Hess said, "To make this funeral a Roy Schaeffer event, a bull elk should whistle." Elk were Roy's specialty, and if he had had the skill to write about it, he could have revealed many secrets of this remarkable animal. But when Roy was buried, the elk were high in the Wallowas and no whistle was heard in the graveyard.

But one interesting thing did happen. Just as the casket was being lowered into the grave, a cock pheasant crowed. Henry Hess remarked, "That was a touching farewell, for like the elk and deer, the birds of the valleys and mountains were kin to Roy."

He knew them, he never killed wantonly, he slept in the snow with the birds, and like St. Francis, considered them his friends.

Roy's funeral brought back to me a flood of memories. I had never visited the Wallowas, which lie close to the Idaho line in eastern Oregon, until I took my seat on the Court. That first summer I made a trip there, met Roy, went with him on a pack trip into the deep recesses of those wondrous mountains, and began to acquire a love for them second only to my feelings for the Cascades.

Roy and I were returning from this trip on a warm August afternoon, when a few miles from Lapover—Roy's dude ranch—he stopped to adjust a saddle. At that stop I told Roy I wished I could buy some property there and build a cabin—but the Wallowas were a national forest. The only building sites I had seen were down in the valley.

Soon we mounted and headed for Lapover. Shortly before reaching it, Roy left the trail and stopped the packtrain on a bench above the Lostine River, right under Flagstaff Point on the opposite ridge. Turning to me, he said, "I'll give you this piece," and on he went.

We later talked about it. Roy had purchased an old mining claim of over a thousand acres that was deep in the forest. He figured the tract he sold me was perhaps five acres, which a survey I made showed it to be.

"The price?" I asked.

"Nothing," he said.

I rejected his offer of a gift and we shortly agreed on the price and shook hands. In time I got the deed for one of the loveliest spots God ever created, a tract with three cabins which I gave to Millie and Bill and the grandchildren.

Chapter XVI

Goose Prairie

I eventually established my own home in Goose Prairie, Washington. Goose Prairie is my place in a sense that Washington, D.C., never could be. My roots are deep in the Prairie. I am a part of the rhythm of the place—of the mornings just before and just after sunrise, when grass, shrubs, and trees are bejeweled; of the evenings when the grosbeaks swoop low and feed on insects, and the doe deer and the porcupine silently emerge from the woods to visit the clover. My home—Prairie House—seldom hears any roar of traffic; the air is pure, and on a clear night the stars just barely tip the peaks of the Cascades.

I came to know Goose Prairie first as a boy when I started backpacking. It used to cost a dime to ride the train from Yakima to Naches, fourteen miles distant, and from Naches, it was forty-eight miles to Goose Prairie by road. Today the way is paved, but in the days of which I speak it was a dirt road. When I left the train at Naches, I always made sure I had a dime to catch the train back home. I kept that dime in the watch pocket of my trousers, and fastened the pocket with a huge safety pin.

Naches is rimmed by sagebrush hills; like Yakima, it is scorching hot. The road goes west along the Naches River, and one travels about fifteen miles before he comes to any conifers. On the first day's hike of about twenty-five miles, we would see white oaks, thistles, sagebrush, and rattlesnakes and much bare basalt rock. Our destination was always the

Anderson Ranch, a homestead in a fertile valley rimmed by low hills covered with ponderosa pine, black pine, and white fir. When I first saw the ranch as a boy I promised myself that one day I would buy it.

The trail we took skirted the edges of the ranch and we would make camp in a sheltered glade at its western end. The nearby Naches River gave us trout for dinner and for breakfast, and a few more that we cooked and carried in a knapsack for lunch.

From the Anderson Ranch to Goose Prairie is only about twenty-three miles, and it is easy going, out of the blistering sun. The road was now narrow for much of the way, the roaring river on our left, towering cliffs on our right.

Goose Prairie is 3,400 feet above sea level, between two mountain ranges that are about a mile and a half apart. The summer temperatures may reach eighty degrees or more by day, but it is always cool at night, forty degrees or lower.

The Prairie had probably once been a lake, and like most lakes, had completed its cycle and filled in. The water table in the center is still very high, but the northern edges are higher, and it was on a stretch of these edges that I built my home fifty years or more after my first boyhood visit.

At the time I first saw it, as a young boy, Tom Fife, a homesteader, owned the whole of Goose Prairie. He raised potatoes and rhubarb, kept a cow and some sheep, and tried to make a few honest dollars prospecting. He was gruff and uncommunicative, but friendly. His favorite dish was red-squirrel mulligan and, I must say, it was quite a sight to a child of eleven to look into a steaming cauldron and see the bright eyes of bobbing squirrels looking back at him.

Goose Prairie was a friendly haven partly because of Tom Fife and partly because it was, in a way, my home base, from which I could head in any direction of the compass for camping, for fishing, for blueberries. Mornings in the Prairie were dazzling. The dew glistened on the grass and on the shrubs and trees. It was worth getting up with the sun just to see the glory of the morning. And that is true to this day. (I was also relieved to get to the Prairie when I was a youngster because it was above the zone of the Northern Pacific rattlesnake, the species that inhabits that area. There are water snakes, but nothing at that altitude to harm a small boy.)

As the years passed, Goose Prairie changed. A Reclamation Service dam was built where a jewel of a lake once drained into the Bumping

River. Jack Nelson and his wife Kitty became its caretakers. Jack was not a wilderness man, but he was a poet, a romantic soul who reveled in the beauty of the Prairie. Kitty was the fisherman, hunter, and trapper. Jack, a great storyteller, later wrote his memories of the Prairie in a book called *We Never Got Away*. Its theme is that the place held them so tightly, what with the otters in wintertime, the berries in August, and the elk in the fall, that no trip they planned ever took place. When I was a boy Jack would hail me, offer me coffee and a doughnut and regale me with stories as I passed his home on the trail leading to Fish Lake, sixteen miles distant.

Goose Prairie, a bare dot even on the few maps on which it appears, is notable for its people as well as its wilderness atmosphere. It is a real neighborhood. A host of people, many now gone, march by in my memories: grimy, ill-shaven miners who worked the shafts at Copper City; a Chinese cook with a broad smile who gave me greetings; Tom Fife, Jack and Kitty Nelson—friends who put tender arms around me as a boy.

As the years passed, Billy McGuffie, the sheepherder who had a marble in his throat that turned every phrase into Scottish dialect, always took front and center stage. Billy, a great storyteller, never ran in short supply because he could invent his tales as he went along.

Ira and Bess Ford have lived in the Prairie for forty-seven years. Their door is never locked; on weekends and holidays they have dozens of visitors who come to pass the time of day. Ira can, in a wink, build a barn or a fence or make an engine run or repair a vacuum cleaner or a garbage-disposal unit. But he has so little faith in modern technology that when he acquires a new carburetor, he always punches a hole in it. He can also cut your hair, and if you are trusting, fix you a drink. Ira still snowshoes around Goose Prairie in the winter, though he is almost eighty.

He raised a family of two boys and a girl by trapping. That was winter work, which meant that if he wanted pine marten, he had to lay traps along the cornice of snowdrifts high on Mount Baldy to the south. Ira loves to talk politics; he's a Republican and his wife, Bess, shares his political opinions. I often ask her how she can reconcile her low opinion of Hubert Humphrey and her high opinion of her husband when, of all the people I know, Ira talks more like Hubert than anyone else. In answer, Bess simply smiles and waves me away.

Ira, who is around eighty, never seems to worry. Does he know about the atomic bomb? Watergate? The kind of men around the world who have access to the button that could destroy all life on the planet? The thieving and corruption that have infected high places? He says he knows all about them and worries about them.

"What happens to your worries?" I asked.

"Well, I don't worry very long before I'm sound asleep."

Some thirty years ago Kay Kershaw, who was born and grew up in Yakima, bought some land in the Prairie, erected a ranch house, brought up horses, and opened one of the very few dude ranches in the state. It is a ranch for people who really love the wilderness, not for those who litter the trails or who look at trees trying to estimate the board feet in them or who appraise the high alpine basins as motel sites serviced by helicopters. Kay Kershaw's ranch—called Double K—reverently introduces people to the area, hoping they will love it. Kay acquired a partner, Isabelle Lynn, born in the East but a real wilderness zealot now and the best cook both west as well as east of the Cascades. Isabelle's hobby of botany and ornithology places her with the best. Moreover, she writes, lobbies, speaks, and carries on active correspondence around the nation on the importance of conserving the wilderness. She is the Northwest representative of the National Parks Association and was recently elected one of its directors.

I find this militant Double K group inspirational but Ira and Bess are not so sure in which direction the good life is to be found. In my speeches I often refer to Goose Prairie as composed of eight people—Kay, Isabelle, two Fords, Bob and Bennie Bosler, and the two Douglases. "Two are for progress; six are against it. That is why Goose Prairie is the loveliest place in America."

When Tom Fife died in 1922 his executor surveyed the 160-acre homestead and had it mapped into one-acre plots. I waited too long to do my purchasing and so I paid a higher price than I need have, but I bought some twelve acres, mostly on the high ground adjoining Double K on the east. One evening, at sunset, I stood on the stump of a tree close to the Forest Service line and picked the site of my house, facing south and looking out on Old Scab, Buffalo, and Baldy—three peaks in the range of seven thousand-plus feet.

With the aid of "water witchers," I drilled two wells, one for the house and one for irrigation. Isabelle, who discovered she has the "power," "witched" one well by means of a metal coathanger. I had doubted her at first, and so she asked me to walk with her, holding her right hand with my left and the coathanger with my right. I did so, and when the coathanger turned, pointing the hook downward, it was impossible for me to stop it.

Howard (Lucky) Gallant, Ira's son-in-law, "witched" the irrigation well, and he not only spotted the place where water would be found but predicted its cubic-feet discharge per minute if I drilled twenty-five feet. And he hit it right on the nose. So I became a convert to water witching.

The architect of Prairie House was Tom Hargis of Yakima, who designed it as a Swiss-chalet type. The roof has a steep pitch, for the snowfall averages twenty feet a year at Goose Prairie; the gable runs north and south so that the low winter sun will melt the snow evenly on each side of the roof. The shingles are thick red cedar. The chimney and three fireplaces are built out of Vantage Ferry basalt, a trade name for the volcanic rock that splits naturally into long, thin pieces and gives a sense of movement to the surface of a structure. The house is built around the big chimney—the kitchen, dining room, and living room occupy three sides. There is a small porch opening off the dining room on the south side. From that spot the surrounding three peaks seem close enough to touch.

Around the house I set in plants identified with the Cascades—the mountain ash, Canadian dogwood, mountain azalea, Oregon grape, and the like. I transplanted the old lilac bush that was outside my window in our old Yakima home, and it grew and survived; but it never would bloom, the altitude is too high and the winter temperature is too low. So I got a Siberian lilac, that our people had brought to this country, which is acclimated to severe cold and high altitudes.

As Prairie House was being built, I spent my time planting the meadow around the house and watering it. This was land that my predecessor had cleared of pine and fir. Soil in these forests is notoriously poor, so I decided to sow white clover. In that way I would build nitrogen into the soil and attract a wide variety of grasses that elk and deer love.

One day as I sowed the seed I heard the baying of hounds on American Ridge to the north. Before long I felt something touch my leg, and turning, I saw a doe deer standing close to me. Her eyes were dilated, she was breathing heavily, and she dripped with perspiration. Obviously she was near exhaustion, and she had come to man for help. I had heard of such things before but had never believed them.

I hesitated but a second, and then depositing my bag of seed on the ground, said to the deer, "Come with me," and I started walking the half-mile or so to Bumping River. She kept at my heels like a puppy dog.

When we reached the river I gave her a pat on the rump; she entered the water and slowly swam to the opposite shore, where she stopped, looked back as if to say good-by, and entered a stand of alder. In an instant the dogs had arrived, baying frantically as they tried to find the scent that had disappeared at the river's edge.

At Goose Prairie, in our meadow, are the biggest, liveliest toads I ever saw. They thrive on mosquitoes and other insects. We work together to keep the Prairie clean and habitable.

The weasel is another inhabitant of the Prairie. Ira Ford says that when old-timers raised chickens here, the hens and rooster ate right alongside the weasel—which contradicts common New England folklore. The otter, a member of the same family, is found at the Prairie also, but not in large numbers. In the winter it plays on the snowbanks surrounding Bumping Lake; and Ira Ford, in his trapping days, followed its trails clear over American Ridge and down to the American River on the north side.

The pileated woodpecker has a two-foot wingspread and hammers away on old fir trees. Three types of grouse—Richardson's, ruffed, and the blue—live at various levels of the surrounding ridges. Pine siskin cling to dandelion stalks, eating the seeds. Over seventy species of birds frequent the Prairie. The hermit thrush is here, along with the veery and willow thrush. A few golden eagles frequent the peaks and the ferruginous hawk sweeps the valley looking for the golden-mantled ground squirrel. The camp robber, Clark's crow, is here, and suddenly appears whenever I broil steaks out of doors, occasionally making off with one of them if I'm not watchful. Stellar's jay—cobalt blue—is much in evidence, scolding loudly. The rufous hummingbird is found in force by late spring. People tend to make their feeders too sweet. Honey is fatal to the bird and any mixture of sugar and water sweeter than one-to-eight is harmful to them. These hummingbirds are interesting to watch. When the fireweed blooms in July, they and the honey bees migrate to the slopes of Old Scab, where the fireweed is thick, and feed on its delicate nectar.

The horned owl lives in Goose Prairie, as does the snowy owl. One day on an American Ridge trail, Lucky, the springer spaniel who stands guard over the Double K Ranch, was intent on following a scent he had picked up. Out of the blue appeared a snowy owl and noiselessly came down within a few inches of Lucky, trying to determine if he was too big for it to carry. The owl's decision was in Lucky's favor, though the dog never knew the peril that threatened him.

. . .

Trails lead up to high country on three sides of the Prairie. Atop American Ridge, behind our home, are spectacular views of Mount Rainier. Atop the opposite ridge are equally spectacular views of Mount Adams and the Goat Rocks. Both trails, as well as the old trail up the valley, lead to the wondrous top country of alpine meadows and dozens of lakes. This area will hopefully soon be converted into the Cougar Lakes Wilderness Area.

The Prairie is, of course, distant and hard to get to, but these days the summer traffic is great, and by Friday night all campgrounds are taken. When I first knew Goose Prairie, a dirt road ran to it all the way from Naches. From American Falls west to Chinook Pass, a distance of nineteen miles, there was only a trail. It was a wondrous one—broad, smooth, and low at a gentle grade. A back-packer had to cross American River twenty-two times in these nineteen miles. But getting one's feet wet or damp was never a burden.

I was teaching at Yale when news came that a road would take the place of the trail. I almost wept at the thought of pot-bellied, cigar-smoking men roaming through a sacrosanct valley and polluting it with the noise and fumes of cars. I wrote, I protested, complained, but progress won out, as it usually does.

People by the hundreds fish the Bumping River, which the state keeps stocked with rainbow and Eastern brook trout. As I have said, since there are more people than fish, I have come out on the side of the fish. When darkness settles over the Bumping, however, there are a few spots where I can still catch fine trout, but I do so only *in extremis,* such as when I have a distinguished visitor. That happened when Eric Sevareid of CBS came to interview me on TV in 1972. On his last evening I took him to my spot, but fish are nervous and fishing is a very delicate procedure. Eric knew the art, but the number of CBS personnel and cameramen with flashbulbs put an end to fishing prospects that night.

At Goose Prairie there is mail delivery six days a week, but no telephone. The mailman is the redoubtable Lyle Hall of Naches. Once I had left on a trip where I had to dress black-tie. I forgot my black shoes, so I telephoned Lyle at night and the next day he found the hidden key to our house, collected the shoes, packaged them and mailed them by air to me in San Francisco, and they arrived in time. Who says our postal system is no good?

In the summer there are deer in the clover every evening. Porcupines also appear to nip the sweet flower heads. The lawn, which really is a meadow, is filled with the golden-mantled ground squirrel, the anchor man in the food chain for predators. Hawks patrol my meadow for their fare, and the pine martens, who specialize in squirrels, have converted my meadow into a happy hunting ground. Now that the grasses in my meadow are high, Richardson's grouse live there, hatching their eggs and raising their young.

The ground squirrels are hibernators. But in the spring before they return to the top side, they actively eat away underneath at any roots in existence. One day Bess Ford, sitting by a window saw an iris plant of of hers slowly being swallowed up. In a few hours it did indeed disappear into the earth, consumed by ground squirrels. These animals did the same to one of my choice lilac plants. Bears occasionally come to the Prairie in search of garbage, and one such yearling visited us in 1972. Cathy—expert with the camera—maneuvered and maneuvered, first inside the jeep, then on top of it, then under it, getting marvelous camera shots of the bear. But at the height of all this, a teen-ager who lives in the Prairie, imagining himself a brave junior Daniel Boone, hid in a trailer and shot the unsuspecting bear at a distance of six feet. He kept the carcass on display, as a sign of his own virility.

Elk usually move to the high country by late spring. But now that my white clover meadow is lush, one herd never quits the valley. From midnight until dawn they graze in groups of five or six or twenty or twenty-five. The bulls frequently fight, and the stomping of the herd often wakes me at night. When they quit the place, they go in a hurry. While deer always go under a fence, elk jump over it. They make an easy clearance of my six-foot red-fir pole fence. The herd lingers on through October, and then, as if by prearranged schedule, they leave the valley only a few days before the hunting season opens.

The toad, the deer, the elk, and the grouse are guardians of Prairie House.

King, my horse, is now about eighteen years old. He is supposed to be a quarter horse, though he is a bit oversized for that class. He is steady and friendly and always hungry, which is his failing. Mila Repa, Cathy's horse, is a domineering mare named after a thirteenth-century Buddhist monk who lived for years in a cave in the Himalaya eating boiled thistles. His only possession was an earthen pan in which he cooked his thistles. One day he stumbled and broke the pan. Thereupon he said he was at last "free"—free of all earthly possession. So Mila Repa is a constant reminder to Cathy that credit cards and charge accounts are no good, that the path to happiness is Mila Repa's path.

Goose Prairie is a bit of heaven in all seasons. In winter, when the snow possesses it, it has a quiet and solitude that I have never known elsewhere. We are about sixteen miles, as the crow flies, from the crest of the Cascades, so we receive the drippings from the storms that come in from the West. The snowfall averages about twenty feet a year and it packs down to about eight feet, and stays with us a couple of months. The greatest snow comes from January to March, but the hold of winter on the mountains is not broken in one swift stroke. There is an old saying, "Spring is born slowly and laboriously at Goose Prairie," but when the western tanager appears, the labor is about over.

There is much life at Goose Prairie in the winter. A Douglas squirrel chatters from a treetop. In the late sixties the Douglas squirrel virtually disappeared, perhaps decimated by illegal hunters, perhaps by a virus. Its disappearance was a tragedy, for it is the squirrel who, as John Muir related in his writings, cuts the pine cones loose from a tree and later collects the nuts from the cones and buries or conceals them in his storehouse. In the Cascades the cones were a source of livelihood for people, who would collect the cones in gunnysacks and sell them to the Forest Service and nurseries for seeding. But as I write, in 1973, the Douglas squirrel seems to be returning.

Two kinds of pollution threaten Goose Prairie. The increasing number of visitors and campers has caused the river to become polluted, its water unsafe for human use except after boiling. The septic tanks in most cabins are inadequate, and the water table in the Prairie is so high that proper sanitary disposal of sewage is expensive—though it can be done.

Noise is another factor. The tote goats, small motorized vehicles, race up trails and scare the wildlife as well as saddle horses during the summer. Though the Forest Service bars them from most trails, there are not enough rangers to police the entire area.

Noise pollutes the Cascades even in winter. Snowmobiles are everywhere. They are a menace to game; elk, chased by snowmobiles, cannot survive. These are devilish machines which invade and destroy privacy and repose. They make a constant whine; it is as though a chain saw were operating for hours on end right outside one's study window, destroying the quiet and solitude. Drastic steps need to be taken if taut nerves are to have the quiet needed for their repair.

Yet a snowmobiler, who was only one short jump from a gorilla, confided in me that until that machine came along, he was going mad on winter weekends for lack of anything to do. Shakespeare, Mozart, Bernstein, Darwin, Veblen, Thoreau—and the great outdoors—were all unknown to him.

The sonic boom is another problem in the wilderness. It raised havoc with horses and their riders in eastern Washington. The noise would come without warning, startling the animals, and our horses always jumped two feet into the air and several feet sideways. That was not disastrous when we were in an open place. But once we were on a narrow trail looking into an abyss, and the risk of injury was great. So I started writing letters about planes that caused this problem, finally sending one to LBJ. He replied that limiting operations so as to eliminate the boom would be "impractical at best and even perilous in the long run."

He added: "I am further told that your area is ringed by Air Defense Command interceptors—another possible source of sonic disturbance. These planes are often bent on intercepting unidentified aircraft detected by radar. The clear urgency of their mission demands the most direct routing at any hour of day or night. To detour around even the smallest locality could invite a delay or error of possibly disastrous consequences to us all."

When I replied, asking if we could have "say, two hours a week during daylight to ride horses in June, July, August, and September," he referred the letter to Air Force Secretary Harold Brown, who wrote me: "To tie these forces to a timetable of any sort is to ignore the unpredictability of the enemy threat."

I then wrote LBJ suggesting that one day a week from eight in the morning to noon, or even from ten to noon be set aside, telling Kosygin of the plan and asking if he would like to have an equal time for horseback riding free of the sonic boom. I suggested that perhaps we and the Russians could settle on a sonic-boom-free period when anyone here or in the Soviet Union could ride safely. I also suggested that such a plan might be a small step toward ending the Cold War. But no reply ever came to that letter.

The planes sent by LBJ to probe the Pacific in search of Russian planes produced a sonic boom of only 1.3 pounds per square foot of pressure. The proposed new SST would produce 2.5 to 3.5 pounds of pressure per square foot. That would be enough to make a horse uncontrollable, not to mention the long-range effect on humans.

The episode illustrated, however, how LBJ was still living in the age of Stalin and walking to the measure of fear. That LBJ thought the Russians actually were aiming, or were likely to aim, missiles at us in 1967 and 1968 was to me unthinkable, knowing, as I did, how fearful the Russians were of nuclear war. The Russians by the 1960's were looking eagerly for an embrace from a friendly American. But LBJ, raised on the Cold War, loved to make political capital out of it.

Goose Prairie now is part of a technological society which may in time destroy it. But the values of the Prairie are so precious, so unique—that all who love the Goose Prairies of this continent will put up a valiant fight to preserve them.

Chapter XVII

Millie and Bill

Few people I have known are competent to be parents. Dr. Draper once said that the only qualification ninety percent of women have to be mothers is biological. I think he was right, and in my view, the way we make a fetish of motherhood is sheer nonsense. In a lesser way, the same is true of fatherhood. The child who survives being brought up by the two and emerges as an integrated person is an accident.

I remember a young female patient of Draper's who was always brought to his office by her mother. Finally, one day the mother asked, "What in the world is wrong with Nancy? You've seen her enough. You should know."

His answer was simple and direct: "You." And of course he lost that patient.

The child unfolds slowly, and it takes great wisdom to help him or her understand the segment of the world that is revealed in each time sequence. It takes wisdom and courage to let the child find his own levels of interest and not to force him to become this or become that according to the tastes of the parent. It takes planning to expose the child to good music, fine arts, interesting conversation, controversial ideas, the harmony and the wildness of nature without at the same time forcing a cult or idea or principle down his throat.

I doubt if I rated high as a father although I did receive a Father of the Year award once.

I think it is a near-impossibility for a child of a celebrity to be "normal." The son of a coal miner or the daughter of a charwoman has no competition, the sky being the limit. But what chance did FDR's sons have? Or Abe Lincoln's? Unless of course they move in a different path from their fathers'. I was therefore happy when my son Bill decided not to go into law.

When Millie was two years old I took her to the Maine woods; together we explored the mysterious operation of the pitcher plant, which closes its leaves on insects and gets its food supply from them. By the time she was three Millie was in love with horses. I found her one day in the barn of a friend in Connecticut, both arms wrapped around the rear leg of a horse; the animal was trembling with fear. In the summer of her fourth year Millie began learning to swim. One July day we were both sitting on the edge of our dock at Lake Wentworth, New Hampshire, when she pushed me off. I swam out a hundred feet or so, turned, and could not see Millie. Realizing she must have fallen into the water, I raced back to the dock, dived, and found her on the bottom of the lake. I applied artificial respiration, and within the hour, after she had calmed down, made her reenter the water and try to swim, for I knew by my own experience the terror that can build up as a result of that kind of experience. She eventually became a fine swimmer.

By the time Millie was in high school she was a "soda jerk" after school hours and on Saturdays at a drugstore in the Washington, D.C., area. In the summers we went to Oregon, to our cabin in the Wallowa Mountains, adjacent to Roy Schaeffer's dude ranch. At thirteen years of age Millie worked for Roy as a wrangler and packer. She loved horses, and her Lightning, a gelding, was the fastest-walking horse I ever knew. Millie, riding Lightning, packed many dudes into the high basins, set up their camps, and then packed them out a week or two later. Millie could tie a diamond hitch and lead a packtrain of twenty horses. She could set up a camp in a jiffy, pitching tents, blowing up air mattresses, starting a fire, cooking dinner.

When Millie was fifteen she was in charge of a twelve-string packtrain belonging to Roy Schaeffer. I was in the party, and our last camp was in the North Minam Meadows in the Wallowas. It rained that night and a drizzle continued the next morning as we broke camp. It was an eleven-mile ride up over one ridge and down the far side to Lapover. When we reached the top of the ridge, snow and sleet were falling and we were quickly soaked through. Since it was August, Millie had not brought her long underwear and wore only Levi trousers, a cotton shirt, a Levi jacket, and a hat. Her clothes were soon frozen. She stopped the packtrain, dismounted, walked to the rear where I was, and said, "Dad, I'm only fifteen and you said I couldn't have a cocktail until I'm eighteen. But I'm almost dead of cold and I know you have a bottle in your saddlebags." Her face was blue and the plea was too moving to deny.

Millie is a well-organized, most efficient person at whatever she does. If she had gone to Harvard Business School, Wall Street, Detroit, or Pittsburgh, she would have risen high in the business or financial world. She now teaches in a British school. She had a perfectly good college degree from Whitman, but since this wasn't accepted in the British school system, she went back to college in England and got another degree. Millie is married to a Britisher, Norman Read, and between Millie and Norman, they have nine children.

When Bill was only four years old he and I went back-packing. The trail, of course, was easy and his pack was light. Bill made the fire, brought water from the creek, helped cook dinner, and learned how to make a fine mattress out of the flat branches of the white fir. That was his first night out under the open skies. He told me later that it took him a long time to fall asleep—he was first startled by the myriad of stars and then so fascinated with them, he could not close his eyes. In time he became an inveterate back-packer.

Eventually Bill became a skilled fly fisherman. On one trip we were camped at Long Lake in the mountains above Lapover and had gone for a day of fishing to Steamboat Lake.

Bill and I had been fishing in the lake with dry flies. Bill, who was fourteen at the time, had caught several Eastern brook trout of from ten to thirteen inches and a rainbow or two around ten inches. But the going was slow. So I started him on mastery of the roll cast. He was standing on the southern shore at the edge of a rock that was wide as a paved street and sloped gently into the water. Suddenly a swarm of grasshoppers came over our shoulder from the southwest. They covered the rock. A high wind blew them out on the water. Then began an extensive, an amazing rise.

The water immediately in front of us became alive with fish. Big trout—two- or three-pounders—rolled under the grasshoppers, sucking them under with a swirl. Smaller trout left the water, jumping again and again for the fresh bait, gorging themselves. There were literally hundreds of swirls and splashes extending farther and farther into the lake as the wind carried the hoppers away from the shore. It would have been impossible to draw a circle three feet in diameter that did not include a rising trout.

The temptation at such a moment is to give the fish what is being offered—to bait hooks with grasshoppers or even to add a grasshopper to a fly hook. But a grasshopper on a hook does not sit as nicely on the water as a grasshopper with his freedom. So I decided on a different course, and asked Bill to try the Hallock killer and to fish it dry. The underbody of the Hallock killer has a yellow-green tinge that is very close to the color of the grasshopper. It was this underbody that the trout would see.

He greased his Hallock killer with mucelin and cast out. It rode high and saucily on the surface, bobbing with the riffle that the wind had kicked up. It was soon surrounded by live grasshoppers, a half-dozen grasshoppers within inches of our flies. In a flash he had a strike and shouted for joy. The trout chose the Hallock killer over the real thing. Bill caught trout as fast as he could cast. He caught trout as long as the grasshoppers pulled trout to the surface. The largest was an eighteen-inch Eastern brook. In view of the angle of decline of the rock into the water, I decided against the use of a net. So Bill beached it. It was wholly out of water on the rock when the hook became disengaged and Bill captured it by falling on it. It was fully eighteen inches long and any fair-minded jury would concede it two pounds.

Bill and I were fishing Silver Creek, Idaho, one September day when he was about fifteen years old. On the upper reaches was a large slough, some thirty yards wide and a quarter-mile or more long. There we took our positions, side by side, he up to his armpits, I well over my waist.

It was a squally day, fifteen minutes of gusty wind followed by a half-hour of quiet. When there was no wind the surface of the slough was glassy. Then conditions were too delicate for fly-fishing, for the shadow of the line sounded an alarm to the rainbow. In those periods of quiet we would get out of the water, work our way up the bank that bounds the slough on the south, and study it. What we saw at one such time startled us. A school of two dozen or more rainbow swam by us on a lazy cruise not more than twenty-five or thirty feet away. There were eight fish better than thirty inches long, a half-dozen more were over twenty-four inches and the rest from sixteen to eighteen inches. It was an armada thrilling to behold.

When the next breeze came, we waded quietly into the water and cast toward the spot where we imagined the cruising rainbow to be. We were fishing dry and had changed from a gray hackle to a bucktail coachman. Within an hour I had three of those big fellows on. There would be a swirl under the fly and the hook would be set. But I was either a trifle slow or a trifle fast. Not once did I set the hook securely. There would be a run, a dorsal fin cutting the water, a jump, a surge—and then a slack line.

At last I was discouraged, and decided to forsake the slough for the stream. Bill promised to follow me shortly. Several hours passed and he had not showed up. Slightly concerned, I started upstream where I had seen him last. Pretty soon someone came running, and shouted, "Your son needs help. He's got a big one on."

"How big?" I asked.

"About ten pounds, I think" was the reply.

Waders are ungainly even for walking. They never were designed for running. But run in them I did. I stopped only once in the half-mile or more, and that was to borrow a net from another fisherman.

But I arrived too late for the battle. There was Bill, wet to the neck, with a grin on his face and a rainbow that was slightly over sixteen inches in length hanging on his right thumb.

When I left him he had forsaken the fly. He waded the neck of the slough in water up to his chin, changed to a reel with nylon line and salmon eggs, and fished as Sandy Balcom, my old friend from Seattle, had taught us.

Bill played the rainbow he caught with salmon eggs for at least forty minutes, and when the last ounce of energy was gone from the rainbow's stout heart, he turned on his side. Bill then slipped a finger through the gill and the battle was over.

As we walked through the willows to the road where our car was parked, I saw in my son's eyes an excitement I had not seen before. I knew there had been awakened in him an instinct that has been carried in the bloodstream of the race since man first lowered a net in the ocean or first stood by a pool with a spear waiting for the flash that heralded the arrival of a salmon or trout.

Bill found himself about his senior year at Whitman. He learned then that he was destined for the theater, and studied under Marcel Marceau at the Sorbonne before he returned to Hollywood. My son is passionately independent, refusing help even from such friends of mine as Jack Benny, the late Edward G. Robinson, and the late Spencer Tracy. But Max Gordon, the famous Broadway producer, once told me that Bill was destined to be one of the great "character actors" of this century.

Bill taught and acted at the Repertory Theatre in San Francisco, at the Little Theatre in Berkeley, and in the Napa Valley theater at Oakville. He also directed plays. He had his own mime show and traveled the lecture circuit with it. Bill has three children, Seana, Pierre, and Eva Marie, all of whom are very creative.

As for Bill, I love, admire, and respect him more than any man I ever knew. One episode will reveal the reason—a story he never told me, but one that I learned from a *New York Times* reporter.

One night about 10:00 P.M. Bill left his apartment in Hollywood to go to a delicatessen to get milk, cheese, bread, and cold cuts. As he was walking along Sunset Boulevard, a patrol car pulled up at the curb, a policeman shouting at him, "Hey, there." Bill walked over and said, "What do you want?" A policeman said, "What's your name?"

Bill replied, "None of your business."

The cop jumped out of the car, saying, "Wise guy, eh?"

Bill repeated his answer.

The cop replied, "We've been looking for you."

"What have I done?" asked Bill.

"You know" was the answer.

Bill, who was getting tired of the whole thing, turned on his heel and started toward the delicatessen, telling the cops where he was going and why. The two cops grabbed him and took him back to the car and drove him to the precinct office.

"Empty your pockets," said the sergeant at the receiving desk.

"Everything except my billfold," said Bill.

"The billfold too."

"Never."

"Why not?"

"Then you'll know who I am."

"Who are you?"

"None of your business."

Bill never surrendered his billfold. They photographed him and fingerprinted him, and at 7:00 A.M.—nine hours later—released him, never knowing that he was the son of a Supreme Court Justice. They released him because the photograph and the fingerprints proved it was a case of mistaken identity. But the cynicism of the police was emphasized by the fact that they booked Bill for "vagrancy"—when his only "crime" was going to the delicatessen at ten o'clock for food for a late supper.

The last words Franklin D. Roosevelt spoke to me were "How are Thunder and Lightning?" This happened at a Sunday luncheon at the White House three weeks before his death. Luncheon was over and he had transferred to his wheelchair. The attendant was wheeling him away when he turned and asked the question.

Thunder and Lightning were horses—Thunder belonging to my son

Bill, and Lightning to my daughter Millie. I told in *Of Men and Mountains* how Millie had acquired Lightning from Roy Schaeffer, and Bill, Thunder from Dan Oliver. They were gifts from two old friends. I had told FDR the story the following winter, his comment being "You're doing all right for a Scotsman."

"Not as well as I would like."

"You mean you are looking for a third horse for nothing?" he asked.

"Exactly, Mr. President. And when I thought of people who might give *me* a horse, I kept thinking of you." He threw back his head and laughed in his hearty way.

Millie to this day is an accomplished horsewoman; and riding bareback in the mountains is probably her highest moment. Bill also still loves horses, but his preference for experiencing the wonders of a wilderness is to go back-packing. He likes to take off with a friend or a dog and listen to the quiet sounds of the woods. His specialty in the mountains is the mushroom. When the fall comes, Bill is out looking for morrels and shaggy manes and he is not averse to mild experimental dishes even with the calves' brain or the icicle mushroom.

Either of my children can be dropped by parachute anywhere in our temperate zone and survive, though there are no matches, knives, or food in their pockets.

Chapter XVIII

The Securities and Exchange Commission

I had been active in Democratic politics in Connecticut, though long registered in Yakima, Washington. I finally registered in Connecticut, paying my poll tax and voting in all elections. Francis Maloney of Meriden, Connecticut, who was in Congress, and I became fast friends. Frank wanted to be senator and Fran Smith, Richard J. Smith, and I, as a volunteer committee of three, undertook to make him such. By then I was working in Washington, D.C., full time, but I taught an occasional course at the Yale Law School and during the fall of 1934 tried to spend my weekends in Connecticut working for Frank.

My role was to deliver the Yale vote. I arranged a huge luncheon at which Frank was to answer questions from the faculty, and I nervously presided, knowing how unpredictable and difficult professors could be. The time for questions came, and the first one was a humdinger. No one could possibly repeat it, it was so long and involved; no one could possibly understand it, it was so obfuscated. Frank quickly replied, "May I ask you a question before I try to answer yours?"

"Certainly" was the reply.

"Are you for me or against me?"

That retort brought down the house, ended the luncheon, and carried Yale overwhelmingly for Frank. A special word needs to be said about Frank Maloney. He became one of the closest friends I ever had in Washington, D.C. He helped me enormously on legislative matters before the Congress and advised me conscientiously on momentous SEC decisions. And in time he became one of my foremost champions when FDR sent my name to the Senate for the Brandeis seat on the Court.

Frank served in the Senate until his death in 1945. He did not bring his family to Washington, but lived alone at the Willard Hotel, working late every night. He was the most conscientious public servant I ever knew. He worked himself to death, dying in 1945 at the young age of fifty-one.

Frank was a devout Catholic and ached when anyone criticized his church. Senator Tom Heflin of Alabama, sometimes called Tom Tom, was known as a Catholic-baiter while Frank was in the House from 1933 to 1935. Hearing that Heflin was going to speak, Frank went to the Senate floor and listened to a tirade against Catholics. Heflin, who liked Frank, joined him as he left the chamber, put his arm around him, and said, "Tell me, Frank, how did you like my speech?" Frank, with his eyes full of sadness, said, "Senator, it made my heart sick to hear you say what you said. You see, I'm Irish and I'm a Catholic." Heflin, as quick as a rattlesnake, replied, "Bless you, Mr. Congressman. I was not speaking of the Irish Catholics. I was after those damn Roman Catholics."

The first chairman of the Securities and Exchange Commission was Joseph P. Kennedy. I did not know Kennedy at the time, but my name came to his attention through my activities at Yale and Harvard and through my writing of numerous popular and technical articles on high finance, predatory practices, protective committees, and bankruptcy or receivership rackets.

One of Kennedy's associates at the SEC was James M. Landis, who had finished Harvard Law School the year I graduated from Columbia, and was in Washington on leave as the dean of Harvard Law School. I had met Jim socially. He was an able, intense, and humorless man. In 1934 Joe Kennedy had Landis call me in New Haven to ask if I would join the staff of the SEC. Congress, by paragraph 211 of the Securities Act, had directed the commission to make a study of protective and reorganization committees, which were creating new scandals in their manipulations of bankruptcies and receiverships, and to report the findings and recommendations to Congress. At Kennedy's suggestion, I was to head up that study.

I consulted with President Angell of Yale and Charlie Clark, the dean, and got a semester's leave of absence and headed for Washington, leaving my little family in New Haven. I reported to Kennedy bright and early one morning. He was friendly but brusque.

"What instructions do you have for me?" I asked.

"Instructions? If I knew what to do, why in hell would I get you down here?"

"What's my budget?"

"Your budget is fifty thousand dollars. Mr. Brassor, the secretary, will find quarters for you."

"Fifty thousand? You mean five hundred thousand, Mr. Chairman."

"You heard me," he replied. And after a pause, he added, "Well, what in hell are you waiting for? Get going."

That was the Joe Kennedy of those days. I did get going. I got an office equipped with carpet, desk, chair, and telephone. I got an adjoining office for a secretary and another for an assistant. The Civil Service sent over as secretary a young lady, Edith Waters, who later married William B. Allen, now a lawyer in Woodstock, Virginia. She stayed with me twenty-three years and was an amazingly efficient, friendly person through all those troublesome times.

The first man I hired was Abe Fortas, who had been my prize student at Yale. Abe and I decided that the next person we should hire was Alger Hiss—Holmes' law clerk and an outstanding lawyer at the Department of Agriculture. We dined with Hiss at the Carleton Hotel, and before we had finished the meal, he turned us down. That was the first and last I ever saw of the man. But as troubled days came upon him, I wondered whether fate would have served him differently if he had chosen Wall Street and predatory finance as his specialty rather than agricultural and, later, foreign affairs. Abe and I next hired Samuel Clark of New Haven, and Martin Riger of New York, a brilliant recent graduate of Columbia Law School, recommended by Max Lowenthal. With that combination, we went into business.

About that time I met Robert E. Kittner, who was then a young newspaperman, working for the New York *Herald Tribune*. He soon was to become a partner with Joseph Alsop, writing a column. He later became president of NBC. Kittner practically cut his eyeteeth on stories about the SEC and wrote scintillating articles, each one painstakingly accurate. In those days he got twenty-five dollars for a Sunday feature. He went to Joe Kennedy to ask his advice on one of them. Joe said, "I got a couple goddamn professors down on the fourth floor—Bill Douglas and Abe Fortas. Why not pick their brains?" And that was the beginning of a long, warm friendship with Bob Kittner.

The $50,000 budget Joe had allocated for the committee was much too small for my SEC project, and I did, in fact, get it increased a short time later to $500,000. We held hearings in 1934 and 1935, and I requested and got repeated leaves of absence from Yale. We eventually submitted eight reports to the Congress. The two specific legislative results of the study were Chapter X of the Bankruptcy Act of 1938 (52 Stat. 840), which Walter Chandler of Memphis, Tennessee—then a congressman—Abe Fortas, and I wrote together, and the Trust Indenture Act of 1939 (53 Stat. 1149), which Abe and I wrote and which Senator Alben Barkley sponsored. Chapter X of the Bankruptcy Act made the SEC the financial advisor of the federal courts in charge of reorganizing corporations. The Trust Indenture Act raised by a notch the fiduciary responsibility of those corporate agencies.

The hours of investigation were endless and the days long. We subpoenaed hundreds of witnesses, holding most of our hearings in Washington. We would start at 9:00 A.M. and run until 5:00 P.M. or later. One of my first witnesses was my old boss, Robert T. Swaine, of the Cravath firm. He had engineered many reorganizations in Wall Street, and we got the anatomy of them from his lips. He told me later, "You stood me on my head and shook all the fillings out of my teeth."

There was, however, no bitterness between us in this regard. The investigations were not conducted as publicity stunts. They were calm and detached and they helped unravel many complex situations.

Burton K. Wheeler, a Democrat, was chairman of the Foreign Relations Committee of the Senate, and while serving in this job, had agreed to be counsel to a committee representing Cuban bondholders, a committee of which Senator Gerald P. Nye was chairman. When our committee went into that situation, Burt's friends objected. But as I understood the Congressional mandate, I was to investigate protective and reorganization committees, not merely Republican miscreants in the field. So I committed the unpardonable sin of revealing Burt's activities; as a result, I was opposed by Wheeler's friends when my nomination to the Supreme Court later came before the Senate.

Burton Wheeler had been a valiant campaigner. He carried Montana even though six of the seven leading newspapers were owned by Anaconda Copper, his main opponent. He had a rousing campaign phrase: "Be sure to vote against me if you ever see my picture on the front page of an Anaconda paper." Burt Wheeler was the man who dug and dug and dug, and finally helped unearth the Teapot Dome scandal. In retaliation he was prosecuted for taking money from an oil man to pull political strings at the Department of the Interior. The Senate gave him a clean bill of health prior to the prosecution, and the jury acquitted him. But Burt experienced the sting of political reprisal, where the whole power of the federal government was laid on him. By the time I arrived in Washington, Burt was a legendary figure. He was one power behind the regulatory measures which I later administered. And it was his driving force and Hugo Black's in the Senate and Sam Rayburn's in the House that got the Public Utility Holding Company Act of 1935 through by a squeak.

Max Lowenthal—a Wall Street lawyer—came to me when we first set up the committee and said he had a friend who could help me in my investigation. He gave me the man's name and concluded by saying, "If there is anyone who will take Holmes' place in the law, it is this man."

Lowenthal was an honest, able lawyer whom I often called "a private SEC," for he represented plaintiffs in suits against Wall Street interests engaged in various forms of skulduggery. But the manner of Lowenthal's approach to me this day made me wary. So I called in my staff and asked them to start an investigation of the man he had recommended. We found that he was up to his ears in questionable reorganization practices and soon had him on the stand.

John Foster Dulles was another witness at the SEC hearings. As I have already related, when I was a brash youngster, I had interviewed him for a job and he seemed, even then, to be sanctimonious. Later I knew him in Wall Street as a person who for a fee would stand for almost anything. When Ivar Krueger, known as the Swedish match king, committed suicide in 1931, and his Krueger and Toll empire collapsed, protective committees were formed in this country to represent the debenture holders. One committee, formed by the bankers who had sold the securities, had John Foster Dulles as its counsel. Another committee, formed in opposition to the bankers and with a view to suing them for fraud in the sale of the securities, had Samuel Untermeyer* as its counsel. The Dulles committee had a majority, about thirty million, of the debentures on deposit. The Untermeyer group had less than a million. Dulles and Untermeyer were at each other's throats—until they agreed on a "treaty." The "treaty" was not in writing; it was an informal oral arrangement. It called for cooperation and collaboration between Dulles and Untermeyer, and the "consideration" was an understanding that so

* Untermeyer had been very prominent on the public side of financial shenanigans as a counsel to the famous Pujo Committee of Congress investigating the Money Trust in 1911.

far as practical, the legal work and legal fees would be equally divided between Dulles and Untermeyer. It had, in other words, nothing to do with the merits of the claims of the debenture holders against the bankers; it had only to do with "predatory" law practice.

I had Dulles on the stand for two days. He was the suave, smooth person the public later knew as Secretary of State. He posed as one wise enough, generous enough, and good enough to be able conscientiously to represent any number of conflicting interests. He was so unctuous and self-righteous that from then on we at the SEC called him a "Christer." He took the churchman's holy position that as an attorney he unfortunately had to do business with the underworld.

Our committee at once issued a subpoena for Untermeyer. A quick response came from his doctor, saying that a summer trip to Washington, D.C., when the humidity and the temperature were soaring, would most assuredly kill the man. That I did not want to do, but I did want Untermeyer's version of the John Foster Dulles story. I talked with Joe Kennedy, and he authorized a hearing at Untermeyer's country home at Hastings-on-Hudson. The day and hour were set. My old friend Thurman Arnold—lawyer, former mayor of Laramie, Wyoming, Dean of Law in West Virginia, and then on the faculty of the Yale Law School—was the hearing examiner. I arranged with Dr. George Draper to come along as my medical advisor, since I was sure Untermeyer would feign illness. Draper agreed to cancel all his engagements for the day and be at Hastings-on-Hudson at 9:00 A.M.—all for a fee of five hundred dollars, which I agreed to pay.

We met there at the appointed hour and I walked up the steps with Draper. Untermeyer was in a wheelchair under an arbor. I introduced myself and then introduced Dr. Draper as "my medical advisor." Untermeyer—smart, daring, witty—gave me a dark look. The hearing started, I doing the examining. I read from the Dulles transcript, bringing the events down to the fee-splitting agreement. Untermeyer passed out—his head to one side, his mouth open, his eyes closed, his breathing heavy. I motioned to Draper, who came over with his stethoscope. In a minute Draper turned to me and gave me a wink—the signal that all was well. In a few moments Untermeyer opened his eyes and I resumed the examination. Once again I came to the vital question as to the fees. At once Untermeyer "passed out" again. Once more I motioned for Draper. Once more he examined Untermeyer and gave me the wink. This happened several times, and each time I thanked the Lord for Draper. But for him I could see the hostile headline: "New Dealer Kills Untermeyer."

Finally Untermeyer stopped playing the game and took the center of the stage. He once more assumed the role of the champion of the underdog. He denounced all the John Foster Dulleses of the world, though finally admitting the churchman's payoff. The legal fees of the Dulles firm were $540,000; those of Untermeyer, $272,500. They were of course paid for services rendered, but their arrangement reflects the struggle not for fair treatment of security holders but for a division of the spoils among the lawyers.

I asked Draper afterward how he could be so sure that Untermeyer was not really sick. He said that his stethoscope could not pick up even the heartbeat, as Untermeyer had a cork type of chest, but Draper got his clue from the pulse, which at all times was steady.

I paid Draper the five hundred dollars by check and sent a bill to the commission, which was in due course rejected by the Comptroller General in a stinging opinion: "Why a lawyer at the SEC needs a doctor to help him make an investigation is a mystery. Moreover, there is no provision in the budget or the regulations authorizing it." I was never reimbursed.

Occasionally I spent an evening with Ferdinand Pecora and his assistant, David Schencker, whom I had known in Law School. Ferd had been counsel to the Fletcher Committee of the United States Senate Committee on Banking and Currency, investigating high finance and stock market manipulations prior to the 1929 market break that introduced the Big Depression. On those evenings I got an inquest on his earlier hearings.

Those hearings, thoroughly prepared, were quite unlike the ones later launched in the 1940's and continued during the fifties and sixties. Pecora, once aware that a witness would invoke the Self-Incrimination Clause of the Fifth Amendment, never asked the question.

I adopted the same policy respecting our SEC investigation of protective and reorganization committees under paragraph 211. Though I had few occasions to apply the policy, I never put a question to which I knew there would be a constitutional objection. When the forties, fifties, and sixties arrived, witnesses were put on the stand merely to see how many times they would invoke the Fifth Amendment. That practice ridiculed and debased rather than dignified the Bill of Rights.

I had been in Washington only a short time when the late Joseph Davies, then chairman of the National Democratic Committee, called all the "faithful" to luncheon at the Metropolitan Club, social headquarters of the Establishment. The faithful were, of course, Democrats holding public office in the federal government. The occasion of the luncheon, it turned out, was not fraternal but financial. The party needed funds, and the place to start raising them was with the faithful. At the end of the luncheon Davies made a pep talk, telling of the needs of the party. He closed by saying that he himself had contributed $40,000.

Turning to the man on his right, Davies asked him for his contribution. As I recall, it was $10,000. Twenty people later, my turn came. So far no one had contributed less than $5,000. I arose and said, "Mr. Davies, my devotion to the party is probably no less than that of anyone present. I pledge fifty dollars."

I felt as small as a mouse, but $50 was to me a spendthrift pledge. My young growing family was then costing me $3,000 more each year than my $10,000 annual salary, and the deficit was being financed by loans on my life insurance policies, a deficit that was to increase to over $15,000 during my five years at the SEC.

I spent a good deal of time, during my early years in Washington, with Joe Kennedy, who had brought his family to Washington. They lived in a manor in Maryland, where I spent many an evening getting to know all the children. Bobby was then nine years old; Jack, seventeen; Joe, Jr., nineteen. It was quite a clan. I never knew a closer-knit family. Each was interested in the other's activities; each was a fan as well as a critic. Their achievements were joint; so were their sorrows or mishaps. Joe was gruff; Rose was tender, tempering Joe's severity. There were usually outsiders at the dinner table, giving perspective to the conversation. Priests, educators, financiers—and professors, like myself. Each evening was a seminar. I could not help contrasting those evenings with my own in Yakima, where food was gulped, everyone too busy for dinner-table conversation.

Joe and I liked each other, became warm friends. Joe left the SEC in September, 1935, and Jim Landis was appointed chairman, but when there was a vacancy on the commission later that year, Joe Kennedy told me he wanted to get "the Boss" to name me to the office. So he took me over to see FDR, who greeted me warmly and said, "You're my man." Frank Maloney endorsed me, and my name went up for nomination. I was confirmed on January 23, 1936, and served from February, 1936, to September, 1937—taking a new leave of absence from Yale.

When my name was sent to the Senate, the Yakima *Republic* on January 29, 1936, editorialized as follows:

WALL STREET TAKE NOTICE

It is not every day that a Yakima boy can make the first page of the *Wall Street Journal* with a column article on his career, but W. O. Douglas made it. In his Yakima days he was known as Orville, later "the fellers called him Bill," but it was as William O. Douglas that the President sent his name to the Senate for confirmation as a member of the Securities and Exchange Commission.

He is traveling in pretty big company and takes Joseph P. Kennedy's place on the commission, though not as chairman. The latter is one of the big financial shots of Wall Street, who was drafted by the President to organize the commission which has for its major task that of keeping common people from getting their fingers burned in buying securities.

"Liberal" Douglas—another of his numerous appellations—is reported as having had six cents when he arrived at Columbia University. The chronicle does not state whether he spent it in high living, but he seems to have acquired a mastery at corporation law which has put him right up near the top of the entire list. Chairman Landis of the SEC is credited with the statement that Douglas has contributed more to the development of corporation law than anyone else in the country. That is covering a pretty wide territory for a man of thirty-seven years.

He was a small boy, a big boy and a high school teacher in Yakima, and he was a top-notcher in all those lines. He got his college work at Whitman and when he wanted a degree from one of the big universities, he rode the rails to New York and started to work on his law course.

Whether he reforms the world of finance and makes Wall Street a safe place for the lambs is not predictable, but he'll do it if anybody can, and Yakima will always be proud to say he lived here as a boy and started work here as a man, and above all, that he married a Yakima girl.

As I have said, when I became a commissioner, James M. Landis was chairman and the other members of the SEC were Robert E. Healy, George C. Mathews, and J. D. Ross.

Landis was of my vintage, and as a protégé of Frankfurter, had done the research and writing on numerous law-review articles, authored by Frankfurter and Landis. Jokingly we often called Jim "and Landis," which he found only mildly humorous. Jim was sharp-beaked, and his piercing eyes and prominent forehead gave him a forbidding appearance. He was as able as any New Dealer I knew. Some called him diabolical, but he was merely intense, withdrawn, introspective. He was born to be dean of a law school, and he would have had a distinguished career at Harvard in that post were it not for the fact that he fell in love with a woman who was not his wife and a divorce was indicated. Harvard would not countenance that. So he resigned as dean, obtained a divorce, married the other lady, came to Washington, D.C., and headed up the Civil Aeronautics Board until he crossed Truman, and then went to New York City to practice law. Although he was long a protégé of Joe Kennedy, Jim somehow went downhill in later years, finally pleading guilty to failure to file several federal income tax returns, and serving a short term of imprisonment. He died shortly thereafter.

Robert Healy was a Vermonter, and he never lost the salty independent character of the sons of Ethan Allen. He was tall and thin, and his receding hair and prominent forehead gave him a Jovian appearance. Healy would have adorned any chair of law in the United States. He had been on the Supreme Court of Vermont and later was counsel to the Federal Trade Commission, which, under his supervision, conducted an investigation of the abuses of public utilities holding companies. These hearings helped lay the basis for the Public Utilities Holding Act of 1935. Healy had a quiet sense of humor and a bulldog tenacity. He never forsook a position he once accepted and his good humor enabled one to tease him about it. He was a liberal in the Norris and La Follette sense of the word. He was impeccably honest and probably was the most implacable foe of the Establishment in my time. He would say over and over again that the holding-company system, as it had evolved, was a parasite. When Bob lost his temper, he became ash-white and was gentleman enough to leave the room until he regained his composure.

George C. Mathews got flaming red when he lost his temper. He was the opposite of Healy in most ways. He, too, was impeccably honest, but Bud, as we called him, was intellectually and emotionally geared to the Establishment. He came out of Wisconsin, where he was a rate expert and later head of a division of the Public Utilities Commission. He was as able as Healy, and my job when I became chairman was to serve as referee between those two contestants. Each had about the same boiling point. They sat opposite each other at the table, and often one went out one door, ash-white, while the other went out another door, beet-red.

J. D. Ross, who took Ferdinand Pecora's place on the SEC, was a public-power man from my state, Washington. J.D. was a promoter of public power. He built Seattle Public Power, the agency that harnessed the Skagit River, impounding water that formed the long finger of water in the North Cascades that is now called Ross Lake. At the time I thought J.D. was a knight in shining armor. When I later discovered the irreparable damage he had done to a river and its valley, I was disillusioned. Men could have been put to work digging coal in the North Cascades, and steam plants could have been built, saving the lovely Skagit for recreation. In the early SEC days J.D.'s job was a sinecure. He contributed virtually nothing to our SEC deliberations. We needed technicians in the world of high finance, and J.D. was as limited as a Fuller-brush man.

Later, when I became chairman, in September 1937, Healy and Mathews continued in office. I got FDR to name Jerome Frank to the commission. Jerry was a Chicago lawyer who had had a vivid experience in psychoanalysis and produced the famous book *Law and the Modern Mind.* He had left Chicago for the greener pastures of New York City, and gave up his practice there for service under the banner of FDR. Jerry had lost the battle of the sharecroppers at the Department of Agriculture under Henry Wallace, and was now a refugee. He found the SEC a stimulating spot. He knew corporation finance, having practiced in Chicago and in New York. He was as competent a person as any who ever came to Washington, D.C.

The fifth member of the commission was John W. Hanes, whom FDR was under great pressure to name in order to "protect" the interests of Wall Street. Hanes had been a securities broker in New York City, with a Stock Exchange seat. He was a hale and hearty Yale graduate with roots in North Carolina and long associations with the tobacco business and with the commodity exchanges. Johnny was a splendid person, very emotional, very protective of high finance, and very inexpert when it came to the ins and outs of high (or low) finance.

Our first general counsel was John J. Burns, who at thirty had been the youngest man ever to sit on the state bench in Massachusetts. Johnny—Irish, Catholic, quick-witted—was the leavening yeast in a serious-minded group. His humor was like a shaft of light penetrating a thickening gloom. He was the best dialect storyteller I ever knew—his Yiddish, Swedish, Italian, and Russian brogue equaling his Irish. He was also an accomplished lawyer of great integrity, who never trafficked in dirty tricks and brought high distinction to the Bar. Johnny left the SEC shortly to practice law in New York City, and tragically, fell on a busy street one night, unconscious but not dead. He might have been saved, but there was not one item of identification in his pockets. So he lay for three days in a city hospital, dying, when one telephone call would have brought the best doctor to his bedside.

Johnny had been the first to predict that FDR would run for a third term. "Sure and who wouldn't want to stay in a nice white house like that with the rent free?"

After Johnny left, in 1936, we had Alan Stroock, whose staff was replete with talent, including Louis Loss, later a Harvard Law professor and author of the monumental tract *Securities Regulation.*

Each division had a head, one of the ablest being Ganson Purcell, who headed Trading and Exchange, and his associate Walter Louchheim. Walter was an amazing man. His father had had a seat on the New York Stock Exchange, and Walter worked there after graduating from Harvard. The firm was Louchheim and Minton, one of the few companies that survived the debacle of 1929. It did so because Walter's father had a hard and fast policy—no partner would ever own any stocks.

After his father's death Walter sold the seat, left the Street, and returned to his first love—philosophy. He entered Columbia to get a doctorate in Aristotelian logic and metaphysics. But he never completed his doctorate, for when the SEC was formed, he was lured down to Washington about the time I went there, and became one of our truly able and preeminent advisors on stock-exchange problems. He served there until 1953, when he entered the investment-counseling business.

His wife, Katie, wrote the fascinating book *By the Political Sea.* She was for years very active in Democratic politics. Walter gave much of himself to civic and cultural affairs, establishing the Katie and Walter Louchheim Fund for chamber music at the Library of Congress. Yet to the end, his philosophy library was still his favorite.

He and John Harlan of the Court were both fastidious men, with a love of the good things of life and a passion for civilized standards. One of my last talks with Walter ran something like this. "Walter, I have known you for nearly forty years. Every time I started discussing finance with you, you cleverly shifted the conversation to Aristotle, philosophy, and logic. Here I am—a man who gave his best years to the government and never acquired a single security of any kind. Yet I was always associating with you, an investment genius who could have made me rich."

His eyes danced as he replied, "We both missed the greatest of all opportunities. In the fifties we should have bought all the islands in the Caribbean. By now we'd be so rich that Katie would never speak to me—and you, the leftist chairman of our old commission, would be so wealthy you would have become a Republican and have written reactionary Court opinions. Now do you understand why over the years we kept talking of philosophy?"

Walter many times had said I should be President, and I always smiled and waved him away. On this last talk he brought it up again. I said, "Walter, you and I are poles apart ideologically. Why in the world have you for years promoted me for the White House?" "It's simple," he replied, "you are a Scot and the only man I know who would have balanced the budget."

We were rich in talent at the SEC; and the energies of the men seemed endless. We would all work until six, take two hours out for dinner, be back at eight, and work until midnight or later, reporting by nine o'clock the next morning for another day.

The SEC had a staff of eighteen hundred men and women, and I was proud of them all. There were no "fixers" on the staff, and if one was suspected, he was quietly dropped. These were honest, idealistic, hard-working, and loyal men and women to the nth degree.

The industry never took them to lunch or dinner. All invitations by industry-connected people to spend weekends on yachts off Long Island or elsewhere were politely turned down. We were not holier-than-thou; we simply did not desire to get entangled in social affairs with those we were regulating, and thus unwittingly blunt the edges of the law. In my five years at the SEC only one man was dismissed, not because he had taken a bribe but because he exuded his susceptibility.

The SEC early became quite popular in government circles. We had of course plenty of antagonists, but no taint of unethical conduct ever touched it, nor did partisan politics motivate it. Above all else, the commission's performance was highly professional. Forty years after the SEC was established it still had the best professional staff of any agency in Washington. And it was not until 1973 that the first whiff of scandal touched it.

I took Gerhard Gesell, just out of law school, and pitted him against Dean Acheson in the New York Stock Exchange investigation—which started with the Whitney defalcation and reached into the mechanisms that made such acts easy. Gerry came out the winner, and in time was on the federal bench.

Abe Fortas had graduated from Yale in 1934. He came down to Washington that summer and worked with Jerome Frank at the Department of Agriculture. When I went to the SEC in October, 1934, Fortas became my right-hand man, as I have said, and he worked with me for five years. Abe, in commenting on our hard work schedule at SEC, would say, "We can at least outwork the opposition." And we all did, for the opposition was made up of middle-aged lawyers who got sleepy and tired come ten o'clock.

Abe and Martin Riger did yeoman service with the commission, as did David Ginsburg, later to be my first law clerk at the Court, Milton Freeman, Sigmund Timberg, Robert Page, Roger Kent, and many others.

I had two exceptionally able law clerks when I was a member of the SEC: one, Margaret Giorchino Corbin, now practicing law in Greenwich, Connecticut; the other was Quigg Newton, later mayor of Denver, president of the University of Colorado, and candidate for the U.S. Senate, and now head of the Commonwealth Foundation.

Louis Dabney, a Virginian with a bulldog's tenacity, did a very special job for me. Howard C. Hopson was head of the Associated Gas & Electric Company. Hopson was a lawyer and accountant extraordinary. He spun off affiliate after affiliate in the AG&E system, transferring assets from one to another and keeping firm though attenuated control of a whole family of companies. Showing AG&E to Lou Dabney was like giving a hound dog a glimpse of possum. Lou spent years tracking down his prey. I saw Lou only once in a while, yet every day he seemed to be resolving some mystery and reducing the anatomy of AG&E to understandable proportions. I think Hopson died before Lou finished his work. Lou's chronicles of the maneuvering were classic to hear, especially when he had a glass of bourbon and branch water and an entire evening to perform.

Two other sleuths were extraordinary. One was tall, thin, quiet, studious, and retiring. The other was corpulent, talkative, and gregarious. I would not see them for months on end, but eventually they would come in from the field with enough data to start civil suits against many promoters, and criminal cases against others. They did not pursue the Harvard, Yale, and Princeton men who dotted Wall Street. Their job was to go after the more disreputable but little-known promoters who sold even ten-cent shares of stock operating out of the "boiler rooms."

My mainstay against the elite was Pat Dowd. Pat was gentle or tough, as circumstances required. He was an expert accountant who could catch the biggest swindlers in the Street in no time.

I was proud of the youngsters of that day. Washington, D.C., became a young man's and a young woman's town. Some came to the capital to put on a better "feed bag" than they could get at home. Some left comfortable outposts where they were paid well to defend the status quo because the excitement of change was in the air and because they felt a responsibility to participate in the revolution. Some wished to escape the treadmill of trivial and repetitive legal work. The sense of freedom, the feeling of power over people and events, the desire for an all-out effort, the excitement of adventure—all these and more made lawyers, sociologists, economists, and political scientists march to the beat of the new drum that was echoing across the land. They poured in from all over the country, coming by freight and bus and Pullman cars, some hitchhiking, some walking. They were filled with idealism and fervor. The best of our men and women were available by the thousands. They literally begged to work for us at the SEC. They swarmed into the nation's capital, taking any available job. The air was filled with great expectation for a great crusade. FDR's voice galvanized people, as the gravelly voice of Harry Truman was later to drive them away.

The commission had three Acts to administer in the early years: the 1933 Act, which regulated the offer and sale of securities; the 1934 Act, which regulated stock exchanges and various practices of brokers and dealers; the 1935 Act, which called for the dissolution of public utility holding companies and the geographical integration of gas and electric systems.

In 1938, largely because of the leadership of my friend Senator Frank Maloney of Connecticut, the 1934 Act was amended to allow, under general supervision of the commission, the self-government of brokers and dealers on the over-the-counter market (which we facetiously called under-the-counter market).

In the 1930's we had figures showing that of the seven million separate holdings of common stock in the two hundred largest industrial corporations, eighty-eight percent were of a hundred shares or less; that less than one percent of the total number of stockholders held fifty percent of all securities listed on stock exchanges; ten percent of all shareholdings amounted to twenty-five percent of the value of all listed common stock and about seventy percent of the value of all listed preferred stock (by the 1960's one out of eight adults owned shares in publicly owned corporations in this country).

The large percentage of stockholders on the small side accentuated the need for investor protection. The problem reminded me of the golden-mantled ground squirrel in the Cascades who is the anchor man in the food chain. He is to predators what hamburger is to man. His enemies are many, including the coyote. In the capitalistic system the unsophisticated small stockholder is the ground squirrel, and the coyote had always been numerous. In the Far West coyotes, however, were for years poisoned or trapped.

The two SEC Acts mentioned provided only fair warning of the approach of the predator through full disclosure. This full disclosure was probably not important to the average small stockholder, as he was not able to analyze what he read, but the flow of truthful information reached the investment counselor who in turn could enlighten the unsophisticated. Hence the spotlight of publicity which we promoted had a cleansing effect.

So far as stock ownership was concerned, we felt that equally important was the disclosure of vital facts in proxy statements. While the country has had a wide popular base of stock ownership, the dispersion of ownership divorced the people from control. In most large corporations control lies in the management, which retains it by proxy solicitations. The management usually has to sin grievously to lose control. Vital facts disclosed in our proxy regulations were central to the new system of full and pitiless publicity.

Both prior to and during my SEC days I had promoted the idea of having "public" directors of our large corporations. (I wrote about this subject in my book *Democracy and Finance*, published in 1940.) The reason was that, by and large, directors tend to become subservient to the management, courteously serving its interests, which are not necessarily consistent with the interest of stockholders or compatible with the public reputation of the company. New Jersey adopted such a requirement for insurance companies and the history of its administration proved that at least some of the directors of our large corporations must not be subservient to management. This was a policy which the SEC had power to enforce. Under our federal administration corporate hierarchies were under the control of the states. And some states, conspicuously Delaware, have been a haven for companies with a bent toward shenanigans and inside operations for the benefit of insiders.

The commission was an integrated working mechanism unlike anything I had seen before or was to experience again. It had five members, and those five sat in session about eight hours a day, discussing problem after problem. The staff presented questions; sometimes they brought in protesting brokers, dealers, underwriters, corporate officials, or their lawyers. Concrete questions would be presented. For example, could a registration statement containing false statements be voluntarily withdrawn by the company in order to escape the stigma of an SEC stop order to prevent the sale of any securities under it? Or could we use the stop order as a prophylactic measure? That was a stirring issue in the mid-thirties and eventually the question reached the Supreme Court.

The SEC early ruled that a registrant who filed a statement governing the sale of securities could not withdraw the statement when the commission smelled fraud, and that the SEC could issue a stop order. In 1936 the Court, by a six-to-three decision, held that the registrant could withdraw the statement and avoid the sting of a stop order, saying that the SEC was acting like the notorious Star Chamber in the seventeenth century. Sutherland wrote for the Court; Cardozo dissented with Brandeis and Stone.

Cardozo said: "A commission which is without coercive powers, which cannot arrest or amerce or imprison though a crime has been uncovered, or even punish for contempt, but can only inquire and report, the propriety of every question in the court of the inquiry being subject to the supervision of the ordinary courts of justice, is likened with denunciatory fervor to the Star Chamber of the Stuarts. Historians may find hyperbole in the sanguinary simile."*

Most of our rulings did not have have the emotional content that propelled that case into the limelight. In case after case we had to determine whether registration statements filed contained false statements of material facts. Some representations were transparent—stock would be issued to promoters for services rendered and then returned to the company, which entered as assets on its books the value of the services allegedly contributed by the promoters. Ownership of nonexistent timber or mineral resources was advertised in these statements. Certification of the fiscal accounts of the company was made by an "independent" accountant, who was in fact only an undisclosed officer of the company. These and thousands of other artifices and devices had been historically used to

* *Jones v. Securities Commission,* 298 U.S. 1.

mulct the public, and in the early years of the 1933 Act the mettle of the new agency was tested over and again—as the early volumes of its decisions show.

The 1934 Act entailed the registration of brokers and dealers, and in the early years brought dozens of cases raising questions concerning the effect of prior criminal convictions and prior civil suits on the qualifications of the registrants. The suspension of their registration and their revocation of it were recurring questions. Registering securities on stock exchanges and delisting them involved nice questions of judgment, and the allowance of markets for unlisted securities often presented very complicated issues. What is a "security"? Is an oil royalty such? Was there "manipulation" of the market when securities were being offered? Were the prices "pegged" or "stabilized" in violation of the Act while an issue was being offered? What standards govern delisting of securities on an exchange? What standards govern a security's suspension?

More and more we became involved under the 1933 Act not only in the independence of accountants but in the reach of an accountant's certificate. What is the standard for a complete audit? What about securities listed or assets actually held in escrow? Can footnotes making full disclosure rectify falsehoods in registration statements? What contingent liabilities need be disclosed? When can property received for stock be carried at the par value of the stock? When can capitalization of the excess of total expenses over total income be treated as an asset? Can securities of no apparent value be carried at their face value as an asset, and later be written off against a reserve for losses?

The problem is an ongoing one. In 1973 the SEC proposed a rule that would require a financial statement as to whether more than one accounting principle had been used in the previous two fiscal years, significantly affecting net income. Battle lines have been drawn with the oil industry, as some companies write off the costs of drilling unsuccessful wells immediately as expenses, while others use "full costing." That means that those costs are amortized year by year over the life of the producing reserves. A shift from one method to another might producing startling results.

The role of the SEC in accounting matters has an interesting history. In 1936 and 1937 Robert E. Healy and I thought the commission should take the lead in formulating accounting principles as it was empowered to do under the 1933 Act. No one in the commission thought it should abdicate this responsibility. All of us had seen partners even in the best firms walk perilously close to the line both as respects civil and criminal liability. James Landis, in his speech of December 4, 1936, before the

Investment Bankers, said that our experience with accountants led us to conclude that the form of financial statements should not be left "to professional responsibility alone," that the SEC had a responsibility to see to it that financial statements were not misleading.

Our chief accountant, Carmon A. Blough, stated on December 13, 1937, that immediate SEC action on statements was required, but the commission often did not have time to do the extensive research necessary to formulate the correct accounting principles in a given case. Even though the prevalent practice seemed "improper," the commission (over my dissent and Healy's) often accepted a statement, provided there was in a footnote a "complete disclosure of the questionable matters."

On February 12, 1938, the commission appointed an intra-agency committee to work on "rules prescribing accounting practices and procedures."

Healy's view and mine were reflected in a Commission Release No. 4 on April 25, 1938:

> In cases where financial statements filed with this commission pursuant to its rules and regulations under the Securities Act of 1933 or the Securities Exchange Act of 1934 are prepared in accordance with accounting principles for which there is no substantial authoritative support, such financial statements will be presumed to be misleading or inaccurate despite disclosures contained in the certificate of the accountant or in footnotes to the statements provided the matters involved are material. In cases where there is a difference of opinion between the commission and the registrant as to the proper principles of accounting to be followed, disclosure will be accepted in lieu of correction of the financial statements themselves only if the points involved are such that there is substantial authoritative support for the practices followed by the registrant and the position of the commission has not previously been expressed in rules, regulations, or other official releases of the commission, including the published opinions of its chief accountant.

Healy had anticipated that ruling in an address on December 27, 1937, before the American Accounting Association, when he said the commission was undertaking "to express a few standards as to principles which we believe are accepted by a majority of good accountants, especially those who do not assume the role of special pleaders for their more lucrative clients."

One example he gave was preferred stock issued at eighty dollars a share with a par value of forty. On its balance sheet the company showed forty dollars a share for the preferred and ten dollars a share as "paid-in surplus." The company claimed the ten dollars could be used to pay dividends to the common stock. Healy denounced that practice. He listed other cases of like gravity and gave instances where the commission was divided, the majority clearing registration statements, though in Healy's view and in mine they were misleading. It was our contention that "if an earnings statement and a balance sheet reflect the results of improper accounting, they amount to misrepresentative and misleading statements in violation of the Security Act."

Healy said that "the commission will continue its efforts to develop a body of accounting principles through its decisions."

What happened in my time was a common-law development of precedents—case by case. Some principles were established by commission rulings, others by opinions of the chief accountant.

The Holding Company Act of 1935 presented a host of technical problems quite different from those under the two other Acts. Holding companies in the utility field were the top of a lush Christmas tree. Beneath were many money-machines controlled by the top figurine.

The top company might hold just enough voting stock in one company to control it, while the latter controlled a string of lower companies. The top company's control of a host of subsidiary or affiliated companies would be complete. Or it might issue nonvoting stock to the public, keeping the voting stock in its corporate family. Down at the bottom would be retail gas and electric companies.

The top pyramid of companies would place all sorts of charges on the retail companies. The top company or some other company in the hierarchy would enter into contracts with the retail companies to perform various services for them. Those services might include management, engineering, accounting, or tax or legal work and the like. The amount of the fees would be determined by the top company, not by competitive market prices. Through exaggerated fees, the top company saddled operating companies with enormous charges, which operating companies paid and which in turn were paid by the consumers of the gas and electricity.

The operating companies were regulated by state agencies; the holding companies were unregulated. They would buy operating properties having, say, annual earnings of $400,000 with bonds or debentures having annual charges of $3,000,000. The securities sold to finance the purchase would be siphoned through various companies in the hierarchy and gullible Mr. and Mrs. Public would end up buying them.

The value of securities of companies in the holding-company structure would be almost impossible to measure. Companies having common stock, preferred stock, and debentures would hold as assets securities in related or affiliated companies. The only real values were way down below in the operating companies. Estimating those values as represented in stock or debentures several companies removed was impossible.

Due in large part to Howard Hopson and Samuel Insull, the holding company in the utility field had become a monster, bleeding operating companies, selling stocks at fantastic prices, living only for the benefit of a few insiders and the investment bankers who serviced them. The insiders held the more secure or safe securities and those that gave control. Mr. and Mrs. Public held the speculative and nonvoting ones. The profits were enormous, but they went largely to the insiders.

The 1935 Act imposed a pervasive method of control on the system. Sales of securities were strictly controlled; corporate structures were simplified; intercompany contracts were screened; far-flung empires were reduced to integrated geographical units; holding companies were eliminated through the commission's authorization to permit not more than two tiers of holding companies over an operating utility.

The Act was bitterly fought. Though the abuses had been blatant and widely recognized, the financial community operating under the legal command of John Foster Dulles stood firm, decided that this New Deal measure was unconstitutional, and refused to make any move to live under it. I went among the investment bankers, whose main interest is money, and pointed out to them the great financial rewards available to those who took over the job of redesigning and reorganizing these systems and floating the new securities. But for once, principle transcended greed. The bankers thought FDR was doing them in, that he had crossed the forbidden constitutional line, and they would not knuckle under to him.

It was John Foster Dulles who, when the Holding Company Act of 1935 was passed, rallied the opposition. He summoned the heads of the major holding-company systems to a meeting and gave them the following advice: "The men who drafted and promoted this law obviously do not know the law or the Constitution. I can assure you that it violates basic constitutional guarantees and that the Supreme Court will strike it down. My strong advice to you gentlemen is to do nothing. Do not comply; resist the law with all your might, and soon everything will be all right."

A man who was present during this meeting told me what happened, and said that after Dulles' speech he was content to ride along with the status quo.

But the back of the opposition to the Act was broken by three Supreme Court decisions, the first decided in 1938 in an opinion written by Chief Justice Hughes sustaining the constitutionality of the provisions of the 1935 Act requiring public utility holding companies to register with the commission.* The second and third cases, decided in 1946 in opinions written by Mr. Justice Murphy, sustained the so-called "death sentence" provision of the Act which in general limited the number of tiers of holding companies over any public utility operating company—decisions in which I took no part, though I was on the Court, because I had been in hot pursuit of the villains in the areas at the SEC.

My friend who had heard Dulles' reassurances on the unconstitutionality of the Act was disillusioned. When I talked to him years later he made the following observation, rather philosophically:

"I came to distrust John Foster Dulles' judgment completely, so much so that when he was proclaiming against Vietnam and Peking in the 1950's and indulging in spectacular brinkmanship wherever the spheres of communism and democracy touched, I thought of his advice to us respecting the Holding Company Act of 1935. Since he was so wrong on it, how can I have any confidence that he is right on these more complex and less understood international problems?"

My friend was Cyrus Eaton of Cleveland, Ohio, philanthropist, organizer of the Pugwash Conference, utility and railroad giant.

There was strategy on both sides of the controversy. I had, as I recall, two hundred court injunctions against me, one federal judge in Maryland holding that the 1935 Act was unconstitutional—even the commas in it. We decided not to fight the injunctions at the time, but to select the best case for test litigation. Electric Bond & Share was chosen. We agreed with the Department of Justice that no criminal suits would be brought while the test case wound its way upward.

There were then over 140 registered holding companies controlling over fifteen hundred subsidiaries. By June 30, 1972, there were only seventeen holding companies controlling 184 subsidiaries, with assets of over twenty six billion dollars, constituting nearly twenty percent of the gas and electric industry in this country. Eliminated were the vast conglomerates and a maze of affiliated companies, some including properties in thirty-two states (such as Bond & Share) and some in over twenty five states (such

* *Electric Bond & Share Company v. SEC*, 303 U.S. 419.

as Associated Gas). The break-up established independent utility systems. The SEC finished its main job under the 1935 Act, and by the sixties was supervising securities issues by those systems which in 1972 equaled nearly three billion dollars.

In the 1930's America had not yet been introduced to the regime of politics for "destruction." Amiable, though rigorous, treatment was given the opposition. Somewhere at the SEC there is a file filled with material that might easily have resulted in an indictment of John Foster Dulles for perjury. But we decided to forget it and get on with the business of the day—which was not destroying people, but getting the work of the world done.

Many opinions were written at the SEC, all unsigned and mostly unanimous. They were published in the manner of court opinions and soon added up to a considerable shelf of books. They were drafted by the staff or by our law clerks, but carefully manicured by the commission, usually while we were in session.

Beyond those formal rulings were less formal considerations; the view of the commission would be sought as to whether a company would be in trouble if it took a specified step or course of action. There were in addition opinions of the General Counsel for reading, debate, and revision. Over and above all that was the drafting of rules and regulations. Those were new Acts and we were writing on clean slates. The ground rules for a particular industry had to be laid. Day after day, week after week we argued and debated, sending the staff back over and again for a revision. Finally, when we approved them, the set of rules would be made public and put down for a public hearing so that the people affected would have a chance to appear and be heard. That chance to be heard before the agency acted was, I thought, a healthy device for cooperative democratic solutions. It proved to be just that, adding to the luster and prestige of the commission.

At the SEC, I had established a small unit that scrutinized every bill introduced into the Senate or the House bearing directly or indirectly on SEC problems. One category of problems was bankruptcy, and our surveillance soon bore fruit. A staff member brought in a bankruptcy bill in 1936 that seemed to make neither heads nor tails. It looked innocuous. But what end would it serve?

It was H.R. 8940, 74th Congress 2d Session. It provided that only creditors who held a minimum of five percent of the total amount of all the indebtedness of the described type of corporation could put that corporation into bankruptcy reorganization. Further, it had a retroactive clause that would make it clearly applicable to the Associated Gas & Electric Company. The bondholders of that company would have to represent over thirteen million bonds in order to satisfy the five-percent clause. It was through this innocuous-looking loophole that the attorneys for Associated Gas & Electric hoped to evade the searching reorganization which the company was immediately facing. In other words, the bill fit one company and in the main benefited one company only—the American Gas & Electric Company.

I checked with the Congress and was told that the bill had been passed by the House and been rushed through the Senate earlier that morning. I raced across town in a taxi, went to the Senate cloakroom, and asked to see Senator Hugo L. Black, whom I had never met although I knew him as a champion of the Holding Company Act and as an enemy of corporate chicanery. When Black met me in the cloakroom, I introduced myself and said, "Senator, you have just done American Gas & Electric Company the greatest possible favor."

He flared up, saying, "Never in my life."

"This very day," I replied, and referring to the Senate bill by number, I added, "You voted for it."

"But it has nothing to do with American Gas & Electric."

"Yes, it does, Senator. By that bill, AG&E will be out of bankruptcy."

"Are you sure?"

"Yes."

"Positive?"

"Absolutely."

"Wait right here."

He literally trotted back onto the floor, to return in a few minutes to thank me and to say the Senate would recall the bill. The Senate did recall the bill and referred it back to the Judiciary Committee for an investigation. Senator O'Mahoney, Democrat of Wyoming, held hearings,* and I was there while O'Mahoney chastened the AG&E lawyers for foisting special legislation on an unsuspecting Senate.

After I became a commissioner I was much closer to the pulse of the agency than I had been as head of the Protective Committee Study, which now became the Reorganization Division or Bureau of the SEC.

* See Hearing, Subcommittee, Committee of Judiciary, U.S. Senate, 74th Congress, 2d Session on H.R. 8940, May 21, 1936.

As a result of complaint after complaint, episode after episode, encounter after encounter, the issue was posed whether the New York Stock Exchange as then constituted would ever rise to the occasion and adopt the kind of system visualized by the 1934 Act. The Landis view was that it was up to the Exchange. My view was that it was up to the commission. The only stout ally I had on the commission was Healy and it looked as if we would lose out.

Nineteen thirty-seven, however, rolled around and Landis had to leave the chairmanship to return to Harvard, where he was going to be dean of the Law School. He was in no hurry to leave; he apparently thought that if he could outstay me in Washington, the chairmanship wouldn't be decided.

I had recently been elected dean of the Yale Law School, and I planned to return there in September unless I was made chairman. My problem was that I had to report to Yale one or two days *before* Landis had to be at Harvard. The very last moment I could leave Washington was by the ten o'clock train on a Thursday morning. I had seen Joe Kennedy the night before and told him that I had lost out on the waiting game and would not be chairman. He said, "Let's wait and see."

I was having breakfast at the Cosmos Club at eight the following morning, September 21, 1937, when Joe called to say that I might be getting a very important call from the White House within the next few minutes—that he had just left Roosevelt and he thought that everything was back on the track. Sure enough, in a few minutes a call came from FDR, who said, "I hear you are leaving town." I replied, "Yes, I am just finishing breakfast and plan to catch the ten o'clock train for New Haven." Roosevelt replied, "Unpack your bag—you are the new chairman of the Securities and Exchange Commission." Once more it was Joe Kennedy who intervened with FDR.

I owed a very special debt to him, for by extending my government service in the Executive branch, he was indirectly responsible for the judicial appointment that came two years later. For if I had gone back to Yale, I would have been out of the mainstream and would not have been appointed to the Court.

The protective committee hearings lasted through 1935, and in time resulted in eight volumes, the report to Congress. The last few volumes were finished by the staff (principally Martin Riger) after I had taken my seat on the Court. Years later I went through those volumes and was amazed at the detail with which the anatomy of high finance and predatory practices on and off the financial markets had been set forth. Those eight volumes were never read, so far as I know, except by Vern Countryman—who was one of my first law clerks at the Court and who later joined the Harvard Law Faculty. He read them not for me, and not because he had been one of my law clerks, but because he was doing a book on the subject.

But the impact of the report was nonetheless considerable. It resulted in the Trust Indenture Act of 1939, 53 Stat. 1149, which in general raised the fiduciary standards of trustees acting under deeds of trust under which securities are issued. It also produced Chapter X of the Bankruptcy Act of 1938, 52 Stat. 833, under which the fairness and feasibility of reorganization plans of companies in bankruptcy were analyzed and reported on by the commission. The SEC had no authoritative voice; all decisions remained with the federal court, but under Chapter X the commission became the advisor of the court.

There were fine citizens as well as rascals who came to my office in the SEC days. One of the best was Harrison Williams, head of the North American Utility system. (He was the husband of the best-dressed woman in the United States.) In his dealings with me he was forthright and honest. While we did not always agree, we understood each other, and he cooperated to the best of his ability in working under the new law.

Robert Wood, former General of the Army and then head of Sears, Roebuck, was another. While Williams was suave, Wood was rough and grumpy. But Wood, too, had decided to live under the law, and he and I worked together to achieve that result amicably.

William Cavalier of San Francisco and Paul Shields of New York City were brokers and dealers and they, too, came with friendly attitudes; with these two I formed warm intimate friendships that lasted until they died.

Hopson of AG&E, already mentioned, was of a different breed—elusive, noncooperative, and hostile. Wendell Willkie, whom I met during this period, was an Indiana lawyer. He headed Commonwealth & Southern, a public utility that fought TVA.

Willkie was steering for politics and eventually became the Republican Presidential nominee. His political strategy was to attempt to make the New Deal appear to be paralyzing the economy and to make us New Dealers seem stupid. Willkie and his Commonwealth & Southern Company had a host of problems with the SEC and he came in often to see me. I would always politely rise as he entered and offer him a chair. He never would take my proffered seat; instead he would walk across the room, pull up a chair, sit down with his back to me, put his feet on the window sill, and bellow at me. What interested me most was that he kept his hat on—better to show his contempt. His approach was indeed juvenile. But it happened over and over again; so I knew it was a studied effort probably to make me lose my head and say indiscreet things. But I never followed suit, nor did my staff. Willkie in our eyes was an adolescent.

But Willkie was also smart and able. I remember particularly one day at lunch when the two of us were alone. Usually he did all the talking. This day I held forth on automation, big steel, big business, and who would eventually have control. He listened to every word, completely immersed. He asked only one question: "Did you send this up as a trial balloon?" I shook my head, and he, I realized, was subtly telling me something I already knew.

At the SEC we always thought Willkie outsmarted David Lilienthal, who from 1941 to 1946 was chairman of TVA, and prior to that, was one of its directors. That agency bought the power lines of Commonwealth & Southern. Willkie drove a hard bargain, to which Lilienthal bowed. Perhaps he was politically smart in paying the high price. We at the SEC thought Willkie got paid for a lot of phony assets, and we told Lilienthal as much. But he sealed the bargain and closed an ugly political row. We were surprised when David Lilienthal offered Willkie about eighty million dollars for the system, an offer which Willkie accepted. It seemed far too generous a figure by our standards. The generous offer did not reflect on Lilienthal's character, for it was impeccable; rather it was a question of judgment.

I had been chairman only a few days when the New York Stock Exchange went into great decline. Black Tuesday, September 7, 1937, was the day leading stocks went off as much as ten points. Black Friday was September 10, 1937, when some stocks went off twenty points, *The New York Times* index dropping 5.98, industrials dropping 9.65. The following Monday, prices on the New York Stock Exchange went off again.

Charles Gay, the Exchange president, called me every hour on the hour. "You must close the Exchange." I had the power to do so, but I knew if I did, the SEC would never recover from it. For the legend would be established that the New Deal was responsible for the market not operating. So I always told Gay, "Close it if you want to. I never will."

"But it's going down dangerously fast and will take all of America with it."

"I admit I don't know much about markets, coming as I do from

Yakima," I told him, "but I always assumed that markets were supposed to go down as well as up."

So the argument between Gay and me continued, day after day. Finally, FDR called me from Warm Springs, Georgia.

"What about this market?" he asked.

"Markets are two-way streets," I replied.

"But this one is going down as a result of a conspiracy."

"Whose conspiracy?"

"Business and Wall Street against yours truly."

"Mr. President," I replied, "you are dead wrong. The market is going down because you cut spending."

A few months earlier, in June, 1937, FDR had indeed slashed public spending sharply. He had cut public payrolls and curtailed public works. The budget had been balanced, and as a result, the 1937 recession ensued. Marriner Eccles of Federal Reserve, the Keynesian influence in the administration, was telling FDR the same thing as I was. Finally, in April, 1938, Harry Hopkins, recently out of the Mayo Clinic after a stomach operation, went to Warm Springs and sold FDR on deficit spending. On April 14, 1938, FDR scuttled his budget-balancing program and sent a message to Congress asking for a resumption of large-scale spending. So the 1937–1938 recession was finally overcome, all over Harry Morgenthau's dogged opposition and his insistence that a loss of "business confidence" had caused the recession.

Ganson Purcell of my staff made a brilliant analysis of the anatomy of the market in those desperate days. He painstakingly reconstructed this anatomy, showing the critical "inside" sales at the critical times. FDR was wrong, there was no conspiracy. But what was wrong was that the short sellers were pounding the market, accelerating its downward course. Purcell's devastating report, which I later made public, raised the question of the need for a better short-sale rule. The Exchange would not act; it was recalcitrant and utterly opposed to the regulatory scheme. If there were to be a short-selling rule, the commission would have to promulgate it. But we were not traders and had little practical experience in the trading mechanism of the market.

My one excursion into security buying had taken place years earlier, when I was practicing law at Cravath's. In those days every office in the Street was filled with rumors, echoes of rumors, "inside" information, tips, and the like. Every day I received whispered messages to buy this or sell that. Finally I succumbed.

The story I heard was that Southern Preferred A, then selling at eight, would go up to twenty-eight. I scraped together what I could. I sold an old phonograph, a war bond or two, and cashed in on a savings account. I raised, all told, about four hundred dollars and took it to a brokerage house, directing that Southern Preferred A be purchased on margin, which was then ten percent. About five hundred shares were bought, and since those shares held all my worldly goods, I kept my eye glued to market reports. At lunchtime I ate a sandwich while I watched the ticker. I bought every edition of the newspapers. I was exhausted by the time the market closed each day.

The first day Southern Preferred A went up three points; the second day it rose several more; by the end of the week it was over twenty. The following week it edged slowly upward until it reached twenty-eight. I rushed down the block to my broker and said, "Sell at the market price." He sold my block at twenty-eight and a quarter. Thereafter the price declined, until in a few days it was back at eight. What a fool I am, I kept saying to myself. Plainly a pool had been operating, insiders unloading shares as the market climbed. But I was not a pool member. I, in my ignorance, might just as well have bought at twenty-eight and sold at eight. This, my one "fling" in the market, had made money for me, but I knew enough never to go back.

So, when in late 1937 I was confronted with the need to write a short-selling rule, I sought expert advice. The man I first talked with was James Forrestal of Dillon, Reed, whom, at that time, I knew only casually. I came to trust him implicitly; he was frank and honest. Jim achieved national prominence shortly after our early acquaintance and he and I became very close friends.

In 1940, FDR was planning to run for a third term, breaking a precedent. He talked very little about his decision, his strategy, or his prospects. Those of us close to him gathered the drift of his thinking largely by intuition.

I spoke mostly to Tom Corcoran and Ben Cohen about the third term, though I also talked with "Pa" Watson, FDR's military aide, a good-humored, tight-lipped man who had taken a special liking to me. (I later learned that I had been Watson's choice to succeed FDR.)

This small group thought that if FDR was not going to run, he'd have said something to someone. We knew everyone of importance to whom he might have confided and he had not spoken a word on the negative side. Nor had he said anything on the positive side.

In the late spring of 1940 I was asked by Marguerite Alice (Missy)

LeHand, the President's secretary, to come to the Oval Room early the following day. When I walked in, a group of about six people were present, including FDR, Tom Corcoran, Harry Hopkins, Alben Barkley, and, I believe, Jimmie Byrnes. The talk was cheerful and casual for a few minutes and then Tom said, "Alben should give the keynote address."

FDR said neither yes nor no, but turning to Alben, said, "Alben, how are your vocal cords these days? I haven't heard you for months. How great it must be to be able to speak as you do."

And then he went off into trivialities about speakers, crowds, stage versus radio until Missy came in and said, "Your next appointment is here, Mr. President."

And as we trailed out of the room, FDR took my arm and said, "Always nice to see you, Bill." As we gathered outside before dispersing, our group stopped, and turning first to Tom and then Alben, I said, "You guys now have your marching orders."

The die really was cast before June, 1940. FDR decided to put on a new protective coloration by realigning himself in the public eye. Prominent and respectable Republicans had to come into the Cabinet and other places of responsibility. Henry L. Stimson, Wall Street lawyer, was avidly promoted by Felix Frankfurter. Who sponsored Frank Knox, I do not know, but on June 20, 1940, FDR appointed Stimson and Knox, respectively, as Secretary of War and Secretary of the Navy.

By that time James Forrestal was also being considered for a high-level job. He was not only receptive, he was putting out feelers. Paul Shields, of Shields and Company, a Wall Street brokerage house, approached me. He also had been go-between for Forrestal when I was wrestling with the New York Stock Exchange problems. Shields, I learned, always spoke for Forrestal.

Forrestal had expressed to Shields his desire to get out of the Street and into the Washington maelstrom. Shields thought this idea terrific and called me, asking my view. I said, "Sure. This is a great place for seminars in the area of adult education."

I spoke to Tom Corcoran, who nominally was attached to Jesse Jones and the RFC but who had been for some years FDR's "hatchet man." He had run numerous errands for FDR around the country and on the Hill. Tom had scouted universities and law firms for talent and was always recommending personnel to FDR and the various Cabinet officers. He "sniffed" out everyone coming to town whom he himself had not picked to see if they were all right. He had sniffed me out, concluding that I was far too conservative to be in charge of matters at the SEC—an opinion he changed only slowly.

Tom knew Jim Forrestal and thought it would be great to have him at the White House. Tom, essentially conspiratorial in his technique, and I, more blunt and outspoken, each in his own way took the message to FDR. Our plea was that Forrestal in the White House would help FDR acquire the conservative coloration he needed to win against Willkie, the businessman's choice, who even by June, 1940, seemed the likely Republican candidate.

FDR made Forrestal the fourth of six newly created administrative assistants in the White House. They were the so-called "secret six," who agreed to serve FDR with "a passion for anonymity." Forrestal first was assigned to Latin-American economic problems. But he worked there only from June 23, 1940, to August 5, when he was moved to the new office of Under Secretary of the Navy on August 5, again on urgings from Tom Corcoran. And when Knox died suddenly in 1944, Forrestal, at the urgings of many of us, was named Secretary of the Navy.

From June 23, 1940, until March 2, 1949, when under pressure from Truman he resigned as Secretary of Defense, Jim Forrestal and I were on close terms. I saw him very often, lunched and dined with him at least once a week, and was in frequent telephone contact. I mention this only because the public records of the day show only a casual relation between us. The reason was that while I was Jim's confidant, it would in his eyes have hurt his public image to be identified with me.

The River Club and Wall Street in New York City were Jim's spiritual headquarters, and I was not a favorite in either place. Jim never embraced me publicly; indeed, he sought to dissociate himself from me in the public eye. Since his own closest ties were with the Establishment, his psyche demanded that *It* think well of him. Yet he rebelled against it, and I was an expression of his rebellion. It came to pass, as crises in his life mounted, that I was with him night after night, pacing the floor, trying to help him untangle the imaginary skein of troubles and woes that seemed to encompass him. This man, with unflinching physical courage, who landed with the Marines at Iwo Jima, was not at home in the world of psychological warfare. He left white-tie dinners to walk with me in the dark, unburdening himself, transferring his problems to me. He left family and friends to telephone me at any hour of the night. He would say, "Bill, something awful is about to happen to me."

I never failed him except the night he died.

Jim leaned on me heavily, but he felt he couldn't introduce me to his friends at the River Club because they would consider me a pariah. He didn't realize that *they* were the pariahs. Still, Jim's attitude did not bother me. I had no ambitions he could help me to achieve.

He was a strange man who was, in many respects, very brave. For example, as I have said, he would go out to the South Pacific and participate in Marine landings and, apparently, not think of the dangers. One Friday afternoon during the war he called me and said, "I'm leaving for Iwo Jima on Tuesday. Would you like to come?"

I looked at my calendar, saw that the Court would not be sitting, and agreed to go. Then, on Monday night, he called to say that the plane was full and there would be no room for me. Thus, I missed the landing of the Marines at Iwo.

When Truman eased Jim out as Secretary of Defense in favor of Louis Johnson, Jim was outwardly calm but inwardly in turmoil. He had called me over to the Pentagon one night and the two of us had a long session. Louis Johnson's friends in the press were laying down a barrage on Jim, and he could not stand that kind of pressure. The rumors spread that Jim had psychological difficulties which made it imperative that he leave government. But that was only Louis Johnson propaganda. Jim was as stable and in as good health as he'd ever been.

One afternoon at about five o'clock I drove to the Pentagon to see Jim once more, and we had another long, long talk of several hours. I laid out a program of counterattack whereby he would answer Johnson. "This is war, Jim," I said. "It's like Iwo Jima, but it's newsprint, not bullets, that's being used against you."

I had a public relations man in mind who could do the job—James Allen, who was my buffer at the SEC. Jim almost agreed, but then rejected the idea. In a few days he was eased out of office, attended a dinner in Johnson's honor, and left for Florida. In Florida he got worse and worse, and obviously needed hospitalization and psychiatric care. He came back to Washington and checked into the Bethesda Naval Hospital on the outskirts of the city. He seemed to be getting better, and as a result, the hospital surveillance of him was lifted.

But on the night of May 23, 1949, Jim Forrestal died. Apparently he had planned to strangle himself by tying one end of a sheet to the radiator of his room, the other end around his neck. He slipped out of the window and hung briefly—but the sheet slipped its knot and Jim Forrestal fell fourteen stories to the ground. I wept, for I had been on my way to the hospital and might have saved my friend's life. It hurt me very deeply. I felt I had let my friend down.

Back in 1937, when I had asked Jim for advice on drafting a short-selling rule, he told me he would have someone see me, provided, *first*, the meeting was secret, and *second*, no one would know, when the rule was announced, who my advisor had been. I pledged my word, and Jim said, "Your man is my partner, Clarence Dillon; he will see you next Sunday night at his Park Avenue apartment. Be there promptly at nine in the evening."

So I was to meet the man known as the "Wolf of Wall Street." I could hardly believe it. When I had been at the Cravath firm, Robert T. Swaine had gone to see Dillon to get the Dillon-Reed account. Dillon kept Swaine waiting two hours, until Swaine, also a proud man, stormed out. So I expected to be kept waiting. And I was. Dillon's liveried butler offered me a Scotch and soda at nine o'clock, another at nine-fifteen, and a third at nine-thirty. Then Clarence Dillon swept into the room with the dignity and grace of a Barrymore. He knew what my mission was and swore me to secrecy. I handed him a sheet on which we had written three possible short-selling rules. He was lost in thought for perhaps five minutes; then he stood up, handed me the paper, and said, "If you want to do an effective job, take the first one of those three rules."

I thanked him, caught the sleeper back to Washington, and in the morning, after swearing my colleagues to secrecy, announced the promulgation of a famous short-selling rule, which was, in substance: no one may sell short at less than one-eighth above the last sale price. That rule has governed the market for over thirty-six years.

Not many weeks passed before the Stock Exchange was delivered into my hands. Charles Gay came down one afternoon to announce that Richard Whitney, president of the Exchange, had misappropriated a client's securities. I at once got hold of Pat Dowd, chief investigator in New York City, to get the relevant records at the crack of dawn the next day.

I broke the news to FDR while he was having breakfast in bed. He and Whitney had been at Groton together but Whitney had become the symbolic head of the Establishment that opposed Roosevelt. When I told him that Whitney had been arrested, he said, "Not Dick Whitney!"

"Yes," I replied, "Dick Whitney."

"Dick Whitney—Dick Whitney," he kept repeating. "I can't believe it."

The Old Man, as we affectionately called FDR, came close to tears. The news did not elate him. Rather, it greatly saddened him. He only added, "You'll know what is best to do."

Whitney's brother was the House of Morgan, *the* Establishment. This felony charge was a blow to it. Thomas E. Dewey had been elected district attorney in New York in 1937 and telephoned me in the morning that Whitney would be arraigned that afternoon, plead guilty, and be sentenced.

"That's the end of the matter," Dewey insisted.

"It's the beginning," I replied.

"Give me all the records your people have."

"When I have finished."

"We must close this whole nasty business out today."

"We must have a full-fledged investigation."

We had such an investigation, and I named Gerhard Gesell to conduct it. Though he was just out of law school, he did a masterful job, disclosing the whole anatomy of Wall Street chicanery and corruption. The Exchange's counsel was Dean Acheson—the suave counterpart of John Foster Dulles—not as garrulous, but like-minded. Acheson was elegant, able, fastidious, and conservative. He served briefly as Under Secretary of the Treasury and graciously bowed out when his conflict with FDR over the gold policy developed into a head-on collision. (He recounted that brief career in *Morning and Noon,* published in 1967.)

Acheson was a spokesman of the Establishment in 1937 and continued as such even when, later, he was Secretary of State under Truman. His advocacy in that position tragically fostered the Establishment as the image of America that was seen by the world in the postwar years.

When the news of Whitney's defalcation was made public, I announced that we were going to reorganize the New York Stock Exchange. The board of the Exchange sent me William Jackson, who was a partner in FDR's old law firm, Carter, Ledyard and Milburn. He was smooth, suave, and severe.

"Now that you are going to take over the Exchange, perhaps you'll need some technical advice. It's not self-operating. It needs manpower and brains. Perhaps I can help you."

I remained silent for a while, pretending to be deep in thought. Finally I said, "There is one thing you can do for me. Tell me where you keep the paper and the pencils."

The message was clear. We meant business. Soon Jim Forrestal called, saying that Paul Shields would see me. Paul was on the board and leading the fight for reform. Would I work with him? My reply was that I would if he were serious. He assured me that he and his minority bloc were just that. So we laid our plans first to make the management of the Exchange less like that of a club and more like that of a public institution; and second, to revise all the rules necessary to take away the insider's advantage over the public.

Dissident Exchange members like William Cavalier of San Francisco also came to see me. Paul reported to me after every board meeting. The board hired John W. Davis for his legal and strategic advice. They had public relations men galore, snowing us under with adverse publicity. In time the Shields group got control of the board and elected William McChesney Martin of St. Louis as president. Bill was a young, bespectacled broker who was a whiz at tennis. In time he became head of the Federal Reserve Board. He was at all times a public-spirited, honest man, and we got along well.

Shortly after the Exchange reform, I went to New York City to address the masters of Wall Street at a big dinner. I wished them well in their new administration, saying I stood by "with a police escort." That made some of them angry and others troubled. Free enterprise, which had converted the stock exchanges into modern Augean stables, was still fighting for opportunities to exploit the unsuspecting public. We were there to make sure they did not succeed.

On March 17, 1938, the Board of Governors of the Stock Exchange voted to expel Richard Whitney from membership. The same day it approved a report of a committee headed by Carle C. Conway, a handsome man who was chairman of the Board of Continental Can Company, which recommended, *inter alia,* that three representatives of the public be made members of the thirty-man Board of Directors. One of these three public members was my friend, Robert M. Hutchins, who served only briefly. His letter of December 15, 1938, to the new "reform" President William McC. Martin read as follows:

> As I intimated at the board meeting yesterday, I must resign as a representative of the public on the Board of Governors of the New York Stock Exchange.
>
> In the hearings before the Securities and Exchange Commission there was evidence tending to show that members of the

> Exchange or their partners knew of Richard Whitney's criminal conduct or of the condition of his firm some months before its failure. The public interest, the good name of the Exchange, and the good name of the members referred to all require the Board of Governors to institute proceedings in which the question of the responsibility of these members may finally be disposed of. The decision of the board yesterday to take no action compels me to present my resignation.

Hutchins was clearly right in his protest. The Exchange, though "reformed," was still a cozy club.

The sordid details are all revealed in our 1938 report on the Richard Whitney matter, which resulted from the investigation made for the SEC by Gerhard A. Gesell. This investigation and report revealed the names of various Exchange members who knew of Whitney's wrongdoing before the news broke. But nothing was ever done by the Exchange to discipline or censure any of these members.

As the months went by, FDR took the Whitney matter more lightheartedly. It came about that as I walked in to see him from time to time, he would rub his hands and say in his exuberantly devilish manner, "Bring me another victim so that I can disembowel him." And then he would feign disappointment when I announced I had no such victim for him that day.

In those days Sidney J. Weinberg of Goldman, Sachs and Company, one of Wall Street's leading investment bankers, would come into my office with a worried look on his face; it seemed that he was worrying because I had done him a grievous wrong. "What's the problem?" I'd ask. And he would say, "Can't you let us have a daily volume of trading on the Big Board of six hundred thousand shares?"

I asked him what I had to do with the volume of trading, and his reply was that until the New Deal, everything had been fine, the volume was up, and brokers could live on their fees. But now, he asserted, it was different; it had to sell at least six hundred thousand shares a day for brokers to break even. And so we went, round and round.

Sidney Weinberg was called Mr. Wall Street. He was bright, amiable, and as conservative as Adam Smith. We later served for years together as members of the Visiting Committee of the Harvard Business School. At every meeting he spoke an aside, accusing me of ruining the country. Once we met just after the case had been argued concerning the constitutionality of Truman's seizure of the steel mills. "The Court hasn't got the guts to hold it unconstitutional," he said in a loud aside. Although we did so hold,* I am sure it made not a whit of difference in Sidney Weinberg's opinion of anyone having anything to do with the New Deal.

One policy consideration kept us from a lot of trouble and embarrassment. Eager beavers on the SEC staff wanted me to sign subpoenas in blank so that without further ado they could fill in anyone's name and any documents or other files they wanted to obtain. But we always denied those requests, believing that subpoenas had to be closely delimited, and in the interests of even corporate privacy, only select documents should be subpoenaed.

Another practice that existed when I came to Washington, and which still continues, is the use of the stamp marked "secret." I had such a stamp, but I never used it, for I believed it was only a device to cover the footprints of a bureaucrat. Over the years I became amazed at the easy use to which the "secret" stamp was put and at how sacrosanct documents so stamped became.

There doubtless are "secrets" in government, such as the codes we use to transmit delicate diplomatic discussions, which need protection. But the whole device has been carried so far as to sweep what any administrator wishes to call "national security" under the rug.

That is largely hogwash. For example, when the Pentagon Papers came to court, resulting in a famous decision, I read all of them, those published as well as those in camera. They did not contain any significant fact I had not known all along. I had no CIA or FBI working for me, but I had made numerous trips to Vietnam, had written a book (*North from Malaya*) about it, had numerous Vietnamese friends, and read *The Vietnamese Times.* (This newspaper was published in Saigon by Gene Gregory, our only expert on Vietnam, who had been released by the Eisenhower-Nixon administration in 1953 because he was a "poor security risk." The risk was that Gene, like myself, had thought that the United States should not support the French in Vietnam.)

I had also known Ngo Dinh Diem, stayed with him on my trips to Saigon, and seen him on his visits to Washington, D.C. So the Pentagon Papers contained no "news" for me. If I, sitting on the sidelines, knew every detail, certainly the "enemy," whoever that might be, knew it long before I did.

. . .

* *Youngstown Sheet and Tube Co. v. Sawyer*, 343 U.S. 579 (1952).

I seldom got into court in SEC days. John Burns, Alan Stroock, and other staff lawyers attended to these details. Once, however, I appeared before Judge John P. Nields of the federal District Court in Wilmington, Delaware. Delaware was a tobacco-producing and a tobacco-chewing state in the thirties. Judge Nields' courtroom was adorned with spittoons about two feet high, made of copper and highly polished each day by a caretaker. The spittoons were placed up and down the aisles, and lawyers and others in the audience would take aim at one eight or ten feet away and always hit it, causing it to emit a slight hum. This day I was engrossed not in the case Judge Nields was hearing, but in the aim of men who were champions in tobacco-juice-spitting.

The case then being tried ended, and Judge Nields said he would entertain a motion in another case. The lawyer was a woman, who was obviously a bit flustered and nervous as she came up the center aisle, thumbing through her papers as she walked toward the bench. She had almost reached it when she stumbled over a spittoon. Down she went with her papers, and out of the spittoon came a generous portion of tobacco juice. I helped the lady up, righted the spittoon, and took my seat. Down came the gavel of Judge Nields, and turning to the lady lawyer, he gave profuse apologies with the grace of any man endowed with Southern manners. Turning to the bailiff, he directed that all spittoons be banished now and forever from his courtroom. Thus does law, I thought, edge slowly and hesitantly toward a regime of justice.

The old SEC days with which I was once familiar marked the "horse-and-buggy" era of American finance, having little relationship to the nature and complexity of today's corporate and financial problems. By the seventies the financial community had changed considerably, presenting problems of vastly different proportions. The growth of social security at the governmental level had been paralleled by the growth of pension plans in the private sector. Pension-plan funds alone totaled roughly thirty billion dollars. Control of these funds was in the hands of a half-dozen banks. The total institutional funds in the stock market was at least two hundred billion. The presence of these vast funds dislocated the capital market, starving some blue chip companies and putting others under new systems of control. It may even have driven the individual more and more out of the market and changed the nature of the process of obtaining capital contributions to industry. The big banks offered checking-account customers plans whereby they could buy stocks from a list, say, of twenty-five securities, and pay for them by automatic deductions from their checking accounts. The protests of brokerage houses were vociferous; and the extent to which the activities of banks in securities transactions is barred by Acts of Congress is not yet fully resolved.*

Moreover, the depreciation of the dollar overseas led to its easy acquisition. The vast expenditures being made by us in Middle-Eastern oil led to the acquisition of controls of American corporations by the new Middle East capitalists.

Purchase of interests in American companies is the ploy not only of Arabian sheiks but of Japanese businessmen as well. Japanese capital is already building a steel mill in Auburn, New York; the Japanese have purchased West Coast canneries and are buying into various American businesses. Numerous facets of the reality of One World are developing.

The multinational corporation emerges more and more as a new political force. The temptation to dabble in overseas politics, as ITT did in Chile, will increase. Foreign interests, investing in our companies, will seek to manipulate our policies just as ITT sought to maneuver Allende of Chile into defeat.

My own feelings about the changes in the financial world were summed up when the SEC celebrated its twenty-fifth anniversary. It was 1959 and Dwight Eisenhower was President. The dinner was a gala affair, many of the old staff were on hand and most of the new. An early speaker had mentioned the big drives in "boiler rooms," the covert switchboards where a bevy of high-powered salesmen worked over sucker lists for sales of securities that had no more realizable value than the blue sky above us.

Many other speeches were made, and when it came my turn the hour was late and I made it short.

I said, "The main difference I see between the old SEC and the new one is that we put in prison a much higher type of person."

Will those who control government policies be brave and wise enough to put in prison or out of business the new buccaneers who operate in the traditions of Vesco, ITT, and those of like ilk?

McCloskey, in *American Conservatism*, published in 1951, asserts that the entrepreneurs who emerged after the Civil War "acknowledged no morality but pecuniary success." In this century big business has been anti-free enterprise. Acquisition of wealth and power took priority over

* 401 U.S. 617.

the development of the moral capacities of the individual. Big business behaved like bandits raiding a frontier. The gospel of wealth was equated with man's dignity before God; exploiting the community became a way of life. Material values were bedecked with moral or ethical values. The "liberty" of industrial giants to become heads of powerful principalities with great political clout was honored by the courts though these giants had no technical competence to do anything except to make money. It is indeed ironical that in this technological age industry cannot make a pollution-free car or mine sulfur in smokestacks rather than in the ground.

Chapter XIX

The Bureaucracy

The great creative work of a federal agency must be done in the first decade of its existence if it is to be done at all. After that it is likely to become a prisoner of bureaucracy and of the inertia demanded by the Establishment of any respected agency. This is why I told FDR over and over again that every agency he created should be abolished in ten years. And since he might not be around to dissolve it, he should insert in the basic charter of the agency a provision for its termination. Roosevelt would always roar with delight at that suggestion, and of course never did do anything about it.

After experience with administrative agencies at the federal level, it seemed to me that most agencies become so closely identified with the interests they are supposed to regulate, eventually they are transformed into spokesmen for the interest groups. That I think is demonstrably true of the Interstate Commerce Commission, the Civil Aeronautics Board, the Maritime Commission, the Federal Communications Commission, the Bureau of Mines, and the Federal Power Commission. The Public Health Service met the same fate by a different route. It became in effect a satellite of state public health agencies, which were in turn controlled by the industrial polluters and other members of the Establishment. The Federal Trade Commission escaped that fate by spending its time, energies, and budget only on the trivialities of business affairs rather than on the really serious problems.

The SEC was not like this in the early days, probably due to a number of exceptional circumstances. It was new, its personnel fresh, and their dedication to the purposes for which the agency had been created was less likely to be tempered by years of pressure from interest groups than was the case with those in older, more established agencies. Finally, the SEC had in the 1930's the strong backing of the President, something not always true in other eras.

FDR was usually willing to back us up whenever the SEC really needed it. Often we were subject to intense political pressures from the same individuals and groups who had a vested interest in SEC activities. One such incident involved our investigation of Transamerica, a Giannini company in the Bank of America nest of companies.

I knew that A. P. Giannini had been a heavy contributor to the Democratic party. So, before cracking down, I went to see FDR.

"Is the front door to the White House closed when I move in on Transamerica?"

"Absolutely," he replied.

"Mr. President, how about the back door?"

FDR roared with laughter and said, "The back door, too, is closed."

Transamerica's trading activities had caught our eye in 1936 and 1937 and we followed them closely. We were then looking into market manipulations on the West Coast, and some such scheme by Transamerica was clearly under way. In 1938 we entered a formal order of investigation, and the wrath of Giannini, a towering giant of a man, descended.

He came to Washington to try to dissuade me, but without success. Not being able to deflect the investigation, in spite of his generous contributions to the Democratic party, Giannini took another tack. He hired a public relations man in the nation's capital, paying him, according to the scuttlebutt, a fee of $100,000. This man's role was to denounce and discredit the SEC, and me in particular—to snow me under. I was followed and investigated for scandalous views. When nothing came of that, the public relations man held regular press conferences in which he subjected both the SEC and me, in particular, to vindictive verbal barrages.

We made immediate rejoinders. My mainstay in this regard was James Allen, who had been on the staff of *The New York Times* and came down to Washington "for the duration." Jimmy, who was later to go high up in the electronics industry in the Northrop Corporation, prepared press releases for me. And so the battle of words went on for some months, until A. P. Giannini tired of that game. During those months I developed what I called "calluses." I had always been thin-skinned, quick to resent criticism and very sensitive to brutal frontal attacks as well as to more subtle ones. Thanks to Giannini, I became almost immune, and the calluses I acquired under his assaults were to stand me in good stead in the rough days ahead.

Giannini never really gave up, he only changed his tactics, wearing out my investigators. I remember one tough hombre I hired, whom I was sure no one could deflect. I sent him to Los Angeles to man the Western front against Giannini. Two days later I saw on the front page of the *Los Angeles Times* a picture of my tough hombre with his arm around A.P., and Eleanor Roosevelt on the other side. But despite the pressure, we finished the job on Giannini and eventually cleaned up an unwholesome situation.

One evening in Washington, D.C., I got a call from Missy LeHand, the President's secretary; she said that a New York Stock Exchange committee was going to Hyde Park to see FDR at noon the next day. (My relationship with Missy was close and trusting. She knew he liked me and that I would never take personal advantage of him.) She asked if I would come. Since things were stacked up high on my desk, I asked if FDR had suggested that I be there.

"Certainly," she replied. "They are coming up to have him fire you!"

I took the sleeper to New York City and caught an early-morning train to Poughkeepsie. From there I went to Hyde Park by taxi, arriving before ten o'clock. Having two hours on my hands, I decided to take a hike. I walked mostly on the roads and soon found myself in a tunnel under the bluffs of the Hudson. The lane was so narrow that I had to stand flat against the wall when two cars passed. When an extra-wide truck met a car, I actually had to pull in my stomach to avoid injury, and even so, the side of the truck brushed my lapels.

When I walked into FDR's office with the Stock Exchange committee at noon, I complained about the hazards of hiking in Hyde Park. I then told the story in detail.

Roosevelt took my story as a cue to filibuster the committee. For one half-hour he held forth on the hazards of travel, the hazards of tunnels, and the hazards of trains and automobiles. He told a weird, rambling story of his experience on a freight train somewhere in Montana. He went on and on, lighting one cigarette after another. Then, at twelve-thirty, Missy walked in, saying, "Sorry, Mr. President, but your next appointment is waiting."

I stood up, as did the members of the committee, and went to the desk where FDR sat, to say good-by. He took each of us by the hand, squeezing it fraternally, and saying with a smile, "Be sure to come up any time anything bothers you."

FDR gave me a wink and we all left. The Stock Exchange committee members had never had a chance to say even one word, and they gave me dark looks as we filed out. I stopped by to tell Missy that apparently the committee had changed its mind about having me fired!

Frank W. Boykin of Alabama was another of those who tried to put pressure on the SEC. Boykin was in Congress in the 1930's, and retired in the 1960's only after having been convicted in a federal court in Maryland under the conflict of interest statute.* When I was chairman of the SEC, Boykin came to me, protesting our order that stopped the sale of securities of a company organized to exploit mahogany in Mexico. Our field investigation showed the scheme to be fraudulent, there being no mahogany trees in the area described.

Boykin was in my office the next day demanding that the stop order be lifted. The promoters were honorable men, he said, "real Americans who make the wheels of industry turn, not like some bureaucrats I know." He pounded the desk, demanding immediate action. I quietly told him the stop order would never be lifted as long as I was chairman.

"Then we'll get a new chairman." Putting on his hat, he added, "Young man, you'll be fired within the hour."

As he walked out, I followed him.

"Where are you going?" he demanded.

"To the White House with you to be present when I'm fired. It's an event I wouldn't miss for anything."

At that time the SEC was located in the southeast corner of Pennsylvania Avenue and 18th Street N.W., so we had only one long block to go. We walked in silence until we came to the northwest gate, where I turned in. But Boykin kept on going.

"Hey, Mr. Congressman," I called. "Aren't you going to get me fired?"

"Oh, go to hell," he shouted as he continued down the avenue.

Another episode of political pressure on the SEC involved the White House more directly. One day Charles Schwartz, a man in his forties, came in to see me. He was the man who had cultivated Mrs. Dodge of the Dodge Motor Company and obtained an option from her for her Dodge stock. He sold the option to Dillon Reed for five million dollars and Reed reorganized the Dodge Motor Company, taking out as its fee

* 337 F. (2d) 180, 184.

thirty million dollars in the process. By 1938 Schwartz was looking for new worlds to conquer. The day of his meeting with me, his arrival was announced from the White House. An official car was meeting him at the airport and delivering him directly to my office.

Schwartz appeared on schedule and wasted no time putting his proposition to me. He desired to arrange with each holding-company executive in the electric-power field to be its representative before the SEC. If I had problems with these utilities—North America, American Gas & Electric, Commonwealth and Southern, or any of the rest—all I would have to do was call him.

I was astounded and suspicious, and as soon as Schwartz left, I sent at once for Harrison Williams, who was head of North American. (Williams, dark, well groomed, was a real gentleman. He was one of the first to realize that blood chemistry was the key to health, and he had a New York doctor who kept close tabs on him.) I saw him often, and while his company had tremendous problems under the Public Utility Holding Company Act of 1935, he was anxious for cooperative action. He realized that the time had come for all public-utility holding companies to put their houses in order. I did not trust Willkie; I suspected most of the other utility heads. But I trusted Harrison Williams and believed he would tell me the truth.

What Williams told me shocked me. He had been called by the White House operator and told to come to Washington, where he was met by a White House car and presented to Charles Schwartz in the Executive Offices. Schwartz told him that for $100,000 a year he would handle and solve all of North American's problems with the SEC. Holding-company executive after holding-company executive was called or approached, according to Williams, and each was offered the same proposition. Schwartz would have fees of at least thirty times $100,000 a year. It was becoming apparent that Schwartz and Jimmy Roosevelt hoped to get my approval of that working arrangement. They thought that if the major utilities had already been lined up, it would facilitate matters with me.

The White House car and the Executive Offices meant to me that the White House was deeply implicated in what could be, up to that time, the biggest scandal since Teapot Dome.

I told Williams he would be a fool to pay Schwartz even ten cents. My door was always open and it cost nothing to come in. Moreover, no one had an "in" with the SEC; there was no "fix" in existence, or possible. After he left I dictated a letter to each holding-company president, stating that fact, and sent it off with commission approval:

> Neither Mr. Schwartz nor any other person is the intermediary between this commission and the utility companies. He is not on our payroll; he has never been on our payroll. He has not received any authorization from us. Nor are we relying upon him for advice or counsel in any of the problems pertaining to the Public Utility Holding Company Action of 1935, or any other matter. In other words, he is in no sense whatsoever, either an intermediary between the commission and the utility industry, nor a representative of this commission. Nor does the commission have any other intermediaries.
>
> I can tell you, as I have told other officers and representatives of utility companies, that if they desire to consult the commission, they should do so directly with members of the commission or members of its staff, and not rely at all on any representations made by persons not falling in those categories.

Schwartz came back in a few days, fuming. Who was I to interfere? Then, James Roosevelt, the President's son and an administrative assistant to the President, called to speak a good word for Schwartz. Jimmy soon came to my office, raising the roof. He said that any stupid fool would know that the only time Democrats could make money was when they were in power: "What chance do we have when the Republicans take over?" I reminded Jimmy that I was not in public office "to make money"; and he stormed out of the office.

Finally, the plot had so thickened that I went over to see FDR, tendering my resignation as chairman. I told him what had happened, and that it seemed to me I stood in the way of ambitious people, that the White House was deeply implicated, and that I no longer could serve. FDR put his head on his arm and cried like a child for several minutes. Finally, wiping away his tears, he said with a faint smile, "Jimmy! What a problem he is. Thanks for telling me. Now get back to your desk. Of course you're not resigning."

I felt very relieved. Shortly after, I saw the President about something else. He never mentioned the matter and neither did I.

The most worrisome problem at the SEC concerned criminal prosecutions. We had no authority to prosecute, only the Department of Justice had that power. But my staff prepared many detailed case histories and we would refer them to the Department of Justice for prosecution. The man in charge of the Criminal Division then was Brian McMahon, later to become senator from Connecticut.

Some of the stormiest sessions I had at the SEC were, curiously, not with Wall Street but with Brian McMahon. Time after time he cast our reports into the dustbin. As a result, many of our field reports came to naught. I did not always know the reason, except that I supposed it usually involved political considerations. I cast no aspersions on Brian McMahon, who later served his nation well in the Senate. He was only a part of the system—a subordinate of Homer Cummings. Somewhere in the background was a powerful figure with money and political connections.

As I observed the Washington scene over the years, I learned that that was the fate of many lost causes, whether the Democrats or the Republicans were in power. Much though we boast of government of laws and not of men, a great deal turns on the discretion of the prosecutor. In that respect it is the man, not the law, that is supreme. Only later did I come to the shattering realization that while the grand jury was designed as a barrier between the people and an oppressive government, the grand jury had become by the late sixties and early seventies a tool of the prosecutor. Witnesses summoned before a grand jury were actually summoned to the prosecutor's office, where they were questioned, intimidated, coerced, or threatened. The result is that a federal prosecutor, if he tells the truth, must admit that he can get a grand jury to indict almost anyone of some crime. This is one hideous aspect of the gargantuan growth in governmental power.

Pressure from those with vested interests was not the only enemy we faced in attempting to carry out public policy. Another problem was the tendency of bureaucrats, large and small, to increase the powers of their fiefdoms in as many ways as possible.

The Cabinet heads and agency heads were all overlords of principalities. They proved the validity of Parkinson's Law over and over again, their ambition being ever to expand and grow larger, to occupy bigger buildings and to have larger budgets. FDR probably would have been a match for them had he chosen to challenge them, but he usually let them go their way, reining them in only occasionally.

I remember one episode involving Jesse Jones, who was an empire builder. He had a principality of his own—the Reconstruction Finance Corporation—and ran it like a feudal lord. Jesse was an able banker, and he had an organization that was not only honest but politically on its toes. He had able men working for him—Tom Corcoran, Ben Cohen, and Stanley Reed, soon to be Solicitor General. Reed, a kind, courtly man—the most perfect gentleman I have known—was later appointed to the Court in 1938, and but for Frankfurter's machinations, might have been Chief Justice in lieu of Fred Vinson almost a decade later.

Jesse Jones' empire-building included designs on the SEC. He wanted it as one of his bureaus. In the winter of 1938–1939 Jesse took me aside at some social function and said he had admired me and my work at the SEC, but he thought that I had never received proper recognition for my efforts.

"What do you suggest?" I asked.

"I want to build you an office building. We can call it the Douglas Building or the SEC Building, or anything you desire." he replied.

Knowing Jesse, I understood he always exacted payment. "And the price?" I asked.

"We'll make the SEC the biggest bureau in the RFC," he replied.

I thanked him for his kind thought of me but told him I thought the independent commission was the best.

He then commented on our quarters. "That's a ratty place to occupy," Jesse said. "You deserve a splendid place."

"It might ruin us, Jesse," I replied, and we parted. But over and again he brought the matter up, and told me when I went on the Court that I had passed up the chance to get the finest building in the city. As a result, the SEC twenty-five years later was independent but still in third-class quarters.

Jesse was under tremendous political pressure on the Hill to take as an advisor everyone's half brother, and he designed a formula for handling the problem. He filled one floor of the RFC building with desks, chairs, phones, and a few secretaries. Every political hack he had to hire to placate a senator or congressman was put in that big room. The new employee would find *The New York Times* on his desk every morning, but he was given nothing to do. He could dictate letters back home, he could telephone to his heart's desire, his monthly check for eight hundred dollars or so never failed to arrive—and he never gummed up Jesse's business.

All of us had occasional political appointments to make. I took the brother of one congressman into the SEC as a rehabilitation measure. The man was a convict, having served a prison sentence for embezzlement. He served me well and supported his family honorably. I took others for patronage reasons—a few from Sam Rayburn's bailiwick—and they all worked out well. But no one in Washington, D.C., handled the problem en masse the way Jesse Jones did.

Jesse's iron control of his own agency was brought home to me very directly in the early SEC days. Under the Holding Company Act of 1935, the SEC was to simplify corporate structures and develop sound regional electric systems. Simplification meant endless corporate reorganizations—a job made to order for the investment bankers and their lawyers. I tried to show the investment bankers the challenging opportunity presented, but they were so ideologically opposed to the "death sentence" law, as it was known, that they refused even to get rich complying with it. I went to Jesse for help, but he would have nothing to do with it. I asked FDR to get Jesse to move. Roosevelt sent for Jesse and me, and in my presence, read "the riot act" to Jesse, so to speak, ending with the admonition, "Now, Jesse, you get together with Bill and work this out."

Jesse and I left the White House together—I to walk back to my office, Jesse to travel a block farther in his big black RFC limousine. As he got into the car, I asked, "Jesse, when shall we get together? How about now?"

"Not now, not tomorrow, never," he replied. Taking off his hat, he pointed to his gray hair and said, "When your hair gets the color of mine, you'll be wise. You will know by then that the President is a very busy man. He's so busy that he'll never even remember this talk we've had."

With that he drove off, and we never did have the conference.

Roosevelt took somewhat the same attitude in an encounter I had with Henry Wallace. My investigations of bankruptcies and receiverships frequently led to commodity speculation, and the more I saw of the exchanges generally, the more convinced I became that the commodity boys needed a thorough going-over. Under Wallace, then the Secretary of Agriculture, the chief beneficiaries of the farm-aid program had been the big operators, the packing houses, the commodity merchants, and the commodity workers. We had no authority at the SEC to regulate commodity exchanges, however, and were not looking for that authority. Agriculture, we thought, should do it. Two other commissioners agreed: Jerome Frank, my mainstay and friend from Agriculture, and Robert E. Healy, stout-hearted Vermonter.

We frequently found stockbrokers who were in financial trouble, caught in a web of commodity transactions, often including "puts and calls." I told FDR that the commodity exchanges needed stricter regulation with respect to manipulative practices. (Puts and calls were later closely regulated in our commodity exchanges.)

After I talked with FDR, he had Missy LeHand set up an appointment for Wallace and me to see him. On the scheduled day an unsuspecting Wallace and I walked in together. FDR had my briefing, and gave Wallace the lecture of his life—issuing a mandate that the commodity exchanges be cleaned up, reorganized, and regulated. Wallace, however, was adamant in his position. He squared away with FDR and flatly refused to have anything to do with such a program. He said he knew the commodity exchanges and would not even make an investigation of them. Wallace was angry because of my presence and because he was on the spot. For the first time I saw the bulldog in Henry. He defied Roosevelt, and the commodity markets went their own way.

Wallace jealously protected his principality in Agriculture. He had over thirty bureaus and agencies to administer. The Pure Food and Drug Act, which contained some controls over pesticides, was under the supervision of Agriculture during the 1930's. But Wallace seemed incapable of making up his mind to ban a pesticide. When such a crisis would come up, he usually left town, leaving Rex Tugwell as Acting Secretary. Rex promptly signed all those orders.

The bureaucracy I saw burgeoning in Washington, D. C., made me shudder to think what would happen under socialism. I had admiration for Norman Thomas, whom I knew. He was, I think, honest and true blue, but it takes more than honest men to run the bureaucracy that socialism spawns. I was for TVA when it was launched, but what I saw of it in the next decade appalled me. TVA was viable in purpose but run by men over whom the people had a very remote, attenuated control. These administrators fulfilled the legal standard of the "public interest" by applying their own personal conceptions of the public good. They were inspired to perpetuate their regime and make it bigger and more powerful by building dams endlessly and branching out in numerous similar fields. Later when I got to communist lands, I saw monolithic bureaucracy in all its crushing power; it exploited the common man and was beyond effective control even by the Politburo.

But my experience in the SEC, in the Executive branch of our own government, convinced me that controls on capitalism were obviously necessary: monopoly power could end all competition, and competition is, by my lights, the important ingredient in the free-enterprise system. Brandeis helped crystallize my views on this matter. He talked many times and at great length about the inability of one person to command efficiently more than one area, one process, one problem. In addition to the obvious economic abuses resulting from monopoly control, Brandeis said that inefficiency resulted when industry was piled on industry, making up into huge monopolies or conglomerates. Since his time merger after merger has taken place, creating gargantuan companies, some with larger budgets than the national budget of France.

Some New Dealers abhorred Brandeis' view. They called it "turning back the clock." Yet antitrust regulation only entailed close supervision over mergers and acquisitions, the release of some units from the monopolistic hold of conglomerates, and the elimination of price-fixing and related evils. As I got deep into the subject, I realized that Teddy Roosevelt, famous as a trust-buster, had only a token force at work on the problem. And as one regime followed another, there were few who put their hearts into real trust-busting. So we witnessed a steady growth in size and power of business units; as I told FDR, I was sure that in time they could become so big and so powerful, government would have to take them over. Because of the greed of some men we would be destined in the long run to have socialism. Yet preservation of free enterprise seemed to me to be the best. I had no personal stake in it, for I never owned securities except government bonds. Yet I was convinced that free enterprise in the Jeffersonian sense freed the spirit and loosed all men's creative energies.

The trend, however, has been in the opposite direction. There was a big splurge in mergers and acquisitions in manufacturing and mining prior to the 1929 crash, but the number had markedly declined by 1934, when the SEC was founded. There were only 101 in that year as compared with 1,245 in 1928. In 1968 statistics showed 2,407, and of that total, there were 207 mergers in which the acquired assets were about fourteen billion dollars. Since 1950 the growth of conglomerates has mounted, many having anticompetitive effects, yet popular feeling in America, I believe, is antimonopolistic. The Sherman Act of 1890, basic in our antitrust arsenal, was passed fifty-two to one in the Senate, the sole opponent being Rufus Blodgett, Democrat of New Jersey. Monopoly and restraints of trade make the American mind uneasy in spite of the blue-ribbon credentials which monopolists display. The Jefferson-Brandeis influence is still strong.

I saw a menace to freedom in the growing bureaucracies of Washington. They stifled men's energies; they were so far removed from the local problems that they did not understand them. I came out of my five-year tour of duty in the Executive branch convinced that while national standards were needed to eliminate discrimination, produce equality, and raise the level of our county courthouses, the driving forces should be local. The standards, in other words, should come from the center—whether it be setting minimum wages on one hand, or the ban on warrantless arrests, or the prohibition of coercive tactics of the police on the other. But the execution had to be local.

Riding high above all these issues was freedom of speech and of the press. The First Amendment seemed to me to be the most important guarantee of freedom that we had. Perhaps we could have its freedom even if we turned socialist, but I doubted it. For then the power of the government would be so great as to make it tempting to still all debate or discussion and to permit only paeans of praise for those in power.

Along with belief in the First Amendment was my conviction that the state existed for the individual, not the individual for the state—putting human rights first. Human rights included the right to own property and enjoy it, as well as the right to stand for radical as well as rightist views and the right to become a vagabond. Government to me was an agency of the people, a priesthood of a very special kind. A man in government need not take his policies from the mob, for the mob is a formless, illiterate organ. He takes his policies from the law as legislatures write it and as the Constitution conceives it. His priesthood requires a faithful commitment to law over and above all else. It is his task to tell the people what the national conscience—the Constitution—requires. The people can change it if they desire. But the main job of the Keepers of the Conscience is to make clear in a fearless way what the demands of civilization are.

Free enterprise is not guaranteed by the Constitution, as are free speech and a free press. But the First Amendment and free enterprise seemed to me to go hand-in-hand in a practical way.

FDR constantly wanted to increase the jurisdiction of the SEC to give it additional things to do. I fought those proposals at every step, knowing that we already were doing all we possibly could do well. That is one quarrel I had with FDR. Another was over his desire to consolidate bureaus and agencies. For example, Roosevelt was always urging me to take on more duties, more responsibilities, to enlarge the SEC.

I told FDR, "Give me twice the amount of responsibility, and someone else will have to do the thinking. I won't be able to know all the facts or make good decisions. That's what's wrong with what you're doing elsewhere in the government."

The President's warm ally in this regard was my friend, Harold Ickes, Republican from Illinois, who headed the Department of the Interior.

Harold was an empire builder, whose aim was an ever-bigger Interior Department. On the same day he got the Bituminous Coal Commission, July 1, 1939, he also acquired the Bureau of Insular Affairs, Bureau of Fisheries, Bureau of Biological Survey, and the Mount Rushmore Commission—and he was made chairman of the Migratory Bird Conservation Commission as well.

Harold was hungry for bureaucratic power. He wanted the Forest Service transferred from the Department of Agriculture to the Department of the Interior, and used every artifice to have it done. He would often greet me with a smile, saying that FDR had promised it would be done. Weeks later he would scowl, saying ugly things about the President and his failure to give Forestry to Ickes.

Harold was a bulldog battler for his ideas. He became obsessed with wanting the Forest Service so that the national forests could be run under the same control as the National Park Service. But most of us who were concerned about conservation were opposed. We knew what was happening to other areas in the public domain. The Bureau of Land Management under Ickes had long been a disgrace, pretty much the tool of the cattle and sheep barons. The National Park Service—shrouded in mystic idealism—was becoming a great "developer" of wilderness areas, destroying the national parks by crisscrossing them with highways and even building villages and towns inside them, as at Yellowstone, rather than keeping civilization on the perimeter. The Forest Service was not perfect; it, too, sometimes bowed to commercial pressures, but Lyle Watts, Chief Forester from 1943 to 1952, was carrying on in the best Pinchot tradition.

Pinchot, my hero of earlier days, was opposed to Ickes' plan for the transfer, both openly and with FDR in private. Ickes, to strike at Pinchot, published an article in the May 25, 1940, issue of *Saturday Evening Post*, entitled "Not Guilty." This article reopened the old Ballinger-Pinchot controversy dating back to 1908 and the years immediately following. At that time there was a great argument as to which of the two—Ballinger or Pinchot—was responsible for the demise of some public lands in Alaska. A Morgan-Guggenheim syndicate, working through one Clarence Cunningham, had filed claims on coal lands on the Bering River in Alaska. Louis R. Glavis, a federal employee, became suspicious of these claims, some thirty in number, for they were to be consolidated after title had been issued, contrary to the requirements of the National Coal Lands Act. Richard A. Ballinger, who was then Secretary of the Interior, ordered Glavis to suspend his investigation. Pinchot was then

Chief Forester, in Agriculture. The resulting scandal led to a Congressional investigation in which Louis D. Brandeis represented Glavis, and George Wharton Pepper represented Pinchot. There was no charge of bribery or corruption, only wrongdoing in giving away public property to private interests in violation of the Coal Lands Act. The committee majority gave Ballinger a clean bill of health. The cries of the dissenting minority became a strong conservation issue, which resulted in the firing of Pinchot by Taft. The issue helped elect Hiram Johnson as governor of California, and widened the breach between Taft and Teddy Roosevelt —a schism that gave Woodrow Wilson the Presidency in 1912.

These were among the wounds that Ickes opened when in 1940 he defended Ballinger against Pinchot. Ickes wrote that Ballinger had not been involved in a corrupt practice. That was never the issue. The issue was whether private interests through subterfuge could defeat the public land policy. Bulldog Ickes would have been the first to attack any Ballinger of his day. In 1940 he was defending Ballinger only to attack Pinchot.

Ickes was the beneficiary of many of FDR's "efficiency" moves. The President liked charts, pointing out pyramids into which agency after agency had been nestled. I told FDR it was a poor way "to run a railroad," my point being that such consolidation made for irresponsible government. I gave as an illustration the Bituminous Coal Commission, a five-man board standing on its own. The board made the decisions and defended them. If an error was made, everyone knew whom to blame. If credit was due, praise would be given. But if that independent agency was swept under the rug of the Department of the Interior, the identity of the policy-maker would disappear. Harold Ickes would thereafter announce a decision, but it would already have been made by a faceless person in the bureaucracy. FDR would get a pretty chart but we would get irresponsible government. Roosevelt was inclined to agree, but he nevertheless went ahead with his "efficiency" plans. The problem was that every head of every independent agency needed to see the President in order to function.

"I counted over three hundred people the other day in that position," he said. "If I did nothing but see them, I'd have a full day. This way I can see you—and the Cabinet officers—and let it go at that."

I made a counterproposal, and that was to make Henry Wallace, by now the Vice-President, the man for the administrative agencies to see. "Put Henry to work," I urged.

"Henry?" he exclaimed. "Would you like to see Henry instead of me? What would Henry know about all those matters?"

"There's only a heartbeat between him and the Presidency."

"Yes. But before we do what you say, let's get someone other than Henry."

Ickes' bureaucratic tendencies were of course not all bad. He watched over every penny in the Public Works Administration, and was properly called "Honest Harold." When a public power dam was being built, he had a federal inspector testing every ton of concrete that was poured. That practice made the contractors of the day angry and irritated, but the job was honestly done. And that is more than could be said for the fifties and sixties, when some contractors in my part of the country actually built their own private homes with federal supplies, Uncle Sam footing the bill under guise of subcontract on a big dam on the Columbia or on some other federal project. Eisenhower, Johnson, and Nixon badly needed an "Honest Harold."

In those days Daniel W. Bell headed the Bureau of the Budget, and he and his efficient staff checked up on us once a year. None of us resented this, knowing that the Bureau served a purpose useful to the President in keeping an overall account of what was happening among the ever-multiplying agencies. But the Bureau at that time had assumed a policy-making position that has continued to this day. One instance of this concerned our expanding role in connection with over-the-counter brokers. Over-the-counter dealers were not brokers on a stock exchange; their dealings were wholly unregulated by the federal government, and there were many abuses due to the lack of ethical standards and rules of conduct with an appropriate legal code. We were moving into the area, and additional funds were needed to hire a staff of enforcement officials. To the best of my recollection, the extent of the new items in the budget called for perhaps $100,000, certainly no more. Dan Bell presided at the meeting at which I tendered our new budget. Dan, with his blue pencil, struck it out completely, saying, "That's something you guys need not get into." I was at once on my feet, protesting, saying, "Danny, you don't know a thing about this over-the-counter area. I do, and we must have the money."

"We've got to cut down on spending" was the reply.

"And when I'm on the carpet for doing nothing about swindles by under-the-counter guys, where will you be? Defending me? Not by a long shot."

And so the argument continued, to no avail, with the result that I went to FDR and got Dan Bell overruled.

Dan Bell was mirroring the big-business attitude. The powers-that-be wanted a hands-off policy when it came to their preserve. The Bureau of the Budget may have been reflecting only its own prejudices, or it may have been responding to pressures from the Establishment. Whatever the reason, my rebellion was instant. The bureau had no rightful concern with policy. It had no expertise in the manifold phases of the financial world, which was under our jurisdiction. It had no responsibilities for day-to-day surveillance and regulation. Yet it set about to determine SEC policy. My position was that the Bureau of the Budget could tell us how much we had to spend in the next fiscal year but that it was up to us to determine how that amount was to be expended. The battles were intense and recurring. I always won in the end, but I usually had to go to the President for help.

This perversion of the function of the Bureau of the Budget has persisted throughout recent history. One example relates to federal control over pollution. President Eisenhower in 1960 vetoed the Federal Water Pollution Control Act because, he said, "Water pollution is a uniquely local blight." John Kennedy and Lyndon Johnson reversed that policy, and with the help of Senator Edmund S. Muskie of Maine, fashioned a vast system of federal control and assistance. But even in the late 1960's the Bureau of the Budget was sabotaging the national program because it had an advisory committee of industrialists, made up of the main polluters, advising it on water pollution and its remedies.

Thus does an agency extend its domain, establish its prestige, and sit at the controls largely as an independent sovereign, like the head of an absolute monarchy.

When I was at the SEC, it would have been unthinkable for one of us to have left the agency to head a utility company, a brokerage house, or a stock exchange—or to have left to become counsel to one of them. The reason was simple: if that were the goal, even in the subconscious, regulation would suffer. The federal agent would then face the job less objectively. In form, he would be serving the public interest; in fact, he would be proving his worth to a future employer.

The sad truth is that in time one SEC employee became president of a stock exchange. Others became heads of public utilities or counsels to utilities. And there were those who were not associated with the SEC but with other federal agencies who drifted into powerful positions with the Establishment and made fortunes. They became Establishment spokesmen and the advocates of the new conservatism that swept the country. They became architects of the "cold war" that kept Moscow and Washington, D.C., apart, when they should have been searching endlessly for a consensus on the dozens of problems that, unresolved, could lead to a nuclear conflict. They did nothing illegal; they were not dishonest within legal definition. They were, however, the symbol of the vast corruption that followed the New Deal. The knights in shining armor sold their souls and became rich; and they in turn showed their new associates how to corrupt the administrative and legislative process.

The same kind of corruption exists whenever a member of the Forest Service leaves the federal employ to take a job with a lumber company. When that system of rewards is established, the public interest suffers. For the regulated have captured the regulators. And that is precisely what has happened in most federal areas.

This is the topic I once debated on television with General Omar Bradley. It was and is the practice for Pentagon generals, upon retirement, to become presidents or vice-presidents of great corporations that have important business with the Pentagon. The Pentagon's procurement contracts are in the billions each year. A friendly, docile procurement officer will certainly be rewarded on his retirement. An aggressive, non-cooperative procurement officer will not be. This was part of the problem about which Eisenhower spoke in his Farewell Address, January 17, 1961.

In my day I saw big government corrupted by big business—working partly through ex-New Dealers. The corruption was not venal; money was not paid for administrative decisions, but the future was bright for the man or woman with brains who knew the master's voice.

I do not mean to intimate that all New Dealers went eagerly for the fleshpots after the New Deal ended. That was occasionally done but by no means always. New Dealers who were lawyers practiced law, and those who were accountants pursued their profession. That of course is what they should have done. The question is, What broad public interest did they serve in their total lives? The answer can be best illustrated by citing the work of Abe Fortas and Thurman Arnold: They practiced law in Washington, D.C., but they also stepped forward to defend innumerable unpopular people when the witch hunt obsessed the nation. They appeared with their clients before congressional committees and tried to make certain that due process of law was administered. More often than not, due process was lacking, and it was common to find Fortas and Arnold carrying these cases to court. One of the most notorious involved

Dorothy Bailey, and another was the case of Owen Lattimore (discussed in the chapter on the witch hunt). Dorothy Bailey lost her job because of the secret testimony and information supplied the loyalty board by an anonymous person. Dorothy Bailey never knew who her accuser was, and therefore was unable to meet him face to face and to show his bias or the reasons for his desire to destroy her. The reason given by the government for this anonymity was that informers would not come forward unless they were protected—the excuse that through the centuries has made informers notorious perjurers. Dorothy Bailey lost her case in the courts, the Supreme Court dividing four to four (341 U.S. 918), at a time when federal employment was considered only a "privilege"* that could be taken away at the whim or caprice of a superior, and not a "right" with the overtones of "property."† Abe Fortas and Thurman Arnold, lawyers for this victim of the witch hunt, did not stop when Dorothy Bailey was thrown to the wolves but worked hard to find her employment in the new regime of disorder that had possessed us. These two old associates of mine brought to law practice in the forties and fifties the "public interest" concept that was to take hold in law offices across the land in the sixties and seventies.

Under Eisenhower, corruption took on an appearance of propriety, for the actors were men of high standing and prestige. When Eisenhower took office he announced that private power should be encouraged to take the place of public power. One of the first things done was to eliminate from the budget TVA funds for construction of a new generating plant. The power needed was for the Atomic Energy Commission, and the search for a private utility to build a plant for that purpose got under way. Two private utilities, one headed by Edgar H. Dixon and the other by Eugene A. Yates (from which the controversy soon took its popular name), submitted a proposal. Questions arose concerning its soundness, and Adolphe H. Wenzell, who worked for the underwriters of the project, was brought in to give advice. He remained on the underwriters' payroll, became a consultant for the Bureau of the Budget with no salary but with a per diem plus transportation. A plan for financing the new private utility was prepared, the underwriter whom Wenzell represented getting 60 percent of the fee.

As criticism of the plan became public, the underwriter waived the fee.

* See separate opinions of Black, Frankfurter, Douglas, and Jackson in *Anti-Fascist Committee v. McGrath*, 341 U.S. 123.

† *Slochower v. Board of Education*, 350 U.S. 551; *Garrity v. New Jersey*, 385 U.S. 493; *Percy v. Sindermann*, 408 U.S. 593.

But when the private utility brought suit for sums due under the contract, a defense was made under an old Civil War statute making it a crime for one who has an interest in a company doing business with the United States to act "as an officer or agent" of the United States "for the transaction of business" of that company—an Act based on the Biblical principle that no man may serve two masters. The Court held that this use of the so-called dollar-a-year man was a conflict of interest and violated the Act, thus making the resulting contract unenforceable (364 U.S. 520).

Edward N. Gadsby was chairman of the SEC under Eisenhower. By 1968 Gadsby and his firm were registered lobbyists for our largest groups of mutual funds and were the front men for Richard Nixon, who was campaigning for the Presidency on grounds, *inter alia*, that free enterprise needed greater freedom than existing security laws provided. These "front men," coming to their tasks with SEC credentials, gave undeserved prestige to promoters of some of the greatest exploitive interests of the age. Gadsby did nothing illegal, but his activities demonstrated that service in federal agencies had fallen far short of the priesthood.

When he became President, Nixon named Roy L. Ash to make a report on the independent regulatory agencies. The report was filed in 1971. It dealt only with organizational problems. It did not touch on the basic problem that the regulators are more sensitive to the welfare of the regulated than to the general public, and therefore, on the whole, make socially undesirable policy.

Roy Ash was a controversial figure. The charge was made that he, as head of Litton Industries, had claims against the government that his position compromised. Whether that was true, I do not know. The point here is only that the Ash Report dealt only with superficial aspects of the problem of administrative fiat. The basic problems will be solved not by redesigning the charts but by programs for appointing commissioners who are in tune with the requirements of consumers, not solely with the welfare of the regulated company. By the late sixties and early seventies the industrial and financial powers were completely in control of the regulatory machines.

Chapter XX

FDR

Before Joe Kennedy left his post as chairman of the SEC, he said, "Bill, you have to get to know the Boss." He took me with him to some business talks, and from that time, I was on the periphery of the White House circle.

By 1936 FDR had begun to invite me to his regular poker parties. These invitations increased after I became chairman of the SEC in September, 1937. I also spent weekends with him at his Maryland retreat, Shangri-La (now known as Camp David), and aboard the Presidential yacht, the *Williamsburg,* cruising the Potomac. Previously I had occasionally helped to write speeches for him; now the assignments became more frequent.

These new and increasing personal contacts with the White House put FDR and me on a new basis. I realized that his entourage was made up mostly of sycophants who sang his praises. He had few around him except Eleanor who told him when he was wrong. She was his antenna, and gave him what the press called his "fifth sense." She traveled extensively, and on her return home, would barge in on him wherever he was or whatever he was doing, and give her report. I heard her say over and again "Franklin, you are wrong" about various matters. And I noticed he usually followed her advice. I decided I would also play that role with him.

One time after Eleanor had returned from a trip to North Carolina, she said, "Franklin, it's really true that the public schools for the Negroes are inferior to those for the whites—inferior in libraries, inferior in faculties, inferior in facilities."

Another time, after she had come back from Alabama and Georgia, she said, "Franklin, we must do something about those sharecroppers. Wallace and Tugwell brag about their farm program, but I tell you, Franklin, the beneficiaries are *not* the men who do the work but only those who own the property."

Her diatribes were not against a particular section or against a particular group. She had a keen perception for any social injustice. Returning from a tour through some New England states and Pennsylvania, she spoke at some length about minimum wages. "They are awful, Franklin. Simply awful. Why, people can't live on them and raise a family as they should."

On February 5, 1937, apparently out of the blue, FDR made a proposal that came to be known as the Court-packing plan. None of us close to the President (except Homer Cummings, the Attorney General) had any inkling of his intention. Usually FDR would send up a trial balloon about a new proposal in order to take a measure of the public attitude. This time he did no such thing. The Court had been striking down some of his New Deal legislation, and flushed with an overwhelming victory in 1936, the President dropped his bombshell. With this action, he would spend a great deal of his political good will and political capital in the following year.

Under the plan, FDR proposed increasing the number of sitting Justices on the Court. For every member over seventy years of age, FDR wanted to name one more, until there were fifteen Justices on the Court.

There were several other aspects of his recommendation. One was that no injunction against the enforcement of a federal statute be issued without previous and ample notice to the Attorney General and an opportunity for him to present evidence to be heard. FDR also recommended that in cases in which any court first determined a question of the constitutionality of an Act of Congress, there should be a direct and immediate appeal to the Supreme Court. In addition, he suggested that a new office be created and filled by the Supreme Court to supervise the administration of the business of the lower federal courts, a function which up to that time had resided in the Department of Justice.

But the heart of the recommendation was that the number of judges in all the federal courts be increased without exception "where there are incumbent judges of retirement age who do not choose to resign."

In his message Roosevelt said, "If an elder judge is not in fact incapacitated, only good can come from the presence of an additional judge in the crowded state of the dockets; if the capacity of an elder judge is in fact impaired, the appointment of an additional judge is indispensable. This seems to be a truth which cannot be contradicted."

But the truth which also could not be contradicted was that this would give him six new appointments to the Supreme Court, one appointment for every Justice over seventy.

The hearings on these recommendations started before the Senate Committee on the Judiciary on March 10, 1937. Lawyers, judges, professors, legislators poured into Washington by the dozen. Among the active proponents were Hugo Black, Robert Jackson, Judge Henry Edgerton, Irving Brant, Ferdinand Pecora, Edward S. Corbin, and many, many others.

The essence of the viewpoint of those favoring the plan was put by the then dean of the Notre Dame Law School, Thomas F. Konop:

> The cry is that the President is usurping the power of the Supreme Court; that he is a dictator and an autocrat; that he wants to destroy our liberties, our free speech and press, freedom of religion, trial by jury, and so forth . . .
>
> Who's usurping? It is the Supreme Court that is usurping the power of Congress and the President. It is the Supreme Court that has been destroying laws providing for a better life, more liberty and equality, social justice, and the pursuit of happiness of 130,000,000 people.
>
> Who is the dictator? One man, not elected by the people, but appointed for life. The fifth Justice of the Supreme Court is the dictator.
>
> What about five-to-four decisions of the Supreme Court of the United States? What about the power of one man, the fifth Justice, to thwart the will of the people as expressed through their representatives? May there not be dictatorship in that?

Irving Brant, famous journalist, took up the same theme: "I am merely stating that it is disastrous to leave the destinies of the United States in the hands of five men who have usurped the policy-making functions of government while remaining totally ignorant of the tremendous political forces which enter into public policy. That is not government; it is absolutism at work."

But the proposal, if adopted, would have made possible a court of fifteen members instead of nine, and that might result in eight-to-seven decisions, as the smaller Court rendered five-to-four decisions. At the hearings on the Court-packing bill the following colloquy took place:

SENATOR O'MAHONEY. The bill does not affect the power?

MR. KONOP. No, I don't think it does.

SENATOR O'MAHONEY. It does not obviate five-to-five decisions?

MR. KONOP. No.

SENATOR O'MAHONEY. Or eight-to-seven decisions?

MR. KONOP. No.

If the votes of five can be overturned by adding to the Court's membership, then the vote of eight could be changed by adding another three, and so on. Every President coming to power would be apt to have his own constitutional philosophy; and if he could manipulate the Court's membership to fit his philosophy, the idea of an independent judiciary would evaporate.

Of course, as Senator Burton K. Wheeler testified, the new appointees might not live up to expectations:

"If you put six men upon the Supreme Bench, what assurance can you have that the legislation which you pass will be affirmed by them? I voted against Mr. Chief Justice Hughes. He has been one of the most liberal members of that Court. All the liberals voted for Mr. Justice Roberts. He turned out to be one of the more conservative members."

Tinkering with the Court's membership is a game that any President can play; a "conservative" can also use it in an attempt to get rid of noxious "liberal" decisions.

Robert H. Jackson, leader of the assault on the Court, made his case around the point that the Court had been in angry collision with the most dynamic and popular President in our history. In other words, the Executive and the Legislative branches should have their way. But I thought then, and still think, that an independent judiciary was created to protect the individual against executive or legislative action.

As Congressman Lemke of North Dakota said:

"Let us assume that some of us are arrested in violation of the Constitution or the Bill of Rights. How could the Supreme Court be of any service to us if they were not permitted to find that the act of Congress was unconstitutional? It could not be done."

That was my philosophy. A court was needed to protect the individual against those kinds of executive and legislative action that were banned by the Constitution. The Justices might construe these guarantees against the popular will or passion. But if their judgments were to be revised by the political branches, a great bulwark of freedom would be lost.

None of us close to FDR was in on the idea of Court-packing. If the President had asked me for my advice, I would have told him I was opposed. The Attorney General, Homer Cummings, sold the plan to him one night in a solo performance at the White House. Cummings may have gotten the idea from a recommendation made by a previous Attorney General, James Clark McReynolds, whom Wilson later named to the Court in 1914.

When Cummings proposed the Court-packing plan to FDR, I am certain that he must have had in mind James Clark McReynolds. I don't suggest that the plan was aimed at "Old Mac," as we affectionately called McReynolds, but rather at the group of which he was a member. For McReynolds was a conservative, and a sturdy advocate of the substantive due process school of thought, which had dominated the Court since the 1880's. I doubt, however, that FDR ever knew that McReynolds, when he was Attorney General, had made substantially the same proposal. It is to be found in the Annual Report of the Attorney General for 1913, and reads as follows:

> Judges of the United States courts, at the age of seventy, after having served ten years, may retire upon full pay. In the past many judges have availed themselves of this privilege. Some, however, have remained upon the bench long beyond the time when they were capable of adequately discharging their duties, and in consequence the administration of justice has suffered. The power of Congress to correct this condition is limited by the provision of the Constitution that judges shall hold their offices during good behavior. I suggest an act providing when any judge of a federal court below the Supreme Court fails to avail himself of the privilege of retiring now granted by law, that the President be required, with the advice and consent of the Senate, to appoint another judge, who shall preside over the affairs of the court and have precedence over the older one. This will insure at all times the presence of a judge sufficiently active to discharge promptly and adequately the duties of the court.

How FDR would have chortled if he could have gone on the radio and announced to the people that he was taking his cue from the staid and conservative Mr. Justice McReynolds!

Like Hugo L. Black, who campaigned vigorously for FDR's plan, I was opposed to the expansive meaning the Court had given to the due process clauses of the Fifth and Fourteenth Amendments. The Court had been using those clauses to strike down laws that shocked their sensibilities. The Fourteenth Amendment says that "No state shall deprive any person of life, liberty, or property without due process of law." The Fifth Amendment places the same restraint on Congress. The old Court construed "liberty" in such an expansive way as to make it virtually impossible for the government to enact social legislation that interfered with the freedom of the owner of a business—corporate or otherwise—to run it as he chose. Even regulation of prices of theater tickets had been struck down.* And Congress had been stymied in its efforts to prohibit child labor by the Court's interpretation of the Commerce clause, which in 1916 was held not broad enough to allow Congress to make a law preventing the interstate movement of the products of child labor.†

The Supreme Court had over the years used the concept of due process in the substantive sense. It would hold that a statute such as one limiting work hours for women violated due process, because it limited the women's right to work and the employer's right to hire them. The Court held that this sort of law deprived a person of his liberty without due process. The liberty it was protecting had to do with working under miserable conditions for more hours than were physically healthy, with a lack of sanitary facilities, etc.

That use of the due process clauses in the Fifth and Fourteenth Amendments injected into the constitutional definition of "liberty" the laissez-faire philosophy of Adam Smith. What it came down to was the individual judge's opinion of the "wisdom" of the law. Holmes, Brandeis, Stone, and Hughes regularly dissented, saying, "Control of working conditions are within the reach of the police power of the state."

The old Court did in fact sit as a superlegislature over Congress and the states. To that, I was opposed. Yet displacing judges whom one did not like with those who shared the ideology of the incoming administration was a dangerous precedent. If FDR could do it because he had a different view of due process, a less benign President could follow the same precedent because he had a different view of the First Amendment. The Justices were old men and would soon pass on. Far better that time rather than political maneuvering rectify their errors.

The way to get these Justices to retire would have been to inaugurate

* *Lochner v. New York* 198 U.S. 45, in 1905.

† *Hammer v. Dagenhart* 247 U.S. 251.

a retirement program. While FDR made no such proposal in his Court-packing plan, the opposition in the Congress rushed through such a program for members of the Supreme Court.

Holmes had resigned on January 12, 1932. He said," The condition of my health makes it a duty to break off connections that I cannot leave without deep regret after the affectionate relations of many years and the absorbing interests that have filled my life. But the time has come and I bow to the inevitable. I have nothing but kindness to remember from you and from my brethren. My last word should be one of grateful thanks."

Hoover in accepting the resignation told Holmes, "No appreciation I could express would even feebly represent the gratitude of the American people for your whole life of wonderful public service, from the time you were an officer in the Civil War to this day—near your ninety-first anniversary. I know of no American retiring from public service with such a sense of affection and devotion of the whole people."

When Holmes left the Bench, members of lower federal courts could "retire" receiving the same salary for life. Members of the Supreme Court could not get a pension by retiring. They could, however, "resign" having reached the age of seventy and having served at least ten years and receive their regular salary for life (45 Stat. 1423). At the time of Holmes the salary was $20,000. So when Holmes resigned, he received a pension of that amount. In a year or so Congress went on an economy binge and reduced Holmes' pension, as I remember, to $10,000. I recall how shocked I was that Congress should be so callous, and many members of the Bar and Bench felt the same way. The Constitution afforded no protection except a guarantee against the diminution of judges' pay "during their continuance in office." The opponents of the FDR Court program, therefore, made a strategic move when they passed the Retirement Act of March 1, 1937.

The idea of "packing" the Court stuck in the public craw. Bob Jackson—to whom FDR promised the Chief Justiceship once Hughes retired—was the knight in shining armor who carried the battle on this issue, and later, in 1941, wrote a book about it, *The Struggle for Judicial Supremacy*. But a few of us around FDR were saddened by the Court-packing project.

As I have said, I had been much opposed to many of the rulings of the old Court that struck down social legislation because in its opinion it violated the due process clauses of the Fifth and Fourteenth Amendments. I made speeches at Yale and elsewhere, denouncing the Justices who added their personal social philosophy of laissez-faire to the Constitution. But I did not favor the Court-packing plan. The President never asked me what I thought of it, he never asked me to help him promote it. And once the President had acted or taken a public position on an issue, I never went to him to offer unasked-for advice.

His lieutenants in the fight—notably Tom Corcoran—used me indirectly. When they were bringing men to Washington, and lining them up as witnesses before the Senate committee, they would occasionally deposit one of those clients in my office at the SEC. I gave the man a comfortable chair and reading material.

"No one is going to tell me what I must say as a witness," one visitor from Notre Dame thundered at me.

I assured him he need have no fear, and so he nervously used my facilities. But I never broached the subject matter to him, nor to any other prospective witness.

I had assumed that Frankfurter was a proponent of the plan. But he assured me he was not. One night we both barely caught the sleeper out of Washington—he for Cambridge, and I for Yale. We sat for a long while in a large smoking room talking about FDR and his plan. Frankfurter was steamed up against the old Court and its due process decisions, but he expressed strong disapproval of the President's plan.

I was to learn years later, from Max Freedman's book *Roosevelt and Frankfurter*, that what Frankfurter told me was not the truth. He was heavily involved in helping FDR promote the plan—efforts which he tried to hide. But his dissemblance was in time made clear.

As *Time* magazine later said:

> What made Frankfurter's performance particularly questionable, however, was that FDR had long since promised him that he would some day be appointed to the Supreme Court. As if with that promise in mind, Frankfurter even told his closest friends that he had no role in the Court-packing scheme. For the Senate Judiciary Committee that was to confirm his appointment, Frankfurter even prepared a statement saying that he had been both silent and neutral. The statement never had to be used. But the fact is that Frankfurter was ready to use it. All his brilliance on the bench, his great capacity for friendship, his loyalty to the President, cannot quite erase this shortcoming of character.

In those days Justice Owen J. Roberts was known in the press as the "swing man." In 1923, prior to the appointment of Roberts, the Court had held in a five-to-three decision in the *Adkins* case that the Washington, D.C., minimum wage law was unconstitutional (261 U.S. 525). In 1936, after Roberts was on the Bench, the Court, in a five-to-four ruling, followed the *Adkins* decision in holding unconstitutional New York's minimum wage law (298 U.S. 587). Roberts was with the majority. Then, on March 29, 1937, he was one of the five Justices overruling the 1923 decision and upholding Washington's minimum wage law (300 U.S. 379). The next day, March 30, 1937, Frankfurter wrote FDR: "And now, with the shift by Roberts, even a blind man ought to see that the Court is in politics, and understand how the Constitution is 'judicially' construed. It is a deep object lesson—a lurid demonstration—of the relation of men to the 'meaning' of the Constitution."

As noted, in 1936 a New York minimum wage law was challenged in *Morehead v. Tipaldo* (298 U.S. 587). Roberts was on the Court and he was one of the five declaring the Act unconstitutional, Hughes, Brandeis, Stone, and Cardozo dissenting. The majority seemed to lean on *Adkins*. Roberts explained his joinder of the majority opinion in the New York case on the ground that no litigant had asked that *Adkins* be overruled. The opinion in its final form, however, reaffirmed *Adkins* in principle. Even so, Roberts stood by it, recording later that he did not propose to reexamine *Adkins* until a new case required that it be done.*

The *West Coast Hotel* case was argued in December 1936 and voted on at a conference held during that month. As Hughes relates in his *Autobiographical Notes*,† the conference vote was Hughes, Brandeis, Roberts, and Cardozo to sustain the state law and overruling *Adkins*. Stone was absent from the bench because of illness from October 14, 1936, to February 1, 1937, and therefore missed the argument. The practice of Hughes was, at the start of an argument, when one Justice was absent, to ask counsel if they would "vouch" him into the case—in other words, treat him as if he were present. Counsel always agreed and thus Hughes avoided putting the case down for reargument. The *West Coast Hotel* case was held for Stone, who returned to the Bench on February 1 and at the next conference of the Court voted to sustain the Act, thus making the decision 5 to 4 in favor of constitutionality. But it took over a month to write and process the majority opinion (written by Hughes) and the dissenting opinion (written by Sutherland), which meant that they did not come down until March 29, 1937.

* Frankfurter, "Mr. Justice Roberts," 104 *Univ. Penn. L. Rev.* 311, 315 (1955).

† Harvard University Press, 1937, p. 312.

FDR's Court plan was announced on February 5, 1937, and many assumed that it was that announcement that changed the result in the *West Coast Hotel* case. Such was not the fact. Stone's view was already known; it had been expressed in his dissent in *Morehead v. Tipaldo* (298 U.S. 587, 631). Roberts' view had crystallized in December 1936 when he cast his vote, weeks before FDR's Court plan had been conceived. Thus do journalists and others on the sidelines often jump to wrong conclusions.

Frankfurter in his March 30, 1937, letter had referred to a letter Hughes wrote to Senator Burton K. Wheeler on March 21, 1937. Hughes said in part:

> An increase in the number of Justices of the Supreme Court, apart from any question of policy, which I do not discuss, would not promote the efficiency of the Court. It is believed that it would impair that efficiency so long as the Court acts as a unit. There would be more judges to hear, more judges to confer, more judges to discuss, more judges to be convinced and to decide. The present number of Justices is thought to be large enough so far as the prompt, adequate, and efficient conduct of the work of the Court is concerned. As I have said, I do not speak of any other considerations in view of the appropriate attitude of the Court in relation to questions of policy.
>
> I understand that it has been suggested that with more Justices the Court would hear cases in divisions. It is believed that such a plan would be impracticable. A large proportion of the cases we hear are important and a decision by a part of the Court would be unsatisfactory.
>
> I may also call attention to the provisions of article III, section I, of the Constitution that the judicial power of the United States shall be vested "in one Supreme Court" and in such inferior courts as the Congress may from time to time ordain and establish. The Constitution does not appear to authorize two or more Supreme Courts or two or more parts of a supreme court functioning in effect as separate courts.
>
> On account of the shortness of time I have not been able to consult with the members of the Court generally with respect to the foregoing statement, but I am confident that it is in accord with the views of the Justices. I should say, however, that I have been able to consult with Mr. Justice Van Devanter and Mr. Jus-

> tice Brandeis, and I am at liberty to say that the statement is approved by them.

Frankfurter said of this Hughes letter:

> That was a characteristic Hughes performance—part and parcel of that pretended withdrawal from considerations of policy, while trying to shape them, which is the core of the mischief of which the majority have so long been guilty. That Brandeis should have been persuaded to allow the Chief to use his name is a source of sadness to me that I need hardly dwell on to you.

But every word Hughes spoke was the truth. The only prevaricator was Frankfurter, who had been promised a seat on the Court and was swinging along with FDR as the price of getting it. Several years passed before it dawned on Roosevelt that his "friend" had chameleonlike qualities—no one told him; he found it out for himself. And the realization of it was shattering.

When Frankfurter first came to town, Harold Ickes greatly admired him. When Frankfurter's name went to the Senate as Associate Justice, Harold had an afternoon champagne party in his office. Harold was convinced that day that long after FDR, long after Ickes, Frankfurter would keep the fires of liberalism burning in Washington, D.C. But it was not long before Ickes announced that his old hero was a real conservative who embraced old precedents under the guise of bowing to "the law," but who actually chose the old precedents because he liked them better. Ickes left in his dictated memoranda bitter comments about Frankfurter.

Lyndon B. Johnson—a tall, thin, gangling, gregarious Texan—came to town on the Court-packing plan, one of the few men in history to make political "hay" out of FDR's proposal. He ran for office on that issue and won. FDR, therefore, had a special feeling toward Lyndon. The only other person who, according to FDR, made political capital out of his Court-packing plan was Hughes, the Chief Justice. Hughes never uttered a word against it; he kept an austere silence, walking with dignity under the blows rained down upon him and his colleagues. Yet Hughes, by silence, grew in stature as the issue was allowed to fade.

"He's the best politician in the country," FDR told me.

During those tense days the annual call that the Court made on the President, usually in November, was discontinued. This yearly visit by the Justices had long been traditional, but after FDR proposed the Court-packing plan, Hughes merely refrained from asking for the appointment. So in 1937 and 1938 there was no call, but by the winter of 1939 feelings had changed and Hughes suggested it be resumed. FDR responded generously and we all met him at four-thirty in the Oval Room. (I was on the Court by that time.) FDR and Hughes repaired to a sofa, where they engaged in animated conversation. When six o'clock came, they were still at it. Missy LeHand got me aside and said, "The Boss has a six o'clock appointment. How do I get rid of the Chief Justice?"

"There's one lesson you must learn, Missy," I replied. "One never gets rid of a Chief Justice."

This practice of the Court's annual call on the President continued when Truman took over. But the year the Court held that Truman had acted unconstitutionally in seizing the steel mills during the Korean War, neither the White House nor the Court tried to arrange a meeting. Under Eisenhower, the visits were made, with no exception. President Kennedy continued the custom, but Johnson and Nixon did not.

Nothing very serious was discussed at these sessions; they were merely social occasions. Under President Eisenhower, Chief Justice Earl Warren had each member of the Court sit on the sofa with Eisenhower for a few minutes, and after about a half-hour or so we all promptly left.

I do remember, however, two rather humorous incidents that happened during our Eisenhower visits. The first occurred after the Court had held that baseball was exempt from antitrust laws, and later that football was not exempt from the antitrust laws. Felix Frankfurter and I had trouble restraining ourselves when Ike asked Earl Warren what the difference in antitrust law was between baseball and football. Of course, there was no difference, and Warren had to explain to Ike how the baseball decision was rendered by Justice Holmes before the Commerce clause was fully developed. The football decision was made at a later point in history, when different judicial constructions prevailed. It was a seminar pretty much over Eisenhower's head.

The last time the members of the Court visited President Eisenhower was just before he was about to leave the White House. I put to him the question: "Mr. President, what do you consider your outstanding achievements in the eight years of your Presidency?" Ike was visibly upset at this, and explained that he had had a hostile Congress and therefore was not able to get through the legislation he wanted. Finally, having searched his mind, he said that the admittance of Alaska and Hawaii to the Union was his most outstanding achievement.

FDR had a somewhat sharper wit than Mr. Eisenhower. Out of one of my poker games with FDR came a letter written by him to Frankfurter, dated November 21, 1939.* This letter, on its face, would be virtually meaningless to an outsider. It reads:

> I am secretly disturbed to find that one so young as Mr. Justice William O. Douglas has so soon taken advantage of the old subterfuge of quoting from obiter dicta of his colleagues and law school professors, expressed through letters, editorials in the *New Republic*, and 1937 speeches by a recent Harvard Law School don.
>
> Because of your seniority, I suggest that you hold a seminar for Bill, asking him to apply to the vivid rules of life in place of the musty rules of law and get him to answer in language which even the President can understand the simple query "Do Baptists play poker?"
>
> In the utmost confidence, in view of your recent assertion to me that you are about to take a freshman course in that ancient and honorable game, you will perhaps be good enough, again in the utmost confidence, to tell me whether we can muster five votes for the game as the Court is now constituted. I am deeply interested because, as you know, there is a vacancy in your honorable body.

FDR delighted in needling people, and his needle was a long one. He was needling Frankfurter in this letter. The reference to Baptists playing poker was a reference to Hughes, who was a Baptist and who, in FDR's eyes, had given him a thrashing on the Court-packing plan. The letter said, in effect: Why not invite Hughes to play some hands of regular poker, since he had shown his poker-playing capacities when he helped to defeat the Court plan?

I had jokingly promised the President a legal opinion on the question of whether Baptists do play poker. He knew how close Felix and I were at that time and that we both had come to Washington from law

* This letter is published without comment in Max Freedman's book *Roosevelt and Frankfurter*, p. 506 (Little, Brown, 1967).

faculties. His "Law School don" was a reference to Felix, who frequently wrote unsigned editorials for the *New Republic*. The "1937 speeches" was a dig at Felix, who, during the critical Court-packing argument, did not come out publicly for the plan but worked for it behind the scenes. Thus, FDR was saying to Felix that he did not want from me a devious Felix-type opinion on this momentous question.

Poker with FDR was usually announced by a telephone message: "There will be a command performance Saturday night."

Typical notice of a "command performance" was the telephone message my secretary, Edith Waters, sent me December 8, 1942: "Secy Morgenthau's office telephoned to say that there is a 'command performance' at 7:00 p.m. on Thursday, December 10. That is the night of the Norris dinner at the Mayflower which you promised to attend. I told the Secretary's office that I would call back."

I broke the engagement for the Norris dinner and told my secretary to tell Morgenthau that "I will be on deck."

The time was always the same, 7:00 P.M. The place varied. Usually the game took place at the home of Harold Ickes in Olney, Maryland, or at Henry Morgenthau's home on 30th Street. The participants, apart from FDR and myself, were usually Harold and Henry, Edwin M. (Pa) Watson and Steve Early. Occasionally FDR's physician, Admiral Ross T. McIntyre, was along. It was a simple game of poker, the stakes limited. No one could bet more than two dollars. As a result, no one ever won or lost more than fifty dollars. We had many variations of old hands. Pa Ferguson, the impeached governor of Texas, had a game named in his honor—four cards down and three up, the low hole card being wild. Ma Ferguson, who succeeded him as governor, had one named in her honor —the same as her husband's except there were three cards down and three up.

I introduced a variation when I told FDR about the Gooks. There are three Gooks—the one-eyed jack of clubs, the one-eyed jack of spades, and the one-eyed king of diamonds—known as Oswald, Inwald, and Clarence, respectively. So, with the Gooks and with the low hole card wild, there was a possibility, with Pa Ferguson, of a hand having seven wild cards. That possibility was never realized with us, but with the Gooks wild and the low hole card wild, one was foolish to bet on anything short of a Royal Flush. The game was so devastating that FDR had to invent a new name. Pa Ferguson was too tame. One night he came up with it—Mr. Justice McReynolds.

Old Mac was typical of the legal mentality and philosophy that FDR abhorred. He represented the plantation system of life in which a few favored folks lounged on wide verandas being served mint juleps by other people, most of whom were Black. Hence it was with delight that FDR, using the prerogatives of "dealer's choice," usually dealt the poker hand—"Mr. Justice McReynolds." What a game it was!

These poker games had an atmosphere of relaxation and gaiety. Anyone who brought up business was never invited back. A serious word was taboo because these were the President's nights out—free of worries and concerns. "Two Dollar" Watson was made to order for jibes by FDR. Pa Watson was keen, discerning, and responsible. He was a healthy influence around FDR; he had a warm heart and generous laugh that infected every crowd. Never did his voice carry the icy tinge of ill-will or malice. Steve Early—tense, and highly professional—worked hard to relax on these occassions. Harold Ickes, filled with a hundred favors he wanted to ask the President, was on edge because the rules banned all serious talk. Morgenthau was Henny Penny to FDR—a dignified, able, loyal servant. Henry did not drink much and was always in the role of the butler who stayed unostentatiously in the wings. McIntyre was soft-spoken, shy, and retiring. It was, all in all, a happy crowd, with FDR and Pa Watson in the center of the stage.

These parties continued up to FDR's death in 1945. Just before the 1944 election we played at the Ickes home, and the President was the loser. He lost fifty dollars and I won fifty dollars. He hated to lose, and therefore, winning from him was a special joy. As I picked up the money I said, tongue-in-cheek, "Mr. President, you can't imagine how sorry I am to do this to you, knowing how you hate to lose at poker."

"Not at all," he replied. "I'm happy that I lost tonight."

Everyone roared, until he added, "One can't be lucky in poker and politics the same time. There's a big election coming up next week."

A year earlier—January, 1943—I had been at a poker party at the Morgenthaus' when FDR was in a serious mood, anxious to discuss matters of state. As we sat together at a small table at a buffet dinner, he asked me if I were not going to ask him who was going to be the next Supreme Court Justice, taking the place vacated by James F. Byrnes. I said I would not, because if I did, I would violate the basic rule forbidding the discussion at these poker sessions of affairs of state. He said if I questioned him, he would not consider it a violation. I countered, saying that others might, however. He finally said, "Aren't you curious as to the appointee?"

"I'm bursting with curiosity, Mr. President."

"Then ask me."

"No, I'll not ask you that question. But I will ask you who is not going to be appointed."

He threw back his head and laughed in his typical robust way. "That's a good question and I'll answer it. Learned Hand is *not* going to be appointed."

Learned Hand had had a distinguished career both on the District Court and on the Court of Appeals. So I replied, "You are passing by a fine man, Mr. President."

"Perhaps so. But this time Felix overplayed his hand."

The President put down his fork and turned to me, saying, "Do you know how many people asked me today to name Learned Hand?" Pausing only a second, he added, "Twenty, and every one a messenger from Felix Frankfurter." Pausing for another second, he thrust out his jaw and added, "And by golly, I won't do it."

His Dutch was up; he was boiling over at this effort to snowball him. After a few minutes' quiet, he asked, "Well, aren't you going to ask who it will be?" After more sparring, he said, "Let's see if you can guess. And I'll give you a clue. His name is famous in Supreme Court history."

My mind was a blank. I could not guess. So he finally told me—Wiley Rutledge. And sure enough, the Rutledge name went up the next Monday, January 11, 1943. (The prior Rutledge on the Court was John Rutledge, who sat as Associate Justice 1790 to 1791 and briefly in 1795 as Chief Justice on a recess nomination that was never confirmed.)

I asked him why he had chosen Wiley. He said that just before leaving the office for this party, Missy LeHand had come in and said that Irving Brant of the St. Louis *Post Dispatch* wanted to see him for a minute. Brant—whom FDR greatly admired—stayed five minutes and convinced him that Rutledge was his man. The President was in the mood to be convinced because of the Frankfurter barrage.

I frequently visited the President at Hyde Park, and was with him there when he completed the plans for the Roosevelt Library. I would tour the estate with him, and he would show me his latest project—for example, the young Christmas trees, which were turning into a good business venture for him. We had many discussions on the spacious porch of the Hyde Park house, where, but for his wife Eleanor, George Draper, and Louis Howe, FDR would have been sentenced to life.

At one point Father Divine, the well-known Black spiritual leader, had bought a palatial place opposite Hyde Park across the Hudson. The scuttlebutt in the village was that the owners had sold it to Father Divine to annoy FDR. The Old Man laughed hilariously at that story.

FDR was a very complicated man. He had a wide range of interests, a lively mind, a great sense of the earth. He was a great storyteller and loved risqué stories. I became identified in his mind with tales he should never hear.

"Well, Mr. Justice," he'd say, "I suppose you've got another of your untellable stories tonight."

I would answer, "I don't want to pollute your ears with it, Mr. President."

"Oh, come on, pollute me" was the answer.

I'd tell the story then and FDR would almost break a rib laughing.

The President loved a joke and when he could turn away from the enormous trials of his office, we tried to be light-hearted with him.

If I needed to see FDR, I would call Missy LeHand or Grace Tully in the evening and she would schedule me to see the President in his bedroom at seven-thirty or eight the following morning. That way, there wouldn't be any one else around and we could talk. I'd usually see him while he was having breakfast in bed or just after the tray had been taken away. Then he was always bubbling over with good humor; it was the best time, I discovered, for quiet talks.

Depending on his mood, or on his schedule, either we would discuss my SEC problem and I would leave, or else the President might be feeling very talkative and say, "Pull up a chair and let's talk."

He might discuss a speech someone made the day before, or he might say, "The Missus says I'm not emphasizing enough social security. What do you think?"

These early-morning visits tended to be short, but sometimes, when I would go out with him on the Presidential yacht, the *Williamsburg*, we'd be alone all afternoon and evening, and then we would talk about everything and everyone—perhaps about James Farley, or Huey Long, or Churchill.

The yacht was used quite a bit because the President had trouble sleeping. He slept best on a boat—if it was running. So we would go down the Potomac, and when we reached a point in the river where the water was deep enough, the *Williamsburg* would go in a circle, round and round, from ten in the evening until seven the following morning.

In FDR's time Camp David was called Shangri-la. The President preferred the Potomac River to Shangri-la, but he did make use of his mountain retreat. I spent many a weekend there with him. I had rather a lonely time at Shangri-la because FDR was holed up doing homework on endless problems—he would read, then doze, then dictate, then read, then doze. I was company-in-waiting, ready to mix his favorite cocktail or to join him for idle chitchat, and of course to eat the noon and evening meals with him. When I was there alone I had hours for hiking the countryside, which, by the way, had at least one marvelous stream where seven-pound brown trout could be caught.

The long hours at Shangri-la gave me time to perfect the dry martini—FDR's favorite cocktail. I fathomed the secret and became his favorite bartender. The martini had to be cold but not watery. That meant the mixer had to be chilled and any ice that was put in taken out quickly. The glasses too had to be frozen. One never shakes a martini, only stirs it. The ratio of gin to vermouth is important but not measurable. Noilly Prat was FDR's favorite vermouth, and holding the mixer up to the light I put in just that touch of vermouth that gave a very slight yellowish tinge to the gin. The rim of the crisp, cold glass would be rubbed with a piece of lemon; a lemon peel would be added; and then the drink would be poured.

More often than not I was taken to Shangri-la as a companion for some other guest, my function being to stick with the guest while FDR worked. On those weekends I got a new insight into Washington, D.C., life and politics. Men hungry for power, position, and publicity ate out their hearts to get a blessing, an approval, an assignment from FDR. Their happiness turned on his smile, his nod, his handshake. I came to realize how oppressive it must be to be dependent on another person's smile or approval. I realized how immune my life had been to such influences, how lonely had been the trail I walked. I wanted nothing from any man. I had my own dreams; and they were dependent solely on me, not on the whim or caprice of another. So it was in sorrow that I saw the parade of ambitious men at Shangri-la.

I remember particularly a weekend with Nelson Rockefeller. I knew Nelson and liked him and thought he had a brilliant future in public service. He wanted at that time to be the Assistant Secretary of State in charge of Latin American affairs. He talked about it as we hiked the countryside and I expressed my support of his ambition.

"Will the Boss offer me the job?" he kept asking me.

I was not in on the secret but I did know FDR. So when on our return to quarters late that afternoon, Nelson asked me what I thought his chances were, I replied, "Nelson, if FDR was going to make you Assistant Secretary of State he would not bring you down here for a weekend, keeping you full of suspense."

"Then why was I invited?"

"I do not know for sure, but I think it is a consolation prize. FDR is about to appoint someone else but wants you to know that he is fond of you. This weekend is really a fond farewell."

That was precisely what happened.

I often was with FDR on weekends as well as at other times when speeches had to be written or when he wanted me merely to spend an evening with him watching a movie. Betsy Roosevelt, James Roosevelt's wife and one of the finest women I ever knew, was often present, sitting quietly in a corner, reading or knitting. "What are you doing here?" I'd ask. She would smile and whisper that the President asked her not to leave him alone. "A real queen," he often said of her.

For speechwriting he usually sat facing a ring of a few of us: Lauchlin Currie, Steve Early, Tommy Corcoran, Robert Sherwood, Ben Cohen, Isadore Lubin, and Harry Hopkins. The anchor man was Samuel I. Rosenman, a New York judge whose quiet presence was FDR's mainstay, for Sam stayed on after everyone else left.

It would be announced before we met that the speech was to be given at a certain place and on a certain subject. FDR would begin by reading aloud a rough draft, and would then call on the people in the room for suggestions. Each of us had a partial draft we would hand up, and FDR read each aloud. He might say, "We'll, I don't think I ought to get into that," or "Use that, Sam." Then he would dictate a paragraph or so to a secretary and resume the out-loud reading of other morsels that various people had sent in. Thus a speech was built, section by section. By 11:00 P.M. or so the first draft of the finished product was ready. Each of us had a copy and would approve or disapprove. These speechwriting sessions usually took place in the Oval Room, as FDR slept next door. He was in shirt sleeves, relaxed, and in good humor. Speechwriting to him was like a house-raising "bee" on the frontier.

These sessions were intense and fast, usually over in less than an hour. At the end of the meeting the notes would be turned over to Sam Rosenman, who would work up a final draft. The rest of us were scriveners.

At that time the White House staff, those immediately around FDR, was an interesting, dedicated group.

Marvin H. McIntyre, a Presidential assistant from 1933 to 1942, was a thin wraith of a man, who always seemed to have a cigarette cough. He was quietly efficient and a strong ally.

Missy LeHand—tall, gracious, quiet, and efficient—was a lovely lady who had worked with FDR when he was in Albany, and prior to that, when he ran for the Vice-Presidency in 1920. She knew his tastes and moods, and her catalogue of those he liked, tolerated, and disliked was complete. She was therefore an effective alter ego. She lived on the third floor of the White House and was a superconfidential secretary. Missy died tragically in 1944 at the age of forty-seven of a cerebral hemorrhage.

Grace Tully, with blue eyes and a broad Irish grin, worked with Missy and took over as secretary when she died. She was a more outgoing person than Missy—loquacious and friendly, with a sparkling humor and a very incisive mind. Grace, in 1949, wrote her tender memoirs—*F.D.R. My Boss.*

Pa Watson was a graduate of West Point and had been heavily decorated in active service. He was a major general and aide to FDR beginning in 1939. He died shortly before Roosevelt, in 1945 at the age of sixty-two. Pa Watson was a friendly, gracious man with all the amenities which his Alabama upbringing had bred in him. He loved to tell and to hear stories; his laugh was infectious. He guarded FDR jealously—not from those who would assault him, but from those who would annoy him or seek to take advantage of him. He was known as "Two Dollar" Watson, since he was always willing to bet that amount on his poker hand. FDR used to tease him about his brilliant military record: "The Lord always takes care of drunks and major generals."

Stephen Early, who died in 1951 at the age of sixty-two, was a brilliant newsman and news executive, who was with the President at the White House from 1933 to 1945, and after his death, became special assistant to Truman. He was a hard-playing golfer who drove a stiff bargain to get extra strokes or a bisque or two. Early's sole dedication was to FDR and he was most protective of his interests. Once William Clark, a federal judge, came to see the President to tender his resignation because he wanted to join the Army for a term. Clark handed the letter of resignation to FDR, saying he hated to resign and wished the President would give him a leave of absence. "Of course," said FDR casually as he tossed the letter in the wastebasket. Steve, who was present, knew they'd be headed for trouble if FDR took that course. So when the judge left, Steve Early retrieved the letter and put it in the file, and in due time it became the vital link in the government's case when Clark later brought suit for back pay—and lost.

Ross T. McIntyre was an admiral assigned as White House physician from 1933 to 1945. He was quiet and unobtrusive and very seldom spoke up, but he was extremely able and kept a stern eye on FDR's health.

Harry Hopkins was not on the White House staff in the early days, but by 1942, after the war broke out, he was living in the White House as special assistant and envoy for the President. He was FDR's closest confidant, giving the President advice on a wide range of policies. Earlier in the New Deal, Hopkins had been in charge of unemployment relief, serving as head of various other committees and agencies before he became Secretary of Commerce in 1938.

By about 1936 Hopkins wanted to be President more than anything else. Hence it was difficult for any young, rising star—even myself, who had no political ambitions—to get on with Harry. He was adept at "throwing sand in the gears," as one of my friends stated. In other words, Harry, by whispered warnings to FDR, could keep any young man down.

Hopkins always looked hungry, overworked and unkempt. He smoked cigarettes incessantly. He was as solicitous of FDR's welfare as a watchdog and extremely sensitive to any criticism of him. He was also intensely jealous of those close to the President (which included me).

Hopkins would make cutting remarks to those around the President. He might say something like "God save the nation if anyone like you ever got in charge."

When in 1940 Hopkins resigned as Secretary of Commerce because of ill health, FDR wrote him: "You may resign the office—only the office—and nothing else. Our friendship will and must go on as always."

The last time I saw Harry Hopkins was at FDR's funeral, when he looked like a walking cadaver.

Henry Morgenthau was the most considerate, the most loyal man in FDR's Cabinet. He was the only one—except for Frances Perkins—who had no personal ambitions to satisfy. Morgenthau was a neighbor of FDR's in New York and was his campaign business manager when he ran for governor in 1928. Roosevelt brought him to Washington to head the Federal Farm Bureau, which Morgenthau merged into the Farm Credit Administration. When the Secretary of the Treasury, William H. Woodin, became ill, FDR made Morgenthau Under Secretary and then Secretary. Henry was as meticulous as the day is long. He even kept a record of every daily event. When I attended conferences in his office, the taped record being kept became a bit of a game. A few of us maneuvered the conversations into irrelevancies; we put risqué stories into the machine; we made startling inventions of facts to cause Henry to interrupt the proceedings. Whatever happened to Henry's voluminous records, I do not know. They were in a sense to be preferred over Harold Ickes', who dictated an account of every day's events. Ickes spent hours polishing them and rewriting them, and then put them into deep freeze for later use. Many have appeared in print in the Ickes diaries.

It was Morgenthau who promoted the War Refugee Board finally established by FDR on January 22, 1944, to aid the rescue and relief of European Jews. The liquidation of Jews by Hitler had long been under way. I was not at the center of our efforts with this terrible problem, only on its periphery, but I knew Randolph Paul and Oscar Cox, lawyers who had been helping Morgenthau in this area. I was also aware that Washington, D.C., at the bureaucratic level was "sticky" on the Jewish question. I felt, though I could not prove it, that there was a streak of anti-Semitism in the State Department. It was public knowledge that Hitler was killing Jews, and even the daily rate was fairly well estimated. Still the State Department deferred action, and the British, fearing Arab reaction, were hesitant about sending Jewish refugees to Palestine. All sorts of whispered schemes were afloat, including bribery of Eastern European governments to let Jews escape. The lurid details are now contained in Arthur D. Morse, *While Six Million Died.* Some now fiercely criticize Pope Pius and FDR. Certainly the West was strangely complacent in the face of Hitler's plan for genocide. We were also even more complacent when genocide swept Indonesia in the sixties under the banner of anti-communism. In 1941–1945 FDR certainly was not apathetic. Whether he could have done more, in spite of his paralyzed Department of State, is, perhaps, still an open question.

Henry Wallace, who replaced Garner as Vice-President in Roosevelt's third administration, did not have many friends in official Washington among the professionals. The intellectuals were for him but not the wheel-horses of Washington politics. That, however, was not too meaningful, for he had a large following in the country—and FDR knew it.

Wallace went in for spiritualism, an avocation which almost became a dangerous liability to FDR in the Presidential election of 1940. Roosevelt was running for a third term, and Wallace was his Vice-Presidential nominee. There was a medium in Georgetown who conducted séances.

People would sit holding hands in a darkened room and wait for the spirit to appear in the form of a cloud over the piano. Then questions would be asked and the spirit would reply. The Washington scuttlebutt was that the spirit's answers to Henry's questions determined the price of corn.

Whether or not that was true, Henry's correspondence with the medium came into the possession of the Republican National Committee. FDR, by hook or by crook, got a copy, and having read the letters, sent for me. Henry Wallace and the medium had a code, which I no longer remember, except that FDR was *The Flaming One*. The President was sick at heart when I walked in. He showed me the letters and asked, "How does one get rid of his Vice-Presidential running mate?"

I had no quick answer, saying I'd be back tomorrow.

The next day I told him that if Henry would resign, the National Committee could name a substitute.

"Suppose he doesn't resign?"

"Then you'll have to have another Democratic Convention."

"My God" was all FDR could say.

Harry Hopkins came in and we three discussed the matter. Harry walked out with me, saying, "This may kill the Old Man."

But FDR was rsecued by happenstance. Wendell Willkie, the Republican candidate for President, had a "girl" in New York (a very fine woman whom I later came to know), and his carryings-on were becoming notorious. A tacit agreement was made with the Republican National Committee that nothing would be said about Willkie's girl if the committee did not release the letters of Henry Wallace to Madame Zenda or her letters to him.

Thus did Roosevelt squeak through October, 1940.

I had a deep and abiding affection for FDR. My closest bond with him was not in the work of cleaning up the capitalist system; rather it was in various expressions of his love of the earth—its grasses and trees, its manifold wildlife, its precious sanctuaries.

When he spoke at Mount Vernon on April 14, 1939, on the 150th anniversary of the election of George Washington to the Presidency, he revealed that side of him:

> "Washington was essentially a man close to mother earth. His early training on a plantation, his profession of surveyor, his studies in agriculture and the development of farmlands were never replaced by his outstanding military service under Brad-

dock or as Commander in Chief for the eight years of the Revolution.

"We know that when Mount Vernon came to him by inheritance, here his heart was planted for all time. Here he could talk with his neighbors about the improvement of navigation on the river, about grist mills on the creeks, about the improving of highways, about the dream of a canal to the western country, about sawmills and rotation of crops, about the topsoil, which even then had begun to run off to the sea, about the planting of trees, new varieties of food and fodder crops, new breeds of horses and cattle and sheep."

FDR was such a man. He, too, loved the earth. As I have said, I toured his Hyde Park estate with him in the car with special equipment that enabled him to drive. He was the "squire" who cherished the topsoil, the fields, and forests and saw in soil conservation as well as in the wilderness the salvation of America.

It was FDR who came to grips with the problems of the Dust Bowl. The shelter belts he built still stand as monuments to his conservation instincts, especially in North and South Dakota. These belts are usually composed of two rows of trees about thirty to sixty feet apart. As the trees grew, the space between the two rows became a tangle of wildwood. Birds were attracted, and rabbits and deer as well. The shelter belts helped make the Great Plains abundant in wildlife. They caught the drifting snows of winter; the spring melt watered the lands. They broke the force of the wind; even now, on a hot, dry day, one can see dust curl up and disappear in them, when at an earlier time it would have blotted out the sun.

It was FDR who in 1935 caused the Soil Conservation Service to be created. This service was excellent for a while, but by the sixties and seventies it had run off the track. It began to follow the example of the Corps of Engineers in "channelizing" rivers—that is to say, turning a river into a flume, and spraying the banks with herbicides, with the result that nothing would grow.

The President pleaded for "the reforestation of the great watershed of the nation" and "to cooperate with nature and not to fight her." In 1936 he said, "The history of every nation is eventually written in the way in which it cares for its soil." In 1937 he proposed the creation of seven regional authorities to make plans for flood control, soil conservation, restoration of forest lands and grazing lands, and the promotion of wilderness values. He also proposed a plan for rejuvenating the Great Plains, restoring them to their original grassland condition.

In 1938 he was responsible for the creation of the Olympic National Park in my state—a section long thought by the lumber barons to be their own fief. This is the area of the rain forest, unique in America. Sitka spruce, Western hemlock, and Douglas fir are the dominant trees, and they grow two hundred feet or more in height, locking branches at the top, so that practically no ray of sun touches the ground. Under them grow the big-leaf maple and red alder. Various mosses are abundant; the ferns are lush; the trees are draped with epiphytes. These rain forests start at about five hundred feet above sea level in valleys like the Hoh, which face the ocean and draw up the moist winds that keep the trees constantly dripping. Above the rain forests are alpine meadows and lakes; above them, many glaciers, topped by jagged Mount Olympus, which is not quite eight thousand feet high but is snow-clad the year round. This is land of the black-tailed deer and Roosevelt elk. Mountain goat flourish in the crags. Steelhead and salmon run the rivers for spawning.

For good measure FDR added a three-mile coastal belt about fifty miles long. This land is physically separated from the main body of the park but comprises most of the true wilderness coastline we have left, if one traveling from the straits of San Juan de Fuca in the West follows the shoreline up through Maine in the East.

I helped FDR on this project, but the main drive was supplied by Harold Ickes. Behind the scenes, giving FDR the technical data he needed, was Irving Brant, who at the President's request made a special study of the area.

In 1939 FDR took the first overall step at the federal level to clean up our streams and lakes from the pollution that was possessing them. In the same year he agreed to give the B&O Railroad Company, whose president was the unusually imaginative Dan Willard, credit on the books of the United States for loans made to it in exchange for the historic C&O Canal property extending 180 miles from Washington, D.C., westward to Cumberland, Maryland, along the Potomac River. In time this was to become the C&O Canal National Historic Park.

Roosevelt spoke of his great love for the Pacific Northwest, and he once told me how he almost went out there as a young man. Weyerhauser Lumber Company had offered him a job.

"Think of it," he said. "Franklin Roosevelt a lumber operator, cutting down trees. What would have happened to me?"

"You would have tired easily of doing that. You'd have run for governor, then the Senate, and then for President."

"I wonder. I wonder," he answered. "Streams of history are very difficult to create." Pausing he added, "There is a time and a place for everyone."

Chapter XXI

The New Deal

The Big Depression was on us. The banks were closed. I remember walking the streets of New Haven with the great sum of ten dollars in my pocket. I did not feel panicky; personally, it only appeared that the wheel had turned, taking everyone back to the conditions of poverty I had known in Yakima. The common disaster seemed to bring everyone closer together. There was much reexamination in university circles of where we had been and where we were going. The stock market crash had been awesome to watch from the sidelines. Many men committed suicide when they saw their empires crumble. Some men like Joseph P. Kennedy were selling short; some like Cyrus Eaton were buying the blue chips at or near the bottom. Samuel M. Smith—in later years one of my closest friends, but not known to me in 1929—was a CPA working with receiverships on the West Coast; he was shortly to acquire the fabulous Pittock Block, Portland, Oregon, which later became a veritable gold mine.

Receiverships and bankruptcies were rampant. Protective and reorganization committees were formed to represent various classes of security holders of these bankrupt companies. Lincoln automobiles that were brand-new came on the market for a few hundred dollars; (and I bought one, which I drove for many years thereafter). The ranks of the unemployed mounted; bread lines increased; soup kitchens multiplied; farm products slumped in price and farmers began dumping their milk in the streets in angry protest; freight cars carried thousands of passengers where once they carried only hundreds; dividend payments stopped and interest payments defaulted, leaving trust accounts dry; the income of colleges and universities plummeted.

President Herbert Hoover's plan to mend the economy was to restore the financial strength of industry so that it could reemploy workers. Federal agencies, such as the Reconstruction Finance Corporation, were formed. Financial loans were poured out to industry, but unemployment mounted.

Opposition to Hoover grew. "The greatest engineer in American history," he was called at one Connecticut meeting I attended.

"He dammed, ditched, and drained the entire country," another platform speaker shouted.

Still another speaker explained Hoover's theory of feeding chickens: "First, feed oats to the horses, and in time there will be enough manure to keep the chickens busy." After a pause he thundered, "I say let's feed the chickens first."

As the 1932 campaign got under way, several of us on the Yale faculty were out on the hustings debating the opposition. I remember one night in Hartford when a fiery professor on the Republican side built his hour-long speech around the theme "You can't make water run uphill." He sat down to thunderous applause.

I arose, to reply briefly: "Come out West and I will show you projects where we send water *over* mountain ranges, as well as through them and around them. Engineers make water run uphill every day." My thesis was that all we needed were engineering skills, and that we needed a new engineer in the White House.

FDR was storming the country and soon was elected in a landslide.

There was, throughout the days of the New Deal, a good amount of speculation about the political theory and philosophy of FDR's program. The words "liberal," "progressive," "radical," and "conservative," however, are not too meaningful. It is often difficult to fit any one person neatly into one of these categories. A "conservative" in constitutional law would technically be he who stuck closest to the constitutional structure of 1787. But in modern-day parlance, those who do so are called "left-wingers." A "conservative" in constitutional law has come to mean he who construes the Constitution and Bill of Rights the best to serve the Establishment. The "liberal" has come to mean one opposed to existing practices, although still working within the constitutional framework. The "radical" is one who, if necessary, would dispense with the framework in seeking solutions. After the 1940's the word "progressive" disappeared from our vocabulary.

In American politics FDR was not regarded as a conservative, though his roots, his family, his early associations were all with the conservative group. When he used politics to serve causes beyond that group's interests, he was viewed as a traitor, as was anyone who, though an original member of their group, later used politics, education, the pen, the pulpit, or the law to serve ends they considered hostile. My friend Harry Golden, of North Carolina, who espoused desegregation of the races, was not considered a traitor, since he was not born in the South. The traitor would be the native Southerner who takes a desegregation stance on race. The conservatives of America—members of the Establishment—never forgave FDR for deserting the cause, which they thought was his by reason of birth.

Those of us close to FDR never felt he deserted the conservative cause in principle. Except for the installation of real collective bargaining, he left the social and economic order largely untouched. His energy was spent in cleaning up that order, eliminating its excesses, and making capitalism respectable. FDR was, in American terminology, more a progressive than a liberal. He worked in the La Follette tradition. Probably no politician can survive who moves left from that position, for the United States has usually been conservative in its inclinations.

During the New Deal days the people were prisoners of their own illusions, as Robert M. Hutchins once put it. The major delusions, to use his categories, were: the budget should be balanced annually; currency must be "sound"; the gold standard was untouchable; socialism was a menace; free enterprise could provide a job for everyone, if it were left alone; the states were supreme, the federal government largely impotent. As Hutchins has said, these "received ideas" were alien to the new world that was in the making. These are the reasons why, I think, the New Deal has become largely meaningless to the subsequent generation.

FDR's embrace of capitalism and most of the basic tenets of the Establishment were made evident by his NRA (National Industrial Recovery Act), which was enacted in 1933 and expired in 1935. This was the Blue Eagle scheme whereby industry was given the power to make the rules governing competition and prices. The NRA stemmed from Rex Tugwell's effort to get Roosevelt to give business the authority to fix its own prices and to put such restrictions on production as it chose. Tugwell, an advisor to FDR, was trying to persuade him, even prior to the nomination, as to the merits of "economic self-government." (Tugwell describes that idea in his book *The Brain Trust.*) Tugwell was opposed to the Wilson-Brandeis view that the Sherman Act and Clayton Act, restricting monopolies and restraint of trade, were desirable, that big units should be broken into small components and kept that way. He thought that the antitrust laws prevented "any sort of social management" and kept competition "at a destructive level." He saw that monopoly in electric power was inevitable and competition impractical, but from that example, he argued with FDR that if "power production could not be fractionalized, neither could other similar industries." Tugwell thought that prices could be controlled in ways other than fractionalization and competition, by government responsibility for the planning of production. Tugwell proposed "an orderly mechanism that might enable industry to produce a cooperation now considered illegitimate."

Tugwell did not make much headway in selling the idea to FDR prior to the 1932 election. His plan, as submitted, was in the form of a proposal for a White House Economic Council whose job would be to reorganize industry on the model of the Federal Reserve System in banking. "The antitrust acts can be repealed and each industry can be encouraged to divide itself into suitable regional groups on which will sit representatives of the Economic Council."

In these early years FDR tried to placate business, and he was still in that mood when I reached Washington, D.C., in 1934. I remember his speech to the American Bankers Association that fall, when the audience cheered him to the echo. He proposed an alliance of business, banking, agriculture, labor, and industry to achieve "business recovery." He added, "What an all-American team that would be!" Of all the measures FDR proposed and got enacted in the first year, two were most crucial to business. One was the Agricultural Adjustment Act, which was to make a few farmers rich and make the plight of the sharecroppers more serious. The other was the NRA, which allowed businessmen to control production and fix prices.

Hugo L. Black, then in the Senate, made a prophetic speech:

"This bill, if it shall pass and become law, will transfer the lawmaking power of this nation, insofar as the control of industry is concerned, from the Congress to the trade associations. There is no escape from that conclusion. That is exactly what has happened in Italy, and as a result, the legislation passed by the parliamentary body of Italy, as expressed by one economist, has reached the vanishing point." (77 Congress Rec 5284)

Under the NRA, the President, on application of "one or more trade or industrial associations or groups," was empowered to "approve a code or codes of fair competition for the trade or industry or subdivision thereof, represented by the applicant or applicants." Once a code was approved, its provisions "shall be the standards of fair competition" for the particular trade or industry, any violation of which carried sanctions both civil and criminal.

There are those who still say that NRA was FDR's fling with socialism, but it had no resemblance to any school of socialist thought. NRA was an attempt to grant to industry the power to set production quotas and prices. It was a grant of monopolistic power to private industry, placing the making of the rules governing business in the hands of business itself.

As Black had said, this Act thus placed lawmaking in the hands of private industry subject to Presidential approval. Tugwell was an economist, not a lawyer, but New Dealers who blessed this monstrosity cannot be excused. They certainly knew better. And it is difficult, even after long reflection, to grasp the mentality of Tugwell, an extremely able man, in conceiving an industrial system under which the biggest, the most powerful units in business laid down the rules of price and competition for the group. The result would obviously be a vicious form of cartel, in which a few companies would determine the destinies of the smaller entrepreneurs.

The project was declared unconstitutional by a unanimous Court in 1935,* a Court that included Brandeis and Cardozo, Butler and McReynolds. Any Supreme Court that ever sat would have so ruled, because lawmaking under the Constitution is a matter for Congress, not for private parties. That proposal of FDR's would have made a structural change in capitalism that would have strengthened the Establishment and taken us a long way down the road to the corporate state.

FDR exploited the old liberal clichés, but he never touched the basic problems of the ghettos—the citadels of the bankers, real estate brokers, moneylenders, and the city officials whom they control. He multiplied agencies, but never aimed at permanent control of basic industries. He never reached the race problem. Personally he worried about it, but politically he aligned himself with the powers-that-be in the South so far as Black people were concerned. And during his administrations he never even effected complete integration of the races in the Armed Forces.

In this regard, one day my secretary announced the presence of a Black

* *Schechter Poultry Corporation v. United States*, 295 U.S. 495.

woman who had come with credentials from my old classmate Paul Robeson. When the woman was escorted in, I offered her a chair, but she remained standing and asked, "Who am I?"

"You are kin to my friend Paul Robeson."

"I know my name. But who am I?"

I shook my head.

She replied, "I am the bastard daughter of the brother of a former Supreme Court Justice."

What she was conveying to me was that she was in the Supreme Court building as a matter of right. Her demand was that I persuade FDR that there should be an immediate desegregation of the races in the Armed Forces.

I talked with FDR about this lady's idea. He did not laugh, scoff, or scorn. He listened intently and with approval and said, "We'll see." After a long pause he added, lighting a cigarette, "You know they call the Missus a nigger-lover. Perfectly dreadful what they say." He reminisced about the strong hold that the South had on the Congress and how his old wheelhorses (meaning people like Jimmie Byrnes and Joe Robinson) had a deep racial bias. And then he passed to other things, and we never did get back to integration in the Armed Forces. When at last integration was achieved under Truman, white officers, who had commanded Black troops, said it was the best thing that had ever happened, for though loyal and a physical part of the Armed Forces, Black troops were understandably sullen and resentful as long as they remained segregated.

Yet in spite of FDR's moderate stance on race and on capitalism, he had a host of bitter enemies. The rancher for whom I had worked in the wheat fields in my early years in the State of Washington was one of them. When I was a field hand, Ralph Snyder was close to bankruptcy. His lands were heavily mortgaged, he was paying at least eight percent interest at the banks, the price of wheat was up and down, making the business extremely hazardous, as the costs were fixed.

Years passed and I did not see Ralph. Finally, in the forties, we met at my log cabin up the Lostine River in the Wallowas Mountains of eastern Oregon. Ralph was then prosperous. His mortgages had been refinanced at an interest rate of about three percent. There was a floor under his wheat. He had tens of thousands of dollars in the bank. Yet for the first half-hour he did nothing but curse FDR.

"How can you be so critical?" I asked. "You are one of the beneficiaries of FDR's farm program. You should be praising him, and all you do is denounce him."

He thought awhile and then gave a most revealing answer. "It is true I am much better off. But let me ask you something—did you ever meet the rancher down the road from me? Well, he's no good—lazy, shiftless, a poor manager. I'd call him worthless. What's happened to him? He's on easy street. He never had it so good. This Roosevelt program makes a no-good guy rich. How can we expect America to be strong if men who couldn't make it on their own are hoisted up by government?"

This same attitude prevailed against practically all New Deal measures. The guarantee of bank deposits is another good example: the banks had closed during the Depression, and some never reopened. The federal guarantee of deposits was to cover a hundred percent of the first $10,000 of deposits, seventy-five percent of the next $40,000, and fifty percent of all deposits over $50,000. Men white with rage argued the merits of this proposal: it will weaken the character of bankers, making them less efficient because they will know that their mistakes will be underwritten by Uncle Sam; it will make people more and more dependent on government, when what is needed is strong and independent men; it is a form of socialism that is dangerous; free enterprise cannot remain free if its mistakes are underwritten by a government; the harsh economic issues sweeping the world will then move in and take over. This was the essence of the hard-core reaction against FDR.

One New Deal reform that was basically liberal gave labor the power of collective bargaining. Up to that time strikes by laborers had been illegal under a rule created by judges, who rather enthusiastically extended the Sherman Act to cover labor. Thus the Pullman strike was broken in 1894. In time judges revised the rule to allow strikes called either to raise wages or to reduce hours of work. They often disallowed strikes to unionize a shop, or strikes that were secondary boycotts aimed at products made by firms engaged in unfair labor practices. In 1914 Congress attempted to change these judge-made rules through the Clayton Act. Though the language of that Act was broad and seemingly all inclusive, judges, in construing it, once more read their antilabor prejudices into the Act and applied it narrowly. By 1933, when FDR took office, one of the main ingredients of industrial strife was the failure of industry to recognize and utilize the theory and practice of collective bargaining.

Collective bargaining was therefore included, even if temporarily, within the codes of fair competition authorized by the NRA. And collective bargaining was permanently included in the Wagner Labor Relations Act creating the National Labor Relations Board in 1935.

The power of industry to fix prices was well established. The power of labor to negotiate for wages somewhat restored the balance. The other liberal reform of the New Deal involved the transfer of the financial center of the United States from Wall Street to Washington. Wilson had warned in 1911, "The great monopoly in this country is the money monopoly." The Pujo Committee, dating from 1912, concluded that the great danger was "the control of credit" by private groups.

The Federal Reserve Act of 1913 remedied part of the problem by establishing the Federal Reserve Board in Washington. As FDR said when he dedicated the lovely Federal Reserve Building in 1937, that board, a governmental, not a private, agency exerts "a powerful influence upon the expansion and contraction in the flow of money through the channels of agriculture, trade, and industry."

But the board did not solve the entire problem. Brandeis discussed the matter in his study, *Other People's Money,* published in 1913:

> The dominant element in our financial oligarchy is the investment banker. Associated banks, trust companies and life insurance companies are his tools. Controlled railroads, public service and industrial corporations are his subjects. Though properly but middlemen, these bankers bestride as masters America's business world, so that practically no large enterprise can be undertaken successfully without their participation or approval. These bankers are, of course, able men possessed of large fortunes; but the most potent factor in their control of business is not the possession of extraordinary ability or huge wealth. The key to their power is Combination—concentration intensive and comprehensive . . .

It was this citadel that the SEC assaulted. Our basic laws—the Securities Act of 1933, the Securities Exchange Act of 1934, and the Public Utility Holding Company Act of 1935—helped move the power away from the investment bankers.

This transfer of financial power was both painful and exciting. The Federal Reserve Board, with its able chairman, Marriner Eccles, who advocated deficit spending, raised alarming specters in the financial community. I saw another example of this alarm when in 1938 I went to Chicago to address the Chicago Bond Club. After the speech I was followed from the room by an irate investment banker, who kept shouting, "Why are you trying to destroy America?"

My answers did not satisfy him, so as we passed through an ornate room on our way to the elevator, I stopped, and pointing to the paintings on the walls, said, "We are doing nothing more destructive to America than would be done to this room if we moved the pictures around."

Trembling with anger, my questioner shouted, "Why in hell do you want to move the pictures around?"

The PWA (Public Works Administration) was the most visible embodiment of the new economic program. Men were at work raking leaves, digging ditches, building roads, planting trees, paving streets, erecting buildings, and so on. There they were—the miserable unemployed people—at long last back on a payroll. Some of them were undoubtedly shiftless; some may have been freeloaders; but many were engineers, salesmen, and clerks temporarily out of work. They were a motley lot, and at the cocktail hour in those days they were the customary subject of conversation. I recall one predinner reception in New York where I was to speak.

A banker of prestige, power, and great physical presence fairly bellowed at me, as if I were Harry Hopkins, head of PWA, "Do you know what I saw? PWA men on a job. What were they doing? Leaning on their shovels. How do you justify spending public money to let worthless men lean on shovels? If they want to lean, I say take them off the payroll of the public and let them lean against a building."

The Puritan ethic, which holds that a sound society requires a nation of people who work, soon won out. FDR viewed federal relief as only a temporary expedient. He had created, as part of the NRA, the WPA (Works Progress Administration) and out of it spun CWA (Civil Works Administration) to employ people. In order to do so, work had to be created. Public buildings were constructed or renovated, thousands of miles of roads and a hundred thousand bridges and viaducts were built. Unemployed writers were put to work cataloguing the contents of American archives, researching the history of various monuments, and writing historical tomes. I knew some of them, and was proud of their work. Teachers were employed to teach new skills. Actors were employed to man improvised theaters.

The story of the work of these authors and artists is told in Jerry Mangione's book, *The Dream and The Deal,* The Federal Writers Project 1935–1954. The entire project cost twenty-seven million dollars—a sum not large enough to buy the bombs necessary to reduce even a small nation to the Stone Age. Applicants had first to be certified as paupers; starving people had to live in a city a prescribed length of time before they could be so certified. But those who got work cards escaped the scrap heap of the unemployed and were transfigured. Since the Depression began, many people had been earning only a few dollars a week. With a work card they received the munificent salary of a hundred dollars a month.

Exciting chronicles were written, though some were never finished. Somewhere in the labyrinths of Washington, D.C., those manuscripts are stored, unfortunately still unpublished. Critics charged that the Reds controlled the project. Middle America conceived of it as boondoggling. Political pressures caused writers to be dropped and sit-in strikes followed, headed by unions the press denounced as left-wing or Red. There were bloody affairs in the wake of the seemingly innocuous effort to put starving members of the fourth estate to work. These people had a song:

Roosevelt! You're my man.
When the time comes
I ain't got a cent
You buy my groceries
And pay my rent
Mr. Roosevelt, you're my man.

A guide to each state was produced, including the state's most interesting historic figures. Accounts of minorities were published, as were some thousand pamphlets, brochures, and books. Across the land other publishers, especially in the South and in New England, became interested. State historical societies published some manuscripts.

The Writers' Project was laughed at, booed, and denounced, but it did produce a lot of interesting Americana. While the communist-oriented writers were talking about this ugly earthly existence and the good times coming, these starving writers wrote about the greatness of America and its future, and at the same time they unfrocked phony figures, promoted racial understanding, and made articulate the lower third of this society.

This was a time when fear stalked the land. As some brokers and bankers were driven to suicide, so were penniless writers who were deprived of their work cards. Throughout the country there was a haunting fear of the loss of jobs. Never in American history had the total collapse of employment, of confidence, of hope been so complete. Only one who lived close to the edge in those days could ever appreciate the powerful impact in FDR's words spoken at his First Inaugural in 1933: "All we have to fear is fear itself."

Well before the time of FDR's election in 1932, people were suffering badly. Unemployment figures were mounting. In the East there were men and women on street corners selling apples, with the hope of getting enough profit to buy some milk for their children. People were being fed at fire stations and public schools and at any available feeding stations. The cities, largely restricted to property taxes for revenue, were unable to meet the financial need. Begging increased; Salvation Army refuges were full; states were getting into relief work but complaining that they did not have the money to meet the demand. And they certainly did not, in light of their existing tax structure. They clamored for federal assistance. Hoover came out against the "dole"; and dole became an ugly four-letter word. Will Rogers said of FDR during the worst of the Depression, "If he burned down the Capitol we would cheer and say, 'Well, we at least got a fire started, anyhow.'"

The Democrats had carried the House in 1930 and the Senate was evenly split. Robert F. Wagner of New York introduced legislation in 1931 which called for one billion dollars for federal public works and federal employment services. The bill passed Congress, but Hoover vetoed it. Wagner's proposal for unemployment insurance also was voted down by the Senate. Robert La Follette and Edward Costigan in the Senate introduced a bill calling for a federal grant of some millions of dollars to the states for unemployment relief. It, too, was voted down by the Senate. Even Hugo Black, then a senator from Alabama, voted against it, speaking at length before the vote was taken. He was strongly in favor of federal money being used to feed and clothe people but he was opposed to the creation of a new bureaucracy to do so. He was only against the creation of a federal agency to disburse the funds. He thought existing state machinery should be used.

Many other people thought relief was a state, not a federal, matter. FDR, who at that time was the governor of New York, led the way by establishing a state program to supplement local relief funds and by the end of 1932 twenty-four states were providing some money to local agencies for relief.

In 1931 Congress overrode a Hoover veto and passed an Act giving the RFC (Reconstruction Finance Corporation) power to lend three hundred million dollars to the states to supplement local relief funds. But that sum was barely a token: the Senate hearings before its Committee on Manufactures tell the gripping human story. My friend Frank Murphy, then the mayor of Detroit, testified that his city had run out of money, and cut off 1,200 families from welfare. Within a few months 300 of them could not be found; they apparently had quit the city in desperation. From 1931 to 1932, 150,000 people left Detroit. The fate of the group which had been deprived of relief was related by Murphy:

"We found 270 of the families were cared for by their next-door neighbors in the block; that 170 were cared for by relatives; that fifty-six percent of them were in arrears in everything—all their bills, groceries, rent, light, and so forth; that there were a few suicides; that forty families had separated, either sent their children to some home and the husband went one way and the wife another, and that the average income of the family heads was $1.56 per week per person for the family. Having in mind that the standard of wages in Detroit, prior to the Depression, was $7 per day, you may see what that means."

Relief in those days was only for "survival." A single adult got $2 a week, an adult couple $3.60; a child under sixteen got 75¢ a week, and 3½ quarts of milk; a child sixteen and over got $1.25 a week.

Economic conditions were so bad that by the time of FDR's First Inaugural, many banks in the country had closed, which led him to say "the money changers have fled from their high seats in the temple of our civilization." I heard this particular speech on the radio in New Haven and I felt that I was one with the President on his social program for taking care of the needy.

A host of legislation was hammered through Congress in the first hundred days of the Roosevelt administration to provide at least temporary relief. Most of the funds went not to breadlines, soup kitchens, or food stamps, but was apportioned among projects that were designed to create "work." Of the four billion dollars of "emergency relief" authorized in 1935, the allocation was as follows: highways and grade crossings, eight hundred million dollars; rural relief, water diversion, irrigation and reclamation, five hundred million; rural electrification, eleven hundred million; housing, four hundred and fifty million; assistance for education, professional and clerical persons, three hundred million; Civilian Conservation Corps, six hundred million; loans or grants to local agencies for self-liquidating projects, nine hundred million; sanitation, erosion, flood control, reforestation, three hundred and fifty million.

Overall, the federal government paid about seventy percent of all relief during that three-year period. Harry Hopkins, as the administrator of the Emergency Relief Act, was a good social worker, but was largely ignorant of broader national needs and knew very little about the rest of the world. He made a study of workers on relief in seventy-nine cities, and found that on the average, they had been unemployed for more than two years. But Hopkins, sensing FDR's opposition to direct payments, parroted the view that only work, not handouts, gave men dignity. He was wont to say that "his" WPA workers looked with disdain on those who received relief.

By the time I reached Washington, in 1934, WPA could provide jobs for only about one in four. The situation worsened when federal direct relief was withdrawn and the unemployed were forced back on state and local agencies.

WPA was only one "work relief" project. The CCC (Civilian Conservation Corps) was another. It provided jobs largely in national forests at subsistence wages, but it could give work to only 250,000 of the 15,000,000 unemployed. I saw these CCC boys at work in the woods, and the exposure of a lad from the Bronx to the wilderness had a permanent effect on him. But what they did to the forests was largely a calamity. They made the interior of the wilderness areas—the sacred sanctuaries, in my mind—easily available to the masses. And that was a curse which was to follow us into the seventies. I told FDR as much, and he understood what I was saying. His response was an expression of his desire to put everyone to work, if possible. "Work is a wonderful therapy," he said. And of course I had to agree. "Cutting down all the shade trees in Hyde Park or in Yakima is also work," I said. "But it would be destructive of other values."

"Let's see what we can do about it," he answered, turning to more pressing things.

The NRA, as noted, had in it a provision for collective bargaining. Industry tried to capture that clause by forming company unions, and as a result, labor became inflamed. By 1934 ugly strikes were sweeping the nation. Bloody battles ensued—strikers against the police, strikers against the National Guard.

FDR stood behind labor and collective bargaining, and that really spelled the end of his desired alliance with business and finance. The alienation was accentuated by his promotion of the Securities Exchange Act in 1934. Business had tasted its "oats" in NRA and saw in labor relations and the increase in federal regulation the twin forces which it must destroy.

By the time the 1934 Congressional election took place, the FDR business-and-financial alliance was dead. Of the thirty-five Senate seats contested, twenty-five were won by Democrats. In the House, the Democrats increased their number from 312 to 322.

FDR, who always had a keen ear and eye for the grassroots, asked for work relief, rather than direct relief. The unemployed, he said, should be preserved not only from "destitution" but also should work for their "self-respect, their self-reliance and courage and determination." At the same time he proposed a social security measure, which in due course was enacted and sustained in 1937 by a Court decision written by Mr. Justice Cardozo (301 U.S. 548).

The "work" relief was denounced by the financial world as a menace to private enterprise, which claimed, first, that it invaded fields traditionally reserved for business. Even ditchdigging, some said, was such an invasion, and certainly road and bridge building, and all construction work. Second, it was said, all relief should be local—a revival of the old cry of states' rights.

A farmer wrote FDR: "I wouldn't plow nobody's mule from sunrise to sunset for 50 cents a day, when I could get $1.50 for pretending to work on a ditch." Protests from the privileged were numerous. Henry Ford got into the act, talking about the boys who rode the rods, how good it was for them. "Why, it's the best education in the world for these boys, traveling around."

I had been on the rods dozens of times and wondered what Henry would have said or done had he been my companion.

Those criticisms had an impact on FDR, who had not yet forged the political alliance that was to thrive for a time between the liberals of the North and the Democrats of the South. The 1936 election, however, was a landslide; only Maine and Vermont went Republican. The Social Security Act had been a target of the Republican party, which claimed that it was the end of the workingman's individuality; henceforth, they said, the worker would have not a name but "a New Deal number." During the campaign FDR had said, in a radio speech, that business and finance were "unanimous in their hate for me—and I welcome their hatred. I should like to have it said in my first administration that in it the forces of selfishness and of lust for power met their match. I should like to have it said of my second administration that in it these forces met their master."

Jim Landis and his wife, Estelle, had invited me to their home in Virginia to listen to the broadcast. The room was filled, most everyone sitting on the floor. They all cheered and applauded. I did not cheer, nor did I applaud. I sat in silence, and shortly left. I loved FDR, but I thought his boast that he would be the "master" did not fit America. I thought then—and still think—that America is a complex and diverse pluralistic society and that there is room for everyone, even the brokers and dealers, who, I had discovered, were a species of leeches in the economy. Capitalism, I thought, was better than socialism, a conviction that was strengthened when I started my world travels. For in a socialist state such as Russia there was a suffocating bureaucracy, no First Amendment, no right to protest, no right to strike, no right to denounce the President, the Congress, or the Court. One who was a "master" of business and finance, like one who was a "master" of labor, read the group he "mastered" out of society. Later, I realized that FDR, of course, was using only a figure of speech and did not literally mean what he said. He was "master" in the adroit political way, not "master" in the sense I feared.

Despite FDR's great popularity there were powerful forces of rebellion working in the years preceding the election in November, 1936. Father Charles E. Coughlin was one; he would broadcast on the radio from the Shrine of the Little Flower in Detroit. I never met him, but I listened to him regularly. He said the contest for world domination was between Christ and communism, yet he also denounced capitalism and the international bankers. He thought the government should own the banking system. FDR knew Coughlin, and had Frank Murphy and Joe Kennedy act as intermediaries for him in seeking political friendship. At times they brought Coughlin to the White House. He generally approved FDR's program in 1933 and 1934 and testified before committees of the Congress on some measures, supporting them. Yet while he might support the President one week, he denounced him the next. He was for assistance to business one day, against competition the next day, for government ownership another time. As I listened to him week after week, I decided he was at heart a fascist. What FDR felt, I never quite knew. His tactics were to placate Coughlin, never to antagonize him, and to leave the White House door open to accommodate the man.

A second force of some moment—yet milder and of a completely different character than Coughlin's—was Francis E. Townsend, a doctor in California who became incensed at seeing hungry old people going through garbage cans looking for morsels. He was a tall, thin man without the dynamic force that motivated Coughlin. I knew him only slightly and heard him speak infrequently. His plan was to give every citizen over sixty years old a pension of two hundred dollars a month, provided he or she not be gainfully employed and provided also that he or she spent the money in thirty days. The latter condition was a gimmick of the times, stressing the importance of spreading money around to grocers, clothiers, and other merchants. The first condition was to placate the business group. Townsend Clubs seemed to spring up like mushrooms, and as I read the papers and listened to the radio, the movement seemed to be shaping up as a major political force. But when I talked with FDR about it, he would smile and seem unperturbed—which was, from his position, a good political stance.

At about this time a right-wing organization, the American Liberty League, was formed. I was sick at heart because one of my heroes—the great Alfred E. Smith—was a founding member. I admired Smith, who was governor of New York when I was at law school. I would go downtown to hear him speak, and later, when he was running for President, I made campaign speeches for him. Al Smith, a Catholic, was defeated for the Presidency by a bigoted America. I always thought that a man, whether Catholic or Protestant, Jew, or Hindu, should be judged on his merits.

Another force concerned FDR greatly: Huey Long of Louisiana. The Kingfish had been governor of Louisiana and used politics with a vengeance. He built magnificent hospitals and schools; his road-building program was very ambitious. But on my visits to his state I would see a new concrete highway end at a county line, pick up again only at the far side of the county. In between one would bog down in muddy ruts and miserable dirt roads. The reason was that the interim county had voted against the Kingfish in the last election.

Long supported FDR in 1932 and for a part of 1933. Thereafter he was on and off, for and against. Long was law-trained, and according to Senator Frank Maloney, as a senator, was the ablest man on the Hill. I saw Huey Long in action in the Senate, but never knew him. Hugo Black thought Long was a powerful politician, a great debater, and a terrific filibusterer. Late in 1933 Long announced a Share the Wealth program under which every family would be guaranteed an annual income of five thousand dollars. Like the Townsend Plan, the program seemed to spread like a prairie fire, though this seeming popularity was in large part Long's propaganda.

FDR was very concerned about Huey Long, but he never denounced the man, even in private conversation with me. He spoke of him gently, praising his political skills. Everyone has always said that Roosevelt was a very astute politician. It seems to me that one of the best bits of evidence is that he never once, in my presence, said anything against his political opponents. About Huey Long he might say, "Well, the man is certainly fervent," or, "He is a really forceful speaker." FDR was a clever politician, but he never practiced the politics of destruction.

FDR was consumed with curiosity as to what Long would do next. His counter to the Kingfish Share the Wealth plan was to ask for an increase in inheritance and income taxes, coupled with a program for social security.

When Huey Long was assassinated in Louisiana in the fall of 1935, I sensed that FDR felt relieved. Huey had been planning to run for the Presidency in 1936, and no one knows whether or not he would have made a formidable race. He was, however, the only opponent that FDR saw on the scene. In retrospect it seems obvious that it wasn't the assassin's bullet that eliminated the Kingfish as a real political threat to FDR—it was FDR's cool and calculated moves to counteract Long's proposals.

Harry Hopkins thought the WPA project or programs like it had become a permanent fixture by 1936, that the clock would not be turned back; he expressed that view in his book *Spending to Save: The Complete Story of Relief*. But Harry's book was hardly out before WPA rolls were drastically reduced. The agency picked up again when a new recession hit the nation in 1938, but in 1939 Congress required that anyone who had been on WPA for eighteen consecutive months should be removed. Yet only a small percentage of those laid off—never more than about twelve percent—were able to get private jobs.

WPA did not suit Middle America, nor did direct relief by the federal government. Federal relief would undermine the very low wage structure that existed in some areas, particularly the South. Moreover, as we have discussed, states' rights was a rallying point: if the local agencies lost their control, the Blacks might get on relief. And think how terrible that would be in an area that had a caste system!

This was the kind of infighting that took place in the mid-thirties, and it became a matter of conversation at the White House and on social occasions. Many a time, when I was talking with FDR alone or with others, Eleanor Roosevelt would come in, having just returned from a trip.

"Franklin," she'd say, "I have just returned from [say, North Carolina] and I have discovered something you should know about."

Then she would give him advice. Sometimes it was about racial discrimination. At other times it concerned the inadequacies of local relief and the need for federal standards. Again it might be the use of local relief to keep the Blacks out of the breadlines.

FDR would always listen patiently and with interest, and he would always thank her. Then she would usually say, "Franklin, you must do something about it."

He would smile and say, "We'll see what can be done."

In spite of FDR's efforts, the social security system which emerged from legislation covered only the "impotent poor," as Priven and Cloward, in *Regulating the Poor*, called them. They were the old, the blind, and the orphaned. The able-bodied poor who could not find employment were left out. Potential workers were kept in the labor pool, though they were starving. Though unemployment insurance was eventually enacted, it was not until 1961 that the Social Security Act was amended to give federal grants-in-aid to the states for families with unemployed fathers. Even so, because of the strict eligibility restrictions few such families got relief under this provision.

In the thirties, federal funds actually subsidized the operation of sweatshops, which could keep their wages at two dollars or three dollars a week because local agencies refused relief to anyone who would not take such a job. Under FDR's leadership, minimum wage laws eventually raised such salaries, but one inheritance of that system was the practice of deducting from relief clients any money they earned. The hearings before the Subcommittee of the Senate Committee on Manufactures in 1933 unearthed, for instance, the following: A man in Pennsylvania on relief was getting $3.50 a week. His wife got a job in a factory, where she worked fifty-four hours a week, for which she received $1.60. The local board deducted the $1.60 from the husband's relief payment, so the wife quit her job and his check went back to $3.50. That pattern has continued to this day. The welfare system in America in practical effect, if not in design, is to keep the poor people poor.

Business that gets a federal subsidy is not penalized if it makes huge profits. Farmers who are paid not to plant certain crops are not penalized for making as much money on the side as they can. Only the poor are penalized. And the same policy extends to social security paid to those under seventy-two years of age, whose payments are also reduced in proportion to their earnings.

FDR's administration left behind a program that never did fit the Jeffersonian design for America. I refer to the policies of the AAA (Agricultural Adjustment Act), sired by Henry Wallace and Rex Tugwell. Land was taken out of production and farmers were subsidized for not growing crops. I have summarized in my book, *Points of Rebellion*, how the agro-business units get public largesse, while the poor and hungry get little or nothing; the agro-business unit also gets vast tax advantages that the small farmer does not enjoy. The error of AAA was in limiting production of food in a nation and in a world of starving people. The aim should have been the creation of means of the distribution of food to the needy until normal purchasing power would take up the slack. Moreover, the processors were not being regulated and they were the ones mulcting the public.

Another evil of AAA was its disregard of the sharecropper. When land was taken out of production, it was the sharecropper who usually was the first to be affected. That often meant the Blacks. FDR was not colorblind, nor did he have a streak of racism in him. But his political alliance with the liberals of the North and the southern Democrats made him freeze when it came to taking positive measures for the Black sharecroppers. FDR could not overrule his leader in the Senate, Joe Robinson of Arkansas.

The sharecropper problem was made worse when benefits were paid out in exchange for plowed acreage. The question of division of the payment between landlord and sharecropper remained, with the planters receiving about ninety percent of the subsidy. Landlords were anxious to get rid of sharecroppers, and since landlords dominated administration of the Act (it was euphemistically called "grassroots democracy" by Tugwell), the displacement of sharecroppers continued.

It was around the processors and the sharecroppers that Jerome Frank and others in the Department of Agriculture made their fight, and they lost on both issues. As to the tenants or sharecroppers, the Farm Security Administration worked hard to render help. But in Washington, D.C., such help was considered "relief," while payments to the planters were "business." "It was the Hoover philosophy of the RFC applied in the South by the dominant planter-political caste," said Denis W. Brogan in *The Era of Franklin D. Roosevelt.* By 1938 sharecroppers were included in the definition of "farmers" in the instructions for holding referenda on cotton and tobacco marketing quotas, and they have been included since that time in all the crops—rice and peanuts as well as tobacco and cotton.

Jerome Frank helped write an opinion for AAA which provided that during the life of a contract with a producer, the landlord must retain not the same number of tenants but the same individuals as tenants during the life of the contract. That memo or opinion went out to the industry when Chester Davis, director of AAA, was out of town. Davis was outraged when he returned and demanded that Frank and his group be discharged. Wallace discharged them, and FDR stood behind Wallace.

Jerome Frank also lost out in his fight for regulation of the processors. Thus AAA truly enthroned the business interests in agriculture and perpetuated the producer-politician caste that has plagued the country ever since.

The most devastating weapon of the New Deal was the RFC. This agency was Hoover's creation and an inheritance that FDR greatly exploited. Under Jesse Jones, it bailed out distressed corporations and in its day did a commendable job, free of suspicion of taint or fraud. But the conceptions that it exploited grew and flourished. Business and finance, which were opposed to relief for the poor or even the modest and largely ineffectual WPA, quickly learned that the public trough was an attractive place to wallow. The policy spread, and many other agencies in time became dispensers of the public purse for the rich. By the 1960's and 1970's "socialism for the rich" seemed to have become our way of life.

There are some of my generation who say in retrospect that business in the 1930's was "the enemy." Business was, of course, mainly aligned against FDR in his political campaigns, and big business fought tooth and nail against most New Deal legislation. But business was not the enemy from the point of view of those of us who were the regulators. The Stock Exchange, for example, was cleaned up, but its destruction as an institution was never in our discussions. Nor had we arrived at a point where any talk of its "nationalization" took place. Such talk—when it did occur—was not aimed at business generally but at select, key industries such as steel. The few of us who urged FDR in that direction were thinking in terms that the British Labour party later espoused. But we had not advanced as far in our thinking as the late Hugh Gaitskell when he proposed "controlled" stock ownership rather than complete nationalization. Our ideas concerning nationalization were indeed embryonic and we never interested FDR to the point where he said, "Let's have a memo on it."

Deficit spending was a recurring topic of conversation in the New Deal days. I, too, was a Keynesian to the extent that I thought government spending was the only practical political course FDR could take to meet what promised to be a recurring economic crisis. But I did not believe it was the best long-range remedy. FDR and I talked about it. The idea of deficit spending was a worry that kept revisiting him, and when he expressed his concern and asked what I thought, I gave him my views. I told him I thought it was hard to beat the American free-enterprise system because it turned loose the genius and energy of hundreds of thousands of people in a frenzy of economic and technological activity. But the concentration of power was a matter of concern. (It was then not nearly as ominous as it is now.) Steel, I pointed out, was even then the fulcrum; automobiles were becoming secondarily critical. My idea was that the federal government would have to sit at the controls at least over steel. How? Not by regulation, for steel would soon run the regulators.

The federal government would have to own steel or own a c interest in it, so that production would be geared to the public n not to profit alone.

Moreover, in my view, deficit spending should be used to develop the public sector. We all grew up on—or were fed—the mythology that the private sector was adequate to produce full employment if left alone. Business needed "confidence." Businessmen should not be hampered in their planning. They needed protection from rapacious competition and from the overbearing demands of labor. I felt this business mythology was false.

Though FDR engaged in deficit spending, it had little effect on unemployment. While there were over seven million unemployed in 1931 and nearly twelve million in 1933, there were still approximately ten million in 1938, nine million in 1939, and seven million in 1940. The percentage of unemployed among the national work force varied up and down from 22.71 percent in 1932 to 16.33 percent in 1939 and 13.08 percent in 1940. It took World War II to change the picture.

FDR's refusal to create an economic public sector made the New Deal only a makeshift, compromising arrangement. There was, of course, a big difference under the New Deal in that people no longer starved. They were fed and temporary jobs were created. But no public sector was permanently created, and FDR never entertained the idea seriously.

Neither FDR nor any President who followed him really faced up to the critical problem of unemployment, which has always been part of the American economy except during periods of war. It is, however, a sorry reflection on any society which builds its affluence upon the four to twenty percent of the population which is, at various stages, out of work.

Only through a public sector can self-reliance and hard work be assured, as the Peking regime eloquently illustrates. We must develop a public sector to operate alongside a private sector; and that public sector must include the professions—law, medicine, and the arts—as well as industry and its allied skills.

The dimensions of the New Deal soon became clear. It was not a program that was in any sense radical. Rather it was a collection of makeshift devices to shore up the capitalistic system. FDR expressed over and again to me as well as publicly, his amazement at the charges of business that he was its enemy, that he was out to "sovietize" the United States, and so on. He truly thought that he was capitalism's best friend, pointing out the way for its survival. That was indeed the narrow area in which he worked. Rex Tugwell's dream of an America living under a cartel system was in a sense a "planned" society, and FDR was "sold" on it in a superficial way. His immediate reaction was to express criticism of the Court that struck the NRA down. But he soon seemed relieved that Hugh Johnson, the agency's administrator, and his Blue Eagle had been swept out. The new targets became the acute problems such as unemployment insurance, minimum wages, and hours of work.

The radicals were disappointed, but in the long run they for the most part accepted the narrow range of choice of New Deal reforms that Middle America would accept. Though more extreme measures were tendered by communists on the left and fascists on the right, the radicals, I knew, wanted basic reforms to come about by constitutional amendments. They never merited the scary headlines they often received.

There were many conservative influences in the New Deal. Dean Acheson, who served briefly, was one. Bernard Baruch—famous as a Wall Street operator—was another. Baruch nursed his fortune during the Depression and knowing FDR, came to Washington, where he held court every morning in Jackson Park, which faces the White House. Baruch was free and easy with his advice to anyone who would listen. He took a kindly liking to me, and was less vain and more able than most conservatives who took a hand in New Deal affairs. But Bernie was not an idea man, only one who would give you a tranquilizer so that you could see industry or high finance through rosy and sympathetic spectacles.

Lewis Douglas, another friend of mine, had been elected to Congress from Arizona four times and was in Congress when FDR took office. FDR made him Director of the Budget on March 4, 1933, with the aim of soliciting conservative support for his program. Lew lasted only until August, 1934, when he resigned in protest to FDR's "pump priming" program. He was out supporting Willkie in 1940. But by the time of World War II, Lew was back in various posts overseas, administering parts of our foreign aid policies, and Truman in 1947 made him ambassador to England.

There were many, many others who lasted through these long years, fighting the New Deal from the inside. The forthright, outgoing reformers did not last long.

Republican Fiorello La Guardia had been in Congress until 1932, but in that election he was swept out in the Roosevelt landslide. He was soon to become mayor of New York, where his voice would still be heard over the land. In Washington, D.C., La Guardia had been a George Norris type of radical—the George Norris that I came to love. He and Norris got the famous Norris-La Guardia Act (47 Stat. 70) through Congress, outlawing the yellow-dog contract. La Guardia called for public works, unemployment insurance, protection of farmers against foreclosures, public power, the forty-hour week. I knew La Guardia and admired him greatly. He was a fiery speaker, flamboyant, smart, and capable of being a demagogue, which he plainly was at times.

My main contact with the radical group in the mid-thirties was Maury Maverick of San Antonio, a lawyer who served in the House as a congressman from Texas from 1935 to 1939. Maury was short and stocky, in that respect very much like La Guardia. Maury also employed the same platform antics—he was flamboyant, cocky, witty, and pugnacious, depending on the need of the situation. He was a radical, not a socialist—and far from being a communist. Maury had his heroes, and they were mine too: Norris and La Follette. He tried to state his radicalism in their idiom. He formed a group of some thirty radicals in the House, one of whom, Mon Wallgren, was from my state, Washington. Mon would mouth Maury's words and ideas, but he soon wilted, carrying the reform banner for only a short time.

Maury admired Huey Long, not for his vicious streak, but for the human causes he championed. Maury used to defend Long, saying the forces he denounced were "the gods of oil and sulphur." As Long's list of gods to be denounced grew and grew, so did Maury's.

Maury Maverick used to tell me his theory of American radicalism: "We Americans want to talk, pray, think as we please—and eat regular."

I suppose I clung to Maury essentially because my own radicalism, if such it could be called, was precisely of his brand. In 1935, when business and finance turned against FDR, it was Maury and his group who told the President that they knew all along that reform could not be based on business support.

Once FDR got that message, he moved ahead with Senator Bob Wagner's labor bill, which guaranteed collective bargaining and established the nature of unfair labor practices; with the Public Utility Holding Company Act; with social security, with unemployment insurance promoted by Secretary of Labor Frances Perkins; with the Banking Act promoted by Marriner Eccles; and with other related bills putting segments of business under regulation.

I often thought that the real driving force behind this legislation was Hugo Black, who as chairman of a special Senate committee to investigate lobbying (1935–1936), and as head of a special Senate committee investigating ship subsidies and airline subsidies (1933–1934), did more than research historical facts. He used the Congressional hearing as it had never been used before, making it an instrument to achieve reform. He pursued financial chicanery, helped to quicken the conscience of America and to mold public opinion to the need for reforms. He expended an intensity of effort seldom seen.

Black dug deep for facts and was as relentless as a terrier pursuing a rat. He was charged with being unfair, but he never trafficked in innuendos and slurs, as did some Senate and House investigators who followed him. His standards were high, as they always had been. He did not emerge from Alabama through the usual hierarchy of politics. He announced what he stood for and campaigned relentlessly for it. Hugo Black never tried to destroy a man or a woman, only ideas. And through his investigative committees he exposed ideas that he thought were hostile to democratic principles. It was largely Black who made possible FDR's reforms in the financial world.

As Professor Gerald T. Dunne wrote in an article,* Hugo Black almost got his thirty-hour bill through Congress during FDR's Hundred Day legislative drive. Had he succeeded, it might well have aborted Tugwell's unconstitutional NRA, which parceled lawmaking out to those who were supposed to be regulated.

The famous Brain Trust of the New Deal was a figure of speech, not a working entity of a fixed group of individuals. Advisors came and went. Hugh Johnson—later to head up the NRA—was in on the ground floor before FDR's election. I knew him only slightly and rated him as a man distinguished only by his invective and by his high-handed management of the draft in 1917. Johnson's mentor was Bernard Baruch.

Many so-called experts came in to advise FDR casually or on an irregular basis. Others were attached to different agencies of government. Ben Cohen was first with PWA and then with the National Power Policy Commission; Rex Tugwell was at Agriculture. Raymond Moley in the early days was a part-time advisor to FDR.

Berle, and Rex Tugwell, both active at the start of the New Deal, were interesting contrasts, though neither lasted for long in FDR's close circle. In 1936 Tugwell resigned his federal posts and became a planning commissioner in New York City. As FDR told me, he wanted to get Rex "out of town." In 1941 FDR made him governor of Puerto Rico (the island did not acquire self-government until 1952).

Tugwell performed a unique service as governor of Puerto Rico (1941–

* *American Bar Association Journal*, December, 1972.

1946). There were young leaders emerging at that time—Luis Muñoz Marín, Jesus Pinero,* Luis Negrón Fernandez, Jaime Benitez, and others. The young leaders were liberal and idealistic, but they had had no experience in actually operating a government. Tugwell introduced them to the art of administration—the use of civil service, the role of a planning board, and so on. As a result of the Tugwell influence, the new men who took command of the affairs of the Commonwealth performed brilliantly and efficiently, in contrast to inexperienced leaders of other nations who came to the practical problems of government without training and insight.

By the time Tugwell had reached eighty, he had drafted a new federal constitution for the United States, commissioned by the Fund for the Republic. In it, of course, he put all the elements of his old NRA, giving constitutional sanction to government by cartels, turning over to industry complete controls over production and pricing—the device he had persuaded FDR to try out and which the Court struck down. Few provisions of the Bill of Rights survived. In an "emergency" a President could suspend free speech and free press across the land. Governors could do the same for their respective states. The Senate was a lifetime group, composed of figureheads. The Chief Justice could remove any judge for any reason. All aspects of an independent judiciary would disappear, and judges—even at the federal level—would be rubber stamps for the Executive.

Tugwell, after years of reflection, in his book *In Search of Roosevelt*, apparently concluded that FDR was qualified by "temperament" to be President, but not by "intelligence." The only evidence Tugwell gave of this lack of intelligence was FDR's disagreement with Tugwell. I saw some of the underlying papers behind the Tugwell constitution, and can say they would shock even the average right-wing lawyer. Tugwell, whose company I always enjoyed, never had the insight into American history which FDR possessed. FDR lacked neither the temperament nor the intelligence necessary for the Presidency. On both counts he was the most qualified in our long history.

What Tugwell failed to recognize was that he had played only a minor

* My friend Saul Haas of Seattle visited Pinero, and every so often he would say, "Jesus, how about another drink?" Finally one day Saul said, "I can't begin to tell you what it does to me, a Jew, to ask Jesus for another shot of whiskey. Do you mind if I call you Jim?" And that is why Jesus Pinero became Jim Pinero.

role in FDR's political scheme of things. FDR was a sailor used to "tacking," so as to make headway without directing his sailboat head-on against the winds and tide. That is why he got rid of most of the so-called Brain Trusters.

Adolph A. Berle, Jr.,* whom many people despised, brought a large measure of Keynesian theory to Roosevelt's administration. He was on a consulting basis at the RFC and at Treasury for a spell. FDR found stimulating Berle's ideas on Latin-American affairs, and eventually made him Assistant Secretary of State in 1938, where he served until 1944.

In college my own main preoccupation had been literature and my great heroes were Shakespeare, Browning, Wordsworth, and Parrington of the University of Washington, who combined literature on the one hand and economics, sociology, and politics on the other. I read Parrington, and in economics, my other major, I discovered Thorstein Veblen, whose ideas Berle was to popularize when he joined the Columbia Law faculty about the time I left there for Yale. What Berle wrote in the shadow of Veblen, Galbraith was to portray later in *The Modern Industrial State.*

Berle gave the impression that he had a mighty ego. At Yale one night he spoke at a dinner. The dining room was at the street level, and because it was a warm evening the windows were open. Berle was explaining the banking crisis of the early thirties and his role in it. He described a meeting of the experts in Washington that lasted way into the night. According to the story the advice he tendered was not accepted, and the meeting broke up. When everyone else had left, he said, he stepped onto the balcony of the Treasury Building and watched a golden moon rise over the city.

"As I stood there," he said, "the words of Goethe came back to me."

At that point in his speech to us at Yale a drunk on the street stuck his head into a window and let loose a rather vulgar "Phooey."

Berle paused a half-minute, then continued, "Perhaps the gentleman is right." And then he went on to explain the Keynesian theory that ultimately prevailed in Washington.

Berle was brilliant, creative, and the essence of integrity. He had graduated from Harvard Law School at an unbelievably young age. He

* For his diaries, see *Navigating the Rapids, 1918–1971,* from the Papers of Adolph A. Berle, edited by Beatrice Bishop Berle and Travis Beel Jacobs, Harcourt Brace Jovanovich, New York, 1973.

took and passed Frankfurter's course on public utilities, and the next year kept coming back to the same class. As one lecture ended, Frankfurter asked him if he had not been in the course the previous year, and Berle replied in the affirmative.

"Then why are you back?"

"Oh, I wanted to see if you had learned anything since last year."

Frankfurter despised Berle from that day on.

Berle was incensed at the impeachment threats against Abe Fortas in 1969 and he was further infuriated when Fortas resigned under fire. Judges should stand up and face their detractors, Berle thought. I knew that Fortas had never committed an impeachable offense; the most heinous thing he could be accused of was his friendship with Lyndon Johnson.

Berle and Tom Corcoran were bitter rivals for FDR's attention in the early days. Tom was primarily a political operator and FDR got rid of him in 1940, when he was running for a third term, because he thought that Tom, in a coalition setting, would be an irritant. I did not agree, because Tom was a good top sergeant who always obeyed his master's voice.

Tom had a similar experience earlier in his career. He had gone to Brown University and then to Harvard Law School, where he had been a protégé of Felix Frankfurter. Later he was Justice Holmes' law clerk. Tom, too, had written articles published as "Frankfurter and Corcoran." Tom and Felix parted company when Tom wanted to be Solicitor General. He had excellent backing for the post, but Frankfurter vetoed the appointment with FDR, calling Tom a "fixer," not a lawyer. And so a long, bitter feud grew.

After he resigned, Tom formed a law firm in Washington and practiced law with zeal. As FDR put it, he was willing to have Tom back in the administration "if he wears a top hat and tails." He meant by that that he wanted Tom back, if at all, as a regular bureaucrat, not as a conspirator. I canvassed numerous federal agencies, trying to find a spot for Tom, but no agency head spoke up for him.

Ben Cohen—brilliant, retiring, self-effacing—was the brain that put most of the pieces together. Ben was the best and most intelligent man in the New Deal. He put the ideas and the philosophy of the period into legislation. After 1950 his vast talents went largely unused, but he above all others most honored the ethical and intellectual ideals for which FDR stood.

In retrospect, the New Dealers, apart from my own associates at the

SEC, were a handful of men and women at the Executive level. Some of these—Harry Hopkins, Ben Cohen, Tom Corcoran, and Henry Wallace have already been mentioned.

Frances Perkins, Secretary of Labor from 1933 to 1945, should also be included. Miss Perkins was a large woman, formidably dressed, with a pleasant face and a facile mind. She was always calm and subdued, even when she expressed ideas that had cutting edges. Like Eleanor Roosevelt, she was a wonderful make-weight for FDR on the side of the poor and the oppressed.

Robert Moses said of Miss Perkins, "The attitude of both labor and employer [toward her] is a good deal like that of habitués of a water-front saloon toward a visiting lady slummer—grim, polite, and unimpressed."

She had been a social worker and promoted industrial and labor legislation in various parts of New York. She was Industrial Commissioner of New York when FDR was the governor. Once an effort was made to impeach her. The male chauvinists of that day thought she was weak and ineffective, but Frances Perkins kept the conscience of America bright in an office that previously had indulged in oppressive practices. She resigned as Secretary of Labor in 1945 after FDR's death.

Frances Perkins was not Harold Ickes' dish. When it was proposed to make Ikes the Secretary of Labor when Frances left in 1945, I teasingly suggested he'd love the big easy chair that she had occupied for so many years. He fairly exploded with words that would alienate him from all Women's Lib movements. The idea of Harold Ickes occupying a female's chair aroused him greatly. Harold did, indeed, have many Victorian attitudes, not all of which were ill-suited to responsible service in a thriving bureaucracy.

There was no one in FDR's time or later who was better at "unfrocking" a person than Harold Ickes. In 1944, speaking of Tom Dewey running for President and John Foster Dulles running for the Senate from New York, Ickes bellowed over the airwaves, "We are facing one of the most serious times in the history of our country. In a period when we need integrity and reliability, we are confronted by these two synthetic adventurers, Tiptoe Tom and Stepladder John—the DDT's—the Dewey-Dulles twins of American politics."

Harold Ickes was a dear friend of mine who spent his later years writing and rewriting his diary. He was honest and ambitious and hard-hitting. His campaign speeches that came over the radio were masterpieces of political diatribe. Ickes said of Dewey before the nomination in

1944 that Tom "had finally thrown his diaper into the ring." In the 1940 campaign Harold dubbed Willkie a "simple, barefoot Wall Street lawyer." FDR, a good stage director, would send Harold way out to a remote town, say, in Montana, to denounce the opposition—and how Harold loved it. Harold was crotchety and he loved to be called the Old Curmudgeon. He lived near Olney, Maryland, where he and his wife, Jane, raised turkeys. He was a Bull Moose Republican who loved FDR's leadership, and Harold watched over his nest at Interior like a mother hen over her brood.

Among the so-called New Dealers, there were two others whom I greatly admired. One was Warren Madden, who had been dean of the West Virginia Law School and later a professor who taught Property Law at Pittsburgh Law School. When the National Labor Relations Board was created in 1935, FDR brought Madden to Washington and made him chairman of NLRB. He followed Lloyd Garrison, dean of the University of Wisconsin Law School, and Francis Biddle, later Attorney General, each of whom served only briefly. Madden's acceptance of that post was his first venture into public life, and his arrival at NLRB was like being dipped in hot oil.

Labor problems were the hottest public issues of the day. Unionists were denounced as communists. The feelings of management ran very high, and so did the emotions of labor. Previous to passage of the Wagner Act, most unions were instruments of the companies, without the power to negotiate freely. The Act legitimatized the independent union, and in so doing, greatly antagonized the corporations.

Madden served as chairman until 1948, and during most of that time he was the most despised man in Washington. He always stood firm and met the charges fearlessly. He was denounced more severely than any federal officer in my time, yet he did yeoman service in honest, hard-headed administration, as a result of which both Hugo Black and I told FDR he should name Madden to the Court.

FDR did not name him only because, thinking of conservatives like Jimmy Byrnes, he thought Madden would never be confirmed because of the hostility his job had engendered. Instead in 1941 FDR named Madden to the Court of Claims, where he served until he retired in 1961. Later, when Madden sat as a retired judge on various cases in the Court of Appeals, I began to get a different view of him. He had defended the Wagner Act in stalwart fashion and stood firm against all assaults, but as a retired judge sitting on the Court of Appeals he took a dim view of certain provisions of the Bill of Rights, such as the self-incrimination clause of the Fifth Amendment. I mention this only to illustrate why Presidents very often make mistakes in naming judges. A President may see in an individual one trait or characteristic that he greatly admires and thus nominate him, yet on the vital issues of the future the nominee may not be in ideological harmony with the President or with the Constitution.

My admiration for Warren Madden was not dimmed by his later decisions on the Court of Appeals. He was devout, honest, and dedicated. A professor who taught Property Law can be excused for not knowing the history of the Bill of Rights as thoroughly as a Hugo Black.

Another man of the New Deal I greatly admired was Cliff Durr of Alabama. Cliff and his wife, Virginia, were Southern conservatives until Virginia's sister, Josephine, married Hugo Black. Both Cliff and Virginia had come from families with slave-owning backgrounds; they were planters and Presbyterians who were quite paternalistic to Blacks. As Cliff once said, all Blacks at that time "were treated alike, which was very bad, but which all accepted as part of the unchanging order of God."

Cliff had been a Rhodes scholar, studying law at Oxford for three years and returning to work for a firm representing the Alabama Power Company. Cliff Durr and Hugo Black, now related through marriage, began to see a lot of each other. They got into terriffic arguments on many occasions, Hugo arguing for public power, higher wages, shorter work weeks, with Cliff being opposed to all. But Cliff and Virginia became slowly convinced they were on the wrong side.

When the Depression of the early thirties hit, Cliff took the position that his law firm should not fire the clerks, stenographers, and younger associates. Rather, it should see the staff through by having the partners reduce their withdrawals of the partnership take. The battle was bitter, and Cliff lost. Not only were the lesser lights discharged, Cliff Durr also was asked to resign, and he found himself out on the street in the middle of the Depression.

Hugo Black was then in the Senate and got Cliff a job at the RFC, where he worked with Stanley Reed on a Save the Banks plan. But as the New Deal program got under way, Cliff was shocked. People were literally starving all over the nation when Henry Wallace was proposing that corn and cotton be plowed under and that the supply of livestock be reduced by killing little pigs. Cliff had come to Washington resolved to save the system; now he began to think that the Wallace-Tugwell-Jesse Jones method of shoring it up was shocking. He lost faith in the system, although he never became socialist or a communist. Like Hugo Black and myself, he became fearful of the concentration of power which socialism could beget. He also believed in freedom of speech and press, due process of law that radiates justice, and law and order in the true meaning of the words. He believed in political and constitutional rights, and in a differently structured economy whereby the basic needs of people would be supplied.

At the RFC, Cliff Durr shifted his interest from banks to defense plants. In 1940 he helped organize a Defense Plant Corporation to help get the country prepared for the war. Jesse Jones was reluctant to sponsor this program because in those days he was saying, "I could do business with Hitler." Defense plans were lagging because the industrialists were on a sit-down strike, so to speak, not wanting to build plants without orders to fill and unless costs and profits were guaranteed. Cliff Durr got FDR to overrule Jesse Jones and defense plants were built.

In 1941 Durr was made a member of the Federal Communications Commission on nomination by FDR. At the FCC he was largely responsible for the creation of an educational radio network, which in time grew into public broadcasting. His creative work at FCC came to an end for a reason most Americans would deem curious.

In January, 1943, Eugene Cox of the House introduced a resolution to investigate the FCC. A battle royal followed, in which Cliff Durr forced defeat of the proposal on proof of a charge that Cox had accepted a $2,500 fee to get a constituent's radio license renewed.

In 1943 Martin Dies let loose a barrage against Goodwin B. Watson, chief analyst at FCC, charging Watson with having communist views and affiliations with communist front organizations. Dies also condemned William E. Dodd, Jr., of the FCC, accusing him of being a member of a group which was "subversive." Robert M. Lovett, who worked in the Virgin Islands, was affiliated with numerous communist groups, charged Dies.

The list Dies presented to the House was long. Watson's salary at FCC was $6,500; Dodd's salary there was $3,200. Watson, Dodd, and Lovett were named in an appropriation bill as not entitled to any salaries under that bill.

Cliff Durr came to the defense of Watson and Dodd, and as a result, an intensive investigation was made of Durr himself. Meanwhile FDR expressed the view that the provision of the bill taking individual employees off the payroll was unconstitutional, but he did not veto the bill because it would have killed other appropriations the government urgently needed. The employees sued in the Court of Claims.

Francis Biddle, the Attorney General, thought the proviso unconstitutional and therefore worked out an arrangement with the Congress to have its own counsel argue the case. The Congress thereupon named John C. Gall to represent it.

The Court of Claims allowed recovery. The Supreme Court took the case on the petition of the United States and affirmed, holding that the bill barring these men from salaried federal positions was a bill of attainder, that is to say, a determination of guilt and the affixing of a stigma on men by a legislative act, not a judical hearing with all the safeguards of due process (328 U.S. 303).

Under the loyalty and security program launched by Harry Truman, a government agency had to exact a loyalty oath from all its employees. These oaths, designed to catch subversives, were of course meaningless to communists. But Cliff Durr felt they were a monstrous invasion into matters of conscience and belief which are protected by the Constitution. So in 1948, rather than take the oath, Cliff refused reappointment to FCC.

Cliff worked for a while with Jim Patton and the Farmers Union. He testified before Congress, opposing the Truman Doctrine. He was against the Korean War and our conversion of Taiwan into an airport for our bombers, ready to strike Peking. He was opposed to our use of force in the Caribbean.

Durr became ill and returned to Alabama with a severe case of arthritis; he was bedridden for two years. In 1952 he opened a law office in Montgomery, Alabama. At that time he, a white, and two other lawyers, Blacks, were the only ones in the area who would take civil rights cases; and he was one of the stalwarts who supported Martin Luther King in the boycott cases.

Cliff Durr, like Hugo Black, thought that Americans were entitled both to bread and freedom of mind and spirit. He was always worried lest they give up freedom for bread *and* jam. But, as this is written, his health is restored, there is hope in his eyes, and he walks with dignity and pride. He never was tempted by the Golden Gravy Train, and spent his mature years living by his ideals, which were truly Jeffersonian.

While we were at the SEC together, my friend Jerry Frank and I often discussed the possible changes that might result from new technology. The ideas of "work" or even "unemployment" might soon be anachronisms. When buttons could be pushed and the job accomplished without human hands, how would the Keynesian theory work? Would not the time come when unemployment would be normal and not occasional; the regular pattern, not a mere emergency?

Jerry and I knew all about Howard Scott and his technocracy. Scott had borrowed from Thorstein Veblen, who wrote a manifesto for technocracy in *The Engineers and the Price System.* Technocracy was said to be neither communist nor fascist. It became known as a dictatorship of engineers, because machines could produce an abundance for everyone; the main problem lay in distribution. The technocrats proposed getting rid of the price system and supplying everyone with the basic necessities and lifetime personal security. Central planning was proposed. Their plan really was in the mainstream of socialist thought, but the technocrats were not harnessed to political action. Technocracy did not die in the thirties, it continued on into the sixties. The only one associated with the movement whom Jerry Frank and I knew was Stuart Chase, who was a fine person. But Jerry and I thought the movement had no thought-out program. Moreover, in 1938 Howard Scott, its leader, was acclaiming the military as "the only efficient and disciplined bodies, and the least affected with business values" and he added that should any minority, "racial, religious, or economic," stand in its way, youth "will concede nothing short of that minority's annihiliation." That announcement gave technocracy a Hitlerian connotation which made Jerry Frank and me lose all confidence in it.

Jerry Frank had discovered Norbert Weiner in the late 1930's. Where he had come across him, I do not know, since Wiener was not publishing much before 1948 and one of his earliest books, *The Human Use of Human Beings*, did not appear until 1950. But Jerry Frank found him and brought his ideas into our circle. It was then we began thinking of society in new dimensions—the day when the machine would do the work. Who would own the machine? A cartel? Government? The people? That was the center of our concern.

Beer and radio would not be enough for the new leisure day. An automated society could give to those who had hobbies endless hours of joy. My hobby was the outdoors—hiking, climbing, fishing, botany, geology, the play of sunsets and sunrises, the feel of white waters under me and a canoe at my command. Others would paint or play the fiddle or do carpentry or discover a "green thumb" in gardening. But how about the men and boys I knew who frequented the pool halls and beer joints in Yakima? They liked an occasional woman on the side. They reveled in off-color stories of the barnyard variety. They found that alcohol was an escape—from the nagging wife, from a frustrated ego, from indecision, from defeat in the struggle against the cruel forces of a cruel world. What would happen to them when there were no "productive" jobs? No assembly-line positions, no stations in a potato-chip factory, not even a job packing cherries—which women did better than men, after all?

And so we faced the horrible prospect of Norbert Weiner's new society, which we knew was coming. Would the new serfs sell "dope"? Would their new occupation be as procurers? What would this do to society?

The Protestant ethic drilled into me in Yakima as a boy held that industry and hard work won out; that frugality in the long run was rewarding; that a man or woman with high ethical standards eventually prevailed. But we began to think that those endowed with this ethic were doomed as far as work was concerned.

These were some of the most disturbing years in my life. What would become of us? Free enterprise had disappeared, or would soon do so. Automation would make every factory the equivalent of a post office. There might be jobs, but they would be state jobs. Their prospectus would be drawn by bureaucrats, whom the Russians would call "commissars." A man or woman who wanted to be an actor, for example, would have to apply to a government bureau. The bureau, sensitive to political overtones, would be unlikely to hire an offbeat person, perhaps even more unlikely than a director in a capitalist society would be. So the list of unemployables would grow—unless individuals conformed to the state pattern—as many of them probably would.

These were the imponderables Jerry Frank and I discussed in those days. And when we examined the programs of the Manufacturers' Association or the Democratic or Republican National Committee, we realized that they were no more prepared to meet the realities of the modern world than the American Legion had been able to cope with the IWW's whom I had known as a boy.

FDR never debated these issues, but he always listened to us. He felt that America was basically very conservative and our people would not readily embrace new concepts. His judgment of these matters was, I felt, better than mine, but, as I told him, "You can conduct a national seminar by radio and educate the voters."

He never said yes and he never said no. But before long, he spent most of his energies conducting national radio talks not on nationalization of steel or on automation, not on a public sector that would end unemployment, but on the dangers of the Nazis and Adolf Hitler and, soon, the mobilization for actual war.

Chapter XXII

The Witch Hunt in the New Deal

In the 1930's we had come to a crossroads. My IWW friends of the earlier Yakima years had not gone the Russian way. They may have been misguided, and they did some ugly things, but most Wobblies were patriots who fought for justice within the framework of our system. Now we were faced with competition from an entirely different way of life.

Communists had been active in Washington, D.C., in the aftermath of the Depression. Franklin Roosevelt did not bring them there; the country, racked with economic problems, had collapsed and gone temporarily to the edge of the abyss. Hungry, bitter people joined all sorts of causes. After recognition of the Soviet Union, Russian agents operated more freely, and when innocent Americans joined groups or committees to promote friendship between the two nations, communists sometimes infiltrated them.

Some Americans joined the Communist party; I was certain that a few people I knew had done so, though I had no proof of it. Their interest, as far as I could tell, was not in bloody overthrow, but in select phases of the Russian experiment such as medical care, collective farms, and social security. In this country individual members of our political parties do not always endorse all the plans and precepts of the party of their choice. The same was true—I thought then and still do—of those who joined the Communist party. In the thirties it was not uncommon for invitations to join the party to be extended to the intelligentsia at cocktail gatherings. I was never asked, but in the winter of 1938 at one gala affair in Georgetown my old friend Saul Haas was asked if he was interested. The people I thought were members did not include Alger Hiss, and though Hiss later received an overwhelming volume of adverse publicity, he was never tried or convicted of espionage or sedition, only of perjury.

Hiss was tried twice, the first jury being unable to agree. The second jury returned a verdict of guilty on the perjury counts. Reed and Frankfurter, while members of the Court, testified at the first trial as character witnesses. So when the Hiss case reached the Court on a petition for certiorari, Reed and Frankfurter, being disqualified, did not vote. Neither did Justice Tom Clark because he had had some connection with the case when he was with the Department of Justice. That left six Justices, a bare quorum, for by statute fewer than six may not act as a Court. Normally it takes four votes out of nine to grant a petition for certiorari. But if there are only seven Justices qualified to sit, the votes of three are enough to grant a petition. And certainly three votes would be ample if only six Justices were qualified.

The following is a copy of the docket sheet I entered when the Hiss case was voted upon in March, 1951 (N.P. meaning not participating).

	Cert.		Jurisdictional Statement				Merits		Question		Absent	Not Voting
	G	D	N	Post	Dis	Aff	Rev	Aff	No	Yes		
Minton, J.		✓										
Clark, J.	N.P.											
Burton, J.		✓										
Jackson, J.		✓										
Douglas, J.	✓											
Frankfurter, J.	N.P.											
Reed, J.	N.P.											
Black, J.	✓											
Vinson, Ch. J.		✓										

U. S. GOVERNMENT PRINTING OFFICE 16—52708-3

Thus a six-man Court, with only Black and me voting to grant, denied the petition.* If either Reed or Frankfurter had not testified at the trial, we would doubtless have had three to grant; and in my view no Court

* 340 U.S. 948.

at any time could possibly have sustained the conviction.

A central weakness in the government's case was the failure to comply with the special federal rule governing prosecutions for perjury. The Court had redefined that special rule in 1945 in a unanimous opinion written for the Court by Justice Black in *Weiler v. United States.** In perjury cases more than the testimony of a single witness is required. His testimony must be corroborated by other trustworthy evidence. The reason is not only that man's memory of past events is notoriously poor; beyond that is the need to protect "honest witnesses from hasty and spiteful retaliation in the form of unfounded perjury prosecutions."†

The Hiss case presented that issue in a dramatic fashion, as Hugo Black and I concluded from our review of the record. Whittaker Chambers, who implicated Hiss, was an ex-Communist. All such characters in the forties and fifties had the halo of those who had "come to Jesus." They easily "fingered" prominent people or people like Hiss who had been close to public figures such as FDR. Their word was almost sacrosanct, though as the cases developed, it appeared that many were notorious liars. According to the *Weiler* decision, corroborated evidence had to supply "independent proof of facts inconsistent with the innocence of the accused." Probably the evidence most damaging to Hiss was the fact that some of the incriminating documents were typed on a typewriter once owned by Hiss. There was no evidence that Hiss or Mrs. Hiss did the typing. The typing might have been done by Chambers or by any stooge of Chambers. It was not even certain that at the relevant times the old typewriter was even owned by Hiss or was under his control. Certain it is that the inference that Hiss was "framed" was strong. The case illustrates the wisdom of having two witnesses on a perjury charge or if there is only one, as in the Hiss case, that the court ride herd on the nature of the corroborative evidence to make certain it has that "trustworthy" character which will prevent one accused of perjury from being "framed."

Moreover, on a later motion for a new trial, there was offer of proof that the typewriter—the one said to belong to Hiss—was itself a "forgery," manufactured to have all the characteristics of the old Hiss typewriter. Review of a denial of that motion was also denied‡ by the Court, this time I being the only one voting to grant.

* 323 U.S. 606.

† *Id.* 609.

‡ 345 U.S. 942.

	CERT.		JURISDICTIONAL STATEMENT				MERITS		QUESTION		ABSENT	NOT VOTING
	G	D	N	POST	DIS	AFF	REV	AFF	NO	YES		
Minton, J.		✓										
Clark, J.	n	P										
Burton, J.		✓										
Jackson, J.		✓										
Douglas, J.	✓											
Frankfurter, J.	n	P										
Reed, J.	n	P										
Black, J.		✓										
Vinson, Ch. J.		✓										

Apart from the legal issues never conclusively resolved, the result of the Hiss case was to exalt the informer, who in Anglo-American history has had an odious history. It gave agencies of the federal government unparalleled power over the private lives of citizens. It initiated the regime of sheeplike conformity by intimidating the curiosity and idealism of our youth. It fashioned a powerful political weapon out of vigilantism.

In the thirties and forties there were bookshops in Washington, D.C., where a wide range of "radical" literature, including, on the one hand, the writings of Karl Marx and, on the other, Thomas Jefferson, was obtainable. These shops were not sinister in appearance; everyone knew what they were or could easily find out. They had lists of patrons, but I always refused invitations to be one, because, not being a joiner, I was reluctant to be a part of any organization; and because in the bookshop situation I had strong suspicions that some of the promoters were communists. In hearings many years later, it was asserted that these shops were convenient "drops" for mail between members of the underground. But Americans in general are joiners, and many were in the bookshop groups merely as an expression of good will toward Russians, not because they believed in the communist creed of violent overthrow.

In many other situations, ad hoc or standing committees of Americans were infiltrated by communists, especially in connection with labor union activities and in matters concerning international policies or programs.

Those who joined these groups usually did so innocently, unaware that they were associated with actual communists. The joiners commonly were not suspicious for the following reasons: first, the Litvinov agreement contained an express promise on the part of Russia not to use the techniques of infiltration and subversion in this nation. Second, there was an enthusiastic desire to cooperate in a new era that envisioned international cooperation, not conflict. Yet these innocent associations were before long used to pillory people who in the utmost good faith had cooperated in these projects.

Some who cooperated with infiltrated groups knew that there were communists in their midst. But the clear teachings of Jefferson and Madison were that one's beliefs were sacrosanct and a person could not be constitutionally reprimanded unless he stepped over the line and acted subversively. The fact that one believed in the communist philosophy never was a crime in this nation.

As the years passed and Hitler came to power, many people fled Germany and sought shelter in the United States. Public opinion here was on the side of the refugees, and no ideological sifting was undertaken. Yet years later federal officials were criticized for allowing communists to enter our ports from Germany.

When Hitler invaded Russia and we, in turn, entered World War II, Russia became our ally. There followed a great outburst of sympathy for that country, followed by many acts of cooperation: shipment of food, lend-lease materials, training of Russian naval officers, and the like.

Yet when the war was over, many who participated in those cooperative projects were mercilessly persecuted by investigating committees. Man's memory is very short, and soon almost the entire press and mass media were in full hue and cry against the alleged miscreants.

The same thing happened in the Asian theater, where Chiang Kai-shek was our ally. Those who believed—and reported—corruption of Chiang's regime were publicly ridiculed and, in some cases, ostrasized. They should have been honored for their vision in seeing that Peking—to whom we finally made gestures of friendship in 1972—would be the wave of the future in Asia. Instead, the hysteria of the day resulted in the excesses of the House Un-American Activities Committee and, in the years following the New Deal, the devastating loyalty and security programs launched by Truman and continued by Eisenhower. Men like Owen Lattimore, occasionally a State Department advisor, John Stewart Service, and John Paton Davies, Jr., were cast into the outer darkness, though years later they were exonerated.

When America stumbled into World War II, it was hardly conscious of the diverse forces loose in the world and wholly unaware that we were about to be captured by one of them—the Kuomintang, which collected millions of American dollars, established the China Lobby, and for two decades brainwashed us all with radio and television programs, with lecturers, and with bought-and-paid-for articles in our leading publications. Twenty years later Averell Harriman, then with the State Department, asked me rather sadly, "How *do* we stop being a satellite to Chiang Kai-shek?"

Meanwhile the hearings before investigating committees went on relentlessly. Harry Dexter White—an unusually able man in monetary and financial matters and long associated with the Treasury—was hounded. Reading the charges against White in the 1950's makes one today ashamed of the nature and quality of the witch hunt. Even after White's death, there were more hearings: all of his papers, including a communist songbook, were introduced into the record. His great "crime" was knowing people the investigators thought were communists.

Parallelism was really the high crime. If one believed in free medical care, he was a communist because Russia had that system. If one proposed disarmament, as Henry Wallace often did, he was a communist because Russia proposed it too. Whenever one's own conviction coincided with a temporary or permanent position of Moscow, that was evidence that he had communist leanings. If he voiced his convictions that disarmament led to peace at the time Russia was clamoring for disarmament, that was nearly conclusive proof that he was a communist.

Owen Lattimore was a man who knew China in the twenties and thirties, as a merchant and trader, as a reporter, as a research student and scholar. Years later, when I visited Outer Mongolia in 1961, I discovered that he had preceded me by a month or so. A member of the Academy of Science in that country told me that Lattimore addressed them for an hour in Ulan Bator, speaking Mongolian. He paid Lattimore the highest compliment possible: "If I had closed my eyes and listened, I would have sworn the speaker was Mongolian."

Lattimore was one of our few Far Eastern experts. He was so out of step with the thinking of the forties that he was dubbed a "subversive" and was investigated over and again by Congressional committees.

I came to know Lattimore in Washington in the forties, first meeting him at one of Leila Pinchot's dinners. He was able and brilliant and held an eminent chair at Johns Hopkins. He and his wife arranged for a Living Buddha from Outer Mongolia to come to Johns Hopkins, one of the clerics who fled his country when the communists took over. I entertained both him and the Lattimores, and learned from them something of Buddhism as practiced in modern Central Asia.

Lattimore, having seen Asian problems and Asian political forces first-hand, refused to revise his theories so as to make them palatable to the prejudices of the America of the forties and fifties. He was therefore hounded by investigating committees, on the stand for hours at a time and for days on end. After one long siege his wife took me aside and said she must get her husband away where he could rest. Did I know a place? I had a fishing lodge on the Quillayute River, where steelhead and cut-throat trout ran. It was far west of Seattle and only a mile or so from the ocean. I offered it to the Lattimores and they accepted.

That was the beginning of a new ordeal. The newspapers tracked the Lattimores down and besieged the place. Learning that the cabin was mine, the papers also hunted me down. "Why are you harboring a communist?" "How can you reconcile being on the Court and putting a communist in your house?"

Lattimore, of course, had done nothing illegal. He had committed no crime. He was not a spy or a foreign agent. On Asian matters he was a member of the avant-garde, saying that the days of Chiang Kai-shek and the other corrupt and reactionary warlords were over, that new revolutionary forces were waking up. This was before the communist takeover of China. And when that happened and Lattimore's prophecy came true, the prophet came to be considered the main conspirator, the cause of it all.

Lattimore was finally indicted for perjury, the charge being that he lied when he denied he was a "follower of the communist line," the proof being his writings and statements between 1935 and 1950. Another count charged perjury in denying he "promoted communist interests."

The District Court, in dismissing the indictment in 1955, said:

> The charges here serve only to inform the defendant that his sworn statements are to be tested against all his writings for chance parallelism with, or indirect support of, communism regardless of any deliberate intent on his part. They demonstrate that the government seeks to establish that at some time, in some way, in some places, in all his vast writings, over a fifteen-year period, Lattimore agreed with something it calls and personally defines as following the communist line and promoting communist interests (127 F. Supp. 405).

Joseph O'Mahoney (along with Abe Fortas and Thurman Arnold) defended this case. The judge was Luther Youngdahl, who was a Republican and three times governor of Minnesota. He was so popular a political figure in Minnesota and so dangerous to Hubert Humphrey that the latter induced Truman to make Youngdahl judge of the U. S. District Court in Washington, D. C. He was one of the best district judges in my time, not merely because of his ruling in the Lattimore case but for his long record of fearless, independent decisions. He was a great immovable rock over which the waves of passion broke and spent themselves.

Lattimore had been tagged with an active association with the Institute of Pacific Relations, which launched a publication in 1927 to study and report on the conditions of people in the Pacific. Senator Pat McCarran had his Senate Internal Security Subcommittee devote the years 1951 to 1952 to IPR and it finally reported that it was "a vehicle used by the communists to orient American Far Eastern policies toward communist objectives." McCarran got Internal Revenue to withdraw IPR's tax-exempt status. Thereupon Internal Revenue assessed IPR for social security contributions for its employees for the year 1955. IPR paid the few hundred dollars demanded and sued for a refund. Another brave federal judge—David N. Edelstein of New York—gave judgment for IPR, finding that it had not carried on propaganda or attempted to influence legislation. Thus a magazine that only strove to present the many-sided aspects of the troubled Asian situation survived and Lattimore was cleared.

Among the stormiest of hearings during this period were those concerning the movie industry. Films had been produced showing the romantic and idealistic side of the Russian people. One such movie (*Mission to Moscow*) was based on a book by Joseph E. Davies, whom FDR had made our Moscow ambassador. These movies did not portray the ugly aspects of the Russian regime. Seldom, indeed, did films we produced show this seamy part of American life. Russia had lost over twenty million people in World War II and thousands of villages and towns had been leveled. They had suffered in a way we Americans had never known, for we have never experienced an actual invasion. So Russia, as our war ally, had our sympathies. Movies are and were primarily entertainment, not political propaganda. Yet the committees went after the producers and script-writers with hammer and tongs.

Jack Warner, whom I knew, properly maintained that if *Mission to Moscow* was a subversive activity, then American ships and their naval escorts that carried food and grain to Russia were also subversive. Louis B. Mayer stoutly defended *Song of Russia,* which, he said, was "a pat on the back" for our then ally. The low ebb was reached when the committee investigated the movie *None But the Lonely Heart*. In this film a mother ran a store, and her son said, "You are not going to get me to work here and squeeze pennies out of little people poorer than I." This line was taken as evidence that the movie was designed to criticize the free-enterprise system, to make people lose faith in it, so that the communists would take over. The agent for Ginger Rogers testified that they had turned down movies that were "just as open propaganda as *None But the Lonely Heart.*" Ronald Reagan, now governor of California, testified that the best way to oppose communism was "to make democracy work"; and he added, "We have spent a hundred and seventy years in the country on the basis that democracy is strong enough to stand up and fight against the inroads of any ideology."

Attempts were made to tie the movie "propaganda" to FDR—either through Henry Wallace, Harry Hopkins, or Lowell Mellett of the Office of War Information. But these efforts failed.

These investigations of subversives neither started in the New Deal nor ended with it. The first Un-American Activities Committee in the House during the days of the New Deal was created in 1934 and headed by John McCormack. Martin Dies of Texas, who had long sought the creation of an Un-American Activities Committee under his own leadership, had his wish fulfilled in 1938. The chairmanship has changed from time to time, but the search for subversives has been continuous.

My friend Jerry Voorhis was made a member of the Dies committee, and many liberals of that day—including myself—criticized him for becoming associated with the witch hunt, as Maury Maverick called the activities of that committee. Jerry gives the details of the episode in his book *Confessions of a Congressman.* He never supported the communist cause, and he was convinced that the case of infiltration of hard-line communists into our system was established—"copper-riveted," as he put it. But what led him to leave the committee in a few years was its disregard of procedural regularities and the easy smearing of anyone by the unverified accusations of eager informants. He discovered, for example, that the chairman was holding sessions, taking the testimony of his own investigators in secret, and then publicizing the results.

Jerry was always my hero because he lived in the tradition of Jefferson and Madison. It is tragic that in spite of his steadfast stand for constitutional principles and procedures, he went down to defeat in 1945, charged with being a communist tool.

In the New Deal days it was customary, once the hue and cry for subversives went up, for Congress to appropriate funds so that the FBI could investigate the cases referred to it by the Dies Committee or by others. In one group of 662 who were investigated, four people were discharged from federal employment on the basis of FBI reports, and in two instances, administrative action other than dismissal was taken. That amounted to one percent of the total number of people under suspicion. In another group of 3,472, forty-three were separated from federal service and twenty-six cases were disposed of without dismissal. The other reports resulted in the discharge of employees or their removal to less sensitive positions, and affected one percent to less than three percent of the thousands investigated.

The gravity of the charges is not known. Whether any were communists —or if so, how many—is not known. Guilt by association was, however, so prevalent and indiscriminate a standard that it is doubtful if hard-core communists were the victims. The victims, I believe, were the offbeat and nonconformists who, for example, joined those who supported Soviet brigades in Spain, not because they were minions of Stalin but because they despised Franco. Or, as I have said, they may have joined a communist "front" group because they believed in the cause being promoted, which seldom was Soviet supremacy, but more likely things as "subversive" as peace, free medical care, and the like.

However that may be, the spectacle of thousands of civilians put through the mill sent fear through those who waited for their names to be called as well as those who had been investigated. It became dangerous to be a free-wheeling, innovative person. Only those wearing homburgs and neat clothes and thinking in Legionnaire terms were beyond reach. Thus did this early witch hunt have a great leveling effect, driving some of our best men and women out of the federal service.

Much later—in 1947—the Attorney General started preparing lists of subversive organizations, which included fascist as well as communist ones. No hearings were held, and the members of such groups usually suffered loss of jobs in government posts as well as in private industry. States joined in and produced their own lists, New York being in the forefront.

In time those federal lists reached the Court. Several organizations, which on the face of the record were engaged solely in charitable or insurance activities, sued to have their subversive designation declared unconstitutional. The Court so ruled, holding that due process required notice and a hearing before any such "pseudo-bills of attainder" could constitutionally be imposed.* The damage suffered by the label "sub-

* *Anti-Fascist Committee v. McGrath*, 341 U.S. 123.

versive" was considerable—meeting places became difficult to obtain; tax exemptions were revoked; licenses to solicit funds were denied.

Some states required employees who were members of groups on the Attorney General's list to take loyalty oaths for state jobs. The Court held that requirement unconstitutional,† because it penalized membership that might have been wholly innocent.‡ Moreover, as stated by Mr. Justice Black: "Our own free society should never forget that laws which stigmatize and penalize thought and speech of the unorthodox have a way of reaching, ensnaring, and silencing many more people than at first intended. We must have freedom of speech for all or we will in the long run have it for none but the cringing and the craven. And I cannot too often repeat my belief that the right to speak on matters of public concern must be wholly free or eventually be wholly lost."*

Out of the hearings of the Un-American Activities Committee came various "blacklists." These started with the ten "unfriendly" witnesses from Hollywood, as related by John Cogley in *Report on Blacklisting.* Most of these ten did not invoke the Fifth Amendment, only the First. They were later to find support in a dissent of Mr. Justice Black* in 1950, involving a provision of an act of Congress which barred the Labor Board from entertaining complaints of unions unless each officer of the union had filed with the board a "non-communist" affidavit. The Court sustained the act. I did not sit, as I was ill, and, therefore, Justice Black was the sole dissenter in this case, saying, "Like anyone else, individual communists who commit overt acts in violation of valid laws can and should be punished. But the postulate of the First Amendment is that our free institutions can be maintained without proscribing or penalizing political belief, speech, press, assembly, or party affiliation. This is a far bolder philosophy than despotic rulers can afford to follow. It is the heart of the system on which our freedom depends."†

Even later the Court‡ put beyond the reach of investigative committees personal political beliefs, philosophies, thoughts and attitudes. As Justice Black early maintained, one's actions or deeds, not one's beliefs, are legitimate matters of governmental investigation.

† *Wieman v. Updegraff,* 344 U.S. 183.

‡ *Id.* 190.

* *Id.* 193.

* *American Communications Association v. Douds,* 339 U.S. 382.

† *Id.* at 452–453.

‡ *Watkins v. United States,* 354 U.S. 178, 188, 197–198.

The Hollywood Ten were held in contempt and jailed, and Hollywood, responding to the pressures of its financiers in Wall Street, told the committee, through Eric Johnston, that the ten would be fired and that the industry would not employ communists in the future.

In Hollywood most people were recruited for the Communist party during the years 1936 to 1939, when the party was anti-Nazi, anti-Franco, pro-labor, and anti-Jim Crow. The recruitment suffered from 1939 to 1941, the period of the Hitler-Stalin pact, and revived when Hitler attacked Russia. Soon new blacklists appeared. The American Legion prepared a list of three hundred people who worked in Hollywood films. Private tests in studios were prepared, busybodies writing in their accusations of individuals.

People were named merely because they had signed *amicus* briefs on behalf of those they thought were unjustly charged. Some were listed because they criticized—as did Hugo Black and myself and many other judges as well—the use of loyalty oaths. There were many blacklists that actually consisted of individuals against whom a particular employer or a designated industry would discriminate when it came to employment. And anyone who was on a blacklist was usually denied employment in other industries as well. The Cogley *Report on Blacklisting* notes how a grocer in Syracuse put pressure on his suppliers to get rid of subversives in their factories and plants—*or else*. No sponsor of a product wanted to have it associated with controversy, let alone subversion. Blacklisting, as a result of these activities, became not only "patriotic" but economically justifiable.

Congress, in due course, passed an act, over Truman's veto, that made it unlawful for a member of a communist-action organization to be employed in any defense facility. A defendant named Robel was indicted for working in a shipyard in Seattle, Washington. The Court, speaking through Chief Justice Warren, held that the provision of the act was unconstitutional by reason of the First Amendment.*

> That statute casts its net across a broad range of associational activities, indiscriminately trapping membership which can be constitutionally punished and membership which cannot be so proscribed. It is made irrelevant to the statute's operation that an individual may be a passive or inactive member of a designated organization, that he may be unaware of the organization's unlawful aims, or that he may disagree with those unlawful aims.

* *United States v. Robel,* 389 U.S. 258.

> It is also made irrelevant that an individual who is subject to the penalties of . . . [this statute] may occupy a nonsensitive position in a defense facility. Thus, . . . [the statute] contains the fatal defect of overbreadth because it seeks to bar employment both for association which may be proscribed and for association which may not be proscribed consistently with First Amendment rights.*

Hence the blacklists—insofar as they included only people with communist beliefs as distinguished from communist action—were illegal.

I knew none of the Hollywood Ten who were condemned. But years later I came across one of these people, a writer who survived because he took a nom de plume. He wrote for years under that name and received three Academy Awards for his brilliant work.

The Hollywood Ten were held in contempt of Congress (by a vote of 240 to 16), tried, and convicted. They were sentenced to one year in prison and a $1,000 fine. The case worked its way up the appellate ladder to the District of Columbia Court of Appeals† which held that Congress had the power to abridge First Amendment rights when it thought the "national welfare" required it and that a witness who refused to say whether he was "a believer in Communism" could be punished.‡ Those ideas were appalling to me and to Black. That decision was made in June, 1949. Frank Murphy, who had been appointed to the Court in 1940, died July 19, 1949. Wiley Rutledge, who took his seat in 1941, died September 10, 1949. The petition for certiorari reached the Court in the spring of 1950. By that time Sherman Minton had taken Rutledge's place; and Tom Clark, Murphy's seat. It takes four votes to grant a petition. No one knows how Murphy and Rutledge would have voted. But they always held the First Amendment in high esteem. Justice Clark, who had been Attorney General when the convictions were obtained, took no part in those cases. The Hollywood Ten on April 10, 1950, got only two votes under the Vinson regime—Hugo Black's and mine.§

The Hollywood Ten had long served their sentences and suffered under the blacklist before the Court, under the Warren regime, ruled in 1957 that investigating committees were restrained by the First Amendment.||

* *Id.* at 265–266.

† 176 F 2nd 49.

‡ *Id.* at 52.

§ 339 U.S. 934.

|| *Watkins v. United States*, 354 U.S. 178.

Once, during the Joseph McCarthy days, a senator of a different stripe joined his committee. Thinking that he would be jolted at his new experience, I asked him a few weeks later how he enjoyed the assignment. He laughed as he replied, "It's like shooting fish in a barrel." That attitude fairly reflected the mood of Washington, and sad to say, it was a favorite indoor sport.

It was to me a sordid spectacle, for it was driving innovative people out of government, out of the news media, out of Hollywood. The bureaucracies, both inside and outside of government, became more staid, more like-minded, less imaginative, and much, much less courageous. I gathered that mainly from observation of the current scene; I saw innocent and wonderful people seared and driven from public life by the awful ordeals they were subjected to in the Un-American Activities Committee hearings, and in the loyalty and security program that Truman fastened onto this nation and which became even a greater scourge under Eisenhower.

Helen Gahagan Douglas of California, who was in the House in 1947, was very conscious of the dangers of the inquisition that our people were suffering. She was far from being a communist. As it was for Jerry Voorhis the Bill of Rights was part of her very being. She saw the First Amendment, fair hearings, and due process as basic to the American way of life. And so she introduced bills to give every person coming before an investigating committee the right to counsel, and to give to that counsel the right to cross-examine witnesses who denounced or defamed a person who, by being summoned before a committee, stood as one accused.

But committees were more interested in publicity than in the truth; they thrived on accusation and made it the basis for casting a citizen into the outer darkness. In the eyes of the committee, counsel would only slow down the proceedings or defeat the purpose of the committee. So Helen Douglas' bill never passed.

She also introduced legislation to make confidential the sources from which an investigative reporter had obtained his news story. The issue finally reached the Court in 1972,* the Court holding in a five-to-four decision that the newsman had no privilege of nondisclosure. That was an old issue, not a new one. Alfred Friendly, of the *Washington Post,* had written about the antics of Clare Hoffman, a one-man subcommittee of the House Labor and Education Committee. His hates were conspicuous, the foremost being labor. And when Al Friendly wrote a story telling how Clare Hoffman had single-handedly broken up a meeting

* *Branzburg v. Hayes,* 408 U.S. 655.

where the Mediation Service was trying to end a three-month strike, Hoffman issued a subpoena to Friendly and demanded to know his sources. That was the trigger for Helen Gahagan Douglas' legislative proposals.*

I had a few personal experiences with witch-hunting. For example, my old friend, David Lawrence of *U. S. News & World Report,* liked to make tables showing what Justices were the most pro-communist. The score was made by rulings in favor of a defendant who was accused of being a communist, and the method of scoring overlooked the constitutional mandate of equal treatment of all persons whether honored or despised. Dave usually rated both Hugo Black and me as ninety percent communist. But once he gave Black a ninety-one percent rating and me only ninety percent. When I next saw Hugo, I teased him about getting one percentage point ahead of me.

This type of experience was, of course, humorous, but one that happened to me in Forks, Washington, was not.

On my travels abroad I took many movies and stills. The movies were 16-mm. colored, and the stills were mostly Kodachromes. I would offer to show them gratis, provided someone would contribute a room without charge and provided further that no tickets would be sold, but instead a free offering would be solicited for a local benefit. Once, for example, an operating table for a hospital in Enterprise, Oregon, was bought from the proceeds. One night the benefit was for the library of the new college at Port Angeles. This night I showed Kodachromes of communist lands I had visited. The hall was about filled and it was only a few minutes before eight, when the lecture was scheduled.

Suddenly the door burst open and a contingent of the local American Legion marched in. They set up a microphone at the lectern and plugged in their huge tape recorder. My permission was not asked. No courtesy of any request was made to any member of the committee. It was the old storm-trooper technique. Since I had harbored Owen Lattimore in my cabin, I must be a subversive.

And so the lecture started, running over an hour; then came questions from the crowd. At the end of the meeting the American Legion committee departed with their microphone and tape recorder, repaired to the Legion hall, and played the tape to another assembled group. A friend of mine among them said that at the end the group dispersed, all rather shamefaced and no one saying a word. The main message from my travels in communist lands was that we have here the precious heri-

* *Washington Post,* March 24, 1973, Op. Ed.

tage of the First Amendment, which neither the communists nor our own vigilantes respect. Yes, I said, communists here should have the right to speak, for the First Amendment covers the entire spectrum of ideas. To select the "good" from the "bad," to sift out First Amendment garbage would install censorship by government. And that is what Jefferson and Madison feared, and that is precisely where the communists and the extreme right find common ground.

During the days of the New Deal when Abe Fortas and I were closely associated at the SEC, we would often comment about those whom we knew in Washington who were probably members of the Communist party. Laughingly Abe asked me one day, "I wonder why neither you nor I have been asked to join." We joked about it over the years, concluding that men, like other animals, have subtle ways of determining what other members of the species are congenial.

This is not to intimate that the infiltration of communists was not a problem. It was a major one, not in government but in special groups. Walter Reuther, a close personal friend, was head of the UAW (United Automobile Workers) and battled long and hard to wrest control of the union from a few communists. They were closely knit, highly disciplined, and ever-vigilant. Walter noticed that they would continue a meeting until two in the morning, or even three or four if necessary, to get the vote they wanted. So Walter trained his men to outwait the communist members and outmaneuver them—which in time UAW did.

Another early friend of mine was Cord Meyer, Jr., whose book *Waves of Darkness* was a moving account of his World War II experiences in which he lost an eye. Cord and I worked together at one time on a world government project. Each of us was for a time associated with the United World Federalists. Cord's book *Peace or Anarchy* sponsored that idea. Cord also became active in the affairs of the American Veterans Committee. He soon discovered that communists had infiltrated that organization, and battles royal at the parliamentary level ensued, one meeting lasting until 7:00 A.M. Cord finally won out, but the experience, as he related it, was a searing one.

Somewhere in this period I researched the Lenin-Stalin tracts dealing with techniques for gaining control of meetings. The details escape me now, but they were vivid and specific. One of them came into prominence when at a later time Khrushchev addressed the United Nations. At one point he took off his shoe and used it to pound the lectern. That precise technique is in one of the texts the Russian communists use in the training of advocates.

Chapter XXIII

International Outlook

My old friend and hiking companion in Yakima, Douglas Corpron, had been in China as a medical missionary. Doug, who received his M.D. in 1921 from the Cincinnati Medical College, sailed for China in 1923, where he served until 1927, financed by the Christian Church of Yakima. He served again in China from 1929 to 1936, from 1939 to 1941, and from 1947 to 1948—all at his hospital at Hofei. Through Doug, China became my new absorbing interest.

I read all I could about China, and Doug's letters kept my interest alive. Doug was a good observer and a discerning reporter, and his heart and that of his wife, Grace, were filled with love for the Chinese people. And his letters confirmed all I had heard about this ancient regime. Over the years, his work was constantly disrupted—by Chinese bandits and the Japanese army.

China was a place where the people lived at a low subsistence level—lower than anything we in Yakima had known. They had no doctors, no schools, no drugstores, no opportunities to escape poverty, malnutrition, ignorance, and oppression. For those in the ivory towers of the universities, for members of the court, for the ruling Kuomintang party, China was a nation of great culture. For the people at the bottom, China was a land of misery. Their only joys were in the intimacies of family life and in the great devotion one family member had for the others.

I knew, of course, that China—and Southeast Asia—had never known democratic traditions. Familial tradition—some called it ancestor worship

—was dominant, and it was reflected in the power exercised by the head of a family, whether he be Chiang Kai-shek or a village peasant. Those at the top named all subordinate officials. Villagers had no say in any affairs of government. Confucius had said, "While a man's father is alive, look at the bent of his will; when his father is dead, look at his conduct. If for three years he does not alter from the way of his father, he may be called filial."

Doug's letters, written over a twenty-five year period ending about 1948, gave a graphic picture of the old China. Chiang Kai-shek had purchased vast good will in the West by endorsing the Christian missions in China. But China was in fact convulsed at the time by separatist movements represented by war lords. The Japanese army was present. Everyone was stealing from those who had food, livestock, or other forms of wealth. China was plagued by disease, by droughts, by famine, by pillaging. Cholera, meningitis, and malaria swept the country. There were no adequate medical facilities, no adequate supply of doctors and nurses. Famines came in regular cycles, it seemed, forcing peasants to try to survive by peeling the bark off trees and cooking it, or by boiling weeds in a spot of grease or oil. Baby girls were usually drowned at birth. Even boys if they were harelipped were cast aside. There was a vast distance between the 10 percent at the top and the 90 percent at the bottom. Society functioned only for the 10 percent.

Doug's letters also confirmed for me the fact that China had never developed Western legal procedures and traditions. There was no jury. Only a judge sat to determine guilt or innocence. The accused had no lawyer. If mercy was shown, it was by the judge. Doug's descriptions of Chinese trials were as shocking as the bloody events which preceded our Fifth Amendment, which protects a man against self-incrimination.*

One of Doug's letters described such a trial:

> The magistrate sat on a podium. The bandits were brought in—in chains—and questioned by the magistrate. When they would not admit their guilt, they were tied up—kneeling on hard boards, with their arms lashed to a crosspiece which passed back of their necks. In this awkward and painful position they would be given stripes with bamboo whips from time to time until finally they confessed. After the confession they were untied. But the magistrate did not stop with the confession under

* Jerome Cohen has shown the way this procedure has evolved (79 Harvard Law Review Y69).

> duress. He continued to interrogate the bandits, obtaining new evidence from them until he was satisfied that he had the right men and that they did not confess just to put an end to the third-degree punishment to which they had been subjected. The next afternoon the three were beheaded in public on the parade grounds.

Franklin D. Roosevelt did not know Asia from personal experience, but he knew it intuitively. As foreign crises mounted in the thirties and forties, China and Russia became more important to us, but they remained enigmatic. Roosevelt would tell me of his talks with the British, including Churchill, who kept referring to the Chinese as "the pigtails." This term offended FDR and he so admonished his British friends, but the British were colonials who had held a rather firm hand over China for a century, and while tolerant of minorities at home, looked with disdain upon "natives" abroad.

Churchill was of the view that China was the "enemy":

> I believe that as civilized nations become more powerful they will get more ruthless, and the time will come when the world will impatiently bear the existence of barbaric nations who may at any time arm themselves and menace civilized nations . . . I believe in the ultimate partition of China—I mean ultimate. I hope we shall not have to do it in our day. The Aryan stock is bound to triumph.

FDR felt that nations which were largely Caucasian had to be discreet and courteous in their relations with the colored peoples of Asia. Roosevelt took many steps in that direction, including a request in 1943 that the Chinese Exclusion Laws be repealed. And as early as March 2, 1934, FDR had addressed the Congress, urging independence for the Philippines. "After the attainment of actual independence by them," he said, "friendship and trust will live." Harry S Truman proclaimed that independence on July 4, 1946, fulfilling FDR's promise.

Roosevelt was constantly needling Churchill on India, urging that England grant India her independence. Needling may be too strong a word; he *urged* Churchill to take that course.

FDR thought highly of Gandhi as a political leader, as the head of a spiritual mission of freedom. FDR did not know the teeming millions of India, but he sensed the measure of their thinking and knew that the postwar years were to be dominated by them and people like them, the world around. He always tried to "educate" Churchill in these regards, as he put it to me, but he never succeeded in budging the Old Boy. "Winnie's world is different from mine," he once said.

Churchill was the reactionary Tory who saw India as a bright jewel in the British crown, and he was adamant. Churchill said on November 10, 1942, "I have not become the King's minister to preside over the liquidation of the British Empire." When the offer of independence came on July 18, 1946, Churchill registered his strong "dissent." It took the Labour Party and Clement Attlee to grant India her independence on August 15, 1947.

The American formula of government fits us and a few other areas, but it is not necessarily made to order for everyone. People of the world are at various stages of governmental development. They must find their own destinies.

FDR worked hard to establish a bridge between Soviet Russia and the United States. When he recognized the Soviet Union in 1933 and negotiated what was known as the Litvinov-Roosevelt Agreement, many Americans were bitter but most were joyful. The first group saw in Moscow an implacable enemy, resolved to take the path of violence to overcome the United States and to use propaganda to divide and confuse us. The second group saw this recognition as the start of a cooperative world regime; they also saw within that nation a medical program reaching every village and a government that fed and housed everyone. I was among those who were pleased by FDR's recognition of Russia, even though the suppression of minorities within that country went on apace, and even though civil liberties as we knew them here were sadly lacking. Acknowledgment of any nation, no matter how antithetical its system may be to us, provides a basis for trade and international intercourse, for exchanges of students and professors, and for a slow building of bridges of understanding between two governments.

It is difficult in the seventies to re-create the public attitudes toward the Soviet Union in the thirties. When in 1943 the property settlement known as the Litvinov Agreement came before the Supreme Court,* the shudder which communism and confiscatory decrees created in the courtroom was noticeable in the dissent of Chief Justice Stone, with which Justice Roberts concurred.

A favorable trade agreement which FDR made in 1935 also increased

* *United States v. Pink,* 315 U.S. 203.

hostile feelings in some American quarters. Under a commercial pact allowing articles of the Soviet Union into this country—a pact that was renewed annually over and again (49 Stat. 3805)—Russia sent many furs here. As a result, some of my own New England and Far Western friends became bitter enemies of FDR, based not on facts but on Cold War propaganda. They were already Republicans, but the Russian competition in furs made them *bitter* Republicans, as other people became during this period.

One friend was a Mr. Lewis of South Norfolk, Connecticut, who made a good living trapping raccoon and fox in the western part of that state. Mr. Lewis not only trapped; he traded in furs, buying and selling and keeping a large inventory. Another was my neighbor, Ira Ford, who raised a fine family trapping pine marten out of Goose Prairie, Washington. Mr. Lewis and Mr. Ford blamed Roosevelt and the Russians for the downward spiral of fur prices. Perhaps the style in furs changed; certain it is that when coon and fox furs fell out of favor in New England and hurt Mr. Lewis, pine marten fur fell in Goose Prairie, Washington, and hurt Ira Ford.

Actually, the greatest import of Russian furs was from 1923 to 1930, when the Republicans were in power. The imports dropped in 1931 and did not climb again until 1935 and 1936. Even so, fur imports never reached the levels of 1924, 1925, and 1926. But both Lewis and Ford became permanent enemies of FDR. Nearly forty years later they still thought Roosevelt was a bum for favoring Russian furs over their own furs.

FDR's greatness lay in understanding the social and economic formula for America's domestic survival as well as in his realization of her increasing responsibilities as a member of the world community. His greatness lay also in knowing how to implement abstract programs in terms of practical politics.

In the 1920's and 1930's we were predominantly isolationist. Our preoccupation was with internal affairs. My friend, Jerome Frank, who I think had the most creative legal mind of anyone in our time, epitomized that isolationist view in his book *Save America First*. Later he retracted, as did many Americans. The turning point for the majority was probably Roosevelt's Quarantine Speech delivered in Chicago, in the heartland of isolationism, on October 5, 1937. Roosevelt said:

"It is true that the moral consciousness of the world must

> recognize the importance of removing injustices and well-founded grievances, but at the same time it must be aroused to the cardinal necessity of honoring sanctity of treaties, of respecting the rights and liberties of others, and of putting an end to acts of international aggression. It seems to be unfortunately true that the epidemic of world lawlessness is spreading. When an epidemic of physical disease starts to spread, the community approves and joins in a quarantine of the patients in order to protect the health of the community against the spread of the disease."

That "disease," some thought, was communism. Yet I knew by then that there were many diseases: Nazism, anti-Semitism, anti-IWW, anti-Black, anti-Chinese. How would we find the wisdom to avoid false trails? Would America in time see the world as Yakima did the IWW's?

I later saw other diseases, such as feudalism in South America and the Middle East; the absence of medical care and schools in Vietnam; the absence of jobs in India; the absence of agricultural techniques in Pakistan; the absence of consumer credit institutions in the Philippines, Peru, Chile, and Bolivia; the absence of representative government and of fair trials in Iran and Brazil. I learned in the Middle East and in Asia in the forties and fifties that affluent America was not on the same wavelength as the people of the slums of the world.

In 1954 I visited Morocco at a time when that country was still a colony of France. Before leaving Washington, D.C., and also in Madrid, Spain, where I stopped off en route, I met some of the non-communist underground working in and out of Morocco. From these people, I learned the names of the Moroccan nationalists who were imprisoned in their own country by the French. Then, while in Morocco itself, I found out that three of these nationalists were being held in the large prison in the capital, Rabat.

During my visit, the French high commissioner, who served under my friend Mendes-France, expressed his eagerness to help me in any way he could. The favor I finally asked of him was to be allowed to see these prisoners. The man became almost apoplectic with rage, and could hardly talk. All he did was shout, "Communists, communists!" But according to my information, the men were not communists, nor had they committed any crimes. Their only offense was that they clamored for the independence of their country.

After leaving the high commissioner, I went to a confectionery shop and bought three boxes of candies and pastries. I took them at once to the prison, where I knocked on a huge wooden door. There was much creaking of hinges as the door swung slowly open, and when I walked in, a French soldier promptly pressed a bayonet against my belly. So escorted, I entered and was taken to the prison inspector, who, learning my mission, fairly hopped about with anger and threatened to lock me up. I encouraged him in his project, saying it would make interesting headlines in Paris and in Washington if he were to imprison a U.S. Supreme Court Justice. The inspector kept me there an hour, and when I departed I left the three boxes for the three political prisoners—gifts that I am sure they never received.

The grapevine within the prison was so effective, however, that every man in every cell soon knew I had been there. By the time I reached Tangier, preparatory to my return to this country, the French had stirred up our State Department, whose people in Tangier soundly criticized me and said it was time I went home.

To be sure, I was not making friends of the French, but I was making new friends of the Moroccans, who, after ousting the French, were soon to have their own government.

Had I denounced the nationalists during my stay in Morocco, our State Department, which supported the French, would have been happy. There was nothing I had done there that was inconsistent with any of my judicial functions. But for one to exercise his First Amendment rights and disagree with the State Department amounted almost to treason. This happened in 1954, when Eisenhower was President, but Truman's State Department and LBJ's and Nixon's were not any more tolerant of dissent.

Before World War II, I met Jimmie Yen, the dedicated Chinese who had founded the Mass Education Movement. I joined his board. We worked on the mainland of China until driven out in 1948; then we worked in Formosa, and later in the Philippines, Colombia, Guatemala, Thailand, South Korea, and Kenya. Our program was to work through and with local groups on five fronts: improving the livelihood of the peasant; bringing medical care to the villages; introducing modern agriculture; providing schools and eliminating illiteracy; introducing representative government at the village level. But the State Department and AID never welcomed Jimmie Yen. As the Pentagon became more and more dominant in our policies, the United States came to look for military rather than political and sociological solutions to overseas problems.

For many, many years, I had tried to think in terms that offered alternatives to war, such as cooperative world systems. Though never an expert, I had my dreams of a peaceful world order. I made speeches to this effect and attended conferences. My concept, I felt, would lead not to communism, but to cooperative projects that would enable a multiracial, multi-religious, multi-ideological world to survive.

As early as the thirties, people were saying that FDR's big mistake was being friendly with Moscow. Even then, everything communist was considered evil. Most people, in their ignorance, knew little about the Soviets, Soviet history, or the impact of communism on that ancient land. FDR himself was certainly not a student of Russia, but he did know what Alexis de Tocqueville had predicted a century earlier—that Russia and the United States would emerge as the two foremost nations on earth, and could, perhaps, face each other in a gigantic power struggle. Churchill thought that part of the strategy of World War II should have been to contain Russia. FDR felt differently. It was his theory that the peace of the world would depend on the degree to which Moscow and Washington collaborated and worked in harmony. That is why from 1933 on he sought every possible occasion to build bridges of understanding between the two nations. That is why, contrary to the advice of some in his own inner circle, he never "unloaded" on Stalin or "took out after" him. Shortly before FDR's death the rumors were that Stalin had been sending him insulting messages, that Stalin was intractable, that FDR would soon have to air publicly the mounting differences between them. The President denied these rumors to me in private, admitting, however, that Stalin was a difficult man. The test of the new world that would emerge after World War II would be its ability to reconcile the new, deep-seated ideological conflicts and not let the emotions behind the strident voices drown out the needs for collaboration and accommodation.

On October 21, 1944, shortly before his death, FDR spoke of Soviet-American relations:

> "In 1933 a certain lady—who sits at this table in front of me—came back from a trip on which she had attended the opening of a schoolhouse. She had gone to the history and geography class with children eight, nine or ten, and she told me that she had seen there a map of the world with a great big white space upon it—no name—no information. The teacher told her that it was blank, with no name, because the school board wouldn't let

her say anything about that big blank space. Oh, there were only a hundred and eighty to two hundred million people in that space, which was called Soviet Russia. And there were a lot of children, and they were told that the teacher was forbidden by the school board even to put the name of that blank space on the map.

"For sixteen years before then, the American people and the Russian people had no practical means of communicating with each other. We reestablished those means. And today we are fighting with the Russians against common foes—and we *know* that the Russian contribution to victory had been, and will continue to be, gigantic."

FDR had the political genius to call the Dumbarton Oaks Conference and in the fall of 1944, over tremendous opposition, launch the United Nations. I talked with him about that strategy many times and we discussed the errors made by Woodrow Wilson regarding the League of Nations which I as a youth had fervently supported. Knowing those mistakes, FDR attempted to avoid their repetition. He felt that Wilson's main problem was that he had not prepared the country *before* the fact. He said that "the American people have to be brought along slowly."

Roosevelt was a political realist who did not think much of legal technicalities. He talked about the proposal to give veto power to the member nations of the UN Security Council that would render that agency impotent to act unless the vote were unanimous. That veto proposal, by the way, was not a Soviet one, as is commonly imagined; rather, it was American in origin.

FDR shrugged it off as unimportant one way or the other: "If the United States and Russia can work together, the United Nations will be a success. If they cannot work together, the UN will fail—veto or no veto."

One of our last talks relating to the United Nations concerned where its site should be—in the States or in another country. He felt that it should not be located in Geneva, as that place was associated with the ill-fated League of Nations; he was determined that the UN should have its headquarters in this country. "Where in this country?" he asked me one day.

I suggested Kansas.

"Alf Landon's state?" he asked.

I said that a spot in the wide-open spaces of Kansas should be selected and an international community built on it. I pointed out that if the UN offices were located in a metropolitan center, the Black delegates could have severe housing difficulties. Also, in a large city, the delegates would tend to disperse at day's end, while in a secluded Kansas spot they would be together around the clock, getting to know each other, hopefully on a more understanding basis. FDR liked the idea but thought it was not "politically feasible"; he was probably right.

It is, of course, impossible to predict what FDR's management of our Asian policy would have been had he lived. It is, however, very doubtful that he would have agreed to a return of Indochina to the French. He knew something of the strength of the underground and its nationalistic overtones. He talked with me about this.

Ho Chi Minh was part of that underground and so was Ngo Dinh Diem. They were ideologically opposed, but that opposition had not surfaced. FDR would, I believe, have worked out a formula for the independence from foreign domination of Cambodia, Laos, and Vietnam. That was the direction of his thinking. Moreover, he had grave doubts about the Kuomintang and Chiang Kai-shek. When he died, Mao Tse-tung and Chou En-lai were on the ascendancy.

Our Asian specialists leaned toward support of Mao. FDR was moving cautiously. Had he lived, I believe he would have met with Mao Tse-tung and Chou En-lai, taken a measure of the men, and charted his course.

The reason why FDR recognized Russia was a good clue as to why he would have cast in his lot with Mao. He knew that Chiang Kai-shek had been a dismal failure, that China was one of the great powers to reckon with, and that world peace necessitated harmonious collaboration between the United States, Russia, and China. Perhaps my wish dictates this conclusion. As I say, it is quite conjectural.

The whispered justification for the "war" in Vietnam was to countercheck China. FDR would never have swallowed that. Moreover, those of us who knew Asia knew that the Vietnam conflict was doomed from the start. FDR would, I think, have known as much. Moreover, he knew enough about Asia to have more than a premonition that Chiang Kai-shek represented not the wave of the future, but a past that had failed.

Unhappily, the broad outlook that FDR advocated passed with his death. America, in its actions abroad, became more "imperialistic" than the British at their worst. Truman, Acheson, and the Pentagon—and Johnson and Nixon—became the architects of that new American foreign policy. The slogans of American imperialism made good politics at home, and we were soon saturated with fears of communism. The Cold War made anti-communism an easy program to follow blindly. The blueprint drawn in the fifties became the inspiration for disastrous overseas operations in the 1960's and 1970's.

America became quickly regimented and we lost our perspective in world affairs. By the 1960's and 1970's we were "policing" the world; we had become the great moralists, using our Army and Air Force and Navy to let the people of the world know the kind of government we thought they *should not* have. The pundits in Washington, D.C., said we had inherited the role of the British and were now keeping the world "safe." FDR would turn in his grave at the thought of it.

Chapter XXIV

Friends and Acquaintances

I always thought of my SEC assignment as a temporary thing. In fact, I did not give up my appointment at Yale, always planning to go back soon. I had no interest in staying in the capital. I disliked it as a place to live and its social life never meant much to me. Unless they have a home somewhere else, and are well established there, people in Washington are rootless. As for me, I have always considered my own State of Washington to be my home, first Yakima and, now, Goose Prairie.

The newcomer to Washington, D.C., is usually enamored with names, celebrities, and the social whirl. In my early days Evelyn Walsh McLean put on the most interesting functions, mixing up the Left and the Right and fashioning a stimulating potpourri.

She was the owner of the Hope diamond and usually wore it at her dinners. She never would let me touch it. "It brings everyone bad luck," she said. "Look at me—no husband, afraid for my life." She was indeed frightened, so frightened she never went to bed until the sun came up. After her champagne parties broke up around midnight, she would don old clothes and scrape varnish and paint, rub down her floors, or paint her walls. Night after night she toiled until dawn, fearful that if she went to sleep, someone would kill her.

It was at one of the McLean parties that I met the first Mrs. Douglas MacArthur. She talked freely of her ex-husband, who had insisted upon a divorce and had then remarried. Mrs. MacArthur was a most gracious, engaging person. One night, referring to the general, she said, "I taught him how to fight."

Mrs. McLean once put Senator Hiram Johnson and me at the same table at dinner. By then my boyhood hero was quite elderly and feeble. He could not believe his ears when I told him, after the men had gathered for coffee and brandy, what he had meant to me when I was a boy. I was in his eyes the symbol of the New Deal that he hated. He was an embittered old man, angry at the world, and at FDR in particular. That night at Mrs. McLean's he was civil to me, but coolly distant. He had few words to say and seemed offended that one of my ilk admired him. We talked less than two minutes when he turned away and left me standing alone. That was the first and only time I saw my boyhood hero.

I also met Senator William Borah in Washington. I saw him socially and I served with him for a while on the Temporary National Economic Committee (TNEC), organized in 1938 to investigate monopolies. Joseph C. O'Mahoney of Wyoming was the chairman and he called our first meeting to order. When the plans on how to conduct the investigation were opened for discussion, Borah rose and said it was unnecessary for him to stay. Turning to me, he said, "My views on antitrust are well known to you, Douglas. I've made up my mind as to what should be done, and I do not need to make any investigation. But go ahead and investigate to your heart's content. I leave you my proxy."

Borah was later to be one of those who worked for my nomination to the Supreme Court. After I had taken my seat on the Court, I was with him at a big black-tie dinner at the White House one night in January, 1940. We were not yet in World War II, although hostilities were raging in Europe. Borah and I stood in a corner having our after-dinner coffee together. I told him how moved I had been as a boy when he had raced in a railroad locomotive from Boise, Idaho, to Nampa to save a Black from being lynched. That night he told me he thought the conflict in Europe was a "phony" war.

Borah did not understand Hitler. He had not read *Mein Kampf*. He did not know about the terrible things afoot in Germany. He thought FDR was promoting our participation in the war. Borah himself had no conception of the devilish forces loose on the European continent, and he never learned the truth—for that same night he slipped on his own bathroom floor, hit his head, and died shortly afterward.

That night at the White House, I felt sad because my two boyhood heroes—Hiram Johnson and William Borah—had somehow or other missed out in later years, letting history pass them by: Borah because he did not know about the persecution of minorities in Germany, though he had been quick to defend minorities in Idaho; Johnson because he did not recognize the fact that the New Deal was carrying forward the vigorous domestic reform he had once headed in California.

Before Borah's estate was probated, $250,000 in currency was found in his safe deposit box. Why would a man keep money there, rather than in stocks, bonds, savings accounts? What was the source of this great fortune? Borah never used taxis, only streetcars. But that economy would never create so large a fortune in one lifetime. Nor could he have saved a quarter of a million out of his meager Senate salary. Did Borah have something to hide? Did this hero of mine (whose mane of hair and thundering voice represented Good as against Evil) have feet of clay?

Gifford Pinchot's wife, Leila, also held soirées in the capital, in an old but elegant house on Rhode Island Avenue. Leila had a shock of red hair that usually was in disarray. Her interests were wide and her mind was sharp. Social justice, economic justice, political justice—these were her causes. And so her parties were roundups of queer, offbeat people. If she was interested at the moment in conservation or logging practices, she would invite some high official of the reactionary American Forestry Association, with someone like myself to cut him down to size. If she was concerned with migrant labor problems, she would have protagonists on both sides of the issue present. When she started moving around the world and saw Greece and Iran in the raw and the oppressive feudalism of the Arab world, her soirées took on larger proportions. Ambassadors, State Department officials, and others in high command were invited, and all were submitted to her searching, gentle, and seemingly innocent, but telling cross-examination.

She did not give champagne parties in the fashion of Mrs. McLean. There was a bar where one who was interested could pour himself a drink. But the emphasis was less on socializing than on conversation, discourse, debate.

Gifford Pinchot was tall and aesthetic-looking, and his eyes had great warmth. His hair was thinning and his mustache was gray. He sometimes attended these affairs, but more often I found him in his own room engrossed in some project while his wife entertained. I spent fascinating hours with him as he relived his forestry days. It was then that I gathered from him his wilderness recipes: one for cooking grasshoppers in deep fat; another for broiling a chicken hawk, the sweetest, most tender meat of the outdoors.

By then Pinchot was seventy-five, but he was still young. Unlike

Johnson and Borah, life had not passed him by. During World War II, Pinchot was helping the Navy equip rubber life rafts with simple but interesting and effective fishing gear. His hobbies had been as absorbing as his profession, and with the passing years, added to his stature. He entered the twilight of his life still active in the world of ideas.

A third lady who in those days put on large parties was Daisy (Mrs. J. Borden) Harriman, who in 1967 died at the age of ninety-seven. She had a large house in fashionable Georgetown and specialized in Sunday night dinners. She had been a suffragette, a promoter of the old League of Nations, and an advocate of many social causes. The preliminaries, after one received a cocktail, were short; the guests were soon settled at tables in a large room. We were packed in tightly, as in a crowded classroom.

The dining room was indeed a classroom. As dessert was being served, Daisy would rise and announce the topic for discussion and then call the name of the lead-off man or woman who was to speak. Once, I recall, she said, "Tonight we will discuss the President's Court-packing plan, and we would like at the outset the views of Bill Douglas."

Some Sundays the discussion was flat and boring; at other times tense and angry arguments took place. I finally declined all her invitations, partly because most of the topics did not interest me and partly because Sunday nights were becoming very special to me. Hours tramping in the woods along the Potomac made for a good night's sleep, which I found more attractive than Daisy Harriman.

I never felt that I would live permanently in Washington. David Lawrence, syndicated columnist and editor of the *U.S. News* (later *U.S. News & World Report*), offered in the 1930's to sell me his house for $37,000, but I turned it down. Years later it became the Swedish Embassy. Not too long ago I was invited to a reception at the embassy, and I asked the ambassador how much his country had paid for the place. The price was two million dollars. "If you'd accepted David Lawrence's offer," a friend said, "you'd no doubt be a Republican by now."

When I first went to Washington in the thirties, I had the impression that senators and representatives had soft, easy jobs and did little to earn their keep. That was the reputation they had acquired. I quickly changed my mind, for my contacts with the Hill taught me that the members of Congress were, by and large, a group of hard-working, dedicated men and women. There were a few who lived in nearby areas who spent only Tuesdays, Wednesdays, and Thursdays on the job and the other four days back home. Some still do just that, but these congressmen were and are in the minority.

I soon began to realize how extensively constituents use their Congressional delegations. An eighty-dollar veteran's claim or some small amount in social security is too small for litigation, but inquiry to a congressman or senator can set wheels in motion at least to locate the claim and find out what its status is. Such an inquiry can expedite processing the claim and settling it. Or when an agency like Immigration, SEC, Federal Trade, or the like is investigating an individual or a company, the aggrieved person may be bewildered and harassed. His congressman or senator can often help to isolate the precise problem and expedite its resolution.

More delicate questions arise when an agency is performing a judicial function, such as when it must grant a license to one applicant or another, or must extend, or rescind, a permit to do a certain kind of business. The temptation on the part of a few congressmen and senators has always been to bear down on the agency in question on behalf of their constituents. That was tried out on me at the SEC, and it never worked.

Among the great plums in the Washington, D.C., pudding has been the granting of radio and TV licenses. The contests have been tremendous and many political allies have been marshaled in the cause. Even some members of Congress obtained licenses for themselves or their families while in office—a practice that should be forever barred as being beyond the ethical line. The use of White House pressure on the Federal Communications Commission caused Sherman Adams, under Eisenhower, to lose his job. I always felt that Sherman Adams' "sin" was far lighter than those of some other Eisenhower bigwigs.

Certain members of Congress became my good friends in my early days in Washington. Hatton Sumners of Texas was in the House during those years. He and I became very close. His gnomelike stature and dry humor made him a "personality" of the times. He was quite bald and had a noticeable bump on the top of his head. Often when I was going headlong toward an objective that he disapproved of, he would tap his head and say, "I have consulted my bump of caution and advise against it." He was very conservative, very wholesome, and as American as apple pie.

Sumners, then chairman of the House Judiciary Committee, argued for the House in the contempt case against William MacCracken, Jr. The

House was investigating the famous air-mail contracts, and MacCracken was charged with destroying his files after a subpoena had been issued by Congress for their production. The case was argued in January, 1935, and I took some time off from my SEC duties to hear the argument. Sumners was a stout advocate and argued well and persuasively. His side won, Brandeis writing the opinion (294 U.S. 125).

Sam Rayburn, long a Democratic congressman from East Texas, had the same small stature as Congressman Sumners, though Rayburn was not quite as slight; he, too, was bald. Sam was a fine man, though a political conservative. He had fathered the three basic SEC laws, with the result that we called the SEC the Rayburn Commission. He was largely responsible for seeing through the Congress the 1933 and 1934 SEC Acts. In 1935 there was a big battle on the SEC Holding Company Act, which Sam supported; and after I became chairman, great battles over our decisions ensued. But Sam, although proud of his role, was so circumspect that not once did he bring pressure to bear to get a decision from us one way or the other.

At each day's end Sam would hold court in a private-office hideaway in the Capitol. Scotch and bourbon and branch water were available. Old cronies drifted in and out. Often I would go to Sam's office to transact some business with him, and then we would go for dinner at Martin's restaurant on Wisconsin Avenue. We always sat in a room that in time became the Rayburn Room. Sam entertained, stag, about once a month in his apartment, where, with a big white apron tied around his chest, he served as bartender, cook, and waiter. Sam had been married very briefly early in life, was divorced, and never remarried. Many a hostess displayed an eligible blonde, but Sam never nibbled.

Rayburn had the countryman's view that the enemies of the people were the rich. The interest rates were high at that period—eight percent in my home state, Washington—and even the big people in Texas were completely excluded from the world of finance by the Eastern establishment. This situation did not change until Lyndon Johnson's time.

Sam, too, had his bumps of caution; he represented the grasslands of America, where people were not starving. He was honest and dedicated, but he was conservative and thought FDR often went too fast. Sam kept a close temperature reading on his own constituents and judged that they represented all of America, which of course they did not. His speech was full of country colloquialisms. A politician about to take a fatal step was usually "a guy who is about to have a cartload of poles fall on him." Sam's philosophy might be characterized as conservative populism.

At about the time I came to know Sam Rayburn, I met Jack Garner, the Texan who was then Vice-President. I was going to Dallas to make a Jackson Day dinner speech for the Democratic National Committee. Never having been in Texas before, and not knowing the political bigwigs of that area, I went to see Garner for advice and also for ideas as to what I should talk about.

It was about midafternoon when I was ushered into the Vice-President's office. He had his coat off; his vest was open; he had discarded his necktie; and he was in his stocking feet. I introduced myself, and he said, "Young man, before we start talking we have to strike a blow for liberty." He disappeared behind a screen which shielded a sink and I could hear the gurgling of a bottle and the running of water. Pretty soon he came out with two glasses containing the strongest brew I had ever tasted. He downed his in practically one gulp and I tried not to be too slow. But to my dismay I discovered that when I had finished the first drink, he thought that still another "blow" should be struck "for liberty." And so the blows continued for half an hour or more before I was able to broach the subject of my visit.

What he told me was not very responsive to my inquiry, but what he said was very revealing. It showed Jack Garner to be the country banker, the country farmer, and the country cattleman arraigned against the financial and industrial power of the East. He said that the greatest threat to America was the three "M's," meaning the Morgans, the Mellons, and the Mills. The import of this message was that I should talk about these three "M's" when I got to Texas. He went on to elaborate his prejudices against them by talking particularly about high interest rates in Texas and the need for federal credit institutions to help the farmers and the ranchers. After the lecture I could not escape without striking still one more "blow for liberty."

Congressman Clarence F. Lea of California had become chairman of the House Interstate and Foreign Commerce Committee when Sam Rayburn became Speaker of the House in 1940. Lea was therefore the custodian of SEC laws in the House, and the one before whom all suggested amendments came. Lea was a professorial type of person—able, quiet, hard-working.

Another congressman I knew well was Walter Chandler of Tennessee. Walter and I became a close-working team as a result of my protective committee investigation and the reports we wrote recommending new legislation. The entire Bankruptcy Act came up for revision in 1938 and Walter oversaw the process. Various groups, including credit men and referees, worked with us. Our SEC staff prepared Chapter X—the reorganization, as distinguished from the liquidation, part of the Act.

Under Chapter X the SEC was given an advisory role to the federal judge in charge of a reorganization. At that time a judge in a reorganization case had no disinterested advisor. He usually turned for advice to the reorganization managers, who represented the underwriters and had many vested interests to preserve. The SEC had no such financial stake and would be able to help any judge tremendously by giving neutral advice. It was easy enough getting the experts to agree on Chapter X, and it was easy to muster the votes in Congress necessary for its passage. It was difficult, however, to reconcile federal judges to having the SEC as a party in *their* proceedings, as the judges thought of them.

The most important federal district was the Southern District of New York, New York City. If I could get the judges of that district sold on the idea, the country would follow suit. So I arranged to meet them for lunch in Manhattan. I was coolly received and the silence was stony after I had finished speaking. The leader of the opposition was Judge Alfred C. Coxe. It took several years to bring him around, though the others soon accepted the offer of the SEC and used it as an impartial advisor on financial aspects of the reorganization. I had had many experiences with judges prior to that time, but never before had I sat with them in conference. I realized then, and later on, that judges as a whole were the most reactionary group I had encountered, even more reactionary than investment bankers. The bankers were usually open to new ideas; the judges were anchored fast to the past. Precedents were their hallmark. What had once been done was hallowed; what had never been done was suspect.

Emanuel Celler was the other main anchor for the SEC on the House side during the early days. Manny was without doubt the ablest of the Hill people with whom I dealt and the most liberal; and by chance, it was Manny who headed the subcommittee of the House Judiciary Committee to investigate me in the 1969–1970 effort to impeach me.

Manny Celler had an illustrious career in the House, where he served starting in 1923. He was chairman of the Judiciary Committee from 1949 to 1953 and again from 1961 until he left the House in 1972. During all those years he was a staunch supporter of the constitutional rights of the individual, whether the acts of oppression came from a big government or a big business. Manny Celler remained through all that time a courageous, liberal, honest, and vigilant congressman.

He sponsored over two hundred bills, most of which emphasized human rights, equality of economic opportunity, the rights of the poor, the rights of other minorities, and the rights of society. As chairman of the Judiciary Committee he reported out three constitutional amendments which were adopted by the States: the Twenty-third Amendment, which granted representation in the Electoral College to the people of the District of Columbia; the Twenty-fourth Amendment, which abolished the poll tax in federal elections; and the Twenty-fifth Amendment, which provides for transfer of power in the event of the disability of the President.

Celler's voice of protest against Hitler and Nazi anti-Semitism was loud and strong. During the Roosevelt administration Breckenridge Long of our State Department was more responsible than anyone else for keeping desperate Jews from getting visas to come to this country. Thus in 1943 our annual quota for all immigrants was 150,000; during that year we admitted only 25,527, and of those, only 4,705 were Jews fleeing from persecution. Secretary Morgenthau early in 1944 induced FDR to set up a War Refugee Board, independent of State Department control, but by then, at least four million Jews had been liquidated by Hitler. Meanwhile, it was Manny Celler who was publicly denouncing the State Department in general and Breckenridge Long in particular for creating "the tragic bottleneck" in getting visas for Jews. He said, "It takes months and months to grant the visa, and then it usually applies to a corpse."

Representative Lister Hill of Alabama, shortly to move to the Senate, was a liberal in economic matters who came in and out of focus in my range of SEC activities. Racial problems were in the background those days. The "liberal" Lister Hill was soon to become a member of the Southern cabal that fought with tooth and nail every assertion of Blacks that they too were first-class citizens. He sacrificed his career on the altar of Southern prejudice. He was a sad person but an extremely able man.

By happenstance I came to know Representative Carroll Reece of Tennessee, a very conservative, very friendly Republican. He was an artist in telling East Tennessee stories. One I recall was about the man who went to a bank to cash a check. The teller gave him his money in small bills and coins, and the man stood there, counting the money over and over and again. "Did I cheat you?" the teller asked.

"No. But you came damn close to it."

George H. Tinkham of Massachusetts, who served in the House nearly thirty years, was an oddball. He wore a huge, bushy, unsanitary-looking beard. One day Johnny Burns, the SEC counsel, and I were at a reception in the Carlton Hotel, and there, big as life, was Tinkham. Johnny grabbed my arm and whispered, "Look, look." I looked, and both of us saw a starling fly out of Tinkham's beard.

I have mentioned Frank Maloney, my mentor in the Senate, and Senators Borah and Byrnes. I also mentioned in passing Joseph T. Robinson, to whom FDR had promised a seat on the Court. Joe was the most reactionary, stuffiest person I ever knew and I shudder to think what votes he would have cast had he sat on the Court.

Another powerful senator in my SEC days was Pat (Byron Patton) Harrison of Mississippi, who served in the Senate from 1919 to 1941. He was a smooth, smart, cigar-smoking Southerner. He and Robinson and Byrnes controlled the Senate; they were the ones with whom I negotiated on the Hill. How FDR was able to work through them was a mystery. He could do it only by trimming his sails. And these men were, I thought, the real reason why FDR soft-pedaled all racial issues.

Pat Harrison brought George Allen to town. Allen was extremely able, very witty, and a man who used important contacts to work his way to the top in business and finance. He worked hard to get close to FDR, but never quite made it. Truman, however, was a pushover for him. Then after Truman, he sized up Eisenhower, dropped out of Democratic politics, and became Republican.

Eisenhower had two friends who, to use his words, "make me feel better when they walk into the room." One was Allen and the other was TV's Arthur Godfrey. Allen was greatly rewarded with over forty directorships on "blue chip" companies, and his book *Presidents Who Have Known Me* was a best seller. For some reason George took a great dislike to me; and I suppose if he told the truth, he would have said that his greatest achievement was in keeping me from becoming President.

Senator Alben Barkley was a political wheelhorse with an undying ambition to be President. Alben was the man in the Senate to see when SEC matters—whether laws, hearings, or budget—bogged down. He fathered the Trust Indenture Act (53 Stat. 1149), which we of the SEC drafted and promoted. He was a prodigious worker, honest and able, though not brilliant. He was an orator of note and used his lungs to produce a powerful effect.

Barkley's first wife was an invalid who had been bedridden for years. The medical costs were enormous, and to cover them, Alben took on speaking engagements across the country for fabulous fees. He was a storyteller of note; his anecdotes, which filled a volume called *That*

Reminds Me, were legion. I remember a social occasion when Alben held forth on the right of Blacks to vote. He told how a Black man had appeared for registration in a Southern town. The registrar, scanning the application, said, "Please quote the First Amendment to the Constitution."

The Black man shook his head.

"Recite the Fourteenth Amendment."

The man again shook his head.

"Tell me, what is a bill of attainder?"

He shook his head again.

"Does the crime of treason require an overt act?"

The Black shook his head.

The registrar, looking the applicant in the eye, asked, "Tell me, nigger, don't you know anything?"

"One thing" was the reply.

"What is that?"

"No nigger is going to vote in the next election."

Homer Bone, the senator from Washington State, was a fireball at home but rather ineffective in Washington, D.C. Homer came to office on the issue of public power, and he did more than any single person to educate the people on the abuses of the electric power industry. The Yakima papers were strongly opposed to Bone and all he stood for. Colonel William Robinson, their editor and publisher, hammered home one idea—that a private power company was "a taxpayer," and what communities like Yakima needed were taxpayers. Public power, he thundered, would have a tax exemption.

That was the starting point of Bone's address one night in Yakima. Colonel Robinson was in the audience, and Bon zeroed in on him, pointing out the fallacy in the colonel's editorials: the cost of doing business includes any and all taxes that are paid; the rate of return reimburses the utility for costs of doing business and allows in addition a return on investment.

"So," thundered Bone, "who really pays the taxes assessed against the private utilities? The consumers of electricity of course." The question, he said, was whether the consumers should pay for those costs plus profits of a private utility or, alternatively, the costs of running a public utility.

The colonel, who was at heart an amiable fraud, was so impressed with Bone as an orator that he met him afterward, sat up half the night talking with him, and put a bottle in his briefcase as he left.

Harry Truman put Bone on the Court of Appeals in the Ninth Circuit, where Bone turned into a Stone Age conservative. The flaming liberal who had espoused the underdog became the spokesman for the most staid and reactionary thinking in our society when it came to civil rights.

"To hell with the Fifth Amendment," he told me. "A woman has been killed, and by God, the police, if necessary, should be able to torture anyone to get a confession." As a judge, the philosophy and spirit of the secret police of Russia—the MVD—possessed him.

As a member of the Temporary National Economic Committee, I came to know two very different senators, one of whom I respected; the other, despised. The latter was William H. King of Utah, a sharp-beaked, petulant character whose main characteristics were vanity and ignorance. He inveighed against every new idea, every suggestion for improvement. My hours with him were agonizing and defeating.

Joe O'Mahoney was different. He was a smart, knowledgeable lawyer from Cheyenne, Wyoming, who came to the Senate in 1934 after a long House term. We were so close that I was a frequent visitor in his home up to the time of my divorce in the 1950's. After that I was treated like a pariah, because Joe and Agnes, his lovely wife, were devout Catholics.

O'Mahoney and Burt Wheeler were the leaders against FDR's Court-packing plan in 1937. In 1938, while serving in the Senate, O'Mahoney became chairman of the newly formed TNEC. I worked closely with him, and he did a good job. His philosophy was really that of the Populists: he was for competition and economic justice. But his range of vision was as limited as Wyoming.

Joe was defeated for the Senate in the fall of 1952, but stayed in Washington to practice law. During his brief time in practice, he represented the United States Cuban Council, and during the course of his duties as their lawyer, he had to appear before committees on the Hill. Being a stickler for compliance with all legal requirements, he registered as a lobbyist and received an identification card bearing the number 783.

At this time, O'Mahoney, along with Thurman Arnold and Abe Fortas, also represented Owen Lattimore, the Johns Hopkins professor who was undergoing investigation because of his views on China policy. When Joe ran for the Senate again from Wyoming in 1954, the opposition bore down hard. Why elect a person so far Left as to represent the communist Lattimore? Why elect a foreign agent? Whom does he really represent?

One of the ads read:

In Wyoming what can mattamore
Than defending that man
Lattimore
HARRISON FOR SENATOR
What could be more stinko
Than defending Lattimore,
the pinko
HARRISON FOR SENATOR

> Do YOU agree that this man, Joseph C. O'Mahoney—Foreign Agent 783—should be vested with the great responsibilities as United States senator, as YOUR representative in Washington, when he, by his own choice, exiled himself from Wyoming and willingly assumed representation of foreign interests DIRECTLY OPPOSED to those of Wyoming; and when he, again by his own choice and with his eyes open, accepted a man such as Owen Lattimore as his client?
>
> This advertisement bought and paid for by outraged Wyoming citizens, for the Harrison for Senator Club, James Wolfe, Treasurer.

Joe won that bloody contest and served in the Senate until 1961.

In the early Washington years Senator Henry F. Ashhurst of Arizona was one of my benefactors. Later, Ashhurst was chairman of the Senate Judiciary Committee when my name came up for nomination to the Court. Ashhurst had a golden tongue and a gracious manner. No finer, more considerate gentleman ever sat in the Senate. He was everyone's friend and an errand boy for every Arizona citizen's wish. When he was defeated in 1940 he made a farewell speech in the Senate that revealed the quality of the man: "I am sure some of my colleagues expect me to describe the sensation of defeat. The first half-hour you believe that the earth has slipped from beneath your feet, that the stars above your head have paled and faded, and you wonder what the Senate will do without you, and you wonder how the country will get along without you. But within another half-hour there comes a peace and a joy that would be envied by the world's greatest philosopher."

Ashhurst, however, was really so depressed at his defeat that he did not return to Arizona. He had no personal income, so FDR arranged that he be employed by a federal agency. His salary was slight, his job unimportant, and he soon faded out of Washington society, where once he had flourished.

Harry Truman was a more casual acquaintance of mine in those years, though I would see him and his wife, Bess, quite regularly at Sunday night dinners at Barney Nover's apartment. At that time, Barney, a newsman from Buffalo, was on the editorial page of the *Washington Post* and was also a columnist. Barney and his wife brought before their footlights up-and-coming people in Washington, and Truman, then quiet and unobtrusive, was one. Later, as World War II approached, Truman headed the famous committee that investigated America's industrial plant. Two future Justices, whom he was to appoint, were on his committee—Harold Burton of Ohio and Shay Minton of Indiana. Burton, quiet and industrious and very conscientious, was the workhorse of the committee. Each endeared himself to Truman in many ways. For instance, on reaching a city, Shay would turn to Truman and say, "Should we check into the hotel and leave our bags or go direct to the whorehouse?"

Truman had a keen sense of humor that ranged from the earthiness of the barnyard to the light touch of the drawing room. At Barney Nover's one night he told about the farm hand in Missouri who went insane. When I asked why, Truman explained that the chap had a quick attack of diarrhea. "Unfortunately, he was in a round barn and went nuts looking for a corner where he could squat."

Truman adored Pendergast and the other Democratic bosses of Missouri. I would listen to his praises of them and write them off as a form of sophomoric sentimentalism. But when at last I met those men and saw how vulgar, sleazy, and uncivilized they were, I somewhat revised my ideas of my friend Harry.

In these early days there were some Republicans as well as Democrats in the Senate who became mainstays for me. Borah was one; another was Arthur Vandenberg of Michigan, who served from 1928 to 1951. Vandenberg was on the Senate Finance Committee before which I frequently testified as spokesman for the SEC. His bald head and large eyes gave him an owlish appearance. His rapierlike mind never missed a point, and when I got just a little off base in my presentation or plea, he was the first to correct me. He was the "opposition," but he never carried it to partisan extremes. It was Vandenberg who offered FDR a hand on a bipartisan foreign policy. He was one of the most realistic of all senators when it came to understanding world affairs, and was one of the first to whom I ever talked about the need and the prospects for creating a world regime of law to take the place of force in settling international disputes.

Robert La Follette of Wisconsin, son of "Old Bob" La Follette, was a very close friend. I first met him when he came through New Haven in the 1930's on campaign tours. He was a great platform speaker. He was largely immersed in domestic politics and did not much interest himself in world affairs. But he and I together came to know about one tiny slice of it—Latvia, one of the three Baltic states.

The Balts had a long history of insecurity, gnawed at by both the Russians and the Germans for centuries. Latvia was under Russian rule until 1918. She was independent from the end of World War I until 1940, when Stalin moved his armies in. Shortly after I reached Washington, a Latvian Embassy had been opened, headed by Alfred Bilmanis, who spoke English and was exceedingly well educated. Bob La Follette and I cultivated Bilmanis and spent hours with him. He of course wanted to learn about American political trends from us, and we were enthralled at his accounts of developments in Latvia. A truly representative democracy was then in existence there. It had a socialistic quality; there were no great peaks of wealth or pits of poverty. Like the Scandinavian countries, income was fairly well distributed.

As Bob and I listened we got a new vision of a possible world order, where little democracies as well as big ones could flourish. We thought that Latvia could be a pacesetter for the underdeveloped nations of the world—if left alone. Russia, however, looked on neighbors with "democratic" tendencies as the United States looked on neighbors with "communist" tendencies. So Stalin moved in and extinguished a diverging experiment and substituted his own regime, just as we, after that time, moved into the Dominican Republic, displaced a regime we abhorred, and substituted a "safer" one.

When the 1946 elections were getting close, Bob La Follette and I had many discussions about his future. I urged him to leave the Republicans in Wisconsin and join the Democratic party, which had become his spiritual home. He debated the issue pro and con and finally decided against it, largely, I think, because of the great La Follette-Republican tradition in Wisconsin. The tragedy of the decision soon became apparent, for the intolerant Joseph McCarthy defeated him. It was a shock to suffer any defeat; it was a shame to have the idealistic, humane La Follette displaced by the unscrupulous, fascist-minded McCarthy.

That blow was the beginning of the end for Bob La Follette. He could not return to Wisconsin and face the people who turned him out. Friends got him a labor-relations job with the United Fruit Company, managed by the Banana King, Sam Zemurray. That association lasted only a little while, when to the horror of all of us, Bob committed suicide.

About the time I went on the Court, I met William Langer, a maverick senator from North Dakota from 1941 to 1959. I told him of my experiences herding sheep in his state, and it was that episode, I think, that started a close tie between us. Langer, while he was governor of North Dakota, had been convicted of a federal crime involving his administration of the national Emergency Relief Acts. As a consequence he was removed from office by the state Supreme Court in 1934. He was, however, elected governor again, and after that, came to Washington, D.C., as a senator.

Langer had been part of a North Dakota group which adopted a socialist program to solve some of the serious woes of the people of that state. Their business enterprises, banking and other economic measures gave North Dakota a rather far-flung, ambitious socialist program. Some taxpayers objected and brought suit to have the program declared unconstitutional, but a unanimous Supreme Court of the United States held in 1920 that it was not unconstitutional (253 U.S. 233).

Langer, on his visits with me in Washington, would relate various phases of that long struggle and the role he played in masterminding the legal battle. This chapter in our history, little known even to Americans, was one I told later to try to convince foreigners that our country was not reactionary in a constitutional sense, as the propaganda made out.

In any event, Langer was very much of a nonconformist, very much of an offbeat person, who in his Senate term stood pretty steadfast to principles when many were deserting them. He was a veteran campaigner, full of many tricks. The plague of anyone running for office is the person who comes forward with an outstretched hand and says, "I bet you don't remember me." Langer had a standard diversionary tactic. He would say, "Why, hello. How's your father?" And that usually worked.

One night after a speech at Minot, a lady accosted him, saying, "I bet you don't remember me," and Langer retorted in his accustomed way. She replied that her father was dead—and Langer was off the hook. The next night Langer spoke in Williston. The same lady showed up there. She came up after the speech and said, "I bet you don't remember me." Langer, still not remembering her, asked, "Why hello. How's your father?" Backing off, she gave him a steely look and said, "Senator, I told you all about Father last night."

When, under Eisenhower, Langer became chairman of the powerful Judiciary Committee of the Senate, he loved to make the members of the Establishment squirm as he expressed his seemingly radical views.

Earl Warren was a recess appointee to the office of Chief Justice and, normally, a Republican Congress would promptly confirm a Republican President's recess appointments. Not Langer. He had nothing against Warren but plenty against Eisenhower, since the Republican regime did not like him and would not give him the patronage he wanted. So he held out on Warren until Eisenhower gave him the postmasters and judges that he wanted.

Langer had once smoked cigars, but by the time I knew him he never lighted one. He used a brand that came wrapped in cellophane. He would put the cigar in his mouth, cellophane and all, and chew and chew. In an hour both the cigar and the cellophane had disappeared. I often wondered what an autopsy of his stomach would have shown.

John L. Lewis—portly and gruff, with massive eyebrows that made him look like the menace the press depicted—was another close acquaintance of mine. I came to know him early in my Washington days and sometimes joined him for lunch at the Carlton Hotel, where he sat at the same table, day after day. He was a lonely man who lived with his daughter across the river in Alexandria. He had come out of the mines and knew firsthand the lives and limbs it had taken to develop the mines and make stockholders rich. He represented the victims, their widows, and the prospective victims with earnestness and a will of steel. He often told me of early explosions and of the ugly resistance to reform that the owners showed.

It was Lewis who in 1939 called John Garner "a labor-baiting, poker-playing, whiskey-drinking, evil old man."

My friend and physician, George Draper, was suspicious of Lewis. Draper told me that most medical histories of aggressive, pompous, tough men pointed up the fact that they were that way because they had physical deficiencies. I felt that the explanation lay in Lewis' rage and indignation that had smoldered for years over the injustices he and other coal miners had suffered.

Harry Truman, after he became President, thought Lewis was a titan of power who defied the ultimate titan. Fred Vinson, Chief Justice, felt the same way about Lewis and often said that John L. was "too big for his britches," too ambitious to honor a White House or a Supreme Court—an attitude that doubtless crept into Vinson's 1947 opinion for the Court in a case where Lewis and his union where held in contempt (330 U.S. 258) and heavily fined. That was also the view that Harold Ickes had of Lewis, and I can still hear Harold groaning about him.

Lewis was negotiator *par excellence*. He could sit for hours across a table, facing employers, and never say a word. His silence was shattering; his sarcasm was biting. His typical answer to an owner's complaint on an economic phase of a strike was: "We wouldn't know that, since God apparently gave all the coal to people on your side. God gave you the right to exploit this piece of the earth. The men with picks and shovels have no rights. Don't you see? Perhaps we should turn our shovels over to you!"

Coal-mine labor disputes were violent affairs. Whether John L. Lewis was guilty of any of the crimes of violence attributed to him, I do not know. I greatly admired him in the early years for his hard-headed representation of the miners, who had suffered cruelly at the hands of the robber barons. But later my appraisal changed somewhat. Lewis and the owners truly "conspired"; in the end there was no real negotiation—they agreed on the price of coal to consumers and split between them the "raise" that Lewis demanded.

During that early period Carl Sandburg always referred to the Temple of Labor in speaking of trade-union meetings and trade-union discussions. Later Sandburg would ask me, "Temple of Labor? Whatever happened to it?"

A few labor leaders, notably Walter Reuther of the UAW, tried to make labor an important factor in civic affairs and in international affairs. Before the AFL–CIO merger Reuther had committees on conservation and the use of leisure time. Soil erosion, the endless cutting of virgin forests, water pollution—these all came into focus as part of labor's genuine and basic interests. The committees reported to the union membership as well as to the people at large. The interests of labor broadened beyond the question of wages and retirement pay. What kind of a society were we developing? What should our relations be with the rest of the world?

Reuther's union eliminated discrimination against Blacks, who were admitted with full equality. Trade unionism under Walter Reuther became an active agency of change and reform, a voice against injustice, a crusade that included housing, national parks, integrated schools, and all the other burning issues of the day. Organized labor became, indeed, the voice of many minorities, and social legislation and a change in community attitudes were its targets.

But after the merger it was the voice of George Meany, not that of Walter Reuther, which was heard. Meany in the AFL and Hoffa in the Teamsters Union lowered the standards of labor; they were interested only in money, not in civic affairs. Meany cast his weight on the side of military ventures overseas. His voice was the voice of reaction and the *status quo*, and Hoffa's voice was the voice of corruption. Both Meany and Hoffa did great harm to the Temple of Labor.

One of the most durable men to come to Washington was Averell Harriman, whom I respected greatly. He was an admirer and supporter of Wendell Willkie in the 1940 campaign, but hedged his bet by also giving heavily to the Democratic Committee. He was eager and able, but he suffered greatly from an inability to speak from a public platform. I remember sitting next to him on the dais while he suffered out a speech. Words came slowly and he ended in a sweat, exhausted. Harriman eventually took lessons in public speaking and became very accomplished at it, campaigning successfully in New York for the office of governor.

In the early days in Washington, Abe Fortas and his fiancée, Carol Agger, were my closest friends. They soon married and I was the best man at their wedding. She was a brilliant, aggressive lawyer at the Labor Board, and after serving in various government posts, became one of the leading tax lawyers in the nation. She and Abe, I always thought, had the best legal minds of any couple I ever knew.

Jerome Frank succeeded me as chairman of the SEC. He became restless in government by 1941 and decided to return to the practice of law. At that time there was a vacancy on the Court of Appeals, Second Circuit, and I suggested to FDR that he put Jerry there. The President said, however, that Robert Patterson, who resigned from that court in July, 1940, to come to Washington as Assistant Secretary of War, might eventually want his old position back. I told Jerry this, and he at once agreed he would step down from the Bench if FDR later wanted to rename Patterson to the court. I then reported back to FDR, saying Jerry would be "tops" on the Circuit Court and "would render grand service even if he were there only for a year or so." Roosevelt agreed, Jerry was named and confirmed, and he took his seat in May, 1941. Shortly thereafter Robert Patterson was killed in a plane trying to land in Newark.

Jerry as judge was a scintillating figure—a prodigious worker, a synergistic influence. My old friends at Yale knew him and were drawn to his chambers for fascinating conversations. Thurman Arnold would visit there, one conversation with Jerry lasting two hours. Thurman would speak for three or four minutes, expounding some speculative theory, and when he stopped, Jerry would hold forth at length on something equally brilliant but entirely different. And so they continued like two ships passing in the night, neither responsive to the other. When Thurman left, Jerry would turn to his law clerk, Sidney Davis, and say, "I never can understand what Thurman is talking about. Can you? Tell me, what did he have in mind today?" All of which confirms Jim Forrestal's description of the art of conversation: "The patience to wait until the other person stops talking before you start."

Jerry Frank had commodious accommodations in Manhattan, which included an extra bedroom for any old friend from Washington. A lonesome man, he urged his friends to stay with him even though they were arguing before his court. So husband and wife, single men, or single women would check in with Jerry, who was very strait-laced and always observed the strictest proprieties. One day he and Learned Hand were sitting on a panel together, hearing cases. The first one was argued by a beautiful as well as brilliant woman who had come up from Washington the day before and had stayed in Jerry's guest room. She and her husband were old, old friends of Jerry. Learned Hand knew nothing about them, and as I have said, he made a specialty out of exquisite off-color stories. So during the course of the argument Jerry whispered to Learned as he pointed to the lady lawyer, "She stayed with me last night." And instantly Jerry and the lady lawyer rose very high in Learned's estimation, for he gave the episode the most romantic coloration possible.

Jerry made a distinguished record on the Court of Appeals; of all the principles for which he stood, one is outstanding, namely the use of the legal concept of "harmless error." It was the practice of the court he served, when "the smell of the case" was strong, to affirm a conviction even though error had been committed at the trial. Jerry Frank, in a long list of dissents (see, e.g., 155 F (2d) 631, 642-664), pointed out that where the error was substantial and not merely a matter of etiquette, the reviewing court in calling the error "harmless" was in effect giving the defendant a "juryless" trial, for the judge reached the conclusion that guilt had been established "on a record other than that which the jury considered; for the judges are able to and do disregard the improper matter, but it is impossible to know that the jury did" (*Id.*, 648-649).

I thought the peroration of this practical hard-headed judge in one dissent was particularly revealing as to how the legal Establishment grinds down the largely helpless, accused individual:

> "Lawyers may talk rhapsodically of *justice*. They may, in Bar Association meetings, hymn the preeminent virtues of 'our Lady of the Common Law,' prostrate themselves devotedly before the

miracle of the common law's protection of human liberties. But, in the last analysis, there is only one practical way to test puddings: if, again and again in concrete instances, courts unnecessarily take the chance of having innocent men sent to jail or put to death by the government because they have been found guilty by juries persuaded by unfair appeals to improper prejudices, then the praises of our legal system will be but beautiful verbal garlands concealing ugly practices we have not the courage, or have grown too callous, to contemplate."

Jerry once wrote me when he was stung by a critic who deplored the kind of opinions he wrote. He sent the criticism on to me because he was extremely sensitive to denunciations. I replied:

November 16, 1942

Dear Jerry,

I have your recent letters. I was frankly a bit sore that anyone would suggest how you should perform your duty or conduct your personal affairs—and style, etc., is certainly personal. I believe in cultivating one's own garden and not other people's. What is good for you may be spinach to me or vice versa. But what the hell? Because you like gin and bitters, is there any reason why I should not get tight on long drinks of Scotch and soda? Nuts! I would not write lay opinions just for exercise or to kill time. Nor would you. Nor would I try to ape someone else. Nor would I go in for $50 words. But others might. And if they do, it's none of my business no matter how much I dislike it. I would forget the whole episode if I were you. I have heard others say that your opinions were most refreshing and a relief from the dull content of law reports.

As ever—
Bill

I never knew a harder-hitting, more practical politician than the indomitable Fiorello La Guardia, congressman from New York from 1917 to 1919 and from 1923 to 1933. He was no sentimentalist when it came to the poor, but had specific remedies, bills already drafted and ready to introduce. As mayor of New York, from 1934 to 1945, he had put Tammany Hall in its place and given the city a new, hopeful outlook. He was plain, ordinary, homespun. Sunday mornings he read the comic sheets to the people over the radio, making the whole big city laugh. Once I was with him on the reviewing platform in New York City, celebrating Columbus Day. He spoke first in Italian, and the audience cheered. He shifted to English for sober thoughts, but then, for asides, would speak Yiddish, bringing down the house.

When General Douglas MacArthur strode bravely down Constitution Avenue and dispersed the Bonus Army, La Guardia responded fiercely, "These people need bread, not bullets."

My friend Ernest Cuneo was La Guardia's guru as well as his disciple, and the two of them worked wonders in national politics. Cancer leveled Fiorello at a fairly young age, sapping America of some of its great strength.

Ernest Cuneo was assistant to Fiorello La Guardia in the early thirties, and in FDR's second term, was associate counsel to the Democratic National Committee. Cuneo's book *Life with Fiorello* is a moving personal account; his volume *Science and History* is a new approach to the ebb and flow of civilizations.

Ernest was one of the most dynamic and creative people in Washington during the New Deal. But except for a brief tour with the Democratic National Committee, he never was on anyone's payroll.

He lived in a small apartment house called the Hermitage and held forth at the nearby Pierre's Restaurant. He gleaned news for both Walter Winchell and Drew Pearson and wrote drafts of many of their columns and broadcasts. He was closely allied with Tom Corcoran and was an idea man for New Deal improvisations. He in time made a deal with Walter Winchell that netted him a million dollars and gave him the North American Newspaper Alliance.

He usually spoke in parables, so that many people did not understand him. He had played both college and professional football and its strategy colored his figures of speech. He would always cheer on a valiant New Dealer from his seat in the bleachers, but he also participated in many staff meetings where strategy was fashioned. He admired FDR for his skillful political management of the plantation owners of the South and the liberals of the West and North, but he deplored the President's conservatism. When FDR failed to use the occasion of Dick Whitney's defalcation to take over the New York Stock Exchange, Ernest Cuneo proclaimed, "FDR is too goddamn conservative."

Benjamin Cohen was an exceptionally able man. He was the author of the Securities Act of 1933, the Securities Exchange Act of 1934, and the

Public Utility Holding Company Act of 1935, all of which we administered at the SEC. Each was an artistic creation with symmetry and internal harmony. In the early days the commission sat in session all day, listening to problems, agreeing on statutory construction, or perhaps even proposing a rule or regulation for adoption. Working with the Acts in that manner made us realize what works of art they were.

Ben was retiring, quiet, and self-effacing. He lived alone and had few friends, although the few were close. He was never in the forefront, but always worked in a hideaway office in the Reconstruction Finance Corporation, where Jesse Jones furnished space for Cohen and Tom Corcoran. Tom was the "first" man of the team; Ben was the thinker and draftsman *par excellence*. Ben stayed on with FDR working on plans for the then unborn United Nations. He was the key man at the Dumbarton Oaks Conference in 1944 and at San Francisco in 1945. From 1945 to 1947 he was counselor to the State Department. From 1946 to 1952 he served on the American delegation to the United Nations. Then his tour of duty ended and Ben retired to private life. He refused all offers to practice law. His hobby was tennis, and when he wasn't playing tennis, he read and pondered and talked with friends. It was a shame that under Democrats and Republicans alike his talents were not used. They were wasted at a time when the nation needed Ben's sense of history and his long-range measure of the public good.

In addition to friends in political life, I also knew well several journalists in Washington. I have already mentioned Robert Kittner, a young newspaperman working for the New York *Herald Tribune*. Bob soon joined Joseph Alsop in producing a column. Joe, an epicurean when it came to food, gave Sunday luncheons at his Georgetown home, to which I was sometimes invited. This was the setting in which past events were called up and future events were divined. It was an exciting and challenging group that gathered there. Joe—often referred to in later years as an arch conservative—was then a forceful advocate of constitutional government and especially dedicated to the First Amendment.

J. Russell Young, correspondent for the Washington *Evening Star* and White House correspondent from 1920 to 1940, was about the build of FDR and resembled him. Russ was a mimic and learned to do takeoffs of the President. He traveled the campaign trains with FDR, and at whistle stops in the gray dawn before Roosevelt was awake, he occasionally would step to the rear platform and address the crowd in FDR's voice. FDR heard of it and was highly amused; once he got up early just to hear

Russ "take him off," and thought Russ was so good at it that he kiddingly suggested that Russ teach the other reporters how to make public addresses. "Then you all can do the campaigning for me."

That was the start of the J. Russell Young School of Expression. It met once a year for dinner, Jesse Jones picking up the tab. The meetings were in the lower dining room at the Mayflower Hotel. Russ was the dean, dressed in cap and gown. After dinner the graduation exercises were held. New students were given tryouts, their names called by Russ without prior notice. The candidate would walk up to the platform, to be given his topic by Russ, with notice that he had only three minutes. I remember that my topic was "Don't Shoot Until You See the Whites of Their Eyes." I was unimportant enough to pass the speaking test and be admitted. A famous Senate orator, however, would probably flunk. Russ kept some of them dangling year after year. The graduates, in cap and gown, had to sing a song, then form a daisy chain. The dean would address the school as bets were made on the number of steins of beer he would drink during his oration. It was a stag affair, but clean and wholesome, and the dean's annual humorous address was a highlight of Washington life.

As I have written, I always disliked the name Orville, though it followed me like a shadow right through high school. I got mostly rid of it in college and completely so in law school. Yet once in a while it would crop up, always making me cringe. In Washington, in the thirties, I met Charles O. Gridley, Washington correspondent for the Denver *Post*, a tall, broad-shouldered, genial man with a receding hairline. He was a member of the Gridiron Club and on one of its occasions—a white tie dinner—we retreated to a corner and had a long talk. Finally he asked, "What does the 'O' in your name stand for?"

I said, "I'll tell you if you tell me about your 'O'."

We shook hands and I told him. His face lit up and he said, "Brother, I sympathize with you. I, too, am cursed with Orville."

Then and there we formed the Secret O Society; only those with that middle initial would be eligible. We never found another prospect, and the society limited itself to a short annual meeting on the evening when the Gridiron Club put on its yearly dinner and show.

The Gridiron annual affair was largely financed by newspaper publishers. The guests were men prominent in private and public life. The head of the party in power, the President, was always invited and usually came. Someone representing the party out of power spoke for it. In between were skits produced by members of the club, duly costumed.

The Marine Band furnished the music. The solos were sung by hired professional singers. And there were two mock restrictions: women, always present; newsmen, never. Also, the Gridiron might be hot, but it would never sear.

It did, however, sear Frank Murphy, one of the Supreme Court Justices from 1940 to 1949. Frank was a bachelor. He never drank an ounce of liquor in his entire life. His father had known alcohol too well, and Frank took a pledge never to taste it. He was not a playboy, he did not frequent night clubs or burlesques, but he did date pretty girls. So his dating became somewhat of a legend around Washington. The Gridiron memorialized it in a skit to the tune of "Moon Over Miami." While the song was being sung, a male figure in judicial robes danced and jumped and twirled on a half-darkened stage against the backdrop of a full moon, Frank was so hurt he never again attended a Gridiron dinner.

Many interesting political talks were made at these dinners by Presidents and by defeated candidates for that office. Perhaps the best of all was by Thomas E. Dewey in 1949, after his defeat by Harry Truman. When he'd gone to bed on election night he was confident he'd won the Presidency, only to awaken to defeat. So he told this story about an Irish wake:

One participant got drunk and passed out. His friends, as a joke, removed the corpse and put their drunken friend in the coffin. Dawn came and the friend awoke. He felt the silken lining of the box he was in, looked around, and then said, "If I am alive, why am I in a coffin? If I am dead, why do I have to go to the bathroom?"

Tom Dewey, who generally was humorless, brought down the house with that story.

Alfred T. Hobson, secretary of the RFC and a confirmed bachelor, was another of my intimates. He had a house on Avon Place, in Georgetown, where he entertained often. He was an excellent cook and bartender and had a taste for good wine.

Hobby had a massive heart attack in 1946 and ended up on the same floor with me in Doctors Hospital, where I had been taken with virus pneumonia. He retired on a pension because of that disability, briefly ran a cattle ranch in Montana, and then bought a house on the coast at quiet Waldoboro, Maine, where he spent his remaining days. Hobby was the real "liberal" of my time; he saw through the great frauds of the Cold War and was a generation ahead of the times when it came to domestic programs.

The thirties and forties were my own "era of folksongs" and I shared that time with Alfred Hobson. He played the piano by ear and had a fine tenor voice that had won him a place on the Cornell Glee Club years earlier. His songs were countless, from "There was a little spider who went up the waterspout" to "You may kiss me once, you may kiss me twice—or three or four or maybe more. But please don't take advantage of my good nature, for I've got out and walked before." And he also had two classic versions of "The Tattooed Lady"—one of them to the tune of "Alexander's Ragtime Band," which ended "But what I liked best, right across her chest, was my home in Tennessee."

Tom Corcoran was another of Hobby's friends; Tom played the accordion, his specialty being "The Unreconstructed Rebel," a pungent relic of the Civil War.

One night James Conzelman, famous all-American halfback and coach of the Chicago Cardinals, came by and I made a list of over 360 folk songs that we sang without a break. Jimmy contributed a unique one, "The Biscuit Song":

> It's easy enough to take a biscuit apart.
> The difficult thing is to put it back just as it was.

My previous experience with folk songs had come about the time of World War I, when I was, as I have said, for a few months each year part of the restless, unhappy, but stoutly independent group of migratory workers who moved south to north in search of work in the Pacific Northwest.

Meeting places, where a pot of stew would be improvised, were under railroad bridges. It was there I sojourned with IWW's, whose lusty, challenging voices gave "Frankie and Johnny" some lurid verses and made "Hallelujah, I'm a Bum!" a work of art.

Through railroad yards, across wheat fields, and up and down the orchards of the Pacific Northwest, mostly sad songs echoed, songs that Woody Guthrie later called "hurt songs." There was power in his words describing the sharecroppers' plight:

> Thirty days we got to spend in jail
> 'Cause we spoke at a union and we ain't got bail.

We who rode the rods knew what he meant.

I have mentioned Carl Sandburg with whom I sometimes sang almost the whole night through as he strummed his guitar. His songs—later collected in *The American Songbag*—mainly reflected sadness and loneliness. Even

O, the E-ri-e was a-rising
The gin was getting low

had a sad, sad ending:

The lonesomest sound, boys,
I ever heard sound, boys,
On the stroke of midnight
Hear the curfew blow.
My buddy will hang, boys,
On the hangman's rope, boys,
On the gallus pole, boys,
When the curfew blows.

A long time ago I sat way into the night with an Irish friend. The hour of reckoning at the hands of a British executioner in Ireland arrived, and an Irish patriot, whom I did not know, met his death. At the stroke of the clock my Irish friend led us all in the singing of "When the Curfew Blows."

The cowboys I met also sang plaintive songs. They and the Blacks seemed to pour the drudgery and misery of their jobs into their music. The best cowboy singer I knew was Tom Whited of Cle Elum, Washington, who sang the Lord's Prayer beautifully and promised to sing it at my funeral. But Tom died early.

"I Ride an Old Paint" and "Poor Lonesome Cowboy" were two other favorites of his, but the prize was "The Strawberry Roan." Tom Whited, who never smoked, always lit a cigarette at the start of this song, letting it burn freely to the end, then lighting a fresh one from the old, and so on. He sat tilted back on an old kitchen chair as he sang, slightly teetering. Memory of the old chorus still echoes in me:

He goes up in the east and comes down in the west,
Just to stay in the saddle, I'm doing my best.

I had among my friends another sort of cowboy, Gary Cooper, the famous actor, whom I met through his father-in-law, Paul Shields, one of the few Wall Street men to support me in my effort to clean up the Stock Exchange. Gary was a quiet man who lived a simple life; he also died quite young of cancer. He would have been good in law, had that field interested him. His superior talents would indeed have made him excel in any field that caught his imagination. He'd visit me at my office at the SEC. He came once, as I recall, at the peak of a very busy workday and we chatted for perhaps half an hour. I escorted him to the elevator, and when we reached the street floor practically every female in the building was in the lobby waiting. Before leaving the elevator I turned to Gary and said, "I've been in this building for nearly five years and this has never happened to me before."

Gary grinned, squeezed my hand, and gently pushed his way through the adoring crowd and many "Oh boys" and dozens of outstretched hands. Reaching the street, he waved to them, and to me, and went with long strides down the avenue.

Spencer Tracy and I arrived in New York City about the same time, he in March, 1922, and I in September. I met him a few years later at a premiere in New York City when he was on his way up the ladder. A warm friendship was formed instantly. In my SEC days in Washington, he was in and out of the city and usually called me. That kind of relationship continued after I went on the Court in 1939. Though we did not see each other often, we were extremely intimate. Our correspondence was skimpy. The last time I saw him was when *Judgment at Nuremberg* was being filmed in Hollywood. We had lunch together in the studio. When he died in 1967, I felt as though my twin brother had passed away. There was, apparently, a physical resemblance between us. I was frequently taken for him in crowds, and some of my friends attached the nickname "Spence" to me on that account. Once, about twenty years ago, he appeared in the nation's capital for the premiere of one of his movies. By prearrangement, I waited for him at the rear exit. Many people surged into the dimly lit alley, and taking me for him, asked, "Mr. Tracy, will you give us your autograph?"

I obliged, and several dozen took the forgeries home. Most of the crowd had gone when Spencer appeared, and my account of the episode made him chuckle as we sipped a nightcap in a secluded spot.

I never knew anyone more American than he. I realize that the label "American" means various things, even a "vigilante" to some, but Spencer was the opposite. He was Thoreau, Emerson, Frost. His ideas had a wide range; he was no respecter of prejudice; his society was classless except for men and women of talent. To that aristocracy, all were welcome.

Therefore, one was always at ease with him. He emanated warmth and tolerance. I know he never talked bunk. He thought and talked in simple terms. His values were humanistic.

He was utterly unencumbered by nonsense about his remarkable ability as an actor. He filled the role of Darrow in *Inherit the Wind* as easily as he dressed for an outing. He never wore make-up, he told me. He searched for the simple truths out of which great friendships and enduring loves are fashioned.

For over twenty years he was deeply in love with Katherine Hepburn and they lived together. I once asked her what the secret was of his stage and screen success. She replied, "The aim of most artists is to strip away the unessentials—Spence did this. I think that that is why he is so universally admired, because, hopefully, the real truth is universal."

Spencer Tracy in a real sense was on a wavelength with humanity around the globe. He knew the predatory nature of man but searched for the kindlier qualities human beings also have in common. In that search he developed compassion and great insights. Because he extolled the virtues that he found in all men, he himself flowered as a human being and became uninhibited and wholly integrated.

Katherine Hepburn was with him the night he died. She heard him get up and go downstairs. She followed, and walked up to him as he was preparing a cup of tea. Suddenly there was a gasp, and Spence sank to the floor, dead.

He was indeed a rare human being—a man for all people, all faiths, all seasons.

I have mentioned how cool, reserved, and remote the people of New York City seemed to me on my first arrival there and for some years thereafter. By the late fifties through the sixties and into the seventies the situation changed. I could hardly walk a block without being accosted by people who had only a pleasant word for me or who wanted to shake my hand. One lady who stopped me said, "You are son of the manse. You got your Calvin creed from your father. How happy we are that you have lived up to it." I did not tell her the dim view I've had of Calvin but merely thanked her for her kind thoughts of me.

If I walked Madison Avenue or Fifth Avenue or Broadway for an hour's shopping or for exercise, I would be hailed by dozens of people—all strangers. The warm heart and the spontaneity of New Yorkers, which

I had missed in my early years, was very much on display. The following story by Janice L. Booker* gives a fair account of this warmth, as well as of my resemblance to still another famous American:

> We had driven into New York for the evening to meet another couple, dear friends, for cocktails and dinner . . . After dinner we wandered over to the Hilton to have a last drink in their lobby cocktail lounge . . .
>
> About ten minutes after we were seated, my husband, Al, . . . casually remarked, "Isn't that Justice Douglas?" We sprang to attention. Sure enough, just outside our window on Sixth Avenue stood an attractive, older man with a shock of white hair and a lined, craggy face. He was with a group of people, and was immediately surrounded by passers-by stretching out whatever they could find—the back of checkbooks, receipts, scraps from theater programs—for autographs. . . . Imagine! The folk hero of our liberal past standing not ten feet away from us, separated merely by a sheet of thermal pane. Agitation outside the window increased, and our friend, Cy, gestured to one of the crowd, indicating by a nod and a questioning look in his eye a need to verify our conjecture. The stranger nodded, and mouthed through the glass the four syllables we were straining to hear.
>
> "Yes, it is," said Cy intensely. "He said it's Justice Douglas." We watched elatedly as he strode with his entourage to the entrance of the Hilton—and—and—yes, passed through the revolving doors within our sight. My friend, Naomi, grabbed the first thing she could from the table, a small placard indicating who would be playing in the piano bar to entertain us for the next two weeks. I settled for a soggy cocktail napkin and followed her to the entrance. . . .
>
> We approached the old man. Bellhops converged from another direction with outstretched baggage tickets ready for autograph. His white hair, disarrayed from the wind, stood like a beacon to his greatness. His eyes glittered with the excitement of the recognition that surrounded him. How humble he is, I thought, to be so pleased by these accolades. My friend was not so speechless as I. "I would like you to know, sir," she said, "that in 1952 in Drexel Hill, Pennsylvania, my husband and I voted for you for

* From *The Shingle,* vol. 36, p. 83 (April, 1973).

President, the only two votes like that recorded in our area."

"Is that so," he responded looking genuinely impressed. "I'll remember that, and I thank you for it."

As she handed him the back of the card . . . for his autograph, and Cy extolled him for his tenacity in the face of alien administrations, I gingerly touched his blue-suited shoulder and recorded the moment in my mental memoir book. He started to autograph the piece of cardboard, hesitated, and said, "If you voted for me for President, I have to write more than my name. Tell me your names and I'll write something special for you." Naomi's eyes shone. What a memento to show her daughters! What a keepsake for history! She related her name and her husband's, first and last, and he laboriously repeated the spelling, saying he had never been a good speller. I mouthed the words "You don't have to know how to spell, what you have written in the way of decisions is sufficient," but my usually verbose tongue failed me. It took him a while to write the message; we waited breathlessly. He finished, handed it over to Naomi, and left us with a greeting and a wave.

She had the first opportunity to read it, and suddenly shrieked, "Oh, no!" We leaned over her shoulder to see what pearls had elicited that response, and read the following: "To my friends, Naomi and Cyrus Wolfman, best wishes from Casey Stengel."

I never met Casey Stengel. Though Chief Justice Warren gave him occasional luncheons at Court to which I was always invited, I was either out of town or in a hospital at the time and could not attend. Whether Spencer Tracy ever knew Casey, I do not know. But I concluded that for the public to confuse me either with Spencer Tracy or with Casey Stengel was a point of distinction. No two men in my time better illustrated the warm heart and bright conscience of our people.

On one occasion, a gentleman stopped me on 56th Street near Park Avenue, called me by name, and said he had admired me for years because once as a waiter he had served me at a restaurant where I drank in rapid succession four double vodkas. "What a man," he said. "If it had happened to me, I'd have been under the table." I never told him it must have been Casey Stengel or Spencer Tracy, because it probably was not. There doubtless is still another understudy for me in Manhattan on the alcoholic side.

Leonard Lyons, famous columnist, and his wife, Sylvia, were among the most talented couples I ever knew. He started out as a member of the New York Bar. Before long he was writing for the *New York Post,* and in a few years, established his well-known column, "The Lyon's Den." Lennie worked from about eight P.M. to four A.M. covering the various nightspots in New York City, afterward repairing to his office at the *Post* to write his column, and then to bed. Sylvia was also a writer and produced many piercing and humorous pieces for magazines. They had four sons, each one precocious. Douglas Lyons was my godson and took his law at Hofstra, where he was very active as a one-man committee to abolish the death penalty.

In the early years, while I was still in New York, I sometimes went with Lennie on his rounds. He knew all the celebrities, their scandals as well as their other lives, but he never printed the scandals. He had only kind things to say about people. Humor, yes. Inside information, yes. But no malicious tales. He was a wholesome man and brought his segment of journalism to a high level.

Through him I met many of the characters of Broadway and Hollywood—Georgie Jessel, Danny Kaye, Jack Benny, Celeste Holm, Toots Shor, Bob Considine, Robert E. Sherwood, Damon Runyon, Walter Winchell, Katherine Hepburn, Helen Hayes, her husband, Charles MacArthur, Moss Hart, Ethel Merman, John Barrymore, Max Gordon, George S. Kaufman, Rita Hayworth, Dinah Shore, Tallulah Bankhead, and many others.

Someone I particularly admired was Oscar Levant, a complicated, introspective man, and a great musician. He wrote several books, the last one being *The Importance of Being Oscar*. He was also a composer of popular music and of symphonies, and a writer of popular songs. When I first met him he was on the popular radio program *Information Please.* From there he went into movies, one of his best being *Rhapsody in Blue,* the story of his friend George Gershwin. Levant was an artist at the piano, and for me he was at his very best when he gave solo recitals as a pianist-raconteur. An hour with Oscar was an intriguing event. His humor was subtle, impudent, and at times brash; at times it seemed to cloak a worried, morose genius.

Oscar Levant had flashes of insight into social, economic, and political problems that many experts in those fields often lacked. It was from his lips that I think I first heard the phrase "socialism for the rich." It was a light-hearted quip, emphasizing why the captains of industry and finance need federal funds more than do people in the ghettos.

I once met Chico Marx and found him to be an extremely intelligent man, well-versed in national problems. I never met Groucho, my hero, but it was Groucho, not Americans for Democratic Action (ADA) or other liberal groups, who cheered me on for my lone dissent in the Pollack case, in 1952 (343 U.S. 451). Pollack was a lawyer of my brother's vintage who had graduated from Columbia Law and was practicing in Washington, D.C. At that time the District licensed a streetcar company to engage in mass transit. The streetcar company entered into a contract with a local radio station, which for a fee entertained the passengers from morning to night with news, educational programs, and the like. There was no way for a passenger to turn the radio off, and Pollack, a regular customer, brought suit to halt the practice.

The question was whether the government was entitled to drill into the heads of those people—truly a "captive" audience—its particular brand of news, propaganda, politics, and the like. I thought it violated due process and went against the grain of our constitutional philosophy, and I voted against the company. Felix Frankfurter would doubtless have joined me had he sat, but he was so terribly offended by the lower court's decision that he felt he could not be objective and stated as much publicly. The Court, speaking through Justice Burton, held otherwise. The sole letter I received applauding my dissent was from Groucho Marx. He said that pretty soon hostesses would come by on streetcars and buses, spraying each customer with a perfume. Groucho intimated that if we could produce "captive audiences" American manufacturers would be entranced. It was the only letter Groucho ever wrote me, and I often wondered what terminated the correspondence. Certainly Groucho is interested in many more things than captive audiences. The basis of my belief is not conjectural; it was confirmed by the artistically beautiful way in which I saw him disembowel the brilliant William Buckley on Buckley's TV show, *Firing Line*.

Of the theatrical people I met, George Kaufman was probably the wittiest and ablest. One of his classic remarks about a President was "Mr. Wilson's mind, as has been the custom, will be closed all day Sunday."

In an article in *The New Yorker* magazine Kaufman once wrote:

> I went to the trouble of looking up the original text on the income tax law as filed in the Library of Congress. Sure enough, there it was—Paragraph D, Clause 18—just as I had suspected: "The taxpayer, in computing the amount of tax due to the government, may deduct from his taxable income all legitimate

expenses incurred in the course of conducting his business or profession—except in the case of George S. Kaufman."

In Washington, D.C., I met two *Life* photographers who greatly influenced me. One was Lisa Larson, in her early thirties, very active physically and an expert with the Leica camera. I had acquired a Leica and was experimenting with its various lenses. I knew little about cameras, but my interest in the wilderness accentuated my desire to learn photography. Lisa would take me out on the street and explain, first, the desired composition of a given shot, and then the lens to be used and the distance factor. Ours were sporadic encounters, for she was in the city only occasionally. She had a keen competitive drive and had resolved to become the best photographer in the nation. She admired Margaret Bourke-White and Eliot Elisofon, but she wanted to be even better than those two artists. Hence her whole commitment was to photography; it was the same passionate drive I had seen in a few of the elite who went into law and a still smaller group that studied medicine. Lisa was one of the loveliest women I ever knew. She died of cancer; I never even knew she was ill until I received word of her demise from a relative. In my mind's eye I can see her loaded with cameras trudging through the far reaches of the world, oblivious of the rain, the mud, or the heat, and bent only on getting exquisite pictures out of a wasteland. She traveled widely and proposed that I do so also. "You write the book and I'll adorn it with pictures of the suffering humanity you encounter. It will be the best travel book ever written."

Her death terminated that possibility, and on my later journeys, I had a feeling of sadness and helplessness because try as I did, I never could get many superlative pictures.

Later I met Eliot Elisofon, a genius with a camera. In addition to taking pictures, he had acquired in his travels one of the most outstanding collections of African art I ever saw. Like Lisa Larson, he was a humanist, always eager to get the feeling of joy, achievement, sadness, defeat in his photographs.

He came to Washington quite frequently, merely to take a walk "at dawn," as he would say. He took an early interest in Harry Truman and would often walk the same route that Truman had earlier trudged. He gave me many lessons in photography, and I improved. Composition came first with him, as it did with Lisa. "Never take a picture which appears to show a tree growing out of the head of a person," he once said. He taught me that on a picture-taking hike one camera should always be set for the correct light reading and (for wide-angle lenses) the distance be set at eight feet to infinity. So prepared, a photographer could take a picture the instant he saw something that interested him—a person or a scene. His suggestions were numerous and specific. Though I no longer recall all of them, I do remember best his offer to grade my films. He would put one X on every one he liked; a double X on those he loved. I remember one that carried four X's, which meant that in a small, small fraction of photos I was excellent.

Chapter XXV

Brandeis and Black

The time came when I had to tell FDR that I was resigning my SEC position. My salary was $10,000, but with a young family, it cost nearly $15,000 a year to live in Washington. I had been there five years and owed $25,000, largely on my insurance policies. Yale wanted me to rëturn and be dean of the Law School, beginning in the fall of 1939. There was nothing I would have liked more, except one thing, and that was being Solicitor General—the lawyer's lawyer. But the list of aspirants for that position was long, and I could not afford to wait it out in Washington. So I gave up any thought of the S.G. job and accepted the deanship at Yale.

The day I told FDR that I would have to leave by June, 1939, he said rather wistfully, "We'll see." Our relationship was such that I knew he would have the final word and would probably come up with some distasteful assignment which I would have difficulty declining. I had not the slightest idea I would ever be on the Court. It never was a part of my dreams. I had visited the Court, as I liked to watch it in operation, but never once in all my life did it even cross my mind that I might one day sit there.

On occasion I would go across town to hear a case of SEC interest argued. Holmes, whom I last saw as a shriveled, hunched old man, was now gone. There was the Jovian Hughes, the easygoing Roberts, the lean, sour McReynolds, the reserved Sutherland, the professorial Stone, and the bulldog Brandeis.

I visited Stone—my first law professor—regularly at his home, which he had built at 24th Street and Wyoming Avenue, N.W., where he had a spacious office.

I also came to know Brandeis intimately.

I was too modest to search Justice Brandeis out when I went to Washington, though our interests in financial as well as in other matters were so similar. But I had not long to wait to meet him. One day he called—not through a secretary, for he had none. Mrs. Brandeis handled all correspondence that he could not manage by longhand. This call was one he made personally, and in his high resonant voice he asked if I could come by his apartment and see him the next Sunday at four o'clock. He lived on California Street, right off Connecticut, and his apartment, while neat, seemed threadbare.

Nevertheless the Brandeis home was radiant with friendship. The evening meal, when guests were present, was usually soup, followed by boiled chicken from which the soup had been made, and capped with a fruit dessert. The party was over by about ten o'clock, since the Brandeis working day started at five o'clock in the morning.

In those days the Court sat in the old room under the dome of the Capitol. There was no Supreme Court Building, so the Justices worked at home. For his office, Brandeis had an apartment in the same building on the floor above his residence.

After that first day in 1934, I was with Brandeis about once a week. He drew me to him to find out what was going on. My work interested him above that of anyone in the city, for I dealt in high finance, the subject that had absorbed him in his early days. He commented over and again on the parallelism between my investigation and the one made by the Pujo Committee in 1912 to 1913, with which he had been closely connected. He asked me searching questions, making me recite chapter by chapter what I had discovered. He was fascinated with the anatomy of high finance and commented that the sons of those he had investigated were apparently no better than their fathers had been.

In his early days Brandeis had looked into the affairs of the New Haven Railroad and followed the machinations that seemed to plague that road. He exacted a promise from me: that when I finished work at the SEC and returned to Yale, I would write a book exposing the anatomy of the complex money matters of the New Haven. It was a promise I asked him to relieve me of when I was confirmed for the Court, and he did so. That sad chapter in American finance was never written.

I learned about Zionism from Brandeis and caught some of his zeal for the establishment of a Jewish state. Brandeis belonged to a different school of thought than that of those who eventually created the State of Israel. Chaim Weizmann, the Zionist leader, in time became Brandeis' chief opponent. Brandeis, born in America, was not a product of European ghettos and was not steeped in Jewish culture. His commitment to Israel was intellectual rather than emotional. He thought of building a state based on economic and social measures, with the aid of businessmen, whether they were Zionists or not. The Weizmann school eventually prevailed, based on the principle that Israel should be composed of ardent keepers of the faith. Although Brandeis withdrew from active participation in Israeli matters, the pull of Zionism was evident in every talk he had with me.

Brandeis thought that the area of Palestine should be developed for Jews and non-Jews alike. He was not caught up in what inspired some of the other Zionists—the desperate necessity to save the remnants of the Jewish European community. Modernization, the use of technicians and engineers, creation of a society not restricted to Jews—these were his concerns. I suppose one might say that he was less nationalistic and less concerned with religious matters than other supporters of a Jewish state.

He remained, however, an ardent supporter of the Zionist cause despite criticism of him from other people in the movement. Felix Frankfurter, likewise, was enormously involved in these matters.

I was with Brandeis the day Hitler invaded Poland. He saw his people facing new and horrible ordeals under the Nazis. He paced his apartment, old and bowed, his hands behind his back, whispering, "Will England fight?" The Chamberlain motif "Peace in our time" he knew to be a phony, and he wondered when the world would wake up.

Brandeis was not a philosopher like Cardozo or a salesman like Frankfurter. Brandeis was a modern Isaiah. He was a mighty man of action who, having found the facts and determined the nature and contours of the problem, moved at once. He admired Jefferson and talked to me often about him, not only about Jefferson's interest in the First Amendment but also about his inventive genius in creating useful articles. Brandeis also admired Jefferson's philosophy concerning private ownership, small units of business and agriculture, and an active democracy.

While still in law practice, Brandeis became interested in the promotion of state minimum-wage and maximum-hour legislation. Oregon had passed a law prohibiting women from working more than ten hours a day in factories and laundries. Brandeis wrote an *amicus* brief in support of the Oregon law when it came before the Supreme Court in 1908.* The brief became famous overnight, for it contained not a single citation of legal precedent, only citations to social and economic treatises dealing with the subject.

Brandeis was intent on educating judges as to the facts of life—as to why doctors, social workers, and others thought the maximum-hour legislation was essential to the well-being of the workers and of the community where they lived. Why, he asked, should the ultimate wisdom of judges be found in dusty lawbooks? Why should not judges be abreast of life? That type of brief—revolutionary as it was in 1908—came in time to be known as a "Brandeis brief."

While practicing in Boston, Brandeis gave much of his time to public service without payment of a fee—preserving the subway system, devising a sliding scale for the gas system, and promoting the savings-bank life-insurance plan. His investigations into high finance led him to Wall Street, and he teamed up for a while with Samuel Untermeyer to help expose the exploitive power of the money trust. Out of these sorties came his books, *The Money Trust* and *Other People's Money*. He was retained by the Interstate Commerce Commission (ICC), as special counsel to help it pass on the application of Eastern roads to put into effect a horizontal five percent increase of freight rates (31 ICC 351).

Brandeis' role as arbiter in the garment industry led to his creation of the famous "protocol" for a permanent government of labor relations in the industry and his promotion of the preferential union shop.

Brandeis' various activities aroused the ire of the Establishment. So when Woodrow Wilson sent his name to the Senate for a seat on the Supreme Court, the powers-that-be moved in to defeat him. Hearings started February 9, 1916, lasted until March 15, 1916, and resumed again May 12, 1916. Brandeis was finally confirmed June 1, 1916: 47 yeas, 22 nays, and 27 not voting.

Brandeis made many notable contributions to the Bar and to the Bench. One of these has gone largely unnoticed. After he took his seat on the Court, Brandeis began to review petitions for certiorari. (Certiorari is a writ to correct errors in a lower court and, in the Federal system, is discretionary, four of nine Justices being necessary for a grant.)

Many of these petitions for certiorari raised racial questions. Such questions may involve only state law—as when a state antidiscrimination

* *Muller v. Oregon*, 208 U.S. 412.

measure is enforced—and state law questions are governed by the state courts. Federal questions are the only issues in state litigation which are reviewable by the Supreme Court. But in order to be reviewed, they must be raised. Thus a federal problem involved in state litigation cannot be reviewed by the Supreme Court unless it has been raised in a state trial, preserved on appeal through the hierarchy of state courts, and then presented to the Supreme Court of the United States. Brandeis soon discovered that many important federal questions presented with clarity and persuasion before our Court had not been properly raised in lower courts and therefore could not be considered.

This failure was explicable on the grounds that the Black lawyer had not been as well trained as his white opponent, since education in the Black law schools of that day was not what it should have been. So Brandeis got hold of Charles H. Houston, a Black Washington, D.C., lawyer who was one of the best ever to appear before our Court, and whose legal training had been at the Harvard Law School.

This was in the late twenties, when Houston was vice-dean of the Howard Law School. While Howard offered no course in Federal Jurisdiction until about ten years later, the Brandeis proposal won instant approval. Houston put the students in his course on constitutional law to work on specific problems, presenting the question as to how to raise, in a trial court, the precise federal constitutional question that would challenge a housing code, or voting barrier, or other racist measure, and how to preserve it on appeal.

Brandeis, like all judges, received a lot of mail asking help in getting a job, pleading that he intervene in some agency proceeding to protect a person, and the like. Brandeis would write on these letters "J.P.P." and they are so marked in the collection of his papers at the University of Louisville. "J.P.P." meant "Judicial Proprieties Prohibit" and Brandeis would pen a letter in his own hand to that effect and send it back to the person who had asked for help.

Brandeis was not unique in being a man of rectitude, but he became more and more unusual as a man who felt that a public office was a public trust and not a position to exploit for private gain.

Brandeis said in the *Olmstead* case in 1928, "Decency, security and liberty alike demand that government officials shall be subjected to the same rules of conduct that are commands to the citizen. In a government of laws, existence of the government will be imperiled if it fails to observe the law scrupulously. Our government is the potent, the omnipresent teacher. For good or for ill, it teaches the whole people by its example.

Crime is contagious. If the government becomes a lawbreaker, it breeds contempt for law; it invites every man to become a law unto himself; it invites anarchy" (277 U.S. 438, 485).

Since that time government has been recurringly lawless as respects entrapment (an agent inciting a crime); wiretaps, where no appropriate warrant is obtained; pilfering of public monies; flouting of election laws; the circulation of scurrilous literature concerning political opponents; and even the burglarizing of private files for political purposes. Lying and deception have grown as practices of government officials—practices that do more to undermine us than the "subversion" against which we have long inveighed.

In American history, lawlessness by government and the great decline in public morality are not new. They have recurred throughout our history. In the last century and in this one the public treasury has been dipped into through direct as well as devious means. Teapot Dome was the high-water mark of this type of corruption.

Ever since World War I our government has been increasingly lawless as it caters to popular fears, and indeed generates them by cries of "subversion" and "un-Americanism." Such manufactured fears have led to constitutional shortcuts of great dimensions. What Mitchell Palmer, Attorney General for Wilson, did to hapless foreigners in New England in the 1920's was a lasting scar, because it flouted constitutional standards, as one brave judge, George W. Anderson, held (265 F. 17). But from that time to the present the nation drifted slowly from constitutional government to a government subject to the will of the politicians in power. A notorious example of this neglect of the Constitution is found in the Sacco-Vanzetti trial.

Slowly but perceptibly the end came to justify the means. Government agents incited weak people to commit crimes which were then tolerated by the courts because "deceit" was deemed necessary for effective law enforcement. The persistence with which the third degree has survived is another example. Electronic surveillance has evolved from crude eavesdropping to sophisticated technology.

It is this kind of lawlessness that Brandeis feared the most. Brandeis can be understood not in terms of conservatism or liberalism, but in terms of morality: the end never justifies the means. In the area of law enforcement he included government as well as individuals in pleading for the exercise of moral judgments.

Every official in every branch of government is responsbile to the law and to the Constitution. The higher he is, the more important it is that he represent the finest of our constitutional traditions.

To give an example of the wariness a public official must exercise: in 1948, the year Thomas Dewey was running for the Presidency, I was invited to Portland to address the Oregon State Bar Association, which put me up at the Benson Hotel. When I checked out of the hotel, I was told that the bill had been taken care of by the association.

By October of that year I was back in Washington for the opening of Court. The Presidential campaign was getting hotter and hotter, and one day I received a telephone call from a friend, Lindsay C. Warren, the Comptroller General of the United States. He told me he had learned that I had been a guest of the Oregon Bar Association at the Benson Hotel in Portland, and that the association had not paid the bill but had routed it to a shipbuilding company that had a contract with the U.S. Navy. The contractor had in fact paid the hotel bill.

The Comptroller knew about the incident because one of Dewey's own men had been tipped off, and this man checked with Lindsay Warren to make sure the facts were correct. The Comptroller looked into the matter, reported to Dewey that it was all true, and promptly called me. I phoned the Benson Hotel to get the amount of the bill and immediately sent off a check in payment. I also wrote a letter excoriating the president of the Oregon Bar for doing anything that would link a member of the Court with such a highly unethical practice. Although the bill, as I recall, was not much over $50, that story would have made headlines in all the papers. It would even, perhaps, have hurt Truman (who had tried to get me to be his running mate), not because I had done anything immoral but because it could be made to appear that I had. This was politics capitalizing on deceit.

Brandeis thought that people in the public service should be selfless. And so they should be. But there seem to be very few of that breed today. By the time of LBJ personal aggrandizement had become the style. It was, I fear, a part of the return of the herd to a primitive selfishness that could destroy us.

Brandeis would have been appalled to see the use of leverage by a congressman or senator to get a radio or TV license for himself or his family. He would, I think, be appalled at the practice I have mentioned before whereby Pentagon officers step out of their uniforms into positions with private companies doing business with the Pentagon. He would have asked this searching question: "How can an officer who had supervised procurement be a good watchdog for the public if on retirement his reward is going to be a nice, fat job with one of the companies making millions out of government largesse?"

Brandeis would also have been shocked if he had lived to know that William H. Tucker, the man who in 1968 was chairman of the ICC, which approved the Penn-Central merger, shortly resigned and became head of the old New Haven, which was required by the ICC decision to become an integral part of Penn-Central.

Mergers depressed him because they turned entrepreneurs into clerks, independent businessmen into faceless lackeys serving some faceless business bureaucracy. The gravitation of power to the center depressed Brandeis for the same reason. States' rights to him had a very special meaning—they were not to be used as an excuse for the Establishment to keep a minority enslaved. A state was a sovereign political entity, as a member of which, the common man had a chance to be heard and to make his views effective.

The computer world would have depressed Brandeis. He saw the forces of disintegration gathering early in this century and it made him sad. The automobile was part of what he disliked. He spoke to me many times about the transformation it was making—not in urban sprawl alone, but in the character of people. An automobile desensitized the driver, making the polite person crude and aggressive. It is the same with any machine. One person in a bomber high above the earth can wipe out thousands of people without sight of blood and without hearing a child's whimper.

Man becomes transformed when a machine separates him from his fellow-man. Man is at his best when he stands on his own feet—accountable to family, to neighbors, to employers, to God. Man is at his worst running with the herd, for then individual responsibility is ignored and individual achievement is not put to the test.

The small men who followed Brandeis in economic affairs mostly ridiculed him for wanting to turn back the clock. But Brandeis' idea was different: he wanted to put the individual and the individual's privacy first, and to establish only the controls that would keep the individual from being regimented.

This line of thought ran through all of Brandeis' opinions, through all his papers, through all his talk. Brandeis had spiritual links with Jefferson as he did with Isaiah, and he lived every day by the faith he acquired from them.

He would be saddened to death if he could see what happened to his dream for this nation.

There is in Brandeis a universal note. We can reach the moon and top all secrets of the universe and yet not survive if we do not serve the soul of man. We serve the soul of man only when we honor individual achievements and respect individual idiosyncrasies. We serve the soul of man only when a man's worth—not his race, creed, or ideology—becomes our basic value.

The nation or the world can be smothered and controlled by a military-industrial complex or by a socialist regime or by some other totalitarian group. But in time the individual will rebel. Man, though presently enmeshed, will seek freedom just as he does today in Russia and in Czechoslovakia, and just as he did in the Watts area of Los Angeles. The struggle is always between the individual and his sacred right to express himself on the one hand, and on the other, the power structure that seeks conformity, suppression, and obedience. At some desperate moment in history, a great effort is made once more for the renewal of individual dignity. And so it will be from now to eternity.

These ideas of freedom did not of course originate with Brandeis. But through his opinions as well as the example of his life, he articulated them and showed they could be practical. That is why Brandeis will always remain a revolutionary symbol.

When I learned, after the event, that Brandeis had gone to FDR and asked that I be named to take his place on the Court when he retired on February 13, 1939, I was the proudest human alive.

I, of course, never served on the Court with Brandeis, but Hugo Black did. For some reason I do not understand, Black and Brandeis were never close. Brandeis came from a more privileged background than either Hugo or I. We two had been exposed to raw-boned experiences. Brandeis did not grow up with policemen shooting at him. Whether that happened in freight yards or in a ghetto, the experience leaves its mark on a man.

Brandeis and Black served together on the Court from October, 1937, to February, 1939, and perhaps something happened during that time that affected Black's attitudes. Whatever it was, Black kept it to himself.

Yet so far as due process in criminal trials was concerned, and the constitutional impossibility of government ever to play an ignoble role, Black and Brandeis thought pretty much alike. Brandeis probably gave a more robust content to the Fourth Amendment than did Black's construction, but that was a minor difference. They stood together on the First Amendment and on the Fifth.

Hugo Black was fiercely intent on every point of law he presented. He was emphatic, concise, and clear. There was no mistaking where he stood. But there was no fierceness directed to his opposition—only to their ideas. I never heard him say an unkind word about any Justice, no matter how deeply opposed the two were. He never indulged in any personal aspersions, no matter how heated the arguments. I think perhaps Bob Jackson at times thought Hugo was personally insulting, but such was never his purpose—and he had only the highest respect for Bob.

When I was rolled on by a horse and sent to Tucson, Arizona, for a long convalescence, Hugo came out to see me, staying a week. He played tennis each day at the university and loafed with me the rest of the time. I came to have a very close relationship with him as a result of that experience.

Hugo loved company and long conversations. His spacious garden in his exquisite Alexandria home was ideal for that purpose during spring and summer. He loved to entertain there; and when, during the Korean War, the Court held on June 2, 1952, that Truman's seizure of the steel mills was unconstitutional,* Hugo asked me what I though of his idea of inviting Truman to his home for an evening after the decision came down. I thought it a capital idea. So in two weeks Hugo extended the invitation and Truman accepted. It was a stag dinner, and only Truman and members of the Court were present. Truman was gracious though a bit testy at the beginning of the evening. But after the bourbon and canapés were passed, he turned to Hugo and said, "Hugo, I don't much care for your law but, by golly, this bourbon is good." The evening was a great step forward in human relations, and to Hugo Black, good human relations were the secret of successful government.

For years Hugo took off for Florida during the winter recess, as he loved the sun on his back. He loved Washington, D.C., in the summer—even its humidity; and he seldom left the city when vacation time came. He read avidly, marking the pages of books with which he disagreed—a practice that misled the minister who preached Hugo's funeral service. Finding passages concerning the virtues of "natural law" all marked in Hugo's books, the minister assumed that "natural law" was Hugo's dish. Natural law, however, was anathema to him, for he felt that it was the source of the judge-made law concerning substantive due process that the old Court had inflicted on the nation between 1882 and 1937.

Clay County, Alabama, his home county, was very close to Hugo's

* 343 U.S. 579.

heart. So was the state of Alabama, where he had practiced law, served as prosecutor, and run for the Senate. The dominant opinion in Alabama favored school segregation. As a matter of constitutional law, Hugo was against it—being one of the four, the others being Burton, Minton, and I, who voted to reverse when *Brown v. Board of Education* (347 U.S. 483) was first argued in December, 1952.

But Alabama rejected that view. When Hugo Black's law class at the university failed to invite him (the outstanding member of the class) to its fiftieth reunion in 1956, Hugo was crushed. He read with tolerant eyes everything his state did, except those matters that seemed to him to trench on constitutional rights. Then he was very upset, but never rancorous or bitter.

Hugo Black was probably the best storyteller of my time. I regret I never took the time to make notes and work the jokes into a brochure. Like the following joke, they usually pertained to Clay County customs or Clay County law practice.

It seems that a sharecropper was charged with the crime of stealing the mule of the landlord. The latter was rich and domineering, without many friends among the common people. The evidence against the defendant was overwhelming, so much so that he did not take the stand. The judge charged the jury, laying down the law meticulously. In five minutes the jury returned.

"Have you reached a verdict, Mr. Foreman?" asked the judge.

"We have, your Honor."

"Then hand it to the clerk."

The clerk put on his glasses, took the paper, unfolded it, cleared his throat, and said, "We the jury find the defendant not guilty, provided that he returns the mule."

The judge brought his gavel down sharply, saying, "There is no such verdict in the law. The defendant is either guilty or not guilty." After giving the charge all over again the judge told the jury to retire and come back with a lawful verdict.

The jury returned in five minutes and the judge asked the foreman, "Have you reached a verdict?"

"We have, Your Honor."

"Then hand it to the clerk."

The clerk put on his glasses, unfolded the paper, cleared his throat, and read: "We the jury find the defendant not guilty. He can keep the mule."

Hugo Black, like Felix Frankfurter and Harlan Stone, was an ardent proselytizer of his constitutional views, seeking to convert any "wayward" Brother on the Court. In his later years that aspect of his character waned, perhaps due to lack of energy. But in his prime there was no more fervent evangelist than Hugo Black.

He had been a Sunday School teacher for years in Alabama, and that background kept surfacing all his life. He had been an active Democrat, and his personal support of the old historic characters in that party was whole-hearted. Thus he was offended when I told him that in my view William Jennings Bryan was a bag of wind. It was not only his party fealty that made him react in that way. He never had an unkind or uncharitable thing to say about anyone he had ever known in public life. In each of them—Democrat, Republican, Socialist—there was some good, and it was the good that he always mentioned. That is one reason those who knew him well invariably loved him. And those who loved him, as I did, would have gone to the very end of the road for him.

When I came on the Court Hugo Black talked to me about his idea of having every vote on every case made public. In cases taken and argued, the vote of each Justice was eventually known. But in cases where appeals were dismissed out of hand or certiorari denied, no votes were recorded publicly. I thought his idea an excellent one and backed it when he proposed to the conference that it be adopted. But the requisite votes were not available then or subsequently. As a result he and I started to note our dissents from denials of certiorari and dismissal of appeal in important cases. Gradually the practice spread to a few other Justices; and finally I ended up in the sixties noting my vote in all cases where dismissals or denials were contrary to my convictions.

When Hugo was eighty-one he had some cataracts removed and seemed to be in good health. He hit tennis balls one hot day with his wife, Elizabeth, and had a very slight stroke doing so, but when the 1970 term of Court started, he seemed fit. In May, 1971, we had a conference and no one noted that he looked ill. His knees, however, buckled when he was returning to his chambers, and he was put to bed with a high fever. But by the time the Pentagon Papers case was argued on June 26, 1971, he seemed to have regained his old strength and fervor, pouring all of it into one of the best opinions he ever wrote.* Shortly thereafter he was in Bethesda Naval Hospital with temporal arteritis, from which he died on September 25, 1971.

Both Black and I were one with Brandeis in his insight into the cor-

* 403 U.S. at 714.

porate world and its chicanery. We also stood with Brandeis in his passion to protect small and medium-sized companies and for participatory democracy in which all classes took part.

Brandeis was Wilson's spokesman in support of the Clayton Act. His testimony before Congress on that measure should be required reading in government courses. The Sherman Act had been used by the judiciary to break the Pullman strike and ultimately to put Eugene Debs in jail. The Clayton Act took labor out from under the antitrust laws, declaring, "The labor of a human being is not a commodity or article of commerce."

The other major provision promoted by Brandeis was the prohibition of an acquisition of stock of one corporation by another where the effect "may be to substantially lessen competition" or "tend to create a monopoly in any line of commerce."

The hole that Brandeis and the Clayton Act did not succeed in plugging up was to prohibit the acquisition of assets of one company by another, thus producing a like effect. That was not done until the Celler-Kefauver Act of 1950.

But Black and Brandeis saw eye to eye on that problem. They were indeed brothers under the skin. I have written this account only to state why it is that though all my personal associations on the Court have been warm, congenial, and enduring, I was ideologically closer to Brandeis and to Black than to any others.

Chapter XXVI

Appointment to the Court

Ambition can be a gnawing, warping, destructive force. I knew several men whose one ambition was to be on the U.S. Supreme Court. Each would have made a fine Justice. None of them, however, made it. And each was bitter about it. Those running for office can make their campaigns and sell themselves to a constituency. But a Supreme Court appointment is a Presidential prerogative, and Presidents usually have their own ideas about major appointments of that character. Those who receive an appointment from a President must still clear the Senate, and that is not always an easy hurdle, as our statistics show. For between 1787 and 1973, twenty-two appointees to the Court were rejected by the Senate.

So when a young lawyer asks me how to go about becoming a Supreme Court Justice, I tell him what I have just written, and add, "The worst thing is to make it a fixation. The important thing is to stay in the stream of history, be in the forefront of events—and carve out a career that will be satisfying in all other respects. For the chances of being on the Supreme Court, even for a male Caucasian, are one in a million."

I never even dreamed of being there. I did dream of being Chief Forester. I dreamed of being a professor of English literature and, later, dean of the Yale Law School. I dreamed of being simultaneously a professor both at the Harvard Business School and at the Yale Law School. I dreamed of being Solicitor General. I dreamed of being an advocate like Hiram Johnson, William Borah, Louis D. Brandeis.

Mother always wanted me to be a minister and follow in Father's steps. But my reaction to that was always instant and adverse; it got so that I asked Mother please never to mention it again.

I never had a yen for public office—not even for the position of mayor or congressman, let alone governor or senator. Indeed, I grew up holding all such offices in disrespect, as I thought that most officeholders were either corrupt or represented some special, selfish interest. It was not until I was at the SEC and worked with Congress that I came to regard the majority of congressmen and senators as worthy public servants.

For years I had delivered the evening paper to the home of Wesley Jones, United States senator from Washington from 1909 to 1932. I revered him from a distance, but that was more of an emotional than an intellectual response. Although he had brought the first Reclamation Service Dam to water the parched lands of Yakima, he was the voice of the Establishment, as was Boise Penrose and most of the other officeholders I knew by reputation. I respected the office but most of the men I did not. And I had no drive to take over those positions and renovate them. In college we had many debates about the matter; I concluded then that a person, to be a successful politician, had to compromise his principles—sometimes to the point of extinction. Years later I admired FDR although he, too, followed the pattern of bowing to expediency. One thing I credited him for, however, was that his compromises with principle bothered him.

I remember a weekend with FDR on the Presidential yacht, the *Williamsburg*. The two of us were cruising Chesapeake Bay, working on the "dagger in the back" speech he delivered at the University of Virginia on June 10, 1940, indicting Mussolini. He talked at length about his 1932 campaign. At the behest of Raymond Moley and other conservative friends, he had made a speech in Pittsburgh on October 10, 1932, coming out for a balanced budget. In 1940 that Pittsburgh speech still tormented him. The budget could not be balanced and at the same time the social needs met. Hoover could balance the budget, certainly. But balancing the budget by Hoover or by anyone else meant a depression.

"Now I have constantly to eat the words I uttered in Pittsburgh," he said over and again.

I thought FDR had sacrificed principle for expediency in the Court-packing plan. The principle was the maintenance of an independent judiciary. To be sure, the rulings of the Court had been setbacks to the President's political program. But we had only to read the mortality tables to know that new judges would soon take the place of the old ones, and perhaps judges of a different vintage would view the problems differently. I said "perhaps" because, in at least the instance of the invalidation of the NRA, the Court was plainly right and FDR plainly wrong.

When it came to the Court, FDR had an Oedipus complex, as Draper once put it. To many people the Court is a father symbol, and as such, it is either loved or hated. That is why so much discussion of the Court throughout history has been emotional rather than rational. That was one of FDR's blind spots, of which he was never fully conscious.

In 1937 Justice Van Devanter retired. On August 12 of that year Roosevelt named Hugo L. Black of Alabama to take his place. By my lights he could not have chosen a better person. But here again, my view and FDR's were somewhat different. His idea in selecting Black was to throw a "tiger," as he put it, into the Court—an outstanding opponent of all that the old Court had done. Happily, Black had greatness as well, but FDR could hardly be expected to know that.

When Black was named to the Court, Senator Ashhurst was chairman of the Senate Judiciary Committee that cleared the nomination and recommended confirmation. Ashhurst spoke in favor of Black. He reviewed the bitter battle to reject Brandeis some twenty years earlier. Seven ex-presidents of the American Bar Association who had "the courage of their retainers" had urged the Senate to reject Brandeis. Ashhurst predicted what turned out to be true: the nation would soon recognize Black, as it had recognized Brandeis, as a distinguished jurist.

Hugo Black was confirmed but not by acclamation. The Senate is often referred to as a club; but that club was divided over Hugo Black. The final vote was 63 to 16 with 16 not voting, most of the nonvoters being absent. The sixteen opposed were ideological opponents. Some did not like the way he had conducted his investigations. Others said there were rumors that Black had been a member of the Ku Klux Klan, but there was not a bit of evidence before the Senate that the rumor was true. The Senate knew the man Black and knew he was not a racist, that he opposed the growing concentration of economic power but was not out to destroy the system, nor to scuttle the Constitution nor the rights of minorities. The whole focus of his political career had been to create equal opportunities for everyone.

The rumor about Black and the Klan was true. In his early days as a lawyer in Alabama, Hugo, like all trial lawyers, depended heavily upon the favor of the local people who made up the juries. The Klan was the biggest, most powerful club in the South, and Hugo joined it. He was a member for a relatively short time, but Hugo Black never did an ugly thing in all his life. He was no more Klan-minded, ever, than was Martin Luther King, Jr., whom he later greatly admired.

During that period I met a congressman on the street who took me by the lapel and shouted, "Why didn't I kill that son-of-a-bitch Black? We were in the Army together. In the same company. I could easily have shot him—and no one would have known the difference." Still shouting he added, "I was a fool, a goddamn silly fool." (Shortly afterward the congressman died of a heart attack.)

After Black took his seat, an action was sought to be filed by one Levitt who challenged Black's appointment and confirmation because the Retirement Act of 1937 was enacted when Black was senator. The argument was that the Act created a "civil office" or increased the "emoluments" of an existing one, thus barring Black from holding the office by reason of Article I, Section 6, U.S. 2 of the Constitution. The motion was denied, the Court holding that Levitt had no standing to bring the suit.* Black, of course, took no part in the decision.

The next vacancy was Justice Sutherland's seat, to which Stanley F. Reed was named on January 15, 1938. Reed was the able Solicitor General from Kentucky who between 1935 and 1938 had argued the New Deal cases before the Court on behalf of the government.

Stanley Reed, a tall, quiet person, never raised his voice or lost his temper. On the Court he was gracious and friendly to everyone—even to Felix Frankfurter, who Mrs. Reed was convinced pulled wires to keep Stanley from being named Chief Justice. (He would, by the way, have made a good one.)

Stanley was a bit to the right of middle on the Court, and though he dissented in the first few weeks from a decision by Hughes that sit-down strikes were illegal, he never again got quite that far left. He was bothered by high blood pressure and one summer went to Duke University to place himself under the care of a physician who believed in an all-rice diet (supplemented by fruit and lemon juice) that would lower blood pressure. The regimen worked on Stanley Reed, though there were some who believed that any starvation diet would have done the same. Stanley Reed has continued into his eighties on rice, retiring from the Court after nineteen years of service and sitting occasionally on cases in lower courts.

He is a joy to be with and one who could be joshed about his deci-

* 302 U.S. 633.

sions. Never once did he rule in favor of an Indian, and jokingly I would inquire if this record was due to some terrible deed committed against a Reed ancestor by an Indian.

Stanley would always smile at the question and say, "Of course not. I only follow the law."

His all-rice diet, three times a day, day after day, made Reed live in hope that he would get invitations to dinner. He always accepted with alacrity and threw his rice diet to the winds.

Hugo Black also loved Stanley, though he seldom agreed with him in Conference. After Stanley retired from the Court, Hugo and I would, with apparent pain and anguish, inform him whenever one of his reactionary opinions was overruled.

Reed is a prince among men. He was so polite and gracious as to be a foil to the agile, provocative Felix Frankfurter, who made great fun of him behind his back, though never to his face.

Next to retire was Justice Cardozo; Felix Frankfurter of Massachusetts was nominated by FDR to take Cardozo's seat on January 5, 1939. Felix was brilliant and able, friendly yet divisive. He had made the work of the Supreme Court his lifelong specialty and brought great distinction to the Bench. People either loved or hated Felix. He had so many fine qualities it was easy for me to overlook the less admirable ones. He was effervescent, demanding, provocative, and teasing. He loved to work counsel over during argument. As Francis Biddle once said, Felix could swallow a whole record as if it were an oyster. Though diminutive in size, he was a towering advocate of a cause.

The next retirement was Brandeis, who sent his notice to FDR on February 13, 1939. Though I was close to Brandeis, I had no inkling he was going to retire. Nor did I know that he had been in touch with FDR, urging that I be named to take his place. Nor did news of his retirement reach me at the SEC that day. The first I knew of it was when I reached my friend Edmund Pavenstadt's place in Georgetown for cocktails that evening. It was a stag affair, and when I walked in, Pavy called for quiet, saying that Arthur Krock of *The New York Times* had an announcement to make. Arthur raised his glass and said, "To the next Justice of the Supreme Court."

"Who has retired?" I asked.

"Brandeis."

"And to whom are we drinking?"

"To you, of course," said Arthur.

I took him aside in the hallway to find out the "facts." The "facts" were that Brandeis had retired and that a group of my friends, headed by Arthur Krock, was promoting me.

"Tomorrow morning there will be a box on the front page of the *Times*, saying that a White House source says that William O. Douglas will succeed Brandeis," Arthur told me. Arthur Krock and FDR were not close. "He thinks I'm poison," said Arthur, "so, if he knows I'm for you, he'll be against you."

Arthur and the President were not on the same wavelength. There was deep-seated suspicion on both sides. As FDR once said to me, "Arthur Krock, though praising Venus de Milo, would end up with the observation, 'You know, she had a very bad case of halitosis.' "

I shrugged the whole thing off and gave no serious thought to it. Sure enough, the *Times* for February 14, 1939, carried the box item Krock had mentioned. But I dismissed the idea as ridiculous for several reasons. First, there was my youth—I was barely forty. Next was the fact that FDR had intimated publicly that the Far West, which had no representative on the Court, would be taken care of in his next Supreme Court appointment. The last Pacific Coast Justice had been D. A. McKenna of California, appointed in 1898. Van Devanter and Sutherland had been from the mountain states, but their places were taken by Southerners. The Court as constituted in February, 1939, had no member from west of the Mississippi.

Yakima, Washington, had been my home, but as I have stated, in the 1930's I was a registered voter in Connecticut. Western I might be in background and orientation, but Eastern I was in politics. I knew FDR well enough to know he would consider that. And, in truth, when he did send my name to the Senate, he nominated me from Connecticut—the third nominee from that state, the others being Oliver Ellsworth, who served from 1796 to 1800, and William Howard Taft, on the Court from 1921 to 1930.

The other reason I felt sure FDR would not consider me for the post was that Senator Lewis Schwellenbach was a serious contender. Lew was from Washington State; he was close to Hugo Black, having served on Black's Senate investigating committee; he had campaigned vigorously for FDR's Court-packing plan. My prognosis almost turned out to be correct, for one day in March, the President called Frank Murphy, the Attorney General, to the White House and said he had decided to appoint Schwellenbach. Murphy, who did not like the man, asked FDR if he would mind another suggestion. FDR said he would not. So Murphy asked that the matter be held over awhile so that he could report back.

I later learned that Murphy asked for the delay because Arthur Krock had gone to him and suggested that my name be sent up. According to Krock, Murphy's eyes lit up as he said, "Bill Douglas? Why, he's a natural."

That put into play a series of forces that led to Schwellenbach's undoing and to his relegation to the federal District Court in Spokane, where he served from 1940 to 1945, resigning to become Secretary of Labor under Truman. Hugo Black felt that the reason Schwellenbach did not get appointed to the Court was his "little black book." Schwellenbach apparently had such a book and would put down, at the time of the incident, the name of any person who slighted him. Then he would check off the name as he got even with each offender.

Schwellenbach's associate from Washington State in the Senate was Homer Bone, and there was bad blood between the two. What the cause was, I never knew, but Bone—and his campaign manager, Saul Haas—set out to block Lew. I knew Homer, but at that time Saul was a total stranger. One day Haas turned up at my office in the SEC and did a strange thing. He picked up my phone and put in a long-distance call to Olympia, Washington. I protested, saying this was a government line and no personal long-distance calls were permitted. He waved that aside as a minor technicality, and producing some liquor, poured himself a drink while he waited for the call to come through. It came through and he talked with Bruce Blake, at that time Chief Justice of the Washington State Supreme Court.

"Our candidate for the Supreme Court is Bill Douglas. Understand, Bruce? Okay. Send off a telegram to FDR at once."

He hung up, poured himself another drink, and put in another call. I buzzed my secretary, Miss Waters, to keep track of the charges, and she did, reporting at the end that he owed Uncle Sam over ninety dollars (which he promptly paid). He called the presidents of most of the Bar Associations in the State of Washington, giving each the same message and the same instructions. All of this took nearly an hour, during which time he drank a pint of whiskey. After finishing the calls, he slipped out as quietly and mysteriously as he had arrived, his mission accomplished.

In time Saul and I became close friends, but on that day I was upset that he was implicating me and my SEC fiscal account in such a telephone campaign.

Saul and Homer did other things. So did Bob La Follette, then senator from Wisconsin. So did Frank Murphy and Arthur Krock, as well as my old friend Jerome Frank. Jerry and I had become so close over the years that once when I lay at death's door following a harrowing accident with a horse in 1949, Jerry wrote me please to get well, saying, "Without you, life is not worth living."

What all these friends of mine did, I never knew in detail. But I was soon to discover that they had a well-thought-out, comprehensive plan. Their idea was not to sell me to FDR, for he knew me as well as they did. It was to convince him that I was a "Westerner." So they approached William Borah, Republican senator from Idaho, then the ranking member of the Senate Judiciary Committee. Borah was, in a sense, FDR's opposition in the Senate. If Borah endorsed me as a Westerner, the President should be satisfied. Who approached Borah and what was said, I never knew. But one day in March, 1939, Borah held a press conference. The questions were obviously planted, and they all pertained to me. The essence of Borah's replies was that he knew me, that he thought I would be a good appointment to the Court, that in his eyes I represented Idaho as well as Washington, and so on. That story was reported in the *Washington Post* the next morning; and for the first time I began to think that maybe . . . perhaps . . . possibly . . . I was in the competition. But I still felt that Schwellenbach would be named.

March 19, 1939, was a bright, springlike Sunday and I was playing golf at the Manor Country Club. I was not much of a golfer, never having had any lessons and not being endowed with the perfect circle swing. A foursome of us from the SEC usually played at the Manor Club, and I was such a poor player that I could easily get handicap strokes from my opponent. With those strokes plus a bisque or two, I usually could make twenty-five or fifty cents on eighteen holes. My friends, however, urged me to take lessons, and I finally did. The pro at a driving range asked me to drive off twelve balls, and after I did, I turned to him, and asked, "See anything wrong?" He retorted, "I never saw so many things wrong with one golfer."

"How much do I owe you?"

"Aren't you going to take lessons?"

"Not if I'm that bad." And paying him a dollar, I left.

This March day I was playing with my SEC associates, and had reached the ninth hole, when a breathless caddy ran up and said the White House wanted me. I went into the clubhouse and telephoned, to learn that FDR wanted to see me at once. So I cleaned up and drove to the White House, where I was ushered into the Oval Office.

I felt in my bones that FDR was going to offer me another job. As I have said, I had told him I was leaving in June to be dean at Yale and I felt he would try to keep me in Washington a while longer. I knew he had other tough jobs and that my days at the SEC were numbered, even if I did not return to Yale. There was, for example, a vacancy in the chairmanship of the FCC. That agency had been rocked, not with scandal, but with inefficiency, and I had heard the President say he would clean it up. There were other things around town that needed doing. But somehow or other the FCC job was the one I felt I'd be saddled with. All the way in from the Manor Club, I figured and figured how I could turn the Old Man down. The FCC was the last thing in town I wanted. Yet if I were "drafted," what could I do?

These were my thoughts as I walked into the Oval Room to receive his hearty greeting. My worst fears were confirmed.

"I have a new job for you." He paused to let the words sink in. "It's a mean job, a dirty job, a thankless job."

My heart sank, as that described the FCC perfectly.

"It's a job you won't like."

I was sure he was right.

"It's a job you'll detest."

I was in silent agreement as he lit a cigarette.

Then, looking up and smiling, he said, "This job is something like being in jail."

Then I knew it was not the FCC. But I could not figure out what else he had in mind. Even then the Supreme Court never crossed my mind.

Finally he said, "Tomorrow I am sending your name to the Senate as Louis Brandeis' successor."

I was dumfounded. And I walked in a daze until the following noon, when my name went to the Senate. The first thing I did was to send a note to Brandeis by messenger, telling him how proud I was. But even then I did not know that Brandeis had told FDR that I was his candidate for his seat.

My backers in the Senate were Frank Maloney of Connecticut, Bobby La Follette of Wisconsin, and William E. Borah of Idaho.

The spearheads of opposition were such liberals as Gilbert Harrison of the *New Republic*, I. F. Stone, and Max Lowenthal, who all thought I was too conservative.

The rumor was that Burton K. Wheeler, who did not vote on my confirmation, would mastermind my failure to be confirmed and that he would be assisted by Max Lowenthal. It was soon reported that Lowenthal was working hard in Wheeler's office, pounding out the script for the opposition. A messenger carried it to the floor, with instructions that Senator Frazier of North Dakota should read it very slowly so as not to run out of manuscript.

Whether those rumors were true, I never knew. They seemed implausible, as Wheeler and I had always been friendly. Nonetheless, the timing was perfect as Frazier droned on and on.

Frazier said:

> . . . We are considering confirming the nomination of a young man to the Supreme Court of the United States. He is forty or forty-one years of age, as I understand. He probably will have about thirty years of service on the Supreme Bench. As I stated yesterday, so far as I have been able to find, he has not taken any interest in progressive measures affecting the common people, such as labor measures, agricultural measures, or the rights of the common people in general.
>
> These newspaper articles indicate that while the name of Mr. Douglas was being considered, and he was being criticized by some of the liberal magazines for not being as liberal as he was supposed to be, and it was stated that he was lined up with Wall Street, on the fifteenth of March, five days before his nomination came in, he had an opportunity to speak, and he took the opportunity, and made a red-hot criticism of Wall Street interests, and "riled" them very much. The reporter said two or three times that the Wall Street interests "saw red"; and five days later his nomination came to the Senate. Some of the newspapers, of course, said that Mr. Douglas had proved his right to be a liberal by criticizing Wall Street (84 Congress Rec. 3781).

By late 1938 and early 1939 John L. Lewis and the President were at the breaking point. Lewis thought labor had been neglected, that FDR was no friend of labor, that he should not run for a third term, that John L. would be willing to run and take his place, or run on the ticket with him, and so on. I was small potatoes in this scramble, but FDR was a big target, and my nomination as Associate Justice played a part in the fight.

The big news was that someone who hated FDR had made a deal with Lewis, who also hated FDR, and Lewis had agreed to loose a blast against me. Bobby La Follette, who was close to labor, was filled with alarm and immediately conferred with Frank Maloney. Both agreed that if Lewis went overboard the next day, the battle for confirmation would be long and bitter. What Maloney and La Follette did to expedite matters, I do not know, but when Frazier finished reading the Wheeler-Lowenthal manuscript, they were able to get an immediate vote.

I was confirmed by a vote of sixty-two to four on April 4, 1939, the four nays being Frazier, Lodge, Nye, and Reed. Wheeler abstained.

I did not know Frazier, Nye, or Reed. I did know Lodge and I was honored that he opposed me. "With him as an enemy, who needs a friend" was the common saying. Lodge's neo-fascist image came into full focus when he served as ambassador to Saigon in 1963 and 1964. But the Lodge whom I early despised was his grandfather, Henry Cabot Lodge, who worked tooth and nail against American adherence to the League of Nations. World solutions of world problems seemed essential to me when I was eighteen. I was bitter at the prejudices shown by the then Establishment. Perhaps that is one reason why in the sixties and seventies I sided with our youth against the new Establishment that held the reins of power.

My last act at the SEC was to provide for Abe Fortas. He had been my right-hand man in all of the turbulent years at that agency. I had White House protection, while he did not. The opposition to our reforms was so powerful that I thought Abe would be the first target and might even be destroyed in his lonely position. So I went to Harold Ickes, put the problem to him, and asked him to put Abe on his staff. He did so and Abe served as general counsel of the Bituminous Coal Division from 1939 to 1941, then as director of the Division of Power from 1941 to 1942 and later as Under Secretary of the Interior from June, 1942 to January, 1946.

When I left, there was a farewell party at the SEC, the whole staff attending. It was a sad occasion, for an old regime had ended and a new one was about to be launched. We would go different ways, and old friends would now disappear.

And so I came to the Court without personal ambition ever playing a part. I had never cast my eyes its way, never dreamed, let alone wished, that I would sit there. I was of course overwhelmed by the honor. But it was not in any degree a fulfillment, as it would have been to many of my friends who had a deep longing for that position. Not being a fulfillment, it was, in a sense, an empty achievement. At first I did not like the work; it took me a few years to accommodate myself to the daily routine. Perhaps I was too young. Perhaps I had too much excess energy.

As the Court enters the courtroom the Crier always announces, "Oyez, oyez, oyez. All those having business before the Honorable, the Supreme Court of the United States, draw near and give their attention, for the

Court is now in sitting. God save the United States and this Honorable Court." The incoming Justice is escorted to the Clerk's desk, where he takes the oath, and then, while the Justices remain standing, is escorted to his seat—the one for the junior always being on the extreme left. In later years, my friend Thurman Arnold, describing my seating on the Court, would say, "He no sooner reached the Bench than a man jumped up and shouted, 'God save the United States and this Honorable Court.'"

I took my seat on April 17, 1939. The formalities were soon over and the most efficient Chief Justice, Charles Evans Hughes, started the call of the cases and the arguments began.

Hughes had set down for reargument during the first two weeks after my arrival cases in which the Court had divided four-to-four, or cases in which the Court was badly split. He hoped, with a full Court of nine, to get majority opinions. One of the first cases I ever voted on (*O'Malley v. Woodrough*, 307 U.S. 277) affected my entire life.

The old Court had held that federal judges' salaries were not taxable by the federal government. The majority so held in *Evans v. Gore*, 253 U.S. 245, Holmes and Brandeis dissenting. The majority reasoned that since Article III, Section 1 of the U.S. Constitution barred a reduction in a judge's salary during his term of office, it also barred the employer (Uncle Sam) from taking back in taxes with one hand what he had given in salary with the other. Congress thereupon enacted a law that the salaries of all federal judges taking office after June 6, 1932, would be subject to the income tax, and the constitutionality of that levy was before us during my first week. We held that the tax was constitutional, Butler dissenting and McReynolds not sitting. As I entered my vote in the docket book, I decided that I had just voted myself first-class citizenship.

The tradition had been that Justices never even voted in public elections. Brandeis stressed the importance of a Justice being aloof from life. In the long past some Justices may have voted, but by the 1930's most of them followed the Brandeis precept. I took a different course. Since I would be paying as heavy an income tax as my neighbor, I decided to participate in local, state, and national affairs, except and unless a particular issue was likely to get into the Court, and unless the activity was plainly political or partisan. That meant I would register and vote; that I would fight to raise the level of the public schools back home in Yakima County; that I would become immersed in conservation, opposing river pollution, advocating wildlife protection, and the like; that I would travel and speak out on foreign affairs. I would not, of course, campaign, nor would I become involved in activities of the Executive branch. But I would exercise the rights of first-class citizenship to the fullest extent possible.

And so I increased my civic activities and decided to write and speak on public issues. I traveled widely, visiting most nations in the world; I wrote books and articles about them, their people, and their problems. I traveled at home, giving some lectures and expressing my views on our foreign policies.

I attended international conferences. I became absorbed with the idea of developing Rules of Law for nations—since law is the only alternative to force that man has devised, and force is now far too dangerous to use.

I was among the first to suggest that a world agency control the manufacture and use of atomic energy. I helped to draft the 1946 resolution to that effect at the Rollins College Conference.

Conservation was my second interest. I hiked, rode horseback, and took canoe trips through all parts of the United States and often related my experiences in public. I became increasingly alarmed at the pollution of our rivers, at the darkening skies due to smog, at the silting of rivers due to overgrazing and reckless logging practices. I saw our beaches despoiled by industry and Lake Erie turning into a cesspool. I saw highways destroying wilderness areas. I was shocked at the manner in which "development" programs were ruining the wilderness recreational potential of the nation.

I wrote, spoke, and debated these subjects. I joined conservation groups. I marched, hiked, and protested against the despoilers and their tactics.

I did indeed try to be a first-class citizen to the fullest extent compatible with my judicial duties.

A person who follows my course is bound to be criticized. Anyone in public life who deals with controversial issues makes enemies, and an enemy is eager to cut one down for any reason, great or small. As it happened, some of my travels produced writings and statements that inflamed some people.

I have already related that when I visited a prison where Moroccan nationalists were jailed by the French, our State Department was incensed. In time I wrote an article for *Look*, the timing of which made it a catalytic agent that brought the issue of Moroccan independence to a head at the United Nations.

Even attending a reception at the Soviet Embassy often brought down the wrath of the press and of others who voiced anti-communist sentiment. Going to Soviet Russia, which I did in 1955, aroused the lions.

Many people assume that a Supreme Court Justice should be remote and aloof from life and should play no part even in community affairs. But if Justices are to enjoy First Amendment rights, they should not be relegated to the promotion of innocuous ideas.

The press never once criticized a Justice—certainly not Taft or Burton or Jackson—for being on a Board of Trustees of a university. Yet when I became a non-salaried member of the board of the Center for the Study of Democratic Institutions, Santa Barbara, California, the press took loud exception. The Center does not have students or grant degrees. It is a lively intellectual round table—livelier than most universities. It exposes current sociological, economic, technological, and international problems that loom large on the contemporary scene.

It is all right with the press for a Justice to be associated with an institution that deals with staid ideas, but not with one that explores all ideas, whether staid or explosive. The press aligned Justices with the status quo, not with forces of change.

In another area, it seems to me that rules for disclosure of outside interests by federal judges are quite capricious. Although judicial codes of ethics have rather continuously improved over the years, the present code, adopted by the American Bar Association and approved by the Judicial Conference, provides for no disclosure by a judge of his income from investments but does require disclosure of his income from writing, lecturing, teaching, and speaking. Thus the amount of book royalties must be made public but not the amount of interest on bonds and dividends on stock (Canon 6). I have long felt that all income of all federal officials should be made public—income of judges as well as income of senators, congressmen, Cabinet officers, and the like. I never could see the reason for requiring disclosures of the income of judges alone. What the Executive or Legislative members do might also be seen in a new light if their income and its nature were known. Moreover, when it comes to disclosure by judges I never could see any possible justification for requiring Jerome Frank, Learned Hand, Benjamin Cardozo, and Joseph Story to disclose the income from their books, yet not requiring the Stephen J. Fields to disclose the income from their railroad stocks and bonds. Justice Black and I protested these discriminations in our dissent in *Chandler v. Judicial Council* (398 U.S. 74, 138–140). The cloak of immunity is drawn tightly around the portfolio of judges, disclosure alone being required of those who write, lecture, and teach. This is not fair or just.

The prejudices or predilections of a judge may be greatly influenced by his investments. They may be even more revealing than his writings or lectures, for writings or lectures usually have a more philosophic quality and are not related to the sins or virtues of a particular corporation. If they are, then the judge should not sit in a case involving that corporation. But the fact that a judge says in a book or lecture that a corporation is not a person within the meaning of the Fourteenth Amendment should not disqualify him from sitting in all corporate cases.

Judges, like laymen, have philosophies of life; through legal education they may indeed have acquired rather fixed opinions. Hugo Black had a special passion about the First Amendment; some judges have a lesser passion about it. To disqualify a judge of either of those schools would be to rid the Bench of those like Black, Brandeis, Cardozo, Frankfurter, Harlan, Holmes, and Warren.

Many Justices in the past carried on outside activities. They have written books about federal laws, taught in law schools, and given lectures. A paid lecture given before an association or the executive officers of a company would of course disqualify a judge from sitting in any case involving that association or company. Giving lectures at universities or writing books on the wonders of the world reflect the interests of judges. What financial return comes from them should be public knowledge, but I have never understood the reason why discrimination should be made in favor of secrecy of one's financial return from investments but publicity of one's royalties.

A conflict with judicial duties is a different matter. A Justice who pickets an anticonservation project is, of course, disqualified to sit in the case, as is a Justice who owns stock in the project. Throughout our history Justices of the Court have leaned over backward when it comes to disqualifications. Yet many have had hobbies: Justice Story was interested in writing; Taft and Burton in education; Holmes in philosophy; Frankfurter in politics; Brandeis in Zionism; Roberts in dairy farming; Fortas played the violin; and so on.

A man or woman who becomes a Justice should try to stay alive; a lifetime diet of the law alone turns most judges into dull, dry husks. *O'Malley v. Woodrough,* the decision that made me a taxpayer, though it did produce for me a peck of trouble, saved me from that fate.

Senator William Langer, maverick of North Dakota, was one of the few people who stood by me in the days of great travail during my early years on the Court. He even stood by me when I issued the stay of execution in the Rosenberg case in 1953 (346 U.S. 273). One day he put his arm around my shoulder and said:

"Douglas, they have thrown several buckets of shit over you. But by

God, none of it stuck. And I am proud."

I liked Langer and his salty talk, but I never shared the conspiratorial viewpoint which he relished. I never reacted in terms of the David-Goliath syndrome. I disagreed greatly with most of my critics, but I felt that they, though misguided, were entitled to their views. People are emotional and react in hasty ways, from which many, like Langer, infer malice. But for one in public life, charity to one's critics is the only course.

In the oscillating movement of the planets man is a tiny speck—a microcosm. We seek truth, and in that search, a medley of voices is essential. That is why the First Amendment is our most precious inheritance. It gives equal time to my opponents, as it gives to me.

I hope it is always that way in this great land, which, in spite of its shortcomings, is still the hope of mankind across the globe.

Index